899 B.C.E.)

s (c. 460–c. 370 B.C.E.)

Plato (c. 428–347 B.C.E.)

Aristotle (384–322 B.C.E.)

Pyrrho (c. 360–270 B.C.E.)

Sextus Empiricus (second–third centuries C.E.) •

Plotinus (c. 205–270) —

• Diogenes Laertius (third century B.C.E.)

St. Augustine (354–430) —

Hypatia of Alexandria (c. 370–415) —

(c. 485–c. 380 B.C.E.)

Cicero (106–43 B.C.E.)

)–399 B.C.E.)

Aristippus (435–350 B.C.E.)

Plato (c. 428–347 B.C.E.)

• Diogenes (fourth century B.C.E.)

Epictetus (c. 55–c. 135)

Marcus Aurelius (121–180)

• Aesara (c. 350 B.C.E.)

St. Augustine (354–430) —

Aristotle (384–322 B.C.E.)

Epicurus (341–270 B.C.E.)

Zeno of Citium (c. 335–c. 263 B.C.E.)

St. Augustine (354–430) —

• Chuang Tzu (c. fourth century B.C.E.)

Hui Neng (638–713) —

Mencius (c. 371–c. 289 B.C.E.)

Hsün Tzu (298–238 B.C.E.)

W9-CDX-473

(continued on back endpaper)

Philosophy
The Power of Ideas

NINTH EDITION

Brooke Noel Moore

California State University, Chico

Kenneth Bruder

California State University, Chico

McGraw Hill

Connect
Learn
Succeed™

The McGraw-Hill Companies

Connect
Learn
Succeed™

PHILOSOPHY: THE POWER OF IDEAS, NINTH EDITION

Published by McGraw-Hill, a business unit of The McGraw-Hill Companies, Inc., 1221 Avenue of the Americas, New York, NY, 10020. Copyright © 2014 by The McGraw-Hill Companies, Inc. All rights reserved. Printed in the United States of America. Previous editions © 2011, 2008, and 2005. No part of this publication may be reproduced or distributed in any form or by any means, or stored in a database or retrieval system, without the prior written consent of The McGraw-Hill Companies, Inc., including, but not limited to, in any network or other electronic storage or transmission, or broadcast for distance learning.

Some ancillaries, including electronic and print components, may not be available to customers outside the United States.

This book is printed on acid-free paper.

1 2 3 4 5 6 7 8 9 0 DOC/DOC 1 0 9 8 7 6 5 4 3

ISBN   978-0-07-803835-8
MHID   0-07-803835-9

Senior Vice President, Products & Markets: *Kurt L. Strand*
Vice President, General Manager, Products & Markets: *Michael Ryan*
Vice President, Content Production & Technology Services: *Kimberly Meriwether David*
Executive Director of Development: *Lisa Pinto*
Managing Director: *Bill Glass*
Brand Manager: *Laura Wilk*
Marketing Specialist: *Alexandra Schultz*
Managing Development Editor: *Sara Jaeger*
Editorial Coordinator: *Adina Lonn*
Director, Content Production: *Terri Schiesl*
Senior Project Manager: *Lisa A. Bruflodt*
Buyer: *Nicole Baumgartner*
Media Project Manager: *Sridevi Palani*
Cover Designer: *Studio Montage, St. Louis, MO.*
Cover Image: *Fancy Collection/SuperStock*
Typeface: *10/12 Plantin Light*
Compositor: *Aptara®, Inc.*
Printer: *R. R. Donnelley*

All credits appearing on page or at the end of the book are considered to be an extension of the copyright page.

CIP has been applied for.

The Internet addresses listed in the text were accurate at the time of publication. The inclusion of a website does not indicate an endorsement by the authors or McGraw-Hill, and McGraw-Hill does not guarantee the accuracy of the information presented at these sites.

www.mhhe.com

To Marianne Moore, Kathryn Dupier Bruder, and Albert Bruder

Contents

Part Two
MORAL AND POLITICAL PHILOSOPHY

233

Part Three
PHILOSOPHY OF RELIGION: REASON AND FAITH

373

Part Four
OTHER VOICES

Chapter 14   Feminist Philosophy   422

Preface

This is a straightforward ungimmicky introduction to philosophy written especially for first- and second-year university students. It contains separate historical overviews of the main subjects of Western philosophy and includes both the analytic and the Continental traditions. It also covers Eastern philosophy, postcolonial philosophy, and feminist philosophy; and contains a chapter devoted to major philosophical problems. We hope readers will learn that thinking deeply about almost anything can lead them into philosophy.

The following are important changes in the ninth edition:

- A new chapter (Chapter 17) on philosophical problems, which includes the problem of free will, the problem of consciousness, the problem of the gift (ethics of generosity), and problems in aesthetics
- A new section on Judith Butler
- A new section on philosophical issues in quantum mechanics
- A new section comparing philosophy East and West
- Expanded coverage of the objectivism of Ayn Rand
- A new section on zombies
- A brief cultural overview of the nineteenth and twentieth centuries, in connection to philosophy
- New material on Gandhi, the Satyagraha Movement, and Hinduism
- Streamlined coverage of Alain Badiou, Gilles Deleuze, Michel Foucault, Jorgen Habermas, and Martin Heidegger
- A revised and updated first chapter making reference to the case of Trayvon Martin
- Updated visuals
- Updated list of suggested readings (list now online)
- New reading selection from Sam Harris

Philosophy—Powerful Ideas

We concluded years ago that most people like philosophy if they understand it and that most understand it if it isn't presented to them in exhausting prose. In this text we strive to make philosophy understandable while not oversimplifying.

We also concluded years ago that some people just aren't moved by the subject. Worse, we learned that those who aren't moved include a few who are sane, intelligent, well informed, and reasonable and who generally have sound ideas about the world, vote for the right people, and are even worth having as friends. Philosophy is just not for everyone, and no text and no instructor can make it so.

So we do not expect every student, or even every bright student, who comes in contact with philosophy to love the field. But we do hope that every student who has had an introductory course in philosophy will learn that philosophy is more than inconsequential mental flexing. Philosophy contains powerful ideas, and it affects the lives of real people. Consequently, it must be handled with due care. The text makes this point clear.

Philosophy: A Worldwide Search for Wisdom and Understanding

Until the middle of the twentieth century, most philosophers and historians of ideas in American and European universities thought philosophical reflection occurred only within the tradition of disciplined discourse that began with the ancient Greeks and has continued into the present. This conception of philosophy has been changing, however, first through the interest in Eastern thought, especially Zen Buddhism, in the fifties, then through the increasingly widespread publication of high-quality translations and commentaries of texts from outside the Western tradition in the following decades. Of course, the availability of such texts does not mean that unfamiliar ideas will receive a careful hearing or even that they will receive any hearing at all.

Among the most challenging threads of the worldwide philosophical conversation is what has come to be known in recent years as postcolonial thought. The lines defining this way of thinking are not always easy to draw—but the same could be said for existentialism, phenomenology, and a number of other schools of thought in philosophy. In any event, in many cultures and subcultures around the world, thinkers are asking searching questions about methodology and fundamental beliefs that are intended to have practical, political consequences. Because these thinkers frequently intend their work to be revolutionary, their ideas run a higher-than-usual risk of being lost to philosophy's traditional venues. We include in this book a small sample from such writers.

Women in the History of Philosophy

Histories of philosophy make scant mention of women philosophers prior to the latter half of the twentieth century. For a long time it was assumed that lack of mention was due to a deficit of influential women philosophers. Scholarship such as that by Mary Ellen Waithe (*A History of Women Philosophers*) suggests that women have been more important in the history of philosophy than is often assumed. To date, we lack full-length translations and modern editions of the works of many women philosophers. Until this situation changes, Waithe argues, it is difficult to reconstruct the history of the discipline with accuracy.

This text acknowledges the contributions of at least some women to the history of philosophy. We include women philosophers throughout the text in their historical contexts, and we also present a substantially revised chapter on feminist philosophy.

Features

Among what we think are the nicer attributes of this book are these:

- Separate histories of metaphysics and epistemology; the Continental, pragmatic, and analytic traditions; moral and political philosophy; feminist philosophy; and the philosophy of religion
- Coverage of postmodernism and multiculturalism
- A section titled "Other Voices," which contains chapters on Eastern influences, feminist philosophy, and postcolonial thought
- Recognition of specific contributions of women to philosophy
- A generous supply of easy, original readings that don't overwhelm beginning students
- Boxes highlighting important concepts, principles, and distinctions or containing interesting anecdotes or historical asides
- Biographical profiles of many of the great philosophers
- Online checklists of key philosophers, with mini-summaries of the philosophers' leading ideas
- End-of-chapter questions for review and reflection and online lists of additional sources
- A pronunciation guide to the names of philosophers
- A brief subsection on American constitutional theory
- A glossary/index that defines important concepts on the spot
- Teachable four-part organization: (1) Metaphysics and Epistemology, (2) Moral and Political Philosophy, (3) Philosophy of Religion, and (4) Other Voices
- A section on arguments and fallacies
- For instructors, online detailed lecture ideas for each chapter

Online Learning Center

- The password-protected Online Learning Center is available at www. mhhe.com/moore9e. Please ask your McGraw-Hill representative for access information.

- The Student Guide contains chapter main points, lists of key philosophers, self-assessment quizzes, and suggestions for further readings.
- The Instructor's Manual contains chapter main points, detailed lecture suggestions, Power Point slides, and lists of philosophers' main works.

 This book is available as a CourseSmart Ebook. CourseSmart is a new way find and buy eTextbooks. At CourseSmart you can save up to 50% off the cost of a print textbook, reduce your impact on the environment, and gain access to powerful web tools for learning. CourseSmart has the largest selection of eTextbooks available anywhere, offering thousands of the most commonly adopted textbooks from a wide variety of higher education publishers. CourseSmart eTextbooks are available in one standard online reader with full text search, notes and highlighting, and email tools for sharing notes between classmates. For further details contact your sales representative or go to www.coursesmart.com.

Acknowledgments

We want to thank Anne D'Arcy for major help with this edition. D'Arcy crafted the new sections on Judith Butler, The Gift, and Zombies, and helped us write or revise material on Alain Badiou, Gilles Deleuze, Michel Foucault, Jürgen Habermas, Martin Heidegger, and "Philosophy East and West." She also helped us with visuals, epigraphs, and fact checks.

Special thanks go as well to Zanja Yudell for writing a section on philosophical problems in quantum mechanics; and to Rachel Steiner who provided three new nice drawings for this edition.

Many friends and colleagues at California State University, Chico have helped us on this and earlier editions: Maryanne Bertram, Judy Collins-Hamer, Marcel Daguerre, Frank Ficarra, Jay Gallagher, Eric Gampel, Tony Graybosch, Ron Hirschbein, Tom Imhoff, Marie Knox, Scott Mahood, Clifford Minor, Adrian Mirvish, Anne Morrissey, Jim Oates, Richard Parker, Dick Powell, Michael Rich, Dennis Rothermel, Robert Stewart, Greg Tropea, Alan Walworth, and Wai-hung Wong.

Also, for their wise and helpful comments on the manuscript for earlier editions, we thank Ken King, previously Mayfield/McGraw-Hill; John Michael Atherton, Duquesne University; Stuart Barr, Pima Community College; Robert Beeson, Edison State College; Sherrill Begres, Indiana University of Pennsylvania; W. Mark Cobb, Pensacola Junior College; Gloria del Vecchio, Bucks County Community College; Ronald G. DesRosiers, Madonna College; Mark A. Ehman, Edison Community College; Thomas Eshelman, East Stroudsburg University; Robert Ferrell, University of Texas at El Paso; James P. Finn Jr., Westmoreland County Community College; Raul Garcia, Southwest Texas State University; Brenda S. Hines, Highland Community College; Chris Jackway, Kellogg Community College; August Lageman, Virginia Intermont College; Bernal Koehrsen Jr., Ellsworth Community College; Henry H. Liem, San José City College; Kenneth A. Long, Indiana University–Purdue University at Fort Wayne;

Adrienne Lyles-Chockley, University of San Diego; Curtis H. Peters, Indiana University Southeast; Adrienne Regnier, Jefferson Community and Technical College; Richard Rice, La Sierra University; Harry Settanni, Holy Family College; William C. Sewell, Michigan Technological University; Douglas Thiel, Moorpark College/Oxnard College; and Chris Weigand, University of Central Oklahoma.

For the ninth edition, we are indebted to:

Edward M. Engelmann, Merrimack College

William Ferraiolo, San Joaquin Delta College

Daniel G. Jenkins, Montgomery College

Gonzalo T. Palacios, Prince George's Community College

A. J. Kreider, Miami Dade College

James Craig Hanks, Texas State University

Clinton F. Dunagan, Northwest Vista College

Christa Lynn Adams, Lakeland Community College

We also thank the following McGraw-Hill staff and freelancers for their excellent work on the ninth edition: Arpana Kumari, Craig Leonard, Laura Wilk, and Lisa Bruflodt. Special thanks are due to Anita Silvers for putting us in touch with Dominic McIver Lopes, to Ellen Fox for material on feminist philosophy, to Gregory Tropea for material on postcolonial thought, to Mary Ellen Waithe for explaining the thought of important women in the history of philosophy, and to Emerine Glowienka for helping us with Aquinas's metaphysics.

1

Powerful Ideas

Philosophers have a delicate task: squeezing the tacit assumptions and
unnoticed implications out of every ill-considered dogma without lapsing
into nitpicking or caricature.   —Daniel Dennett

On the night of February 26, 2012, volunteer George Zimmerman, 28,
drove his SUV through The Retreat At Twin Lakes, a gated community
near Orlando, Florida. Upon seeing an individual he didn't know walking around
inside the gates, Zimmerman called the local police department. The individual,
17-year-old Trayvon Martin, who was visiting someone in the community with his
father, was on his way back from the local 7-Eleven. Martin was wearing a hoodie
and was carrying a bag of Skittles, a can of iced-tea, and his cell phone. Zimmerman observed Martin "cutting between houses," and walking too slowly for the
inclement weather.

While still on the phone with the police dispatcher, Zimmerman left his car.
There was a fight. When it was over, Trayvon Martin lay dead on the ground, having been shot by Zimmerman once in the chest, at close range.

Although Martin had not been armed, Zimmerman told the police that Martin
had attacked him and that he shot Martin in self-defense. The police detained
Zimmerman, who was bleeding from the nose and from lacerations on the back of
his head, and questioned him for several hours. Then they released him.

The incident received national attention, in part because racist motives for the
slaying and police investigation were raised. Zimmerman is a Hispanic American,
of a multi-racial background, and Martin was an African American.

A Special Prosecutor was appointed to take over the investigation, and eventually she charged Zimmerman with murder in the second degree. Zimmerman
turned himself in, and was placed in custody.

As we write this, Zimmerman has not been brought to trial. When he is, various kinds of questions will be examined. Some of these questions are factual—What exactly happened when Zimmerman left his car? Did Zimmerman accost Martin? Did Martin attack Zimmerman? Cries of help were heard: whose cries were they?

Other questions are legal: did Zimmerman break any laws? The legal questions depend for their answer on the facts, and which facts matter is determined by what laws pertain.

There is a third kind of question, that we want to focus on here. The Zimmerman case will apparently involve Florida's Stand Your Ground law, a controversial law that states that a person may use force to defend himself without an obligation to retreat, where there is a reasonable belief of a threat.

Is this a good or just law? This is a philosophical question. It probably won't be discussed at George Zimmerman's trial, but it has been and will continue to be debated widely and heatedly. And there is a sense in which it is just as important as the other questions. If the Stand Your Ground law enables George Zimmerman to avoid being unjustly convicted of murder, that is a good thing. But if it makes it possible for him to get away with murder, that isn't.

Philosophical questions, like this one, are among the more fundamental you can ask. That of course does not necessarily mean they are pressing questions. "How can I get this computer to run right?"—*that* is an example of a question that can be pressing in a way in which philosophical questions rarely are. You rarely have to drop what you are doing to answer philosophical questions.

But let's look more carefully at this question, how can I get my computer to run right. Notice that the question relates to the *quality* of your life. Not knowing how to get your computer working diminishes your ability to function efficiently. It impacts your life unfavorably.

But *what kind of life should you live in the first place?* This is another philosophical question. And there is a sense in which it is more fundamental than the question about how to get your computer to run right, because there are lives you might live in which you might not own a computer.

Notice now that this question (what kind of life should you live?) implies that the life you live is *up to you*. However, is this really correct? Is it true that the life you live is up to you?

"Excuse me," you may be saying. "What do you mean, is the life I lead up to me? Obviously it is up to me. Whatever I do is up to me. Nobody is making me read this book, for example. I'm reading it because I want to read it."

No doubt most people think our voluntary actions are up to us. That's sort of what it means to say than an action is voluntary. But what about our *desires and values?* Are these up to us? After all, our voluntary actions stem from our desires and values. This question—*are our desires and values really up to us*—is deeply philosophical. As an experiment, you might try to change a desire or a value by an act of will. Will yourself to believe, for example, that it is actually right or good to hurt kittens. Can you do it? No? Well then think of something you desire. Can you make yourself *not* desire it by an act of will? If you try such an experiment, it may not be so clear after all that your desires, values, actions, or the life you lead really is up to you.

If you pay attention to politics or listen to talk radio, you will know that we are venturing into an area that is charged politically. Many believe that people are responsible for their own situation. They take the view that if someone is poor or sick or out of work, it is (with certain exceptions) his or her own fault. They may then subscribe to the idea that it would be wrong to take money from those who have lots of it and give it to people who are in need. Are they correct? How do you know that? These too are philosophical questions.

So you can see that philosophical questions, though not pressing in the sense in which the need to fix your computer might be pressing, are nevertheless important and divisive and arise quite easily in everyday contexts.

DEPARTMENT OF EXPLOSIVES

Some philosophical beliefs are so deeply held that people are ready to die for them. Just before dawn, on March 20, 2003, the United States unleashed an all-out missile and bomb attack on targets in Iraq. U.S. President George W. Bush then appeared on television before the world to state that the attack would free Iraqis from a terrible outlaw regime that threatened the world with weapons of mass murder. An important part of the rationale offered by George W. Bush for attacking Iraq was that Iraqis should be liberated from totalitarianism and should have freedom and democracy. At the time, most Americans assumed, without giving it much thought, that people universally want these things. Many Americans were surprised when supporters of Saddam Hussein, the Iraqi premier at the time, other Iraqi insurgents, and various religious leaders from the region actually denounced democracy, freedom of the press, and freedom of religion and referred to them as "Western perversions." Could it really be, some Americans wondered, that some people actually think totalitarianism is not evil and freedom and democracy are not good? Unfortunately, it became all too clear such "extremists" would stop at nothing to resist having what most Americans assumed all people want and should have.

The American Civil War, which was fought over the institution of slavery, is another example of a clash in values that ended in indescribable bloodshed. Although the Cold War remained cold, it, too, pitted different belief systems—capitalism and communism—against each other. Wars often are fought for ideas. Philosophies matter.

When we are confronted with a stark clash of values such as happened in the Iraq war, the American Civil War, or the Cold War, we might well wonder whether there are objective standards or criteria by which the opposed philosophies might be evaluated. Is democracy *really* a good? Does the United States do the right and proper thing in trying to spread freedom throughout the world? Well, of course, we think so. George W. Bush referred to freedom as "almighty God's gift to each man and woman in this world," which fact, in his opinion, morally required America to spread it.[1]

---

[1] See, for example, Bush's speech on April 4, 2004, in Buffalo, New York.

But those fighting America believe they are commanded by God to resist. Saddam Hussein appeared on television a few hours after the attack on Iraq began and declared that the invasion would be repelled through the grace of God. Both sides cannot be right, and if it is the other side that is mistaken, how do we know that? We might try to settle things by polling the world to see what most people think, but those who regard democracy as a "perversion" won't accept the democratic assumption on which that solution depends.

It is to the philosophy department you must turn for answers to questions like these. As you will discover when you read this book, many philosophical questions are abstract and theoretical, and few would resort to physical methods to defend them. Yet even abstract and theoretical issues can connect to ideas that people will go to extremes to enforce, defend, or spread. The philosophy department, as philosopher Van Meter Ames once said, works with explosive material, dangerous stuff.

WHAT IS PHILOSOPHY?

The word **philosophy** comes from the Greek *philein,* which means "to love," and *sophia,* which means "knowledge" or "wisdom." Because knowledge can be discovered in many fields, the Greeks (who invented philosophy) thought of any person who sought knowledge in any area as a philosopher. Thus, philosophy once encompassed nearly everything that counted as knowledge.

This view of philosophy persisted for more than two thousand years. The full title of Sir Isaac Newton's Principles, in which in 1729 Newton set forth his famous theories of mechanics, mathematics, and astronomy, is *Mathematical Principles of Natural Philosophy.* At that time, physics was still thought of as a variety of philosophy. In fact, at some point nearly every subject currently listed in your university's catalog would have been considered philosophy. If you continue your studies and obtain the highest degree in psychology, mathematics, economics, sociology, history, biology, political science, or practically any other subject, you will be awarded a PhD, the doctorate of philosophy.

However, philosophy can no longer claim those subject areas that have grown up and moved out of it. What, then, is philosophy today? In 2012 the Republican Party of Texas adopted a platform that opposed the teaching of skills that "have the purpose of challenging the student's fixed beliefs and undermining parental authority."[2] The Republican Party of Texas was not targeting philosophy per se, and philosophy has nothing to do with undermining parental authority. But philosophy has everything to do with challenging fixed beliefs. In fact, philosophy *is* the challenging of fixed beliefs, by means of careful thinking and logic. This indeed is as good a definition of contemporary philosophy as one could come up with.

---

[2] http://s3.amazonaws.com/texasgop_pre/assets/original/2012Platform_Final.pdf.

PHILOSOPHICAL QUESTIONS

To understand a subject, we should look at the questions it tries to answer. Is it good to spread freedom? How do we know that? And, by the way, what is freedom? These are questions of philosophy. As you can see, these questions are quite unlike those asked by economists, physicists, historians, communication studies experts, and so forth.

Here are a few other examples of philosophical questions.

- To what extent do we have a moral obligation to people we don't know? For that matter, to what extent do we have a moral obligation to nonhuman living things? How about the environment: do we have a moral obligation to it?
- What are the ethically legitimate functions and scope of government? What form of government is best? What is the proper connection between religion and the state? Questions like these separate Democrats from Republicans, conservatives from liberals, communists from capitalists, and theocrats from democrats.
- Do people have natural rights? If so, how do we know that? Where do they come from? What makes one person's list of rights superior to another person's?
- Is there a God? Perhaps just as important, does it make any difference whether there is or isn't a God?
- Do ends justify means?
- What, if anything, is the self? Is a person more than a physical body? Do people really have free will?
- What is truth? Beauty? Art?
- Is it possible to know anything with absolute certainty?
- Does the universe have a purpose? Does life? Is there order in the cosmos independent of what the mind puts there?
- What is time?
- Could anything have happened before the Big Bang?

Clearly, it is *possible* to go through life without spending a moment wondering about such questions, but most of us have at least occasional moments of reflection about one or another of them. In fact, it is pretty difficult not to think philosophically from time to time. Whenever we think about a topic long enough, if our thinking is the least bit organized we may end up engaged in philosophy. Real-life ethical dilemmas provide an excellent illustration. For example, situations arise in which we must balance our own needs against the needs of others we care about—an aging parent might require care, for instance. Of course, we will try to determine the extent of our obligation. But we may go beyond this and ask what *makes* this our obligation, or even more generally, what makes *anything* our obligation. Is it simply that it strikes us that way? Or is there some feature of situations that requires a certain response? If we are led to questions like these, the rest of the university curriculum will be of little help. Other subjects tell us how things are or how they work or how they came about, but not what we should do or why we should do it. Unfortunately, when most people reach this point in their reflections, they really don't know what to think next.

Of course, ethical dilemmas are not the only questions that lead one into philosophy. For instance, these days a controversy exists as to whether Intelligent Design is a scientific theory on all fours with evolution. Although many scientists are prepared (and qualified) to answer this question, in fact it is *not* a scientific question; you aren't likely to find an article about it in a scientific journal. It is, rather, a question in the *philosophy* of science.

To take quite a different example of how philosophical questions crop up in everyday contexts, sci-fi movies often portray robots that think like people. Will it someday be possible to build a robot than can actually think? The question requires a philosophical response. Of course you might just wait and see what they come up with, but will that help? You can't just go observe whether robots are thinking. Even if scientists succeed in building a robot that walks and talks and acts like Metro in *Real Steel,* one still might reasonably deny that the robot actually thinks. "It isn't made out of flesh and blood," you might say. But then beings from other galaxies might think even though they are not made out of flesh and blood, so why must computers be made out of flesh and blood to think? Is it perhaps because computers don't have "souls" or aren't alive? Well, what is a soul, anyway? Why aren't computers alive? What is it to be alive? These are philosophical questions. Philosophers have spent a great deal of time analyzing and trying to answer them.

As can be gathered from what we have said so far, an important feature of philosophical questions is that they cannot be answered in any straightforward way by the experimental method. For example, in a recent experiment scientists implanted a tiny chip in a paralyzed woman's brain that transmits electrical signals from her brain neurons to a computer. The computer decodes the signals and transmits them to a robotic arm. The woman, whose name is Cathy, cannot move her own arm, but can make the robotic arm move with her thoughts.[3] The question then arises: the computer chip is a physical thing, and so is electrical activity within Cathy's brain; but is Cathy's thought something different or separate from the electrical activity? This is none other than the age old philosophical question about the relation between thought and the brain, and the experiment does not resolve it.

Often, too, philosophers ask questions about things that seem so obvious we might not wonder about them—for example, the nature of change. That things change is obvious, and we might not see anything puzzling in the fact. If something changes, it becomes different; so what?

For one thing, if we have a *different* thing, then we seem to be considering *two* things, the original thing and the new, different thing. Therefore, strictly speaking, shouldn't we say not that something changed but rather that it was *replaced?* If, over the course of years, you replaced every part in the Prius you bought—every part, the engine block, all door panels, each nut, bolt, and piece of steel, glass, rubber, vinyl, battery, or whatever—would you still have the same Prius? If you gathered up all the original pieces and put them together again, would that be the original Prius?

---

[3] http://www.sciencenews.org/view/generic/id/340728/title/Paralyzed_woman_grips%2C_sips_coffee_with_robot_arm.

Perhaps these questions seem to be questions of nomenclature or semantics and of no practical interest. But over the course of a lifetime every molecule in a person's body may possibly (or probably!) be replaced. Thus, we might wonder, say, whether an old man who has been in prison for forty years for a murder he committed as a young man is really the same person as the young man. Since (let us assume) not a single molecule of the young man is in the old man, wasn't the young man in fact replaced? If so, can his guilt possibly pertain to the old man, who is in fact a different man? What is at stake here is whether the old man did in fact commit murder, and it is hard to see how this might be simply a matter of semantics.

Other times, philosophical questions come up when beliefs don't fit together the way we would like. We believe, for example, that anything that happens was caused to happen. We also believe that a cause *makes* its effect happen—if spoiled meat caused you to get sick, it *made* you sick. But we also believe that when we voluntarily decide to do something, nothing made us decide. And that belief seems to imply that our decision wasn't caused. So, which is it? Is every happening caused? Or are some happenings uncaused? Or is it perhaps that decisions aren't actually "happenings"? Do you see a way out of this dilemma? If so, congratulations. You are philosophizing.

MISCONCEPTIONS ABOUT PHILOSOPHY

Incorrect ideas people have about philosophy ought to be discussed here at the outset.

First is the idea that *one person's philosophy is as correct as the next person's* and that *any philosophical position is as good, valid, or correct as any other opinion.* This idea is especially widespread when it comes to values. If one person thinks that one should contribute a major part of one's income to help support an aging parent, and another person thinks a much lower limit is called for, you might say something like, "Well, the first person's view is correct for that person, and the second person's view is correct for the second person." Or let's say you think there is nothing wrong with same-sex marriage, and your roommate doesn't agree. You might be tempted to say something like, "Well, my view is correct for me, and my roommate's view is correct for my roommate."

"My view is correct for me, and my roommate's view is correct for my roommate." What this means is far from clear. Does it mean it would be okay for you to marry someone of the same sex but wrong for your roommate to do so? That proposal probably would not be acceptable either to you or to your roommate. If your roommate thinks gay marriage is wrong, he or she probably thinks it is wrong for *you* as well as for him or her. He or she probably thinks gay marriage is wrong, period. And someone who believes there is nothing wrong with gay marriage probably doesn't think there is anything wrong with either you or your roommate marrying someone of the same sex.

In other words, if you and your roommate disagree as to whether there is anything wrong with two people of the same sex getting married, you cannot both be correct. You and your hypothetical roommate have contradictory opin-ions that *cannot* both be correct. So much, then, for thinking that one person's philosophy is as correct as the next person's or that any philosophical position is as good, valid, or correct as any other opinion. This may hold true for such matters as whether chocolate ice cream tastes good, but it does not hold true for a philosophical thesis.

Another misconception about philosophy is that it is *nothing but* opinion. In fact, we should distance ourselves from this notion, or at least from the "nothing but" part. This is because philosophy *requires opinions to be supported by good reasoning*. If you express your opinion without providing supporting reasoning, your philosophy teacher is apt to say something like, "Well, that is an interesting opinion," but he or she won't say that you have produced good philosophy. Philosophy requires supporting your opinions—which, by the way, can be hard work.

Another idea people sometimes have when they first enter into philosophy is that "truth is relative." Now, there are numerous things a person might mean by that statement. If he or she means merely that people's beliefs are relative to their perspectives or cultures, then there is no problem. If, however, the person means that the same sentence might be both true and not true depending on one's per-spective or culture, then he or she is mistaken. The same sentence cannot be both true and not true, and whatever a person wishes to convey by the remark, "Truth is relative," it cannot be that. Of course, two different people from two different

Does a tree falling in the forest make a sound when nobody is around to hear it? Never mind that! Is there even a forest if there is nobody to observe it?

cultures or perspectives might *mean* something different by the same words, but that is a separate issue.

A different sort of misconception people have about philosophy is that it is light reading, something you relax with in the evening after all the serious work of the day is done. In reality, philosophical writing generally takes time and effort to understand. Often it seems to be written in familiar, everyday language, but that can be deceiving. It is best to approach a work in philosophy with the kind of mental preparedness and alertness appropriate for a textbook in mathematics or science. You should expect to be able to read *an entire novel* in the time it takes to understand just a *few pages* of philosophy! To understand philosophy, you have to reread a passage several times and think about it a lot. If your instructor assigns what seem to be short readings, don't celebrate. It takes much time to understand philosophy.

A PHILOSOPHICAL TOOL KIT

Philosophy isn't light reading, and it isn't mere expression of opinion. Philosophers support their positions with arguments, which (ideally) make it plain why the reasonable person will accept what they say.

Argument

When you support a position by giving a reason for accepting it, you are making an **argument.**[4] Giving and rebutting arguments (itself a form of argument) is the most basic philosophical activity; it distinguishes philosophy from mere opinion. **Logic,** the study of correct inference, is concerned with whether and to what extent a reason truly does support a conclusion.

To illustrate, if you tell someone you believe that God exists, that's not philosophy. That's just you saying something about yourself. Even if you add, "I believe in God because I was raised a Catholic," that's still just biography, not philosophy. If, however, you say, "God must exist because the universe couldn't have caused itself," then you have given an *argument* that God exists (or existed). This remark counts as philosophy.

But if you want to be good at philosophy, you must also consider challenges to and criticisms of your arguments. Such challenges are known as **counterarguments.** Suppose, for example, someone challenges your argument with "Well, if God can be self-caused, then why can't the universe?" You are now being called upon to *defend* your assumption that the universe could not be self-caused. Good philosophizing requires the ability to reason correctly, to defend assumptions, and to anticipate and rebut rebuttals.

---

[4] When you see a word or phrase in bold print in this book, it is defined in the index/glossary at the back of the book.

The Socratic Method

Philosophers have spent much time over the centuries trying to arrive at a proper understanding of several important concepts: truth, beauty, knowledge, justice, and others you will be reading about shortly. One of the most famous of all philosophers, the Greek philosopher Socrates [SOK-ruh-teez] (c. 470–399 B.C.E.), championed a method for doing this, which is now called the Socratic method. To see how this works, imagine that you and Socrates are discussing *knowledge:*

> *You:* You're asking me what knowledge is? Well, when you believe something very strongly, that's knowledge.
>
> *Socrates:* But that would mean that kids who believe in fairies actually know there are fairies, if they believe this strongly.
>
> *Y:* That's a good point. To know something, then, isn't just to believe it very strongly. The belief also must be true.
>
> *S:* That still doesn't sound quite right. That means a mere *hunch* is knowledge, if a person believes it strongly, and it turns out to be correct.
>
> *Y:* Well, you're right again. So, for one to know something, one must believe it strongly, it must be true, AND it must NOT be a mere hunch. In other words, it must be based on good evidence or solid reasoning. . . .

The exchange might continue until you offer an analysis of knowledge with which Socrates cannot take issue.

So, the **Socratic method** as practiced by Socrates involves proposing a definition, rebutting it by counterexample, modifying it in the light of the counterexample, rebutting the modification, and so forth. Needless to say, the method can be practiced by one person within his or her own mind. Clearly, the method can help advance understanding of concepts, but it can also be used to improve arguments or positions.

If you are reading this book as part of a class in philosophy, you may see your instructor utilizing the Socratic method with the class.

Thought Experiments

When we asked you to try to make yourself think, through an effort of willing, that it is good to hurt kittens, we were asking you to conduct a thought experiment. **Thought experiments** are not uncommon in science; in philosophy, they are among the most common methods used to try to establish something. You will encounter thought experiments in this book, and although some of them may seem far-fetched, you shouldn't discount them for that reason. For example, to establish whether time travel is possible, a philosopher might ask us to imagine someone stepping into a time machine, going back in time to before she was born and, while there, accidentally killing her parents. The thought experiment seems to show that, on one hand, the person existed at the time she entered the time machine; but, on the other hand, because her parents never gave birth to her, she could not have existed at that or any other time. The thought experiment thus shows, or seems to show, that time travel leads to contradictions and therefore is impossible.

Reductio ad Absurdum

Philosophers will often attempt to establish a thesis by using the **reductio ad absurdum**—demonstrating that the contradictory of the thesis is or leads to (i.e., "reduces to") an absurdity. The thought experiment about time travel is an example of this method as well as an illustration of a thought experiment.

The most famous *reductio ad absurdum* in the history of philosophy is St. Anselm's ontological proof that God exists. As we shall see in detail in Chapter 13, St. Anselm (c. 1033–1109) began his famous proof by assuming—merely for the sake of argument—that God, a being "greater than which cannot be conceived," does *not* exist. This assumption, Anselm argued, leads to the absurd result that a being greater than which cannot be conceived is not a being greater than which cannot be conceived. In other words, the idea that God does not exist "reduces" to an absurdity; therefore, God exists. Likewise, in the foregoing dialogue between you and Socrates, Socrates argued that the assumption that knowledge is identical with strong belief leads to an absurd result; which means that knowledge is *not* identical with strong belief.

Fallacies

A **fallacy** is a mistake in reasoning. Some mistakes are so common they have earned names, many in Latin. You won't often find philosophers making these mistakes, but you will often find them referring to the mistakes, so you should at least be familiar with the more common specimens.

• **Switching the burden of proof:** Logically, you can't prove your position by asking an opponent to disprove it. You don't prove God exists by challenging a listener to prove God doesn't exist.

• **Begging the question:** These days, you frequently hear people assert that something "begs the question." Generally, when people say this they mean the thing *invites* some question. However, this is not what "begging the question" means to logicians or philosophers. To them, you *beg the question* when you *assume* the very thing you are trying to prove, which means your "proof" doesn't go anywhere. For example, if you want to give a reason for thinking that God exists, and your reason is that "It says so in the Bible, and the Bible is the word of God," you are assuming that God exists, when that is what you were supposed to prove. It's like trying to prove that someone committed a crime because "he was the one who did it."

• *Argumentum ad hominem* (argument against the person): This fallacy amounts to transferring the qualities of a spokesperson to his or her insights, arguments, beliefs, or positions. For example, thinking that a person's *position* is frightening because the person himself is frightening would be an obvious mistake in reasoning, an *argumentum ad hominem*.

It is especially important to note that when someone—Susan, let us say—has changed her mind about something, it doesn't mean that what she now thinks is incorrect. That *Susan* has contradicted herself doesn't mean that what she has just said is contradictory. If a critic of a war supported the war at an earlier time, that fact doesn't mean her criticism is defective. The earlier support and the present criticism are logically unrelated. That someone has changed positions is a fact about the *person,* not his or her position. Confusing these two things is perhaps the most common mistake in reasoning on this planet.

From time to time, you hear someone ask an opponent if he or she really believes what he or she has said. That question is irrelevant to the truth or falsity of what the person has said. In his book *Republic,* Plato portrayed Socrates as conversing with the Athenian general Thrasymachus. Socrates asks Thrasymachus whether he really believes his own argument. Thrasymachus responds by saying,

> What difference does it make to you whether I believe it or not? Why don't you test the argument?[5]

Thrasymachus's response is 100% correct, in response to a question like Socrates's.

- **Straw man:** This fallacy occurs when you think you have refuted a view by distorting, misrepresenting, or exaggerating it. When the Irish philosopher George Berkeley maintained that physical objects really exist only in the mind, the English writer Samuel Johnson "refuted" Berkeley by kicking a rock and proclaiming, "I refute him thus!" But Samuel Johnson misrepresented Berkeley, for Berkeley never maintained that rocks aren't solid; Berkeley's position was that solid things like rocks (and legs and boots) exist only in the mind.

Suppose we argue that there is no such thing as free will, because our decisions are predetermined by our heredity and environment. If an opponent then points out that people obviously can choose what they do, the opponent has brought in a straw man. Our position wasn't that people don't make choices but that choices were predetermined by heredity and environment. What we said was X; our opponent acts as if we had said Y.

- **False dilemma** (either–or fallacy): This is the fallacy of offering two choices when in fact more options exist. Suppose someone says, "Either God exists, or there is no explanation for the universe." This is a false dilemma because it ignores a third possibility, namely, that there is an explanation of the universe that does not involve God.

- **Appeal to emotion:** This is trying to establish a point by arousing pity, anger, fear, and so on. Suppose we try to "prove" that God exists with the "argument" that "if you don't believe in him, you will burn in hell." We haven't really given an argument; we are just trying to scare the listener into agreeing with us.

---

[5] Plato, *Plato in Twelve Volumes,* Vols. 5 & 6, translated by Paul Shorey. Cambridge, MA, Harvard University Press; London, William Heinemann Ltd. 1969.

Philosophy begins in amazement and curiosity.

• **Red herring:** When someone brings an irrelevancy into a conversation, it is called a red herring. As you can see, many of the fallacies just discussed qualify as red herrings.

If you are reading this book as part of a course, there could be lots of discussion in class, and the discussion will involve disagreements. In addition, people will defend their positions with arguments. Perhaps you will find examples of these fallacies among the arguments you hear. You may even find an example or two in the arguments you read in this book.

THE DIVISIONS OF PHILOSOPHY

Most philosophical questions tend to fall into one of these four areas:

• *Questions related to being or existence.* **Metaphysics** is the branch of philosophy that is concerned with these questions. Two basic questions of metaphysics are: What is being? and What are its fundamental features and properties? Some of the questions listed earlier are questions of metaphysics, including: Is there a God? and Do people really have free will? Metaphysics has little to do with the occult or Tarot cards and the like.

• *Questions related to knowledge.* **Epistemology,** the theory of knowledge, is the branch of philosophy concerned with these questions. What is the nature of knowledge, and what are its criteria, sources, and limits? These are basic questions of epistemology, and thus it includes such questions from the list at the beginning of the chapter as: What is truth? and Is it possible to know anything with absolute certainty?

• *Questions related to values.* Included under this heading are primarily (1) **moral philosophy (ethics),** the philosophical study of moral judgments;

(2) **social philosophy,** the philosophical study of society and its institutions; (3) **political philosophy,** which focuses on the state and seeks to determine its justification and ethically proper organization; and (4) **aesthetics,** the philosophical study of art and of value judgments about art.

• *Questions pertaining to the theory of correct inference,* otherwise known as **logic,** which seeks to investigate and establish the criteria of valid reasoning and demonstration.

Part One of this book is devoted to metaphysics and epistemology, which are closely related. Part Two is concerned with questions of values, especially moral and political values. We talked a bit about logic earlier in this chapter.

Although philosophy has four main branches, they do not each contain an equal number of theories or concepts or words. Your library probably has more holdings under political philosophy than under the other areas and the fewest under epistemology or aesthetics.

There are other ways of dividing philosophy. Many universities offer philosophy courses that examine the fundamental assumptions and methods of other disciplines and areas of intellectual inquiry, such as science (philosophy of science), language (philosophy of language), and religion (philosophy of religion). Philosophy of science and philosophy of language are covered in Part One because most of the issues in these two areas are either metaphysical or epistemological issues. Part Three is devoted entirely to the philosophy of religion, especially to the question of whether God's existence can be proved.

WHO SAID PHILOSOPHY HAD
NO PRACTICAL USES?

The fourth part of this book is called "Other Voices," and in it we consider various current themes in philosophy as well as influences and traditions beyond mainstream Western philosophy.

In this edition there is a new chapter, Chapter 17, in which four important philosophical problems are discussed, the problem of free will, what is consciousness, the problem of the gift, and what is art (and related issues in aesthetics).

THE BENEFITS OF PHILOSOPHY

What can you do with a background in philosophy? As our friend Troy Jollimore said, the list of things you *can't* do with a background in philosophy is shorter than the list of things you can do. Life favors people who have the skills philosophy students tend to have in abundance. Just Google something like "scores by majors on LSAT." The LSAT is the law school aptitude test. You may have no intention of becoming a lawyer, but you know that, to be a lawyer, you must first be admitted to a law school, which requires no little mental ability. You will get similar results if you check out scores by major on the Graduate Record Exam (GRE), the Medical College Admission Test (MCAT), or the Graduate Management Aptitude Test (GMAT). Try it! You will find that philosophy majors do much better on these aptitude tests than other majors in the humanities, business majors, political science majors, or just about any other major you can think of. This suggests that philosophy students have exceptional aptitude for some of the most useful of all skills, including analytical thinking, critical thinking, careful reasoning, problem solving, and communication. Now, one of the things you learn when you study philosophy is that cause and effect is difficult to establish, and it is an open question whether studying philosophy makes students better thinkers or whether better thinkers are attracted to philosophy in the first place. But philosophical training does emphasize the aforementioned skills. Finding answers to philosophical questions involves being good at exposition and logic, making nuanced distinctions, recognizing subtle similarities and differences, and detecting unstated assumptions.

More than this, those who have learned their philosophical lessons well may not be as prone as others to superficiality and dogmatism. Philosophy requires objectivity, reasonableness, and an open mind. These general attributes, along with the critical thinking skills that come with the practice of philosophizing, can stand one in good stead when faced with the problems life generously provides.

CHECKLIST	KEY TERMS AND CONCEPTS	

To help you review, a checklist of the key philosophers of this chapter can be found online at www.mhhe.com/moore9e.	aesthetics 14
	appeal to
	  emotion 12
		argument 9
		argumentum ad
		  hominem 11

begging the
  question   11
counterargument   9
epistemology   13
fallacy   11
false dilemma   12
logic   9
metaphysics   13
moral philosophy
  (ethics)   13
philosophy   4

political
  philosophy   14
red herring   13
*reductio ad
  absurdum*   11
social philosophy   14
Socratic method   10
straw man   12
switching the burden
  of proof   11
thought experiment   10

7. Are all philosophical questions unanswerable? How about the question you mentioned in question 4?

8. Does it matter if God exists? Take a position, and defend it with an argument.

9. Does what is true depend on what your society believes is true? Was the world flat when people believed it was flat?

10. "2 + 2 = 4." Was this true before there were people (or other beings) around to think it? Explain.

QUESTIONS FOR DISCUSSION AND REVIEW

1. Why do you want to study philosophy?

2. Now that you've read this chapter, is philosophy what you expected it to be?

3. Why is it that the most advanced degree in so many fields is the doctor of philosophy?

4. Which of the questions raised in this chapter is most interesting to you? What do you think the answer is?

5. Can two people both be correct if one says, "Two members of the same sex should not have the right to get married," and the other says, "Two members of the same sex should have the right to get married"? Defend your answer with an argument.

6. If, by the time you become an adult, every molecule in your body has been replaced with a different one, are you-the-adult the same person as you-the-child?

LINKS

http://www.jimpryor.net/teaching/guidelines/writing.html
  A guide to writing philosophy papers. We strongly encourage you to read it before you write your first paper.

http://www.ditext.com/encyc/frame.html
  This resource enables you to compare topics listed in major Internet encyclopedias of philosophy.

http://plato.stanford.edu/contents.html
  An excellent encyclopedia of philosophy. You can look up most philosophical topics here.

http://www.askphilosophers.org
  Ask a question, get an answer, maybe.

SUGGESTED FURTHER READINGS

Go online to www.mhhe.com/moore9e for a list of suggested further readings.

Part One
Metaphysics and Epistemology: Existence and Knowledge

2

The Pre-Socratics

You cannot know what is not, nor can you express it. What can be thought of and what can be—they are the same.   —Parmenides

It is wise to agree that all things are one.   —Heraclitus

You don't generally find metaphysics and epistemology very far apart. **Metaphysics,** as you now know from reading Chapter 1, is the branch of philosophy concerned with the nature and fundamental properties of being. **Epistemology** is the branch that explores the sources, nature, limits, and criteria of knowledge. These days, when a philosopher makes a metaphysical assertion, he or she will generally consider whether it is the kind of assertion that could possibly be known; that's why metaphysics and epistemology go together. However, the first philosophers were mainly metaphysicians, so we shall begin by discussing metaphysics. When we look at Plato, whose vast philosophy covered all subjects, we shall take up epistemology.

In its popular usage, the word *metaphysics* has strange and forbidding associations. "Metaphysical bookstores," for example, specialize in all sorts of occult subjects, from channeling, harmonic convergence, and pyramid power to past-life hypnotic regression, psychic surgery, and spirit photography. However, the true history of metaphysics is quite different. Given the way in which the term was originally coined, you may find its popular association with the occult somewhat amusing. Here is the true story.

Aristotle (384–322 B.C.E.) produced a series of works on a wide variety of subjects from biology to poetry. One set of his writings is known as the *Physics*, from the Greek word *physika*, which means "the things of nature." Another set, to which Aristotle never gave an official title but to which he referred occasionally as "first philosophy" or "wisdom," was called simply "the books after the books on nature" (*ta meta ta physika biblia*) by later writers and particularly by Andronicus

The Nature of Being

When a philosopher asks, What is the nature of being? he or she may have in mind any number of things, including one or more of the following:

- Is being a *property* of things, or is it *some kind of thing* itself? Or is there some third alternative?

- Is being basically *one*, or are there *many* beings?

- Is being *fixed* and *changeless*, or is it *constantly changing?* What is the relationship between *being* and *becoming?*

- Does everything have the *same kind* of being?

- What are the fundamental *categories* into which all existing things may be divided?

- What are the fundamental *features* of reality?

- Is there a fundamental *substance* out of which all else is composed? If so, does it have any properties? Must it have properties?

- What is the world like *in itself,* independent of our perception of it?

- What manner of existence do *particular things* have, as distinct from *properties, relations,* and *classes?* What manner of existence do *events* have? What manner do *numbers, minds, matter, space,* and *time* have? What manner do *facts* have?

- That a particular thing has a certain characteristic—is that a fact about the *thing?* Or is it a fact about the *characteristic?*

Several narrower questions may also properly be regarded as questions of metaphysics, such as: Does God exist? Is what happens determined? Is there life after death? Must events occur in space and time?

Some of these questions are none too clear, but they provide signposts for the directions a person might take in coming to answer the question, What is the nature of being? or in studying metaphysics. Because the possibilities are so numerous, we will have to make some choices about what topics to cover in the pages that follow. We cannot go on forever.

---

of Rhodes, who was the cataloger of Aristotle's works in the first century B.C.E. The word *metaphysics,* then, translates loosely as "after the *Physics.*"

The subjects Aristotle discussed in these works are more abstract and more difficult to understand than those he examined in the *Physics.* Hence, later authorities determined that their proper place was indeed "after the *Physics,*" and thus *Metaphysics* has stuck as the official title of Aristotle's originally untitled work and, by extension, as the general name for the study of the topics treated there— and related subjects. Aristotle's works are the source of the term *metaphysics,* but Aristotle was not the first metaphysician. As we'll show in this chapter, philosophers before Aristotle had also discussed some of these things.

The fundamental question treated in Aristotle's *Metaphysics,* and thus the fundamental metaphysical question, can be put this way: *What is the nature of being?* A number of different subjects might qualify as "related" to this question, and in contemporary philosophical usage metaphysics is a rather broad and inclusive field. However, for most philosophers it does not include such subjects as astral projection, psychic surgery, or UFOs. Instead, it includes such questions as those in the box "The Nature of Being."

What is the nature of being? One of the authors used to ask his introductory classes to answer that question in a brief essay. The most common response, along with "Huh?" "What?" "Are you serious?" and "How do you drop this class?" was "What do you *mean,* 'What is the nature of being?'" People are troubled by what the question means and are uncertain what sort of thing is expected for an answer.

This is the way, incidentally, with a lot of philosophical questions—it is difficult to know exactly what is being asked or what an answer might look like.

In this chapter, we explore several different approaches that have been taken to this question.

The first philosophers, or first Western philosophers at any rate, lived in Ionia, on the coast of Asia Minor, during the sixth century B.C.E. They are known collectively as the **pre-Socratic philosophers,** a loose chronological term applied to the Greek philosophers who lived before Socrates (c. 470–399 B.C.E.). Most left little or nothing of their own writings, so scholars have had to reconstruct their views from what contemporaneous and later writers said about them.

Experience indicates that it is sometimes difficult to relate to people who lived so long ago. However, the thinking of these early philosophers has had a profound effect on our world today. During this period in Western history—ancient Greece before Socrates—a decisive change in perspective came about that ultimately made possible a deep understanding of the natural world. It was not *inevitable* that this change would occur, and there are societies that exist today whose members, for lack of this perspective, do not so much as understand why their seasons change. We are not arguing for the virtues of advanced technological civilization over primitive life in a state of nature, for advanced civilization is in some ways a mixed blessing. But advanced civilization is a fact, and that it is a fact is a direct consequence of two developments in thought. One of these, which we will not discuss, is the discovery by the Greeks of mathematics. The other, which we are about to discuss, is the invention by the Greeks of philosophy, specifically metaphysics.

THE MILESIANS

Tradition accords to **Thales** [Thay-leez] (c. 625–547 B.C.E.), a citizen of the wealthy Ionian Greek seaport town of Miletus, the honor of being the first Western philosopher. And philosophy began when it occurred to Thales to consider whether there might be some *fundamental kind of stuff* out of which everything else is made. Today we are so accustomed to thinking of the complex world we experience as made up of a few basic substances (hydrogen, oxygen, carbon, and the other elements) that we are surprised there ever was a time when people did not think this. Thales deserves credit for helping to introduce a new and important idea into Western thought.

Thales also deserves credit for helping introduce a nonmythological way of looking at the world. The Greeks thought their gods were in charge of natural forces; Zeus, for example, the supreme god, was thought to sometimes alter the weather. Our own belief that nature runs itself according to fixed processes that govern underlying substances began to take shape about this time, and Thales' philosophizing contributed to this important change in outlook.

What is the basic substance, according to Thales? His answer was that *all is water,* and this turns out to be wrong. But it was not an especially silly answer for him to have come up with. Imagine Thales looking about at the complicated world

According to legend, Thales predicted a bumper crop of olives and became wealthy.

of nature and reasoning: "Well, if there is some underlying, more fundamental level than that of appearances, and some kind of substance exists at that level out of which everything else is made, then this basic substance would have to be something very flexible, something that could appear in many forms." And of the candidates Thales saw around him, the most flexible would have been water—something that can appear in three very different states. So we can imagine Thales thinking that, if water can appear in these three very different forms that we know about, it may be that water can also appear in many other forms that we do not understand. For example, when a piece of wood burns, it goes up in smoke, which looks like a form of steam. Perhaps, Thales might have speculated, the original piece of wood was actually water in one of its more exotic forms.

We are guessing about Thales' reasoning, of course. And in any case Thales did come to the wrong conclusion with the water idea. But it was not Thales' *conclusion* that was important—it was what Thales was *up* to. Thales attempted to explain the complex world that we see in terms of a simpler underlying reality. This attempt marks the beginning of metaphysics and, for that matter, of science. Science is largely just an effort to finish off what Thales started.

Two other Milesians at about this time advanced alternatives to Thales' theory that the basic stuff is water. One of these was **Anaximander** [an-nex-im-AN-der] (610–c. 547 B.C.E.), a pupil of Thales, who maintained that the basic substance out of which everything comes must be even more elementary than water and every other substance of which we have knowledge. The basic substance, he thought, must be ageless, boundless, and indeterminate. From the basic stuff, a nucleus of fire and dark mist formed; the mist solidified in its center, producing the world. The world is surrounded by fire, which we see as the stars and other heavenly bodies, through holes in the mist. The seasons change as powers of heat and cold and wetness and dryness alternate. Anaximander, as you can see, proposed a theory of the universe that explained things in terms of natural powers and processes.

The third great Milesian philosopher was **Anaximenes** [an-nex-IM-in-eez] (fl. c. 545 B.C.E.), who pronounced the basic substance to be air and said that air becomes different things through processes of condensation and rarefaction. When it is rarefied, air becomes fire; when it is condensed it becomes first wind, then (through additional condensation) clouds, water, earth, and, finally, stone. He said that the earth is flat and floats on air. It isn't hard to imagine why Anaximenes thought that air is the basic substance; after all, it is that which enables life to exist. Anaximenes attempted to explain natural occurrences with his theory, and his attempt to identify the basic principles of transformation of the underlying substance of the world continues to this day.

PYTHAGORAS

Quite a different alternative was proposed by **Pythagoras** [puh-THAG-uh-rus] (c. 580–c. 500 B.C.E.) and his followers, who lived in the Greek city of Crotona in southern Italy. The Pythagoreans kept their written doctrines pretty secret, and controversy remains over the exact content of these doctrines. Pythagoras is said to have maintained that things are numbers, and we can try to understand what this might mean. Two points make a line, three points define a surface, solids are made of surfaces, and bodies are made out of solids. Aristotle, a primary source of information about the early philosophers, reported in his *Metaphysics* that the Pythagoreans "construct natural bodies, things that have weight or lightness, out of numbers, things that don't have weight or lightness." However, Theano, the wife of Pythagoras, had this to say:

> Many of the Greeks believe Pythagoras said all things are generated from number. The very assertion poses a difficulty: How can things which do not exist even be conceived to generate? But he did not say that all things come to be from number; rather, in accordance *with* number—on the grounds that order in the primary sense is in number and it is by participation in order that a first and a second and the rest sequentially are assigned to things which are counted.

In other words, things are things—one thing ends and another thing begins—because they can be enumerated. If one thing can be distinguished from another thing, it is because things were countable. Also, in Theano's account, it would not matter whether a thing were a physical object or an idea. If we can delineate it from another of its type—if it can be enumerated—it is a thing; and if it is a thing, it can be enumerated.

PROFILE: Pythagoras (c. 580–c. 500 B.C.E.)

Pythagoras was born on the Greek island of Samos. You may safely disregard the reports that he descended from the god Apollo; he was the son of a prominent citizen named Mnesarchus.

Not much is known for certain about the life of Pythagoras, although it is known that eventually he traveled to southern Italy, where he founded a mystical-scientific school in the Greek-speaking city of Crotona. The Pythagoreans believed in the transmigration of the soul, shared their property, and followed a strict set of moral maxims that, among other things, forbade eating meat.

Unfortunately, the Pythagorean community denied membership to a rich and powerful citizen of Crotona named Cylon. After Pythagoras retired to Metapontium to die, Cylon had his fellow Crotonians attack the Pythagoreans and burn their buildings to the ground. Worse still, from the Pythagoreans' point of view, he had all the Pythagoreans killed except two.

The Pythagorean school was eventually restarted at Rhegium, where it developed mathematical theorems, a theory of the structure of sound, and a geometrical way of understanding astronomy

The Pythagorean theorem: $a^2 + b^2 = c^2$.

and physics. To what degree these ideas actually stem from Pythagoras is a matter of conjecture.

Despite having written nothing, Pythagoras for many centuries was among the most famous of philosophers. Today, outside philosophy, he is remembered mainly for the Pythagorean theorem, which, in fact, the Babylonians had discovered much earlier.

So, according to Theano, Pythagoras meant there is an intimacy between things and numbers. Whatever the thing, whether it is physical or not, it participates in the universe of order and harmony: it can be sequenced, it can be counted, it can be ordered. And in the Pythagorean philosophy, the idea of orderliness and harmony applies to all things.

The Pythagorean combination of mathematics and philosophy helped promote an important concept in metaphysics, one we will encounter frequently. This is the idea that the fundamental reality is eternal, unchanging, and accessible only to reason. Sometimes this notion about fundamental reality is said to have come from Plato, but it is fair to say it originated with the Pythagoreans.

HERACLITUS AND PARMENIDES

Another important pre-Socratic philosopher was **Heraclitus** [hayr-uh-KLITE-us] (c. 540–c. 480 B.C.E.), a Greek nobleman from Ephesus, who proposed yet another candidate as the basic element. According to Heraclitus, *all is fire*. In fixing fire as the basic element, Heraclitus was not just listing an alternative to Thales' water and Anaximenes' air. Heraclitus wished to call attention to what he thought

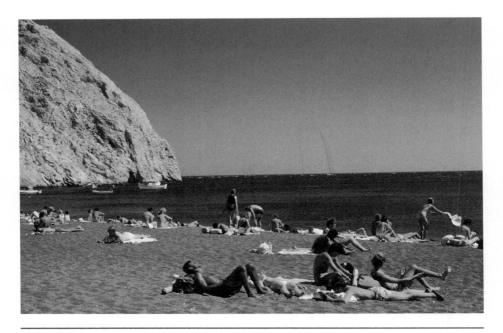

Today tourists flock to Greek beaches, but not necessarily to read philosophy.

was the essential feature of reality; namely, that it is *ceaselessly changing*. There is no reality, he maintained, save the reality of change: permanence is an illusion. Thus, fire, whose nature it is to ceaselessly change, is the root substance of the universe.

Heraclitus did not believe that the process of change is random or haphazard. Instead, he saw all change as determined by a cosmic order that he called the ***logos,*** which is Greek for "word." He taught that each thing contains its opposite, just as, for example, we are simultaneously young and old and coming into and going out of existence. Through the *logos* there is a harmonious union of opposites, he thought.

Heraclitus is famous for the remark attributed to him, "You cannot step in the same river twice." The remark raises the important philosophical **problem of identity** or "sameness over change": Can today's river and yesterday's river be the *same,* since not a single drop of water in yesterday's river is in today's river? The question, obviously, applies not just to rivers, but to anything that changes over time: rivers, trees, chickens, and the World Wide Web. It also, significantly, applies to people, and this is the **problem of personal identity:** you are not *quite* the same person today that you were yesterday, and over a lifetime it begins to seem that we should just drop the qualifying word *quite.* The atoms in George Bush Senior are not the same atoms as in George Bush Junior, and so we have two different people there—but the atoms in George Bush Senior in 2005 likewise are not the same atoms as in George Bush Senior in 1959. So why do we count this as one person and not as two?

Change does seem to be an important feature of reality—or does it? A younger contemporary of Heraclitus, **Parmenides** [par-MEN-uh-deez], thought

On Rabbits and Motion

Parmenides' most famous disciple, **Zeno** [ZEE-no] (c. 495–c. 430 B.C.E.), devised a series of ingenious arguments to support Parmenides' theory that reality is One. Zeno's basic approach was to demonstrate that motion is impossible. Here are two of his anti-motion arguments:

1. For something, let's say a rabbit, to move from its own hole to another hole, it must first reach the midway point between the two holes. But to reach that point, it must first reach the quarter point. Unfortunately, to reach the quarter point, it must reach the point that is one-eighth the distance. But first, it must reach the point one-sixteenth the distance. And so on and so on. In short, a rabbit, or any other thing, must pass through an infinite number of points to go anywhere. Because some sliver of time is required to reach each of these points, a thing would require an infinite amount of time to move anywhere, and that effectively rules out the possibility of motion.

2. For a rabbit to move from one hole to a second hole, it must at each moment of its travel occupy a space equal to its length. But when a thing occupies a space equal to its length, it is at rest. Thus, because the rabbit—or any other thing—must occupy a space equal to its length at each moment, it must be at rest at each moment. Thus, it cannot move.

Well, yes, it seems obvious that things move. Which means either there is a mistake in Zeno's logic or that rabbits, and just about every other thing, are not really the way they seem to be. Zeno favored the second alternative. You, perhaps, will favor the first alternative. So what is the mistake in Zeno's logic?

---

otherwise. Parmenides' exact dates are unknown, but he lived during the first quarter of the fifth century B.C.E.

Parmenides was not interested in discovering the fundamental *substance* that constitutes everything or in determining what the most important *feature* of reality is. His whole method of inquiry was quite unlike that of his predecessors. In all probability the Milesians, Heraclitus, and the Pythagoreans reached their conclusions by looking around at the world and considering possible candidates for its primary substance or fundamental constituents. Parmenides, by contrast, simply assumed some very basic principles and attempted to *deduce* from these what he thought *must be* the true nature of being. For Parmenides it would have been a complete waste of time to look to the world for information about how things really are.

Principles like those Parmenides assumed are said in contemporary jargon to be **a priori principles,** or **principles of reason,** which just means that they are known *prior* to experience. It is not that we learn these principles first chronologically but rather that our knowledge of them does not depend on our senses.

For example, consider the principle "You can't make something out of nothing." If you wished to defend this principle, would you proceed by conducting an experiment in which you tried to make something out of nothing? In fact, you would not. You would base your defense on our inability to *conceive* of ever making something out of nothing.

Parmenides based his philosophy on principles like that. One of these principles was that, if something changes, it becomes something different. Thus, he reasoned, if being itself were to change, then it would become something different. But what is different from being is nonbeing, and nonbeing just plain *isn't.* Thus, he concluded, being *does not change.*

What is more, being is *unitary*—it is a single thing. If there were anything else, it would not be being; hence, it would not be. (The principle assumed in this argument is similar to "a second thing is different from a first thing.")

Further, being is an *undifferentiated whole*: it does not have any parts. Parts are different from the whole, and if something is different from being, it would not be being. Hence, it would not be.

Further, being is *eternal*: it cannot come into existence because, first, something cannot come from nothing (remember?) and, second, even if it could, there would be no explanation why it came from nothing at one time and not at another. And because change is impossible, as already demonstrated, being cannot go out of existence.

By similar arguments Parmenides attempted to show that motion, generation, and degrees of being are all equally impossible. For examples of arguments demonstrating the impossibility of motion, see the box "On Rabbits and Motion."

Heraclitus envisioned being as ceaselessly changing, whereas Parmenides argued that being is absolutely unchanging. Being is One, Parmenides maintained: it is permanent, unchanging, indivisible, and undifferentiated. Appearances to the contrary are just gross illusion.

EMPEDOCLES AND ANAXAGORAS

The philosophies of Parmenides (being is unchanging) and Heraclitus (being is ceaselessly changing) seem to be irreconcilably opposed. The next major Greek philosopher, **Empedocles** [em-PED-uh-kleez] (c. 490–430 B.C.E.), thought that true reality is permanent and unchangeable, yet he *also* thought it absurd to dismiss the change we experience as mere illusion. Empedocles quite diplomatically sided in part with Parmenides and in part with Heraclitus. He was possibly the first philosopher to attempt to reconcile and combine the apparently conflicting metaphysics of those who came earlier. Additionally, Empedocles' attempt at reconciliation resulted in an understanding of reality that in many ways is very much like our own.

According to Empedocles, the objects of experience *do* change, but these objects are composed of basic particles of matter that *do not* change. These basic material particles themselves, Empedocles held, are of four kinds: earth, air, fire, and water. These basic elements mingle in different combinations to form the objects of experience as well as the apparent changes among these objects.

The idea that the objects of experience, and the apparent changes in their qualities, quantities, and relationships, are in reality changes in the positions of basic particles is very familiar to us and is a central idea of modern physics. Empedocles was one of the first to have this idea.

Empedocles also recognized that an account of reality must explain not merely *how* changes in the objects of experience occur but *why* they occur. That is, he attempted to provide an explanation of the forces that cause change. Specifically, he taught that the basic elements enter new combinations under two forces—love and strife—which are essentially forces of attraction and decomposition.

This portrayal of the universe as constituted by basic material particles moving under the action of impersonal forces seems very up to date and "scientific" to us today, and, yes, Empedocles was a competent scientist. He understood the mechanism of solar eclipses, for example, and determined experimentally that air and water are separate substances. He understood so much, in fact, that he proclaimed himself a god. Empedocles was not displeased when others said that he could foresee the future, control the winds, and perform other miracles.

A contemporary of Empedocles was **Anaxagoras** [an-ak-SAG-uh-rus] (c. 500–c. 428 B.C.E.). Anaxagoras was not as convinced of his own importance as Empedocles was of his, but Anaxagoras was just as important historically. For one thing, it was Anaxagoras who introduced philosophy to Athens, where the discipline truly flourished. For another, he introduced into metaphysics an important distinction, that between *matter* and *mind.*

Anaxagoras accepted the principle that all changes in the objects of experience are in reality changes in the arrangements of underlying particles. But unlike Empedocles, he believed that everything is *infinitely* divisible. He also held that each different kind of substance has its own corresponding kind of particle and that each substance contains particles of every other kind. What distinguishes one substance from another is a preponderance of one kind of particle. Thus, fire, for example, contains more "fire particles" than, say, water, which presumably contains very few.

Whereas Empedocles believed that motion is caused by the action of two forces, Anaxagoras postulated that the source of all motion is something called **nous.** The Greek word *nous* is sometimes translated as "reason," sometimes as "mind," and what Anaxagoras meant by *nous* is apparently pretty much an equation between mind and reason. Mind, according to Anaxagoras, is separate and distinct from matter in that it alone is unmixed. It is everywhere and animates all things but contains nothing material within it. It is "the finest of all things, and the purest, and it has all knowledge about everything, as well as the greatest power."

Before mind acted on matter, Anaxagoras believed, the universe was an infinite, undifferentiated mass. The formation of the world as we know it was the result of a rotary motion produced in this mass by mind. In this process gradually the sun and stars and moon and air were separated off, and then gradually, too, the configurations of particles that we recognize in the other objects of experience.

According to Anaxagoras, mind did not *create* matter but only acted on it. Notice also that Anaxagoras's mind did not act on matter for some *purpose* or *objective.* These are strong differences between Anaxagoras's mind and the Judaeo-Christian God, although in other respects the concepts are not dissimilar. And, although Anaxagoras was the first to find a place for mind in the universe, Aristotle and Plato both criticized him for conceiving of mind as merely a mechanical cause of the existing order.

Finally, Anaxagoras's particles are not physical particles like modern-day atoms. If every particle is made of smaller particles, as Anaxagoras held, then there are no smallest particles, except as abstractions, as infinitesimals, as idealized "limits" on an infinite process. For the idea that the world is composed of actual physical atoms, we must turn to the last of the pre-Socratic philosophers, the Atomists.

Mythology

Western philosophy was born on the back of Greek **myths** and not merely in the sense that early philosophers were seeking an alternative, more observationally based, systematic understanding. Thales spoke of all things being full of gods. Xenophanes objected to anthropomorphizing gods within Greek mythology. Heraclitus disliked Homer and Hesiod for using myths that led to misunderstandings about the true nature of things. Conversely, Plato made frequent and fruitful use of myths. The allegory of the cave in the *Republic* (see Chapter 3) provides a key for understanding both his metaphysics and his epistemology. In the *Symposium*, heavenly and earthly love are different, just like the two Aphrodites. Plato's own creation theory in the *Timaeus* is couched in mythical terms.

In the *Principles of a New Science Concerning the Common Nature of All Nations* (1725), Italian philosopher Giambattista Vico placed myths at the early stages of civilization in what he called the "age of the gods." A more scientific approach to the interpretation of myths began in the middle of the nineteenth century and continues to the present day. Western thinking is constantly being renewed by the discovery of new and hidden meanings in the Greek myths. Recent examples include the founding of psychoanalysis by Sigmund Freud, which to no small degree is based on his unique

interpretation of the Oedipus myth. In the United States, the writings on mythology by Mircea Eliade and Joseph Campbell have found a significant following.

THE ATOMISTS

The Atomists were **Leucippus** [loo-SIP-us or loo-KIP-us] and **Democritus** [dee-MOK-rut-us]. Not much is known of Leucippus, although he is said to have lived in Miletus during the mid-fifth century B.C.E., and the basic idea of **Atomism** is attributed to him. Democritus (c. 460–c. 370 B.C.E.) is better known today, and the detailed working out of Atomism is considered to be the result of his efforts. He was also a brilliant mathematician.

The Atomists held that all things are composed of physical atoms—tiny, imperceptible, indestructible, indivisible, eternal, and uncreated particles composed of exactly the same matter but different in size, shape, and (though there is controversy about this) weight. Atoms, they believed, are infinitely numerous and eternally in motion. By combining with one another in various ways, atoms compose the objects of experience. They are continuously in motion, and thus the

The atomic theory of matter originated in Greek philosophy.

various combinations come and go. We, of course, experience their combining and disassembling and recombining as the generation, decay, erosion, or burning of everyday objects.

Some qualities of everyday objects, such as their color and taste, are not really "in" the objects, said the Atomists, although other qualities, such as their weight and hardness, are. This is a distinction that to this day remains embodied in common sense; yet, as we will discuss in Chapter 6, it is totally beset with philosophical difficulties.

Anyway, the Atomists, unlike Anaxagoras, believed there is a smallest physical unit beyond which further division is impossible. And also unlike Anaxagoras, they saw no reason to suppose the original motion of atoms resulted from the activity of mind; indeed, they did not believe it necessary in the first place to explain the origin of that motion. As far as we can tell, they said in effect that atoms have been around forever, and they have been moving for as long as they have been around. This Atomist depiction of the world is quite modern. It is not such an extravagant exaggeration to say that, until the convertibility of matter and energy was understood in the twentieth century, the common scientific view of the universe was basically a version of atomism. But the Atomist theory did run up against one problem that is worth looking at briefly.

The Greek philosophers generally believed that for motion of any sort to occur, there must be a void, or empty space, in which a moving thing may change position. But Parmenides had argued pretty convincingly that a void is not possible. Empty space would be nothingness—that is, nonbeing—and therefore does not exist.

The Atomists' way of circumventing this problem was essentially to ignore it (although this point, too, is controversial). That things move is apparent to sense perception and is just indisputable, they maintained, and because things move, empty space must be real—otherwise, motion would be impossible.

One final point about the Atomist philosophy must be mentioned. The Atomists are sometimes accused of maintaining that chance collisions of atoms cause them to come together to form this or that set of objects and not some other. But even though the Atomists believed that the motion of the atoms fulfills no purpose, they also believed that atoms operate in strict accordance with physical laws. Future motions would be completely predictable, they said, for anyone with sufficient information about the shapes, sizes, locations, direction, and velocities of the atoms. In this sense, then, the Atomists left nothing to chance; according to them, purely random events, in the sense of just "happening," do not occur.

The view that future states and events are completely determined by preceding states and events is called **determinism.** Chapter 17 contains a discussion of the problem of free will. Determinism runs counter to a belief in free will.

To sum up this chapter, despite the alternative theories the pre-Socratics advanced, an important common thread runs through their speculation, and it is this:

> All believed that the world we experience is merely a manifestation of a more fundamental, underlying reality.

That this thought occurred to people represents a turning point in the history of the species and may have been more important than the invention of the wheel. Had it not occurred, any scientific understanding of the natural world would have proved to be quite impossible.

The desire to comprehend the reality that underlies appearances did not, however, lead the various pre-Socratic philosophers in the same direction. It led the Milesians to consider possible basic substances and the Pythagoreans to try to determine the fundamental principle on which all else depends. It led Heraclitus to try to determine the essential feature of reality, Parmenides to consider the true nature of being, and Empedocles to try to understand the basic principles of causation. Finally, it led Anaxagoras to consider the original source of motion and the Atomists to consider the construction of the natural world. Broadly speaking, these various paths of inquiry eventually came to define the scope of scientific inquiry. But that was not until science and metaphysics parted ways about two thousand years later.

CHECKLIST

To help you review, a checklist of the key philosophers of this chapter can be found online at www.mhhe.com/moore9e.

KEY TERMS AND CONCEPTS

QUESTIONS FOR DISCUSSION AND REVIEW

1. Explain the derivation of the word *metaphysics*.

2. Provide possible interpretations of the question, What is the nature of being?

3. Compare and contrast the metaphysics of the three Milesians. Whose metaphysics seems most plausible to you, and why?

4. The Pythagoreans theorized that all things come to be in accordance with number. What does that mean?

5. Compare and contrast the metaphysics of Heraclitus and Parmenides.

6. Explain and critically evaluate Parmenides' arguments that being is unitary, undifferentiated, and eternal.

7. Compare and contrast the metaphysics of Empedocles, Anaxagoras, and the Atomists. Whose views are the most plausible, and why?

8. "The behavior of atoms is governed entirely by physical law." "Humans have free will." Are these statements incompatible? Explain.

9. Is it true that something cannot come from nothing? How do you know?

10. "What can be thought of and what can be are the same." Was Parmenides correct in believing this?

SUGGESTED FURTHER READINGS

Go online to www.mhhe.com/moore9e for a list of suggested further readings.

3

Socrates, Plato

Thus the soul, since it is immortal and has been born many times, and has seen all things both here and in the other world, has learned everything that is. —Plato, *Meno*

Love [is] between the mortal and the immortal. . . . [It is] a grand spirit which brings together the sensible world and the eternal world and merges them into one great whole. —Diotima in Plato's *Symposium*, 202e

I [Socrates] affirm that the good is the beautiful. —Plato's *Lysis*, 216d

If you have heard of only one philosopher, it is probably one of the big three: Socrates, Plato, or Aristotle. These three were the most important philosophers of ancient Greece and in some respects the most important, period. Plato was the pupil of Socrates, and Aristotle was the pupil of Plato. This chapter covers Socrates and Plato; the following chapter, Aristotle.

SOCRATES

In the fifth century B.C.E., the center of Western civilization was Athens, a city-state and a democracy. This period of time was some three centuries after the first Olympic Games and the start of alphabetic writing, and approximately one century before Alexander the Great demonstrated that it is possible to conquer the world or what passed for it then. Fifty thousand citizens of Athens governed the city and the city's empire. Athenians did not settle disputes by brawling but rather by discussion and debate. Power was not achieved through wealth or physical strength or skill with weapons; it was achieved through words. Rhetoricians, men and women with sublime skill in debate, created plausible arguments for almost any assertion and, for a fee, taught others to do it too.

These rhetoricians, the Western world's first professors, were the **Sophists.** They were interested in practical things, and few had patience with metaphysical speculation. They demonstrated their rhetorical abilities by "proving" the seemingly unprovable—that is, by attacking commonly held views. The net effect was an examination and a critique of accepted standards of behavior within Athenian society. In this way, moral philosophy began. We will return to this topic in Chapter 10.

At the same time in the fifth century B.C.E., there also lived a stonemason with a muscular build and a keen mind, **Socrates** [SOK-ruh-teez] (470–399 B.C.E.). He wrote nothing, but we know quite a bit about him from Plato's famous dialogues, in which Socrates almost always stars. (Plato's later dialogues reflect Plato's own views, even though "Socrates" is doing the speaking in them. But we are able to extract a reasonably detailed picture of Socrates from the earlier dialogues.)

Given the spirit of the times, it is not surprising that Socrates shared some of the philosophical interests and practices of the Sophists. We must imagine him wandering about the city, engaging citizens in discussion and argument. He was a brilliant debater, and he was idolized by many young Athenians.

But Socrates did not merely engage in sophistry—he was not interested in arguing simply for the sake of arguing—he wanted to discover something important, namely, the *essential nature* of knowledge, justice, beauty, goodness, and, especially, traits of good character such as courage. The method of discovery he followed bears his name, the Socratic method. To this day, more than twenty centuries after his death, many philosophers equate proficiency within their own field with skill in the **Socratic** (or **dialectic**) **method.**

The method goes like this: Suppose you and Socrates wish to find out what knowledge is. You propose, tentatively, that knowledge is strong belief. Socrates then asks if that means that people who have a strong belief in, say, fairies must be said to *know* there are fairies. Seeing your mistake, you reconsider and offer a revised thesis: knowledge is not belief that is *strong* but belief that is *true*.

Socrates then says, "Suppose the true belief, which you say is knowledge, is based on a lucky guess. For instance, suppose I, Socrates, ask you to guess what kind of car I own, and you guess a Volvo. Even if your guess turns out to be right, would you call that knowledge?"

By saying this, Socrates has made you see that knowledge cannot be equated with true belief either. You must therefore attempt a better analysis. Eventually you may find a definition of knowledge that Socrates cannot refute.

So the Socratic/dialectic method is a search for the proper definition of a thing, a definition that will not permit refutation under Socratic questioning. The method does not imply that the questioner knows the essential nature of knowledge. It only demonstrates that the questioner is skilled at detecting misconceptions and at revealing them by asking the right questions. In many cases the process may not actually disclose the essence of the thing in question, and if

Socrates' prison—or what is left of it.

Plato's dialogues are an indication, Socrates himself did not have at hand many final, satisfactory definitions. Still, the technique will bring those who practice it closer to this final understanding.

The **Delphi Oracle** is said to have pronounced Socrates the wisest of people. (An oracle is a shrine where a priest delivers a god's response to a human question. The most famous oracle of all time was the Delphi Oracle, which was housed in the great temple to Apollo in ancient and Hellenistic Greece.) Socrates thought the pronouncement referred to the fact that he, unlike most people, was *aware* of his ignorance. Applying the Socratic method, one gets good at seeing misconceptions and learning to recognize one's own ignorance.

Socrates was not a pest who went around trapping people in argument and making them look idiotic. He was famous not only for his dialectical skill but also for his courage and stamina in battle. He staunchly opposed injustice, even at considerable risk to himself. His trial and subsequent death by drinking hemlock after his conviction (for "corrupting" young men and not believing in the city's gods) are reported by Plato in the gripping dialogues *Apology, Crito,* and *Phaedo.* These dialogues portray Socrates as an individual of impressive character and true grit. Although it would have been easy for him to escape from prison, he did not do so, because, according to Plato, by having chosen to live in Athens he had implicitly promised to obey the laws of the city.

Richard Robinson summarizes the greatest value of Socrates, as we perceive him through Plato, as lying in Socrates' clear conception of the demands placed on us by reason:

> [Socrates] impresses us, more than any other figure in literature, with the supreme importance of thinking as well as possible and making our actions conform to our thoughts. To this end he preaches the knowledge of one's own starting-points, the hypothetical entertainment of opinions, the exploration of their consequences and connections, the willingness to follow the argument wherever it leads, the public confession of one's thoughts, the invitation to others to criticize, the readiness to reconsider, and at the same time firm action in accordance with one's present beliefs. Plato's *Apology* has in fact made Socrates the chief martyr of reason as the gospels have made Jesus the chief martyr of faith.

PLATO

When we pause to consider the great minds of Western history, those rare individuals whose insight elevates the human intellect by a prodigious leap, we think immediately of Socrates' most famous student, **Plato** (c. 428–347 B.C.E.), and Plato's student, Aristotle (384–322 B.C.E.). Both Plato and Aristotle were interested in practically every subject, and each spoke intelligently on philosophical topics and problems. Platonic metaphysics formed the model for Christian theology for fifteen centuries. This model was superseded only when translations of Aristotle's works were rediscovered by European philosophers and theologians in the thirteenth century A.D. After this rediscovery, Aristotle's metaphysics came to predominate in Christian thinking, although Christianity is still Platonic in many, many ways.

Plato's Metaphysics: The Theory of Forms

Plato's metaphysics is known as the **Theory of Forms,** and it is discussed in several of the two dozen compositions we have referred to as **Plato's dialogues.** The most famous dialogue is the *Republic*, from the so-called middle period of Plato's writings, during which Plato reached the peak of his genius. The *Republic* also gives Plato's best-known account of the Theory of Forms.

According to Plato's Theory of Forms, what is truly real is not the objects we encounter in sensory experience but, rather, **Forms,** and these can only be grasped intellectually. Therefore, once you know what Plato's Forms are, you will understand the Theory of Forms and the essentials of Platonic metaphysics. Unfortunately, it is not safe to assume Plato had *exactly* the same thing in mind throughout his life when he spoke of the Forms. Nevertheless, Plato's concept is pretty clear and can be illustrated with an example or two.

The Greeks were excellent geometers, which is not surprising, because they invented the subject as a systematic science. Now, when a Greek geometer demonstrated some property of, say, *circularity*, he was not demonstrating the property of

PROFILE: Aristocles, a.k.a. Plato (c. 428–347 B.C.E.)

Plato was the nickname of an Athenian whose true name was Aristocles. The nickname, which means "broad shoulders," stuck, and so did this man's philosophy. Few individuals, if any, have had more influence on Western thought than Plato.

Plato initially studied with Cratylus, who was a follower of Heraclitus, and then with Socrates. He was also influenced by the Pythagoreans, from whom he may have derived his great respect for mathematics. Plato thought that the study of mathematics was a necessary introduction to philosophy, and it is said that he expelled from his Academy students who had difficulty with mathematical concepts.

Plato founded his Academy in 387, and it was the first multisubject, multiteacher institution of higher learning in Western civilization. The Academy survived for nine centuries, until the emperor Justinian closed it to protect Christian truth.

Plato's dialogues are divided into three groups. According to recent respected scholarship, the

Portrait of Plato. Eyes were not the artist's specialty, perhaps.

earliest include most importantly the *Apology,* which depicts and philosophically examines Socrates' trial and execution; the *Meno,* which is concerned with whether virtue can be taught; the *Gorgias,* which concerns the nature of right and wrong; and the first book of the *Republic.* The dialogues from the middle period include the remaining books of the *Republic, Phaedo, Symposium, Phaedrus, Cratylus, Parmenides,* and *Theaetetus.* In the most famous of these, the *Republic,* Plato explains and interrelates his conceptions of justice, the ideal state, and the Theory of Forms. Plato's later dialogues include most notably the *Timaeus,* which is Plato's account of the creation of the universe; the *Sophist,* which examines the nature of nonbeing; and the *Laws,* which is concerned with what laws a good constitution should contain. The *Laws* is Plato's longest dialogue and the only dialogue in which Socrates is not present.

something that could actually be found in the physical world. After all, you do not find circularity in the physical world: what you find are *things*—various round objects—that approach perfect circularity but are not *perfectly* circular. Even if you are drawing circles with an excellent compass and are paying close attention to what you are drawing, your "circle" is not perfectly circular. Thus, when a geometer discovered a property of circularity, for example, he was discovering something about an *ideal* thing. Circularity does not exist in the physical world. Circularity, then, is an example of a Form.

Here is another example. Consider two beautiful objects: a beautiful statue and a beautiful house. These are two very different objects, but they have *something* in common—they both qualify as beautiful. Beauty is another example of a Form. Notice that beauty, like circularity, is not something you encounter directly in the physical world. What you encounter in the physical world is always some object or other, a house or a statue or whatever, which may or may not be beautiful. But beauty itself is not something you meet up with; rather, you meet up with *objects* that to varying degrees *possess* beauty or, as Plato said, "participate" in the Form *beauty.* Beauty, like circularity, is an ideal thing, not a concrete thing.

You may be tempted to suppose that the Forms are just ideas or concepts in someone's mind. But this might be a mistake. Before any people were around, there were circular things, logs and round stones and so on—that is, things that came close in varying degrees to being perfectly circular. If there were circular things when there were no people around, or people-heads to have people-ideas in, it would seem that circularity is not just an idea in people's heads. It may be more difficult to suppose that there were beautiful things before there were people to think of things as beautiful, but this difficulty might only be due to assuming that "beauty is in the eyes of the beholder." Whether that assumption truly is justified is actually an unsettled question. (It is a question that belongs to the aesthetics branch of philosophy.)

Sometimes Plato's Forms are referred to as *Ideas,* and the Theory of Forms is also said to be the Theory of Ideas. But *Idea* is misleading because, as you can see, Plato's Forms are not the sort of ideas that exist in people. We will stick with the word *Forms.*

Forms have certain important and unusual features. We will begin by asking, How *old* is circularity? Immediately on hearing the question, you will realize that circularity is not any age. Circular things, sand dollars and bridge abutments and so on, are some age or other. But circularity itself has no age. The same thing is true of beauty, the Form. So we can see that the Forms are ageless, that is, *eternal.*

They are also *unchanging.* A beautiful house may change due to alterations or aging, but that couldn't happen to beauty itself. And you, having learned that the circumference of the circle is equal to π times twice the radius distance, aren't apt to worry that someday the circle may change and, when it does, the circumference will no longer equal $2\pi r$.

Finally, the Forms are *unmoving* and *indivisible.* Indeed, what sense would it make even to suppose that they might move or be physically divided?

When you think of these various characteristics of Forms and remember as well that Plato equated the Forms with true reality, you may begin to see why we stated that Plato's metaphysics formed the model for Christian theology. You may also be reminded, we hope, of what Parmenides said about true being (i.e., that it is eternal, unmoving, unchanging, and indivisible). Of course, you should also remember that for Parmenides there is only one being, but for Plato there are many Forms.

But why did Plato say that only the Forms are truly real? A thing is beautiful only to the extent it participates in the Form *beauty,* just as it is circular only if it participates in the Form *circularity.* Likewise, a thing is large only if it participates in the Form *largeness,* and the same principle would hold for all of a thing's properties. Thus, a large, beautiful, round thing—a beautiful, large, round oak table, for instance—couldn't be beautiful, large, or round if the Forms *beauty, largeness,* and *circularity* did not exist. Indeed, if the Forms *oak* and *table* did not exist, "it" wouldn't even be an oak table. Sensible objects—that is, the things we encounter in sensory experience—are what they are only if they sufficiently participate in their corresponding Forms. Sensible objects owe their reality to the Forms, so the ultimate reality belongs to the Forms.

Many people scold philosophers, mathematicians, and other thinkers for being concerned with abstractions and concepts. "That's all very interesting," they say about some philosophical or mathematical theory, "but I'm more interested in the *real* world." By "real world" they mean the world you experience with your senses. On the face of it, at least, Plato makes a convincing case that that world is *not* the real world at all.

The Cave

In the *Republic,* Plato uses a vivid allegory to explain his two-realms philosophy. He invites us to imagine a cave in which some prisoners are bound so that they can look only at the wall in front of them. Behind them is a fire whose light casts shadows of various objects on the wall in front of the prisoners. Because the prisoners cannot see the objects themselves, they regard the shadows they see as the true reality. One of the prisoners eventually escapes from the cave and, in the light of the sun, sees real objects for the first time, becoming aware of the big difference between them and the shadow images he had always taken for reality.

The cave, obviously, represents the world we see and experience with our senses, and the world of sunlight represents the realm of Forms. The prisoners represent ordinary people, who, in taking the shadows to be the real world, are condemned to darkness, error, ignorance, and illusion. The escaped prisoner represents the philosopher, who has seen light, truth, beauty, knowledge, and true reality.

Of course, if the philosopher returns to the cave to tell the prisoners how things really are, they will think his brain has been addled. This difficulty is sometimes faced by those who have seen the truth and decide to tell others about it.

Plato was aware that there is a sense in which the objects we see and touch are real. Even appearances are *real* appearances. But Plato's position is that the objects we see and touch have a *lesser* reality because they can only approximate their Form and thus are always to some extent flawed. Any particular beautiful thing will always be deficient in beauty compared with the Form *beauty.* And, as any particular beautiful thing owes whatever degree of beauty it has to the Form *beauty,* the Form is the source of what limited reality as a beautiful thing the thing has.

Thus, Plato introduced into Western thought a *two-realms* concept. On one hand, there is the realm of particular, changing, sense-perceptible or "sensible" things. This realm Plato likened to a cave (see the box "The Cave"). It is the realm of flawed and lesser entities. Consequently, it is also, for those who concern themselves with sensible things, a source of error, illusion, and ignorance. On the other hand, there is the realm of Forms—eternal, fixed, and perfect—the source of all reality and of all true knowledge. This **Platonic dualism** was incorporated into Christianity and transmitted through the ages to our thought today, where it lingers still and affects our views on virtually every subject.

Now, Plato believed that some forms, especially the Forms *truth, beauty,* and *goodness,* are of a higher order than other Forms. For example, you can say of the Form *circularity* that it is beautiful, but you cannot say of the Form *beauty* that it is circular. So the Form *beauty* is higher than the Form *circularity.* This fact will turn out to be very important when we consider Plato's ethics in the second part of this book. Also, as we shall see in Part Two, Plato connected his Theory of Forms with a theory of the ideal state.

Plato's Theory of Knowledge

The first comprehensive theory of knowledge in philosophy was Plato's. Certainly many of his predecessors had implicit theories of knowledge, and some of them spoke explicitly on epistemological subjects. Some were quite skeptical. A **skeptic**

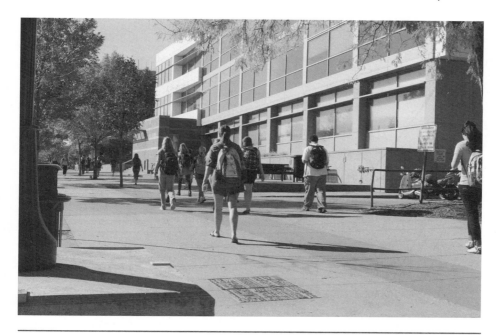

Today's universities all descended from Plato's Academy.

is a doubter, a person who doubts that knowledge is possible. Xenophanes (c. 570–480 B.C.E.) declared that, even if truth were stated, it would not be known. Heraclitus (c. 535–475 B.C.E.), whom we talked about earlier, was a contemporary of Xenophanes. He had the idea that, just as you cannot step into the same river twice, everything is in flux; this theory suggests it is impossible to discover any fixed truth beyond what is expressed in the theory itself. (Heraclitus, however, apparently did not himself deduce skeptical conclusions from his metaphysical theory.) Cratylus, a younger contemporary of Socrates (470–399 B.C.E.), carried this flux theory even further, arguing that you cannot step even once into the "same" river, because with each passing moment there is a new river. And, for that matter, a new "you." As if that were not enough, he said that our words themselves change in their meaning as we speak them, and therefore true communication is impossible. Likewise impossible, one would think, would be knowledge. Cratylus, it is said, largely abstained from conversation and merely wiggled his finger when someone spoke to him, figuring that his understanding of words he heard must necessarily be different from the meaning the speaker intended.

Skeptical themes are also found in the pronouncements of the Sophists. If you were a citizen of Athens and wanted to be influential, you needed to be trained by a Sophist, who could devise an argument to back up any claim. Because the Sophists could make a plausible case for any position, they seemed to show that one idea is as valid as the next, a theory that supports skepticism.

Gorgias (c. 485–380 B.C.E.), one particularly famous Sophist, said: "There is no reality, and if there were, we could not know of it, and even if we could, we

In Plato's Myth of the Cave, a group of prisoners are placed so they can see, on the wall of the cave, only shadows of objects carried back and forth in front of a fire behind them. Because the shadows are all they see, the prisoners assume them to be reality.

could not communicate our knowledge." This statement parallels that of Xenophanes just mentioned.

The best-known Sophist philosopher of all, Protagoras (c. 485–410 B.C.E.), said that "man is the measure of all things." This can be interpreted—and was interpreted by Plato—as meaning that there is no absolute knowledge: one person's views about the world are as valid as the next person's. Plato argued strenuously against this theory. In his dialogue *Theaetetus*, Plato pointed out that, if Protagoras is correct, and one person's views really are as valid as the next person's, then the person who views Protagoras's theory as false has a valid view. To this day beginning philosophy students subscribe to Protagoras's theory (without knowing it is Protagoras's theory), and to this day philosophy instructors use Plato's argument against it.

In the *Theaetetus*, Plato also tried to show that another popular idea about knowledge is mistaken. This is the idea that knowledge may be equated with sense perception. Plato had several reasons for thinking this equation is false.

One reason for thinking that knowledge is not just sense perception is the fact that knowledge clearly involves more than sense perception. For example, sense perception by itself tells us a straight stick stuck in water is bent—*thinking* is required for us to know the stick is actually straight. Further, just to know the stick *exists* or is of a certain *length* involves thought. Visual sensations give you colored expanses, auditory sensations give you sounds, but existence itself is a concept that cuts across several senses simultaneously and is supplied by thought. Judgments of length, for example, involve making comparisons with rulers or tape measures, and comparing is a mental activity.

Another reason knowledge is not just sense perception is that you can retain knowledge even *after* you are no longer sensing a thing. Finally, and even more important, in Plato's view true knowledge is knowledge of what *is*. Because the objects of sense perception are always changing (remember Heraclitus?), sense perception and knowledge cannot be one and the same.

True knowledge, Plato was certain, must be concerned with what is *truly real*. This means, of course, that the objects of true knowledge are the Forms because the objects of sense perception are real only to the extent that they "participate" in the Forms.

This, then, is essentially Plato's theory of knowledge, and he elaborated on it in the *Republic*—especially in a passage known as the **Theory of the Divided Line** and in the **Myth of the Cave.**

The Theory of the Divided Line is used by Plato to contrast knowledge, on one hand, with mere belief or opinion, on the other. Plato illustrates his theory by dividing a vertical line in two parts. The upper part of the line stands for knowledge, and the lower part stands for belief (opinion). Knowledge is concerned with absolutes— absolute beauty, absolute good, and so forth—in short, with the Forms. And this is not unreasonable of Plato. If your "knowledge" of beauty or goodness or circularity or the like is limited to this or that beautiful car or good deed or round plate, then you really do not have knowledge of *absolute* beauty, goodness, or circularity. At best you have a bunch of opinions that, as they are as likely as not to be riddled with error, come closer to *ignorance* than to true knowledge.

In Plato's Divided Line, the upper part of the line represents knowledge and the lower part represents opinion. Plato also subdivided the knowledge section of the line into two parts and did the same for the opinion section. (How these further subdivisions are to be understood is a matter of controversy.) What is essential to remember is that, according to Plato, the highest form of knowledge is that obtained through the *use of reason* because perfect beauty or absolute goodness or the ideal triangle cannot be perceived.

Plato's Theory of Love and Becoming

As mentioned earlier, knowledge is true ultimately because it is knowledge of what is. Plato believed that it is not enough to know the truth; rather, a person must also become that truth. This is where Plato's epistemology, or theory of truth, becomes a metaphysics, or theory of being. To know, for Plato, is to be. The more you know, the more you are and the better you are.

Plato began, as we saw, with the Myth of the Cave, which shows how and why human beings are in the dark about the truth of things. And this ignorance is almost universal—even Socrates admits that he has no knowledge. What allows humans eventually to come into the light of day regarding the truth of things is the Forms. Each individual has in his or her immortal soul a perfect set of Forms that can be remembered (*anamnesis*), and only this constitutes true knowledge. To remember the Forms is to know the absolute truth and simultaneously to become just and wise. Through the Forms, all skeptical doubts are laid to rest and the individual becomes good in the process. This way of thinking is so powerful and compelling that twentieth-century philosopher Martin Heidegger suggested that all Western philosophy since Plato is but a variety of Platonism.

Plato believed in two radically separate spheres: the realm of shadows or imperfect, changing beings and the realm of perfect, eternal, unchanging Forms. The problem is, how do we get out of the cave to the perfect world of Forms? In his dialogue *The Symposium*, Plato postulated the notion of love as the way in which a person can go from the state of imperfection and ignorance to the state of perfection and true knowledge. He defined love as a longing for and a striving to attain the object of longing. Love is that which seeks to possess the beautiful and to recreate in beauty. Human beings love to love: they truly come alive only in seeking a beloved, whether that beloved is another human being or an idea or health or money.

For Plato, love is meant to be the force that brings all things together and makes them beautiful. It is the way by which all beings, but especially human beings, can ascend to higher stages of self-realization and perfection. Plato's love begins as an experience of lacking something. Love provokes both thought and effort in the pursuit of what is lacking. The deeper the thought, the greater the love.

Plato initially mirrored the Athenian view that the deepest human relationships were between two men, usually an older man and a younger one. Women were not only considered the weaker sex but were also thought to be superficial, excitable, and superstitious. Marriage had as its purpose the reproduction and raising of children, and physical lovemaking was considered a low form of love. Plato's love does not exclude physical beauty, but "Platonic love" begins at a higher stage of development, namely, with the sharing of beautiful thoughts with a beautiful person. Plato believed that this kind of love should be experienced while a person is young. It is this intellectual or spiritual love that begins the ascent of love, which may eventually lead to the permanent possession of Absolute Beauty or Goodness.

The love for just one other human, even if that person is as noble as a Socrates, remains a limited form of intellectual eros. It is but the first step in the ascent of philosophical love to Absolute Beauty. To reach the higher stages of love means entering what are called the *mysteries*. Plato had Socrates recount a theory of love given to him by a woman named Diotima. Socrates implies that few may be able to follow this line of reasoning, which he himself has difficulty comprehending, but Diotima's theory of love was this: The higher forms of love express the will to immortality and the will to produce immortal "children," not merely physical children. All love seeks to possess beauty and to reproduce in beauty, but the creation of immortal children (like the writings of Homer) can grant the author immortality. A first step beyond merely loving a beautiful person and begetting beautiful thoughts lies in the realization that beauty in all things is one and the same and that all love is one. A further step involves the recognition of the superiority of intellectual or spiritual beauty over physical beauty. Then love must expand beyond preoccupations with a particular person to an appreciation of the beauty of moral practices and laws. An individual is part of larger social groupings, each with accompanying obligations.

Love here takes the form of appreciating and aptly participating in organizations such as a city-state like Athens. Yet no matter how wide a person's involvement is in the moral and social spheres of love, this still does not represent the highest and most inclusive love. A person begins to glimpse the all-inclusive, all-uniting kind of love by first seeing the beauty of knowledge as a whole or at least many of the different forms of knowledge. This leads to an appreciation and love of the whole realm of beauty or the integrated beauty of everything there is. In the happiness of viewing such vast beauty, a person will have beautiful thoughts and be able to speak beautiful words. Eventually such a person may be able to make the final leap to the beauty and truth, which is beyond all mortal things.

The last and highest stage of love lies in the discovery of the ultimate mystery, Absolute Beauty itself. The beauty of this being contains no change of any kind. It was never born and will never die, nor will it increase or decrease. It is not good in one part and bad in another. It is perfect and one with itself forever. All imperfect things participate in this Beauty, thereby receiving a modicum of fulfillment and self-realization. Plato indicated that once a person has seen Absolute Beauty, then such a fortunate person would no longer be dazzled by mere physical beauty or the other rubbish of mortality. This, for human beings, is the ultimate kind of immortality, he thought.

Thus, love for Plato is the ultimate way of knowing and realizing truth. For mortals, love is a process of seeking higher stages of being: physical love begets mortal children; intellectual or spiritual love begets immortal children. The greater the love, the more it will contain an intellectual component. The lifelong longing and pursuit seeks ever higher stages of love so that it can eventually lead to the possession of Absolute Beauty. This is the pursuit that motivates the highest sorts of human beings and that transforms entire civilizations. To love the highest is to become the best.

SELECTION 3.1

Apology★

Plato

[*In 399 B.C.E., Socrates was sentenced to death by an Athenian court for impiety and corrupting the youth of Athens. This excerpt is from Plato's dialogue* Apology, *in which Socrates is seen defending himself.*]

I will make my defense, and I will try in the short time allowed to do away with this evil opinion of me

★ From Christopher Biffle, *A Guided Tour of Five Works by Plato*, 3rd edition. Mountain View, CA: Mayfield, 2001, pp. 36–40. Based on the nineteenth-century translation by Benjamin Jowett. Copyright © 2001 by The McGraw-Hill Companies, Inc. Reprinted with permission from The McGraw-Hill Companies.

which you have held for such a long time. I hope I may succeed, if this be well for you and me, and that my words may find favor with you. But I know to accomplish this is not easy—I see the nature of the task. Let the event be as the gods will; in obedience to the law I make my defense.

I will begin at the beginning and ask what the accusation is which has given rise to this slander of me and which has encouraged Meletus to proceed against me. What do the slanderers say? They shall be my prosecutors and I will sum up their words in an affidavit. "Socrates is an evil-doer and a curious person, who searches into things under the earth and in the heavens. He makes the weaker argument defeat the stronger and he teaches these doctrines to others." That is the nature of the accusation and that is what you have seen in the comedy of Aristophanes. He introduced a man whom he calls Socrates, going about and saying he can walk in the air and talking a lot of nonsense concerning matters which I do not pretend to know anything about—however, I mean to say nothing disparaging of anyone who is a student of such knowledge. I should be very sorry if Meletus could add that to my charge. But the simple truth is, O Athenians, I have nothing to do with these studies. Very many of those here are witnesses to the truth of this and to them I appeal. Speak then, you who have heard me, and tell your neighbors whether any of you ever heard me hold forth in few words or in many upon matters of this sort. . . . You hear their answer. And from what they say you will be able to judge the truth of the rest.

There is the same foundation for the report I am a teacher and take money; that is no more true than the other. Although, if a man is able to teach, I honor him for being paid. There are Gorgias of Leontium, Prodicus of Ceos, and Hippias of Elis, who go round the cities and are able to persuade young men to leave their own citizens, by whom they might be taught for nothing, and come to them, whom they not only pay but are also thankful if they may be allowed to pay them.

There is actually a Parian philosopher residing in Athens who charges fees. I came to hear of him in this way: I met a man who spent a world of money on the sophists, Callias, the son of Hipponicus, and knowing he had sons, I asked him: "Callias," I said, "if your two sons were foals or calves, there would be no difficulty in finding someone to raise them. We would hire a trainer of horses, or a farmer probably, who would improve and perfect them in their own proper virtue and excellence. But, as they are human beings, whom are you thinking of placing over them? Is there anyone who understands human and political virtue? You must have thought about this because you have sons. Is there anyone?"

"There is," he said.

"Who is he?" said I. "And of what country? And what does he charge?"

"Evenus the Parian," he replied. "He is the man and his charge is five minae."

Happy is Evenus, I said to myself, if he really has this wisdom and teaches at such a modest charge. Had I the same, I would have been very proud and conceited; but the truth is I have no knowledge like this, O Athenians.

I am sure someone will ask the question, "Why is this, Socrates, and what is the origin of these accusations of you; for there must have been something strange which you have been doing? All this great fame and talk about you would never have come up if you had been like other men. Tell us then, why this is, as we should be sorry to judge you too quickly."

I regard this as a fair challenge, and I will try to explain to you the origin of this name of "wise" and of this evil fame. Please attend then and although some of you may think I am joking, I declare I will tell you the entire truth. Men of Athens, this reputation of mine has come from a certain kind of wisdom which I possess. If you ask me what kind of wisdom, I reply, such wisdom as is attainable by man, for to that extent I am inclined to believe I am wise. Whereas the persons of whom I was speaking have a superhuman wisdom which I may fail to describe, because I do not have it. He who says I have, speaks false and slanders me.

O men of Athens, I must beg you not to interrupt me, even if I seem to say something extravagant. For the word which I will speak is not mine. I will refer you to a wisdom which is worthy of credit and will tell you about my wisdom—whether I have any and of what sort—and that witness shall be the god of Delphi. You must have known Chaerephon. He was a friend of mine and also a friend of yours, for he shared in the exile of the people and returned with you. Well, Chaerephon, as you know, was very impetuous in all his doings, and he went to Delphi and boldly asked the oracle to tell him whether—as I said, I must beg you not to interrupt—he asked the oracle to tell him whether there was anyone wiser than I was. The Pythian prophetess answered, there was no man wiser. Chaerephon is dead himself but his brother, who is in court, will confirm the truth of this story.

Why do I mention this? Because I am going to explain to you why I have such an evil name. When I heard the answer, I said to myself, "What can the god mean and what is the interpretation of this riddle? I know I have no wisdom, great or small. What can he mean when he says I am the wisest of men? And yet he is a god and cannot lie; that would be against his nature." After long consideration, I at last thought of a method of answering the question.

MAKING PHILOSOPHY ACCESSIBLE: POP-UP PLATO

S. HARRIS

I reflected if I could only find a man wiser than myself, then I might go to the god with a refutation in my hand. I would say to him, "Here is a man who is wiser than I am, but you said I was the wisest." Accordingly I went to one who had the reputation of wisdom and observed him—his name I need not mention; he was a politician whom I selected for examination. When I began to talk with him I could not help thinking he was not really wise, although he was thought wise by many and wiser still by himself. I tried to explain to him that he thought himself wise but was not really wise. The result was he hated me, and his hatred was shared by several who were present and heard me. So I left him, saying to myself, as I went away: "Well, although I do not suppose either of us knows anything really beautiful and good, I am better off than he is—for he knows nothing and thinks that he knows. I neither know nor think that I know. In this latter, then, I seem to have an advantage over him." Then I went to another who had still higher philosophical pretensions, and my conclusion was exactly the same. I made another enemy of him and of many others besides him.

After this I went to one man after another, being aware of the anger that I provoked; and I lamented and feared this, but necessity was laid upon me. The word of the god, I thought, ought to be considered first. And I said to myself, "I must go to all who appear to know and find out the meaning of the oracle." And I swear to you Athenians, by the dog, I swear, the result of my mission was this: I found the men with the highest reputations were all nearly the most foolish and some inferior men were really wiser and better.

I will tell you the tale of my wanderings and of the Herculean labors, as I may call them, which I endured only to find at last the oracle was right. When I left the politicians, I went to the poets: tragic, dithyrambic, and all sorts. There, I said to myself, you will be detected. Now you will find out you are more ignorant than they are. Accordingly, I took them some of the most elaborate passages in their own writings and asked what was the meaning of them—thinking the poets would teach me something. Will you believe me? I am almost ashamed to say this, but I must say there is hardly a person present who would not have talked better about their poetry than the poets did themselves. That quickly showed me poets do not write poetry by wisdom, but by a sort of inspiration. They are like soothsayers who also say many fine things, but do not understand the meaning of what they say. The poets appeared to me to be much the same, and I further observed that upon the strength of their poetry they believed themselves to be the wisest of men in other things in which they were not wise. So I departed, conceiving myself to be superior to them for the same reason I was superior to the politicians.

At last I went to the artisans, because I was conscious I knew nothing at all, and I was sure they knew many fine things. In this I was not mistaken, for they did know many things of which I was ignorant, and in this they certainly were wiser than I was. But I observed even the good artisans fell into the same error as the poets. Because they were good workmen, they thought they also knew all sorts of high matters, and this defect in them overshadowed their wisdom. Therefore, I asked myself on behalf of the oracle whether I would like to be as I was, having neither their knowledge nor their ignorance, or like them in both. I answered myself and the oracle that I was better off as I was.

This investigation led to my having many enemies of the worst and most dangerous kind and has given rise also to many falsehoods. I am called wise because my listeners always imagine I possess the wisdom which I do not find in others. The truth is, O men of Athens, the gods only are wise and in this oracle they mean to say wisdom of men is little or nothing. They are not speaking of Socrates, only using my name as an illustration, as if they said, "He, O men, is the wisest who, like Socrates, knows his wisdom is in truth worth nothing." And so I go my way, obedient to the gods, and seek wisdom of anyone, whether citizen or stranger, who appears to be wise. If he is not wise, then in support of the oracle I show him he is not wise. This occupation quite absorbs me, and I have no time to give either to any public matter of interest or to any concern of my own, but I am in utter poverty by reason of my devotion to the gods.

There is another thing. Young men of the richer classes, who have little to do, gather around me of their own accord. They like to hear the pretenders examined. They often imitate me and examine others themselves. There are plenty of persons, as they soon enough discover, who think they know something, but really know little or nothing. Then those who are examined by the young men, instead of being angry with themselves, are angry with me. "This confounded Socrates," they say, "this villainous misleader of youth!" Then if somebody asks them, "Why, what evil does he practice or teach?," they do not know and cannot tell. But so they may not appear ignorant, they repeat the ready-made charges which are used against all

philosophers about teaching things up in the clouds and under the earth, and having no gods, and making the worse argument defeat the stronger. They do not like to confess their pretense to knowledge has been detected, which it has. They are numerous, ambitious, energetic and are all in battle array and have persuasive tongues. They have filled your ears with their loud and determined slanders. This is the reason why my three accusers, Meletus and Anytus and Lycon, have set upon me. Meletus has a quarrel with me on behalf of the poets, Anytus, on behalf of the craftsmen, Lycon, on behalf of the orators. As I said at the beginning, I cannot expect to get rid of this mass of slander all in a moment.

This, O men of Athens, is the truth and the whole truth. I have concealed nothing. And yet I know this plainness of speech makes my accusers hate me, and what is their hatred but a proof that I am speaking the truth? This is the reason for their slander of me, as you will find out either in this or in any future inquiry.

SELECTION 3.2
Republic★

Plato

[*Plato's dialogue* Republic *is one of the most widely read Western books of all time. In this selection, Plato compares Goodness (or the Good) to the sun, sets forth his famous Theory of the Divided Line, and explains the Myth of the Cave.*]

Glaucon: But, Socrates, what is your own account of the Good? Is it knowledge, or pleasure, or something else? . . .

              . . .

S: . . . First we must come to an understanding. Let me remind you of the distinction we drew earlier and have often drawn on other occasions, between the multiplicity of things that we call good or beautiful or whatever it may

be and, on the other hand, Goodness itself or Beauty itself and so on. Corresponding to each of these sets of many things, we postulate a single Form or real essence, as we call it.

G: Yes, that is so.

S: Further, the many things, we say, can be seen, but are not objects of rational thought; whereas the Forms are objects of thought, but invisible.

G: Yes, certainly.

S: And we see things with our eyesight, just as we hear sounds with our ears and, to speak generally, perceive any sensible thing with our sense-faculties.

G: Of course.

S: Have you noticed, then, that the artificer who designed the senses has been exceptionally lavish of his materials in making the eyes able to see and their objects visible?

★ From *The Republic of Plato*, translated by Francis McDonald Cornford (Oxford: Clarendon Press, 1941). By permission of Oxford University Press.

G: That never occurred to me.

S: Well, look at it in this way. Hearing and sound do not stand in need of any third thing, without which the ear will not hear nor sound be heard; and I think the same is true of most, not to say all, of the other senses. Can you think of one that does require anything of the sort?

G: No, I cannot.

S: But there is this need in the case of sight and its objects. You may have the power of vision in your eyes and try to use it, and colour may be there in the objects; but sight will see nothing and the colours will remain invisible in the absence of a third thing peculiarly constituted to serve this very purpose.

G: By which you mean?

S: Naturally I mean what you call light; and if light is a thing of value, the sense of sight and the power of being visible are linked together by a very precious bond, such as unites no other sense with its object.

G: No one could say that light is not a precious thing.

S: And of all the divinities in the skies is there one whose light, above all the rest, is responsible for making our eyes see perfectly and making objects perfectly visible?

G: There can be no two opinions: of course you mean the Sun.

S: And how is sight related to this deity? Neither sight nor the eye which contains it is the Sun, but of all the sense-organs it is the most sun-like; and further, the power it possesses is dispensed by the Sun, like a stream flooding the eye. And again, the Sun is not vision, but it is the cause of vision and also is seen by the vision it causes.

G: Yes.

S: It was the Sun, then, that I meant when I spoke of that offspring which the Good has created in the visible world, to stand there in the same relation to vision and visible things as that which the Good itself bears in the intelligible world to intelligence and to intelligible objects.

G: How is that? You must explain further.

S: You know what happens when the colours of things are no longer irradiated by the daylight, but only by the fainter luminaries of the night: when you look at them, the eyes are dim and seem almost blind, as if there were no unclouded vision in them. But when you look at things on which the Sun is shining, the same eyes see distinctly and it becomes evident that they do contain the power of vision.

G: Certainly.

S: Apply this comparison, then, to the soul. When its gaze is fixed upon an object irradiated by truth and reality, the soul gains understanding and knowledge and is manifestly in possession of intelligence. But when it looks towards that twilight world of things that come into existence and pass away, its sight is dim and it has only opinions and beliefs which shift to and fro, and now it seems like a thing that has no intelligence.

G: That is true.

S: This, then, which gives to the objects of knowledge their truth and to him who knows them his power of knowing, is the Form or essential nature of Goodness. It is the cause of knowledge and truth; and so, while you may think of it as an object of knowledge, you will do well to regard it as something beyond truth and knowledge and, precious as these both are, of still higher worth. And, just as in our analogy light and vision were to be thought of as like the Sun, but not identical with it, so here both knowledge and truth are to be regarded as like the Good, but to identify either with the Good is wrong. The Good must hold a yet higher place of honour.

G: You are giving it a position of extraordinary splendour, if it is the source of knowledge and truth and itself surpasses them in worth. You surely cannot mean that it is pleasure.

S: Heaven forbid. But I want to follow up our analogy still further. You will agree that the Sun not only makes the things we see visible, but also brings them into existence and gives them growth and nourishment; yet he is not the same thing as existence. And so with the objects of knowledge: these derive from the Good not only their power of being known, but their very being and reality; and Goodness is not the same thing as being, but even beyond being, surpassing it in dignity and power.

(Glaucon exclaimed with some amusement at my exalting Goodness in such extravagant terms.)

It is your fault; you forced me to say what I think.

G: Yes, and you must not stop there. At any rate, complete your comparison with the Sun, if there is any more to be said.

S: There is a great deal more.

G: Let us hear it, then; don't leave anything out.

S: I am afraid much must be left unspoken. However, I will not, if I can help it, leave out anything that can be said on this occasion.

G: Please do not.

S: Conceive, then, that there are these two powers I speak of, the Good reigning over the domain of all that is intelligible, the Sun over the visible world—or the heaven as I might call it; only you would think I was showing off my skill in etymology. At any rate you have these two orders of things clearly before your mind: the visible and the intelligible?

G: I have.

S: Now take a line divided into two unequal parts, one to represent the visible order, the other the intelligible; and divide each part again in the same proportion, symbolizing degrees of comparative clearness or obscurity. Then (A) one of the two sections in the visible world will stand for images. By images I mean first shadows, and then reflections in water or in close-grained, polished surfaces, and everything of that kind, if you understand.

G: Yes, I understand.

S: Let the second section (B) stand for the actual things of which the first are likenesses, the living creatures about us and all the works of nature or of human hands.

G: So be it.

S: Will you also take the proportion in which the visible world has been divided as corresponding to degrees of reality and truth, so

that the likeness shall stand to the original in the same ratio as the sphere of appearances and belief to the sphere of knowledge?

G: Certainly.

S: Now consider how we are to divide the part which stands for the intelligible world. There are two sections. In the first (C) the mind uses as images those actual things which themselves had images in the visible world; and it is compelled to pursue its inquiry by starting from assumptions and travelling, not up to a principle, but down to a conclusion. In the second (D) the mind moves in the other direction, from an assumption up towards a principle which is not hypothetical; and it makes no use of the images employed in the other section, but only of Forms, and conducts its inquiry solely by their means.

G: I don't quite understand what you mean.

S: Then we will try again; what I have just said will help you to understand. (C) You know, of course, how students of subjects like geometry and arithmetic begin by postulating odd and even numbers, or the various figures and the three kinds of angle, and other such data in each subject. These data they take as known; and, having adopted them as assumptions, they do not feel called upon to give any account of them to themselves or to anyone else, but treat them as self-evident. Then, starting from these assumptions, they go on until they arrive, by a series of consistent steps, at all the conclusions they set out to investigate.

	Objects		States of Mind
Intelligible World	**The Good**		
	Forms	**D**	Intelligence (*noesis*) or Knowledge (*episteme*)
	Mathematical Objects	**C**	Thinking (*dianoia*)
The Visible World	**The Sun**		
	Actual Things	**B**	Belief (*pistis*)
	Images	**A**	Imagining (*eikasia*)

G: Yes, I know that.

S: You also know how they make use of visible figures and discourse about them, though what they really have in mind is the originals of which these figures are images: they are not reasoning, for instance, about this particular square and diagonal which they have drawn, but about *the* Square and *the* Diagonal; and so in all cases. The diagrams they draw and the models they make are actual things, which may have their shadows or images in water; but now they serve in their turn as images, while the student is seeking to behold those realities which only thought can apprehend.

G: True.

S: This, then, is the class of things that I spoke of as intelligible, but with two qualifications: first, that the mind, in studying them, is compelled to employ assumptions, and, because it cannot rise above these, does not travel upwards to a first principle; and second, that it uses as images those actual things which have images of their own in the section below them and which, in comparison with those shadows and reflections, are reputed to be more palpable and valued accordingly.

G: I understand: you mean the subject-matter of geometry and of the kindred arts.

S: (D) Then by the second section of the intelligible world you may understand me to mean all that unaided reasoning apprehends by the power of dialectic, when it treats its assumptions, not as first principles, but as *hypotheses* in the literal sense, things "laid down" like a flight of steps up which it may mount all the way to something that is not hypothetical, the first principle of all; and having grasped this, may turn back and, holding on to the consequences which depend upon it, descend at last to a conclusion, never making use of any sensible object, but only of Forms, moving through Forms from one to another, and ending with Forms.

G: I understand, though not perfectly; for the procedure you describe sounds like an enormous undertaking. But I see that you mean to distinguish the field of intelligible reality studied by dialectic as having a greater certainty and truth than the subject-matter of the "arts," as

they are called, which treat their assumptions as first principles. The students of these arts are, it is true, compelled to exercise thought in contemplating objects which the senses cannot perceive, but because they start from assumptions without going back to a first principle, you do not regard them as gaining true understanding about those objects, although the objects themselves, when connected with a first principle, are intelligible. And I think you would call the state of mind of the students of geometry and other such arts, not intelligence, but thinking, as being something between intelligence and mere acceptance of appearances.

S: You have understood me quite well enough. And now you may take, as corresponding to the four sections, these four states of mind: *intelligence* for the highest, *thinking* for the second, *belief* for the third, and for the last *imagining*. These you may arrange as the terms in a proportion, assigning to each a degree of clearness and certainty corresponding to the measure in which their objects possess truth and reality.

G: I understand and agree with you. I will arrange them as you say.

S: Next, here is a parable to illustrate the degrees in which our nature may be enlightened or unenlightened. Imagine the condition of men living in a sort of cavernous chamber underground, with an entrance open to the light and a long passage all down the cave. Here they have been from childhood, chained by the leg and also by the neck, so that they cannot move and can see only what is in front of them, because the chains will not let them turn their heads. At some distance higher up is the light of a fire burning behind them; and between the prisoners and the fire is a track with a parapet built along it, like the screen at a puppet-show, which hides the performers while they show their puppets over the top.

G: I see.

S: Now behind this parapet imagine persons carrying along various artificial objects, including figures of men and animals in wood or stone or other materials, which project above the parapet. Naturally, some of these persons will be talking, others silent.

G: It is a strange picture, and a strange sort of prisoners.

S: Like ourselves; for in the first place prisoners so confined would have seen nothing of themselves or of one another, except the shadows thrown by the fire-light on the wall of the Cave facing them, would they?

G: Not if all their lives they had been prevented from moving their heads.

S: And they would have seen as little of the objects carried past.

G: Of course.

S: Now, if they could talk to one another, would they not suppose that their words referred only to those passing shadows which they saw?

G: Necessarily.

S: And suppose their prison had an echo from the wall facing them? When one of the people crossing behind them spoke, they could only suppose that the sound came from the shadow passing before their eyes.

G: No doubt.

S: In every way, then, such prisoners would recognize as reality nothing but the shadows of those artificial objects.

G: Inevitably.

S: Now consider what would happen if their release from the chains and the healing of their unwisdom should come about in this way. Suppose one of them set free and forced suddenly to stand up, turn his head, and walk with eyes lifted to the light; all these movements would be painful, and he would be too dazzled to make out the objects whose shadows he had been used to see. What do you think he would say, if someone told him that what he had formerly seen was meaningless illusion, but now, being somewhat nearer to reality and turned towards more real objects, he was getting a truer view? Suppose further that he were shown the various objects being carried by and were made to say, in reply to questions, what each of them was. Would he not be perplexed and believe the objects now shown him to be not so real as what he formerly saw?

G: Yes, not nearly so real.

S: And if he were forced to look at the fire-light itself, would not his eyes ache, so that he would try to escape and turn back to the things which he could see distinctly, convinced that they really were clearer than these other objects now being shown to him?

G: Yes.

S: And suppose someone were to drag him away forcibly up the steep and rugged ascent and not let him go until he had hauled him out into the sunlight, would he not suffer pain and vexation at such treatment, and, when he had come out into the light, find his eyes so full of its radiance that he could not see a single one of the things that he was now told were real?

G: Certainly he would not see them all at once.

S: He would need, then, to grow accustomed before he could see things in that upper world. At first it would be easiest to make out shadows, and then the images of men and things reflected in water, and later on the things themselves. After that, it would be easier to watch the heavenly bodies and the sky itself by night, looking at the light of the moon and stars rather than the Sun and the Sun's light in the day-time.

G: Yes, surely.

S: Last of all, he would be able to look at the Sun and contemplate its nature, not as it appears when reflected in water or any alien medium, but as it is in itself in its own domain.

G: No doubt.

S: And now he would begin to draw the conclusion that it is the Sun that produces the seasons and the course of the year and controls everything in the visible world, and moreover is in a way the cause of all that he and his companions used to see.

G: Clearly he would come at last to that conclusion.

S: Then if he called to mind his fellow prisoners and what passed for wisdom in his former dwelling-place, he would surely think himself happy in the change and be sorry for them. They may have had a practice of honouring and commending one another, with prizes for the man who had the keenest eye for the passing shadows and the best memory for the order in which they followed or accompanied one another, so that he could make a good guess as to which was going to come next. Would our released prisoner be likely to covet those prizes or to envy the men exalted to honour and power in the Cave? Would he not feel like Homer's Achilles, that he would far sooner "be on earth as a hired servant in the house of a landless man" or endure anything rather than go back to his old beliefs and live in the old way?

G: Yes, he would prefer any fate to such a life.

S: Now imagine what would happen if he went down again to take his former seat in the Cave. Coming suddenly out of the sunlight, his eyes would be filled with darkness. He might be required once more to deliver his opinion on those shadows, in competition with the prisoners who had never been released, while his eyesight was still dim and unsteady; and it might take some time to become used to the darkness. They would laugh at him and say that he had gone up only to come back with his sight ruined; it was worth no one's while even to attempt the ascent. If they could lay hands on the man who was trying to set them free and lead them up, they would kill him.

G: Yes, they would.

S: Every feature in this parable, my dear Glaucon, is meant to fit our earlier analysis. The prison dwelling corresponds to the region revealed to us through the sense of sight, and the fire-light within it to the power of the Sun. The ascent to see the things in the upper world you may take as standing for the upward journey of the soul into the region of the intelligible; then you will be in possession of what I surmise, since that is what you wish to be told. Heaven knows whether it is true; but this, at any rate, is how it appears to me. In the world of knowledge, the last thing to be perceived and only with great difficulty is the essential Form of Goodness. Once it is perceived, the conclusion must follow that, for all things, this is the cause of whatever is right and good; in the visible world it gives birth to light and to the lord of light, while it is itself sovereign in the intelligible world and the parent of intelligence and truth. Without having had a vision of this Form no one can act with wisdom, either in his own life or in matters of state.

G: So far as I can understand, I share your belief.

S: Then you may also agree that it is no wonder if those who have reached this height are reluctant to manage the affairs of men. Their souls long to spend all their time in that upper world—naturally enough, if here once more our parable holds true. Nor, again, is it at all strange that one who comes from the contemplation of divine things to the miseries of human life should appear awkward and ridiculous when, with eyes still dazed and not yet accustomed to the darkness, he is compelled, in a law-court or elsewhere, to dispute about the shadows of justice or the images that cast those shadows, and to wrangle over the notions of what is right in the minds of men who have never beheld Justice itself.

G: It is not at all strange.

S: No; a sensible man will remember that the eyes may be confused in two ways—by a change from light to darkness or from darkness to light; and he will recognize that the same thing happens to the soul. When he sees it troubled and unable to discern anything clearly, instead of laughing thoughtlessly, he will ask whether, coming from a brighter existence, its unaccustomed vision is obscured by the darkness, in which case he will think its condition enviable and its life a happy one; or whether, emerging from the depths of ignorance, it is dazzled by excess of light. If so, he will rather feel sorry for it; or, if he were inclined to laugh, that would be less ridiculous than to laugh at the soul which has come down from the light.

G: That is a fair statement.

S: If this is true, then, we must conclude that education is not what it is said to be by some, who profess to put knowledge into a soul which does not possess it, as if they could put sight into blind eyes. On the contrary, our own account signifies that the soul of every man does possess the power of learning the truth and the organ to see it with; and that, just as one might have to turn the whole body round in order that the eye should see light instead of darkness, so the entire soul must be turned away from this changing world, until its eye can bear to contemplate reality and that supreme splendour which we have called the Good. Hence there may well be an art whose aim would be to effect this very thing, the conversion of the soul, in the readiest way; not to put the power of sight into the soul's eye, which already has it, but to ensure that, instead of looking in the wrong direction, it is turned the way it ought to be.

G: Yes, it may well be so.

S: It looks, then, as though wisdom were different from those ordinary virtues, as they are called, which are not far removed from bodily qualities, in that they can be produced by habituation and exercise in a soul which has not possessed them from the first. Wisdom, it seems, is certainly the virtue of some diviner faculty, which never loses its power, though its use for good or harm depends on the direction towards which it is turned. You must have noticed in dishonest men with a reputation for sagacity the shrewd glance of a narrow intelligence piercing the objects to which it is directed. There is nothing wrong with their power of vision, but it has been forced into the service of evil, so that the keener its sight, the more harm it works.

G: Quite true.

S: And yet if the growth of a nature like this had been pruned from earliest childhood, cleared of those clinging overgrowths which come of gluttony and all luxurious pleasure and, like leaden weights charged with affinity to this mortal world, hang upon the soul, bending its vision downwards; if, freed from these, the soul were turned round towards true reality, then this same power in these very men would see the truth as keenly as the objects it is turned to now.

G: Yes, very likely.

S: Is it not also likely, or indeed certain after what has been said, that a state can never be properly governed either by the uneducated who know nothing of truth or by men who are allowed to spend all their days in the pursuit of culture? The ignorant have no single mark before their eyes at which they must aim in all the conduct of their own lives and of affairs of state; and the others will not engage in action if they can help it, dreaming that while still alive, they have been translated to the Islands of the Blest.

G: Quite true.

S: It is for us, then, as founders of a commonwealth, to bring compulsion to bear on the noblest natures. They must be made to climb the ascent to the vision of Goodness, which we called the highest object of knowledge; and, when they have looked upon it long enough, they must not be allowed, as they now are, to remain on the heights, refusing to come down again to the prisoners or to take any part in their labours and rewards, however much or little these may be worth.

G: Shall we not be doing them an injustice, if we force on them a worse life than they might have?

S: You have forgotten again, my friend, that the law is not concerned to make any one class specially happy, but to ensure the welfare of the commonwealth as a whole. By persuasion or constraint it will unite the citizens in harmony, making them share whatever benefits each class can contribute to the common good; and its purpose in forming men of that spirit was not that each should be left to go his own way, but that they should be instrumental in binding the community into one.

G: True, I had forgotten.

S: You will see, then, Glaucon, that there will be no real injustice in compelling our philosophers to watch over and care for the other citizens. We can fairly tell them that their compeers in other states may quite reasonably refuse to collaborate: there they have sprung up, like a self-sown plant, in despite of their country's institutions; no one has fostered their growth, and they cannot be expected to show gratitude for a care they have never received. "But," we shall say, "it is not so with you. We have brought you into existence for your country's sake as well as for your own, to be like leaders and king-bees in a hive; you have been better and more thoroughly educated than those others and hence you are more capable of playing your part both as men of thought and as men of action. You must go down, then, each in his turn, to live with the rest and let your eyes grow accustomed to the darkness. You will then see a thousand times better than those who live there always; you will recognize every image for what it is and know what it represents, because you have seen justice, beauty, and goodness in their reality; and so you and we shall find life in our commonwealth no mere dream, as it is in most existing states, where men live fighting one another about shadows and quarrelling for power, as if that were a great prize; whereas in truth government can be at its best and free from dissension only where the destined rulers are least desirous of holding office."

G: Quite true.

S: Then will our pupils refuse to listen and to take their turns at sharing in the work of the community, though they may live together for most of their time in a purer air?

G: No; it is a fair demand, and they are fair-minded men. No doubt, unlike any ruler of the present day, they will think of holding power as an unavoidable necessity.

S: Yes, my friend; for the truth is that you can have a well-governed society only if you can discover for your future rulers a better way of life than being in office; then only will power be in the hands of men who are rich, not in gold, but in the wealth that brings happiness, a good and wise life. All goes wrong when, starved for lack of anything good in their own lives, men turn to public affairs hoping to snatch from thence the happiness they hunger for. They set about fighting for power, and this internecine conflict ruins them and their country. The life of true philosophy is the only one that looks down upon offices of state; and access to power must be confined to men who are not in love with it; otherwise rivals will start fighting. So whom else can you compel to undertake the guardianship of the commonwealth, if not those who, besides understanding best the principles of government, enjoy a nobler life than the politician's and look for rewards of a different kind?

G: There is indeed no other choice. One who holds a true belief without intelligence is just like a blind man who happens to take the right road, isn't he?

SELECTION 3.3
Meno*

Plato

[*In this selection from the dialogue* Meno, *"Socrates" explains another of Plato's theories about knowledge: Knowledge about reality comes from within the soul through a form of "recollection" rather than from without through being taught. The passage also serves to show that, in Plato's opinion, the soul is immortal. In the dialogue, Socrates has a boy who knows nothing of geometry construct a square twice the size of a given square. After one or two failed attempts, the boy succeeds without having been taught how to do it by Socrates. How could he succeed if knowledge of geometry were not already within his soul?*]

Meno: But how will you look for something when you don't in the least know what it is? How on earth are you going to set up something you don't know as the object of your search? To put it another way, even if you come right up against it, how will you know that what you have found is the thing you didn't know?

Socrates: I know what you mean. Do you realize that what you are bringing up is the trick argument that a man cannot try to discover either what he knows or what he does not know? He

* From *Plato, Protagoras and Meno,* translated by W. K. C. Guthrie (London: Penguin Press, 1956), pp. 128–139. Translation copyright © W. K. C. Guthrie, 1956. Reproduced by permission of Penguin Books Ltd.

would not seek what he knows, for since he knows it there is no need of the inquiry, nor what he does not know, for in that case he does not even know what he is to look for.

M: Well, do you think it a good argument?

S: No.

M: Can you explain how it fails?

S: I can. I have heard from men and women who understand the truths of religion—(*Here he presumably pauses to emphasize the solemn change of tone the dialogue undergoes at this point.*)

M: What did they say?

S: Something true, I thought, and fine.

M: What was it, and who were they?

S: Those who tell it are priests and priestesses of the sort who make it their business to be able to account for the functions which they perform. Pindar speaks of it too, and many another of the poets who are divinely inspired. What they say is this—see whether you think they are speaking the truth. They say that the soul of man is immortal: at one time it comes to an end—that which is called death—and at another is born again, but is never finally exterminated. . . .

Thus the soul, since it is immortal and has been born many times, and has seen all things both here and in the other world, has learned everything that is. So we need not be surprised if it can recall the knowledge of virtue or anything else which, as we see, it once possessed. All nature is akin, and the soul has learned everything, so that when a man has recalled a single piece of knowledge—*learned* it, in ordinary language—there is no reason why he should not find out all the rest, if he keeps a stout heart and does not grow weary of the search; for seeking and learning are in fact nothing but recollection.

We ought not then to be led astray by the contentious argument you quoted. It would make us lazy, and is music in the ears of weaklings. The other doctrine produces energetic seekers after knowledge; and being convinced of its truth, I am ready, with your help, to inquire into the nature of virtue.

M: I see, Socrates. But what do you mean when you say that we don't learn anything, but that what we call learning is recollection? Can you teach me that it is so?

S: I have just said that you're a rascal, and now you ask me if I can teach you, when I say there is no such thing as teaching, only recollection. Evidently you want to catch me contradicting myself straight away.

M: No, honestly, Socrates, I wasn't thinking of that. It was just habit. If you can in any way make clear to me that what you say is true, please do.

S: It isn't an easy thing, but still I should like to do what I can since you ask me. I see you have a large number of retainers here. Call one of them, anyone you like, and I will use him to demonstrate it to you.

M: Certainly. (*To a slave-boy.*) Come here.

S: He is a Greek and speaks our language?

M: Indeed yes—born and bred in the house.

S: Listen carefully then, and see whether it seems to you that he is learning from me or simply being reminded.

M: I will.

S: Now boy, you know that a square is a figure like this?

(*Socrates begins to draw figures in the sand at his feet. He points to the square* ABCD.)

Boy: Yes.

S: It has all these four sides equal?

Boy: Yes.

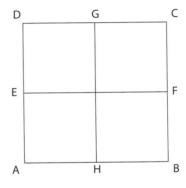

S: And these lines which go through the middle of it are also equal? (*The lines* EF, GH.)

Boy: Yes.

S: Such a figure could be either larger or smaller, could it not?

Boy: Yes.

S: Now if this side is two feet long, and this side the same, how many feet will the whole be? Put it this way. If it were two feet in this direction and only one in that, must not the area be two feet taken once?

Boy: Yes.

S: But since it is two feet this way also, does it not become twice two feet?

Boy: Yes.

S: And how many feet is twice two? Work it out and tell me.

Boy: Four.

S: Now could one draw another figure double the size of this, but similar, that is, with all its sides equal like this one?

Boy: Yes.

S: How many feet will its area be?

Boy: Eight.

S: Now then, try to tell me how long each of its sides will be. The present figure has a side of two feet. What will be the side of the double-sized one?

Boy: It will be double, Socrates, obviously.

S: You see, Meno, that I am not teaching him anything, only asking. Now he thinks he knows the length of the side of the eight-feet square.

M: Yes.

S: But does he?

M: Certainly not.

S: He thinks it is twice the length of the other.

M: Yes.

S: Now watch how he recollects things in order— the proper way to recollect.

You say that the side of double length produces the double-sized figure? Like this I

mean, not long this way and short that. It must be equal on all sides like the first figure, only twice its size, that is eight feet. Think a moment whether you still expect to get it from doubling the side.

Boy: Yes, I do.

S: Well now, shall we have a line double the length of this (AB) if we add another the same length at this end (BJ)?

Boy: Yes.

S: It is on this line then, according to you, that we shall make the eight-feet square, by taking four of the same length?

Boy: Yes.

S: Let us draw in four equal lines (*i.e., counting* AJ, *and adding* JK, KL, *and* LA *made complete by drawing in its second half* LD), using the first as a base. Does this not give us what you call the eight-feet figure?

Boy: Certainly.

S: But does it contain these four squares, each equal to the original four-feet one? (*Socrates has drawn in the lines* CM, CN *to complete the squares that he wishes to point out.*)

Boy: Yes.

S: How big is it then? Won't it be four times as big?

Boy: Of course.

S: And is four times the same as twice?

Boy: Of course not.

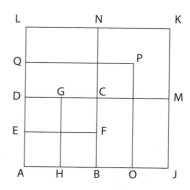

S: So doubling the side has given us not a double but a fourfold figure?

Boy: True.

S: And four times four are sixteen, are they not?

Boy: Yes.

S: Then how big is the side of the eight-feet figure? This one has given us four times the original area, hasn't it?

Boy: Yes.

S: And a side half the length gave us a square of four feet?

Boy: Yes.

S: Good. And isn't a square of eight feet double this one and half that?

Boy: Yes.

S: Will it not have a side greater than this one but less than that?

Boy: I think it will.

S: Right. Always answer what you think. Now tell me: was not this side two feet long, and this one four?

Boy: Yes.

S: Then the side of the eight-feet figure must be longer than two feet but shorter than four?

Boy: It must.

S: Try to say how long you think it is.

Boy: Three feet.

S: If so, shall we add half of this bit (BO, *half of* BJ) and make it three feet? Here are two, and this is one, and on this side similarly we have two plus one; and here is the figure you want. (*Socrates completes the square* AOPQ.)

Boy: Yes.

S: If it is three feet this way and three that, will the whole area be three times three feet?

Boy: It looks like it.

S: And that is how many?

Boy: Nine.

S: Whereas the square double our first square had to be how many?

Boy: Eight.

S: But we haven't yet got the square of eight feet even from a three-feet side?

Boy: No.

S: Then what length will we give it? Try to tell us exactly. If you don't want to count it up, just show us on the diagram.

Boy: It's no use, Socrates, I just don't know.

S: Observe, Meno, the stage he has reached on the path of recollection. At the beginning he did not know the side of the square of eight feet. Nor indeed does he know it now, but then he thought he knew it and answered boldly, as was appropriate—he felt no perplexity. Now however he does feel perplexed. Not only does he not know the answer; he doesn't even think he knows.

M: Quite true.

S: Isn't he in a better position now in relation to what he didn't know?

M: I admit that too.

S: So in perplexing him and numbing him like the sting-ray, have we done him any harm?

M: I think not.

S: In fact we have helped him to some extent towards finding out the right answer, for now not only is he ignorant of it but he will be quite glad to look for it. Up to now, he thought he could speak well and fluently, on many occasions and before large audiences, on the subject of a square double the size of a given square, maintaining that it must have a side of double the length.

M: No doubt.

S: Do you suppose then that he would have attempted to look for, or learn, what he thought he knew (though he did not), before he was thrown into perplexity, became aware of his ignorance, and felt a desire to know?

M: No.

S: Then the numbing process was good for him?

M: I agree.

S: Now notice what, starting from this state of perplexity, he will discover by seeking the truth in company with me, though I simply ask him questions without teaching him. Be ready to catch me if I give him any instruction or explanation instead of simply interrogating him on his own opinions.

(*Socrates here rubs out the previous figures and starts again.*)

Tell me, boy, is not this our square of four feet? (ABCD.) You understand?

Boy: Yes.

S: Now we can add another equal to it like this? (BCEF.)

Boy: Yes.

S: And a third here, equal to each of the others? (CEGH.)

Boy: Yes.

S: And then we can fill in this one in the corner? (DCHJ.)

Boy: Yes.

S: Then here we have four equal squares?

Boy: Yes.

S: And how many times the size of the first square is the whole?

Boy: Four times.

S: And we want one double the size. You remember?

Boy: Yes.

S: Now does this line going from corner to corner cut each of these squares in half?

Boy: Yes.

S: And these are four equal lines enclosing this area? (BEHD.)

Boy: They are.

S: Now think. How big is this area?

Boy: I don't understand.

S: Here are four squares. Has not each line cut off the inner half of each of them?

Boy: Yes.

S: And how many such halves are there in this figure? (BEHD.)

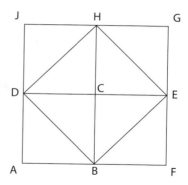

Boy: Four.

S: And how many in this one? (ABCD.)

Boy: Two.

S: And what is the relation of four to two?

Boy: Double.

S: How big is this figure then?

Boy: Eight feet.

S: On what base?

Boy: This one.

S: The line which goes from corner to corner of the square of four feet?

Boy: Yes.

S: The technical name for it is "diagonal"; so if we use that name, it is your personal opinion that the square on the diagonal of the original square is double its area.

Boy: That is so, Socrates.

S: What do you think, Meno? Has he answered with any opinions that were not his own?

M: No, they were all his.

S: Yet he did not know, as we agreed a few minutes ago.

M: True.

S: But these opinions were somewhere in him, were they not?

M: Yes.

S: So a man who does not know has in himself true opinions on a subject without having knowledge.

M: It would appear so.

S: At present these opinions, being newly aroused, have a dream-like quality. But if the same questions are put to him on many occasions and in different ways, you can see that in the end he will have a knowledge on the subject as accurate as anybody's.

M: Probably.

S: This knowledge will not come from teaching but from questioning. He will recover it for himself.

M: Yes.

S: And the spontaneous recovery of knowledge that is in him is recollection, isn't it?

M: Yes.

S: Either then he has at some time acquired the knowledge which he now has, or he has always possessed it. If he always possessed it, he must always have known; if on the other hand he acquired it at some previous time, it cannot have been in this life, unless somebody has taught him geometry. He will behave in the same way with all geometrical knowledge, and every other subject. Has anyone taught him all these? You ought to know, especially as he has been brought up in your household.

M: Yes, I know that no one ever taught him.

S: And has he these opinions, or hasn't he?

M: It seems we can't deny it.

S: Then if he did not acquire them in this life, isn't it immediately clear that he possessed and had learned them during some other period?

M: It seems so.

S: When he was not in human shape?

M: Yes.

S: If then there are going to exist in him, both while he is and while he is not a man, true opinions which can be aroused by questioning and turned into knowledge, may we say that his soul has been for ever in a state of knowledge? Clearly he always either is or is not a man.

M: Clearly.

S: And if the truth about reality is always in our soul, the soul must be immortal, and one must take courage and try to discover—that is, to recollect—what one doesn't happen to know, or (more correctly) remember, at the moment.

M: Somehow or other I believe you are right.

S: I think I am. I shouldn't like to take my oath on the whole story, but one thing I am ready to fight for as long as I can, in word and act: that is, that we shall be better, braver and more active men if we believe it right to look for what we don't know than if we believe there is no point in looking because what we don't know we can never discover.

M: There too I am sure you are right.

CHECKLIST

To help you review, a checklist of the key philosophers of this chapter can be found online at www.mhhe.com/moore9e.

KEY TERMS AND CONCEPTS

Delphi Oracle 34	Myth of the Cave 41
Forms/Theory of	Platonic dualism 38
Forms 35	Plato's dialogues 35

skeptic   38
Socratic/dialectic
  method   33

Theory of the Divided
  Line   41

QUESTIONS FOR DISCUSSION AND REVIEW

1. Can you step into the same river twice? Once?

2. Plato's metaphysics incorporates ideas from some of the earlier philosophers mentioned

in Chapter 2. Identify those philosophers and their ideas.

3. Give an example of a Platonic Form not mentioned in the text. Explain whether it really exists, and why.

4. Does a world of Forms exist separately from the world of concrete, individual things? Explain.

5. What is the Myth of the Cave?

6. Is sense perception knowledge?

7. Can beauty be in more than one object at one time? Explain.

8. Are appearances real for Plato? Are they real in fact?

SUGGESTED FURTHER READINGS

Go online to www.mhhe.com/moore9e for a list of suggested further readings.

4

Aristotle

Motion being eternal, the first mover, if there is but one, will be eternal also.
—Aristotle

Plato's most distinguished pupil was **Aristotle** (384–322 B.C.E.), on whom Plato had a tremendous influence. Aristotle was eventually hired to teach Alexander the Great, and Alexander attributed his happiness to his teacher, Aristotle. Nevertheless, it is a good bet that Alexander, who conquered the world, was not preoccupied with philosophy.

We noted earlier we owe the term *metaphysics* to Aristotle, or at least to those who cataloged his works. But metaphysics formed just a part of Aristotle's interests. Aristotle was interested in every subject that came along, and he had something reasonably intelligent to say about all of them, from poetry to physics, from biology to friendship.

Aristotle's books are more systematic than are Plato's, which provides evidence of his more painstaking attention to nature. It should tell you something, however, that, although Plato is a main staple of any decent literature program, Aristotle is not. Cicero did praise Aristotle for his "copious and golden eloquence," but many find Aristotle a bit tedious. Maybe that is because what we have from Aristotle is mainly lecture notes edited by some of his students.

Nevertheless, Aristotle was a careful observer and a brilliant theorizer, and his thought influenced philosophy in the future. Some fifteen centuries after his death, he was considered the definitive authority on all subjects outside religion, a fact that may have impeded more than it helped scientific progress because science, to get anywhere, cannot assume that something is so solely because some authority says that it is so, even if that authority is Aristotle.

What we call metaphysics Aristotle called "first philosophy." First philosophy, in Aristotle's view, is in some sense more abstract and general than are the specific

PROFILE: Aristotle (384–322 B.C.E.)

Clip art, supposedly of Aristotle.

Aristotle was not correct about everything. He thought the brain is a minor organ compared with the heart and that eels are spontaneously generated from mud. He also thought that parsnips cause erections and that women are an inferior product.

But he did know a great deal. In fact, Aristotle systematized all that was then known, and, as if that were not sufficient, he extended the limits of knowledge in virtually every existing subject, including biology, psychology, zoology, physics, and astronomy as well as in those areas that today are deemed the province of philosophy, including ethics, politics, aesthetics, metaphysics, and logic. His work was of enormous and lasting significance.

Aristotle was born in Stagira, a Greek colony along the Macedonian coast. His father, Nicomachus, was the physician of the king of Macedonia, Amyntas II. When he was eighteen, Aristotle went to Athens, where he studied under Plato at Plato's Academy for some twenty years. Plato may ultimately have come to resent Aristotle, and Aristotle eventually discovered that he disagreed with important Platonic doctrines, but Aristotle always retained a great respect for his teacher.

In 342 Aristotle was hired by Philip of Macedonia to tutor his son, Alexander, who was thirteen at the time. Alexander, of course, went on to conquer most of the then civilized world, but we suspect that none of this was the result of anything Aristotle taught him. Whatever Alexander learned from Aristotle, he repaid by sending Aristotle zoological specimens from his many travels and by funding his studies.

In 335 Aristotle formed his own school at the Lyceum, in Athens, and some of the sharper members of the Academy joined up with Aristotle. Because of his practice of lecturing in the Lyceum's walking place, or *peripatos,* Aristotle's followers became known as the peripatetics, the "walkers."

Aristotle emphasized the importance of direct observation of nature and believed that you must obtain factual data before you can begin to theorize. He also maintained that knowledge of things requires description, classification, and causal explanation. This is, of course, the modern scientific view, although (as is explained in the text) Aristotle emphasized a different aspect of causation from that stressed in modern science.

Aristotle's works are often classified under five headings: the *Organum,* which consisted of six treatises on logic; the *Rhetoric* and the *Poetics;* his works on natural science, including most importantly the *Physics* and *De Anima* (On the Soul); *Metaphysics;* and the works on ethics and politics, which include the *Nicomachean Ethics, Eudemian Ethics,* and *Politics.*

sciences, and it considers the most basic questions of existence. The most basic question of existence is, What is it to be? So we will begin there.

WHAT IS IT TO BE?

In Aristotle's opinion, to be is to be a particular thing. And each thing, Aristotle maintained, is a combination of *matter* and *form.* A statue, for example, is a chunk of marble with a certain form. It is the same with other things too. There is some stuff out of which each thing is made, and there is the particular form this bit of stuff takes. Without the stuff, the thing would not exist, because you cannot have a thing made out of nothing. Likewise, without form, the thing would not exist. Without form, the stuff would not be some *particular kind of thing;* it would just be stuff. The form determines what the thing is; it is the essential nature of the thing.

For example, the marble of the statue is the same marble as it was when it was cut into a block at the quarry. But now it has a new form, and that form is what distinguishes the marble now from the marble in the block in the quarry. Yes, the marble has always had *some* form or other, but its transformation to this particular form is what makes it a statue. Thus, the form is what determines what a thing is, and for this reason Aristotle equated a thing's form with its essence.

According to Aristotle, you need both form and matter to have a thing, and, with the exception of god (discussed later), neither form nor matter is ever found in isolation from the other.

Things do change, of course: they become something new. Thus, another basic question is, What produces a change? In Aristotle's opinion each change must be directed toward some end, so just four basic questions can be asked of anything:

1. *What is the thing?* In other words, what is its form? Aristotle called this the **formal cause** of the thing. We do not use the word *cause* that way, but Aristotle did, and we just have to accept that.
2. *What is it made of?* Aristotle called this the **material cause.**
3. *What made it?* This Aristotle called the **efficient cause,** and this is what today we often mean by "cause."
4. *What purpose does it serve?* That is, for what end was it made? This Aristotle called the **final cause.**

Consider again a statue, Michelangelo's *David,* for example. What it is, (1), is a statue. What it is made of, (2), is marble. What made it, (3), is Michelangelo (or Michelangelo's chisel on the marble). And (4), it was made for the purpose of creating a beautiful object. Of course, natural objects were not made by humans for their purposes, but they still do have "ends." The end of an acorn, for instance, is to be a tree.

But consider the acorn example more closely. The acorn is not actually a tree, only potentially so, correct? Change can therefore be viewed, according to Aristotle, as movement from potentiality to actuality. Because actuality is the source of change, *pure actuality* is the *ultimate* source of change. Pure actuality is the unchanged changer or unmoved mover or, in short, god. It should be noted that the pure actuality that Aristotle equated with god is not God, the personal deity of the Jewish or Christian religions.

It sometimes is difficult to perceive the ancient Greek metaphysicians as all being concerned with the same thing. But Aristotle explained that his predecessors were all concerned with *causation.* Thales, for example, was concerned with the stuff from which all is made: the material cause of things. Empedocles and Anaxagoras were concerned with why there is change, with efficient causation. In his Theory of Forms, Plato considered formal causation. It remained for Aristotle himself, Aristotle thought, to present an adequate explanation of final causation. So Aristotle gave us a handy way of integrating (and remembering) ancient Greek metaphysics.

ACTUALITY AND POSSIBILITY

Aristotle delineated the different kinds of imperfect, changing beings in terms of possibility and actuality. At one extreme is matter, which consists only of possibility. Matter, as we saw, is that which must be moved because it cannot move or form itself. At the other extreme is god as pure actuality, which can only move things without god being moved or changed in any way. God is the unmoved mover. Any movement on god's part would imply imperfection and is therefore impossible. Nature (*physis*) and all the things of the universe exist between these two poles. Things move and are moved as a process of actualizing some of their potentialities. There is a penchant in each being to take on ever-higher forms of being in an effort to approach the unmoving perfection of god. It is things' love of and longing for perfection or god that moves the universe. God remains the unmoved mover.

Aristotle maintained that the stars, having the most perfect of all shapes, were beings with superhuman intelligence. Being much closer to god in the hierarchy of beings, they are incarnated gods unto themselves. Because their actions are much more rational and purposeful than those of the lower order beings on the earth, stars exercise a benevolent influence on earthly matters. Today many people read their astrology charts in the newspaper every day, and some political leaders even organize their programs around them. In this regard, Aristotle has not been the only one seeing stars.

To Aristotle, the earth is a mortal sphere. Things on it come to be and then cease to be. Earthly things are in a constant, unsettled state of becoming. As a consequence, earthly things and earthly matters long for the fixity and quietude that perfection allows. And although they strive mightily to become as perfect and god-like as possible, they never exhaust their own potentiality. Since god alone is pure act and perfect actualization, changes in the natural world go on without ceasing.

ESSENCE AND EXISTENCE

Aristotle was the first philosopher to discuss being in terms of **existence** and **essence** or, more exactly, in terms of existence and **substance** (***ousia***). The first judgment to be made regarding a thing is whether or not it exists. Then, further judgments need to be made. Therefore, a judgment regarding existence is but a first step. Further judgments need to be made regarding a thing's substance and its characteristics. If a thing is, what is it? Aristotle gives the term "substance" a double meaning. "Substance" refers first of all to the individual, particular thing. For example, humans are given proper names, which mark them out as singular. Aristotle called this quality of uniqueness "this-thereness" (*tode ti*). "Substance" secondarily refers to what a thing is in common with other things. In English, this is known as the thing's essence, or that by virtue of which it is the sort of thing it is. Each thing has an essence or definition, which it often shares with other like things. We, for example, share the essence of human beings or rational animals as Aristotle

Athens today. Ancient Greece gave us Plato and Aristotle, systematic mathematics, the Olympics, and (last but not least) democracy.

defined us. Aristotle believed these essences to be fixed species, which can be determined and hierarchically ordered. For example, the physical world can be divided into mineral, vegetable, and animal genera. To be a specific thing is to have a set potential that is more or less realized at any given time and is in a continuous process of actualization. This forming process constitutes a thing's being and allows it to become a whole individual. Happiness, for example, is one way of measuring to what degree a human is succeeding at fulfilling his or her potential. Other key ways of measuring fulfillment of potential include truth, beauty, oneness, and justice.

TEN BASIC CATEGORIES

Aristotle thought that there were yet other ways that humans use to think about things. These are the ten basic categories of being, which he developed. Besides substance itself, humans make judgments regarding things in terms of their quantity, quality, relationships, place, time, posture, constitution, passivity, and activity. Aristotle thought that all possible predicates, or what we can attribute to things, could be subsumed under these basic categories or classifications. These categories allow us to comprehend various aspects of any thing's being. Not only do we want to know that a thing is; we want to know what it is and how it functions. Aristotle, like his teacher Plato, believed that the more we know about things, the better off we will be. Your instructor may ask you to see if you can come up with a better list of basic categories. We think Aristotle's list is pretty good.

Aristotle defined human beings as rational animals. The soul (**psyche**) is the form of the body and that which prevents humans from falling apart. The human soul also provides the purposes and the ultimate end that human beings pursue. Part of this is the natural penchant of humans to try to fulfill as much of their potential as possible. Curiously, Aristotle thought that the principal organ of the soul was the heart, whereas the brain, he thought, was concerned with cooling the overheated blood.

THE THREE SOULS

In fact, Aristotle believed humans have three souls, which form a single unity. The first is the vegetative soul, the source of nourishment and reproduction. The second, the animal soul, is the basis of sensation as well as the ability to move. It is the animal soul that gives humans the ability to experience feelings of pleasure and pain. It also allows humans to avoid or to pursue pleasure and/or pain. The third soul is the *nous,* or the intelligent or spiritual soul. This soul is pure and immortal. It does not share the mortality of the body but is much more akin to the gods. Certain psychic processes are common to animals and humans and have their root in the animal soul. But there is likewise a higher speculative way of thinking that is unique to the human soul and gives rise to the human interest in ethics, epistemology, and metaphysics. The human soul alone can know the nature of being-as-a-whole and can intimate what god's nature must be.

ARISTOTLE AND THE THEORY OF FORMS

It is an important fact that Aristotle took great issue with Plato's Theory of Forms. For Plato, two or more items—coins, let's say—can both be said to be circular if they participate in a third thing, the Form *circularity*. According to Plato, the Form *circularity* exists apart or separately from individual coins and other circular things, and they are dependent on it for their existence as circular things, as explained earlier. But according to Aristotle, this talk of participating is metaphorical and meaningless. Further, he thought that Plato was mistaken in holding that, although individual circular things depend for their existence as circular things on the Form *circularity*, the reverse does not hold true. For in fact (believed Aristotle), the reverse does hold true: if there were not individual circular things, there would be no such thing as the Form *circularity*.

One of Aristotle's most compelling arguments against the Theory of Forms is known as the **Third Man argument.** It goes like this. Plato said that what ties

Aristotle and Plato on Forms

These coins are all circular. Plato thought they are all circular because they "partake" in *circularity*, which, Plato said, existed apart and separately from particular coins. Aristotle thought that Plato's theory was metaphorical and meaningless. He held that universals like circularity have no independent existence apart from particular things.

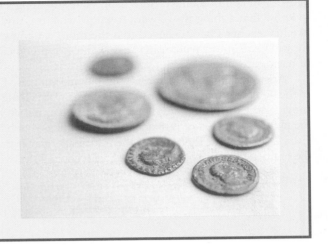

two circular coins together, what they have in common, is the Form *circularity*. But what, Aristotle asked, ties the coins together *with* the Form *circularity*? Some *further* form? Well, what ties this further Form together with the first Form, yet *another* Form? You can see the problem.

Aristotle's own view is that the Forms are **universals**—something that more than one individual can be. Many different individual things can be beautiful or circular or large or green; so beauty, circularity, largeness, and greenness are universals. But only one thing can be you, and only one thing can be Aristotle; so you and Aristotle are not universals but particulars. Universals, Aristotle insisted, do not exist separately or apart from particulars. Circularity and greenness, for example, have no independent existence apart from particular round things and particular green things (see the box "Aristotle and Plato on Forms").

Aristotle is fairly convincing when he tells us what is wrong with Plato's Theory of Forms, but he is less helpful in explaining just what universals are. The apparent failure of Aristotle (and Plato and their contemporaries) to produce a satisfactory theory of universals and their relationship to particulars resulted in an obsession with the problem through many centuries.

Now, a short summary statement of the differences between Plato's and Aristotle's metaphysics is bound to be a grotesque oversimplification, unless the sentences are very complicated. Nevertheless, the oversimplified difference comes to this: According to Plato, there are two realms. One is the realm of particular, changing, sensible things, and the other is a separate and superior realm of eternal, fixed, and unchanging Forms to which the particular things owe their reality. According to Aristotle, forms are found only within particular things, which are an embodiment of both form and matter. Aristotle did not disdain having knowledge of particular, sensible things, and because these things are always changing, Aristotle was much concerned with change itself. This concern led him to his theory of the four causes that underlie change.

ARISTOTLE'S THEORY OF KNOWLEDGE

Most things, for Aristotle, are known through sense experience and are thought about using discursive reasoning, or reasoning from one thing or aspect to another. For example, Aristotle sought to define things by determining how a thing is similar to other things (**genus**) and how it is specifically different (species, or **specific difference**). Such discursive reasoning defines things by way of their limitations, sameness, and differences. Chains of related things can build up a composite picture of things based on cause and effect, on subject and object, on possibility and actuality. This kind of thinking works well in the changing, imperfect world of which we humans are so much a part. Discursive reasoning is the basis of the natural sciences but also provides a way of understanding ourselves and our everyday lives. But Aristotle believed that there is an entirely different kind of thinking that is at times necessary, namely, intuition. Intuition is an immediate, direct seeing of a certain truth. For example, that which is absolutely simple, namely god, needs ultimately to be known via intuition. God's existence and nature can be roughly intimated as the cause of the natural world. But a deeper, more compelling comprehension of god requires intuition. Also, the highest principles of knowing must be known intuitively, as they can never be adequately known or proven via discursive reasoning. This includes the most fundamental of all logical and epistemological principles, the principle of noncontradiction, which, expressed informally, states a thing cannot both be and not be at the same time and in the same respect. Without this fundamental principle, no discursive reasoning is even possible.

LOGIC

Before we end this chapter, one other aspect of Aristotle's philosophy needs to be mentioned. Aristotle made a great contribution to the history of logic. To be specific, it was Aristotle who first *made a study of the principles of sound reasoning,* especially those involved in one of the most important forms of inference—the syllogism.

What is inference? To *infer* one proposition from other propositions is to see that the first one *follows from* the others. For example, the proposition "Some philosophers are Greeks" follows from (and thus may be inferred from) the propositions "Some philosophers were born in Greece" and "All philosophers who were born in Greece are Greeks."

This particular inference is a syllogism, which means that in it one proposition is inferred from two others. The syllogism is an absolutely fundamental form of inference, and Aristotle made the first complete analysis of the syllogism. His analysis was so brilliant and thorough that it is still taught in universities throughout the world, just as Euclid's examination of the fundamentals of geometry still serves as the basis for beginning courses in that subject. Aristotle's treatment of the syllogism is the basis for beginning courses in logic, and Aristotle is known as the father of logic.

Aristotle examined other important areas of logic as well, and he attempted to define the *forms of thought,* or ways in which we think about reality. Because

Aristotle assumed that the ways in which we think about reality represent the way reality is, there is tight linkage between Aristotle's logic and his metaphysics—but Aristotelian logic is a subject for another book.

SELECTION 4.1

Metaphysics*

Aristotle

[*This selection will enable you to understand why, for Aristotle, metaphysics is the examination of the most general features of being. In the selection, Aristotle is not trying to prove some overall thesis but, rather, is only describing various important and interesting aspects of the process of change. Included are the relation of form to matter, the nature of forms, and the types of generation (i.e., the ways things come into existence).*]

The Process of Change

Everything which comes into being is brought about by something, that is, by a source from which its generation comes. And it is composed of something. Now this latter is best described not as the absence of the thing but as the matter from which it comes. And it becomes a particular thing, as a sphere or a circle or some other thing. Now one does not "make" the material—as the bronze—of which a thing is composed; so one does not make the sphere, except in a secondary sense, in so far as the bronze circle is a circle and one makes it. For the act of making a particular thing is a process of making it out of some material in general. I mean that to make the bronze round is not to make the "round" or the "sphere," but quite a different thing—that of putting this form into what did not have it previously. If one made the "form," one would make it out of something else, for this would underlie it, as when one makes a sphere out of bronze. This is done by making of a particular kind of substance, namely bronze, a special sort of thing, namely a sphere. And if one makes this "sphere" also in the same way, it is evident that he will make it in the same manner, and the process of origination will go on to infinity. It is evident therefore that

the form, or whatever one ought to call the shape of the perceived object, is not "made." It does not "become," nor does it have an origin. Nor is there any for the essential conception of a thing. For this is what is implanted in another entity, either by training or by nature or by force. But one does cause the "bronze sphere" to *be*. For one makes it out of bronze and the form of "sphere." One puts the form into this matter, and it is then a bronze sphere. But if there is an origin for "the idea of sphere in general" it will be something generated from something else. That which is generated will have to be analyzed again in turn, and each reduced to something further, then that to something else; I mean in one aspect into matter, in another into form. A sphere is a figure whose surface is everywhere equally distant from a center. One aspect of it is the material into which the form is to be put; the other the form which is to be put into it. The whole is what results, namely, the bronze sphere.

It is evident from what we have said that the part which is spoken of as the form or the essence does not originate; but the combination which derives its name from this does; and in everything which originates there is matter, and it is now this thing, now that. Is there then a "sphere" beside the particular spheres? Or is there a "house" beside the houses of brick? Or would there never be any particular things if this were so? The genus gives the general character, but is not a definite particular thing. But one makes and produces such and such a thing out of "this" particular substance. And when it has been produced it is "this thing of such and such a kind." This concrete existing thing is "Kallias" or "Socrates," just as the other was "this bronze sphere," but it is man and animal in general just as the other was a bronze sphere in general. It is evident then that the formal principle, as some are accustomed to speak of forms, if they are something aside from the particulars and beside the acts of eration and the essences, is of no use. For not by virtue of them would there be particular instances of them. In some cases indeed it is evident that that which causes is the same sort of thing as that which is caused, yet not identically the same, nor one numerically, but in form—as in the case of the products of nature. Man begets man, (and so it is), except where something arises of different nature, as when a horse begets a mule. Yet these cases also are really similar to the others; but what is common to a horse and an ass has not been given a name as a "proximate genus"; perhaps it would be "mule."

So it is evident that it is not at all necessary to supply forms as patterns (for they would have to be found in these cases especially, since these are certainly substances). The begetter is adequate to the production of the effect and to the embodiment of the form in the matter. And the compound—such and such a form in this flesh and these bones—is Kallias or Socrates. They differ because of their matter, for it is different, but they are the same in form. For the form is indivisible.

Of things which come into existence some are generated by nature, some by art, some by chance.

And all things which are generated are generated by something and from something and as some particular thing. Some particular thing, I mean with respect to each category, such as substance, quantity, quality or place. Origination by nature occurs in the case of those things whose origin is through the processes of nature. The substance of which they are formed we call matter; the source from which they arise is some thing in nature; the kind of thing which they become is "man" or "plant" or some other thing of the kind which we are especially accustomed to call "substances." All things which have an origin, whether by nature or by art, have a material part. Each of them might exist or not exist; and the seat of this double possibility is the material part of them. In general that out of which and in accordance with which they arise is some natural thing. For that which comes into being has some natural character as that of a plant or an animal. And that under the influence of which it arises is a natural object which with reference to its form may be said to be homogeneous. And this form is found in another individual; as one man begets another man. In this way arise the things which come about by nature.

CHECKLIST

To help you review, a checklist of the key philosophers of this chapter can be found online at www.mhhe.com/moore9e.

KEY TERMS AND CONCEPTS

existence and essence 63	*nous* 65
	psyche 65
formal, material, efficient, and final causes 62	substance (*ousia*) 63
	Third Man argument 65
genus and species-specific difference 67	universals 66

QUESTIONS FOR DISCUSSION AND REVIEW

1. What are the four Aristotelian causes of a baseball?

2. Aristotle believed that if individual horses did not exist, there would be no such thing as the Form *horse*. Is this correct?

3. Are universals real? In what sense?

4. Can there be essences without existence?

5. What are the two kinds of substance?

6. Explain what Aristotle means by "intuition." Do humans have intuition?

7. Do you agree with Aristotle that every change is directed toward some end?

8. Explain why pure actuality is the ultimate source of change, for Aristotle.

9. Why is god the unmoved mover, according to Aristotle?

10. Review Aristotle's ten categories of being. Could alien intelligences think about things in terms of different categories?

SUGGESTED FURTHER READINGS

Go online to www.mhhe.com/moore9e for a list of suggested further readings.

5

Philosophers of the Hellenistic and Christian Eras

Though philosophers disagree on the nature of things, and the mode of investigating truth, and of the good to which all our actions ought to tend, yet on these three great general questions, all their intellectual energy is spent.   —St. Augustine

Before he died in 323 B.C.E. at age thirty-two, Aristotle's student Alexander the Great, son of the Macedonian king Philip II, had conquered the entire civilized Western world and made a statement by naming every other city after himself. The Macedonian domination of the Greek-speaking world, known as the **Hellenistic age** (*Hellene* means "Greek"), was a period of major achievements in mathematics and science.

Having started with Alexander around 335 B.C.E., Macedonian hegemony was carried forth by the families of three of Alexander's generals and lasted about a century and a half, until Philip V of Macedon and Antiochus III of Syria were each defeated (around 190 B.C.E.) by a new ascending power: Rome. From that time on, for approximately the next seven hundred years, the Western world *was* the Roman Empire, built on plunder and the power of the sword.

For two centuries, beginning in 27 B.C.E. with the reign of Julius Caesar's grandnephew Octavian, who was known as "Augustus, the first Roman emperor and savior of the world," the Roman Empire enjoyed peace, security, and political stability. But eventually, after the reign of Marcus Aurelius (161–180 C.E.), conditions deteriorated into chaos. Nevertheless, the ultimate fall of the empire was postponed by Diocletian, who divided the empire into eastern (Byzantine) and western (Roman) halves, and by Constantine I, who granted universal religious

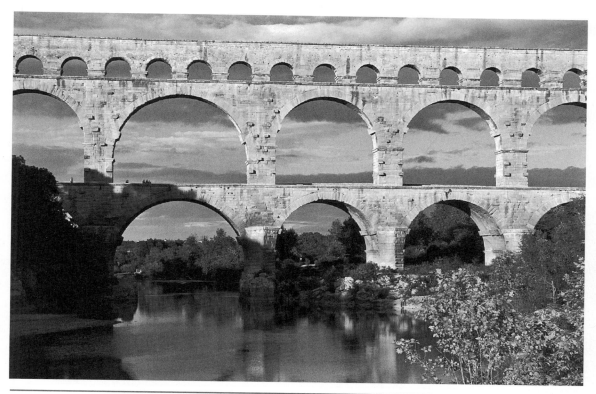

A Roman aqueduct today. Perhaps great-great-great-grandparents of contemporary Italians swam here.

tolerance, thus in effect recognizing Christianity. Finally, however, internal anarchy opened the Roman frontiers to the barbarians. Although the (Eastern) Byzantine Empire survived until the fifteenth century, in 476 the last emperor of the (Western) Roman Empire was deposed by the Goths. The Dark Ages followed.

The engineering feats of the Romans are astonishing. They built aqueducts and underground sewers and and were the first to have windows made of glass. Wealthy Romans had central heating and running water. Roman highways were paved with concrete and squared stone. Roman roads and bridges are still used today, and some may outlast today's highways. They are, however, bumpy.

Perhaps the most important contribution of Roman thought to our society is in law: Roman law is the basis for modern civil law. Of course, the Romans also excelled at warfare, which explains why so many of our epic movies feature Roman battles. Romans also enjoyed watching men fight each other—or animals—to death, and unlike Hollywood, the combatants weren't faking it.

METAPHYSICS IN THE ROMAN EMPIRE

During the Hellenistic and Roman periods, there were four main traditions or "schools" of philosophy; three arose around the time of Alexander and were in fact products of Greek culture, not Roman. Two of these—Stoicism and Epicureanism—were concerned with the question of how individuals should best conduct their affairs. If there had been supermarkets at the time, Stoic and Epicurean advice would have been available in paperbacks for sale at the checkout counters. In metaphysics, the Stoics subscribed to the idea that all existence is corporeal; in epistemology they believed that knowledge could be had through sense perception checked by reason. The Stoics also made important contributions to logic, which are beyond the scope of this book. Most importantly, perhaps, the concept of natural law, as a principle of rationality that infuses the universe and to which human behavior ought to conform, comes directly from the Stoics, as we discuss in Chapters 10 and 11.

The third school—**Skepticism**—(to which we will turn shortly) was concerned with the possibility of knowledge. The remaining school, unlike these other three, did arise during Roman times, but this school was for all intents and purposes a revision of Plato's philosophy. It is known as **Neoplatonism,** and it had considerable influence on the metaphysics of Christianity.

Plotinus

The great philosopher of Neoplatonism was **Plotinus** [pluh-TYE-nus] (205–270 c.e.). During Plotinus's lifetime, the Roman Empire was in a most dismal state, suffering plague, marauding barbarian hordes, and an army incompetent to do anything but assassinate its own leaders. Civilization was tottering dangerously near the abyss. Plotinus, however, was inclined to ignore these earthly trifles, for he had discovered that by turning his attention inward, he could achieve union with god.

Now think back for a moment to Plato. According to Plato's metaphysics, there are two worlds. On one hand, there is the cave, that is, the world of changing appearances: the world of sensation, ignorance, error, illusion, and darkness. On the other hand, there is the light, that is, the world of Forms: the world of intellect, knowledge, truth, reality, and brightness whose ultimate source of existence and essence is the Form *the Good*. Plotinus further specified this ultimate source or reality as god or the One. For Plotinus, god is above and beyond everything else—utterly transcendent.

But Plotinus's god, like Plato's Good and unlike the Christian God, is not a personal god. God, according to Plotinus, is indefinable and indescribable, because to define or describe god would be to place limitations on what has no limits. About god it can be said only that god is. And god can be apprehended only through a coming together of the soul and god in a mystical experience. This mystical "touching" of god, this moment in which we have the "vision," is the highest moment of life.

PROFILE: Plotinus (205–270 C.E.)

Plotinus's interest in philosophy began when he was twenty-eight in Alexandria (the most famous Alexandria, the one in Egypt). His first teacher was Ammonius, the "Sack Carrier," who was so called because he earned his living as a gardener.

About 244, Plotinus traveled to Rome and founded what came to be a renowned school of Neoplatonic philosophy. Even the emperor Gallienus and his wife, Salonina, patronized the school. Plotinus tried to get his students to ask questions for themselves; consequently the discussions were lively and sometimes almost violent. On one occasion, Plotinus had to stop a particularly ugly confrontation between a senator and a rich man; he urged both parties to calm themselves and think rather only of the One (about which see the text).

Plotinus himself was a quiet, modest, and selfless human being. He was thought to possess an uncanny ability to penetrate into the human character and its motives, and so he was sought out for all manner of practical advice.

He would not, however, acknowledge his birthday. This is because, at least according to Porphyry, who wrote a biography of Plotinus, Plotinus was ashamed that his immortal soul was contained in a mortal body, and the event of his soul entering his body was therefore something to be regretted. He also would not allow his face to be painted or his body to be sculpted. In fact, his long disregard of his body eventually caused him to lose his voice, and his hands and feet festered with abscesses and pus. Because Plotinus greeted his students with an embrace, the net result was a falling off in enrollment.

Plotinus's philosophy had a great influence on St. Augustine and other doctors and fathers of the Church. Christian theology is unthinkable without the mystical depth that comes from Plotinus.

THE RISE OF CHRISTIANITY

As mentioned in the accompanying Profile, Plotinus's thought was very influential on the last of the great ancient philosophers, Augustine, who also happens to be one of the two or three most important Christian theologians of all time. Eventually, the predominance of Christianity in Europe came to define the framework within which most Western philosophizing took place. Not long after Plotinus, the great philosophers of the western part of the Roman Empire, or what became of the western part, were almost without exception Christians.

The original Christians, including Jesus and his followers, were Jews. Christianity gradually evolved from a Jewish sect to a separate religion. Now, the Romans were generally pretty tolerant of the religious ideas and practices of the various peoples under their subjugation, but the Jews, including members of the Christian splinter sect, were not willing to pay even token homage to the Roman emperor-deities. The Christians, moreover, were unusually active in trying to make converts. Thus, to Roman thinking, the Christians were not only atheists who ridiculed the Roman deities but also, unlike more orthodox Jews, fanatical rabble-rousers who attempted to impose on others what to the Romans counted as gross superstition. As a result, for a couple of centuries or so the Christians were persecuted from time to time by assorted Roman emperors, sometimes rather vigorously.

PROFILE: St. Augustine (354–430 C.E.)

Augustine grew up in northern Africa. His father was a successful man of the world, and Augustine was expected to follow a similar path. Accordingly, he studied rhetoric in Carthage. While there, however, he fell in with a group of students known as the "rebels," who found amusement in such pastimes as attacking innocent passersby at night. Augustine, to his credit, did not participate in these episodes, though he did steal fruit from a neighbor's tree for the sheer perversity of doing so.

As a young man, Augustine also indulged in many love affairs. He took a concubine, and the union produced a son. He came to have doubts about his lifestyle, however, and eventually these doubts began to take the upper hand. With the encouragement of his family, he became engaged to a young woman of a prominent family. But Augustine grew impatient and took a new lover.

In the meanwhile, Augustine's studies had taken him to Rome and to Milan, where he became a professor of rhetoric. His mother, Monica, had already become a Christian. Through her encouragement and through Augustine's exposure to St. Ambrose, the celebrated preacher, Augustine was baptized into Christianity at the age of thirty-three. He returned to northern Africa and soon thereafter was called on to serve as Bishop of Hippo.

As bishop, Augustine used his rhetorical abilities to the full in fiercely attacking what he perceived to be the many heresies of the time. His thinking was dominated by two themes, the sinfulness of human beings and the inscrutability of God. At the age of seventy-two, he withdrew from the world and died in self-chosen solitude.

Nevertheless, of the numerous cults that existed during the first couple of centuries of the Common Era (C.E.), Christianity eventually became the most popular. Its followers became so numerous and, thanks to the administrative efforts of Paul of Tarsus (later St. Paul), so well organized that, by the early part of the fourth century, the emperor Constantine announced its official toleration.

Specifics of Christian doctrine need not concern us, and its central beliefs are well known: Jesus is the son of God, and Jesus's life, crucifixion, and resurrection are proof of God's love for humans and forgiveness of human sin; in addition, those who have faith in Christ will be saved and have life everlasting. The God of Christianity is thought (by Christians) to be the creator of all; and he is also thought to be distinct from his creation.

St. Augustine

St. Augustine [AUG-us-teen] (354–430 C.E.), who came from the town of Tagaste, near what is today the Algerian city of Annaba, transferred Platonic and Neoplatonic themes to Christianity. Transported down through the ages to us today, these themes affect the thought of both Christian and non-Christian.

"Whenever Augustine," Thomas Aquinas later wrote, "who was saturated with the teachings of the Platonists, found in their writings anything consistent with the faith, he adopted it; and whatever he found contrary to the faith, he amended." Through

Augustine on God and Time

The *ex nihilo* theory (God created the world out of nothing) invites a troublesome question for Christian theology: Why did God choose to create the world at the time he did and not at some other? Thanks to Plato and Plotinus, Augustine was able to provide a potentially reasonable answer to this question.

According to Augustine, the question rests on a false assumption, that God (and his actions) exists *within* time. On the contrary, Augustine maintained, God does not exist in time; instead, time began with the creation by God of the world. God is *beyond* time. In this way the timeless attribute of Plato's Good and Plotinus's One was transferred by Augustine to the Christian God.

But what exactly, Augustine wondered, is time? Here Augustine broke new philosophical ground by coming forth with a very tempting answer to this question.

"What, then, is time?" he asked. "If no one asks of me, I know; if I wish to explain to him who asks, I know not." On one hand, only the present exists, for the past is no more, and the future is not yet.

But, on the other hand, certain things did happen in the past, and other things will happen in the future, and thus past and future are quite real. How can the past and the future be both real and nonexistent?

Augustine's answer to this almost hopelessly baffling question is that past and future exist only in the human mind. "The present of things past is memory; the present of things present is sight; and the present of things future is expectation."

Augustine's analysis of time is that it is a subjective phenomenon. It exists "only in the mind." (Thus, before God created us, there was no time.) As will be discussed in Chapter 7, the idea that time is subjective was later developed by the eighteenth-century philosopher Immanuel Kant into the theory that time, space, causation, and other basic "categories" of being are all subjective impositions of the mind on the world. The same idea was then carried to its ultimate conclusion by the Absolute Idealists, who said that the world *is* mind.

Augustine's views on time can be found in the eleventh book of his *Confessions*.

Augustine, Christianity became so permanently interwoven with elements of Platonic thought that today, as the English prelate William Inge said, it is impossible to remove Platonism from Christianity "without tearing Christianity to pieces."

St. Augustine regarded Plotinus and Plato as having *prepared* him for Christianity by exposing him to important Christian principles before he encountered them in scripture. (But neither Plato nor Plotinus was Christian.) Augustine had a very strong inclination toward skepticism and was tempted to believe that "nothing can be known." Plato and Plotinus enabled Augustine to overcome this inclination.

Today we take for granted the concept of a separate, immaterial reality known as the transcendent God. Even those who do not believe in God are familiar with this concept of God's immateriality and are not inclined to dismiss it as blatant nonsense (though some, of course, do). But careful reflection reveals that there is not much within experience that gives rise to this concept, for we seem to experience only concrete, physical things. Through the influence of Plato and Plotinus, St. Augustine perceived that belief in a distinct immaterial reality was not the blindly superstitious thing that it might seem. And through Augustine's thought, the Christian belief in a nonmaterial God received a philosophical justification, a justification without which (it is arguable) this religion would not have sustained the belief of thoughtful people through the ages. (Other explanations of the durability of the Christian belief in God are, of course, possible.)

Augustine accepted the Platonic view that "there are two realms, an intelligible realm where truth itself dwells, and this sensible world which we perceive by sight and touch." Like Plato before him, St. Augustine thought that the capacity of the human mind to grasp eternal truths implied the existence of something infinite and eternal apart from the world of sensible objects, an essence that in some sense represented the source or ground of all reality and of all truth. This ultimate ground and highest being Augustine identified with God rather than with Platonic Forms.

Augustine, however, accepted the Old Testament idea that God created the world out of nothing. This idea of **creation *ex nihilo*,** creation out of nothing, is really quite a startling concept when you think about it, and Greek thinkers had had trouble with it. Their view had been that getting something from nothing is impossible. (The box "Augustine on God and Time" describes Augustine's thinking about creation.)

Augustine also accepted the Gospel story of the life, death, and resurrection of Jesus Christ and believed that God took on human form in the person of Jesus. Thus, Augustinian theology gives God a human aspect that would have been unthinkable for Neoplatonists, who thought that the immaterial realm could not be tainted with the imperfection of mere gross matter.

It is sometimes said that St. Augustine was the founder of Christian *theology*. Certainly his influence on Christian thought was second to none, with the exception of St. Paul, who formulated a great deal of Christian doctrine. One very important aspect of St. Augustine's thought was his concept of evil, in which the influence of Plato and Plotinus is again evident. (We will say something about this in Chapter 10.)

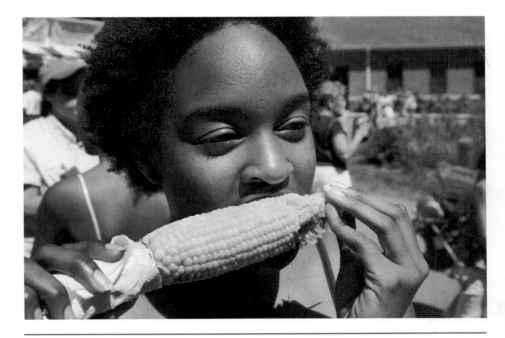

Can this girl know she is eating corn? Academics and Pyrrhonists say no. Augustine says yes.

PROFILE: Pyrrho (c. 360–270 B.C.E.)

Not a great deal is known about Pyrrho, after whom the Pyrrhonist tradition is named, for he left no writings. Diogenes Laertiús, a third-century Greek biographer (whose tales about the ancient philosophers, despite their gossipy and sometimes unreliable nature, are an invaluable source of history), reported that Pyrrho was totally indifferent to and unaware of things going on around him. A well-known story told by Diogenes Laertiús is that once, when Pyrrho's dear old teacher was stuck in a ditch, Pyrrho passed him by without a word. (Or perhaps this story indicates that Pyrrho was quite aware of things around him.) According to other reports, however, Pyrrho was a moderate, sensible, and quite level-headed person.

It is at any rate true that Pyrrho held that nothing can be known about the hidden essence or true nature of things. He held this because he thought every theory can be opposed by an equally sound contradictory theory. Hence, we must neither accept nor reject any of these theories but, rather, must suspend judgment on all issues. The suspension of judgment, **epoche,** was said by Pyrrho to lead to **ataraxia,** tranquility or unperturbedness. Pyrrho's fame was apparently primarily a result of his exemplary **agoge** (way of living), though there are differences of opinion about what that way of life actually was.

Augustine and Skepticism

Total skeptics maintain that nothing can be known or, alternatively, profess to suspend judgment in all matters. **Modified skeptics** do not doubt that at least some things are known, but they deny or suspend judgment on the possibility of knowledge about particular things, such as God, or within some subject matter, such as history or ethics. In the Hellenistic and Roman periods after Plato, two schools of skepticism developed, and they were something like rivals: the **Academics** (who flourished during the third and second centuries B.C. in what had earlier been Plato's Academy) and the **Pyrrhonists** (the disciples of **Pyrrho** [PEER-row] of Elis, c. 360–270 B.C.E.). The Academics and the Pyrrhonists were both total skeptics; the main difference between them seems to be one of phrasing. The Academics held that "all things are inapprehensible"—that is, nothing can be known. The Pyrrhonists said, in effect, "I suspend judgment in the matter, and I suspend judgment on all other issues I have examined too." In short, Pyrrhonists maintained that they did not know whether knowledge was possible.

The most famous skeptic of all time was the last great Pyrrhonist skeptic, **Sextus Empiricus** [SEX-tus em-PEER-uh-kus], who lived in the second to third centuries C.E. Although Sextus's writings are extensive and constitute the definitive firsthand report on Greek skepticism, little is known about Sextus himself. We do not know where he was born or died or even where he lived. We do know, however, that he was a physician.

In Sextus's writings may be found virtually every skeptical argument that has ever been devised. Sextus set forth the **Ten Tropes,** a collection of ten arguments by the ancient skeptics against the possibility of knowledge. The idea behind the Ten Tropes was this. Knowledge is possible only if we have good grounds for believing that what is, is exactly as we think it is or perceive it to be. But we do not have good grounds for believing that what is, is exactly as we think it is or perceive

Sextus's Asterisk

In a seventeenth-century play by the great French comic playwright Molière called *The Forced Marriage,* a skeptic is beaten in one scene. While he is being beaten, the skeptic is reminded that skeptics cannot be sure that they are being beaten or feel pain. Molière, evidently, did not view skepticism as a serious philosophy.

In defense of Sextus, we might mention that Sextus placed a small asterisk beside his skepticism.

He said that he did not "deny those things which, in accordance with the passivity of our sense impressions, lead us involuntarily to give our assent to them." That I am in pain is an *involuntary* judgment on my part and therefore does not count, Sextus would say.

We leave it to you to determine if this line of defense enables Sextus to escape Molière's criticism.

---

it to be. For one thing, we never are aware of any object as it is independent of us but only as it stands in relationship to us. Therefore, we cannot know how any object really is in itself.

For example, think of a wooden stick. The qualities we think it has are those we perceive by sense—but not so fast! Does the stick have *only* those qualities that it appears to us to have? Or does it have *additional* qualities that are unknown to us? Or does it have *fewer* qualities than appear to us? The senses themselves cannot tell us which of these options is correct, and Sextus argues that because the senses cannot tell us, the mind cannot either. (The seventeenth-century French comic playwright Molière famously made fun of this theory, as you can see in the box "Sextus's Asterisk.")

Now, back to St. Augustine. During the Christianization of the Roman Empire, skepticism waned, but St. Augustine was familiar with Academic Skepticism through the description by the Roman historian Cicero. Augustine concluded that total skepticism is refuted in at least three ways.

First, skepticism is refuted by the **principle of noncontradiction,** which we explained earlier more informally. According to this principle, a proposition and its contradiction cannot *both* be true—one or the other must be true. The propositions "The stick is straight" and "It is false that the stick is straight" cannot both be true. Thus, we at least know that the stick cannot be both straight and not straight. However, not all contemporary philosophers are convinced by this argument of St. Augustine's, and it does not exactly confront the line of reasoning employed by Sextus Empiricus.

Second, Augustine held that the act of doubting discloses one's *existence* as something that is absolutely certain: from the fact *I am doubting,* it follows automatically that *I am.* (The famous French philosopher René Descartes elaborated on a similar refutation of skepticism, which will be described in Chapter 6.) Some contemporary philosophers, however, are unconvinced by this maneuver as it too does not quite address the specific line of reasoning employed by Sextus.

Finally, Augustine also held that sense perception itself gives a rudimentary kind of knowledge. Deception in sense perception occurs, he said, only when we "give assent to more than the fact of appearance." For example, the stick appears bent at the point it enters the water. If we assent only to the appearance of the stick and say merely that it *looks* bent, we make no mistake. It is only if we judge that the stick actually *is* bent that we fall into error.

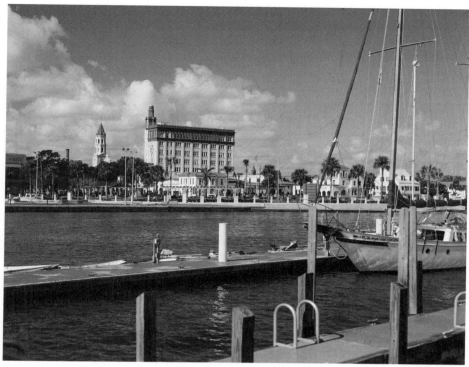

Saint Augustine, Florida, America's oldest city, founded in 1565, more than a thousand years after St. Augustine died.

Augustine saw these three insights as a refutation of skepticism and regarded this refutation as highly important, but he did not try to derive anything else of great importance from them. The most important truths for Augustine are received by revelation and held on faith, and this doctrine was assumed throughout the Christian Middle Ages.

Hypatia

Another important figure of this period was **Hypatia** [hy-PAY-sha] (c. 370–415). Recent scholarship discloses that Hypatia's influence on Western thought was significant, especially through her teaching and her work on astronomy in what was at the time a center of culture and learning, Alexandria.

Hypatia and her father, Theon, a famous mathematician and astronomer, taught the astronomy of Ptolemy. Claudius Ptolemy was a second-century scholar whose work was the definitive treatment of astronomy (and would remain so for well over a thousand years, until the sixteenth century, when the Ptolemaic system was overthrown by Nicholas Copernicus). Hypatia was the last major commentator on Ptolemy's work.

Hypatia was hardly a skeptic. She and her father prepared an updated edition of Ptolemy that included thousands of astronomical observations that had been recorded in the centuries after Ptolemy's death. Ptolemy's theory, which postulated the earth as the center of the universe and the sun going around the earth, gave pretty accurate predictions of celestial events, but not 100 percent accurate predictions, and the farther away in time an observer was from Ptolemy, the less accurate were the predictions. Hypatia improved the theories, extending computations to many additional place values (using an abacus!). This greater accuracy improved the predictability of astronomical calculations. She tinkered with Ptolemy's theory, using more sophisticated algebra and geometry than he had, to make astronomical facts a better fit with his theory and with theories of mathematics and geometry that he had relied on to develop his theory of astronomy. She tried to improve the rigor of theorems by finding and filling gaps to achieve greater completeness. Sometimes she improved the soundness of proofs by devising direct proofs where only indirect proofs had existed before.

Especially important, Hypatia found errors in the part of Ptolemy's theory that showed how the sun revolved around the earth. (This was important from both the Christian and the pagan standpoints—Hypatia was a pagan—because from either standpoint philosophically the earth must be the center of the universe.) Equally important philosophically, she tried to demonstrate the *completeness* of Ptolemy's astronomy and Diophantus's theory of algebra (Diophantus was an important Greek mathematician). A theory is "complete" when it explains everything within its scope. There are difficulties in proving completeness, but mostly they have not been understood until this century. In Hypatia's time nobody knew how to show that a theory was complete. Hypatia's approach was to introduce as many refutations and counterexamples to a theory as she could think up.

For Hypatia, mathematics and astronomy were ways of checking metaphysical and epistemological features of Plato's, Aristotle's, and Plotinus's philosophies against the physical universe. For example, Aristotle held that the circle is the most perfect shape. If the circle is the most perfect shape, then its ideal Form, in Plato's sense of Form, must be that which is reflected by god's perfect creation, the universe. Plato's and Aristotle's thought could be checked against astronomical theories and findings about the shape of the universe.

Philosophically, Hypatia was sympathetic to Plotinus's metaphysics and to Stoicism (see Chapter 10). She and all good Plotinians believed that the solution to the mystery of the One, the ultimate source of reality, would explain everything. It would explain the nature of god, the nature of the universe, and our place in it.

For Hypatia, philosophy was more than an abstract intellectual exercise: it implied personal ethical and religious knowledge, a way of living. Hypatia introduced beginning students to Plato's metaphysics and to Plotinus's interpretations of Plato to make a difference in their daily lives. Mathematics and astronomy were considered essential ingredients in preparation for a study of metaphysics. Consequently, she prepared careful, symmetrical expositions of elements of mathematical and astronomical proofs for her students.

We are not sure which later astronomers noticed Hypatia's commentary on Ptolemy, because apparently only two copies of it have survived. Both were obtained during the Renaissance by the Lorenzo di Medici library. Thus, her work could have

PROFILE: Hypatia of Alexandria (c. 370–415 c.e.)

Hypatia taught in Alexandria, Egypt, at what was called the Museum. Back then, philosophy was still a pretty wide field, and philosophers like Plotinus and Hypatia were not about to impose distinctions (as we now do) among such subjects as religion, mathematics, astronomy, and the slice of philosophy known as metaphysics.

Hypatia became famous when she was very young. By 390, students were coming to her from throughout northern Africa. (Europe was still an uncivilized place, but Alexandria was late antiquity's equivalent of Silicon Valley.) Every decent scientist and philosopher passed through Alexandria.

Hypatia was a pagan, but she had a lot of students who were Christians and maybe even a few Jewish students. Considering that by 410 relationships among different religious groups were so bad that there were frequent riots, Hypatia must have made sense to lots of people with very different orientations. One came from Cyrene (in Libya) to become her student and went on to convert to Christianity, becoming first a priest and then a bishop.

Over the past thousand or so years, when anybody has bothered to write about Hypatia, the chronicler has invariably told the story of how she dealt with sexual harassment by one of her male students. She supposedly threw the fifth-century equivalent of a used sanitary napkin at him—and never heard from him again. (Apparently, the Museum did not have procedures for dealing with sexual harassment.)

Until this century, it was thought that Hypatia wrote only three books and that all of them were lost. Can you imagine your copy of this book being found fifteen centuries from now, and its being discovered to contain the last surviving fragment of Descartes' *Meditations?* That is what happened to all of Hypatia's works! From what we know now, it looks as if Hypatia prepared about half a dozen scholarly writings of various lengths. Some of those writings have only recently been identified by scholars as being by her. Her works were copied, edited, translated, retranslated, incorporated into other people's writings, bought, sold, and traded by scholars from Rome to Baghdad to Britain for more than a thousand years. Versions of her different works exist in Greek, Latin, Hebrew, and Arabic—but not in English. Writings by Hypatia include an edition of Diophantus's *Arithmetica,* a work based on Archimedes' *Sphere and Cylinder;* an anonymous work on one-sided figures; a commentary on Archimedes' *Dimension of the Circle;* a commentary on Apollonius Pergaeus's *Conics* that formed the basis for later commentaries, including one by the astronomer Edmund Halley (of Halley's Comet fame); and a commentary on part of Ptolemy's *Syntaxis Mathematica.*

In 415, Hypatia was savagely murdered, allegedly by a gang of monks. Her corpse was then hacked into pieces and burned.

been seen over a thousand years later by the young graduate student Nicholas Copernicus, who was traveling around Italy trying to read all the Ptolemy he could find. But we don't know whether Copernicus actually saw Hypatia's work or whether it influenced him to rethink the geocentric model of the universe.

THE MIDDLE AGES AND AQUINAS

Augustine died in 430, some forty-six years before the date usually assigned as the end of the (Western) Roman Empire. The final centuries of the empire had witnessed the spread of Christianity through all classes of society and eventually an alliance between the Church and the state. They also had seen a growing belief in demons, magic, astrology, and darker superstitions. After the abdication of the last Roman emperor in 476, the light of reason was all but extinguished in Europe. These Dark Ages lasted to about 1000. Compared with the shining cultures of the East at the same time, Europe barely qualified as a civilization.

Precipitating the fall of the empire were barbarian invasions, and after the fall ferocious hordes swept across the land, replacing the empire with Germanic kingdoms. In the next century (i.e., the sixth), Justinian, the Byzantine emperor, partially reconquered the Western Empire; but shortly after his death Italy was invaded by the Lombards, and Syria, Egypt, and Spain were conquered by the Muslims. The Carolingian Franks under Charlemagne restored stability for a brief time, bringing into existence (on Christmas Day, 800) what later was called the Holy Roman Empire, although subsequent invasions by the Vikings and Muslims again spread chaos and destruction. During this period Slavic conquests of the Balkans separated Greek and Latin cultures, and the Greek and Latin churches also gradually drew apart.

Though in general philosophy during the Dark Ages was not fresh or ground breaking, there were exceptions. Boethius in the sixth century (who was executed for treason) and John Scotus in the ninth (whose work was posthumously condemned), were both philosophers of remarkable ability. The thought of both men, though basically Neoplatonic, was original and profound.

By about year 1000, invasions had become few and far between. Northern invaders had been Christianized, and the instable kingdoms were replaced with somewhat more stable states. The pope and secular rulers were more or less equal in power and authority.

However, during the High Middle Ages, as the next few centuries are called, the pope became the most powerful leader in Europe. The Church was the unifying institution of European civilization, and monarchs were averse to defying it.

In the growing security and prosperity that followed the Dark Ages, urban centers grew, and intellectual life, centered in the great universities that arose under the auspices of the Church, was stimulated through commercial and military contact with Greek, Arabian, Jewish, and (more indirectly) Indian cultures.

Still, independent or unorthodox thinking was not without its hazards, especially if it laid any foundation for what Church authorities perceived to be a heretical viewpoint. During the medieval Inquisition, those accused of heresy were brought to trial. The trials, however, were secret, and there was no such thing as the right to counsel. One's accusers were not named, and torture was used in service of the truth. An interesting practice was that of torturing not only the accused but also those speaking on behalf of the accused. As might be imagined, one was apt to find few witnesses on one's behalf. It was not unusual for heretics to recant their sins.

Despite all this, the High Middle Ages was a period of growing personal liberty, literacy, and intellectual vigor. One philosophical problem that was important to thinkers of the time—as it had been to Aristotle (see Chapter 4) and to contemporary analytic philosophers (see Chapter 9)—was the delicious problem of **universals.** This, put simply, is the question whether a term (a noun or noun phrase) that applies to more than one thing (a "universal" term) denotes something that

During the High Middle Ages, several universities were founded, including, famously, the University of Paris. This is a photograph of the Sorbonne, one of the most famous colleges making up the original university. It was founded in 1247 by a French theologian, Robert de Sorbon.

exists outside the mind. For example, when we say "Barack Obama is a man," the first term, the name *Barack Obama*, names something that exists out there independent of the mind. But what about the term *man?* Those who think that universal terms like "man" denote something that exists outside the mind subscribe to **realism;** those who think they correspond only to concepts in the mind subscribe to **conceptualism.** Those who think you can account for universal terms without invoking universals either as real things out there in the world or as concepts in the mind subscribe to **nominalism.** Which of these theories, if any, is correct is a question of perennial interest among philosophers. Perhaps your instructor will ask you to tackle it.

Contact with the Arabic world during the High Middle Ages led to a rekindling of interest among European church leaders in the philosophy of Aristotle. Through the centuries the Muslim world had enjoyed greater access to ancient Greek philosophy than had the Christian, and many Christian thinkers first encountered Aristotle's philosophy through Arabian commentaries on Aristotle and through Latin translations of Arab translations of Greek texts. Because Aristotle's repudiation of Plato's realm of Forms seemed at odds with Christian philosophy, which was Augustinian and Platonic in outlook, some Church thinkers (notably one named Bonaventura, c. 1217–1274) thought it necessary to reject Aristotle. Others (notably one called Albert the Great, 1193–1280) came to regard Aristotle as the greatest of all philosophers and concluded that there must be an underlying accord between Christian principles and Aristotle's philosophy.

The most important of those who belonged to the second group was **St. Thomas Aquinas** [uh-QUYNE-nuss] (1225–1274), whose philosophy was deemed by Pope Leo XIII in 1879 to be the official Catholic philosophy. To this day Aquinas's system is taught in Catholic schools as the correct philosophy, and so Aquinas's thought continues to affect living people directly.

Aquinas had access to translations of Aristotle's works that were directly from the Greek (not Latin translations of Arab translations), and his knowledge of Aristotle was considerable and profound. In a manner similar to that in which Augustine had mixed Platonic philosophy with Christianity, Aquinas blended Christianity with the philosophy of Aristotle, in effect grafting the principles and distinctions of the Greek philosopher to Christian revealed truth. The result was a complete Christian philosophy, with a theory of knowledge, a metaphysics, ethical and political philosophies, and a philosophy of law. Expect to encounter Aquinas again in this book.

Another way in which Aquinas is important is this. In Aquinas's time a distinction was finally beginning to be made between *philosophy* and *theology*. No person was more concerned with tracing the boundaries of the two fields than was Aquinas. His main idea was that philosophy is based on precepts of reason and theology on truths of revelation held on faith.

Aquinas was convinced that there is a real external world ordered by law and that human beings truly can have knowledge of that world. He did not believe that reality was a product of the human mind, nor was he sympathetic to attacks on the value of the sciences. However, Aquinas held that even though we can have true knowledge of the natural world, such knowledge is insufficient. It does not take into account the other realm—namely, the realm of supernatural truth. Large portions of this realm are inaccessible by human reason, Aquinas held, including the most profound aspects of Christian belief: the Trinity, God's taking on human form, and Christ's resurrection. Such mysteries are beyond our ability to adequately comprehend through reason.

Although such mysteries were *beyond* human reason, Aquinas believed they were not *contrary* to human reason. He held that there can be only one truth, part of which is accessible to human reason and part of which requires faith. Human reason, for Aquinas, could know of the existence of God and also that there can be but one God. However, other aspects of God's being are less available to human reason. In the end, philosophy serves as a handmaiden for theology—and reason as an instrument of faith.

Some of the main points of Aquinas's metaphysics may be summarized as follows. *Change*, Aquinas thought, can be explained using the Aristotelian four-cause theory: the efficient cause is that which produces the change; the material cause is the stuff that changes; the formal cause is the form the stuff takes; and the final cause is what explains why there was a change. (See the box "Why Do Humans Stand Upright?")

Why Do Humans Stand Upright?

For four reasons, said Aquinas:

1. Animals use their sense organs for seeking food. Because the sense organs are located mostly in the face, their faces are turned to the ground. Humans, by contrast, also use the senses to pursue truth, and for this purpose it is better that they are able to look up and about.

2. The brain functions better when it is above the other parts of the body.

3. If we walked on all fours, our hands would not be available for other purposes.

4. If we walked on all fours, we would have to take hold of food with our mouths, which would require our lips and tongue to be thick and hard, hindering speech.

In short, we walk erect because certain purposes (communicating, seeking truth, using our hands and brain) are best served by doing so. This is a **teleological explanation,** the type of explanation that we mentioned in connection with Aristotle in Chapter 4.

All physical things are composed of matter and form, he said, following Aristotle. Matter, which remains constant throughout a change, is that which a thing is made out of, and form is that which determines what sort of thing it is. By virtue of being separate clumps of matter, these two rocks are different, and by virtue of having the same form, these two rocks are both rocks and thus are the same. Contrary to the Platonic–Augustinian tradition, Aquinas held that the form of a thing cannot exist apart from matter.

But Aquinas went beyond Aristotle to point out that, besides the composition of matter and form in things, there is also a composition of its essence (matter plus form) and its existence. *What* something is (its essence) is not the same as *that* it is (its existence); otherwise, it would always exist, which is contrary to fact. Further, if existing were identical with any one kind of thing, everything existing would be only that one kind—again, contrary to fact. Aquinas made a unique contribution to metaphysics by highlighting that existence is the most important actuality in anything, without which even form (essence) cannot be actual.

Moreover, Aquinas also emphasized that nothing could cause its own existence, because it would already need to exist (as cause) before it existed (as effect), which is a contradiction. So anything that begins to exist is caused to exist by something already existing and, ultimately, by an Uncaused Cause of Existence, God. Thus, Aquinas went beyond Aristotle's concept of God as Pure Act (because God is changeless, without beginning or end) to an understanding of God as Pure Act of Existence.

Some aspects of God's nature can be known. We can know that God is the perfect being that exists in himself yet is the source of the known universe. It is only through the scriptures, however, that humans can know how creation represents the realization of the Divine Ideas (Plato in substantially changed form).

Thomistic *cosmology* (theory of the universe as an ordered whole) is based on a geocentric view of the universe, and this is also true of Aquinas's psychology. The earth is the center of the universe, and the human being is the center of the earth's existence. Remember that Aristotle believed that matter is passive and that the

According to the philosophy of Aquinas, these rocks are separate and distinct clumps of *matter*, but they all have the same *form* and thus are all rocks. Likewise, all physical things are composed of *matter* and *form*. Further, *what* something is (its *essence:* matter plus form) is distinct from the fact *that* it is (its *existence*).

form is the effective, active principle of a thing. For Aquinas, the "essential form" of the human body is the soul. The soul, of course, is nothing physical; it is a pure form without matter. As a pure form, the soul is indestructible and immortal. It is, indeed, the principle of activity and life of the person. In addition, the soul is immortal in its individual form: Each person's soul, unique to her or him, is immortal. Each soul is a direct creation of God and does not come from human parents. It stands in a relationship of mutual interdependency relative to the body. A human being is a *unity* of body and soul. Aquinas taught that without the soul the body would be formless and that without a body the soul would have no access to knowledge derived from sensation.

Aquinas's epistemology was built on Aristotle's notion of three powers of the soul, namely, the vegetative (e.g., reproduction), the animal (e.g., sensation), and the human (e.g., the understanding). Aquinas also agreed with Aristotle's idea that human knowing is relatively passive and receptive. Knowledge is reached when the picture in the understanding agrees with what is present in reality (*adaequatio rei et intellectus*). Such knowledge is empirical in that it has its source in experience and is based on sense perceptions rather than on participation in the Divine Ideas. However, sense experience always accesses individually existing things; what leads to knowledge is the discovery of the essence of things that represents their definition. The discovery of essences requires imagination and human intelligence.

A final consideration of Aquinas's thinking concerns his proofs for the existence of God. We will examine them in detail in Chapter 13 but mention here that the proofs are variations on the idea that things must have an ultimate cause, creator, designer, source of being, or source of goodness: namely, God. Our knowledge of God's *nature*, however, is in terms of what God is *not*. For example, because God is unmoved and unchangeable, God is eternal. Because he is not material and is without parts, he is utterly simple. And because he is not a composite, he is not a composite of essence and existence: his essence is his existence.

Aquinas believed that the task of the wise person is to find both order and reason in the natural world. It is in the systematic ordering of the complexities of reality that human greatness can be found. Aquinas created a philosophical–theological system during the zenith hour in the power of the Church and of the pope, and interest in it experienced a strong revival in the nineteenth and twentieth centuries. These ideas continue to play a vital role in the Church as an institution and in religion as a governing factor in daily life.

SELECTION 5.1
Confessions*

St. Augustine

[*When you think about it, neither the past nor the future exists, and the present has no duration. What, then, is left of time? In this famous selection from his* Confessions, *Augustine presents his thoughts on these and related puzzles—and offers a solution to them.*]

Book XI—Time and Eternity

What is time? Who can explain this easily and briefly? Who can comprehend this even in thought so as to articulate the answer in words? Yet what do we speak of, in our familiar everyday conversation, more than of time? We surely know what we mean when we speak of it. We also know what is meant when we hear someone else talking about it. What then is time? Provided that no one asks me, I know. If I want to explain it to an inquirer, I do not know. But I confidently affirm myself to know that if nothing passes away, there is no past time, and if nothing arrives, there is no future time, and if nothing existed there would be no present time. Take the two tenses, past and future. How can they "be" when the past is not now present and the future is not yet present? Yet if the present were always

present, it would not pass into the past: it would not be time but eternity. If then, in order to be time at all, the present is so made that it passes into the past, how can we say that this present also "is"? The cause of its being is that it will cease to be. So indeed we cannot truly say that time exists except in the sense that it tends towards non-existence. . . .

xx (26) What is by now evident and clear is that neither future nor past exists, and it is inexact language to speak of three times—past, present, and future. Perhaps it would be exact to say: there are three times, a present of things past, a present of things present, a present of things to come. In the soul there are these three aspects of time, and I do not see them anywhere else. The present considering the past is the memory, the present considering the present is immediate awareness, the present considering the future is expectation. If we are allowed to use such language, I see three times, and I admit they are three. Moreover, we may say, There are three times, past, present, and future. This customary way of speaking is incorrect, but it is common usage. Let us accept the usage. I do not object and offer no opposition or criticism, as long as what is said is being understood, namely that neither the future nor the past is now present. There are few usages of everyday speech which are exact, and most of our language is inexact. Yet what we mean is communicated.

---

* From *St. Augustine: Confessions*, translated by Henry Chadwick. Copyright © Henry Chadwick 1991. By permission of Oxford University Press.

xxi (27) A little earlier I observed that we measure past periods of time so that we can say that one period is twice as long as another or equal to it, and likewise of other periods of time which we are capable of measuring and reporting. Therefore, as I was saying, we measure periods of time as they are passing, and if anyone says to me "How do you know?" I reply: I know it because we do measure time and cannot measure what has no being; and past and future have none. But how do we measure present time when it has no extension? It is measured when it passes, but not when it has passed, because then there will be nothing there to measure.

When time is measured, where does it come from, by what route does it pass, and where does it go? It must come out of the future, pass by the present, and go into the past; so it comes from what as yet does not exist, passes through that which lacks extension, and goes into that which is now nonexistent. Yet what do we measure but time over some extension? When we speak of lengths of time as single, duple, triple, and equal, or any other temporal relation of this kind, we must be speaking of periods of time possessing extension. In what extension then do we measure time as it is passing? Is it in the future out of which it comes to pass by? No, for we do not measure what does not yet exist. Is it in the present through which it passes? No, for we cannot measure that which has no extension. Is it in the past into which it is moving? No, for we cannot measure what now does not exist. . . .

xxiv (31) Do you command me to concur if someone says time is the movement of a physical entity? You do not. For I learn that no body can be moved except in time. You tell me so, but I do not learn that the actual movement of a body constitutes time. That is not what you tell me. For when a body is moved, it is by time that I measure the duration of the movement, from the moment it begins until it ends. Unless I have observed the point when it begins, and if its movement is continuous so that I cannot observe when it ceases, I am unable to measure except for the period from the beginning to the end of my observation. If my observing lasts for a considerable time, I can only report that a long time passed, but not precisely how much. When we say how much, we are making a comparison—as, for example, "This period was of the same length as that," or "This period was twice as long as that," or some such relationship.

If, however, we have been able to note the points in space from which and to which a moving body passes, or the parts of a body when it is spinning on its axis, then we can say how much time the movement of the body or its parts required to move from one point to another. It follows that a body's movement is one thing, the period by which we measure is another. It is self-evident which of these is to be described as time. Moreover, a body may at one point be moving, at another point at rest. We measure by time and say "It was standing still for the same time that it was in movement," or "It was still for two or three times as long as it was in movement," or any other measurement we may make, either by precise observation or by a rough estimate (we customarily say "more or less"). Therefore time is not the movement of a body. . . .

Nevertheless we do measure periods of time. And yet the times we measure are not those which do not yet exist, nor those which already have no existence, nor those which extend over no interval of time, nor those which reach no conclusions. So the times we measure are not future nor past nor present nor those in process of passing away. Yet we measure periods of time.

(35) "God, Creator of all things"—*Deus Creator omnium*—the line consists of eight syllables, in which short and long syllables alternate. So the four which are short (the first, third, fifth, and seventh) are single in relation to the four long syllables (the second, fourth, sixth, and eighth). Each of the long syllables has twice the time of the short. As I recite the words, I also observe that this is so, for it is evident to sense-perception. To the degree that the sense-perception is unambiguous, I measure the long syllable by the short one, and perceive it to be twice the length. But when one syllable sounds after another, the short first, the long after it, how shall I keep my hold on the short, and how use it to apply a measure to the long, so as to verify that the long is twice as much? The long does not begin to sound unless the short has ceased to sound. I can hardly measure the long during the presence of its sound, as measuring becomes possible only after it has ended. When it is finished, it has gone into the past. What then is it which I measure? Where is the short syllable with which I am making my measurement? Where is the long which I am measuring? Both have sounded; they have flown away; they belong to the past. They now do not exist. And I offer my measurement and declare as confidently as a practised sense-perception will allow, that the short is single, the long double— I mean in the time they occupy. I can do this only because they are past and gone. Therefore it is not

the syllables which I am measuring, but something in my memory which stays fixed there.

(36) So it is in you, my mind, that I measure periods of time. Do not distract me; that is, do not allow yourself to be distracted by the hubbub of the impressions being made upon you. In you, I affirm, I measure periods of time. The impression which passing events make upon you abides when they are gone. That present consciousness is what I am measuring, not the stream of past events which have caused it. When I measure periods of time, that is what I am actually measuring. Therefore, either this is what time is, or time is not what I am measuring.

. . . Who therefore can deny that the future does not yet exist? Yet already in the mind there is an expectation of the future. Who can deny that the past does not now exist? Yet there is still in the mind a memory of the past. None can deny that present time lacks any extension because it passes in a flash. Yet attention is continuous, and it is through this that what will be present progresses towards being absent. So the future, which does not exist, is not a long period of time. A long future is a long expectation of the future. And the past, which has no existence, is not a long period of time. A long past is a long memory of the past.

SELECTION 5.2

Summa Theologica: **Questions on God***　　　*St. Thomas Aquinas*

[*First question (Article 12): Can we know God by reason? After presenting both sides, Aquinas states his view in the Reply. Second question (Article 13): Can we gain a deeper knowledge of God through grace? Aquinas again presents both sides and gives his reply.*]

Article 12: Can we know God by our natural reason in this life?

1. It seems that we cannot know God by our natural reason in this life. For Boethius says, "reason cannot grasp simple forms." But God, as I have shown, is a supremely simple form. So, we cannot gain knowledge of him by natural reason.

2. Moreover, according to Aristotle the soul understands nothing by natural reason without images. But since God is incorporeal our imagination can have no image of him. So, we cannot know him by natural reason.

3. Both good and bad people have natural reason since they each have a human nature. But only the

good have knowledge of God. As Augustine says, "The weak eye of the human mind is not fixed on that excellent light unless purified by the justice of faith." So, we cannot know God by natural reason.

On the contrary, St Paul says, "What is known about God [i.e. what can be known about him by natural reason] is manifest in them."

Reply: The knowledge that is natural to us has its source in our senses and therefore extends just so far as it can be led by sensible things. But our understanding cannot reach to a vision of God's essence from these, for sensible creatures are effects of God which are unequal to the power of their cause. So, knowing them does not lead us to understand the whole power of God, and we do not thereby see his essence. Yet they are effects which are causally dependent, so we can at least be led from them to know of God that he exists and that he has whatever must belong to him as the first cause of all things, a cause that surpasses all that he causes.

So, we know about God's relation to creatures (that he is the cause of them all), and about the difference between him and them (that he is not a part of what he has caused). We also know that the difference between God and his effects is not due to any deficiency in him but to the fact that he vastly surpasses them all.

---

* From Thomas Aquinas, *Summa Theologiae, Questions on God,* edited by Brian Davies and Brian Leftow, pp. 134–137. Reprinted with permission of Cambridge University Press.

Hence:

1. By reason we can know *that* a simple form is, even though we cannot succeed in understanding *what* it is.

2. God is known to natural reason through the images of his effects.

3. Knowledge of God through his essence belongs only to the good since it is a gift of grace. But the knowledge we have by natural reason belongs to both good and bad. Augustine says in his *Reconsiderations*, "I now disapprove of what I said in a certain prayer, 'O God who wants only the clean of heart to know truth . . .' for one could reply that many who are unclean know many truths" (i.e. by natural reason).

Article 13: Besides the knowledge we have of God by natural reason, is there in this life a deeper knowledge that we have through grace?

1. It seems that by grace we do not have a deeper knowledge of God than we have by natural reason. For Dionysius says that those best united to God in this life are united to him as to something utterly unknown. He says this even of Moses, who received great graces of knowledge. But we can come to be joined to God by natural reason without knowing what he is. So, grace gives us no greater knowledge of God than natural reason does.

2. Moreover, by natural reason we only come to know God through images in the imagination. Yet the same is true of the knowledge we have through grace, for Dionysius says: "It is impossible for the divine ray to shine upon us except as screened round about by the many-coloured sacred veils." So, by grace we have no fuller knowledge of God than we have by natural reason.

3. Again, our minds adhere to God by the grace of faith. But faith does not seem to be knowledge, for Gregory says we have "faith and not knowledge of the unseen." So, grace adds nothing to our knowledge of God.

On the contrary, St Paul says, "God has revealed to us through his Spirit" a wisdom which "none of this world's rulers knew"—and a gloss says that this refers to philosophers.

Reply: We have a more perfect knowledge of God by grace than we have by natural reason. The latter depends on two things: images derived from the sensible world, and the natural intellectual light by which we make abstract intelligible concepts from these images. But human knowledge is helped by the revelation of grace when it comes to both of these. The light of grace strengthens the intellectual light. As is clear in the case of prophetic visions, God gives us images better suited to express divine things than those we receive naturally from the sensible world. Moreover, God sometimes gives us sensible signs and spoken words to show us something of the divine—as at the baptism of Christ, when the Holy Spirit appeared in the form of a dove and the voice of the Father was heard saying, "This is my beloved Son."

Hence:

1. Although in this life revelation does not tell us what God is and so joins us to him as if to an unknown, nevertheless it helps us to know him better in that it shows us more and greater works of his and teaches us things about him that we can never arrive at by natural reason, as for instance that God is both three and one.

2. The stronger our intellectual light, the deeper the understanding we derive from images, whether these are received in a natural way, from the senses, or formed in the imagination by divine power. Revelation provides us with a divine light which enables us to attain a more profound understanding from these images.

3. Faith is a sort of knowledge in that it makes the mind assent to something knowable. Yet the assent here is not due to the vision of the believer but to the vision of the one who is believed. So, in so far as it lacks the element of seeing, faith fails to be knowledge in a strict sense of the term, for such knowledge causes the mind to assent through what is seen and through an understanding of first principles.

CHECKLIST

To help you review, a checklist of the key philosophers of this chapter can be found online at www.mhhe.com/moore9e.

KEY TERMS AND CONCEPTS

Academics 77	Pyrrhonists 77
agoge 77	realism 83
ataraxia 77	Skepticism 72
conceptualism 83	teleological
creation *ex nihilo* 76	explanation 85
epoche 77	Ten Tropes 77
Hellenistic age 70	total versus modified
Neoplatonism 72	skeptic 76
nominalism 83	universals 82
principle of	
noncontradiction 78	

QUESTIONS FOR DISCUSSION AND REVIEW

1. Compare and contrast the views of the Academics and the Pyrrhonists.

2. "Nothing can be known." What is a powerful objection to this claim?

3. "I do not know whether knowledge is possible." Defend or attack this claim.

4. Defend some version of total skepticism.

5. What is creation *ex nihilo?* State a reason for thinking that creation *ex nihilo* is impossible.

6. Explain the difference between realism, conceptualism, and nominalism. Which theory is the most plausible, and why?

7. Billy the Kid cannot be in more than one place at a given time. Can Billy the Kid's *height* (five feet, four inches) be in more than one place? Explain.

8. Can we say only what God is not?

9. Give a teleological explanation of why polar bears have white fur.

SUGGESTED FURTHER READINGS

Go online to www.mhhe.com/moore9e for a list of suggested further readings.

6

The Rise of Modern Metaphysics and Epistemology

Every part of the universe is body, and that which is not body is not part of the universe.   —Thomas Hobbes

Wood, stone, fire, water, flesh . . . are things perceived by my senses; and things perceived by the senses are immediately perceived; and things immediately perceived are ideas; and ideas cannot exist outside the mind.
     —George Berkeley

The transitional period between medieval and modern times was the Renaissance (fourteenth through sixteenth centuries). Through its emphasis on worldly experience and reverence for classical culture, the Renaissance helped emancipate Europe from the intellectual authority of the Church. The modern period in history (and philosophy) that followed lasted through the nineteenth century. Its interesting cultural and social developments include, among other things, the rise of nation-states, the spread of capitalism and industrialization, the exploration and settlement of the New World, the decline of religion, and the eventual domination of science as the most revered source of knowledge. The last development is the most important to a history of metaphysics and epistemology and is briefly described in the box "The Scientific Revolution."

The Scientific Revolution

Modern science began with the Scientific Revolution. That commenced when Copernicus (1473–1543) broke with long tradition and proposed (mid-sixteenth century) that the earth is not the center of the universe but in fact revolves, with the other planets, around the sun. The essence of the revolution lies in several ideas: (1) it is *important* to understand how the world works; (2) to do that, you have to *examine the world itself* rather than read Aristotle or consult scripture; (3) a fruitful way to examine the world is through *experimentation*—this is an idea expressed most clearly by Francis Bacon (1561–1626); and (4) the world is a *mechanical system* that can be *described mathematically*—this is an idea expressed most clearly by René Descartes (1596–1650). The details of the mechanistic Cartesian picture of the universe were filled in (to a degree) by the observations and findings of (among others) Tycho Brahe (1546–1601), Johannes Kepler (1571–1630), Galileo Galilei (1564–1642), and, most important, Sir Isaac Newton (1642–1727), who combined the various discoveries into a unified description of the universe based on the concept of gravitation.

Certain newly invented instruments aided the early scientists in their study of the world, including, most famously, the telescope, the microscope, the vacuum pump, and the mechanical clock. And by no means were the findings of the new science limited to astronomy and the dynamics of moving bodies. There were, for example, William Harvey's (1578–1657) discovery of the circulation of the blood, William Gilbert's (1540–1603) investigations of electricity and magnetism, and the various discoveries of Robert Boyle (1627–1691)—the father of chemistry—concerning gases, metals, combustion, acids and bases, and the nature of colors.

Another important idea that came to be characteristic of the Scientific Revolution was that the fundamental constituents of the natural world are basically corpuscular or atomistic—things are made out of tiny particles. The modern scientists (in effect) declared that Democritus had gotten things right.

To most educated Westerners today, it is a matter of plain fact that there exists a universe of physical objects related to one another spatiotemporally. These objects are composed, we are inclined to believe, of minute atoms and subatomic particles that interact with one another in mathematically describable ways.

We are also accustomed to think that in addition to the spatiotemporal *physical* universe there exist human (and perhaps other) observers who are able to perceive their corner of the universe and, within certain limits, to understand it. The *understanding,* we are inclined to suppose, and the *minds* in which this understanding exists, are not themselves physical entities, though we also tend to think that understanding and minds depend in some sense on the functioning of physical entities such as the brain and central nervous system. They, the understanding itself and the minds that have it—unlike physical things such as brains and atoms and nerve impulses and energy fields—exist in time but not in space. They, unlike physical things, are not bound by the laws of physics and are not made up of parts.

Thus, today it seems to be a matter of plain common sense that reality has a dual nature. The world or the universe, we believe, consists of physical objects on one hand and minds on the other. In a normal living person, mind and matter are intertwined in such a way that what happens to the body can affect the mind

Galileo being tried for heresy before a papal tribunal.

and what happens in the mind can affect the body. The clearest examples of mind–body interaction occur when the mind, through an act of will, causes the body to perform some action or when something that happens to the body triggers a new thought in the mind.

So this *commonsense metaphysics,* as we have been describing it, is dualistic. It supposes that two different kinds of phenomena exist: physical and mental (often called "spiritual"). *Dualism* is essentially the "two-realms view" invented by Plato, incorporated with changes into Christianity by Augustine and others and transmitted to us in its contemporary form by early modern philosophers.

Although our commonsense metaphysics is dualistic, it did not have to be that way; we might have adopted an alternative metaphysical perspective. Here are the main possibilities:

- **Dualism.** This view holds that what exists is either physical or mental ("spiritual"); some things, such as a human person, have both a physical component (a physical body) and a mental component (a mind).
- **Materialism,** or physicalism. This view holds that only the physical exists. Accordingly, so-called mental things are in some sense manifestations of an underlying physical reality. (Do not confuse metaphysical materialism with the doctrine that the most important thing is to live comfortably and acquire wealth.)

- **Idealism.** This view holds that only the mental (or "spiritual") exists. Accordingly, so-called physical things are in some sense manifestations of the mind or of thought. (Do not confuse metaphysical idealism with the views of the dreamer who places ideals above practical considerations.)

- *Alternative views.* Some theorists have held that what exists is ultimately neither mental nor spiritual; still others have believed that what exists is ultimately both mental and physical. How could it be both mental and physical? According to this view, sometimes called **double aspect theory,** the mental and physical are just different *ways of looking at* the same things—things that in themselves are neutral between the two categories.

Thanks to the legacy of Greek and Christian influences on Western civilization, dualism continues to command the assent of common sense. Increasingly, however, the march of science seems philosophically to undermine metaphysical dualism in favor of materialism. At stake here are three important questions:

1. Does an immaterial God exist?
2. Do humans have free will?
3. Is there life after death?

Unfortunately for those who would prefer the answer to one or another of the questions to be "yes," a scientific understanding of the world tends to imply the materialist view that all that exists is matter. This is one major reason why modern metaphysics may be said to be concerned with powerful stuff: riding on the outcome of the competition among the perspectives just listed (dualism, materialism, idealism, and alternative views) is the reasonableness of believing in God, free will, and the hereafter.

Let us therefore consider each of these perspectives as it arose during the modern period of philosophy.

Chronology of Postmedieval History

Here, for easy reference, are the dates of the major periods in postmedieval history mentioned in the text:

The Renaissance: the fourteenth through sixteenth centuries

The Reformation and Counter-Reformation: the sixteenth century

The Scientific Revolution: the seventeenth century (though that revolution still continues)

The Enlightenment or *Age of Reason:* the eighteenth century

The Industrial Revolution: the mid-eighteenth to mid-nineteenth centuries

The Romantic Period: the late eighteenth to very early nineteenth centuries

The Age of Technology: the twentieth century to the present

DESCARTES AND DUALISM

Many European thinkers of the sixteenth century began to question established precepts and above all to question the accepted authorities as arbiters of truth. That so-and-so said that something was true was no longer automatically accepted as proof of that something, no matter who said it or what the something was. This tendency to question authority effectively set the stage for the Scientific Revolution and modern philosophy, both of which are products of the seventeenth century. (For a chronology of postmedieval history, see the box above.)

Modern philosophy is usually said to have begun with **René Descartes** [day-KART] (1596–1650), mathematician, scientist, and, of course, philosopher. Descartes' importance to Western intellectual history cannot be overestimated. Other thinkers we have mentioned may have equaled him in significance, but none has surpassed him. He made important contributions to physiology, psychology, optics, and especially mathematics, in which he originated the Cartesian[1] coordinates and Cartesian curves. It is thanks to Descartes that students now study analytic geometry; he introduced it to the world.

Descartes was a Catholic, but he also believed there are important truths that cannot be ascertained through the authority of the Church. These include those truths that pertain to the ultimate nature of existing things.

But what, then, he wondered, is to be the *criterion* of truth and knowledge in such matters? What is to be the criterion by which one might separate *certain knowledge* about matters of fact from inferior products such as *mere belief?*

Such questions were not new to philosophy, of course. During the Renaissance, the classical skeptical works, notably those by Sextus, were "rediscovered," published, and taken quite seriously—even contributing to the controversies during the Protestant Reformation about the knowability of religious beliefs. In addition, in the sixteenth and seventeenth centuries, various new skeptical writings appeared. Especially noteworthy in this resurgent skeptical tradition were Pierre Gassendi (1592–1655) and Marin Mersenne (1588–1648), who separately used a variety of

---

[1] *Cartesian* is the adjective form of Descartes.

PROFILE: René Descartes (1596–1650)

Descartes had the great fortune to be able to transform his inheritance into a comfortable annual income on which he lived. And he did not waste his time. Before he died, he had made important advances in science, mathematics, and philosophy. Descartes founded analytic geometry and contributed to the understanding of negative roots. He wrote a text in physiology and did work in psychology. His work in optics was significant. His contributions in philosophy are of enormous importance.

As a youth, Descartes attended the Jesuit College at La Flèche and the University of Poitiers. When he was twenty-one, he joined the Dutch army and, two years later, the Bavarian army. His military experience allowed him to be a spectator of the human drama at first hand and granted him free time to think. In 1628 he retired to Holland, where he lived for twenty years in a tolerant country in which he was free from religious persecution.

Descartes was a careful philosopher and a cautious person. Although he took great issue with the medievalist thinking of his teachers, he did not make them aware of his reactions. Later, when he heard that the Church had condemned Galileo for his writings, he decided that he would have his works published only one hundred years after his death. He subsequently changed his mind, though he came to wish that he had not. For when he did publish some of his ideas, they were bitterly attacked by Protestant theologians; Catholic denunciations came later. This caused Descartes to say that, had he been smarter, he would not have written anything, so he would have had more peace and quiet to think.

Two unconnected incidents in Descartes' life are always mentioned in philosophy texts. One is that the insights that underlay his philosophy came to him in dreams after he had spent a winter day relaxing in a well-heated room while in the army in Bavaria. The other is that he accepted an invitation, with some reluctance, to tutor Queen Christina of Sweden in 1649. This was a big mistake, for the cold weather and early hour of his duties literally killed him. We can only speculate what the queen learned from the episode.

Descartes' principal philosophical works are *Discourse on Method* (1637), *Meditations on First Philosophy* (1641), and *Principles of Philosophy* (1644).

skeptical arguments (which we do not have the space to discuss) to establish the unknowability of the true nature of things. Both believed, however, that a study of the appearances of things could yield information useful for living in this world.

Descartes was vitally concerned with skeptical questions as to the possibility of knowledge, but he was no skeptic. His interest in mathematics strongly affected his philosophical reflections, and it was his more or less lifelong intention to formulate a unified science of nature that was as fully certain as arithmetic.

He did, however, employ skepticism as a method of achieving certainty. His idea was simple enough: I will doubt everything that can possibly be doubted, he reasoned, and if anything is left, then it will be absolutely certain. Then I will consider what it is about this certainty (if there is one) that places it beyond doubt, and that will provide me with a *criterion* of truth and knowledge, a yardstick against which I can measure all other purported truths to see if they, too, are beyond doubt.

Skepticism as the Key to Certainty

Let's see how Descartes' *doubting methodology* worked.

To doubt every proposition that he possibly could, Descartes employed two famous conjectures, the **dream conjecture** and the **evil demon conjecture.** For all I know, Descartes said, I might now be dreaming—that is Descartes'

Descartes' Conjectures

For all I know, I might now be dreaming. This is Descartes' dream conjecture, and it is easy enough to disprove, correct? I just pinch myself. But then again . . . am I just dreaming that I pinched myself? Might not any evidence I have that I am now awake just be dream evidence? Can I really be certain that I won't find myself in a few moments waking up, realizing that I have been dreaming? And thus can I really be sure that the things I see around me, this desk and book, these arms and legs, have any existence outside my mind?

Well, you may say, even if I am dreaming, there are still many things I cannot doubt; even if I am dreaming, I cannot doubt, for instance, that two and three are five or that a square has four sides.

But then again—and this is where Descartes' evil demon conjecture comes in—of course, it seems absolutely certain to me that two and three make five and that a square has four sides. But *some* propositions that have seemed absolutely certain to me have turned out to be false. So how can I be sure that *these* propositions (that two and three make five and that a square has four sides), or any other proposition that seems certain to me, are not likewise false? For all I know, a deceitful and all-powerful intelligence has so programmed me that I find myself regarding as absolute certainties propositions that in fact are not true at all.

Descartes thought that these two conjectures combined in this way to force him "to avow that there is nothing at all that I formerly believed to be true of which it is impossible to doubt."

dream conjecture. And further, he said, for all I know, some malevolent demon devotes himself to deceiving me at every turn so that I regard as true and certain propositions that are in fact false. That supposition is Descartes' evil demon conjecture.

Yes, these two conjectures are totally bizarre, and Descartes was as aware of that as you are. But that is just the point. What Descartes was looking for was a measure of certainty that escapes even the most incredible and bizarre possibilities of falsehood.

And what he discovered, when he considered everything he thought he knew in the light of one or the other of these two bizarre possibilities, is that he could doubt *absolutely everything, save one indubitable truth:* "I think, therefore I am"—*cogito, ergo sum.* Remember this phrase, which is from Descartes' *Discourse on Method.*

What Descartes meant is that any attempt to doubt one's existence as a thinking being is impossible because to doubt is to think and to exist. Try for a moment to doubt your own existence, and you will see what Descartes meant. The self that doubts its own existence must surely exist to be able to doubt in the first place. (For further description of this line of reasoning, see the box "Descartes' Conjectures.") Like Augustine, Descartes had found certain truth in his inability to doubt his own existence.

The "Clear and Distinct" Litmus Test

Descartes went much further than Augustine. Having supposedly found certain knowledge in his own existence as a thing that thinks, he reasoned as follows:

I am certain that I am a thing that thinks; but do I not then likewise know what is required to make me certain of a truth? In this knowledge of my existence as a thinking thing there is nothing that assures me of its truth, excepting the clear and distinct perception of that which I state, which would not indeed suffice to assure me that what I say is true, if it could ever happen that a thing that I conceived so clearly and distinctly could be false. And accordingly it seems to me that already I can establish as a general rule that all things that I perceive very clearly and very distinctly are true.

In other words, Descartes examined his single indubitable truth to see what guaranteed its certainty and saw that any other proposition he apprehended with identical "clarity and distinctness" must likewise be immune to doubt. In short, he had discovered in the certainty of his own existence an essential characteristic of certain truth: anything that was as clear and distinct as his own existence would pass the litmus test and would also have to be certain.

Using this **clear and distinct criterion,** Descartes found to his own satisfaction that he could regard as certain much of what he had initially had cause to doubt. This doubting methodology was like geometry, in which a theorem whose truth initially only *seems* true is demonstrated as absolutely certain by deducing it from basic axioms by means of rules of logic. Descartes' axiom was, in effect, "I think, therefore I am," and his rule of logic was "Whatever I perceive clearly and distinctly is certain."

And so Descartes, having armed himself with an absolutely reliable litmus test of truth, discovers first that he has certain knowledge that God exists. (We shall go over the details of Descartes' proof of God's existence in Part Three.) Also, Descartes finds that he knows for certain, and that therefore it is the case, that God would not deceive the thinking mind with perceptions of an external world—a world of objects outside the mind—if such did not exist. Thus, for Descartes, there are, beyond God, two separate and distinct substances, and reality has a dual nature. On one hand is *material substance,* whose essential attribute is **extension** (occupancy of space), and on the other hand is *mind,* whose essential attribute is **thought.** Because a substance, according to

Oliva Sabuco de Nantes and the Body–Soul Connection

Descartes speculated that the mind interacts with the body in the pineal gland. Sixty or so years before Descartes, **Oliva Sabuco de Nantes** [sah-BOO-ko] (1562–?) proposed that, as the properties of the mind (or "soul," as she called it) are not physical properties, they cannot be physically located in some specific spot. Thus, she reasoned, the connection between body and soul occurs *throughout* the brain. The brain and the rest of the body "serve the soul like house servants serve the house," she maintained. She argued that a person is a microcosm (a miniature version) of the world, and this discloses that, in the same way as God activates, rules, and governs the world, the soul governs the "affects, movements, and actions of humans."

It is worth mentioning that Sabuco also believed that the intimate connection between soul and brain means there is a close relationship between psychological and physical health and between morality and medicine. For example, as soon as a negative emotion such as *sorrow* begins to affect our body, she said, we must control it before it becomes unmanageable *despair*. Virtuous passions promote good health, she said; immoral passions cause sickness and disease. As an illustration, she cited excessive sexual activity, which causes (she believed) excessive loss of an essential brain fluid, resulting in brainstem dehydration and the insanity found in advanced cases of syphilis and gonorrhea. There exists, she reasoned, a natural, medical basis for moral sanctions against sexual promiscuity. (It is pretty easy to think of a modern illustration of this thesis.)

Sabuco, born in Alcaraz, Spain, published her important book, *New Philosophy of Human Nature,* when she was only twenty-five years old. This was at the tail end of the Spanish Inquisition—not the most congenial of times for objective scholarship—and Sabuco was taking something of a risk as a woman writer of philosophy. Nevertheless, she was highly knowledgeable about ancient and medieval thinkers, and her book was cleared by the Church with only a few changes. It became quite influential and was published several times during her lifetime and in every century after her death.

Certainly, Sabuco did not solve the problem of mind–body interaction, but she anticipated by several hundred years today's holistic medicine with its emphasis on the intimate connection between mental and physical well-being.

Descartes, "requires nothing other than itself to exist," it follows that mind and matter are totally independent of each other. Still, he thought that in a living person the mind and the material body interact, the motion of the body being sometimes affected by the mind and the thoughts of the mind being influenced by physical sensations.

This is, of course, familiar stuff. Our commonsense metaphysics is pretty much the dualistic metaphysics of Descartes. (However, see the box on Oliva Sabuco.) Unfortunately, there are embarrassing difficulties in the Cartesian dualistic metaphysics. These difficulties vexed Descartes and have yet to be plausibly resolved. In Chapter 9 we explain these difficulties in some detail.

To anticipate what is said there, Descartes thought:

1. Material things, including one's own body, are completely subject to physical laws.

But he also thought:

2. The immaterial mind can move one's body.

The difficulty is that, if the immaterial mind can do this, then one's body evidently is *not* completely subject to physical laws after all. It seems contradictory to hold both (1) and (2). Do *you* hold both (1) and (2)?

Descartes also found it difficult to understand just how something immaterial *could* affect the movement of something material. He said that the mind interacts with the body through "vital spirits" in the brain, but he recognized that this explanation was quite obscure and almost wholly metaphorical. It was, in short, a dodge.

Some of Descartes' followers proposed a solution to the problem of how the immaterial mind interacts with the material body, given that the body is supposed to be subject to physical laws. The solution is called **parallelism.** The mind, they argued, does not *really* cause the body to move. When I will that my hand should move, my act of willing only *appears* to cause my hand to move.

What actually happens is two parallel and coordinated series of events: one a series of mental happenings, and the other a series that involves happenings to material things. Thus, my act of willing my hand to move does not cause my hand to move, but the act of willing and the movement of the hand *coincide.* Hence, it *appears* that the willing causes the moving.

Why do these events just happen to coincide? To account for the coinciding of the mental happenings with the physical happenings, Descartes' followers invoked God. God, they said, is the divine coordinator between the series of mental happenings and the series of material happenings. (In a variant of parallelism known as **occasionalism,** when I will my hand to move, that is the occasion on which God causes my hand to move.)

This theory of parallelism seems far-fetched, true. But perhaps that only illustrates how serious a difficulty it is to suppose both that material things, including one's body, are completely subject to physical laws and that the immaterial mind can move one's body.

To date, a satisfactory explanation of the problem of interaction still has not been found.

Despite these problems, Descartes thought he had succeeded in establishing metaphysical dualism as absolutely certain. He also thought he had shown that the mind, because it is not in space and hence does not move, is not in any sense subject to physical laws and therefore is "free." The metaphysical dualism that survives today as mere "common sense," though it originated with Plato and was incorporated into Christianity by Augustine, survives in the form developed by Descartes. Yesterday's philosophy became today's common sense.

Notice Descartes' overall approach to metaphysical issues. Instead of asking, "What is the basic stuff?" or "Of what does reality consist?" Descartes took an indirect approach and asked, in effect, "What do I know is the basic stuff?" and "Of what can I be certain about the nature of reality?" Descartes tried to discover *metaphysical* truth about what *is* through epistemological inquiry about *what can be known.*

We will call this approach to metaphysical truth the **epistemological detour.** After Descartes, and largely because of him, modern philosophy has attached considerable importance to epistemology, and metaphysical inquiry is often conducted via the epistemological detour.

Unfortunately, maybe the least debatable part of Descartes' overall reasoning is the two skeptical arguments (the dream conjecture and the evil demon conjecture) he advanced at the outset, which seem to make it a live issue whether what passes for knowledge genuinely is knowledge. After Descartes, the philosophers of the seventeenth century became divided about the power of reason in overcoming skepticism. This division is summarized in the box later in this chapter (page 113) titled "Rationalism and Empiricism."

HOBBES AND MATERIALISM

Thomas Hobbes (1588–1679) read Descartes' *Meditations* before its publication and raised several criticisms, which, together with Descartes' rejoinders, were published by Descartes. About ten years later, in 1651, Hobbes published his own major work, *Leviathan.*

Hobbes was on close terms with many of the best scientists and mathematicians of the period, including most significantly Galileo, and their discoveries seemed to him to imply clearly that all things are made of material particles and that all change reduces to motion. Accordingly, the basic premise of Hobbes's metaphysics is that *all that exists is bodies in motion,* motion being a continual relinquishing of one place and acquiring of another. Because, according to Hobbes, there are two main types of bodies, physical bodies and political bodies, there are two divisions of philosophy, natural and civil. Here we are concerned with Hobbes's natural philosophy. Later we will examine his civil, or political, philosophy, which was enormously important.

Now, this business that all that exists is bodies in motion might sound plausible, until you consider such things as thoughts or acts of volition or emotion. Can it really be held that *thought* is just matter in motion? That *emotions* are? That *hatred* is? "Yes," said Hobbes.

Perception

Hobbes's strategy was to show that there is a basic mental activity, **perception,** or, as he called it, "sense," from which all other mental phenomena are derived and that perception itself reduces to matter in motion.

Perception, he maintained, occurs as follows: Motion in the external world causes motion within us. This motion within (which Hobbes called a "phantasm") is experienced by us as an external object (or group of objects) having certain properties. The properties do not *really* exist in the objects, Hobbes said; they are just the way the objects *seem* to us:

> The things that really are in the world outside us are those motions by which these seemings are caused.

So motion outside us causes motion within us, which is a perception. If the internal motion remains for a while even after the external object is no longer present, it is then *imagination* or *memory.* And *thinking,* he said, is merely a sequence of these perceptions. (There are subtleties in his account of thinking we won't now bother with.)

Now, humans, unlike animals (Hobbes said), are able to form signs or names (words) to designate perceptions, and it is this ability that allows humans to reason. In Hobbes's view, *reasoning* is nothing but "adding and subtracting of the consequences of general names." Reasoning occurs, for example, when you see that the consequences of the name *circle* are, among other things, that if a straight line is drawn through the center of a circle, the circle has been divided into two equal parts.

As for *decisions* and other voluntary actions, such as walking or speaking or moving our arms, these are all movements of the body that begin internally as "endeavors," caused by perceptions. When the endeavor is toward something that causes it, this is *desire;* when away from it, it is *aversion.* Love is merely desire, and hate merely aversion. We call a thing "good" when it is an object of desire and "bad" when it is an object of aversion. *Deliberation* is simply an alternation of desires and aversions, and *will* is nothing but the last desire or aversion remaining in a deliberation.

We've left out the finer details of Hobbes's account, but this should show you how Hobbes tried to establish that every aspect of human psychology is a derivative of perception and that perception itself reduces to matter in motion.

This theory that all is matter in motion may well strike you as implausible, maybe even ridiculous. Nevertheless, as you will see in Chapter 9, it expresses in a rudimentary form a view that is quite attractive to many contemporary philosophers and brain scientists, namely, that every mental activity is a brain process of one sort or another.

THE ALTERNATIVE VIEWS OF CONWAY, SPINOZA, AND LEIBNIZ

So much, then, for Descartes and dualism and Hobbes and materialism. We still need to discuss the remaining two perspectives listed at the beginning of this chapter, idealism and "alternative views." Since historically idealism was introduced last, we turn now to these alternative views—the three alternative metaphysical systems of Anne Conway, Benedictus de Spinoza, and Gottfried Wilhelm, Baron von Leibniz. It must be said that Spinoza and Leibniz had the greatest influence on subsequent developments, but we shall treat the three in chronological order.

The Metaphysics of Anne Conway

The metaphysical system that **Anne Conway** (1631–1679) developed is a *monadology:* a view that all things are reducible to a single substance that is itself irreducible. (This is roughly what atomic theory was until the discovery of subatomic particles in the twentieth century.) The most famous monadology in the history of philosophy is that of Leibniz. Leibniz was familiar with Conway's metaphysics, and scholars believe Conway's philosophy was a forerunner of Leibniz's.

In Conway's view, there is a kind of continuum between the most material and the most mental or "spiritual" substances. All created substances ("Creatures,"

PROFILE: Anne Finch, The Viscountess Conway (1631–1679)

Like most women of the seventeenth century, Anne Conway, as she is usually called, had no formal education. Her father, who was speaker of the House of Commons, died a week before Anne was born. But her family remained influential, her half-brother becoming lord high chancellor in England. So Anne Finch grew up knowing some of the most important and influential English intellectuals of her time. At home, she somehow managed to learn French, Latin, Hebrew, and Greek. She also studied mathematics and philosophy. She was critical of the work of Descartes (or "Cartes," as he was sometimes called), Hobbes, and Spinoza. And she discussed philosophy with some fairly well-known philosophers who lived in or visited England during her lifetime. The philosophical community was a small one there, and everybody in it seems to have known everybody else. She worked closely with some influential philosophers known as the Cambridge Platonists.

Anne Conway suffered from migraine headaches, and that is supposed to account for the unreadable scrawl with which she penciled her book, *The Principles of the Most Ancient and Modern Philosophy*. Depending on which scholar you read, she wrote it either between 1671 and 1674 or between 1677 and 1679. She died without having a chance to correct or revise it. Her husband was away in Ireland at the time; and Francis Mercury von Helmont, her friend and one of the colleagues with whom she often discussed philosophy and religion, preserved her body in wine until her husband could return for the funeral.

Von Helmont had Conway's work translated into Latin and published in 1690. Two years later, it was translated back into English by somebody whose initials were J. C. Now, von Helmont was a good friend of Leibniz and showed him Conway's book. Scholars who have studied Conway's philosophy consider her to have been a forerunner of Leibniz in many ways. However, in the words of Sarah Hutton, writing in 2003 in the *Stanford Encyclopedia of Philosophy*,[*]

> although she was unusual as a female philosopher of the seventeenth century, by virtue of the fact that her philosophy achieved publication, the anonymity of her work has ensured that she has suffered the same neglect that has been the lot of most pre-modern female philosophers.

A digital copy of *The Principles of the Most Ancient and Modern Philosophy* is available online at http://digital.library.upenn.edu/women/conway/principles/principles.html.

---

[*] http://plato.stanford.edu/entries/conway.

Conway called them) are both mental and physical to some degree or other. Conway also argued that all created substances are dependent on God's decision to create them. Moreover, she said that all such Creatures have both an individual essence (what makes one thing different from another) and an essence that is common to all. This essence in common is what later came to be known as *de re* modality. The idea of *de re* essentially means that a property (in this case, the property of being both mental and physical) must be a property of anything that is created by God; otherwise, it ceases to be what it is. It could not exist except that it is necessarily both mental and physical. Everything—persons, animals, plants, inanimate objects (furniture)—is a substance. And everything is partly physical and partly mental, and could not be otherwise.

God, of course, is another matter, Conway believed. God is nonmaterial, nonphysical; God is also all-perfect. Therefore, the one thing God cannot do is change his mind about being spiritual. To change his mind and be physical one moment, spiritual the next, and maybe back again, would imply that one state or the other was less than perfect. What possible reason could God have to want to change? What's not to like? Now, that does not mean that God cannot be physical; he just does not *want* to be and never would want to be because that would suggest that he was not perfect before the change. And we all know that if God is anything, he is perfect. God created Christ (making God older than Christ), and Christ, God's first physical manifestation of himself (his first Creature), always had some degree of physical essence and some degree of mental or spiritual essence.

Because God is perfect, Conway held, he is changeless and therefore exists outside the dimension of time. Conway's concept of time is less technical than, but philosophically much like, that articulated recently by the great contemporary physicist Stephen Hawking in his book *A Brief History of Time*, according to whom (roughly) time is the succession of events. Conway called events "motions" and "operations" of created objects (Creatures). Understood this way, time is the measure of changes in things. Because creating (making Creatures) is part of God's primary essence (a necessary property—the way God defines himself, as creator), Conway's God is an eternal creator. The universe is therefore not something that was made at some specific time: it always existed because God always existed and he was always creating. Past and future are all God's present.

Conway's book, *The Principles of the Most Ancient and Modern Philosophy*, reminds one of Spinoza's *Ethics* (see the following section) and Leibniz's *Monadology* (see pages 108–109) in that Conway begins with a series of assumptions or "axioms" (though she did not refer to them as such) and then derives from them various philosophical conclusions or "theorems" (though, again, she did not refer to them as such). If you read these three works, you are apt to be struck by how difficult it is to dispute the writer's conclusions if you accept the assumptions.

Spinoza

God also played an important role in the philosophy of **Benedictus de Spinoza** [spin-O-zuh] (1632–1677), even though Spinoza was considered an atheist. About the time Hobbes was sending his work to Amsterdam for publication, Spinoza was completing his major work, *Ethics*, in that city. Holland during this period of history was the most intellectually tolerant of all European countries, sort of a seventeenth-century Berkeley, California. It was probably also the only country in which the government would have tolerated Spinoza's opinions, which, like Hobbes's, were considered atheistic and repulsive.

Spinoza's *Ethics* consists of some 250 "theorems," each of which he attempted to derive by rigorous deductive logic from a set of eight basic definitions and seven self-evident axioms. Given his axioms and definition of substance (that which depends on nothing else for its conception, i.e., that which is self-subsistent), Spinoza was able to prove that there are no multiple substances, as Descartes thought, but

PROFILE: Benedictus de Spinoza (1632–1677)

The gentle Spinoza was among the most ethical men ever to have lived. "As a natural consequence," twentieth-century philosopher Bertrand Russell observed, "he was considered, during his lifetime and for a century after his death, a man of appalling wickedness."

Spinoza's family was one of many Jewish families that fled Portugal for Holland to escape the terrors of the Inquisition. His serious nature and love of learning were appreciated by all until he pointed out that the Old Testament and biblical tradition were full of inconsistencies. This produced a venomous wrath in the Jewish community. At first Spinoza was offered an annual pension for concealing his doubts. When this failed, the logical next step was taken: an attempt was made to murder him. He was finally, of course, excommunicated from the synagogue.

For a time, Spinoza lived in the house of his Latin teacher, though he later rented a room in a tiny house in Rhynsburg, now a suburb of Leyden, where he earned a sparse living by grinding glass lenses. He lived a modest and frugal existence and preferred to work on his philosophy than to do anything else.

Spinoza became known despite his quiet and retiring existence, and at one point he was offered a professorship at Heidelberg. He declined the appointment, realizing that there would be restrictions on his academic freedom and fearing that his philosophy might draw sharp reactions in German society. In that suspicion he was probably correct, if the fact that many German professors referred to him as "that wretched monster" is any indication.

Still, after his death, some of the greatest thinkers eventually came to appreciate his depth. Hegel went so far as to say that all subsequent philosophy would be a kind of Spinozism.

Spinoza died when he was forty-four, from tuberculosis. His condition was aggravated by the glass dust that he was forced to breathe in his profession. Today, the society for out-of-work American philosophers is called The Lensgrinders.

only one infinite substance. Spinoza equated this substance with God, but we must not be misled by his proof of God. Spinoza's "god" is simply *basic substance:* it is not the personal Judaeo-Christian God; rather, it is simply the sum total of everything that is. It is reality, nature. Although Spinoza was considered an atheist, he was not. On the contrary, he was a pantheist: god is all.

Because there is only one substance, according to Spinoza, thought and extension are not the attributes of two separate and distinct substances, mind and matter, as Descartes had thought. What they are, in Spinoza's system, are different attributes of the one basic substance—they are alternative ways of conceiving of it.

So a living person, from Spinoza's point of view, is not a composite of two different things. The living person is a single unit or "modification" of substance that can be conceived either as extension or as thought. Your "body" is a unit of substance conceived as extension; your "mind" is the selfsame unit of substance conceived as thought.

Because, according to Spinoza, the infinite substance is infinite in all respects, it necessarily has infinite attributes. Therefore, thought and extension are not the only attributes of substance. They are just the only attributes we know—they are the only ways available to us of characterizing or conceiving substance. They are, so to speak, the only "languages" in terms of which we can speak and think about reality or substance.

Accordingly, for Spinoza there is no problem in explaining how the mind interacts with the body, for they are one and the same thing. Wondering how the mind and the body interact is like wondering how your last glass of *wine* and your last glass of *vino* could mix with each other. The mind and the body are the same thing, conceptualized from different viewpoints.

In Spinoza's system, there is no personal immortality after death. Further, free will is an illusion; whatever happens is caused by the nature of substance. Material bodies are governed by the laws of physics, and what happens to them is completely determined by what happened before. Because the mental and the material are one and the same, what happens in minds is as inevitable as what happens in bodies. Everything was, is, and will be exactly as it must be.

There is certainly more to Spinoza's philosophy than this, but this is enough for our purposes here. Where Descartes had postulated two separate substances, both Hobbes and Spinoza postulated only one. For Hobbes, however, what exists is only material; a nonmaterial mental realm does not exist. For Spinoza, what exists is both material and mental, depending on how it is conceptualized. Thus, although neither Hobbes nor Spinoza was faced with Descartes' problem of explaining how two realms, the mental and the material, interact, Hobbes was faced with a different problem, that of *explaining away* the mental realm. We are inclined to ask Hobbes just how and why this illusory mental realm seems so clearly to be real when in fact it is not. For Spinoza, the mental realm is real, and there is nothing that he needs to explain away.

Before leaving Spinoza, we should mention that his philosophy is interesting not merely for its content but for its form as well. Spinoza attempted to geometrize philosophy to an extent unequaled by any other major philosopher.

Euclid began his *Elements* with a set of basic definitions and unproved postulates, and from them he logically derived a set of geometric theorems. Likewise, Spinoza began with definitions and seemingly self-evident axioms and proceeded to derive theorems or "propositions" from them.

For example, Spinoza's Proposition III states, "Things which have nothing in common cannot be one the cause of the other." And under that proposition Spinoza gives a proof that refers back to two of his axioms. Thus, giving Spinoza his definitions, and assuming his axioms are beyond doubt and that he made no mistakes in logic, every one of Spinoza's propositions—his *entire* philosophy—is beyond doubt! Spinoza, unlike Descartes, did not take the epistemological detour by explicitly asking, "What can be known?" But by geometrizing his philosophy, Spinoza attempted to provide a metaphysical system that could be known with certainty to be true.

Leibniz

Many recent scholars qualified to make such a judgment think that **Gottfried Wilhelm, Baron von Leibniz** [LIBE-nits] (1646–1716), was the most brilliant intellect of his age. This judgment is made specifically with the fact in mind that Leibniz was the contemporary of a very bright light, Sir Isaac Newton (1642–1727). Leibniz and Newton, independently of each other, developed the calculus—and at the time, there was bitter controversy over who did so first. Leibniz's calculus was

Newtonians, Metaphysicians, and Émilie du Châtelet

One of the important intellectual controversies of the eighteenth century was whether there could be such a thing as action at a distance. On one hand were the Cartesians (followers of Descartes), who said that, if an object is to move, another object must *come up against it and push it.* On the other hand were the Newtonians (followers of Sir Isaac Newton), who believed in action at a distance—for example, two objects will attract one another through the force of gravity, even though they are separated by space. Cartesians generally viewed the concept of action at a distance, and the forces postulated to explain such action, as mystical and bizarre.

This controversy was just a minor skirmish in a broader conceptual battle, that between Newtonian empirical physics, which was based on observation and experimentation, and speculative metaphysics, which was grounded to a large extent purely on reason and was represented by the Cartesians and, most important, the brilliant Leibniz. According to the metaphysicians, even if Newtonian science described *how* the universe operates, it did not show *why* the universe must operate in that way. The metaphysicians felt that Newtonian physics lacked the rational grounding or certainty found in the systems of a Descartes or a Leibniz.

The metaphysical group had other problems with Newtonianism, too, such as how God fit into the Newtonian picture of the universe. If the universe is a vast physical machine, couldn't God change his mind and destroy it—maybe make a different machine? How could there be human free will if the Newtonians were right and humans are just small parts in God's big machine? Do humans have free will, can they do what they choose, or are they nothing more than bodies, moving in reaction to immaterial forces?

A major participant in the disputes between science and metaphysics was **Émilie du Châtelet** [SHA-ta-lay] (1707–1749). Du Châtelet, a colleague (and lover) of Voltaire, was both a scientist and a philosopher, and her writings were respected by both camps. Her two-volume annotated translation of Newton's *Mathematical Principles of Natural Philosophy* (1759) remains to this day *the* French translation of Newton.

In her three-volume work, *Institutions de Physique* (1740), du Châtelet sought to answer some of the metaphysicians' complaints about Newtonianism. She did this essentially by adapting Leibniz's metaphysical principles (for example, the principle of sufficient reason and the principle of the identity of indiscernibles) to Newtonian science in such a way as to provide, she hoped, a vigorous metaphysical foundation for it and to allay fears that Newtonianism required abandoning important theological tenets. Although du Châtelet perhaps did not resolve all the problems, it is safe to say that she did as much as anyone to bring into focus exactly what the bones of contention were.

published in 1684, a few years before Newton's, but Newton had been slow in publishing his work. (Another controversy between the followers of both thinkers is discussed in the box "Newtonians, Metaphysicians, and Émilie du Châtelet.")

Because Leibniz's philosophy is highly technical and difficult to characterize or summarize in a brief passage, we won't go into it in detail. Basically, it is a complicated metaphysical system according to which the ultimate constituents of reality are indivisible atoms. But Leibniz's atoms are not indivisible units of matter, for, because matter is extended, a piece of matter, however tiny, is always further divisible. Instead, Leibniz's atoms are what he called **monads,** which are indivisible units of force or energy or activity. Here, Leibniz anticipated by a couple of centuries the views of contemporary physics, according to which material particles are a form of energy. Leibniz, however, believed the monads to be entirely *nonphysical* and often referred to them as "souls," though he distinguished them from souls in the ordinary sense.

Leibniz's philosophy is not just haphazard or idle speculation. His entire metaphysical system seems to follow from a few basic and plausible assumptions, or basic principles. One of these principles, for example, the **principle of the identity of indiscernibles,** says that, if two beings have exactly the same set of properties, then they are identical with one another. Another principle, known as the **principle of sufficient reason,** says that there is a sufficient reason why things are exactly as they are and are not otherwise. Leibniz also used this principle as a proof of God, as we shall see in Chapter 13.

Leibniz's most famous work is the *Monadology,* available online at http://www .rbjones.com/rbjpub/philos/classics/leibniz/monad.htm.

THE IDEALISM OF LOCKE AND BERKELEY

Descartes, Hobbes, Conway, and Spinoza all belonged to the lively seventeenth century, the century that produced not only great philosophy but also some of the most important scientific discoveries of all time. The seventeenth century, you may recall from your history books, was also the century of the Thirty Years' War (1618–1648), which was the most brutal European war before this century, and the English Civil War. It also witnessed the Sun King (Louis XIV of France), the opening of Harvard, the founding of Pennsylvania, and the popularization of smoking.

In England the most important philosopher of the time was **John Locke** (1632–1704). In his great work, *An Essay Concerning Human Understanding,* Locke wished to inquire into the origin, certainty, and extent of human knowledge. Many of his views will almost certainly be shared by most readers of this book. Locke's epistemology is indeed so widely accepted that much of it is now thought to be so much common sense. You should be prepared, however—terrible philosophical difficulties attend Locke's basic position, as commonsensical as it will probably seem.

John Locke and Representative Realism

Locke's fundamental thesis was that all our ideas come from experience. The human mind at birth, he wrote (echoing Aristotle), is essentially a *tabula rasa,* or blank slate. On this blank slate, experience makes its imprint. External objects impinge on our senses, which convey into the mind ideas, or, as we might prefer to say today, perceptions, of these objects and their various qualities. In short, sensation furnishes the mind with all its contents. *Nihil in intellectu quod prius non fuerit in sensu*—nothing exists in the mind that was not first in the senses. This, of course, is familiar and plausible.

These ideas or perceptions of some of the qualities of external objects are accurate copies of qualities that actually reside in the objects, Locke said. This is what he meant. Think of a basketball. It has a certain size, shape, and weight, and when we look at and handle the ball, our sensory apparatus provides us with accurate pictures or images or ideas or perceptions of these "primary" qualities, as Locke called them.

Locke's theory: According to Locke, when we say we are looking at an external object, what we are really doing is attending to the perceptions or "ideas" of the object in our mind. Some of these perceptions, such as those of a basketball's size and shape, accurately represent qualities in the object itself. Other perceptions, such as those of the basketball's color and odor, do not represent anything in the object.

The basketball also has the power to produce in us ideas of "secondary" qualities, such as the brown color, the leathery smell, the coolness we feel when we hold it, and so forth. Are these qualities really in the basketball? Well, not exactly, you will say. And that is exactly what Locke said. These secondary qualities exist in the basketball only as the power of the basketball to produce in us ideas of color and taste and so forth—but the color and taste are purely subjective and exist in us merely as ideas. In other words, in Locke's view—and we will bet that this is your view as well—if all sentient creatures were removed from the proximity of the basketball, there would not *be* any brownness, leathery odor, or coolness, but only an object of a certain size and shape and weight, composed of minute particles that collectively would smell leathery and feel cool and look brown if any creatures with sense organs then came into existence and held and looked at and sniffed the ball.

This theory that Locke accepted is often called **representative realism.** In a sentence, it is the theory that we perceive objects *indirectly* by means of our "representations" or ideas or perceptions of them, some of which are accurate copies or representations or reflections of the real properties of "external" objects, of objects "outside the mind." This theory is widely held and is probably regarded by most people as self-evident. Open almost any introductory psychology text, and you will behold implicit in its discussion of perception Locke's theory of representative realism.

Now, we said a moment ago that terrible philosophical difficulties attend to this very nice, down-to-earth, commonsense theory known as representative realism, and it is time for us to explain ourselves. As justifiable as Locke's theory may seem, it is subject to a powerful objection, stated most eloquently by the Irish bishop and philosopher George Berkeley.

George Berkeley and Idealism

If Locke is correct, then we experience sensible things, things like basketballs and garden rakes, *indirectly*—that is, through the intermediary of our ideas or perceptions. But if that is true, **George Berkeley** [BAR-klee] (1685–1753) said, then we cannot know that *any* of our ideas or perceptions accurately represent the qualities

PROFILE: George Berkeley (1685–1753)

Berkeley was born in Ireland and studied at Trinity College, Dublin. He was made a Fellow of the College in 1707. His *Treatise Concerning the Principles of Human Knowledge* (1709) was a great success and gave Berkeley a lasting reputation, though few accepted his theory that nothing exists outside the mind.

Berkeley eventually obtained a post that included a lucrative stipend. But he gave up the post in what proved to be a futile attempt to establish a college in the Bermudas to convert the Indians in North America. He was made Bishop of Cloyne in 1734.

Berkeley was known for his generosity of heart and mind, and also for his enthusiasm for tar water (water made from pine tar). He especially liked the fact that tar water did not have the same effects as alcohol. His writings about the health benefits of drinking tar water actually caused it to become a fad in English society for a time.

Berkeley's main works, in addition to the one already mentioned, are *Essay Towards a New Theory of Vision* (1709) and *Three Dialogues between Hylas and Philonous* (1713).

of these sensible things. Why can't we know this? Because, Berkeley argued, if Locke is correct, we do not directly experience the basketball (or any other object) itself. Instead, what we directly experience is our *perceptions* and *ideas* of the basketball. And if we do not have direct experience of the basketball itself, then we cannot compare our perceptions or ideas of the basketball with the basketball itself to see if they "accurately represent" the basketball's qualities.

Indeed, given Locke's position, Berkeley said, we cannot really know that a thing like a basketball or a garden rake even *exists*. For according to Locke's theory, it is not the *object* we experience but rather our *perceptions* or *ideas* of it.

This, then, is Berkeley's criticism of Locke's theory. As satisfying as it might seem to common sense, Locke's position is the short road to skepticism. If we accept Locke's theory, then we cannot know that "sensible things," things like basketballs and rakes and even our own hands and feet, actually exist.

Berkeley began his criticism of Locke's theory by noting that the objects of human knowledge consist of "ideas" (1) conveyed to the mind through the senses (sense perceptions), (2) perceived by the mind when the mind reflects on its own operations, or (3) compounded or divided by the mind with the help of memory and imagination. "Light and colors, heat and cold, extension (length) and figures (shapes)—in a word the things we see and feel—what are they but so many sensations, notions, ideas, or impressions on the sense?"

There exist, therefore, Berkeley said, ideas and the minds that have them. However, Berkeley observed, people have the strange opinion that houses, mountains, rivers, and all sensible objects have an existence outside the mind. But that is a contradictory opinion, Berkeley suggested. "For what are the forementioned objects but the things we perceive by sense? And what do we perceive besides our own ideas or sensations? And is it not plainly contradictory that any one of these, or any combination of them, should exist unperceived?"

At this point, John Locke's theory kicks in and says that our ideas of *primary* qualities (extension, figure, motion, and so on) *represent* to us or *resemble* properties that exist outside the mind in an inert, senseless substance called matter. "But it is evident," Berkeley wrote, "that extension, figure, and motion are only ideas existing in the mind and consequently cannot exist in an unperceiving substance."

Common sense, of course, tells us that the so-called secondary qualities such as tastes, odors, and colors, exist only in the mind because, after all, what tastes sweet or smells good or seems red to one person will taste bitter or smell bad or seem green to another person. But, Berkeley argued, "let anyone consider those arguments which are thought to prove that colors and tastes exist only in the mind, and he shall find they may with equal force prove the same thing of extention, figure, and motion." In other words, extension, figure, and motion are relative to the observer, too. A cookie, for example, might taste sweet to one taster and bitter to another; but its shape will be elliptical to an observer viewing it from the side and round to an observer viewing it straight on, and its size will be smaller to an observer farther away.

Of course, our inclination is to distinguish the *perceived* size and shape of a cookie from the size and shape that are the cookie's "true" size and shape. But Berkeley pointed out that size and shape (and the other qualities) *are* perceived qualities. Talking about an *unperceived* size or shape is nonsense. It is like talking about unfelt pain. And thus sensible objects, because they are nothing more than their qualities, are themselves only ideas and exist only in the mind.

But, you may still insist (in frustration?), surely there are material things "out there" that have their own size, shape, texture, and the like! Well, Berkeley has already responded to this line of thought: it is contradictory to suppose that size, shape, texture, and so on could exist in unthinking things. Size, shape, texture, and so on are *ideas*, and it is silly to suppose that ideas could exist in unthinking things.

Material Things as Clusters of Ideas

This theory of Berkeley's is *idealism*, the last of the four metaphysical philosophies. There are other versions of idealism, but in Berkeley's version, sensible things, such as tables, chairs, trees, books, and frogs, are not material things that exist outside the mind. They are, in fact, groups of ideas and as such are perceived directly and exist only within the mind. Because they are ideas, we can no more doubt their existence than we can doubt our own aches and pains (which also, indeed, are ideas).

Berkeley's idealism does not mean, however, that the physical world is a mere dream or that it is imaginary or intangible or ephemeral. Dr. Samuel Johnson (1709–1784), the famous English literary critic and scholar, believed that he had refuted Berkeley by kicking a stone, evidently thinking that the solidity of the stone was solid disproof of Berkeley. In fact, Johnson succeeded only in hurting his foot and demonstrating that he did not understand Berkeley. A stone is just as hard an object in Berkeley's philosophy as it is to common sense, for the fact that a stone exists only in the mind does not make its hardness disappear.

Rationalism and Empiricism

A doctrine that St. Thomas Aquinas (see Chapter 5) accepted and attributed to Aristotle, and that John Locke also accepted, is *nihil in intellectu quod prius non fuerit in sensu;* that is, there is nothing in the intellect that was not first in the senses. This doctrine is called **empiricism.** Another doctrine, known as **rationalism,** holds that the intellect contains important truths that were not placed there by sensory experience. "Something never comes from nothing," for example, might count as one of these truths, because experience can tell you only that something has never come from nothing so far, not that it can never, ever happen (or so a rationalist might argue). Sometimes rationalists believe in a *theory of innate ideas,* according to which these truths are "innate" to the mind—that is, they are part of the original dispositions of the intellect.

The empiricist is, in effect, a type of modified skeptic—he or she denies that there is any knowledge that does not stem from sensory experience. Most rationalists, by contrast, do not deny that *some* knowledge about the world can be obtained through experience. But other rationalists, such as Parmenides (see Chapter 2), deny that experience can deliver up any sort of true knowledge. This type of rationalist is also a type of modified skeptic.

Classical rationalism and empiricism in modern philosophy were mainly a product of the seventeenth and eighteenth centuries. Rationalism is associated most significantly during that time period with Descartes (1596–1650), Spinoza (1632–1677), and Leibniz (1646–1716). These three are often called the *Continental rationalists* and are contrasted with Locke (1632–1704), Berkeley (1685–1753), and Hume (1711–1776), the *British empiricists.* (We discuss Hume in the next chapter.) Philosophers from other periods, however, are sometimes classified as rationalists or empiricists depending on whether they emphasized the importance of reason or experience in knowledge of the world. Those earlier philosophers treated in this book who are usually listed as rationalists are, among others, Pythagoras, Parmenides, and Plato. Those who are often listed as empiricists are Aristotle, Epicurus, and Aquinas. Immanuel Kant (1724–1804), also discussed in the next chapter, is said to have synthesized rationalism and empiricism because he believed that all knowledge *begins* with experience (a thesis empiricists agree with) but also believed that knowledge is not limited to what has been found in experience (a thesis rationalists agree with).

Modern epistemology, as you will see, has been predominantly empiricist. This is because the Continental rationalists, and later rationalists too, were primarily metaphysicians. That is, they were generally less concerned with discussing the possibility of knowledge and related issues than with actually coming to propose some philosophically important theory about reality. The great exception is Descartes, a rationalist who concerned himself explicitly with the possibility of knowledge.

As for the stones found in dreams, Berkeley distinguished unreal dream stones from real stones just the way you and we do. Stones found in dreams behave in an irregular and chaotic manner—they can float around or change into birds or whatever—compared with those found in waking life. And Berkeley distinguished stones that we conjure up in our imaginations from real stones by their lack of vividness and also by the fact that they, unlike real stones, can be brought into existence by an act of our will.

Berkeley and Atheism

So Berkeley's position was that sensible things cannot exist independent of perception—to be is to be perceived (***esse est percipi***). What, then, happens to

Telegraph Avenue in Berkeley, California. The city was named after George Berkeley because of his line of poetry, "Westward the course of empire takes its way."

this desk when everyone leaves the room? What happens to the forest when all the people go away? What happens to sensible things when no one perceives them?

Berkeley's answer was that the perceiving mind of God makes possible the continued existence of sensible things when neither you nor any other people are perceiving them. Because sensible things do not depend on the perception of humans and exist independently of them, Berkeley wrote, "There must be some other mind wherein they exist." This other mind, according to Berkeley, is God.

Berkeley believed that the greatest virtue of his idealist system was that it alone did not invite skepticism about God. Dualism, he thought, by postulating the existence of objects outside the mind, made these objects unknowable and was just an open invitation to skepticism about their existence; skepticism about the existence of sensible objects, he thought, would inevitably extend itself to skepticism about their creator, God. Materialism, he believed, made sensible objects independent of God; and thus it, too, led to skepticism about God. His own system, he thought, by contrast made the existence of sensible objects undeniable (they are as undeniable as your own ideas). This meant, for Berkeley, that the existence of the divine mind, in which sensible objects are sustained, was equally undeniable.

So, for Berkeley, the fact that sensible things continue to exist when we do not perceive them is a short and simple proof of God's existence. Another similar proof, in Berkeley's view, can be derived from the fact that we do not ourselves cause our ideas of tables, chairs, mountains, and other sensible things.

We would say the railroad tracks *appear* to grow smaller and closer together. Berkeley thought the tracks *really* did grow smaller and closer together.

"There is therefore," he reasoned, "some other will or spirit that produced them"—God.

Berkeley was aware that his theory that what we call material things are ideas both in God's mind and in our own raises peculiar questions about the relationship between our minds and the mind of God. For example, if a mountain is an idea in God's mind and we perceive the mountain, does that mean we perceive or have God's ideas?

With Berkeley, Hobbes, Descartes, and Spinoza, the four basic metaphysical perspectives of modern philosophy were set out: reality is entirely physical (Hobbes), *or* it is entirely nonphysical or "mental" (Berkeley), *or* it is an even split (Descartes), *or* "matter" and "mind" are just alternative ways of looking at one and the same stuff (Spinoza). See the box "Mind–Body Theories."

An alternative, epistemological classification of these philosophers is given in the box "Rationalism and Empiricism" a bit earlier in this chapter.

Mind–Body Theories

Matter	Mind		
+	+	Both matter and mind	Descartes' dualism
+	−	Only matter, no mind	Hobbes's materialism
−	+	No matter, only mind	Berkeley's idealism
−	−	No matter, no mind	Spinoza's alternativism

SELECTION 6.1

Meditations on First Philosophy*

René Descartes

[*Descartes'* Meditations on First Philosophy *is among the most widely read books of all time—right up there, almost, with Plato's* Republic. *In this selection, Descartes is trying to doubt everything that can be doubted and finds that almost everything that he previously thought he knew for certain is actually open to question.*]

Reason persuades me that I ought no less carefully to withhold my assent from matters which are not entirely certain and indubitable than from those which appear to me manifestly to be false. . . .

All that up to the present time I have accepted as most true and certain I have learned either from the senses or through the senses; [and], although the senses sometimes deceive us concerning things which are hardly perceptible, or very far away, there are yet many others to be met with as to which we cannot reasonably have any doubt. . . .

For example, there is the fact that I am here, seated by the fire, attired in a dressing gown, having this paper in my hands and other similar matters. And how could I deny that these hands and this body are "mine[?] . . ."

At the same time I must remember that . . . I am in the habit of sleeping and in my dreams representing to myself the same things. . . . How often has it happened to me that in the night I dreamt that I found myself in this particular place, that I was dressed and seated near the fire, while in reality I was lying undressed in bed! At this moment it does indeed seem to me that it is with eyes awake that I am looking at this paper. . . . But in thinking over this I remind myself that on many occasions I have in sleep been deceived by similar illusions, and in dwelling carefully on this reflection I see . . . that there are no certain indications by which we may clearly distinguish wakefulness from sleep. . . .

At the same time we must at least confess that . . . whether I am awake or asleep, two and three together always form five, and the square can never have more than four sides, and it does not seem possible that truths so clear and apparent can be suspected of any falsity.

Nevertheless . . . how do I know that I am not deceived every time that I add two and three, or count the sides of a square, or judge of things yet simpler, if anything simpler can be imagined? . . . Possibly God has not desired that I should be thus deceived, for He is said to be supremely good. . . . But let us . . . grant that all that is here said of a God is a fable. . . . I shall then suppose, not that God who is supremely good and the fountain of truth, but some evil genius not less powerful than deceitful, has employed his whole energies in deceiving me; I shall consider that the heavens, the earth, colors, figures, sound, and all other external things are nought but the illusions and dreams of which this genius has availed himself in order to lay traps for my credulity; I shall consider myself as having no hands, no eyes, no flesh, no blood, nor any senses, yet falsely believing myself to possess all these things. . . .

[Yet even if] there is some deceiver or other, very powerful and very cunning, who ever employs his ingenuity in deceiving me[,] then without a doubt I exist also if he deceives me, and let him deceive me as much as he will, he can never cause me to be nothing so long as I think that I am something. So that after having reflected well and carefully examined all things, we must come to the definite conclusion that this proposition: I am, I exist, is necessarily true each time that I pronounce it, or that I mentally conceive it.

But what am I, now that I suppose that there is a certain genius which is extremely powerful, and, if I may say so, malicious, who employs all his powers in deceiving me? Can I affirm that I possess the least of all those things which I have just said pertain to the nature of body? I pause to consider, I revolve all these things in my mind, and I find none of which I can say that it pertains to me. It would be tedious to

---

* René Descartes, "Meditations on First Philosophy" from *The Philosophical Works of Descartes,* translated by Elizabeth S. Haldane and G. R. T. Ross, Vol. 1 (Cambridge: The University Press, 1911).

stop to enumerate them. Let us pass to the attributes of soul and see if there is any one which is in me? What of nutrition or walking [the first mentioned]? But if it is so that I have no body it is also true that I can neither walk nor take nourishment. Another attribute is sensation. But one cannot feel without body, and besides I have thought I perceived many things during sleep that I recognised in my waking moments as not having been experienced at all. What of thinking? I find here that thought is an attribute that belongs to me; it alone cannot be separated from me. I am, I exist, that is certain. But how often? Just when I think; for it might possibly be the case if I ceased entirely to think, that I should likewise cease altogether to exist. I do not now admit anything which is not necessarily true: to speak accurately I am not more than a thing which thinks, that is to say a mind or a soul, or an understanding, or a reason, which are terms whose significance was formerly unknown to me. I am, however, a real thing and really exist; but what thing? I have answered: a thing which thinks. . . . What is a thing which thinks? It is a thing which doubts, understands, [conceives], affirms, denies, wills, refuses, which also imagines and feels. . . .

. . . [I]n the little that I have just said, I think I have summed up all that I really know, or at least all that hitherto I was aware that I knew. In order to try to extend my knowledge further, I shall now look around more carefully and see whether I cannot still discover in myself some other things which I have not hitherto perceived. I am certain that I am a thing which thinks; but do I not then likewise know what is requisite to render me certain of a truth? Certainly in this first knowledge there is nothing that assures me of its truth, excepting the clear and distinct perception of that which I state, which would not indeed suffice to assure me that what I say is true, if it could ever happen that a thing which I conceived so clearly and distinctly could be false; and accordingly it seems to me that already I can establish as a general rule that all things which I perceive very clearly and very distinctly are true.

[*At this point in the* Meditations, *Descartes proves to his own satisfaction that he perceives clearly and distinctly that God exists and that God would never permit Descartes to be deceived as long as Descartes forms no judgment except on matters clearly and distinctly represented to Descartes by his understanding. He then continues:*]

Because I know that all things which I apprehend clearly and distinctly can be created by God as I apprehend them, it suffices that I am able to apprehend one thing apart from another clearly and distinctly in order to be certain that the one is different from the other, since they may be made to exist in separation at least by the omnipotence of God . . . and therefore, just because I know certainly that I exist, and that meanwhile I do not remark that any other thing necessarily pertains to my nature of essence, excepting that I am a thinking thing, I rightly conclude that my essence consists solely in the fact that I am a thinking thing . . . [and as] I possess a distinct idea of body, inasmuch as it is only an extended and unthinking thing, it is certain that this I is entirely and absolutely distinct from my body, and can exist without it. . . .

There is certainly further in me a certain passive faculty of perception, that is, of receiving and recognising the ideas of sensible things, but this would be useless to me, if there were not either in me or in some other thing another active faculty capable of forming and producing these ideas. . . . [A]nd since God is no deceiver, [and since] He has given me . . . a very great inclination to believe that [these ideas] are conveyed to me by corporeal objects, I do not see how He could be defended from the accusation of deceit if these ideas were produced by causes other than corporeal objects. Hence we must allow that corporeal things exist. . . . [And] we must at least admit that all things which I conceive in them clearly and distinctly, that is to say, all things which, speaking generally, are comprehended in the object of pure mathematics, are truly to be recognised as external objects. . . .

[O]n the sole Ground that God is not a deceiver . . . there is no doubt that in all things which nature teaches me there is some truth contained. . . . But there is nothing which this nature teaches me more expressly than that I have a body which is adversely affected when I feel pain, which has need of food or drink when I experience the feelings of hunger and thirst, and so on; nor can I doubt there being some truth in all this.

Nature also teaches me by these sensations of pain, hunger, thirst, etc., that I am not only lodged in my body as a pilot in a vessel, but that I am very closely united to it, and so to speak so intermingled with it that I seem to compose with it one whole. For if that were not the case, when my body is hurt,

I, who am merely a thinking thing, would not feel pain, for I should perceive this wound by the understanding only, just as the sailor perceives by sight when something is damaged in his vessel. . . .

[T]here is a great difference between mind and body, inasmuch as body is by nature always divisible, and the mind is entirely indivisible. For, as a matter of fact, when I consider the mind, that is to say, myself inasmuch as I am only a thinking thing, I cannot distinguish in myself any parts, but apprehend myself to be clearly one and entire; and although the whole mind seems to be united to the whole body, yet if a foot, or an arm, or some other part, is separated from my body, I am aware that nothing has been taken away from my mind. And the faculties of willing, feeling, conceiving, etc.,

cannot be properly speaking said to be its parts, for it is one and the same mind which employs itself in willing and in feeling and understanding. But it is quite otherwise with corporeal or extended objects, for there is not one of these imaginable by me which my mind cannot easily divide into parts, and which consequently I do not recognise as being divisible. [T]his would be sufficient to teach me that the mind or soul of man is entirely different from the body, if I had not already learned it from other sources.

I further notice that the mind does not receive the impressions from all parts of the body immediately, but only from the brain, or perhaps even from one of its smallest parts, to wit, from that in which the common sense is said to reside.

SELECTION 6.2
Ethics*

Benedictus de Spinoza

[*This excerpt will give you a good idea of Spinoza's geometric method in which metaphysical certainties ("Proportions") are deduced from a short list of "Definitions" and self-evident "axioms."*]

Definitions and Axioms

Definitions   I. By that which is *self-caused,* I mean that of which the essence involves existence, or that of which the nature is only conceivable as existent.

II. A thing is called *finite after its kind,* when it can be limited by another thing of the same nature; for instance, a body is called finite because we always conceive another greater body. So, also, a thought is limited by another thought, but a body is not limited by thought, nor a thought by body.

III. By *substance,* I mean that which is in itself, and is conceived through itself: in other words, that of which a conception can be formed independently of any other conception.

IV. By *attribute,* I mean that which the intellect perceives as constituting the essence of substance.

V. By *mode,* I mean the modifications of substance, or that which exists in, and is conceived through, something other than itself.

VI. By *God,* I mean a being absolutely infinite—that is, a substance consisting in infinite attributes, of which each expresses eternal and infinite essentiality.

Explanation.—I say absolutely infinite, not infinite after its kind: for, of a thing infinite only after its kind, infinite attributes may be denied; but that which is absolutely infinite, contains in its essence whatever expresses reality, and involves no negation.

VII. That thing is called free, which exists solely by the necessity of its own nature, and of which the action is determined by itself alone. On the other hand, that thing is necessary, or rather constrained, which is determined by something external to itself to a fixed and definite method of existence or action.

VIII. By *eternity,* I mean existence itself, in so far as it is conceived necessarily to follow solely from the definition of that which is eternal.

* From *The Chief Works of Benedictus de Spinoza,* Vol. 2, revised edition, translated by R. H. M. Elwes (London: George Bell & Sons, 1901), 45–48.

Explanation.—Existence of this kind is conceived as an eternal truth, like the essence of a thing, and, therefore, cannot be explained by means of continuance or time, though continuance may be conceived without a beginning or end.

Axioms   I. Everything which exists, exists either in itself or in something else.

II. That which cannot be conceived through anything else must be conceived through itself.

III. From a given definite cause an effect necessarily follows; and, on the other hand, if no definite cause be granted, it is impossible that an effect can follow.

IV. The knowledge of an effect depends on and involves the knowledge of a cause.

V. Things which have nothing in common cannot be understood, the one by means of the other; the conception of one does not involve the conception of the other.

VI. A true idea must correspond with its ideate or object.

VII. If a thing can be conceived as non-existing, its essence does not involve existence.

Seven Propositions on Substance

Propositions   PROP. I. *Substance is by nature prior to its modifications.*

Proof.—This is clear from Defs. iii. and v.

PROP. II. *Two substances, whose attributes are different, have nothing in common.*

Proof.—Also evident from Def. iii. For each must exist in itself, and be conceived through itself; in other words, the conception of one does not imply the conception of the other.

PROP. III. *Things which have nothing in common cannot be one the cause of the other.*

Proof.—If they have nothing in common, it follows that one cannot be apprehended by means of the other (Ax. v.), and, therefore, one cannot be the cause of the other (Ax. iv.). *Q.E.D.*

PROP. IV. *Two or more distinct things are distinguished one from the other, either by the difference of the attributes of the substances or by the difference of their modifications.*

Proof.—Everything which exists, exists either in itself or in something else (Ax. i.),—that is (by Defs. iii. and v.), nothing is granted in addition to the understanding, except substance and its modifications. Nothing is, therefore, given besides the understanding, by which several things may be distinguished one from the other, except the substances, or, in other words (see Ax. iv.), their attributes and modifications. *Q.E.D.*

PROP. V. *There cannot exist in the universe two or more substances having the same nature or attribute.*

Proof.—If several distinct substances be granted, they must be distinguished one from the other, either by the difference of their attributes, or by the difference of their modifications (Prop. iv.): If only by the difference of their attributes, it will be granted that there cannot be more than one with an identical attribute. If by the difference of their modifications—as substance is naturally prior to its modifications (Prop. i.),—it follows that setting the modifications aside, and considering substance in itself, that is truly (Defs. iii. and vi.), there cannot be conceived one substance different from another,—that is (by Prop. iv.), there cannot be granted several substances, but one substance only. *Q.E.D.*

PROP. VI. *One substance cannot be produced by another substance.*

Proof.—It is impossible that there should be in the universe two substances with an identical attribute, i.e., which have anything common to them both (Prop. ii.), and, therefore (Prop. iii.), one cannot be the cause of another, neither can one be produced by the other. *Q.E.D.*

Corollary.—Hence it follows that a substance cannot be produced by anything external to itself. For in the universe nothing is granted, save substances and their modifications (as appears from Ax. i. and Defs. iii. and v.). Now (by the last Prop.) substance cannot be produced by another substance, therefore it cannot be produced by anything external to itself. *Q.E.D.* This is shown still more readily by the absurdity of the contradictory. For, if substance be produced by an external cause, the knowledge of it would depend on the knowledge of its cause (Ax. iv.), and (by Def. iii.) it would itself not be substance.

PROP. VII. *Existence belongs to the nature of substance.*

Proof.—Substance cannot be produced by anything external (Corollary Prop. vi.), it must, therefore, be its own cause—that is, its essence necessarily involves existence, or existence belongs to its nature.

SELECTION 6.3

Treatise Concerning the Principles of Human Knowledge

George Berkeley

[*Berkeley's philosophy—that what we call material objects are really just ideas in the mind—strikes newcomers to philosophy as bizarre and preposterous. In this selection, Berkeley defends his view through a series of arguments and rebuttals to those who would disagree with him. Enjoy Berkeley's direct, powerful, elegant English.*]

It is evident to anyone who takes a survey of the objects of human knowledge, that they are either ideas (1) actually imprinted on the senses, or else such as are (2) perceived by attending to the passions and operations of the mind, or lastly (3) ideas formed by help of memory and imagination, either compounding, dividing, or barely representing those originally perceived in the aforesaid ways. By sight I have the ideas of lights and colors, with their several degrees and variations. By touch I perceive hard and soft, heat and cold, motion and resistance, and of all these more and less either as to quantity or degree. Smelling furnishes me with odors, the palate with tastes, and hearing conveys sounds to the mind in all their variety of tone and composition. And as several of these are observed to accompany each other, they come to be marked by one name, and so to be reputed as one thing. Thus, for example, a certain color, taste, smell, figure, and consistence, having been observed to go together, are accounted one distinct thing, signified by the name "apple." Other collections of ideas constitute a stone, a tree, a book, and the like sensible things. . . .

2. But besides all that endless variety of ideas or objects of knowledge, there is likewise something which knows or perceives them, and exercises divers operations, as willing, imagining, remembering, about them. This perceiving, active being is what I call mind, spirit, soul, or myself. By which words I do not denote any one of my ideas, but a thing entirely distinct from them wherein they exist, or, which is the same thing, whereby they are perceived; for the existence of an idea consists in being perceived.

3. That neither our thoughts, nor passions, nor ideas formed by the imagination, exist without the mind, is what everybody will allow. And it seems no less evident that the various sensations or ideas imprinted on the sense, however blended or combined together (that is, whatever objects they compose), cannot exist otherwise than in a mind perceiving them. . . .

4. It is indeed an opinion strangely prevailing amongst men, that houses, mountains, rivers, and in a word all sensible objects, have an existence, natural or real, distinct from their being perceived by the understanding. But with how great an assurance and acquiescence soever this principle may be entertained in the world, yet whoever shall find in his heart to call it in question may, if I mistake not, perceive it to involve a manifest contradiction. For what are the forementioned objects but the things we perceive by sense? and what do we perceive besides our own ideas or sensations? and is it not plainly repugnant that any one of these, or any combination of them, should exist unperceived?

5. Light and colors, heat and cold, extension and figures—in a word the things we see and feel—what are they but so many sensations, notions, ideas, or impressions on the sense? And is it possible to separate, even in thought, any of these from perception? . . .

8. But, say you, though the ideas themselves do not exist without the mind, yet there may be things like them, whereof they are copies or resemblances, which things exist without the mind in an unthinking substance. I answer, an idea can be like nothing but an idea; a color or figure can be like nothing but another color or figure. . . . Again, I ask whether those supposed originals or external things, of which our ideas are the pictures or representations, be themselves perceivable or no? If they are, then they are ideas and we have gained our point; but if

you say they are not, I appeal to anyone whether it be sense to assert a color is like something which is invisible; hard or soft, like something which is intangible; and so of the rest.

9. Some there are who make a distinction betwixt primary and secondary qualities. By the former they mean extension, figure, motion, test, solidity or impenetrability, and number; by the latter they denote all other sensible qualities, as colors, sounds, tastes, and so forth. The ideas we have of these they acknowledge not to be the resemblances of anything existing without the mind, or unperceived, but they will have our ideas of the primary qualities to be patterns or images of things which exist without the mind, in an unthinking substance which they call matter. By matter, therefore, we are to understand an inert, senseless substance, in which extension, figure, and motion do actually subsist. But it is evident from what we have already shown, that extension, figure, and motion are only ideas existing in the mind, and that an idea can be like nothing but another idea, and that consequently neither they nor their archetypes can exist in an unperceiving substance. Hence, it is plain that the very notion of what is called matter, or corporeal substance, involves a contradiction in it.

10. They who assert that figure, motion, and the rest of the primary or original qualities do exist without the mind in unthinking substances, do at the same time acknowledge that color, sounds, heat, cold, and such-like secondary qualities, do not; which they tell us are sensations existing in the mind alone. . . . Now, if it be certain that those original qualities are inseparably united with the other sensible qualities, and not, even in thought, capable of being abstracted from them, it plainly follows that they exist only in the mind. But I desire anyone to reflect and try whether he can, by any abstraction of thought, conceive the extension and motion of a body without all other sensible qualities. For my own part, I see evidently that it is not in my power to frame an idea of a body extended and moving, but I must withal give it some color or other sensible quality which is acknowledged to exist only in the mind. In short, extension, figure, and motion, abstracted from all other qualities, are inconceivable. Where therefore the other sensible qualities are, there must these be also, to wit, in the mind and nowhere else.

11. Again, great and small, swift and slow, are allowed to exist nowhere without the mind, being entirely relative, and changing as the frame or position of the organs of sense varies. The extension therefore which exists without the mind is neither great nor small, the motion neither swift nor slow, that is, they are nothing at all. . . .

12. That number is entirely the creature of the mind, even though the other qualities be allowed to exist without, will be evident to whoever considers that the same thing bears a different denomination of number as the mind views it with different respects. Thus, the same extension is one, or three, or thirty-six, according as the mind considers it with reference to a yard, a foot, or an inch. Number is so visibly relative, and dependent on men's understanding, that it is strange to think how anyone should give it an absolute existence without the mind. . . .

14. It is said that heat and cold are affections only of the mind, and not at all patterns of real beings, existing in the corporeal substances which excite them, for that the same body which appears cold to one hand seems warm to another. Now, why may we not as well argue that figure and extension are not patterns or resemblances of qualities existing in matter, because to the same eye at different stations, or eyes of a different texture at the same station, they appear various, and cannot therefore be the images of anything settled and determinate without the mind? Again, it is proved that sweetness is not really in the sapid (i.e. flavorful) thing, because the thing remaining unaltered the sweetness is changed into bitter, as in case of a fever or otherwise vitiated palate. Is it not as reasonable to say that motion is not without the mind, since if the succession of ideas in the mind become swifter, the motion, it is acknowledged, shall appear slower without any alteration in any external object?

15. In short, let anyone consider those arguments which are thought manifestly to prove that colors and tastes exist only in the mind, and he shall find they may with equal force be brought to prove the same thing of extension, figure, and motion. . . . The arguments foregoing plainly show it to be impossible that any color or extension at all, or other sensible quality whatsoever, should exist in an unthinking subject without the mind, or in truth,

that there should be any such thing as an outward object. . . .

18. But though it were possible that solid, figured, movable substances may exist without the mind, corresponding to the ideas we have of bodies, yet how is it possible for us to know this? Either we must know it by sense or by reason. As for our senses, by them we have the knowledge only of our sensations, ideas, or those things that are immediately perceived by sense, call them what you will; but they do not inform us that things exist without the mind. . . . It remains therefore that if we have any knowledge at all of external things, it must be by reason, inferring their existence from what is immediately perceived by sense. But what reason can induce us to believe the existence of bodies without the mind, from what we perceive. . . . It is granted on all hands (and what happens in dreams, frenzies, and the like, puts it beyond dispute) that it is possible we might be affected with all the ideas we have now, though there were no bodies existing without, resembling them. Hence, it is evident the supposition of external bodies is not necessary for the producing of our ideas; since it is granted that they are produced sometimes, and might possibly be produced always in the same order we see them in at present, without their concurrence. . . .

20. In short, if there were external bodies, it is impossible we should ever come to know it;

and if there were not, we might have the very same reasons to think there were that we have now. Suppose (what no one can deny possible) an intelligence without the help of external bodies, to be affected with the same train of sensations or ideas that you are, imprinted in the same order and with like vividness in his mind. I ask whether that intelligence hath not all the reason to believe the existence of corporeal substances, represented by his ideas, and exciting them in his mind, that you can possibly have for believing the same thing?

22. I am content to put the whole upon this issue: if you can but conceive it possible for one extended movable substance, or, in general, for any one idea, or anything like an idea, to exist otherwise than in a mind perceiving it, I shall readily give up the cause. . . .

23. But, say you, surely there is nothing easier than for me to imagine trees, for instance, in a park, or books existing in a closet, and nobody by to perceive them. I answer, you may so, there is no difficulty in it; but what is all this, I beseech you, more than framing in your mind certain ideas which you call books and trees, and the same time omitting to frame the idea of anyone that may perceive them? But do not you yourself perceive or think of them all the while? . . . When we do our utmost to conceive the existence of external bodies, we are all the while only contemplating our own ideas.

CHECKLIST

To help you review, a checklist of the key philosophers of this chapter can be found online at www.mhhe.com/moore9e.

KEY TERMS AND CONCEPTS

QUESTIONS FOR DISCUSSION AND REVIEW

1. Define or explain dualism, materialism, and idealism.

2. Explain and critically evaluate either Descartes' dream conjecture or his evil demon conjecture.

3. Should Descartes have questioned whether there could be thinking without an "I" that does the thinking?

4. "We can think. This proves we are not just mere matter." Does it?

5. "Material things, including one's body, are completely subject to physical laws." "The immaterial mind can move one's body." Are these two claims incompatible? Explain.

6. What does Spinoza claim is the relationship of the mind to the body?

7. Why does Berkeley say that sensible objects exist only in the mind?

8. Are the qualities of sensible objects (e.g., size, color, taste) all equally relative to the observer?

9. Does Berkeley's philosophy make everything into a dream?

10. If all our knowledge comes from experience, why might it be difficult to maintain that we have knowledge of external objects?

SUGGESTED FURTHER READINGS

Go online to www.mhhe.com/moore9e for a list of suggested further readings.

7

The Eighteenth and Nineteenth Centuries

The problem of the relation of the world in the head to the world outside the head constitutes, together with the problem of moral freedom, the distinctive character of the philosophy of the moderns.　　—Arthur Schopenhauer

The eighteenth century ushered in the Enlightenment, and despite the French and American revolutions, the century was marked by comparative peace and stability, an improved standard of living, and an increase in personal freedom. Fewer witches were persecuted, and burning heretics became rare. Religion continued to decline in importance politically, socially, and intellectually. Commerce expanded. Money grew. In short, all was well. Handel composed *The Messiah.*

After George Berkeley, the two most important philosophers of the eighteenth century were David Hume (1711–1776) and Immanuel Kant (1724–1804). Hume and Kant were both very reluctant to allow even the possibility of metaphysical knowledge. Hume believed that all our knowledge is limited to what we experience, namely, sensory impressions. However, he was not willing to agree with Berkeley that sensible objects are just clusters of sensory impressions. Kant was more generous about what we can know, as we shall see.

DAVID HUME

The epistemology of **David Hume** (1711–1776), like that of George Berkeley (see previous chapter), is a development of the empiricist thesis that all our ideas come from experience—that is, from sensation or inner feelings. In some passages Hume displays total skepticism, but mostly he appears as a modified skeptic who focuses his attention on certain narrower issues that have continued to dominate epistemological inquiry since Hume's time.

Much of Hume's epistemology rests on four assumptions. To see whether you agree with them or not, mark "T" or "F" in front of each of these four statements:

1. **T or F** Every claim that something exists is a factual claim. (That is, when you claim that something exists, you are expressing what you think is a fact.)
2. **T or F** Factual claims can be established only by observation or by causal inference from what is observed. (For example, you can tell if an engine is knocking just by listening to it, but to know that it has worn bearings, you have to make an inference about the cause of the knocking.)
3. **T or F** Thought, knowledge, belief, conception, and judgment each consist in having ideas.
4. **T or F** All ideas are derived from and are copies of impressions of sense or inner feelings, that is, perceptions.

If you marked "T" for each of these four statements, you agree with Hume. But what do these four assumptions entail?

The Quarter Experiment

Let's begin with (1) and (2). First, put a quarter in front of you next to this book. The quarter exists, correct? This claim, according to principle (2), can be established—that is, proved or justified—only by observation or by inference from what you observe.

But what is it you observe? The quarter? Well, no, as a matter of fact, that does not seem quite right. Look at what you call the quarter. Leave it on your desk and get up and move around the room a bit, looking at the quarter all the while. What you *observe* as you move about is a silverish object that constantly changes its size and shape as you move. Right now, for example, what you observe is probably elliptical in shape. But a quarter is not the sort of thing that constantly changes its size and shape, and a quarter is never elliptical (unless someone has done something illegal to it). *So what you observe changes its size and shape, but the quarter does not change its size and shape. It follows that what you observe is not the quarter.*

Here you might object. "What I am seeing is a silverish object from various distances and angles," you might say.

PROFILE: David Hume (1711–1776)

David Hume died of cancer at the age of sixty-five. In the face of his own death, he retained his composure and cheerfulness, having achieved the goal of the ancient skeptics, *ataraxia* (unperturbedness). It may be questioned, though, whether his calm good nature resulted from his skepticism, for apparently he exhibited this trait of personality throughout his life.

Born in Edinburgh, Scotland, of a "good family," as he said in his autobiography, Hume was encouraged to study law but "found insurmountable aversion to everything but the pursuits of philosophy and general learning." Before he was thirty, he published *A Treatise of Human Nature,* one of the most important philosophical works ever written. Yet, at the time, Hume's *Treatise* "fell dead-born from the press," as he put it, "without reaching such distinction as even to excite a murmur among the zealots." Convinced that the failure of the work was due more to form than content, he recast parts of it anew in *An Enquiry Concerning Human Understanding* and *An Enquiry Concerning the Principles of Morals.* The latter work, in Hume's opinion, was incomparably his best. Hume's last philosophical work, *Dialogues Concerning Natural Religion,* was published posthumously in 1779. There are differences between Hume's *Treatise* and *An Enquiry Concerning Human Understanding,* his two works in epistemology, and philosophers disagree about the merits of each. Although during his lifetime Hume was primarily known as a historian rather than as a philosopher, his impact on subsequent philosophy, especially in Great Britain and other English-speaking countries, and on Kant was significant.

But, in fact, if you consider carefully what you are observing, it is a silverish object that changes its size and shape. You do not see a silverish disk that looks the same from every vantage point. What you see does change. Thus, it still follows, because the quarter does not change, that what you see is not the quarter.

What is it, then, that you observe? According to Hume, it is your *sense impressions* of the quarter. Thus, if your belief that the quarter exists is to be justified, that belief must be a causal inference from what you observe—that is, from your impressions—to something that is distinct from your impressions and causes them, namely, the quarter. But there is a major problem here: you never experience or are in any way in contact with anything that is distinct from your impressions. Thus, you never observe a connection between your perceptions and the quarter. So how could you possibly establish that the quarter *causes* your impressions? And if you cannot establish that, then, according to Hume, you cannot regard your belief in the existence of the quarter as justified.

Of course, the same considerations apply to a belief in the existence of any external object whatsoever. Here is Hume expressing these considerations in his own words:

> The only existences, of which we are certain, are perceptions. . . . The only conclusion we can draw from the existence of one thing to that of another, is by means of the relation of cause and effect, which shews, that there is a connection betwixt them. . . . But as no things are ever present to the mind but perceptions; it follows that we may observe a conjunction or a relation of cause and effect between different perceptions, but can never observe it between perceptions and objects. 'Tis impossible, therefore, that from the existence of any of the

What you see here is elliptical. Quarters aren't elliptical. Therefore, what you see is not a quarter, right?

qualities of the former, we can ever form any conclusion concerning the existence of the latter.

Now, go back to assumptions (3) and (4). Notice that it follows directly from these two assumptions that there is no knowledge, belief, conception, judgment, thought, or even idea of external objects (things distinct from our sense impressions of them). Here again Hume explained:

> Now, since nothing is ever present to the mind but perceptions, and since all ideas are derived from something antecedently present to the mind; it follows, that 'tis impossible for us so much as to conceive or form an idea of anything specifically different from ideas and impressions. Let us fix our attention out of ourselves as much as possible: Let us chase our imagination to the heavens, or to the utmost limits of the universe; we never really advance a step beyond ourselves, nor can conceive any kind of existence, but those perceptions, which have appeared in that narrow compass.

Hume on the Self

According to Hume, similar careful scrutiny of the notion of the self or mind, supposedly an unchanging nonmaterial substance within us, discloses that we have no knowledge of such a thing. Indeed, we do not really have even an *idea* of the mind, if the mind is defined as an unchanging nonmaterial substance within, Hume held. Our ideas cannot go beyond our sense impressions, and we have no impressions of the mind, except perhaps as a bundle of impressions.

Some philosophers, said Hume, imagine we are conscious of what we call our "self" or "mind" and that we feel its existence and are certain of its "perfect identity and simplicity." But, he asked, "From what impression could this idea be derived?"

> It must be some one impression that gives rise to every real idea. But self is not any one impression, but that to which our several impressions and ideas are supposed to have a reference. If any impression gives rise to the idea of self, that impression must continue invariably the same through the whole course of our lives, since self is supposed to exist after that manner. But there is no impression constant and invariable. . . . There is no such idea. . . .
>
> For my part, when I enter most intimately into what I call *myself,* I always stumble on some particular perception or other, of heat or cold, light or shade, love or hatred, pain or pleasure. I never can catch myself at any time without a perception, and never can observe any thing but the perception. . . . The mind is a kind of theatre, where several perceptions successively make their appearance; pass, re-pass, glide away, and mingle in an infinite variety of postures and situations. There is properly no *simplicity* in it at one time, nor *identity* in different. . . . The comparison of the theatre must not mislead us. They are the successive perceptions only, that constitute the mind.

Hume on Cause and Effect

Because any inference from the existence of one thing to that of another is founded, according to Hume, on the relation of cause and effect (statement 2 on page 125), Hume analyzed that relation carefully. He discovered that experience reveals no necessary connection between a cause and an effect.

At first this thesis—that we experience no necessary connection between a cause and its effect—seems straightforwardly false. The car going by makes the noise you hear, doesn't it? The impact of the golf club drives the ball down the fairway. Disconnecting a spark plug forces the engine to idle roughly. The cue ball moves the eight ball when it hits it. What could be plainer than that in each case the cause necessitates the effect?

Yet by paying attention to what he actually experienced in an instance of so-called causation, Hume discovered that he did not experience the cause actually *producing* the effect. Instead, he discovered one event simply being conjoined with a second event. He saw the cue ball hitting the eight ball, and he saw the eight ball rolling away, but he did not see the cue ball *making* the eight ball move.

If you consider an instance of causation, you may find you agree with Hume. Do you really perceive the car making the noise you hear? Or do you, instead, just see the car and hear the noise? Do you perceive the flame producing heat? Or do you just see the flame and feel the heat? Consider the matter carefully. Which is it? Do you perceive X *causing* Y? Or do you just perceive X *and* Y? Hume found that in every single instance in which he experienced an event X supposedly causing another event Y, he didn't really experience X *causing* Y, but only X *and* Y. He concluded it is really just the **constant conjunction** of X and Y we take for causation. We experience a constant conjunction of flame and heat, and the causation we suppose is in flame is really only in our minds.

Not only that, because so-called causation really boils down to just a constant conjunction of a so-called cause with a so-called effect, there is no real justification for supposing the so-called cause will always be accompanied by the so-called effect. For example, you have experienced a constant conjunction between flame and heat. Are you not then justified in supposing that future experience will show a similar conjunction between flame and heat?

Well, Hume's answer is that you are *not* justified. If you say the next flame you encounter will be accompanied by heat, it is because you assume **the future will resemble the past.** Indeed, all reasoning based on present and past experience assumes the future will be like the past. But that means, Hume saw in a flash, that the assumption itself cannot be proved by an appeal to experience. To attempt to prove the assumption by appealing to experience, he observed, "must evidently be going in a circle."

It is hard to exaggerate the significance of this finding, as a moment's thought will show. The fact that all inference from past and present experience rests on an apparently unprovable assumption (that the future will resemble the past) leads to skeptical conclusions even more sweeping than Hume for the most part was willing to countenance. It means, for instance, that much of what we think we know, we do not really know. Will food and water nourish you the next time you eat and drink? Will our names be the same this evening as they are now? Will the words at the beginning of this sentence have changed meaning by the time you get to the end of the sentence? Evidently the answers to these questions, though seemingly obvious, *are mere assumptions, the truth of which we cannot really know.*

Do we see the pin *making* the balloon pop? Hume maintained that all he saw was just (1) the pin contacting the balloon and (2) the balloon popping. He did not see the pin *making* the balloon pop.

Perhaps you can now understand why, in the conclusion to Book I of *A Treatise of Human Nature,* Hume reflects that what he has written shows that

> the understanding, when it acts alone, and according to its most general principles, entirely subverts itself, and leaves not the lowest degree of evidence in any proposition, either in philosophy or common life.

Thus, Hume said, he is "ready to reject all belief and reasoning, and can look upon no opinion even as more probable or likely than another." This skepticism is not modified: it is uncompromisingly total. Hume said, though, that a true skeptic "will be diffident in his philosophical doubts, as well as of his philosophical conviction." In other words, a true (total) skeptic will doubt his doubts too.

Now that you have looked at the philosophy of David Hume, you will perhaps see why we have given this book the title it has. If Hume's ideas are correct, then must we not in the end despair, as Cratylus did (Chapter 3), and watch the world from a distance, merely wiggling our fingers?

IMMANUEL KANT

It is time now to turn to **Immanuel Kant** [kahnt] (1724–1804). Most scholars regard Kant as one of the most brilliant intellects of all time. Unfortunately, they also consider him one of the more difficult philosophers to read. Difficult or not, Kant provided a significant and ingenious response to Hume's skepticism. In a sentence, Kant believed that certain knowledge does indeed exist, and he set about to show how this could be possible, given Hume's various arguments that pointed in the opposite direction.

The Ordering Principles of the Mind

Think back for a second to Descartes. Descartes believed he could prove to himself that objects like tables and harpsichords and planets and so forth exist outside the mind. But his "proof" of these "external" objects was circuitous. First, Descartes had to prove to himself that he existed. Then he had to prove that God existed. Then he had to argue that God would not deceive him on such an important thing as the existence of tables and harpsichords and other external objects. Perhaps it is not surprising that this "proof" did not win many adherents.

John Locke, as we saw, believed knowledge comes from the sensations or "ideas" furnished to the mind by experience. The problem with this theory, George Berkeley was quick to see, is that it limits our knowledge to our sensations or ideas—which means we cannot know that anything exists except our sensations or ideas. Berkeley essentially accepted this and maintained that tables and harpsichords must just be clusters of sensations or ideas. David Hume, too, agreed that our knowledge is limited to our sensations or ideas, though he didn't think that tables and harpsichords and the like are mere sensations/ideas. Hume thought, "'tis vain to ask whether there be bodies [external objects] or not"—and tried to figure out what caused us to believe in bodies.

PROFILE: Immanuel Kant (1724–1804)

Kant was one of the first modern philosophers to earn his living as a professor of philosophy. Though he hardly ever left Königsberg, his birthplace, his ideas traveled far, and he is considered by many to be the greatest philosopher ever.

Kant's first works were in natural science and secured for him a substantial reputation before his appointment as professor of logic and metaphysics at Königsberg in 1770. After his appointment, he wrote nothing for ten years as he contemplated the issues that eventually appeared in his most important work, the *Critique of Pure Reason* (1781, 2nd ed. 1787). The actual writing of the book took "four or five months," he said, and was done "with the utmost attention to the contents, but with less concern for the presentation or for making things easy for the reader." Readers universally understand what he meant.

The reaction to the work was primarily one of confusion, and this led Kant to publish a shorter, more accessible version of his major work, titled *Prolegomena to Any Future Metaphysics* (1783). This

is an excellent book with which to begin the study of Kant's epistemology and metaphysics. To fix dates a bit, Kant's *Prolegomena* came out in the same year the American War of Independence ended and, incidentally, the first successful hot-air balloon flight was made.

Two years after publication of the *Prolegomena*, Kant's first major treatise on ethics, the *Foundations of the Metaphysics of Morals*, appeared. A comparatively brief work, it is nevertheless one of the most important books ever written on ethics.

Kant's second and third critiques, the *Critique of Practical Reason* (1788) and the *Critique of Judgment* (1790), were concerned with morality and aesthetics, respectively. In addition to the three *Critiques*, the *Prolegomena*, and the *Foundations*, Kant wrote many other, lesser works.

In his last years he suffered the indignity of hearing younger German philosophers say that he had not really understood what he had written, an unusually stupid idea that history has long since laid to rest.

It was scandalous, Immanuel Kant thought, that philosophy was reduced to either the idealism of Berkeley or the skepticism of Hume. Accordingly, Kant offered his own (complicated) proof of external objects. The usual way to try to prove the existence of external objects had been to argue from sensations outward to objects. Kant tried a different approach. His strategy, roughly, was to argue that a stream of sensations could not qualify as experience unless the stream was unified and conceptualized by the mind as the experience of external objects. (Arguments of this sort, which attempt to establish something as a necessary precondition of the possibility of experience, are called "transcendental arguments," and there is much controversy as to what, if anything, they really prove.)

Kant compared himself to Copernicus (1473–1543), who developed the heliocentric theory of planetary motion, which eventually replaced the old view that the sun and planets circle the earth. Before Copernicus, people assumed that the apparent motion of the sun was its real motion. Copernicus realized that the apparent motion of the sun was due to *our* motion, not the sun's motion. Kant had a very similar idea, known sometimes as the **Copernican revolution in philosophy.** According to this idea, the fundamental properties or characteristics of objects in the world outside the mind are due to our minds, not to the objects themselves.

What Kant meant is perhaps best illustrated by thinking of a person wearing blue glasses. The person sees everything in blue. Why? Because the glasses "impose" blueness on the person's sensations. Likewise, all of us experience the world as consisting of external objects. Not only that, we see the objects as existing in space and time and as related to one another causally. Why? Because, Kant theorized, our minds impose these forms on our sensations. Our sense-data are processed by the mind in such a way that we have the sort of experience we do, just as the sense-data of Mr. Blue Glasses are processed by his glasses in such a way that he has the sort of blue experience he does.

Kant's revolutionary theory—that sense-data are processed by the mind in such a way that we have the sort of experience we do have—explains how we can be sure of many of the things we are sure of. For example, according to Hume, we cannot be absolutely certain that the next flame we encounter will be accompanied by heat (maybe the flaming stuff will be some odd, new synthetic substance). Nevertheless, we *can* be certain that the flame will be in space and time. This knowledge could not be derived from experience, because experience informs us only of the way things have been so far, not of the way they must be. We can have this certainty that any flame we encounter will be in space and time, Kant said, only if space and time are "imposed" on our sensory data by the perceiving component of the mind.

Just think of an electric door or a TV camera. Data enter into the device, but it doesn't *experience* anything. The device is sensitive to light—it has "sensations"—but no experience. Likewise, for our sensations to qualify as experience, they must be processed in certain specific ways. First of all, these sensations must be subject to spatial-temporal shaping. That is, the perceiving part of the mind must perceive them as objects existing outside us in space and time. Second, they must also be conceptualized—brought under concepts. For raw sensory stimulation to qualify as experience, it must be organized and recognized as a *person* or *car* or *strawberry* or whatever. Sensory stimulation that isn't conceptualized is "blind," Kant said.

Further, Kant held, to qualify as experience, sensory stimulation must be unified in a single connected consciousness. If it weren't unified, it could never qualify as experience. In addition, he said, unification and conceptualization must conform to rules of cognition, just as perception must conform to spatial-temporal shaping. Thus, sensory stimulation must be organized as the experience of objects in space and time; but, likewise, it must be organized as the experience of objects that conform to cause and effect and other relationships. Change, for example, must be experienced as the change of a permanent substance whose quantity in nature remains constant.

This theory explains nicely, Kant said, how we know that we will *never* experience uncaused change. The only way to explain such certain knowledge is to assume that the mind "imposes" causation on experienced change. To qualify as experienced, a change must be subject to causation—just as to qualify as seen, a thing must be blue to the person who is forced to wear blue glasses.

Things-in-Themselves

In substance, then, this was Kant's response to the challenge David Hume put to epistemology. Hume was partially correct. He was correct in thinking that knowledge begins with experience. But he was not correct in thinking that knowledge is derived from experience. It is better to say that the mind is *awakened* by experience. But once awakened, it doesn't simply receive and store stimulation as would a camera. It actively processes it according to underlying principles and categories, which can be disclosed by careful examination.

However—and this is a big "however"—according to Kant, our knowledge is limited to **phenomena,** or experienceable objects—things that could be the subject of experience. For only things that are experienced are subject to the categorizing and unifying activity of the mind. To be experienced, objects must be in space and time, related to one another by cause and effect, and otherwise subject to the principles of cognition; but we cannot apply these categories and principles to things "as they are in themselves"—**noumena,** or things that exist outside experience. Concerning this "noumenal" world beyond experience, the world of the thing-in-itself, ***das Ding-an-sich*** (as it is said in German), skepticism is unavoidable, for Kant. When rules that apply to the world of experience are applied to a reality-beyond-experience, contradictions and mistakes result. Kant was willing to say that three "ideas of reason"—God, world, self—at least point to *possibilities* in the noumenal realm, but we can have no knowledge of the realm. Kant's epistemology limits legitimate metaphysical reasoning to this world.

So, relative to the world of experience, Kant was not a skeptic. But relative to things-in-themselves, he was. This doesn't mean he made no headway relative to Hume. On Hume's theory, we simply cannot be certain that the future will resemble the past—because Hume assumed all knowledge is derived from experience. But this seems wrong: we can be certain that, in some respects, the future will resemble the past. We can be certain we will never experience an uncaused event (despite the fact that contemporary physicists speak of uncaused events on the subatomic level). We can be certain we will never experience an object that isn't in space or time. We can be certain we will never experience an object that has no properties. Kant's theory seems better able than Hume's to explain these and similar facts.

THE NINETEENTH CENTURY

Kant died in 1804, at the beginning of the nineteenth century. The first part of the nineteenth century was the Romantic era in European arts and letters, which arose in revolt against the rationalism of the preceding century. This was the period that emphasized adventure and spiritual vision in literature, produced huge and noisy symphonies, and stressed exotic themes in the visual arts. Careful reasoning was out; emotional spontaneity was in.

In philosophy, although Kant's successors did not exactly repudiate what he had written, they certainly did stand it on its ear. This dramatic response to Kant was German **Absolute Idealism,** the philosophies of Johann Gottlieb Fichte (1762–1814), Friedrich Wilhelm Joseph von Schelling (1775–1854), and **Georg Wilhelm Friedrich Hegel** [HAY-gul] (1770–1831).

Kant had argued that the mind imposes certain categories on the objects of experience and that this is what makes it possible to have knowledge of the world

PROFILE: Georg Wilhelm Friedrich Hegel (1770–1831)

There was a sort of incredible solemnity about Hegel that earned him the nickname "the old man" while he was still a university student at Tübingen, Germany. He was serious about everything he did and was even somber when he drank. In high school he devoted his time to collecting copious notes concerning what he thought were the ultimate questions of life, a sure sign that he would wind up as a philosopher.

Hegel's fellow university student Friedrich Schelling gained renown in philosophy early in life. But for Hegel it was a struggle. After having served as a private tutor, newspaper editor, and director of a high school, he was given a professorship at Heidelberg and then at Berlin, where, finally, he became famous. His lectures drew large audiences despite his tendency to stop and start and break off in midsentence to page furiously through his notes.

His listeners could sense that something deep and important was happening. Hegel was quite handsome and became popular with the society women of Berlin. All this satisfied him enormously.

Not everyone admired Hegel, however. Arthur Schopenhauer, another famous philosopher we will discuss a bit later, described Hegel as an unimaginative, unintelligent, disgusting, revolting charlatan who ruined the entire generation of intellectuals who followed him. You should bear in mind, though, that poor Schopenhauer attempted to schedule his lectures at Berlin at the same hour as Hegel's—and found himself lecturing to an empty hall.

Hegel's main works are *Phenomenology of Mind* (1807), in which he first presented his metaphysical system, *Science of Logic* (1812–1816), *Encyclopedia of the Philosophical Sciences* (1817), and *Philosophy of Right* (1821).

of experience. His epistemological thesis, as we have seen, is that we can have knowledge *only* of the world of experience and can have no knowledge of things "as they are in themselves." The Absolute Idealists, however, transformed this epistemological skepticism into metaphysical idealism. What could there be such that the mind could not know it? they asked. If it is not knowable, they reasoned, then it is unthinkable; and if it is unthinkable, why, it just plain isn't. So thought, or consciousness, does not merely categorize reality: its categories *are* reality. There cannot be unknowable things-in-themselves, they said, for everything that is, is a product of the knowing mind.

Reality is not, however, the expression of your thought or ours or any other particular person's, they said, for neither you nor any other person created the world of independent external things that exists around us. Rather, reality is the expression of *infinite* or *absolute* thought or consciousness. And when we think or philosophize about reality, this is consciousness becoming aware of itself, that is, becoming infinite.

So, from the perspective of Hegel, the cosmos and its history are the concrete expression of thought. Thus, everything that happens and every field of human inquiry are the proper domain of the philosopher, who alone can understand and interpret the true relationship of each aspect of reality to the whole. Absolute Idealism, as this philosophy is called, attempted to achieve a complete and unified conception of all reality, a conception that gave meaning to each and every aspect in relationship to the sum total. It was the towering pinnacle of metaphysical speculation, and virtually everything that happened subsequently in metaphysics and epistemology happened in reaction to it, as you are about to see.

The Main Themes of Hegel

Hegel's philosophy is difficult, but the main themes are these:

1. "Everything depends on grasping the truth not merely as Substance but as Subject as well." This means that what is true, what is real, is not merely that which is thought *of,* but that which *thinks.* Thus, what is most real—the Absolute—is thought thinking of itself.

2. Hegel's idealism is different from Berkeley's. For Berkeley, the objective world in fact exists in the minds of individuals. For Hegel, the objective world is an unfolding or expression of infinite thought, and the individual mind is the vehicle of infinite thought reflecting on itself.

3. Reality, the Absolute, for Hegel, is not a group of independent particulars or states of affairs, but rather like a coherent thought system such as mathematics, it is an integrated whole in which each proposition (each state of affairs) is logically connected with all the rest. Thus, an isolated state of affairs is not wholly real; likewise, a proposition about this or that aspect or feature of reality is only partially true. The only thing that is totally true (or totally real, because these amount to the same thing) is the complete system.

4. **The Absolute,** the sum total of reality, is a system of conceptual triads. To formalize Hegel's system somewhat artificially: for proposition or concept *A* there is a negation, *not-A;* and within the two there is a synthetic unity, or synthesis, *B. B,* however, has a negation, *not-B,* and within *B* and *not-B* there is a synthesis, *C,* and so on. Thus, the higher levels of the system are implicit in the lower levels—for example, *C* and *B* are both implicit in *A.* In this way the entire system of thought and reality that is the Absolute is an integrated whole in which each proposition is logically interconnected with the rest.

Note that for Hegel this triadic structure is not a method by means of which we discover truth. Instead, it is the way things are: it is the actual structure of thought. Thus, for example, the most basic or fundamental category or concept is *being.* But being is nothing without *not-being,* its opposite. And the synthesis of these opposites is *becoming;* hence, the Absolute is becoming. In similar fashion, at each stage of his exposition Hegel posits a **thesis,** to which there belongs an **antithesis,** and the thesis and antithesis are a unity in a higher **synthesis.** The higher levels of the system are always implicit in the lower levels.

Ultimately, therefore, we come to the apex, or highest triad, of Hegel's system: the synthesis of "Idea" and "Nature" in "Spirit." And Idea and Nature are each, in turn, the synthesis of two lower opposing concepts. Thus, Idea is the synthesis of subjectivity (that which thinks) and objectivity (that which is thought of). What Hegel means by "Idea" is self-conscious thought, which is exactly what you would expect to be the synthesis of that which thinks and that which is thought of. "The absolute Idea," Hegel wrote, "alone is being, eternal life, self-knowing truth, and it is all truth."

The antithesis of Idea is Nature. In other words, on one hand there is self-knowing or self-conscious thought ("Idea"), and on the other there is what we

Ludwig van Beethoven

As you can see, the great German composer Ludwig van Beethoven (1770–1827) lived at almost exactly the same time as Hegel. Beethoven was the link between the controlled and formal Classical era in music and the passionate and tempestuous Romantic era. Hegel's philosophy, for some reason, perhaps because of its grandness and scope, reminds one much more of the music of the Romantic era.

might call the independent world (Nature), the external expression of Idea, or Idea outside itself. (It is in his philosophy of Nature that Hegel attempted to integrate the various concepts of science into his system.)

So Nature and Idea, as thesis and antithesis, have their own synthesis. As we said, this is the synthesis of the main triad of Hegel's entire system and is what Hegel called "Spirit." We might translate "Spirit" as "thought knowing itself both as thought and as object" or as "the Idea returning into itself." We did not say that Hegel is easy.

The philosophy of Spirit also has three main subdivisions: subjective spirit and its antithesis, objective spirit, with the synthesis as Absolute Spirit. Subjective spirit is the realm of the human mind; objective spirit is the mind in its external manifestation in social institutions. Hegel's analysis of objective spirit contains his social and political philosophy, in which he attempts to display the relationships (always more or less triadic) among such various concepts as property, contract, crime, punishment, right, personality, family, society, and the state.

In the end, therefore, we come to know the part played by every aspect of reality in the whole, and we are led to understand that the highest conception of the Absolute is as Spirit.

So Hegel's system is really a grandiose vision of the history of the universe and the history of human consciousness as a necessary unfolding of infinite reason. It purports to be a complete conceptual framework for each aspect of reality and for every component of human thought and history. This system represents the towering summit of metaphysical speculation.

Arthur Schopenhauer

Reactions to Hegel's Absolute Idealism were swift and strong. Karl Marx (1818–1883) tried to turn Hegel on his head by interpreting the evolutionary progress of the species as being due to economic factors. (We cover the details of Marx's theory in Chapter 11.) Søren Kierkegaard (1813–1855) poured scorn on Hegel's grandiose scheme. Friedrich Nietzsche (1844–1900) rejected Hegel's idealism and all similar metaphysics. (We cover Kierkegaard and Nietzsche in the next chapter.) However, the most famous attacks on Hegel's exuberant rationalism came from **Arthur Schopenhauer** [SHOW-pun-owr] (1788–1860). Schopenhauer regarded Hegel personally as an opportunistic charlatan and viewed him philosophically as a dud. For Schopenhauer, Hegel's "reason" was an exercise in philistine

We don't think Schopenhauer had a shoulder holster (like this person), but he did sleep with a pistol under his pillow

self-deception; his attempt to paint the world in rational terms, pathetic and misguided. Schopenhauer didn't stop with Hegel: science and the humanities as a whole have been mustered, he believed, to picture the universe as reasonable, governed by laws under the master of the rational human intellect. Reality, he maintained, is very different.

Specifically, for Schopenhauer human beings are rarely rational in their actions. On the contrary, they are blindly driven by will to pursue selfish desires. Reason is invoked after the fact as a way of rationalizing what has been done from impulse, he held. Schopenhauer's world is peopled with vicious little men who commit atrocities in pursuit of trifling objects. It is a world in which no one can be trusted and security requires sleeping with a loaded pistol under the pillow. Their willfulness makes humans a violent part of a grotesque scenario that has neither sense nor reason, in Schopenhauer's view.

Believe it or not, Schopenhauer took his point of philosophical departure to be Kant, who had argued that the phenomenal world is structured by the understanding. However, according to Schopenhauer, it is the *will* that does the structuring. This, very roughly, is his theory.

How do you come to know yourself? You come to know your character through your decisions and choices, correct? Well, these are the result of willing. Further, from the perspective of the will, the act of willing and the bodily act that we ordinarily say is *caused* by that act are one and the same thing: "The action of the will is nothing but the act of will objectified, that is, translated into perception," Schopenhauer wrote.

Certainly this theory is plausible enough, and it enabled Schopenhauer to regard not just one's body but all phenomena as the objectification of will. Further, according to Schopenhauer, the will is the force that makes plants grow, forms crystals, turns magnets toward the North Pole—in short, does everything.

Schopenhauer's theory is difficult at this point because he, like Kant, made a distinction between phenomena and noumena. Schopenhauer distinguished between cosmic, impersonal, will-in-itself and its manifestation in the phenomenal world. Will-in-itself is the originating source of everything that happens and, as such, is not determined by anything else. It is, one might say, blind and purposeless. Each person is a manifestation of will-in-itself and subject to unceasing striving. Accordingly, the world is in disarray and is a sorry sight, because we are witless lackeys of this errant, cosmic will. One can achieve a measure of peace and happiness, according to Schopenhauer, only to the degree one escapes the tyranny of will. This can be done by moving beyond knowledge of one's own will to objectivity and understanding of will-in-itself, in which state the world of phenomena becomes a kind of nothingness. He spoke of this detached state as one of ecstasy and rapture and thought it could be glimpsed through art, music, and aesthetic experience.

Sigmund Freud (1856–1939), who read Schopenhauer, based psychoanalysis on the concept that human actions stem not from rationality but from unconscious drives and instincts in what he called the *id*, or "it" part of the self. The influence of Schopenhauer is evident.

Friedrich Nietzsche also read Schopenhauer and became convinced that the world is driven by cosmic will, not by reason. However, that is a story for our next chapter.

SELECTION 7.1

An Enquiry Concerning Human Understanding*

David Hume

[*In* An Enquiry Concerning Human Understanding, *David Hume argued that the contents of the mind fall into only two categories: thoughts or ideas, and "impressions"—the material given to us by our senses and experience. The difference between ideas and impressions, he says, is solely that ideas are less vivid or forceful than impressions. In this passage Hume argued that the creative power of the mind is nothing more than the power to compound and transpose the material given to us by the senses and experience. Hence, he wrote, when we suspect a word is employed without any meaning or idea, we only have to ask from what impressions the supposed idea comes. If we cannot discover any impressions, that confirms our suspicions. Contrast these views with those of Kant in the following selection.*]

Section II. Of the Origin of Ideas

. . . Nothing, at first view, may seem more unbounded than the thought of man, which not only escapes all human power and authority, but is not even restrained within the limits of nature and reality. To form monsters, and join incongruous shapes and appearances, costs the imagination no more trouble than to conceive the most natural and familiar objects. And while the body is confined to one planet, along which it creeps with pain and difficulty; the thought can in an instant transport us into the most distant regions of the universe; or even beyond the universe, into the unbounded chaos, where nature is supposed to lie in total confusion. What never was seen, or heard of, may yet be conceived; nor is any thing beyond the power of thought, except what implies an absolute contradiction.

But though our thought seems to possess this unbounded liberty, we shall find, upon a nearer examination, that it is really confined within very narrow limits, and that all this creative power of the mind amounts to no more than the faculty of compounding, transposing, augmenting, or diminishing the materials afforded us by the senses and experience. When we think of a golden mountain, we only join two consistent ideas, *gold* and *mountain,* with which we were formerly acquainted. A virtuous horse we can conceive; because, from our own feeling, we can conceive virtue; and this we may unite to the figure and shape of a horse, which is an animal familiar to us. In short, all the materials of thinking are derived either from our outward or inward sentiment: the mixture and composition of these belongs alone to the mind and will. Or, to express myself in philosophical language, all our ideas or more feeble perceptions are copies of our impressions or more lively ones.

---

* David Hume, "An Enquiry Concerning Human Understanding," in *Philosophic Classics: From Plato to Nietzsche,* Walter Kaufmann and Forrest E. Baird, eds. (Englewood Cliffs, N.J.: Prentice-Hall, 1994). We have omitted one of Hume's footnotes.

To prove this, the two following arguments will, I hope, be sufficient. First, when we analyze our thoughts or ideas, however compounded or sublime, we always find that they resolve themselves into such simple ideas as were copied from a precedent feeling or sentiment. Even those ideas, which, at first view, seem the most wide of this origin, are found, upon a nearer scrutiny, to be derived from it. The idea of God, as meaning an infinitely intelligent, wise, and good Being, arises from reflecting on the operations of our own mind, and augmenting, without limit, those qualities of goodness and wisdom. We may prosecute this enquiry to what length we please; where we shall always find, that every idea which we examine is copied from a similar impression. Those who would assert that this position is not universally true nor without exception, have only one, and that an easy method of refuting it; by producing that idea, which, in their opinion, is not derived from this source. It will then be incumbent on us, if we would maintain our doctrine, to produce the impression, or lively perception, which corresponds to it.

Secondly, if it happens, from a defect of the organ, that a man is not susceptible of any species of sensation, we always find that he is as little susceptible of the correspondent ideas. A blind man can form no notion of colours; a deaf man of sounds. Restore either of them that sense in which he is deficient; by opening this new inlet for his sensations, you also open an inlet for the ideas; and he finds no difficulty in conceiving these objects. The case is the same, if the object, proper for exciting any sensation, has never been applied to the organ. . . .

. . . Here, therefore, is a proposition, which not only seems, in itself, simple and intelligible; but, if a proper use were made of it, might render every dispute equally intelligible, and banish all that jargon, which has so long taken possession of metaphysical reasonings, and drawn disgrace upon them. All ideas, especially abstract ones, are naturally faint and obscure; the mind has but a slender hold of them: they are apt to be confounded with other resembling ideas; and when we have often employed any term, though without a distinct meaning, we are apt to imagine it has a determinate idea annexed to it. On the contrary, all impressions, that is, all sensations, either outward or inward, are strong and vivid: the limits between them are more exactly determined: nor is it easy to fall into any error or mistake with regard to them. When we entertain, therefore, any suspicion that a philosophical term is employed without any meaning or idea (as is but too frequent), we need but enquire, *from what impressions is that supposed idea derived?* And if it be impossible to assign any, this will serve to confirm our suspicion. By bringing ideas into so clear a light we may reasonably hope to remove all dispute, which may arise, concerning their nature and reality.

SELECTION 7.2

Critique of Pure Reason*

Immanuel Kant

[*In the previous selection, you saw that Hume thought all concepts are derived from sensory "impressions." To put this point in Kant's language, Hume thought that all concepts are "empirical" and none are "a priori" ("empirical" and "not a priori" mean the same thing). In this difficult selection, Kant argues that time is not empirical (i.e., that time is a priori). In other words, according to Kant, time is not derived from sensory impressions or what Kant calls "intuitions." He also explains what time is.*]

* From Immanuel Kant's *Critique of Pure Reason*, translated by Norman Kemp Smith (London: Macmillan and Company, 1929). Reproduced with permission of Palgrave Macmillan.

Transcendental Aesthetic Section II, Time

§4, Metaphysical Exposition of the Concept of Time

1. Time is not an empirical concept that has been derived from any experience. For neither co-existence nor succession would ever come without our perception, if the representation of time were not presupposed as underlying them *a priori*. . . .

2. Time is a necessary representation that underlies all intuitions. We cannot, in respect of appearances in general, remove time itself, though we can quite well think time as void of appearances. Time is, therefore, given *a priori*. In it alone is actuality of

appearances possible at all. Appearances may, one and all, vanish; but time (as the universal condition of their possibility) cannot itself be removed.

3. . . . Time has only one dimension; different times are not simultaneous but successive (just as different spaces are not successive but simultaneous). These principles cannot be derived from experience, for experience would give neither strict universality nor apodeictic certainty. We should only be able to say that common experience teaches us that it is so; not that it must be so. These principles are valid as rules under which alone experiences are possible; and they instruct us in regard to the experiences, not by means of them.

4. Time is not a discursive, or what is called a general concept, but a pure form of sensible intuition. Different times are but parts of one and the same time. . . . Moreover, the proposition that different times cannot be simultaneous is not to be derived from a general concept. . . .

§6, *Conclusions from These Concepts*

(a) Time is not something which exists of itself, or which inheres in things as an objective determination, and it does not, therefore, remain when abstraction is made of all subjective conditions of its intuition. Were it self-subsistent, it would be something which would be actual and yet not an actual object. Were it a determination or order inhering in things themselves, it could not precede the objects as their condition. . . .

(b) Time is nothing but the form of inner sense, that is, of the intuition of ourselves and of our inner state. It cannot be a determination of outer appearances; it has to do neither with shape nor position, but with the relation of representations in our inner state. . . .

(c) Time is the formal *a priori* condition of all appearances whatsoever. Space, as the pure form of all *outer* intuition, is so far limited; it serves as the *a priori* condition only of outer appearances. But since all representations, whether they have for their objects outer things or not, belong, in themselves, as determinations of the mind, to our inner state; and since this inner state stands under the formal condition of inner intuition, and so belongs to time, time is an *a priori* condition of all appearance whatsoever. It is the immediate condition of inner appearances (of our souls), and thereby the mediate condition of outer appearances. Just as I can say *a priori* that all outer appearances are in space, and are determined *a priori* in conformity with the relations of space, I can also say, from the principle of inner sense, that all appearances whatsoever, that is, all objects of the senses, are in time, and necessarily stand in time-relations.

If we abstract from *our* mode of inwardly intuiting ourselves—the mode of intuition in terms of which we likewise take up into our faculty of representation all outer intuitions—and so take objects as they may be in themselves, then time is nothing. It has objective validity only in respect of appearances, these being things which we take *as objects of our senses*. . . .

Time is therefore a purely subjective condition of our (human) intuition (which is always sensible, that is, so far as we are affected by objects), and in itself, apart from the subject, is nothing.

SELECTION 7.3

The Philosophy of History*

Georg Wilhelm Friedrich Hegel

[*In the previous selection, Kant said that time is a construct of the mind. In this selection, Hegel goes Kant one further: everything, Hegel says, is a construct of* Reason. *Hegel doesn't argue for this thesis in this selection but only asserts that it has been "proved."*]

The only Thought which Philosophy brings with it to the contemplation of History, is the simple conception of *Reason;* that Reason is the Sovereign of the World; that the history of the world, therefore,

* From Georg Hegel, *The Philosophy of History*, translated by J. Sibree (New York: The Colonial Press, 1900). ·

presents us with a rational process. This conviction and intuition is a hypothesis in the domain of history as such. In that of Philosophy it is no hypothesis. It is there provided by speculative cognition, that Reason—and this term may here suffice us, without investigation the relation sustained by the Universe to the Divine Being—is *Substance*, as well as *Infinite Power;* its own *Infinite Material* underlying all the natural and spiritual life which it originates, as also the *Infinite Form*—that which sets this Material in motion. On the one hand, Reason is the *substance* of the Universe; viz., that by which and in which all reality has its being and subsistence. On the other hand, it is the *Infinite Energy* of the Universe; since Reason is not so powerless as to be incapable of producing anything but a mere ideal, a mere intention—having its place outside reality, nobody knows where; something separate and abstract, in the heads of certain human beings. It is

the Infinite complex of things, their entire Essence and Truth. It is its own material which it commits to its own Active Energy to work up; not needing, as finite action does, the conditions of an external material of given means from which it may obtain its support, and the objects of its activity. It supplies its own nourishment, and is the object of its own operations. While it is exclusively its own basis of existence, and absolute final aim, it is also the energizing power realizing this aim; developing in it not only the phenomena of the Natural, but also of the Spiritual Universe—the History of the World. That this "Idea" or "Reason" is the *True,* the *Eternal,* the absolutely *powerful* essence; that it reveals itself in the World, and that in that World nothing else is revealed but this and its honor and glory—is the thesis which, as we have said, has been proved in Philosophy, and is here regarded as demonstrated.

SELECTION 7.4

The World as Will and Representation*

Arthur Schopenhauer

[*Some terminology: By "empirical" Schopenhauer means "capable of being verified by observation and experiment, capable of being encountered in space and time."*

By "ideality" he means the property of existing in consciousness or thought.

By "phenomenon" he means an object of experience in space and time. By "phenomenon of the brain" he means an experience produced by the brain.]

On the Fundamental View of Idealism

In endless space countless luminous spheres, round each of which some dozen smaller illuminated ones revolve, hot at the core and covered over with a hard cold crust; on this crust a mouldy film has produced living and knowing beings: this is empirical truth, the real, the world. Yet for a being who thinks, it is

a precarious position to stand on one of those numberless spheres freely floating in boundless space, without knowing whence or whither, and to be only one of innumerable similar beings that throng, press, and toil, restlessly and rapidly arising and passing away in beginningless and endless time. Here there is nothing permanent but matter alone, and the recurrence of the same varied organic forms by means of certain ways and channels that inevitably exist as they do. All that empirical science can teach is only the more precise nature and rule of these events. But at last the philosophy of modern times, especially through Berkeley and Kant, has called to mind that all this in the first instance is only *phenomenon of the brain,* and is encumbered by so many great and different *subjective* conditions that its supposed absolute reality vanishes, and leaves room for an entirely different world-order that lies at the root of that phenomenon, in other words, is related to it as is the thing-in-itself to the mere appearance.

"The world is my representation" is, like the axioms of Euclid, a proposition which everyone must recognize as true as soon as he understands it, although it is not a proposition that everyone understands as soon as he hears it. To have brought this proposition to consciousness and to have connected it with the problem of the relation of the ideal to the real, in other words, of the world in the head to the world outside the head, constitutes, together with the problem of moral freedom, the distinctive characteristic of the philosophy of the moderns. For only after men had tried their hand for thousands of years at merely *objective* philosophizing did they discover that, among the many things that make the world so puzzling and precarious, the first and foremost is that, however immeasurable and massive it may be, its existence hangs nevertheless on a single thread; and this thread is the actual consciousness in which it exists. This condition, with which the existence of the world is irrevocably encumbered, marks it with the stamp of *ideality*, in spite of all *empirical* reality, and consequently with the stamp of the mere *phenomenon*. Thus the world must be recognized, from one aspect at least, as akin to a dream, indeed as capable of being put in the same class with a dream. For the same brain-function that conjures up during sleep a perfectly objective, perceptible, and indeed palpable world must have just as large a share in the presentation of the objective world of wakefulness. Though different as regards their matter, the two worlds are nevertheless obviously moulded from one form. This form is the intellect, the brain-function. Descartes was probably the first to attain the degree of reflection demanded by that fundamental truth; consequently, he made that truth the starting-point of his philosophy, although provisionally only in the form of sceptical doubt. By his taking *cogito ergo sum* as the only thing certain, and provisionally regarding the existence of the world as problematical, the essential and only correct starting-point, and at the same time the true point of support, of all philosophy was really found. This point, indeed, is essentially and of necessity *the subjective, our own consciousness*. For this alone is and remains that which is immediate; everything else, be it what it may, is first mediated and conditioned by consciousness, and therefore dependent on it. It is thus rightly considered that the philosophy of the moderns starts from Descartes

as its father. Not long afterwards, Berkeley went farther along this path, and arrived at *idealism* proper; in other words, at the knowledge that what is extended in space, and hence the objective, material world in general, exists as such simply and solely in our *representation*, and that it is false and indeed absurd to attribute to it, *as such*, an existence outside all representation and independent of the knowing subject, and so to assume a matter positively and absolutely existing in itself. But this very correct and deep insight really constitutes the whole of Berkeley's philosophy; in it he had exhausted himself.

Accordingly, true philosophy must at all costs be *idealistic;* indeed, it must be so merely to be honest. For nothing is more certain than that no one ever came out of himself in order to identify himself immediately with things different from him; but everything of which he has certain, sure, and hence immediate knowledge, lies within his consciousness. Beyond this consciousness, therefore, there can be no *immediate* certainty; but the first principles of a science must have such a certainty. It is quite appropriate to the empirical standpoint of all the other sciences to assume the objective world as positively and actually existing; it is not appropriate to the standpoint of philosophy, which has to go back to what is primary and original. *Consciousness* alone is immediately given, hence the basis of philosophy is limited to the facts of consciousness; in other words, philosophy is essentially *idealistic*. Realism, which commends itself to the crude understanding by appearing to be founded on fact, starts precisely from an arbitrary assumption, and is in consequence an empty castle in the air, since it skips or denies the first fact of all, namely that all that we know lies within consciousness. For that the *objective existence* of things is conditioned by a representer of them, and that consequently the objective world exists only *as representation*, is no hypothesis, still less a peremptory pronouncement, or even a paradox put forward for the sake of debate or argument. On the contrary, it is the surest and simplest truth. . . .

That the *objective world would exist* even if there existed no knowing being at all, naturally seems at the first onset to be sure and certain, because it can be thought in the abstract, without the contradiction that it carries within itself coming to light. But if we try to *realize* this abstract thought, in other words, to reduce it to representations of perception, from which alone (like everything abstract) it can have content and truth; and if accordingly we attempt to *imagine an objective world without a knowing subject,* then we become aware that what we are imagining at that moment is in truth the opposite of what we intended, namely nothing but just the process in the intellect of a knowing being who perceives an objective world, that is to say, precisely that which we had sought to exclude. For this perceptible and real world is obviously a phenomenon of the brain; and so in the assumption that the world as such might exist independently of all brains there lies a contradiction. . . .

. . . [I]mmediately connected with simple or *Berkeleian* idealism, which concerns the *object in general,* is *Kantian* idealism, which concerns the specially given *mode and manner* of objective existence. This proves that the whole of the material world with its bodies in space, extended and, by means of time, having causal relations with one another, and everything attached to this—all this is not something existing *independently* of our mind, but something that has its fundamental presuppositions in our brain-functions, *by means of* which and *in* which alone is *such* an objective order of things possible. For time, space, and causality, on which all those real and objective events rest, are themselves nothing more than functions of the brain; so that, therefore, this unchangeable *order* of things, affording the criterion and the clue to their empirical *reality,* itself comes first from the brain, and has its credentials from that alone. Kant has discussed this thoroughly and in detail; though he does not mention the brain, but says "the faculty of knowledge." He has even attempted to prove that that objective order in time, space, causality, matter, and so on, on which all the events of the real world ultimately rest, cannot even be *conceived,* when closely considered, as a self-existing order, i.e., an order of things-in-themselves, or as something absolutely objective and positively existing; for if we attempt to think it out to the end, it leads to contradictions. . . .

But even apart from the deep insight and discernment revealed only by the Kantian philosophy, the inadmissible character of the assumption of absolute *realism,* clung to so obstinately, can indeed be directly demonstrated, or at any rate felt, by the mere elucidation of its meaning through considerations such as the following. According to realism, the world is supposed to exist, as we know it, independently of this knowledge. Now let us once remove from it all knowing beings, and thus leave behind only inorganic and vegetable nature. Rock, tree, and brook are there, and the blue sky; sun, moon, and stars illuminate this world, as before, only of course to no purpose, since there exists no eye to see such things. But then let us subsequently put into the world a knowing being. That world then presents itself *once more* in his brain, and repeats itself inside that brain exactly as it was previously outside it. Thus to the *first* world a *second* has been added, which, although completely separated from the first, resembles it to a nicety. Now the *subjective* world of this perception is constituted in *subjective,* known space exactly as the *objective* world is in *objective,* infinite space. But the subjective world still has an advantage over the objective, namely the knowledge that that external space is infinite; in fact, it can state beforehand most minutely and accurately the full conformity to law of all the relations in that space which are possible and not yet actual, and it does not need to examine them first. It can state just as much about the course of time, as also about the relation of cause and effect which governs the changes in outer space. I think that, on closer consideration, all this proves absurd enough, and thus leads to the conviction that that absolutely *objective* world outside the head, independent of it and *prior* to all knowledge, which we at first imagined we had conceived, was really no other than the second world already known *subjectively,* the world of the representation, and that it is this alone which we are actually capable of conceiving. Accordingly the assumption is automatically forced on us that the world, as we know it, exists only for our knowledge, and consequently in the *representation* alone, and not once again outside that representation.

CHECKLIST

To help you review, a checklist of the key philosophers of this chapter can be found online at www.mhhe.com/moore9e.

KEY TERMS AND CONCEPTS

the Absolute   135
Absolute Idealism   133
constant
   conjunction   129
Copernican revolution
   in philosophy   131
das Ding-an-sich   133

"The future will
   resemble the
   past."   129
noumena   133
phenomena   133
thesis, antithesis,
   synthesis   135

QUESTIONS FOR DISCUSSION AND REVIEW

1. Do you ever experience anything other than your own perceptions? Explain.

2. Explain Hume's reasons for questioning the idea of the mind/self.

3. "Necessity is something in the mind, not in the objects." Explain what this means and what Hume's reasons were for holding it.

4. Will the future resemble the past? Can you *know* it will, or must you merely *assume* it will?

5. If knowledge begins with experience, must it also rise from experience? Explain.

6. Is it possible that we may someday experience an event that is in neither space nor time? If not, why not?

7. Is it possible for extraterrestrial aliens to experience things that are not in space or time?

8. Do infants have *experience,* or do they just have sensations? Do cats? Do fish? Explain.

9. Can we have knowledge of things-in-themselves? Be sure to clarify what you mean by the phrase.

10. "Everything depends on grasping the truth not merely as Substance but as Subject as well." Who said this, and what does it mean?

SUGGESTED FURTHER READINGS

Go online to www.mhhe.com/moore9e for a list of suggested further readings.

8

The Continental Tradition

I rebel; therefore I exist.　　—Albert Camus

The first half of the nineteenth century was still very much under the sway of the French Revolution (1787–1799). Democratic, egalitarian ideals were on the march. Monarchies and authoritarian regimes were under threat. Sharing this optimistic turbulence was the dominant cultural movement of the century, romanticism. It preferred adventure, excitement, and a sense of infinite possibility. Beethoven (1770–1827) demanded that the artist achieve perfection and not only in musical composition. The French painter Eugene Delacroix (1798–1863) battled for liberal ideas which could be manifested at their best in free, personal expression. The primacy of the subject/artist led to sublime works of art such as the musical compositions of the Vienna three, Hadyn, Mozart, and Beethoven, not to mention Schubert, Schumann, Chopin, and Brahms. In Weimar, it was the classic writings of Goethe (1749–1832) and Schiller (1759–1805) which had philosophical depth and vision. Absolute perfection in art was thought possible, and was regarded as the crowning achievement of humanity. The romantic poet, Johann Friedrich Holderin (1770–1843), an associate of Hegel, described the poet as half deity.

In America in the early nineteenth century, literature was also full of a sense of adventure as well as whimsical fun as expressed in the writings of James Fenimore Cooper Herman (1789–1851) and Washington Irving (1783–1859). But it was only with Melville's *Moby Dick* (1851) that America hit its stride and found a whale to match its terrors and ambitions.

The second great historical event determining the nineteenth century in Europe was the Industrial Revolution. The first half of the nineteenth century was dominated by Britain, which became the leading manufacturing country in the world with its development of steam engines driven by coal. In the second half of the nineteenth century Germany gradually became the leader of a "second Industrial Revolution," namely, of steel, electricity, the internal combustion engine, and chemicals. It also developed a vastly expanded network of "invisible" exports: banking, insurance, and shipping.

Industrial development brought with it social problems as well as opportunities. Cities became overcrowded, polluted, and ugly. Workers were often poorly paid and had to work long hours. Accidents were rife. Child labor was accepted as a necessity and packaged as an opportunity. This changing nature of society led to cultural movements very different from romanticism. Naturalism was an art and literary movement which began in France around 1830 and then spread to Germany and Italy. It involved showing the world as constantly changing and full of contradictions and ugliness as well as beauty. It conveyed melancholy and despair owing to humanity's hopeless struggle against the overwhelming forces of nature.

The second half of the nineteenth century was dominated by social thinking and, in particular, by the positivism of Auguste Comte (1798–1857) and the *Communist Manifesto* of Karl Marx (1818–1883). The social plight of the poor was depicted by painters like Gustave Courbet (1819–1877) and by writers like Emile Zola (1840–1902), Honore de Balzac (1799–1850), and Gustav Flaubert (1821–1880). This movement, known as realism, rejected classical and romantic optimism and hubris and replaced these with an exact depiction of reality and real social conditions. Henrik Ibsen (1828–1906) did something similar in drama. Human life was perceived as an epic struggle, not a fairy tale with a happy ending.

However, prosperity at the end of the nineteenth century resulted in the so-called Gilded Age in America, the Victorian and Edwardian eras in the United Kingdom, and the *belle epoque* (beautiful era) in France—all of which too soon gave way to the slaughter and horrors of World War I. The competition among European countries for world markets and resources ended in a tragic self-immolation, whereby Europe lost both economic and cultural domination of the world. War literature came to the fore, headed by Erich Maria Remarque's *All Quiet on the Western Front* (1927). After 1917 and the overthrow of the Czar in Russia, the fear of communism and social and economic revolution terrified the European upper classes. Art and literature sought ways of expressing disgust at the old ways of thinking and of showing the new much harsher reality. After all, during World War I the most civilized countries of the world showed themselves to be the most barbaric. Avant garde movements arose such as Dadaism, Surrealism, Futurism, and the *Neue Sachlichkeit* (New Objectivity) in Germany. Shock became the new method of expression. To adequately show the new situation, Bertolt Brecht (1898–1956) recommended "distancing" the play from the audience so that facial identification of the actors would not be possible. The Depression of 1929 had an additional sobering effect on life in the United States, and also in Europe.

Between the world wars, young American thinkers, writers, composers, and artists sought meaning and truth in Europe, especially in Paris. Some of them became known as the "Lost Generation": Gertrude Stein (1874–1946), Ernest Hemingway (1899–1961), F. Scott Fitzgerald (1896–1940), and Henry Miller (1891–1980). T. S. Eliot, an American expatriated to England, wrote "The Waste Land" (1922), which depicted the distress of the post–World War I, pre–Depression world of the twenties. Most of these individuals were depicted in Woody Allen's 2011 smash hit movie, *Midnight in Paris*.

After World War II, existentialism (which will be discussed below) became popular in philosophy and influenced art and the theater. In America, the existential shift took the form of the Beat Generation. Jack Kerouac (1922–1969), influenced by Henry Miller, traveled across the United States and wrote *On the Road* in 1951. Allen Ginsburg wrote "Howl" in 1955, likewise expressing the exasperation and desperation of the young in what was perceived to be an absurd world.

World War II had also meant the decimation of Europe and had led to Europe's loss of world markets and colonies. War literature and preoccupation with war again became influential culturally in Europe and in the United States. Norman Mailer published *The Naked and the Dead* in 1948. Joseph Heller's *Catch-22* followed in 1961. Both expressed the depressed mood of the times and the stupidity and irrationality of war. After the war the so-called Cold War set in with the overhyped tensions between the two "superpowers," the United States and the Soviet Union. Economic colonialism continued to replace colonialism via armed intervention and military presence.

Now looking back once again at the junction between the *nineteenth* and *twentieth* centuries, philosophy split, as we have said, into two traditions, the Analytic tradition, found mostly in English-speaking countries and Scandinavia, and the Continental tradition, originating on the European continent. Within **Continental philosophy** may be found various identifiable schools of philosophical thought: existentialism, phenomenology, hermeneutics, deconstruction, and critical theory. Two influential schools were existentialism and phenomenology, and we will begin this chapter with them.

Both existentialism and phenomenology have their roots in the nineteenth century, and many of their themes can be traced back to Socrates and even to the pre-Socratics. Each school of thought has influenced the other to such an extent that two of the most famous and influential Continental philosophers of the last century, Martin Heidegger (1889–1976) and Jean-Paul Sartre (1905–1980), are important figures in both movements, although Heidegger is primarily a phenomenologist and Sartre primarily an existentialist.

EXISTENTIALISM

Some of the main themes of existentialism are the following:

- Traditional and academic philosophy is sterile and remote from the concerns of real life.
- Philosophy must focus on the individual in her or his confrontation with the world.

- The world is irrational (or, in any event, beyond total comprehending or accurate conceptualizing through philosophy).
- The world is absurd, in the sense that no ultimate explanation can be given for why it is the way it is.
- Senselessness, emptiness, triviality, separation, and inability to communicate pervade human existence, giving birth to anxiety, dread, self-doubt, and despair.
- The individual confronts, as the most important fact of human existence, the necessity to choose how he or she is to live within this absurd and irrational world.

The existentialists do not guarantee that this **existential predicament,** as it might be called, can be solved. What they do say is that without utter honesty in confronting the assorted problems of human existence, life can only deteriorate—that without struggling doggedly with these problems, the individual will find no meaning or value in life.

Now, many of these themes had already been introduced by those brooding thinkers of the nineteenth century, Arthur Schopenhauer (see previous chapter), Søren Kierkegaard, and Friedrich Nietzsche. All three had a strong distaste for the optimistic idealism of Hegel—and for metaphysical systems in general. Such philosophy, they thought, ignored the human predicament. For all three, the universe, including its human inhabitants, is seldom rational, and philosophical systems that seek to make everything seem rational are just futile attempts to overcome pessimism and despair.

Søren Kierkegaard [KEER-kuh-gard] (1813–1855) scorned Hegel's system, in which the individual dissolves into a kind of abstract unreality. By contrast, Kierkegaard emphasized the individual and especially the individual's will and need to make important choices. Where Hegel was abstract to a degree rarely found outside, say, mathematics, Kierkegaard was almost entirely concerned with how and what the individual actually chooses in the face of doubt and uncertainty.

For Kierkegaard, existence in this earthly realm must lead a sensitive person to despair. Despair, Kierkegaard held, is the inevitable result of the individual's having to confront momentous concrete ethical and religious dilemmas *as an individual.* It is the result of the individual's having to make, *for himself and alone,* choices of lasting significance.

According to Kierkegaard, despair is the *sickness-unto-death* and is the central philosophical problem. Is there anything in this world or outside it to which the individual can cling to keep from being swept away by the dark tides of despair? This, for Kierkegaard, is the fundamental question. His eventual conclusion was that nothing earthly can save a person from despair. Only a subjective commitment to the infinite and to God, not based on abstract intellectualizing or theoretical reasoning, can grant relief.

Kierkegaard emphasized the theme of the irrationality of the world in opposition to Hegel's belief in its utter rationality. The earth, Kierkegaard thought, is a place of suffering, fear, and dread. Of these three, dread, according to Kierkegaard, is the worst because it has no identifiable object or specifiable cause. Dread renders

PROFILE: Søren Kierkegaard (1813–1855)

Søren Kierkegaard, Danish philosopher and religious thinker, was virtually unknown outside Denmark until the twentieth century. Ultimately, however, his thought had a profound impact on existentialist philosophy and Protestant theology.

Kierkegaard's life was outwardly unexciting. He attended the universities of Copenhagen and Berlin and was much influenced by German culture, though he made polemical attacks on Hegel, whose metaphysics he regarded as totally inapplicable to the individual.

As for his inward life, Kierkegaard professed himself to have been, since childhood, "under the sway of a prodigious melancholy," and his grim outlook was made even gloomier by the confession of his father—himself no carefree spirit—that he had sinned and had even cursed God. Finding himself without moorings, Kierkegaard regarded dread and despair as the central problems of his life, and he learned that he could escape their grasp only through a passionate commitment of faith to God and the infinite.

Although Kierkegaard became engaged to marry, he found it necessary to break off the engagement, apparently because God occupied the "first place" in his life, though his own writing about the subject is murky. The episode, at any rate, was so momentous that even the sketchiest biography of Kierkegaard is obliged to mention the woman's name: Regine Olsen. The agony of choosing between God and Regine, a choice Kierkegaard felt he had to make, affected him profoundly.

Kierkegaard defined three types of life: the aesthetic, the ethical, and the religious. These correspond to what English philosophy professor Ray Billington has called the life of the observer, the life of the follower, and the life of the initiator. The "aesthetic" life is dominated by impulse, emotions, and sensual pleasures and does not truly involve making choices. The "ethical" life does involve making choices, but those who live this life make choices on the basis of some kind of moral code, which they in effect fall back on as a sort of crutch. But at a higher and much more difficult plane, that of the "religious," individuals realize that they must decide all issues for themselves. They face the agony of having to rely on their own judgment while never knowing whether this judgment is correct. The despair one faces at this level is overcome only by a "leap of faith," that total and infinite commitment to God.

Some of Kierkegaard's most important philosophical works, *Either/Or* (1843), *Philosophical Fragments* (1844), and *The Concluding Unscientific Postscript* (1846), were published under pseudonyms.

us almost helpless to resist it. Kierkegaard regarded with disdain the idea that philosophy should be concerned with general or ideal "truths" and abstract metaphysical principles. Philosophy must speak to the anguished existence of the individual who lives in an irrational world and who must make important decisions in that world.

Friedrich Nietzsche [NEE-cheh] (1844–1900) read Arthur Schopenhauer (1788–1860 see Chapter 7) and became convinced that the world is driven by cosmic will, not by reason. Nietzsche rejected Hegel's idealism and all similar rationalist metaphysics. However, he disagreed with Schopenhauer as to the nature of the cosmic will. For Nietzsche, the world is driven and determined by the **will-to-power.** However, according to Nietzsche, Western society had become

PROFILE: Friedrich Wilhelm Nietzsche (1844–1900)

Nietzsche was the son of a Lutheran minister. His father died of insanity when Nietzsche was four, and Nietzsche was raised until he was fourteen in a household of women, consisting of his mother, sister, grandmother, and two maiden aunts.

After studying at the universities of Bonn and Leipzig, Nietzsche, whose genius was evident from the beginning, was appointed associate professor of classical philology at the University of Basel at the unheard-of young age of twenty-four without even having written a doctoral thesis. Within two years he had become a full professor. In 1879, however, he was forced by ill health to resign his chair, and by 1889, he, like his father earlier, had become irretrievably insane. Nietzsche's insanity, however, may have been caused by medication.

Two of the principal intellectual influences on Nietzsche's life were the writings of Schopenhauer and the music of Richard Wagner, which Nietzsche compared to hashish in its ability to relieve mental pressure. For a period Nietzsche and Wagner—one of the century's most brilliant philosophers and one of its most brilliant composers—were friends, though this friendship did not last.

Nietzsche's writings have been enormously influential in Continental philosophy. Nietzsche saw himself as an active nihilist whose role was to tear down the old "slave morality" of Christian civilization. He looked to the *Übermensch*, whose will-to-power would set him beyond conventional standards of morality, a line of thought that later was seized upon, misinterpreted, and misused by defenders of Nazism.

Nietzsche's widespread popularity outside philosophical circles owes much to the power of thought expressed in numerous infamous quotations. "Which is it," Nietzsche asked in one of these, "is man one of God's blunders or is God one of man's?"

increasingly decadent. People had come to lead lives largely devoid of joy and grandeur. They were enslaved by a morality that says "no" to life and to all that affirms it. They had become part of a herd, part of a mass that is only too willing to do what it is told. The herd animal, he held, is cowardly, reactionary, fearful, desultory, and vengeful. The mediocrity of Western civilization, he believed, was a reflection of these qualities. Only the rare and isolated individual, the Superman, or ***Übermensch***—a famous concept in Nietzsche's philosophy—can escape the triviality of society.

The Superman, according to Nietzsche, embraces the will-to-power and overthrows the submissive and mediocre "slave" mentality that permeates society and dominates religion. In his embrace of the will-to-power, the *Übermensch* not only lives a full and exciting life but creates a new, life-affirming morality as well. He creates rather than discovers values. God, whom the meek and compassionate worship as the source of values, is just simply "dead."

Nietzsche also believed we have no access to absolute truths—such things as Plato's Forms and Kant's a priori principles of knowing. Indeed, he believed there are no facts, only interpretations. We will discuss a recent development of this idea later in this chapter when we encounter Jacques Derrida, a deconstructionist.

Metaphysics is difficult for those who believe there are no facts, and Nietzsche's philosophy is consciously antimetaphysical. Nevertheless, Nietzsche did subscribe to one metaphysical concept, "the eternal recurrence of the same." This is the theory that what happens recurs, exactly the same, again and again. Those with the slave mentality despise their lives and have a deep resentment for most everything that happens. They long to escape this life and hope that some afterlife will provide a modicum of happiness and fulfillment. They would look with horror and regret on the idea that what happens recurs again and again. The *Übermensch*, by contrast, affirms and celebrates life and bends it to his will. Having no regrets, he would relish the idea that life would happen again and again in exactly the same way.

Nietzsche, Kierkegaard, and Schopenhauer signaled that the smug self-satisfaction of nineteenth-century European philosophy—and culture—camouflaged emptiness and decadence. Their concern for the situation of the individual person; their disdain for abstract, remote, and (in their view) meaningless systems of thought; their denial of the rationality of the world and the people within it; their awareness of a vacuity, triviality, and pettiness within human existence; their efforts to find a reason for not despairing entirely—these themes spread rapidly into *belles lettres* (literature) as a whole in the late nineteenth and early twentieth centuries. Art movements such as Dadaism, Surrealism, and Expressionism expressed disenchantment with the established life of the bourgeoisie and its culture and values and sought to break out of the straitjacket of worn-out ideas and safe lifestyles. A sense that life is meaningless and empty, that the individual is alone and isolated and unable to communicate with others except on the most trivial of levels, permeated the thinking of the intellectuals and literati of the time and has persisted in art, literature, and philosophy until today.

Another persistent theme in twentieth-century literature pertains to the horror of coping in an absurd world—a world in which there is no apparent reason why things happen one way and not another. The characters in the stories and novels of Franz Kafka (1883–1924), a Czech whose mother tongue and the language in which he wrote were German (a fact itself suggestive of human dislocation), invariably find themselves thrust into a situation they do not comprehend but in which they must nevertheless act and be judged for their actions. Nor are they certain that the situation in which they find themselves is not one of their own making. Kafka's parable *The Metamorphosis,* for example, tells of an ordinary salesman who supports his sister and aging parents. One day the salesman awakens at home to find that his body has been changed into that of a giant insect. He does not know why this has happened, and he will die without finding out. At first he is treated compassionately by the other family members, on whom he is of course dependent, but soon they resent his not supporting them and eventually come to regard him as a nuisance as well as an unwelcome family secret. At one point, pieces of fruit thrown by a frustrated and irate family member become embedded in his body and grow infected. Slowly but inevitably, the metamorphosed man loses heart and dies. Kafka presumably thought the story represented to some extent the fate of all human beings.

Psychoanalysis

Other themes in twentieth-century literature and philosophy have their origin in **psychoanalysis,** a psychological theory and therapeutic method developed by **Sigmund Freud** (1856–1939). Ancient Greek philosophers placed reason on a towering pedestal, viewing it as the ultimate standard of truth. "Man is a rational animal," Aristotle stated. Right action, Greek thinkers held, is action subject to review by the high court of reason. Freud offered an alternative concept. According to Freud, the real causes of our decisions and behavior lie deep below the level of deliberate, rational thought or consciousness. One behaves as one does, Freud believed, not because one makes rational decisions but because one is subject to unconscious drives that acquire their shape during childhood. Freud explained these drives by using the stories and characters of ancient mythology. He referred, for example, to the Oedipus complex, after the Greek mythological character Oedipus, who unknowingly killed his father to have sex with his mother. In the words of Adam Phillips, Freud "housed the violent and licentious Olympian gods inside our heads and made us act out all over again their ancient, irreconcilable disputes."[1]

Freud was influenced by Schopenhauer and mentioned him more than any other philosopher. Schopenhauer believed that a dark ground determines most human behavior, a force he identified as the blind and purposeless cosmic will in each of us. Freud, too, thought that we are not conscious of the real source of behavior, which he described in terms of the **id** (Latin for "it")—the raging sea of hidden drives, irrational impulses, forbidden desires, and animal instincts that Freud translated by means of ancient mythology. According to Freud, it is because we are dominated by the unconscious that human behavior is destructive both to self and others. As with Schopenhauer, Freud believed that civilization can be rescued only if we come to understand the subterranean forces underlying human behavior.

Nietzsche also influenced Freud. Freud, too, viewed God as an illusion, a mere reworking of one's human father in superhuman form. However, where Nietzsche believed that the prevailing Judaeo-Christian worldview—a spent, anti-body, anti-life, anti-pleasure mentality—had turned people into its slaves, Freud located the psychological enslavement of humanity in human self-delusion. The truth of one's being, Freud theorized, is withheld via denial, repression, and projection. In place of reality comes a fantasy universe of wishful thinking that punishes us mercilessly through the **superego**—roughly speaking, a combination of conscience and social pressure that leads us to pursue such impossible ideals as utter honesty, absolute truth, eternal love, and perfect happiness.

According to Freud, through psychoanalysis (which is something like a Socratic search for truth undertaken by a patient with the help of the analyst), the patient gradually reveals, and thus learns about, his or her deepest fears, desires, and conflicts. Although psychoanalysis can help a patient discover the causes of anguish and anxiety and can help the person deal with them in a more proactive, intelligent manner, it is a slow, arduous, open-ended process that

---

[1] From *The Penguin Freud Reader,* edited by Adam Phillips. London, Penguin. 2006, p. 592.

(like a Socratic dialogue) never discloses "absolute truth." It can, however, lead to a profound deepening of one's understanding and existence.

The other two great practitioners of psychoanalysis likewise expressed philosophical themes. Carl Gustav Jung (1875–1961) developed an analysis of patients based on the notion of *archetypes*. Jungian archetypes are akin to Plato's Forms, which (according to Plato) are the reality underlying all changing things. Alfred Adler (1870–1937) analyzed patients on the theory that actions are motivated by one's perception of one's defects and are attempts to compensate for them. This tends to result, Adler thought, in overcompensation and many attendant psychic problems. Adler's theory is reminiscent of Socratic theory that love is a lack and an attempt to overcome that lack. It also is reminiscent of Aristotle's notion of God as a final cause of human actions in that we seek godlike perfection.

Theories of psychoanalysis were influential on later Continental philosophy for various reasons, perhaps most notably in bringing forth the idea that we are fundamentally ignorant of our own nature. Psychoanalysis also influenced subsequent Continental philosophy in suggesting that absolute truth, honesty, and happiness are illusory and unattainable ideals that, in fact, make life difficult. The psychoanalysts also emphasized *praxis,* the application of theory to real life, and rooted their theories in concrete cases and the real experiences of patients. The emphasis on praxis is characteristic of much subsequent Continental philosophy.

Another contribution of psychoanalysis was the understanding of human life as an organic process from birth to death, in which early life determines adulthood. According to this view, problems currently experienced more than likely have roots in traumatic events in a person's childhood. The novelist Marcel Proust observed that we come most alive and experience the deepest happiness when we remember past events and relationships. Psychoanalysis tends to see this remembering in terms of becoming conscious of one's anxieties and their origins in infancy. The psychoanalytic view is that, paradoxically, by dealing with psychic pain and trauma consciously, the patient can experience the deepest pleasure and self-realization.

TWO EXISTENTIALISTS

Existentialism as a philosophical movement was something of a direct reaction to perceived social ills and was embraced by artists and writers as much as by philosophers per se. So it is not surprising that two of the greatest existentialist philosophers, Albert Camus and Jean-Paul Sartre, wrote drama, novels, and political tracts as well as philosophical works. Both also thought it important to disseminate their ideas into society as a whole in the hope of having some direct influence. Both were involved in the French Resistance during World War II against the terror of German fascism. Both thought—despite their belief in the absurdity of life—that responsible social action is necessary, as is an understanding of the sociopolitical forces at work in the world.

Literature and Philosophy

There is a big difference between a novel or a poem and a philosophical essay. Still, themes and ideas that might loosely be described as philosophical are encountered throughout the world's great literature. Literature, after all, personifies human perspectives, thoughts, aspirations, values, and concerns. Often it is an immediate response to the current human situation and human needs. For example, beginning in the late nineteenth century, various European writers began to challenge the values of their culture and emphasized the idea that the individual is alone and isolated. Existentialism began this way, and the main themes of the movement, such as absurdity and meaninglessness, were only later thematized and delineated by writer–philosophers such as Camus, Sartre, and de Beauvoir.

The extent to which literature is or contains philosophy is itself a philosophical issue of controversy and substance. However, we can mention several literary approaches or viewpoints or "takes" on life that qualify in obvious ways as philosophical. The first might be described as a viewpoint based on absence. This way of thinking is based on the idea that the world is radically defective in that it is incapable of providing human beings what they truly need to be satisfied and/or happy. Examples of such writers include Franz Kafka, Fyodor Dostoyevsky, Albert Camus, Jean-Paul Sartre, and Samuel Beckett. Such writers take a position on human nature and needs, though they do so implicitly rather than explicitly.

A second basic literary approach is based on fullness. This viewpoint sees life as immeasurably rich and bountiful. Life is to be lived all out, and every moment intensified and enjoyed. This is the traditional bailiwick of Romantics such as Goethe, Nietzsche, and Lord Byron. Goethe wrote, "If you want to create something, you must be something." American examples of this approach to life and literature include the poetry of Walt Whitman and the writings of Ralph Waldo Emerson and Henry David Thoreau. More contemporary examples would be Henry Miller and Anaïs Nin.

A third literary approach is the tragic stance. Here, life for whatever reason is tragic at its best and pathetic at its worst. The underlying pessimism in the plays of Sophocles and the tragedies of William Shakespeare are considered by many

the very height of Western literature and culture. *Oedipus Rex, Hamlet,* and *King Lear* have not been surpassed for their dramatic power and truth telling. Shakespeare powerfully suggests this stance in Hamlet: "To be or not to be, that is the question." The plays of the Swedish writer August Strindberg and the films of Ingmar Bergman are powerful contemporary variations of the tragic stance. Two examples of this approach by American writers are Arthur Miller's *The Death of a Salesman* (1949) and Eugene O'Neill's *Long Day's Journey into Night* (1956). The tragic stance is related to the first viewpoint: the fundamental philosophical question, Camus asserted, is whether there is any reason not to commit suicide.

A fourth literary approach to life is the comic vision. Life here is seen as a comedy, a kind of cosmic joke. It is better to laugh at life than to cry. As Erasmus wrote in the fifteenth century, "The highest form of bliss is living with a certain degree of folly." Erasmus thought that folly is not difficult to find but surrounds us everywhere in our everyday lives. A more modern writer who recognized the absurdity of life yet refused to be defeated by it was Eugene Ionesco. He wrote, "To become conscious of what is atrocious and to laugh at it is to become master of what is atrocious." A potent example of this attitude in American literature can be found in Joseph Heller's *Catch-22.* There are similarities here with Stoicism, covered in Chapter 10.

A fifth approach to life through literature is developed by Martin Heidegger in his interpretations of poets like Hölderlin, Rainer Maria Rilke, and Georg Trakl. This literature, in the view of Heidegger, is the pursuit of the unknown, the unthought, and the unsaid. The poetic thinker's task is to go out into the darkness and experience the human condition in the deepest way possible.

A sixth literary approach uses the medium to provide rules, maxims, and suggestions as to how life ought to be lived. There is the whole genre of coming-to-maturity or growing-up novels in literature, which provide lessons for the young and the not so young. Actually, almost all significant literature includes depiction of the consequences of actions and moral lessons. The examples of such writers are numerous. We will mention only two

Literature and Philosophy *(continued)*

of the greatest. The writings of Cervantes are a veritable storehouse of proverbs and wise sayings, such as, "Never stand begging for that which you have the power to earn." Another writer known for his didactic potency is Charles Dickens. He wrote, for example, "Reflect on your present blessings, of which every man has many, not on your past misfortunes, of which all men have some." Literature can provide the average reader with an initial access to philosophy and deeper questions in life. Hermann Hesse's *Siddhartha* is a classic example of a novel about how to become a noble, even heroic, person.

For a while there, Robert M. Pirsig's *Zen and the Art of Motorcycle Maintenance* was something of a cult novel and continues after three decades to be read by young people who are interested in knowing how Zen, and Eastern philosophy generally, can provide a model for living well in the present. Another fictional work that has been widely read and that has introduced many to the history of philosophy is Jostein Gaarder's *Sophie's World*. Here whole swaths of Western philosophy are presented in an approachable and readable way that also relates them to contemporary life and its problems.

Camus and Sartre are by no means the only existentialist philosophers. Other famous existentialists include Gabriel Marcel and Simone de Beauvoir in France (discussed in Chapter 14), Karl Jaspers in Switzerland, Martin Heidegger in Germany (whose work in phenomenology is discussed later in this chapter), Miguel de Unamuno and José Ortega y Gasset in Spain, and Nicola Abbagnano in Italy. But Camus and Sartre are especially representative of the movement, and we will focus on them. Camus, we might note, was reluctant to be classified as an existentialist because that lumped him together with Sartre, with whom Camus quarreled.

Art of the absurd.

PROFILE: Albert Camus (1913–1960)

Camus was born in Mondovi, Algeria, on November 7, 1913. His French father was a farmworker, and his Spanish mother, a maid. His father died in the war soon after Camus' birth, forcing Camus' mother to move into the impoverished quarter of Algiers at the end of the Casbah. Camus later considered the poverty in which he grew up the great source of his deepest insights. His Spanish pride and intensity as well as his intellectual acumen were noticed by a teacher, Louis Germain, who made sure that Camus could attend a first-rate high school, one normally accessible only to the rich.

Camus was athletic and played goalie for the Racing Universitaire. After one game, he left the playing field in a sweat, which developed into a cold and then into tuberculosis. This meant that he would not be able to become a teacher after he passed his state examination in philosophy. Instead, he turned to journalism, working at first for the *Algeria Republican.* By the age of twenty he was already married and separated and had both joined and quit the Communist Party. He had also formed his own theater group, l'Équipe.

Camus was eventually thrown out of Algeria for writing articles concerning the poverty and backwardness in its provincial areas. During World War II, he was the lead article writer for the French Resistance newspaper *Combat.* After the war, he wrote such major works as *The Stranger, The Rebel,* and *The Plague* and also maintained his involvement with theater groups. In 1957 he received the Nobel Prize for literature. He was killed in an automobile accident in 1960.

Camus was a straightforward, unpretentious person who always had time for his friends, for actors, and for young people starting out. Many looked upon him as a kind of big brother. He dedicated himself to the love and enjoyment of this world. He believed that the secret of the art of living lies in the sun, the sea, and a youthful heart.

Albert Camus

Albert Camus [kah-MOO] (1913–1960) grew up in poverty in Algeria and fought in the French Resistance against the Nazis. He saw much suffering, waste, and death even before the war; perhaps not surprisingly, the principal philosophical question for him was, *Is there any reason not to commit suicide?* Camus believed that this question arises when a person stops deceiving himself or herself and begins seeing the world without preconceived illusions (see the box "Life Is Absurd" on page 158).

Many people, Camus believed, live their whole lives and die without ever seeing things as they really are. More specifically, instead of seeing the "tragic nature of life," they waste their lives in "stupid self-confidence." That is, although they in fact spend their lives in or near despair in an absurd world that continually frustrates true human needs, they mask the fact with a forced optimism. And the more "profitable" such false optimism is, the more entrenched it becomes. In Camus' view, for many of us self-deception has become a dominant mode of being. This implies, as well, that often we are strangers to ourselves and to our own inability to meet our fundamental needs.

Existentialism in European Literature

As we said in the preceding box, starting in the late nineteenth century, some European artists began to challenge the culture and values of their society. In various ways, their works expressed their sense that life is meaningless and empty and that the individual is alone and isolated. A sampling of literature from the late nineteenth through the mid-twentieth centuries shows some of the ways in which those themes were presented.

- "Notes from the Underground" (1864), a story by Fyodor Dostoyevsky, tells how an imperfect society can waste the lives of its best members. The "underground man" lives in a society that prefers and rewards mediocrity. Hence his intelligence, sensitivity, and strength of character are neither needed nor wanted. He is condemned to watch second-rate compatriots surpass him and achieve success while his own superior talents languish unused. He is left with a life of bitterness, hopelessness, and shame. His sole pleasure consists in acts of spite and revenge, more imaginary than real.

- "The Death of Ivan Ilyich" (1884), a story by Leo Tolstoy, provides a powerful and moving example of the meaninglessness and futility of life. Ivan Ilyich had led what he thought was a successful, busy, ambitious life. But when he learns that, though still in the prime of life, he has an incurable and fatal disease, he begins noticing that his wife and family members are really only concerned about the inheritance and that his fellow workers have already begun jockeying to replace him. He sees that no one really cares about him or has any genuine sympathy for his situation. He cannot understand the insincerity and cruelty of others, including that of his own family, and he cannot understand God's cruelty and His absence in time of need.

Above all, Ivan cannot understand why he is so *alone,* abandoned to suffer and die. Has he done something deserving of such punishment? Ivan exclaims, "I am not guilty," but Tolstoy adds that Ivan "is not certain it is so."

- *The Trial* (1925), a novel by Franz Kafka, explores the idea that we can feel responsible—or even *be* responsible—for the situations in which we find ourselves (and whose causes we certainly do not understand). A man, Joseph K., is arrested, convicted, and executed without ever being able to find out what crime he was supposed to have committed. Nor is he conscious of having committed any crime. Yet such is his sense of self-doubt that he is never sure he does not deserve to be condemned.

- *The Bald Soprano* (1950), a play by Eugène Ionesco, is in the dramatic tradition known as "theater of the absurd." Two strangers meet at a dinner party and enter into conversation. Slowly they discover that they had sat in the same train compartment five weeks earlier, live in the same city and house, and both have a daughter with one red eye and one white eye. Ultimately, to their delight, they discover that they are husband and wife.

- *Waiting for Godot* (1953), a play by Samuel Beckett, explores the inability of humans to communicate with one another. Two tramps, Didi and Gogo, wait in a desertlike environment for someone named Godot to arrive, who will tell them what to do. They talk only to pass the time, not because they have anything to say. They seem often to be talking at the same time on entirely different subjects without either one noticing. And it does not matter, for it does not interrupt the emptiness of the words.

What are these basic needs? According to Camus, there are two: the need for clarity or understanding and the need for social warmth and contact. Unfortunately, however, we live in an absurd world, a world in which these basic human needs are unmet. The need for clear understanding of the world founders on the "opaqueness and density of the world"; indeed, it founders on the very fact that the world is absurd and consequently provides no sufficient reason for why things happen one way and not another.

Life Is Absurd

One of Camus' principal theses is that life as we find it is absurd. The notion of absurdity implies that there is no ultimate reason that things are the way they are. It also implies that life is unjust and frustrates human needs. Most important, perhaps, that the world is absurd seems to mean, for Camus, that it provides no absolute or necessary basis of value. That we must make choices and decide how to act in a valueless and absurd world is often called the "existential predicament."

The second essential need, the need for human warmth and contact, also remains unfulfilled, Camus thought. Humans in this violent age tend to remain strangers to one another (as well as to themselves); they live solitary existences in which relationships are matters of convention rather than of mutual sharing and understanding. The absurdity of life in frustrating essential human needs means that hoped-for happiness often turns to misery and despair—even though many hide this tragedy from themselves behind a façade of baseless hopes.

Camus likened life to the fate of Sisyphus in the myth of the same name. Sisyphus had provoked the wrath of the gods and was condemned to roll a huge stone up a hill, only to see it roll back down again. This act repeated itself forever. Human beings, according to Camus, are similarly condemned to lives of "futile and hopeless labor" without reasonable hope of fulfilling their true needs. No matter how hard we try to live a just and meaningful existence, it is unlikely that our efforts will lead to lasting results.

In this context it may easily be understood why Camus considered the question of suicide to be a primary philosophical issue. *Why indeed* should one wish to continue living under such circumstances as Camus has depicted? Nevertheless, Camus regarded suicide as unacceptable. Suicide, he thought, is a kind of weak-minded acquiescence to an unjust destiny. Camus believed, perhaps paradoxically, that by struggling against the Sisyphean fate to the end, by rebelling against the absurdity and tragedy of life, it is possible to give life meaning and value. His position indeed is that only through this struggle with an absurd world can the individual achieve fulfillment, solidarity with others, and "a brief love of this earth."

Increasingly, Camus focused his concern on the grotesque inhumanity and hideous cruelty of a world torn asunder by war and Nazism. Civilization, he thought, certainly with some justification, is suffering from a "plague" of epidemic proportions, a plague that kills many and sickens all. (Perhaps Camus' most famous work was *The Plague*, 1947.) In such an unjust world, one finds oneself committing violent acts *merely to survive*. Camus viewed the world as, in effect, sponsoring an ongoing competition in murder, as a place in which it is difficult to raise a finger without killing somebody. Capital punishment, he thought, is just one example of how the "decent citizen" is reduced to the level of a murderer. And in outright warfare the morality of violence exceeds control and comes into the open.

Camus wrote that "one cannot always live on murders and violence." By living out the values of the lowest animals, the individual is delivered up to the merciless power of despair and cynicism. Camus loathed the "absolute cynicism" of modern society that, he implied, drove humans to desperation and prevented them "from taking responsibility for their own life."

Thus, Camus came increasingly to insist that each individual must spend his or her life fighting the plague—that is, the degeneracy of the world. Each must resist the temptations offered by cunning and violence; what is called for, he thought, is a "revolt" against the existing "order." Perhaps as a way of fighting the plague, Camus' thinking after the war became increasingly concerned with social and political issues. This represents a shift from his early works, which are focused much more strictly on the concerns of the individual.

But Camus thought that the revolt against a revolting world must be "measured" and limited. What Camus means is made clearer in his play *Caligula* (1944), in which the Roman emperor Caligula is presented as an example of a man who discovers the implicit cruelty and viciousness of human existence. In order not to fall victim to this evil, Caligula revolts against it in an unmeasured way, through his own acts of cruelty and viciousness. Such an unmeasured reaction was unacceptable to Camus; it meant becoming more bestial than the other beasts. In short, for Camus, the violence of the world does not excuse or justify violence in response.

Thus, the best that is possible for the individual, Camus implied, is a measured revolt wherein he or she spends life resisting violence and injustice. The effort, he maintained, must be predicated on the assumption that "any mutilation of mankind is irrevocable." The individual must fight for justice and liberty and against all forms of tyranny: "Let us die resisting," he wrote. Yet we must have no illusions or false optimism about the possible results of our action. For it may well be that nothing will improve: in an absurd world, nothing is guaranteed.

Jean-Paul Sartre

Albert Camus was agnostic, maintaining that he did not know whether or not there is a God. **Jean-Paul Sartre** [sartr] (1905–1980) was atheistic. A human being, Sartre said, is *abandoned,* by which "we mean that God does not exist." And according to Sartre, the abandonment of humans—that is, the nonexistence of God—has drastic philosophical implications. Basically, there are four. After you read about them, you might read the box "Is Sartre Only for Atheists?".

First, because there is no God, there is no maker, and no such thing as a divine conception of a human being in accordance with which the individual is created. This means, Sartre thought, that there is no such thing as a human nature that is common to all humans; no such thing as a specific essence that defines what it is to be human. Past philosophers had maintained that each thing in existence has a definite, specific essence; Aristotle, for example, believed that the essence of being human is being rational. But for Sartre, the person must produce her or his own essence, because no God created human beings in accordance with a divine concept. Thus, in the case of human beings, Sartre wrote, "**existence precedes essence,**" by which he meant very simply that you are what you make of yourself. You are what *you* make of yourself.

The second implication of the nonexistence of God is this. Because there is no God, there is no ultimate reason why anything has happened or why things are the way they are and not some other way. This means that the individual, in effect, has been *thrown* into existence without any real reason for being. But this does not mean that the individual is like a rock or a flea, which also (because there is no God) have no ultimate reason or explanation. Rocks and fleas, Sartre would say, have only what he calls "being-in-itself" (in French, *être-en-soi*), or mere existence. But a human being, according to Sartre, not only exists, that is, has being-in-itself, but also has "being-for-itself" (*être-pour-soi*), which means that a human being, unlike an inanimate object or a vegetable, is a self-aware or conscious subject that creates its own future. We will return to this point shortly.

Third, because there is no God and hence no divine plan that determines what must happen, "there is no determinism." Thus, "man is free," Sartre wrote, "man is freedom"; in fact, he is **condemned to be free.** Nothing forces us to do what we do. Thus, he said, "we are alone, without excuses," by which he meant simply that we cannot excuse our actions by saying that we were forced by circumstances or moved by passion or otherwise determined to do what we did.

Fourth, because there is no God, there is no objective standard of values: "It is very troubling that God does not exist," Sartre wrote, "for with him disappears every possibility of finding values . . . there can no longer be any good a priori." Consequently, because a Godless world has no objective values, we must establish or invent our own values.

Consider briefly what these various consequences of our **abandonment** entail. That we find ourselves in this world without a God-given "human nature" or "essence"; that we are active, conscious, and self-aware subjects; that we are totally free and unconstrained (and unexcused) by any form of determinism; and that we must create our own values—these facts mean that each individual has an awesome responsibility. According to Sartre, first of all, we are responsible for what we are. "Abandonment implies that we ourselves choose our being." Second, we must *invent* our own values. And third and finally, because "nothing can be good for us without [also] being [good] for all," in inventing our own values we also function as *universal legislators* of right and wrong, good and evil. In choosing for ourselves, we choose for all. "Thus, our responsibility is much greater than we had supposed it, for it involves all mankind."

This responsibility for oneself and thus for all humankind, Sartre thought, we experience as anguish, and it is clear why he maintained that this is so: our responsibility is total and profound and *absolutely inescapable.* You might perhaps object that many people, perhaps even most, certainly do not seem to be particularly anxious, let alone anguished. It is true, Sartre admitted, that many people are not consciously or visibly anxious. But this merely is because they are hiding or fleeing from their responsibility: they act and live in self-deception or inauthenticity, what Sartre called "**bad faith.**" Further, he said, they are ill at ease with their conscience, for "even when it conceals itself, anguish appears."

It is not difficult to understand why one might seek to avoid shouldering one's responsibility to oneself and thus to others, for as Sartre depicted it, this responsibility is overwhelming. But in Sartre's view something else also contributes to the difficulty of this task: one does not know *what* to choose, because the world is experienced as absurd. It is experienced as absurd, Sartre maintains, because, since God does not exist, it lacks necessity—it lacks an ultimate rhyme or reason

PROFILE: Jean-Paul Sartre (1905–1980)

Jean-Paul Sartre studied philosophy at the École Normale Supèrieure. He also studied the philosophies of Husserl and Heidegger and spent one year in Berlin. While still a graduate student, he met Simone de Beauvoir, who later played a key role in the early phases of the women's liberation movement, especially with her famous book, *The Second Sex* (1948). Their friendship and mutual support lasted until Sartre's death, though in the opinion of historian Paul Johnson, "In the annals of literature, there are few worse cases of a man exploiting a woman." (Sartre never wrote anything about their relationship.)

During World War II, Sartre served in the French army, became a German prisoner of war, escaped, and worked in the Resistance movement. Throughout his life he supported political causes and movements, including the French Communist Party. In 1951, he tried unsuccessfully to found a new political party, radically leftist but noncommunist in orientation.

Sartre's most famous works include the novel *Nausea* (1939), the play *No Exit* (1944), and the philosophical treatise *Being and Nothingness* (1943). In 1964 Sartre declined the Nobel Prize in literature, citing "personal reasons."

When Sartre died, fifty thousand people marched behind his coffin through the streets of Paris. He was indeed a national treasure.

Is Sartre Only for Atheists?

If God does exist, then technically speaking we are not "abandoned." But some of the main problems that arise from abandonment seem also to arise merely if we cannot *know* whether God exists. For if we do not know whether God exists, then we do not know whether there is any ultimate reason why things happen the way they do, and we do not know whether those values we believe are grounded in God really do have objective validity.

In fact, even if we do know that God exists and also know that values are grounded in God, we still may not know which values are grounded in God: we may still not know what the absolute criteria and standards of right and wrong are. And even if we know what the standards and criteria are, just what they mean will still be a matter for subjective interpretation. And so the human dilemma that results may be very much the same as if there were no God.

Nonatheists should not dismiss Sartre too hastily.

for being this way and not that way. The world, therefore, is experienced as fundamentally senseless, unreasonable, illogical, and, therefore, "nauseating." It calls forth both revulsion and boredom. It is "perfectly gratuitous" (*gratuitá parfaite*) and often just simply too much (*de trop*).

Nevertheless, according to Sartre, it is only through acceptance of our responsibility that we may live in **authenticity.** To be responsible, to live authentically, means intentionally to make choices about one's life and one's future. These choices are made most efficaciously, Sartre maintained, by becoming "engaged" in the world and by selecting a **fundamental project,** a project that can mobilize

Bad faith, sort of.

and direct all of one's life energies and permit one to make spontaneous choices. Through this project, in short, the individual creates a world that does not yet exist and thus gives meaning to his or her life.

So Sartre's metaphysics (or antimetaphysics), which stood opposed to the belief in God, determinism, necessity, and the objectivity of values, in effect leaves the human individual in what may plausibly be called an absurd situation. There is nothing that one must do; there is nothing that must be done. To find meaning in life, the individual must create his or her world and its values by making authentic choices. These choices first take the form of intentions directed toward future events. Then they become actions of an engaged being in a world of people, a political (and politically troubled) world. The choices that we make are made for all humankind and are, therefore, in this limited sense "absolute" ethical principles. Although we initially find ourselves in an absurd world not of our choosing, we can remake that world through our choices and actions, and we must do so, as difficult as that may be.

Sartre and Kant on Ethics

"I choose myself perpetually," Sartre wrote. By this he meant that we each are in a continual process of constructing ourselves and our values or ethics. And Sartre believed that when a person determines something to be right for himself or herself, that person is also determining it to be good for all.

This universalization of individual choices is reminiscent of Immanuel Kant's supreme precept of morality, the categorical imperative, according to which you must only act in such a way that the principle on which you act could be a universal law. Kant, however, as we will see in Part Two, grounded the categorical imperative and hence all morality in reason, which he thought determines a priori what is right and wrong. Sartre, however, maintains that there is no a priori moral law and that Kant's formal law is inadequate as a guide for concrete action in everyday life. It is rather what a person does that in fact determines his morality. "In choosing myself, I choose man," Sartre said.

It is perhaps arguable, however, that *this* principle ("in choosing myself, I choose man") is for Sartre a universal principle underlying morality.

You Are What You Do

According to Sartre, you create yourself through your choices. But be aware that, for Sartre, these self-creating choices are not found in mere "philosophical" abstractions or speculations. The choices that count, for Sartre, are those that issue forth in actions. "There is reality only in action," he wrote, "man is nothing other than the whole of his actions."

This means that, according to Sartre, no hidden self or true you lies behind your deeds. If, for example, in your actions you are impatient and unforgiving, it is a fiction for you to think, "Well, if others could see into my heart, they would know that in reality I am patient and understanding." If you are cowardly in your deeds, you deceive yourself if you believe that "in truth" or "deep, down inside" you are courageous. If you have not written great poetry, then it is an illusion for you to believe that you nevertheless have the soul of a great poet.

It is easy to see why Sartre believed that his doctrine horrified many people. Many people think of their behavior as but poorly reflecting their true character, which they believe is in some way superior to the character that displays itself in their actions. Those who think this deceive themselves, according to Sartre.

This exposition of Sartre's thought focuses on his understanding of what might be called the existential predicament. His thinking evolved over time, and he became increasingly concerned—like Camus—with social and political issues. These interests and his fascination with Marxist philosophy led to a modification of his existentialist stance, but we can do no more in this book than mention this. We have also not dealt with his epistemology, his aesthetics, or his views on psychoanalysis.

PHENOMENOLOGY

This impressive-sounding word denotes the philosophy that grew out of the work of Edmund Husserl (1859–1938). In brief, **phenomenology** interests itself in the essential structures found within the stream of conscious experience—the stream of phenomena—as these structures manifest themselves independently of the assumptions and presuppositions of science.

Sartre at the Movies.

Phenomenology, much more than existentialism, has been a product of philosophers rather than of artists and writers. But like existentialism, phenomenology has had enormous impact outside philosophical circles. It has been especially influential in theology, the social and political sciences, and psychology and psychoanalysis. Phenomenology is a movement of thinkers who have a variety of interests and points of view; phenomenology itself finds its antecedents in Kant and Hegel (though the movement regarded itself as anything but Hegelian). Kant, in the *Critique of Pure Reason,* argued that all objective knowledge is based on phenomena, the data received in sensory experience. In Hegel's *Phenomenology of Mind,* beings are treated as phenomena or objects for a consciousness.

What are **phenomena?** It is difficult to convey precisely what is meant by the term, but it may help for you to consider the distinction between the way something is immediately experienced and the way it "is." Place a penny on the table before you, look at it, and concentrate on your experience as you look. The penny-in-experience changes its shape and size as you move your head. Of course you are accustomed to assuming that there is a second penny "beyond" this changing penny-in-experience, the so-called "real" penny. You must ignore this assumption. Forget about the "real" penny, and focus on the penny-in-experience. Indeed, don't restrict your attention to the *penny*-in-experience. Contemplate the table-in-experience, the room-in-experience. Consider your *entire* experience at the moment. And when you do this, ignore your inclination to suppose that there is a second world (the "real" world) lying beyond the world-in-experience. Congratulations: you are now practicing the phenomenological method. Notice that, as long as you limit your attention to the world-in-experience, you can have certain knowledge. The world beyond experience, the "real" world assumed by natural sciences, is a world in which much is unknown and doubtful. But the world-in-experience, the world of pure phenomena, can be explored without the same limitations or uncertainties.

Edmund Husserl

The first great phenomenologist, **Edmund Husserl** [HOO-surl] (1859–1938), attempted to rekindle Europe's waning faith in the possibility of certainty by proposing a universal phenomenology of consciousness, a "science" that studies the structures that are the same for every consciousness. Accordingly, he developed **transcendental phenomenology,** whose purpose it was to investigate phenomena without making any assumptions about the world. To investigate phenomena in this way is to "bracket" or "exclude" one's presupposition about the existence or nature of an "external" or "physical" or "objective" world. Husserl called this process **phenomenological reduction,** and you just did it above. Its purpose is to examine the meaning produced by pure impersonal consciousness and to describe the human "life-world" in terms of those essences (which all human beings share) found within conscious experience.

This sounds a bit like psychology, but Husserl distinguished transcendental phenomenology from regular psychology, which approaches the mind with the assumptions and methods of the other natural sciences in their study of the

Construction on the German Autobahn began in 1931, the year Edmund Husserl published a detailed phenomenological exploration of intersubjectivity in *Cartesian Meditations*. Roughly, intersubjectivity is imagining yourself in another person's shoes.

"objective" world. It (Husserl's phenomenology) also sounds a bit like traditional idealistic metaphysics, in which everything is reduced to thought. But that tradition at least invokes the dualistic worldview of the natural sciences in order to deny it. Phenomenology, in theory, simply explores conscious experience without making any metaphysical assumptions.

Martin Heidegger

In any event, Husserl believed phenomenology opens up for scrutiny a realm that escapes the uncertainty and conditional status of the empirical world, and he called for a "return to the things themselves" (i.e., phenomena). **Martin Heidegger** [HY-dig-ger] (1889–1976) was stimulated by Husserl's call to return to the things themselves and by Husserl's major work, *Logical Investigations* (1900). Heidegger, too, was convinced that it was necessary to look at things with fresh eyes, unshrouded by the presuppositions of the present and past. He, too, wanted rigorously to ground things in a deeper source of certainty. But for Heidegger, this source is not phenomena, as it was for Husserl, or anything subjective at all. On the contrary, for Heidegger, the ultimate source is *Being* itself.

Although Being is continuously manifesting itself in things, according to Heidegger, Being itself has been forgotten. Humans have been caught up in their own ideas. Being has been reduced to a world of "objects" that are manipulated and dominated by human "subjects" through a series of human-made logics. Logic is equated with truth when in fact, according to Heidegger, it is only a means to control and use things after human designs; that is, logic is logistics.

Heidegger believed that it is both arrogant and destructive to assume that humans are the masters of nature or to follow Protagoras's dictum, "man is the measure of all things." This assumption of the absolute power of humanity was for Heidegger the real cause of the cultural destitution and social dissolution within the twentieth century. Heidegger thought that we live in an intellectually impoverished (*dürftig*) time, and that it is likely to become worse until we abandon our presumptuousness and return to the wisdom inherent in Being itself. The return must involve *listening* to Being instead of toying with things arbitrarily.

According to Heidegger, we are basically ignorant about the thing that matters most: the true nature of Being. Our lives are a kind of Socratic search for this lost and unknown source of all things. Consciousness of the priority of Being would mean a new beginning for philosophy as well as for Western civilization, he held.

Heidegger, therefore, initially sought to establish a scientific study of Being as the root of all meaning and necessity in things. This effort broadened out later and became a quest for an even more direct approach to Being itself. Early on—for example, in his first major work, *Being and Time* (1927)—Heidegger's ideas still contained much that is Husserlian and Kantian in approach. He still sought true knowledge in a priori structures found in the human mind. It is only in his later thinking—after he had what he called a fundamental "turning about"—that he sought to uncover Being directly, beyond the a priori categories or structures of human perception and thought. He did so without assurance that any absolute certainty about Being itself is even possible.

PROFILE: Martin Heidegger (1889–1976)

Heidegger was born in the small town of Messkirch near the Black Forest of Germany. Originally he went to the University of Freiburg to study theology, but he soon began studying philosophy. Heidegger studied Husserl's philosophy closely and became personally acquainted with Husserl after the latter took a chair at Freiburg in 1916.

Almost from the beginning, Heidegger stood out—not merely because of his countrified mode of dress but also because of his profound thought. Over the years Heidegger grew increasingly critical of Husserl's philosophy, and, though he was named to Husserl's chair in philosophy at Freiburg in 1928, their friendship came to an end.

Initially Heidegger was quite taken with the National Socialist (Nazi) Party in post–World War I Germany and remained a party member until the end of World War II. This was a prestigious gain for the Nazis, especially when Heidegger was made rector of the University of Freiburg. During Heidegger's brief term as rector (he withdrew after ten months), he made speeches and was otherwise active in support of Hitler and his movement. After the war, Heidegger did not speak out to condemn Nazi atrocities. There is controversy as to what his true sentiments were, however.

Although Heidegger did not teach formally after the war, he remained in Freiburg until his death. His works are in the process of being published—in eighty volumes.

It is usually with reference to his earlier work that Heidegger is sometimes called an existentialist. Heidegger himself resisted this appellation. Yet he was very much influenced by Kierkegaard and Nietzsche, and the concern expressed in his early works with such existentialist themes as fear, dread, meaninglessness, and death is quite evident. Sartre studied in Germany for a brief time in the 1930s and was influenced by Heidegger. Sartre attributed the concept of abandonment to Heidegger, and Sartre and Heidegger both were concerned with the concepts of bad faith, authenticity, a life's project, and others.

Still, in decisive ways, Heideggerian and Sartrian philosophies are dissimilar. Heidegger never did abandon his belief in Being as the basic principle of philosophy, whereas for Sartre individual existence was of paramount importance. Sartre believed that, as a consequence of the nonexistence of God, nothing about Being is necessary; Heidegger believed that Being is absolutely necessary. Politically, Sartre considered himself a Marxist and accepted much of the Marxist view of historical events, whereas Heidegger was not in any sense sympathetic to the Marxist worldview. All in all, Heidegger and Sartre philosophically are quite different, despite the superficial resemblance.

At the heart of Heidegger's *Being and Time* is the notion of **Sinn** (sense, meaning), the absence of which in life was said to be the problem of human existence. For Heidegger, the human being is **thrown into the world** and soon experiences both fear and dread when confronted with forces beyond understanding. The better part of human life, he maintains, needs to be used in *"head-breaking,"* that is, in attempting to discover what the appearances mean—what they suggest and hide.

Further, humans are "beings-in-the-world," which means that they can be open only to what is within the horizons of their world. They exist and are conscious within a world with other beings, but the meaning of human relationships is at first but dimly perceived and poorly understood. As a consequence of their lack of insight and understanding, many humans live ungenuine and inauthentic lives. They do not make adequate or appropriate choices for themselves because they do not understand who they are or what they are confronting. And although they may experience unease living in a world beyond their comprehension, they make too little effort to extend their comprehension. They suffer from a kind of "primitive" being, which Heidegger refers to as **everydayness,** and fail to fulfill their real potential. Thus, Heidegger invoked the concept of everydayness to explain why human beings continue to lead unthinking lives.

Another typical existential theme connected by Heidegger with an everyday existence is an inauthentic mode of communication, namely, *chatter*. Speech is reduced to a meaningless flood of words that camouflages fear, prevents understanding, and precludes any meaningful communication. Nothing truly meaningful is ever said or allowed to be said.

An authentic existence can be found, according to Heidegger, only if one can understand oneself as a totality. And seeing oneself as a whole can happen only by facing the hard fact that one is mortal. We are, Heidegger said, "beings-unto-death." By facing death, we can see and delineate the limits of our being. We begin to see the limited amount of time yet available and begin to realize we must not waste it.

The innermost nature of the human being, according to Heidegger, is caring—a concern for beings in the world. This caring takes place over time. And thinking must do so as well. Thus, for Heidegger, we are essentially *temporal* beings.

According to Heidegger, human thinking is "ecstatic," which means it is directed toward an anticipated future. The most effective way of embracing one's future, he thought, is by throwing oneself open into Being. This project (*Entwurf*) opens the person to the fundamental truth of Being that has been forgotten. Therefore, the individual who has been thrown into the world finds her or his ground and truth in the openness and light of the truth of Being itself.

As noted earlier, Heidegger thought that the cultural and intellectual poverty of the twentieth century was a direct result of the pervasive assumption that the value of things is solely determined by human intelligence and human will (the assumption that the human is the measure of all things). This assumption or metaphysical stance, he thought, has led not only to individual loneliness, alienation, and unfulfillment but to social destructiveness as well. For Heidegger, this metaphysical point of view, which he perceived as having been entrenched in Western civilization since Plato, assumed the superiority of Ideas over any physical reality existing "outside" the mind. In Heidegger's opinion, Nietzsche's will-to-power, whereby the will becomes the absolute determiner of the value of things and of oneself, represented the philosophical culmination of this Platonic metaphysics.

Poetry   According to the later Heidegger, instead of imposing our thought on things, we must think in a quiet, nonimpositional way so that we can catch a glimpse of Being as it shows itself. In contrast to others in the phenomenological tradition, Heidegger believed that thought cannot impose itself on Being because Being makes thought possible. What is required, therefore, he said (in contrast to the existentialists), is a new kind of thinking in which humans look to Being itself for enlightenment and not merely to themselves. This kind of thinking occurs, according to Heidegger, in the best poetry. Poetic thinking can uncover the as-yet unseen, unthought, and unspoken. Therefore, he said, systematic philosophy, with its grandiose schemes, with its mind–body and other dualistic splits, with its metaphysics and metaphysical traditions, must give way to this more original kind of thinking. Through this deeper way of thinking, Heidegger said, we may at long last rediscover the depth of what has been forgotten—Being itself.

Heidegger wrote essays about many poets, including Hölderlin, Rilke, Trakl, and others. But he also wrote poems that suggest how the poet might bring a glimmer of light to the darkness within existence. It is the poet, for Heidegger, who ventures out into the unknown to find the "unique thought" that will bring the necessary light for the coming time.

Eastern Philosophy   Especially later in his life, Heidegger grew interested in Eastern philosophy and especially the philosophy of Lao Tzu (see Chapter 15). Perhaps Heidegger's new way of thinking—listening to Being—represents a coming together of Eastern and Western philosophizing. Certainly there are common currents and themes. Both believed that "nature is not human-hearted" (Lao Tzu) and that what is called human "knowledge" is mostly ignorance. Both felt that "those who care will be cared for" (Lao Tzu). What is necessary, according to both, is to take nature [Being] as a "guide." And it is as Lao Tzu suggested: "In the clarity of a still and open mind, the truth will be revealed."

Emmanuel Levinas

Born in Kaunas, Lithuania, **Emmanuel Levinas** (1906–1995) was the son of a bookstore manager. Levinas, understandably, became an avid reader, especially of classic Russian literature and the Hebraic Bible. In 1923 he went to Strasburg (Germany) to study philosophy and focused on the philosophy of Husserl and Heidegger. Levinas was mainly responsible for introducing phenomenology into France. During World War II his parents were killed by the Nazis, and he himself was interned in a prisoner-of-war camp. After the war, he took up a number of academic posts, culminating in a professorship at the Sorbonne. His principal writings center around two areas of concern: Talmudic commentaries and ethics, understood in the broader sense of being aware of what and how we humans exist in the world.

Martin Heidegger, as you know from what we have written already, had made a radical critique of the whole history of Western metaphysics interpreted as a form of Platonism. Western metaphysics represented, for Heidegger, a devolutionary process that ended in Nietzsche's nihilism and the complete forgetting of Being itself. Heidegger not only declared the end of metaphysics but also attempted to establish a new way of thinking about Being that he initially called ontology.

Levinas based his critique of Heidegger mainly on Heidegger's major early work, *Being and Time* (1927). In stark contrast with Heidegger, Levinas wanted philosophy to break out of the stranglehold of Being. Levinas tried to establish a philosophy rooted in the notions of radical otherness and unbridgeable separateness. Philosophy begins, he believed, with the horrible experiences of our otherness (*alterity*). Other people exist as unovercomable alterity. Time, language, and even existence itself is experienced as other. And God, for Levinas, exists as Absolute Otherness, a separateness never to be breached. True meaning and understanding of ourselves, for Levinas, can only be reached by a meeting with this radical Other in all its strangeness. The attempt to meet with the Other represents an act of transcendence and is the key human event. The Other exists "prior to any act" whatsoever.

Thus, for Levinas, ontology (the study of Being) represented the wrong-headed attempt to reduce this irreducible otherness to sameness, to reduce the Other to a mere object for consciousness. The project is doomed because the Other exists prior to ontology. Instead of starting with Being and trying to explain beings, we must begin with beings in their separateness and otherness. In particular, we must confront other humans in their invisibility and incomprehensibility. The Other remains a puzzle but a puzzle that can nevertheless reveal secrets.

The secrets of the Other both reveal and hide themselves in the human face (*le visage*). The face, for Levinas, is our epiphany into the Other. First of all, the face of the Other throws into question the "I" that we have constructed in our alienation from the Other. To know ourselves, we must know the Other. We are therefore "hostage" to the Other for our being and for our understanding of ourselves.

The Other, for Levinas, is the infinite in the individual self. As encountered in the form of the face, it solicits us to posit ourselves for this Other. It is that which makes communication possible. It opens us up to the transcendent, to the Absolutely Other, to the infinite, to God and to His Law. This takes us to the realm of Levinas's transcendental ethical philosophy. For Levinas, ethics is prior to ontology. The responsibility of thinking is always in response to an unfulfilled and ultimately unfulfillable obligation to the Other.

The Good, for Levinas, is therefore prior to the true. Our primary responsibility is for the Other, and that responsibility trumps even our obligation to ourselves and to the world of things. It is an obligation of self-sacrifice to the Other, an obligation to the infinite. In meeting the Other, we find our own meaning, the "answer" that we are.

This vigilance toward the Other grounds our being and represents the original form of openness to the world. The concomitant forgetting of self leads to real communication and justice. Levinas offers the Hebraic Bible as a model of ethical transcendental philosophy. The Absolute Other to which we are responsible is God or the Most High. By studying the written Law, our obedience to God ruptures our egoism as we respond to God's commandments. This allows us to attain true freedom.

Levinas had a profound influence on French thinkers such as Jean-Paul Sartre (discussed earlier in this chapter) and, as we will see, Jacques Derrida.

AN ERA OF SUSPICION

"My experiences," wrote Friedrich Nietzsche in his posthumously published confessional called *Ecce Homo,* "entitle me to be quite generally suspicious of the so-called 'selfless' drives, of all 'neighbor love' that is ready to give advice and go into action." In the last third of the twentieth century, diverse Continental voices were raised against what they saw as suspicious assumptions about the meaning of right and wrong, the nature of language, and the very possibility of human self-understanding. Some Continental philosophers have been suspicious about Western metaphysical systems that they claim lead to the manipulation of nature or that set up a certain ethnic or cultural perspective as absolute truth. Some voices have raised suspicions about the common assumption that language in some way represents external reality. Still others claim to find deep ideological biases in even the most "neutral" philosophical observations.

Philosopher and sociologist Jürgen Habermas has challenged the legitimacy of some of the rational principles assumed by the human sciences. French philosopher Michel Foucault explored the deeply ingrained social power systems that shape how social institutions deal with the sexuality of their members and with those who are sick, criminal, or insane. Jacques Derrida developed the technique of deconstruction in literary and philosophical criticism to show, he said, that language meanings cannot be "tied down" and that, as a result, claims that certain passages express the "truth" become suspicious indeed. Finally, American philosopher Richard Rorty, deeply influenced by Continental philosophy and the American pragmatism of William James and John Dewey, proposed a new task for philosophy. Because the discipline could never find "the truth," it must be used in the service of human beings to extend one's horizons, one's possibilities.

Jürgen Habermas

Jürgen Habermas [HAHB-ur-mahs] (1929–), a professor at the University of Frankfurt, is one of many thinkers influenced by the critical approach of the Frankfurt School (see box, page 172). In this context, "critical" means reflective, thoughtful, especially on the assumptions of science or philosophy. Science, he points out, is only one way to look at the world and isn't appropriate for the investigation of the mutually shared meanings we experience in our everyday human world. This is because science makes objective findings. Humans should be treated as subjects interacting with other subjects. Habermas discusses the "emancipatory knowledge" that is the concern of **critical theory.** Critical theory makes explicit the controlling ideology of a political or social order. It can bring a kind of freedom or emancipation as people examine their own deeply held assumptions and find them to be false. This emancipation would change the way humans communicate with each other and would thus change society. Habermas proposed a theory of communication he called the **ideal speech situation,** in which persons are free to speak their minds and listen to reason without fear of repercussions. Recent work by Habermas has focused on the rise of countercultural groups, feminism, and various liberation movements and whether they constitute the beginnings of the kind of free society he envisions.

PROFILE: Jürgen Habermas (1929–   )

Habermas was born in Düsseldorf, Germany. He was raised in Gummersbach, where his father was the director of a seminary. When World War II ended, he was sixteen years old. He studied at the University of Bonn and was especially interested in Hegel, Marx, and modern Marxist thinkers. After receiving his PhD in 1954, he became an assistant to Theodor Adorno at the University of Frankfurt. Adorno and Max Horkheimer were the leading figures in the Frankfurt School, renowned for the attempts its followers made to integrate the disciplines of philosophy, psychoanalysis, social science, and

literary criticism. Habermas would make his own substantial contribution to the School's thought. The subject matter of his books varies greatly, but his overall concern has been to free people and thinking from unnecessary and unhelpful rules, categories, and other constraints. He achieved widespread recognition relatively early on with books such as *Theory and Practice* (1962), *The Logic of the Social Sciences* (1967), *Toward a Rational Society* (1971), *Knowledge and Human Interest* (1981), *The Theory of Communicative Action* (1981), and *Theory of Social Action* (1984).

The Frankfurt School

The Institute for Social Research was founded in 1923, affiliated with the University of Frankfurt, and, after exile in New York during the Nazi era, returned to Frankfurt in 1949. Those associated with the school were loosely united in the task of developing from Marxism a critical theory approach to art and the human sciences that would,

on one hand, reject crude materialist determinism as an ideology and, on the other hand, reject positivism and any possibility of a value-free social science. Those associated with the school include Herbert Marcuse (1898–1979), Theodor Adorno (1903–1969), and Jürgen Habermas.

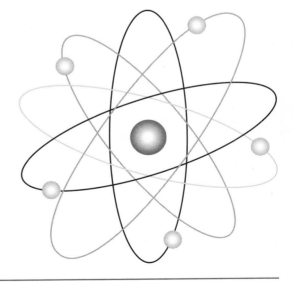

Can empirical science investigate subjectivity?

Philosophical Anthropology

When he was a tender undergraduate, one of the authors traveled to the University of Tübingen in Germany to study. He signed up for a course called *Philosophische Anthropologie*. He had no idea what the course might be about, but he could at least translate its name, which is the main reason he signed up for it. It was the first course in philosophy he had ever taken.

On the first day of class, he sat in the middle of a huge lecture hall—more students were in that one class than were in all the courses in philosophy he took after that, back in America, combined. The Herr Professor walked to the lectern, shuffled through some notes, ripped off his glasses and sucked on them like a pipe, and gazed heavenward for several minutes, deep in thought. "*Was,*" he asked the ceiling, "*ist der Mensch?*"—What is man? This struck your author as a fairly interesting question—at least to get things started—and he waited for the answer.

What is man? What is a human being? This is the fundamental question of philosophical anthropology, which, along with beer, is important in German universities.

The term *anthropology* goes back to the Greeks and has been used ever since to denote the study of humans (*anthropos*) and their societies. Early Church fathers used the term to distinguish the study of humans from the study of God; over the centuries—and especially during the sixteenth to eighteenth centuries—anthropology became increasingly divorced from theology, metaphysics, and the natural sciences. Kant, for example, held that to be worldly wise, we must go beyond the natural sciences and acquire an extensive knowledge of human nature through biographies, histories, travel books, plays, and so forth. For Kant, such an anthropology, though not a science, provided a practical study of what a free and self-determined human being is.

In the nineteenth century, German Romantics (*Romantic* here does not mean "lover"; it denotes a member of the important nineteenth-century movement that emphasized imagination and emotions in literature and art) sought a vision of the total human being. Hegel, however, distinguished between anthropology, which considers humans as they are *potentially*, and philosophy of history, which considers humans as they are *actually*. The Hegelian attack on anthropology and its lack of historical grounding has been carried on by selected German philosophers up to the present, where it lingers in Martin Heidegger's thought and that of the Frankfurt School of social philosophy, both mentioned in this chapter. Today, "philosophical anthropology," as the philosophical study of human nature and existence is called, is moving away from the philosophy of history and seeks to establish itself as an independent discipline. It includes semiotics and structuralism.

Was ist der Mensch? Unfortunately, the professor's answer lasted the entire semester. Unfortunately, too, your author did not understand the answer. In fact, that single question, *Was ist der Mensch?* was the only thing your author understood in the entire course, for his knowledge of German was none too good. (Later, when he read an English translation of the professor's lectures, he found he still was not sure of the answer.)

Michel Foucault

Michel Foucault [foo-KO] (1926–1984) was a French philosopher, social theorist, and historian of ideas. He was intensely suspicious of philosophic and scientific truth claims. In his first period, Foucault considered himself a kind of archaeologist, searching historical data to find the discourses that shape societies. Discourse in this context means how people talk and how they act as a result. He believed he had discovered what he called **epistemes,** "created realities" that are the ground of true and false in each era. But this method is also dependent, as Foucault came to see, on a kind of objectivity on the part of the researcher, so he abandoned it.

PROFILE: Michel Foucault (1926–1984)

Foucault told a group of American philosophers in Berkeley, California, in April 1983 that when Jorgen Habermas visited him in Paris, Foucault "was quite struck by his observation of the extent to which the problem of Heidegger and of the political implications of Heidegger's thought was quite a pressing and important one for him." Habermas interpreted Heidegger as a German neoconservative and Heidegger's Nazism as somehow connected with Heidegger's own philosophical positions.

Foucault told the interviewers that he believed there was "a very tenuous 'analytic' link between a philosophical conception and the concrete political attitude of someone who is appealing to it; the 'best' theories do not constitute a very effective protection against disastrous political choices." But, Foucault added, "I don't conclude from this that one may say just anything within the order of theory, but, on the contrary, that a demanding, prudent, 'experimental' attitude is necessary; at every moment, step by step, one must confront what one is thinking and saying with what one is doing, with what one is."

Before he died on June 25, 1984, of toxoplasmosis-produced lesions on the brain as a result of AIDS,

Foucault was engaged during most of his academic career in a project that attempted to chart the power relations by which societies exclude, lock up, or institutionalize the insane, the prisoner, the homosexual—those persons society defines as "other." Unlike Habermas, Foucault denied that societies could ever free themselves from such exclusionary forces; no "ideal speech situation" was possible.

Foucault himself was something of a scandal to "polite" French society. One biographer writes of the philosopher's sadomasochistic erotic practices, his appearance in public wearing leather clothes, his open affection for men, and his fondness of the gay bathhouses of San Francisco.

Born in Poitiers, France, on October 15, 1926, Foucault was the firstborn son of a surgeon. He was a professor of the Collège de France from 1970. Foucault's major works include *Madness and Civilization* (English translation 1965), *The Birth of the Clinic: An Archaeology of Medical Perception* (1973), *Discipline and Punish: The Birth of the Prison* (1977), *The Order of Things: An Archaeology of the Human Sciences* (1970), and *The History of Sexuality* (3 volumes, English translation 1978–1986).

His second project was what Nietzsche had called **genealogy.** For Foucault, genealogy wasn't about knowledge; it was about power. In his later books, Foucault was less concerned with the language-worlds created by society than with the lived body, the embodied consciousness. Genealogy doesn't prescribe any practices. Instead, it illuminates the everyday social habits that constitute us and express the working power of the body.

Structuralism versus Deconstruction

Structuralism is a methodology that seeks to find the underlying rules and conventions governing large social systems such as language or cultural mythology. It hearkens back to Swiss linguist **Ferdinand de Saussure** [so-SIWR] (1857–1913), who emphasized the study of the language system itself (*langue*) rather than particular speech (*parole*). Saussure was concerned with the "deep structures" of language common to all speakers. He saw linguistics as the study of signs, which he defined as a combination of the *signifier* (the physical thing that signifies) and the *signified* (that which is signified). A sentence is a sequence of signs the meaning of which depends not only on the order of the signs ("I can go" vs. "Can I go?") but also on the contrast of each sign with other signs in the language that are not present. Thus, the "I" in "I can go" contrasts with other possible subjects: she, he, you, and so on. It is the relationship between the "I" and these other signs not present that gives the "I" its meaning because our understanding of "I" takes place with the linguistic system and its interrelationships as background. How the "I" differs from other subjects gives the sign its meaning. Notice here that the emphasis Saussure makes is on the internal linguistic system and its infrastructure; it is of little concern to him whether a given sentence expresses something true about the outside world.

The French anthropologist **Claude Lévi-Strauss** [LAY-vee-STROWSS] (1908–2009) adapted Saussure's methods and applied them to his ethnographic research. Lévi-Strauss was interested in finding the underlying structures of thought in the myths of nonindustrial societies and in human communities generally. Characteristic of Lévi-Strauss's structuralist approach, as shown, for example, in *The Savage Mind* (1962; English translation 1966), is the search for a group of rules or "laws" that accounts for the social complexities of even so-called primitive cultures. Cultures (and literary works) were seen as systems of signs the meaning of which could be found in the particular relationships of signs with other signs in the system itself. The implication is that the individual person is very much a construct of the underlying, impersonal rules of the system.

Jacques Derrida

The analysis of sign systems of various types, from advertising slogans to animal communication, is now called **semiotics** (from the Greek word *semeion*, meaning "sign"); most of the structuralist methodology fits within this "science of signs." But is such a science really possible? That is, are meanings within language or cultural systems stable enough to provide a definitive interpretation of texts or rituals arising from those systems? In the late 1960s, French philosopher and literary theorist **Jacques Derrida** [day-ree-DAH] (1930–2004) said the answers were "no." He maintained that no such stable meanings were possible and that no definitive meaning of a text could ever be established. In fact, the very notion of a "definitive meaning" implied certain unproven (and unprovable) assumptions about texts and language.

Derrida's **deconstructive method** is to lay bare those assumptions about language, to "question" the text about possible multiple meanings, and in so doing to show what he calls the **free play of signifiers.** By this Derrida means that the writer of a word "privileges" that word for a moment; this "privileging" becomes the medium for the play of the signifier—*différence*—rather than any background of a fixed linguistic system (which, according to Derrida, does not exist). This is reminiscent of the Heraclitean tradition that "you cannot step into the same river twice"; only now it means "you cannot step into the same language twice." Because meaning can occur only as experience, our experiences are constantly overriding

PROFILE: Jacques Derrida (1930–2004)

Derrida was born into a lower-middle-class Sephardic Jewish family in El Biar, Algiers. Early on, he was interested in sports and even had the notion of becoming a soccer player. He experienced considerable difficulty with anti-Semitism at the lycée where he studied. While in his teens, he published some poetry in North African journals. After a couple of unsuccessful attempts, he was eventually admitted at the age of nineteen to the prestigious École Normale Supérieure in Paris. He married in 1957. During the sixties, he was part of the political foment in Paris. His fame began to spread during his memorable participation in a colloquium at Johns Hopkins University. He taught there and at Yale University in recent years and published over twenty books.

One curious episode in Derrida's life occurred when he was nominated for an honorary degree at Cambridge University. In a very unusual way, four Cambridge dons expressed their displeasure and disagreement with such an award. A great hullabaloo followed, with nineteen academics publishing a letter in *The Times* decrying his writings as incomprehensible and full of French verbal tricks and gimmicks. The implication was that he was a charlatan. After much furor, a vote was taken, which Derrida won, and he showed up to claim his title. But the row continues, with many in the Anglo-American philosophical world looking on his writings with grave suspicions.

("overwriting") the dictionary definitions of words, effacing those definitions, which in turn are also in flux. A printed dictionary gives the false impression that language has stable meanings, whereas those meanings are continuously "at play" and changing. The use of a word not only goes beyond the dictionary definition but also "effaces" those forces at work that act just beyond the horizon of consciousness. These "forces" are no more available to us than Kant's *Ding-an-sich,* or thing-in-itself (see Chapter 7). From the perspective of deconstruction, then, there are no extralinguistic connections available to anchor meanings within language.

Derrida's comments recall Saussure's system of "differences," but Derrida takes Saussure's observation to its logical extreme: because all things intelligible to human beings must pass through their language system to be understood, they inevitably become "texts." Thus, the meaning of, say, the transcendental Forms can be found only through an exploration of the continual play of signifiers as Plato is interpreted and interpreted again. No ultimate meaning can be found—what Plato really meant, what a Form really is—because, if all human understanding comes through textuality, there is no ultimate meaning to be found.

Derrida's critique of linguistic structuralism and of structural anthropology represents but a part of his thinking. His deepest forays into philosophy concern the metaphysical. Here his thinking is most influenced by Hegel, Husserl, and Heidegger. He most tellingly used his deconstructive method to attack Husserl's transcendental idealism.

Derrida started his critique by agreeing with Heidegger that metaphysics had been reduced to onto-theology, or a metaphysics according to which all beings stem from a divine logos. *Onto-theology* is a term used by Heidegger to describe the development of metaphysics since Plato. Metaphysics has increasingly come to reduce being into beings and the highest and first being, or God. Since Nietzsche's declaration that "God is dead," modern metaphysics has sought to find structures of absolute certainty in human subjectivity and logic. For Heidegger, this has meant that metaphysics is at an end because it has forgotten *being* entirely and has replaced it with a sterile logic and human hubris. Derrida sees this artificial reduction of metaphysics to a supposed transcendental, absolutely certain logic. You may recall the word *transcendental* as referring to Immanuel Kant's idea that consciousness structures sense-data into spatio-temporal objects that are related to one another by cause and effect and other principles. Husserl attempted to ground human knowing in a transcendental science of logic or on a universal phenomenology of consciousness (see earlier in this chapter). Derrida elaborated on this development as a *logocentrism,* and this term is meant to apply to Heidegger's thinking as well. The logocentric worldview is based on a nostalgia for an original state of full being or presence that is now lost. Beings are held to derive their structure and meaning from a divine logos similar to the *logos* Heraclitus first posited in the sixth century B.C.E. *Logos* has many meanings in Greek, such as "word," "speech," "thought," "reason," but for Heraclitus and later thinkers, it is the principle and source of order, necessity, and rationality in the universe. Logocentrism is based on a preference for a stable, hierarchical world of necessary being. The necessity and transcendence of such a world is available only to a few rare persons who are capable of thinking transcendentally. Derrida used the deconstructive method to uncover unfounded assumptions and the artificial oppositions on which logocentric thinking is based.

Thinking and language can never be closed systems of absolutely certain, transcendental concepts. Rather, they should be open ended, if temporally limited. They must in some way be capable of dealing with things' uniqueness—their changeability, uncertainty, and incompleteness. The claims of deconstruction are much more modest, but they can affect reality in a more positive way. Derrida's philosophy is a plea for reason to be used in the realms of metaphysics, anthropology, and linguistics. He further extends this procedure to the realms of politics, ethics, and psychology. In a way, he is the Socrates for the twentieth century, forcing a recognition that most claims of absolute knowledge are full of contradictions and untenable.

Derrida's books include *Of Grammatology* (1967; English translation 1976) and *Writing and Difference* (1967; English translation 1978).

Gilles Deleuze

Gilles Deleuze [jeel-duh-LOOZ] (1925–1995), one of the most important figures in contemporary Continental philosophy, wrote on so many subjects—film,

PROFILE: Gilles Deleuze (1925–1995)

Born in Paris, Deleuze had a typical academic career, and, although as a philosopher he advocated difference and change, he rarely traveled and seemed to lead a very sedate life. He is often characterized as a philosophical outsider, and for several reasons. His interests were not typical of his day: for example, he was always interested in British empiricism (which has never been too popular in France), and he preferred writing about the "minor" thinkers in the philosophical tradition, thinkers who tend to be overlooked: like the Stoics, Spinoza, and Henri Bergson. (Bergson [1859–1941] was another important French philosopher, most famous for tracing the relationship between free will and the subjective experience of time.) Deleuze was also never an adherent of any of the major philosophical movements in twentieth-century France: existentialism, phenomenology, structuralism, and postmodernism. This makes his philosophy idiosyncratic, but few would deny its influence. Indeed, Michel Foucault once wrote, "Perhaps one day, this century will be known as Deleuzian."

Deleuze wrote some of his most famous books with a colleague, Félix Guattari. While the books Deleuze wrote on his own tended to be studies of single philosophers, the books he wrote with Guattari were much more political in orientation and more sweeping in scope. The most famous of these is *Anti-Oedipus*, which was very influential on the young, politically-oriented generation of French students in the early 1970s. *Anti-Oedipus* argues that desire should not be seen as something that lacks what it desires (as has been argued since Plato). Desire is instead something like a "machine"—it links up with things that are outside it. Deleuze and Guattari study the kinds of things desire links up with. Sometimes these are things that restrain desire, such as social institutions, the family, the church, or the military. One of the most important claims in *Anti-Oedipus* is that desire can actively seek its own repression. But desire can also link up with things that take it into uncharted territories. Deleuze and Guattari prefer to see desire doing this and try to find ways in which desire can be helped to make such new and transgressive links.

Deleuze is considered one of the major players in postmodernism. His books include: *Nietzsche and Philosophy* (1962), *Difference and Repetition* (1968), and *The Fold: Leibniz and the Baroque* (1988).

literature, logic, politics—that it's difficult to summarize his philosophy. We'll focus on the one thing that stands out most: the notion of *multiplicity,* i.e., the production of concepts. Deleuze made the study of multiplicity the centerpiece of his thought, claiming that any singular entity, any "one," is abstracted from an original multiplicity. This view led him to be suspicious of claims that anything, any "one," transcends the multiple.

Accordingly, Deleuze believed that the philosophical method—the way philosophy goes about doing things—should be changed. In his critique, he used the model of a tree. Often, he argued, philosophers study things as if they were trees. How so? Well, philosophers often assume that what they are studying is clear, distinct, and well organized. In fact, Deleuze said, this approach doesn't account for multiplicity. Instead, philosophers should use the image of a rhizome, a plant that grows horizontally, not vertically like a tree. Rhizomes spread out, get entangled with other rhizomes and grow over things like grass or climbing ivy does. Deleuze argued that if philosophers would use the rhizome model, they would come up with a very different picture of how things are.

Consider language, for example. Deleuze would point out that English is really a multiplicity of dialects, not a single language, and that so-called "proper" English is only one dialect, one small part of a larger rhizome. This approach to language illustrates Deleuze's main philosophical concern, one that he applied to literature, politics, film, psychoanalysis, and even the arts. Accordingly, his work has been put to use by scholars in the various fields of architecture, urban studies, anthropology, geography, musicology, gender studies, and others.

Alain Badiou

Alain Badiou [uh-LANE-Buh-DEEW] (1937–), once a troublemaker in Deleuze's courses, is also primarily interested in thinking about multiplicity; however, he argues that it is impossible to totalize everything that exists. In fact, what exists, he says, is "infinite," in fact, "infinitely infinite." The topic of infinity is something that sets Badiou apart from most contemporary Continental philosophers, who believe that infinity is something so abstract that we can't even conceive of it. But Badiou points out that even though we are mortal and have no experience of infinity, mathematicians have been thinking about and working with infinity, especially in set theory, for over a century. Philosophers have fallen far behind them. Badiou suggests that philosophers should start looking again at what mathematicians are doing, as they did in Plato's day, and that doing so may lead philosophers to think very differently about *being*.

SELECTION 8.1
Existentialism and Humanism*

Jean-Paul Sartre

[*This is a pretty clear and straightforward explanation of what existentialism is, followed by examples and illustrations.*]

What is this that we call existentialism? . . . Actually it is the least shocking doctrine, and the most austere; it is intended strictly for technicians, and philosophers. However, it can easily be defined. What makes the matter complicated is that there are two kinds of existentialists: the first who are Christian, and among whom I will include Jaspers and Gabriel Marcel, of the Catholic faith; and also, the atheistic existentialists among whom we must include Heidegger, and also the French existentialists, and myself. What they have in common is simply the fact that they think that existence precedes essence, or, if you wish, that we must start from subjectivity. . . .

What does it mean here that existence precedes essence? It means that man exists first, experiences

himself, springs up in the world, and that he defines himself afterwards. If man, as the existentialist conceives him, is not definable, it is because he is nothing at first. He will only be [something] afterwards, and he will be as he will have made himself. So, there is no human nature, since there is no God to think it. Man simply is, not only as he conceives himself, but as he determines himself, and as he conceives himself after existing, as he determines himself after this impulse toward existence; man is nothing other than what he makes himself. This is the first principle of existentialism. It is also what we call subjectivity. . . . Man is at first a project which lives subjectively, instead of being a moss, a decaying thing, or a cauliflower; nothing exists prior to this project; nothing is intelligible in the heavens, and man will at first be what he has planned to be. Not what he may wish to be. . . . If existence really precedes essence, man is responsible for what he is. Thus, the first step of existentialism is to show every man [to be] in control of what he is and to make him assume total responsibility for his existence. And, when we say that man is responsible for

* From Jean-Paul Sartre, *L'Existentialisme est un humanisme* (Paris: Editions Nagel, 1946), translated by Deanna Stein McMahon.

himself, we do not [only] mean that man is responsible for his precise individuality, but that he is responsible for all men. . . . When we say that man determines himself, we understand that each of us chooses himself, but by that we mean also that in choosing himself he chooses all men. Indeed, there is not one of our actions which, in creating the man we wish to be, does not [also] create at the same time an image of the man we think we ought to be. To choose to be this or that, is to affirm at the same time the value of what we choose, for we can never choose evil; what we choose is always the good, and nothing can be good for us without [also] being [good] for all. . . .

This enables us to understand what some rather lofty words, like anguish, abandonment, despair mean. As you will see, it is quite simple. First, what do we mean by anguish? The existentialist readily declares that man is [in] anguish. That means this: the man who commits himself and who realizes that it is not only himself that he chooses, but [that] he is also a lawgiver choosing at the same time [for] all mankind, would not know how to escape the feeling of his total and profound responsibility. Certainly, many men are not anxious; but we claim that they are hiding their anguish, that they are fleeing from it; certainly, many men believe [that] in acting [they] commit only themselves, and when one says to them: "what if everyone acted like that?" they shrug their shoulders and reply: "everyone does not act like that." But really, one should always ask himself: "what would happen if everyone did the same?" and we cannot escape this troubling thought except by a kind of bad faith. The man who lies and who excuses himself by declaring: "everyone does not act like that," is someone who is ill at ease with his conscience, because the act of lying implies a universal value attributed to the lie. Even when it conceals itself, anguish appears. . . .

And when we speak of abandonment, an expression dear to Heidegger, we mean only that God does not exist, and that we must draw out the consequences of this to the very end. . . . The existentialist, on the contrary, thinks that it is very troubling that God does not exist, for with him disappears every possibility of finding values in an intelligible heaven; there can no longer be any good a priori, since there is no infinite and perfect consciousness to think it; it is not written anywhere that the good exists, that we must be honest, that we must not lie, since precisely we exist in a context where there are only men. Dostoyevsky has written, "If God did not exist, everything would be allowed." This is the point of departure for existentialism. Indeed, everything is allowed if God does not exist, and consequently man is abandoned, because neither in himself nor beyond himself does he find any possibility of clinging on [to something]. At the start, he finds no excuses. If, indeed, existence precedes essence, we will never be able to give an explanation by reference to a human nature [that is] given and fixed; in other words, there is no determinism, man is free, man is freedom. Moreover, if God does not exist, we do not find before us any values or orders which will justify our conduct. So, we have neither behind us nor before us, in the luminous realm of values, any justifications or excuses. We are alone, without excuses. It is what I will express by saying that man is condemned to be free. Condemned, because he has not created himself, and nevertheless, in other respects [he is] free, because once [he is] cast into the world, he is responsible for everything that he does. . . .

To give you an example which [will] allow [you] to understand abandonment better, I will cite the case of one of my students who came to see me in the following circumstances. His father was on bad terms with his mother, and moreover, was inclined to be a collaborator. His older brother had been killed in the German offensive of 1940, and this young man, with feelings somewhat primitive but generous, wanted to avenge him. His mother lived alone with him, quite distressed by the semi-betrayal of his father and by the death of her eldest son, and found consolation only in him. This young man had the choice, at that time, between leaving for England and enlisting in the Free French Forces—that is to say, to forsake his mother—or to stay near his mother and to help her [to] live. He fully realized that this woman lived only for him and that his disappearance—and perhaps his death—would cast her into despair. He also realized that, in reality, [and] concretely, each action that he performed with regard to his mother had its surety in the sense that he was helping her to live, whereas each action that he might perform in order to leave and fight was an ambiguous action which could be lost in the sands, to answer no purpose. For example, leaving for England, he might remain indefinitely in a Spanish camp, while passing through Spain; he might arrive in England or in Algiers and be placed in an office to keep records. Consequently, he found himself facing two very different kinds of action: one concrete, immediate, but applying only to one individual; or else an action which applied to a whole [group] infinitely vaster, a national community but which was by that reason ambiguous, and which could be interrupted on the way. And, at the same time, he hesitated between two kinds of ethics. On the one hand, an ethic of sympathy, of individual devotion; and on the other hand a wider ethic but whose effectiveness was more questionable. He had to choose between the two. Who could help him to choose? Christian doctrine? No. Christian doctrine says: "be charitable, love your neighbor, devote yourself to others, choose the hardest way, etc. . . ." But which is the hardest way? Whom must we love as our brother, the soldier or the mother? Which has the greatest utility, the one [which is] definite, to help a definite individual to live? Who can decide it *a priori?* No one. No written ethic can tell him. The Kantian ethic says: "never treat others as [a] means, but as [an] end." Very well; if I remain near [with] my mother I will treat her as an end and not as means, but by this same action, I risk treating those who fight around me as a means; and conversely if I go to rejoin those who are fighting I will treat them as an end, and by this action I risk treating my mother as a means.

If these values are vague, and if they are still too broad for the specific and concrete case that we are considering, it remains for us only to rely on our instincts. This is what this young man tried to do; and when I saw him, he said: "basically, what counts is the sentiment; I ought to choose that which actually pushes me in a certain direction. If I feel that I love my mother enough to sacrifice everything else for her—my desire for vengeance, my desire for action, my desire for adventures—I [will] stay near her. If, on the contrary, I feel that my love for my mother is not sufficient, I [will] leave." But how [do we] judge the weight of a feeling? What constituted the worth of his feeling for his mother? Precisely the fact that he stayed for her. I may say, I love this friend enough to sacrifice such a [certain] sum of money for him; I can say it, only if I have done it. I may say: I love my mother enough to remain with her, if I have remained with her. I can determine the worth of this affection only if, precisely, I have performed an action which confirms and defines it. Now, as I require this affection to justify my action, I find myself caught in a vicious circle.

Further, Gide has said very well, that a feeling which is acting and a feeling which is real are two nearly indiscernible things: to decide that I love my mother by remaining near her, or to act a part which will make me stay for my mother, is nearly the same thing. In other words, the feeling is constituted by the actions that we perform: I cannot then consult it in order to guide myself according to it. What that means is that I can neither seek for in myself the authentic state which will push me to act, nor demand from an ethic the concepts which will allow me to act. At least, you say, he went to see a professor to ask his advice. But, if you seek advice from a priest, for example, you have chosen this priest, you already knew, after all, more or less, what he was going to advise you. In other words, to choose the adviser is still to commit yourself. The proof of it is what you will say, if you are a Christian: consult a priest. But there are priests who are collaborators, priests who wait for the tide to turn, priests who belong to the resistance. Which [should you] choose? And if the young man chooses a priest who is a member of the resistance, or a priest who is a collaborator, he has already decided [on] the kind of advice he will receive. Thus, in coming to see me, he knew the reply that I was going to make to him, and I had only one reply to make: you are free, choose, that is to say, invent. No general ethic can show you what there is to do; there is no sign in the world. The Catholics will reply: "but there are signs." Let's admit it; it is myself in any case who chooses the meaning that they have. . . .

Abandonment implies that we ourselves choose our being. Abandonment goes with anguish. As for despair, this expression has a very simple meaning. It means that we will restrict ourselves to a reliance upon that which depends on our will, or on the set of the probabilities which make our action possible. . . . From the moment when the possibilities that I am considering are not strictly involved by my action, I must take no further interest in them, because no God, no design can adjust the world and its possibilities to my will. . . . Quietism is the attitude of men who say: "others can do what I cannot do." The doctrine that I am presenting to you is exactly opposite to quietism, since it claims: "there is reality only in action." It goes further [than this] besides, since it adds: "man is nothing other than his project, he exists only in so far as he realizes himself, thus he is nothing other than whole of his actions, nothing other than his life." According to this, we can understand why our doctrine horrifies a good many men. Because often they have only one way of enduring their misery. It is to think: "circumstances have been against me, I was worth much more than what I have been; to be sure, I have not had a great love, or a great friendship, but it is because I have not met a man or a woman who was worthy of it. I have not written very good books because I have not had the leisure to do it. I have not had children to whom to devote myself because I did not find a person with whom I could have made my life. [There] remains, then, in me, unused and wholly feasible a multitude of dispositions, inclinations, possibilities which give me a worth that the simple set of my actions does not allow [one] to infer." Now, in reality, for the existentialist there is no love other than that which is made, there is no possibility of love other than that which manifests itself in a love; there is no genius other than that which expresses itself in works of art. The genius of Proust is the totality of Proust's works; the genius of Racine is the set of his tragedies, beyond that there is nothing. Why [should we] attribute to Racine the possibility of writing a new tragedy, since precisely he did not write it? In his life a man commits himself,

draws his own figure, and beyond this figure there is nothing. Obviously, this thought may seem harsh to someone who has not had a successful life. But, on the other hand, it prepares men to understand that only reality counts, that the dreams, the expectations, the hopes allow [us] only to define a man as [a] disappointed dream, as miscarried hopes, as useless expectations; that is to say that that defines them negatively and not positively. However, when we say "you are nothing other than your life," that does not imply that the artist will be judged only by his artworks, for a thousand other things also contribute to define him. What we mean is that man is nothing other than a set of undertakings, that he is the sum, the organization, the whole of the relations which make up these undertakings.

SELECTION 8.2
The Myth of Sisyphus*

Albert Camus

[*Camus begins by asserting that I know only that I and the world outside me exist; the rest of supposed knowledge is mere "construction." (Especially interesting is his view that trying to define or understand himself is nothing but water slipping through his fingers.) He ends with observing how absurd it is that the heart longs for clear understanding, given the irrationality of everything.*]

Of whom and of what indeed can I say: "I know that!" This heart within me I can feel, and I judge that it exists. This world I can touch, and I likewise judge that it exists. There ends all my knowledge, and the rest is construction. For if I try to seize this self of which I feel sure, if I try to define and to summarize it, it is nothing but water slipping through my fingers. I can sketch one by one all the aspects it is able to assume, all those likewise that have been attributed to it, this upbringing, this origin, this ardor or these silences, this nobility or this vileness. But aspects cannot be added up. This

very heart which is mine will forever remain indefinable to me. Between the certainty I have of my existence and the content I try to give to that assurance, the gap will never be filled. Forever I shall be a stranger to myself. In psychology as in logic, there are truths but no truth. Socrates' "Know thyself" has as much value as the "Be virtuous" of our confessionals. They reveal a nostalgia at the same time as an ignorance. They are sterile exercises on great subjects. They are legitimate only in precisely so far as they are approximate.

And here are trees and I know their gnarled surface, water and I feel its taste. These scents of grass and stars at night, certain evenings when the heart relaxes—how shall I negate this world whose power and strength I feel? Yet all the knowledge on earth will give me nothing to assure me that this world is mine. You describe it to me and you teach me to classify it. You enumerate its laws and in my thirst for knowledge I admit that they are true. You take apart its mechanism and my hope increases. At the final stage you teach me that this wondrous and multicolored universe can be reduced to the atom and that the atom itself can be reduced to the electron. All this is good and I wait for you to continue.

---

* From *The Myth of Sisyphus* by Albert Camus, translated by Justin O'Brien, copyright © 1955, copyright renewed 1983 by Alfred A. Knopf. Used by permission of Alfred A. Knopf, a division of Random House, Inc.

But you tell me of an invisible planetary system in which electrons gravitate around a nucleus. You explain this world to me with an image. I realize then that you have been reduced to poetry: I shall never know. Have I the time to become indignant? You have already changed theories. So that science that was to teach me everything ends up in a hypothesis, that lucidity founders in metaphor, that uncertainty is resolved in a work of art. What need had I of so many efforts? The soft lines of these hills and the hand of evening on this troubled heart teach me much more. I have returned to my beginning. I realize that if through science I can seize phenomena and enumerate them, I cannot, for all that, apprehend the world. Were I to trace its entire relief with my finger, I should not know any more. And you give me the choice between a description that is sure but that teaches me nothing and hypotheses that claim to teach me but that are not sure. A stranger to myself and to the world, armed solely with a thought that negates itself as soon as it asserts, what is this condition in which I can have peace only by refusing to know and to live, in which the appetite for conquest bumps into walls that defy its assaults? To will is to stir up paradoxes. Everything is ordered in such a way as to bring into being that poisoned peace produced by thoughtlessness, lack of heart, or fatal renunciations.

Hence the intelligence, too, tells me in its way that this world is absurd. Its contrary, blind reason, may well claim that all is clear; I was waiting for proof and longing for it to be right. But despite so many pretentious centuries and over the heads of so many eloquent and persuasive men, I know that is false. On this plane, at least, there is no happiness if I cannot know. That universal reason, practical or ethical, that determinism, those categories that explain everything are enough to make a decent man laugh. They have nothing to do with the mind. They negate its profound truth, which is to be enchained. In this unintelligible and limited universe, man's fate henceforth assumes its meaning. A horde of irrationals has sprung up and surrounds him until his ultimate end. In his recovered and now studied lucidity, the feeling of the absurd becomes clear and definite. I said that the world is absurd, but I was too hasty. This world in itself is not reasonable, that is all that can be said. But what is absurd is the confrontation of this irrational and the wild longing for clarity whose call echoes in the human heart. The absurd depends as much on man as on the world. For the moment it is all that links them together. It binds them one to the other as only hatred can weld two creatures together. This is all I can discern clearly in this measureless universe where my adventure takes place.

SELECTION 8.3

A Dialogue with Jorgen Habermas: Fundamentalism and Terror*

Giovanna Borradori

[*Selections 8.3 and 8.4 are excerpts from interviews about the attack on the World Trade Center on September 11, 2001, with Jorgen Habermas and Jacques Derrida, two influential Continental philosophers. The interviews are conducted by philosopher Giovanna Borradori, a specialist in the philosophy of terrorism. Although this is not technical philosophy, it will give you a good idea of the thinking of the two men. Habermas* notes that September 11 could be called the first historic world event.]

Borradori: . . . [O]ur topic is terrorism, which seems to have taken up new meaning and definition after September 11.

Habermas: The monstrous act itself was new. And I do not just mean the action of the suicide hijackers who transformed the fully fueled airplanes together with their hostages into living weapons, or even the unbearable number of victims and the dramatic extent of the devastation. What was new was the symbolic force

---

* An excerpt from *Philosophy in a Time of Terror: Dialogues with Jorgen Habermas and Jacques Derrida* by Giovanna Borradori, published by the University of Chicago Press, © 2003.

of the targets struck. The attackers did not just physically cause the highest buildings in Manhattan to collapse; they also destroyed an icon in the household imagery of the American nation. Only in the surge of patriotism that followed did one begin to recognize the central importance the towers held in everyone's imagination, with their irreplaceable imprint on the Manhattan skyline and their powerful embodiment of economic strength and projection toward the future. The presence of cameras and of the media was also new, transforming the local event simultaneously into a global one and the whole world population into a benumbed witness. Perhaps September 11 could be called the first historic world event in the strictest sense: the impact, the explosion, the slow collapse—everything that was not Hollywood anymore but, rather, a gruesome reality, literally took place in front of the "universal eyewitness" of a global public. God only knows what my friend and colleague experienced, watching the second airplane explode into the top floors of the World Trade Center only a few blocks away from the roof of his house on Duane Street. No doubt it was something completely different from what I experienced in Germany in front of the television, though we saw the same thing.

Certainly, no observation of a unique event can provide an explanation per se for why terrorism itself should have assumed a new characteristic. In this respect one factor above all seems to me to be relevant: one never really knows who one's enemy is. Osama bin Laden, the person, more likely serves the function of a stand-in. Compare the new terrorists with partisans or conventional terrorists, for example, in Israel. These people often fight in a decentralized manner in small, autonomous units, too. Also, in these cases there is no concentration of forces or central organization, a feature that makes them difficult targets. But partisans fight on familiar territory with professed political objectives in order to conquer power. This is what distinguishes them from terrorists who are scattered around the globe and networked in the fashion of secret services. They allow their religious motives of a fundamentalist kind to be known, though they do not pursue a program that goes beyond the engineering of destruction and insecurity. The terrorism we associate for

the time being with the name "al-Qaeda" makes the identification of the opponent and any realistic assessment of the danger impossible. This intangibility is what lends terrorism a new quality.

Surely the uncertainty of the danger belongs to the essence of terrorism. But the scenarios of biological or chemical warfare painted in detail by the American media during the months after September 11, the speculations over the various kinds of nuclear terrorism, only betray the inability of the government to at least determine the magnitude of the danger. One never knows if there's anything to it. In Israel people at least know what can happen to them if they take a bus, go into a department store, discotheque, or any open area—and how frequently it happens. In the U.S.A. or Europe one cannot circumscribe the risk; there is no realistic way to estimate the type, magnitude, or probability of the risk, nor any way to narrow down the potentially affected regions. . . .

Borradori: Philosophically speaking, do you consider terrorism to be a wholly political act?

Habermas: Not in the subjective sense in which Mohammed Atta, the Egyptian citizen who came from Hamburg and piloted the first of the two catastrophic airplanes, would offer you a political answer. No doubt today's Islamic fundamentalism is also a cover for political motifs. Indeed, we should not overlook the political motifs we encounter in forms of religious fanaticism. This explains the fact that some of those drawn into the "holy war" had been secular nationalists only a few years before. If one looks at the biographies of these people, remarkable continuities are revealed. Disappointment over nationalistic authoritarian regimes may have contributed to the fact that today religion offers a new and subjectively more convincing language for old political orientations.

Borradori: How would you actually define terrorism? Can a meaningful distinction be drawn between national and international or even global terrorism?

Habermas: In one respect, Palestinian terrorism still possesses a certain outmoded characteristic in that it revolves around murder, around the indiscriminate annihilation of enemies, women, and children—life against life. This is what distinguishes it from the terror that appears in the paramilitary form of guerilla warfare. This form of warfare has characterized many national liberation movements in the second half of the twentieth century—and has left its mark today on the Chechnyan struggle for independence, for example. In contrast to this, the global terror that culminated in the September 11 attack bears the anarchistic traits of an impotent revolt directed against an enemy that cannot be defeated in any pragmatic sense. The only possible effect it can have is to shock and alarm the government and population. Technically speaking, since our complex societies are highly susceptible to interferences and accidents, they certainly offer ideal opportunities for a prompt disruption of normal activities. These disruptions can, at a minimum expense, have considerably destructive consequences. Global terrorism is extreme both in its lack of realistic goals and in its cynical exploitation of the vulnerability of complex systems.

Borradori: Should terrorism be distinguished from ordinary crimes and other types of violence?

Habermas: Yes and no. From a moral point of view, there is no excuse for terrorist acts, regardless of the motive or the situation under which they are carried out. Nothing justifies our "making allowance for" the murder or suffering of others for one's own purposes. Each murder is one too many. Historically, however, terrorism falls in a category different from crimes that concern a criminal court judge. It differs from a private incident in that it deserves public interest and requires a different kind of analysis than murder out of jealousy, for example. Otherwise, we would not be having this interview. The difference between political terror and ordinary crime becomes clear during the change of regimes, in which former terrorists come to power and become well-regarded representatives of their country. Certainly, such a political transition can be hoped for only by terrorists who pursue political goals in a realistic manner; who are able to draw, at least retrospectively, a certain legitimation for their criminal actions, undertaken to overcome a manifestly unjust situation. However, today I cannot imagine a context that would someday, in some manner, make the monstrous crime of September 11 an understandable or comprehensible political act.

Borradori: Do you think it was good to interpret this act as a declaration of war?

Habermas: Even if the term "war" is less misleading and, morally, less controvertible than "crusade," I consider Bush's decision to call for a "war against terrorism" a serious mistake, both normatively and pragmatically. Normatively, he is elevating these criminals to the status of war enemies; and pragmatically, one cannot lead a war against a "network" if the term "war" is to retain any definite meaning.

SELECTION 8.4

A Dialogue with Jacques Derrida: 9/11 and Global Terrorism

Giovanna Borradori

[*See the introductory note to Selection 8.3. In this selection, Derrida displays his keen eye for language by noticing that the event is referred to simply as "September 11." He then considers the philosophical significance of that fact.*]

Borradori: September 11 [le 11 septembre] gave us the impression of being a major event, one of the most important historical events we will witness in our lifetime, especially for those of us who never lived through a world war. Do you agree?

Derrida: Le 11 septembre, as you say, or, since we have agreed to speak two languages, "September 11." We will have to return later to this question of language. As well as to this act of naming: a date and nothing more. When you say "September 11" you are already citing, are you not? You are inviting me to speak here by recalling, as if in quotation marks, a date or a dating that has taken over our public space and our private lives for five weeks now. Something *fait date*, I would say in a French idiom, something marks a date, a date in history; that is always what's most striking, the very impact of what is at least felt, in an apparently immediate way, to be an event that truly marks, that truly makes its mark, a singular and, as they say here, "unprecedented" event. I say "apparently immediate" because this "feeling" is actually less spontaneous than it appears: it is to a large extent conditioned, constituted, if not actually constructed, circulated at any rate through the media by means of a prodigious techno-socio-political machine. "To mark a date in history" presupposes, in any case, that "something" comes or happens for the first and last time, "something" that we do not yet really know how to identify, determine, recognize, or analyze but that should remain from here on in unforgettable: an ineffaceable event in the shared archive of a universal calendar, that is, a supposedly universal calendar, for these are—and I want to insist on this at the outset—only suppositions and presuppositions. Unrefined and dogmatic, or else carefully considered, organized, calculated, strategic—or all of these at once. For the index pointing toward this date, the bare act, the minimal deictic, the minimalist aim of this dating, also marks something else. Namely, the fact that we perhaps have no concept and no meaning available to us to name in any other way this "thing" that has just happened, this supposed "event." An act of "international terrorism," for example, and we will return to this, is anything but a rigorous concept that would help us grasp the singularity of what we will be trying to discuss. "Something" took place, we have the feeling of not having seen it coming, and certain consequences undeniably follow upon the "thing." But this very thing, the place and meaning of this "event," remains ineffable, like an intuition without concept, like a unicity with no generality on the horizon or with no horizon at all, out of range for a language that admits its powerlessness and so is reduced to pronouncing mechanically a date, repeating it endlessly, as a

kind of ritual incantation, a conjuring poem, a journalistic litany or rhetorical refrain that admits to not knowing what it's talking about. We do not in fact know what we are saying or naming in this way: September 11, *le 11 septembre*, September 11. The brevity of the appellation (September 11, 9/11) stems not only from an economic or rhetorical necessity. The telegram of this metonymy—a name, a number—points out the unqualifiable by recognizing that we do not recognize or even cognize that we do not yet know how to qualify, that we do not know what we are talking about.

This is the first, indisputable effect of what occurred (whether it was calculated, well calculated, or not), precisely on September 11, not far from here: we repeat this, we must repeat it, and it is all the more necessary to repeat it insofar as we do not really know what is being named in this way, as if to exorcise two times at one go: on the one hand, to conjure away, as if by magic, the "thing" itself, the fear or the terror it inspires (for repetition always protects by neutralizing, deadening, distancing a traumatism, and this is true for the repetition of the televised images we will speak of later), and, on the other hand, to deny, as close as possible to this act of language and this enunciation, our powerlessness to name in an appropriate fashion, to characterize, to think the thing in question, to get beyond the mere deictic of the date: something terrible took place on September 11, and in the end we don't know what. For however outraged we might be at the violence, however much we might genuinely deplore—as I do, along with everyone else—the number of dead, no one will really be convinced that this is, in the end, what it's all about. I will come back to this later; for the moment we are simply preparing ourselves to say something about it.

I've been in New York for three weeks now. Not only is it impossible not to speak on this subject, but you feel or are made to feel that it is actually forbidden, that you do not have the right, to begin speaking of anything, especially in public, without ceding to this obligation, without making an always somewhat blind reference to this date (and this was already the case in China, where I was on September 11, and then in Frankfurt on September 22). I gave in regularly to this injunction, I admit; and in a certain sense I am doing so again by taking part in this friendly interview with you, though trying always, beyond the commotion and the most sincere compassion, to appeal to questions and to a "thought" (among other things, a real political thought) of what, it seems, has just taken place on September 11, just a few steps from here, in Manhattan or, not too far away, in Washington, D.C.

I believe always in the necessity of being attentive first of all to this phenomenon of language, naming, and dating, to this repetition compulsion (at once rhetorical, magical, and poetic). To what this compulsion signifies, translates, or betrays. Not in order to isolate ourselves in language, as people in too much of a rush would like us to believe, but on the contrary, in order to try to understand what is going on precisely beyond language and what is pushing us to repeat endlessly and without knowing what we are talking about, precisely there where language and the concept come up against their limits: "September 11, September 11, le 11 septembre, 9/11."

We must try to know more, to take our time and hold onto our freedom so as to begin to think [about] this first effect of the so-called event: From where does this menacing injunction itself come to us? How is it being forced upon us? Who or what gives us this threatening order (others would already say this terrorizing if not terrorist imperative): name, repeat, rename "September 11," "le 11 septembre," even when you do not yet know what you are saying and are not yet thinking what you refer to in this way. I agree with you: without any doubt, this "thing," "September 11," "gave us the impression of being a major event." But what is an impression in this case? And an event? And especially a "major event"? Taking your word—or words—for it, I will underscore more than one precaution. I will do so in a seemingly "empiricist" style, though aiming beyond empiricism. It cannot be denied, as an empiricist of the eighteenth century would quite literally say, that there was an "impression" there, and the impression of what you call in English—and this is not fortuitous—a "major event." I insist here on the English because it

is the language we speak here in New York, even though it is neither your language nor mine; but I also insist because the injunction comes first of all from a place where English predominates. I am not saying this only because the United States was targeted, hit, or violated on its own soil for the first time in almost two centuries—since 1812 to be exact—but because the world order that felt itself targeted through this violence is dominated largely by the Anglo-American idiom, an idiom that is indissociably linked to the political discourse that dominates the world stage, to international law, diplomatic institutions, the media, and the greatest technoscientific, capitalist, and military power. And it is very much a question of the still enigmatic but also critical essence of this hegemony. By critical, I mean at once decisive, potentially decisionary, decision-making, and in crisis: today more vulnerable and threatened than ever.

Whether this "impression" is justified or not, it is in itself an event, let us never forget it, especially when it is, though in quite different ways, a properly global effect. The "impression" cannot be dissociated from all the effects, interpretations, and rhetoric that have at once reflected, communicated, and "globalized" it from everything that also and first of all formed, produced, and made it possible. The "impression" thus resembles "the very thing" that produced it. Even if the so-called "thing" cannot be reduced to it. Even if, therefore, the event itself cannot be reduced to it. The event is made up of the "thing" itself (that which happens or comes) and the impression (itself at once "spontaneous" and "controlled") that is given, left, or made by the so-called "thing." We could say that the impression is "informed," in both senses of the word: a predominant system gave it form, and this form then gets run through an organized information machine (language, communication, rhetoric, image, media, and so on). This informational apparatus is from the very outset political, technical, economic. But we can and, I believe, must (and this duty is at once philosophical and political) distinguish between the supposedly brute fact, the "impression," and the interpretation. It is of course just about impossible, I realize, to distinguish the "brute" fact from the system that produces the "information" about it. But it is necessary to push the analysis as far as possible. To produce a "major event," it is, sad to say, not enough, and this has been true for some time now, to cause the deaths of some four thousand people, and especially "civilians," in just a few seconds by means of so-called advanced technology. Many examples could be given from the world wars (for you specified that this event appears even more important to those who "have never lived through a world war") but also from after these wars, examples of quasi-instantaneous mass murders that were not recorded, interpreted, felt, and presented as "major events." They did not give the "impression," at least not to everyone, of being unforgettable catastrophes.

We must thus ask why this is the case and distinguish between two "impressions." On the one hand, compassion for the victims and indignation over the killings; our sadness and condemnation should be without limits, unconditional, unimpeachable; they are responding to an undeniable "event," beyond all simulacra and all possible virtualization; they respond with what might be called the heart and they go straight to the heart of the event. On the other hand, the interpreted, interpretative, informed impression, the

conditional evaluation that makes us believe that this is a "major event." Belief, the phenomenon of credit and of accreditation, constitutes an essential dimension of the evaluation, of the dating, indeed, of the compulsive inflation of which we've been speaking. By distinguishing impression from belief, I continue to make as if I were privileging this language of English empiricism, which we would be wrong to resist here. All the philosophical questions remain open, unless they are opening up again in a perhaps new and original way: what is an impression? What is a belief? But especially: what is an event worthy of this name? And a "major" event, that is, one that is actually more of an "event," more actually an "event," than ever? An event that would bear witness, in an exemplary or hyperbolic fashion, to the very essence of an event or even to an event beyond essence? For could an event that still conforms to an essence, to a law or to a truth, indeed to a concept of the event, ever be a major event? A major event should be so unforeseeable and irruptive that it disturbs even the horizon of the concept or essence on the basis of which we believe we recognize an event as such. That is why all the "philosophical" questions remain open, perhaps even beyond philosophy itself, as soon as it is a matter of thinking the event.

CHECKLIST

To help you review, a checklist of the key philosophers of this chapter can be found online at www.mhhe.com/moore9e.

KEY TERMS AND CONCEPTS

QUESTIONS FOR DISCUSSION AND REVIEW

1. To what extent are we responsible for the situations in which we find ourselves? When does responsibility begin?

2. Can humans communicate with one another? (Do not assume that communicating is the same as talking.) Are people ever really *not* strangers? Explain.

3. What is "bad faith," and how do we recognize whether we have it?

4. Do we live in an absurd world?

5. Explain the myth of Sisyphus. To what extent is this situation an accurate depiction of life?

6. What does it mean to say that we are abandoned?

7. Does a belief in God rescue us from the existential predicament?

8. What does Sartre mean by saying that we are condemned to be free? What does he mean by saying, "I choose myself perpetually"? And what does he mean by saying, "In choosing myself, I choose man"?

9. Do you think it is true that most humans live inauthentic lives?

10. Can having a "fundamental project" save us from a "lost life"? Explain.

SUGGESTED FURTHER READINGS

Go online to www.mhhe.com/moore9e for a list of suggested further readings.

9

The Pragmatic and Analytic Traditions

It is no truer that "atoms are what they are because we use 'atom' as we do" than that "we use 'atom' as we do because atoms are as they are." Both of these claims . . . are entirely empty.   —Richard Rorty

We have no way of identifying truths except to posit that the statements that are currently rationally accepted (by our lights) are true.   —Hilary Putnam

As the twenty-first century gains momentum, we might reflect briefly on all the last one brought us: air travel, Einstein, nuclear weapons, television and computers, clones, photographs of sunsets on Mars, war on civilian populations, genocide, AIDS, the rise and fall of the Soviet Union, racial integration in the United States, and hip-hop. In art and literature, traditional structures and approaches were cast aside with abandon. Schoenberg and Stravinsky brought the world music that lacked fixed tonal centers; Cage brought it music that lacked sound. In Europe existentialist philosophers proclaimed the absurdity of the human predicament. In Russia the followers of Marx declared an end to the existing order; still later, the followers of the followers declared an end to Marx.

In philosophy, on the continent of Europe in the twentieth century, the assault on idealism was begun by the nihilistic attacks of Schopenhauer and Nietzsche (**nihilism** is the rejection of values and beliefs) and by the religious anti-idealism of Søren Kierkegaard. Anti-Hegelianism reached its summit in existentialism, according to which life is not only not perfectly rational, it is fundamentally irrational and absurd. Meanwhile, in Britain and the United States, philosophers were busy with other things, as we explain in this chapter.

PRAGMATISM

The United States' distinctive contribution to philosophy is known as **pragmatism** or, sometimes, American pragmatism. The brightest lights of pragmatism were the "classic" pragmatists **C. S. Peirce** (1839–1914), **William James** (1842–1910), **John Dewey** (1859–1952), and more recently **Richard Rorty** (1931–2007). In general, pragmatists rejected the idea that there is such a thing as fixed, absolute truth. Instead, they held that truth is relative to a time and place and purpose and is thus ever changing in light of new data.

To fine-tune things a bit, in the 1870s, Peirce and James created a philosophy club in Cambridge, Massachusetts, from whose discussions pragmatism sprang. James, however, gave the credit for inventing pragmatism to Peirce. The latter, a logician, thought of pragmatism as a rule for determining a proposition's meaning, which he equated with the practical consequences that would result from the proposition's being true. By this standard, he said, metaphysical propositions are mostly either meaningless or absurd. Truth, he said famously, is the opinion fated to be agreed to by all who investigate.

Despite Peirce's importance, most people probably associate pragmatism with James, an entertaining and colorful expositor of ideas. James thought the whole point of philosophy should be to find out what difference it makes to a person if an idea is true or false. The meaning and truth of an idea, he said, are determined by its usefulness, by its "cash value." The whole purpose of thinking, he held, is to help us relate to our surroundings in a satisfactory way. An idea is a road map, whose meaning, truth, and value lie in its ability to carry us from one part of experience to another part in a secure, simple, and efficient way.

James thought that, in general, ideas that have been verified or falsified by the community of scientific investigators enable us to make the most accurate predictions about the future and therefore may be counted on to possess the highest degree of workability. However, he also believed that, within certain parameters, you can *will yourself to believe* something, and also that, within certain parameters, you are wise to make yourself believe something if doing so benefits you. He didn't mean that you should deceive yourself. If you smoke, he wouldn't advise you to believe that smoking promotes good health because you would feel better if you believed it: in the long run, believing that smoking is healthy won't benefit you. But if you must either accept or reject a belief, and the evidence for and against the belief weighs in equally, then believe as your "vital good" dictates, said James. For example, if the hypothesis that God exists works satisfactorily for you in the widest sense of the word, you are justified in believing it is true. We will consider this theory more carefully in Part Three.

For Peirce, what is true is what investigators agree to; the *sum* of its consequences is what a conception means. James, by contrast, has a much more individualistic concept of meaning and truth: roughly, what is true is what "works" for the individual. Of course, for James, what the community of scientific investigators agree to is what ultimately does work for the individual. So, as a practical matter, for both James and Peirce the same scientific findings will count as true.

PROFILE: John Dewey (1859–1952)

John Dewey lived almost a century. He was born before the American Civil War, and he died during the Korean War. His influence on American life was profound.

Dewey was the third of four children in his family. His father owned a grocery business and then a tobacco business in Burlington, Vermont, where Dewey was raised. Dewey was not considered a brilliant mind as a high school student, but his discovery of philosophy as a junior at the University of Vermont awakened slumbering genius. He received his PhD at Johns Hopkins and taught at Michigan, Minnesota, Chicago, and Columbia. He continued to write, publish, and lecture long after his retirement from Columbia in 1930.

Dewey exerted his greatest influence on society by virtue of his educational theories. He was an effective proponent of progressive education, which opposed formal, authoritarian methods of instruction in favor of having students learn by performing tasks that are related to their own interests. Today, educational practice throughout the United States and in many areas across the world generally follows the fundamental postulates of Dewey's educational philosophy, although his belief that the school is the central institution of a democratic society is not always shared by American taxpayers.

A kind, generous, and modest man, Dewey was also an effective social critic and an influential participant in reform movements. He was utterly fearless in advocating democratic causes, even those, like women's suffrage, that were deeply unpopular. Despite having unreconcilable philosophical differences with philosopher Bertrand Russell (discussed later in this chapter), Dewey was active on Russell's behalf when Russell was denied permission to teach at the City College of New York in 1941 (see the profile on Russell). He was also one of the original founders of the American Civil Liberties Union.

Dewey was not the world's most inspiring public speaker, and one of his students said that you could understand his lectures only by reading your notes afterward. Maybe the popularity of these lectures of his throughout the world despite the stylistic drawbacks is sound indication of the power of Dewey's ideas.

The bibliography of Dewey's works runs over one hundred fifty pages, and his writings touch on virtually every philosophical subject. All told, he wrote forty books and seven hundred articles. His thought dominated American philosophy throughout the first part of the twentieth century. He was and still is America's most famous philosopher.

Among the most famous of Dewey's works are *Reconstruction in Philosophy* (1920), *Human Nature and Conduct* (1922), *Experience and Nature* (1925), *The Quest for Certainty* (1929), *Art As Experience* (1934), *Freedom and Culture* (1939), and *Problems of Men* (1946).

John Dewey's brand of pragmatism is known as **instrumentalism,** according to which, roughly, the forms of human activity, including thought, are instruments used by people to solve practical problems. In Dewey's view, thinking is not a search for "truth" but rather an activity aimed at solving individual and social problems, a means by which humans strive to achieve a satisfactory relationship with their environment.

From Dewey's perspective, metaphysics, like religious rites and cults, has been a means of "escape from the vicissitudes of existence." Instead of facing the uncertainties of a constantly changing world, metaphysicians have sought security by searching for fixed, universal, and immutable truth.

From Dewey's point of view, nature is experience. This is what he means. Objects are not fixed substances but individual things ("existences" or "events," he called them) that are imbued with meanings. A piece of paper, for instance, means one thing to a novelist, another to someone who wants to start a fire, still another to an attorney who uses it to draw up a contract, still another to children making paper airplanes, and so on. A piece of paper is an instrument for solving a problem within a given context. What a piece of paper *is* is what it means within the context of some activity or other.

But when he held that an object is what it means within an activity, Dewey did not mean to equate the object with the thought about it. That was the mistake made by idealism, in Dewey's view. Idealism equated objects with thought about them and thus left out of the reckoning the particular, individual thing. Objects are not reducible to thought about objects, according to Dewey. Things have an aspect of particularity that idealism entirely neglects, he held.

But this does not mean that Dewey thought that there are fixed, immutable substances or things. The doctrine that "independent" objects exist "out there" outside the mind—realism—is called by Dewey the **spectator theory of knowledge.** It is no more acceptable to Dewey than is idealism. On the contrary, his view was that, as the uses to which a thing is put change, the thing itself changes. To refer to the earlier example, a piece of paper is both (1) a particular item and (2) what is thought about it within the various and forever-changing contexts in which it is used.

Given this metaphysical perspective, from which abstract speculation about so-called eternal truths is mere escapism, it is easy to understand why Dewey was primarily interested in practical problems and actively participated in movements of social, political, and educational reform. He was effective as a social activist, too. Few individuals have had more impact on American educational, judicial, or legislative institutions than did Dewey. The educational system in which you most probably were raised, which emphasized experimentation and practice rather than abstract learning and authoritarian instructional techniques, is the result of his influence.

During the twentieth century, pragmatism in many United States university philosophy departments was replaced by analytic philosophy, which had its roots in Britain (as we shall see). However, the pragmatic tradition in America was carried forward by Willard Van Orman Quine, Hilary Putnam, and others, and most famously perhaps by Richard Rorty, who we will turn to next.

Richard Rorty

American philosopher **Richard Rorty** (1931–2007) was suspicious of the traditional claims of philosophy itself to have the method best suited to finding "truth." He adopted the way of American pragmatism exemplified by William James and John Dewey and applied it to the role of literature in society. The "best" literature, Rorty said, can open its readers to new possibilities for constructing a meaningful life. Some philosophical writing falls into this character. He disputed the idea that philosophy's focus should be to determine what we can and can't know. "Truth is not out there," he wrote. In other words, truth is not separate from what we experience in our daily lives. Truth is whatever "survives all objections within one's culture." Nobody can say whether or not (s)he has reached the truth, except in the sense held in one's culture. And "there is no method for knowing one has reached the truth, or when it is closer than before."

In his early career, Rorty worked on mainstream analytical philosophy. In his later years, he sought to combine American liberalism with Continental literature and philosophy. He borrowed from Freud, Nietzsche, Heidegger, Wittgenstein, Quine, and others. Over time, however, he became disenchanted with professorships in philosophy departments and became first a professor of humanities, then a professor of comparative literature at Stanford. In his writings, he drew on Dewey, Hegel, and Darwin, creating a pragmatist synthesized theory to refute some of the givens of traditional philosophy.

Rorty referred to the standards of evidence, reasonableness, knowledge, and truth as "starting points" and described his pragmatic view that standards are relative to one's culture by saying that the starting points are "contingent." If we give up trying to evade "the contingency of starting points," then "we shall lose what Nietzsche called 'metaphysical comfort,' but we may regain a renewed sense of community."

Despite his many critics, Rorty produced an impressive volume of work on thought, culture, and politics, which has won him a place as a much-discussed thinker.

ANALYTIC PHILOSOPHY

To understand analytic philosophy, we first of all have to understand what analysis is.

What Analysis Is

Quite simply put, philosophical **analysis** resolves complex propositions or concepts into simpler ones. Let's take an elementary example. The proposition

Square circles are nonexistent things.

might be resolved by analysis into the simpler proposition

No squares are circular.

This second proposition is "simpler" philosophically because it refers only to squares and their lack of circularity, whereas the first proposition refers to two distinct classes of entities, square circles and nonexistent things.

Moreover, the first proposition is troubling philosophically. It is certainly an intelligible proposition. Hence, it would seem that square circles and nonexistent things must (somehow and amazingly) exist in some sense or another. If they did not exist, the proposition would be about nothing and thus would not be intelligible. (It is precisely this reasoning that has led some philosophers to conclude that every object of thought must exist "in some sense," or "subsist.")

The second sentence contains the same information as the first but does not have the puzzling implications of the first. Not only is it simpler than the second, it is also clearer. Once the first sentence is recast or analyzed in this way, we can accept what the first sentence says without having to concede that square circles and nonexistent things exist "in some sense."

This very simple example of analysis will perhaps help make it clear why many analytic philosophers have regarded analysis as having great importance for the field of metaphysics. Be sure that you understand the example and everything we have said about it before you read any further.

A Brief Overview of Analytic Philosophy

To understand how analysis became so important as a method of philosophy, think back to Kant (Chapter 7). Kant thought that knowledge is possible if we limit our inquiries to things as they are experienceable, because the mind imposes categories on experienceable objects. The Absolute Idealists, Hegel being the prime example, then expanded on Kant's theory and held that the categories of thought *are* the categories of being. Absolute Idealism quickly caught hold in Western philosophy, and even in England clever versions of it flourished in the late nineteenth century. We say "even in England" because prior to this time English philosophy had been firmly rooted in empiricism and common sense.

One Englishman who subscribed to idealist metaphysical principles was **Bertrand Russell** [RUSS-ul] (1872–1970). Russell, however, had taken an interest in philosophy in the first place because he studied mathematics and wanted to find a satisfactory account of numbers and mathematics. He began to think that Absolute Idealist philosophies involve a couple of very dubious and interrelated assumptions: first, that propositions all have the subject/predicate form, and second, that an object's *relationships* to other entities are a part of the object's essence. Russell felt these assumptions were incompatible with there being more than one thing (which was why Absolute Idealist theories all maintained there is but one thing, the Absolute) and thus felt they were incompatible with mathematics. Further, when Russell read what Hegel had to say about mathematics, he was horrified, finding it both ignorant and stupid. So Russell abandoned Absolute Idealism.

What Russell had in mind by saying he wished to find a satisfactory account of numbers and mathematics was this. He wanted to ascertain the absolutely basic, indefinable entities and the absolutely fundamental indemonstrable propositions of mathematics. It might seem to you that the basic entities of mathematics are numbers and that the absolutely fundamental propositions are propositions of arithmetic such as $2 + 2 = 4$. Russell, however, believed that propositions about numbers are only *apparently* or *grammatically* about numbers (just as the proposition we presented was only apparently or grammatically about square circles) and that arithmetical propositions are logically derivable from even more basic propositions.

The theory that the concepts of mathematics can be defined in terms of concepts of logic, and that all mathematical truths can be proved from principles of formal logic, is known as **logicism.** The first part of the theory (that mathematical concepts can be defined in terms of logical concepts) involves our friend analysis:

PROFILE: Bertrand Russell (1872–1970)

Bertrand Russell came from a distinguished background. His grandfather, Lord John Russell, was twice prime minister; his godfather was John Stuart Mill, of whom much mention is made in later chapters; and his parents were prominent freethinkers. Because his parents died when he was young, Russell was brought up in the household of Lord Russell. This side of the family was austerely Protestant, and Russell's childhood was solitary and lonely. As a teenager, he had the intuition that God did not exist and found this to be a great relief.

In the fall of 1890, at a time when several other brilliant philosophers were also there, Russell went to Cambridge to study mathematics and philosophy. Many of Russell's important works in philosophy and mathematics were written during his association with Cambridge, first as a student, then as a fellow and lecturer. His association with Cambridge ended in 1916, when he was dismissed for pacifist activities during World War I. He was restored as a fellow at Cambridge in 1944.

Russell was dismayed by the enthusiasm among ordinary people for the war, and his own pacifism created much resentment. After he was dismissed from Cambridge, he was imprisoned for six months for his pacifism; thereafter, he held no academic position again until he began to teach in the United States in 1938.

Russell thought that without a proper education a person is caught in the prison of prejudices that make up common sense. He wanted to create a kind of education that would be not only philosophically

sound but also nonthreatening, enjoyable, and stimulating. To this end he and his wife, Dora, founded the Beacon Hill School in 1927, which was influential in the founding of similar schools in England and America.

In addition to writing books on education during the period between the wars, Russell wrote extensively on social and political philosophy. His most infamous popular work, *Marriage and Morals* (1929), was very liberal in its attitude toward sexual practices and caused the cancellation of his appointment to City College of New York in 1940. He was taken to court by the mother of a CCNY student, and the court revoked Russell's appointment "for the sake of public health, safety, and morals." Apparently the most damaging part of the evidence against Russell was his recommendation in the book that a child caught masturbating should not be physically punished.

World War II and the Nazi onslaught caused Russell to abandon his pacifism. In 1961, however, he was again imprisoned, this time for activity in demonstrations against nuclear weapons, and in 1967 he organized the so-called war crimes tribunal directed against American activities in Vietnam.

Russell received the Nobel Prize for literature in 1950, one of many honors bestowed on him. In his autobiography he said that three passions had governed his life: the longing for love, the search for knowledge, and unbearable pity for the suffering of humankind. Throughout his life Russell exhibited intellectual brilliance and extraordinary personal courage.

propositions involving numbers must be analyzed into propositions involving logical concepts—just as we analyzed a proposition about squares and nonexistent things into a proposition about squares and their properties. The details of this analysis, and the derivation of mathematical truths from principles of formal logic, are too technical to be examined in a text like this one.

Russell was not the only proponent of logicism. Somewhat earlier the German mathematician **Gottlob Frege** [FRAY-guh] (1848–1925) had devised a "language"—a series of symbols—in which logical properties could be stated precisely and without the ambiguities of ordinary language. Modern symbolic logic is derived from Frege's language—the importance of which Russell may have been the first person other than Frege himself to understand. Frege was concerned not only with the logical foundations of arithmetic but also with the issue of how words have meanings—an issue that was central throughout twentieth-century philosophy. For these reasons, many historians credit Frege even more than Russell with being the "founder" of analytic philosophy. However, Russell's writings were more widely read in English-speaking countries during at least the first half of the century, and in English-speaking countries Russell and Alfred North Whitehead's collaborative work, *Principia Mathematica* (final volume published in 1913), was considered the culminating work of logicism—and was a stunning intellectual achievement in any event.

Under the influence of his friend and colleague at Cambridge University, G. E. Moore (1873–1958), Russell began to conceive of the analytic method as *the* method of philosophy in general, a method that promised to deliver the same apparently indisputable results in other areas of philosophy that it had in the philosophy of mathematics. Around 1910 he began trying to do for epistemology exactly what he had attempted for mathematics: trying to determine the absolutely basic, indefinable entities and absolutely fundamental indemonstrable types of propositions of our knowledge of the external, physical world.

Moore, too, was concerned with our knowledge of the external world and devoted considerable energy to the analysis of some commonsense beliefs about physical objects. Moore also extended the analytic approach to propositions in moral philosophy (more on this in Part Two). Somewhat later, Gilbert Ryle (1900–1976), another important practitioner of analytic techniques, conceived of traditional philosophical problems as resting on "linguistic confusions." He achieved impressive apparent resolutions of several perennially knotty philosophical problems by using analytic techniques. Ludwig Wittgenstein (1889–1951), Russell's student and later a colleague, thought that, by using analysis, philosophy could actually disclose the ultimate, logical constituents of reality, their interrelations, and their relationship to the world of experience. Wittgenstein thought the goal of analysis was to reduce all complex descriptive propositions to their ultimately simple constituent propositions. These latter propositions would consist of "names" in combination, which would represent the ultimate simple constituents of reality.

In the 1920s, Moritz Schlick (1882–1936), a philosopher at the University of Vienna, formed a group known as the **Vienna Circle,** the members of which were much impressed by the work of Russell and Wittgenstein. Referring to their philosophy as **logical positivism,** the group held that philosophy is not a theory but an activity whose business is the logical clarification of thought. The logical positivists proclaimed a "**verifiability criterion of meaning.**" According to this criterion, suppose you say something, but nobody knows what observations would verify what you are trying to say. Then you haven't really made a meaningful empirical statement at all. And thus, the logical positivists held, traditional metaphysical utterances are not meaningful empirical statements. Take, for example, Hegel's thesis that reason is the substance of the universe. How could this be verified? Well, it just could not be. So it is not a genuine factual proposition; it is not empirically meaningful. In a reading selection at the end of the chapter, A. J. Ayer (1910–1989), who was the most famous English member of the Vienna Circle, explains the verifiability criterion of meaning in more detail.

Moral and value statements, the logical positivists said, are likewise empirically meaningless. At best they are expressions of emotions rather than legitimate statements. Philosophy, they said, has as its only useful function the analysis of both everyday language and scientific language—it has no legitimate concern with the world apart from language, for that is the concern of scientists.

The Vienna Circle dissolved when the Nazis took control of Austria in the late 1930s, but to this day many people still equate analytic philosophy with logical positivism. This is true despite the fact that nowadays few philosophers who refer to themselves as analysts subscribe to the verifiability criterion of meaning or accept many other of the basic assumptions of logical positivism.

In fact, today it is doubtful whether many of those who would call themselves analytic philosophers would even describe analysis as the only proper method of philosophy. Indeed, few would even describe their daily philosophical task as primarily one of analysis. There are philosophical tasks one might undertake other than analysis, and some who would still not hesitate to call themselves analysts have simply lost interest in analysis in favor of these other tasks. Others, like Wittgenstein, have explicitly repudiated analysis as the proper method of philosophy. Wittgenstein's about-face was published in 1953 in his enormously influential *Philosophical Investigations.*

Further, it is now widely held that many philosophically interesting claims and expressions cannot intelligibly be regarded as complexes subject to resolution into simpler and less misleading expressions. Certainly, the intent to recast the meaning of an expression into a less misleading form can be carried out only if its "real" or "true" meaning can be ascertained by the analyst. But concerns have been raised, perhaps most notably by W. V. O. Quine (1908–2000), about whether it is ever possible to say in some absolute, nonrelativistic sense what the meaning of an expression is. And for many expressions, it seems inappropriate in the first place to speak of their "meaning." Clearer understanding of many expressions seems to be achieved when we ask how the expression is used or what it is used to do rather than what it means, unless the latter question is taken as being equivalent to the two former questions, as it often is.

So it has become accepted that there are many useful philosophical methods and techniques other than the analysis of language, and it is pretty widely thought that good, substantial philosophical work is by no means always the result of analysis of some sort. Many of today's analytic philosophers would deny being directly concerned with language (though most are concerned with expressing themselves in clear language). Nor could it be said that all analytic philosophers mean the same thing when they speak of analysis. In its broadest sense, a call for "analysis" today is simply a call for clarification, and certainly today's analytic philosophers exhibit (or hope they exhibit) a concern for clarity of thought and expression as well as a great appreciation for detail. Most, too, would be inclined to say that at least some opinions expressed by earlier philosophers reflect linguistic confusions if not outright logical errors, but beyond this it is not the case that all analytic philosophers use some common unique method of philosophizing or have the same interests or share an identifiable approach to philosophical problems. In today's world, philosophers are apt to call themselves "analytic" to indicate that they do not have much training or interest in Continental philosophy as for any other reason.

So, to boil this down, the history of "analytic philosophy" is just the history of a strain of twentieth-century philosophy primarily in English-speaking countries that evolved from the writings and discussions of Russell, Moore, Frege, Wittgenstein, and others.

Language and Science

Frege's interest in the foundations of mathematics and the proper understanding of arithmetical terminology led Frege, and Russell after him, to reflect on broader questions about the nature of language and how language has meaning. Following the lead of Frege and Russell, many twentieth-century analytic philosophers were fascinated with questions of language—how words and sentences can have meaning, what it is for them to have meaning, and how they connect with the world. Many analytic philosophers indeed consider philosophy of language (which is concerned with such questions rather than with providing specific analyses of interesting or important propositions) to be more fundamental and important than metaphysics or epistemology. It is easy to understand why they might take this view. For example, according to the verifiability theory of meaning propounded by the logical positivists, an assertion purporting to be about reality can have meaning only if it is possible to verify it through observation. This theory led the positivists to reject metaphysical assertions as meaningless.

What is it for a word or phrase to have a meaning? If you had to answer this question, you would perhaps begin with the simplest kinds of words or phrases, words or phrases like the name "Mark Twain" or the naming phrase "the author of *Roughing It*" that simply designate things (in this case, a person). This was exactly the starting point of many philosophers of language, and a large literature was generated throughout the twentieth century on the problem of what it is for a name or naming phrase to have a meaning. A large literature was generated not only because such words and phrases are the simplest and most fundamental linguistic units but also because it wasn't clear what it is for such words and phrases to have a meaning. The starting point turned out to be located in rather deep water.

We cannot go into those matters here, but to give you an idea of only elementary difficulties, consider the apparently innocent question, What is the meaning of "Mark Twain"? The apparently obvious answer is that the meaning of "Mark Twain" is the person designated by that name, that is, Mark Twain. This answer will not do, of course: Mark Twain (the person) no longer exists, but "Mark Twain" (the name) still has a meaning. Further, since "Mark Twain" and "Samuel Clemens" designate the same person, according to the theory we are considering, the two names mean the same thing. Hence the theory we are considering absurdly entails that the sentence "Mark Twain was Samuel Clemens" means the same as the sentence "Mark Twain was Mark Twain." If what the theory entails is absurd, the theory itself must be defective.

It seems, therefore, that there is more to the meaning of a name than the thing it designates; but what more? Frege called this additional element the "sense" of the name, and he and Russell said that the sense of a name is given by a "definite description" associated with the name; in the case of "Mark Twain," this definite description might be "the American author who wrote *Tom Sawyer*." Russell then proposed a theory of how definite descriptions can have a reference—a theory that he once said was his most important contribution to philosophy. However, these are technical issues; suffice it to say that the question of how even such elementary linguistic items as names have meaning has not been resolved.

Another seemingly easy question—that also turns out to be quite difficult—is, What is it for a sentence to have a meaning? Take the sentence "Our cockatoo is in its cage"; apparently the sentence must in some way "represent" the fact that our cockatoo is in its cage. But what, then, should we make of a sentence like "Our cockatoo is not in the refrigerator"? Does that sentence represent the "negative" fact of *not* being in the refrigerator? What kind of fact is that? For that matter, what is it for a sentence to "represent" a fact in the first place? And, incidentally, what *are* facts? As we shall see in a moment, Wittgenstein believed that a sentence "pictures" a fact—a belief from which he derived an imposing metaphysical system.

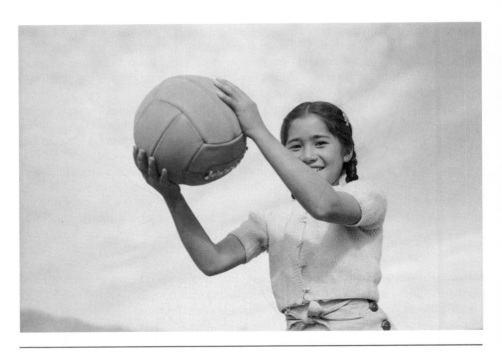

How many objects are in this picture? Two? Really? What about the girl's hair or the seams on the volleyball—are those objects? Analytic philosophy is useful to sort out confusions such as this.

Further, as pointed out earlier, for many expressions meaning seems fixed by how the expression is used more than by what the words in it refer to. A threat or a promise might clearly fall into this category, for example. Some writers, accordingly, have been much concerned with the "pragmatics," or social aspects and uses, of language. All in all, questions of language, meaning, and the connection between language and the world still remain among the most actively discussed in contemporary analytic philosophy.

Another subject of interest for many analytic philosophers has been science. Many of the issues in the philosophy of science were first raised by the philosophers of the Vienna Circle—the logical positivists—who included not only philosophers but scientists and mathematicians as well. What might philosophers think about when they think about science? They might wonder whether and in what sense "scientific entities" (such as genes, molecules, and quarks) are "real" or what relation they bear to sensory experience. They may inquire as to the nature of a scientific explanation, theory, or law and what distinguishes one from the other. Are scientific observations ever free from theoretical assumptions? they might inquire. They may wonder what it is that marks off science from other kinds of inquiry, including philosophy and religion (do they perhaps at some level all accept something "on faith"?)—and from pseudoscience. In a similar vein, they may wonder what kind of reasoning, if any, characterizes science. They may consider the extent to which the natural sciences (if not all the individual sciences) are "reducible" to physics.

An issue with which the logical positivists were concerned was the relation of statements about theoretical scientific entities such as neutrons and protons to statements that record our observations. After all, protons cannot be observed, and according to the verifiability criterion of meaning, a statement that cannot be verified by observations is meaningless. Thus, some of the positivists felt that statements about protons (for example) must be logically equivalent to statements about observations; if they were not, they, too, would have to be thrown out as meaningless gibberish along with metaphysical utterances. Unfortunately, this "translatability thesis" turned out to be doubtful, and the question of the precise relationship between theory and observation is still very much under discussion.

The positivists assumed, in any case, that statements that report observations are directly confirmed or disconfirmed by experience and, in this respect, are unlike theoretical statements. But later philosophers of science, such as, notably, N. R. Hanson, suggested that what one observes depends on the theoretical beliefs one holds, so the distinction between theory and observation is very weak, if it exists at all. Indeed, some theorists questioned whether there are theory-independent "facts" at all.

One philosopher of science, Thomas Kuhn (1922–1996), was especially concerned with scientific activity conceived not as the verification of theories but rather as the solving of puzzles presented within a given scientific "paradigm"—a scientific tradition or perspective like Newtonian mechanics or Ptolemaic astronomy or genetic theory. Because, in Kuhn's view, observations are imbued with theoretical assumptions, we cannot confirm one theoretical paradigm over some other theoretical paradigm simply by appeal to some common and neutral set of observational data; alternative paradigms are incommensurable. As you will see, there are affinities between this view and what is called *antirepresentationalism*, which we discuss later.

One other point deserves mention in this overview of analytic philosophy. It used to be that the history of philosophy was largely the history of the philosophies of specific individuals—Plato's philosophy, Aristotle's philosophy, Kant's philosophy, and so forth. But this changed after Russell, Moore, and Wittgenstein. Twentieth-century philosophy, especially perhaps philosophy in the analytic tradition, tends to be treated as a history of specific ideas, such as those mentioned in this chapter. Historians of twentieth-century philosophy often mention specific individuals only to give examples of people who subscribe to the idea at hand. It is the idea, rather than the philosopher, that is more important.

In addition, although the views of some specific "big-name" philosophers have been enormously influential within analytic philosophy, the course of analytic philosophy has been determined primarily by the journal articles published by the large rank and file of professional philosophers. These papers are undeniably technical, are directed at other professionals within the field, and usually deal with a fairly limited aspect of a larger problem. Articles and books that deal in wholesale fashion with large issues (e.g., What is the mind? Is there knowledge? What is the meaning of life? What is the ideal state? What is truth?) are comparatively rare. For this reason, and perhaps for others, the work of analytic philosophers strikes outsiders as narrow, theoretical, irrelevant, inaccessible, and tedious. The work of twentieth-century mathematicians is doubtlessly equally incomprehensible to laypersons, but the public's expectations are different for philosophers.

Experience, Language, and the World

Analytic epistemology and metaphysics are a maze of crossing paths, but they wind through two broad areas of concern. The first of these is the interrelationship of experience, language, and the world. The second broad concern is the nature of the mind. In this section we consider a specific metaphysical and epistemological theory that resulted from concern with experience, language, and the world.

Analytic philosophy's first major metaphysical theory, **logical atomism,** is associated primarily with Bertrand Russell and his student and colleague **Ludwig Wittgenstein** [VITT-ghen-shtine] (1889–1951). Russell connected to it an epistemological theory known as phenomenalism. Atomists (Russell, Wittgenstein, and others who subscribed to their views) believed that the world is not an all-encompassing Oneness, as Hegelians would have it, but a collection of "atomic facts." To say the world consists ultimately of *facts* is to say it does not consist only of *things* but rather *things having properties and standing in various relations to one another.* Your study area, for example, has a chair and a desk and a lamp and so on standing in a certain arrangement; their being in this arrangement is not a thing, it is a fact.

The most basic facts, atomists like Russell and Wittgenstein believed, are *atomic,* which means they are components of more complicated facts but are not themselves composed of simpler or more basic facts; and it means they are logically independent of every other fact. (*Logically independent* here means

PROFILE: Ludwig Wittgenstein (1889–1951)

So many discussions of Wittgenstein's philosophy were submitted to philosophy journals in the 1950s and 1960s that for a while some journals allegedly were reluctant to accept further manuscripts on his ideas. No other philosopher of the twentieth century had as great an impact on philosophy in Great Britain and the United States.

Wittgenstein was born in Vienna into a wealthy family and studied to become an engineer. From engineering, his interests led him to pure mathematics and then to the philosophical foundations of mathematics. He soon gave up engineering to study philosophy with Russell at Cambridge in 1912–1913. The following year he studied philosophy alone and in seclusion in Norway, partly because he perceived himself as irritating others by his nervous personality. During World War I he served in the Austrian army; it was in this period that he completed the first of his two major works, the *Tractatus Logico-Philosophicus* (1921), which sets forth logical atomism, explained in the text.

Wittgenstein's father had left Wittgenstein a large fortune, which after the war Wittgenstein simply handed over to two of his sisters, and he became an elementary school teacher. Next, in 1926, he became a gardener's assistant, perhaps a surprising walk of life for one of the most profound thinkers of all time. He did, however, return to Cambridge in 1929 and there received his doctorate, the *Tractatus* serving as his dissertation. In 1937 he succeeded G. E. Moore in his chair of philosophy.

During World War II Wittgenstein found himself unable to sit idly by, so he worked for two years as a hospital orderly and for another as an assistant in a medical lab. Time and again Wittgenstein, an heir to a great fortune and a genius, placed himself in the humblest of positions.

In 1944 Wittgenstein resumed his post at Cambridge, but, troubled by what he thought was his harmful effect on students and disturbed by their apparent poor comprehension of his ideas, he resigned in 1947. His second major work, the *Philosophical Investigations,* was published in 1953, two years after his death.

Reportedly, when he became seriously ill in April 1951 and was told by his physician that he was about to die, his response was simply, "Good." When he died a few days later, his last words were, "Tell them I've had a wonderful life."

that any basic or atomic fact could remain the same even if all other facts were different.)

Now, the atomists believed that profound metaphysical implications follow from the truism that we can form true propositions about the world, some of which are complexes of other, simpler, propositions. For a complex proposition must be resolvable into these simpler propositions. As an example, the proposition "The United States elected a Democrat as president" is resolvable, in principle, into propositions about individual people and their actions. But when people vote, they are really just doing certain things with their bodies. So a proposition about a person voting is resolvable, in principle, into propositions about these doings— about going into an enclosed booth, touching a screen or picking up a marking pen and marking a piece of paper, and so forth. Even a proposition such as "John Smith picked up a marking pen" is theoretically resolvable into propositions about John Smith's bodily motions and a piece of plastic that has certain properties; and indeed we are still quite far from reaching the end of this theoretical process of resolving complex propositions into more elementary ones.

Because complex propositions in principle must be resolvable into simpler propositions by analysis, theoretically there must be fundamental and absolutely uncomplex (i.e., simple) propositions that cannot be resolved further. Corresponding to these absolutely simple "atomic" propositions are the fundamental or atomic facts. (The precise nature of the "correspondence" between proposition and fact turned out to be a difficult matter. Wittgenstein thought the proposition *pictured* the fact.) Because every atomic fact is logically independent of every other, idealists were thought to be mistaken in believing that All is One. Further, because atomic facts are logically independent of one another, the propositions that corresponded to them are logically independent of one another.

Now, you may want an example or two of an atomic fact. Just what *is* a basic fact? Are these facts about minds or matter or neutrons or quarks or what? you will ask.

Well, the logical atomists, remember, were *logical* atomists, and this means that not all those who subscribed to logical atomism were concerned with what *actually are* the atomic facts. Some of them, most famously Wittgenstein, were concerned with setting forth what logically must be the basic structure of reality and left it to others to determine the actual content of the universe. Determining the logical structure of reality was enough, no little task in its own right, they thought.

As for Russell, he was always somewhat less concerned about what *actually* exists than with what we must *suppose* exists. For all he knew, he said, all the gods of Olympus exist. But the essential point is that we have no reason whatsoever to suppose that this is so.

As for what we must suppose exists, Russell changed his mind over the course of his long life. But generally he believed that the bare minimum that must be supposed to exist does *not* include many of the things that "common sense" is inclined to say exist, such as physical objects and atoms and subatomic particles. Russell's view was that what we say and think and believe about such things as these—let's call them the objects of common sense and science—can in theory be expressed in propositions that refer only to *awarenesses,* or **sense-data.** His position was that philosophically we do not have to believe in the existence of chairs or rocks or planets or atoms, say, as a type of entity that in some sense is more than just sense-data. Here, on one hand, he said in effect, are "data" actually given to us in sensation; there, on the other, are the external objects we strongly believe are out there and that science tells us so much about. How do we get from knowledge of our sense-data to knowledge of the objects? What we truly *know,* Russell said, are the data of immediate experience, our sense-data. Therefore, he said, what we *believe* exists (physical objects and scientific entities like atoms and electrons) must be definable in terms of sense-data if our belief in physical objects and scientific entities is to be philosophically secure. The affinities of this view with those of the logical positivists discussed earlier will be clear.

This idea—that physical and scientific objects are "definable" in terms of sense-data, or, more precisely, the idea that propositions about such objects in theory are expressible in propositions that refer only to sense-data—is known as **phenomenalism.** During the first forty or so years of the twentieth century, phenomenalism seemed plausible to many analytic philosophers as a way of certifying our supposed knowledge of external objects. But today few philosophers are phenomenalists. There was strong adverse criticism of the theory around the middle of the twentieth century for a number of reasons. First, it became generally accepted that there is no set of sense-data the having of which logically entails that you are experiencing any given physical object. Second, it was unclear that physical-object propositions that mention specific times and places could find their equivalents in propositions that refer only to sense-data. And finally, it was thought that phenomenalists had to believe in the possibility of what is called a **private language,** and the idea of whether such a language is coherent was questioned (see the box "What I Mean by '*Blue*'").

Now, consider the history of epistemology and metaphysics from Descartes onward. One way of characterizing this history is that it has been an extended search for metaphysical truth derived from *incorrigible foundations of knowledge.*

What I Mean by "*Blue*"

"What I mean by *blue* might be entirely different from what you mean by *blue,* and you and I cannot really understand each other."

Possibly most people find plausible the idea that one person does not know what another person means by a given word. They may tend to believe that a word stands for an idea that is the meaning of the word. And therefore, they think, because a word's meaning is locked up in the mind, what each of us means by our words is private to each of us.

In *Philosophical Investigations* (published in 1953 and regarded by many analytic philosophers as the most important philosophical work of the twentieth century), Ludwig Wittgenstein presented (around section 256) a somewhat sketchy series of reflections against the possibility of having a private language, a language that can be understood only by oneself.

The meanings of words lie not inside the mind, Wittgenstein suggested, but in their uses, and these uses are governed by rules. Because the rules are not our own private rules, other people can check the correctness of our usage of a given word. We do not and could not possibly have private languages, for in such "languages" the correctness of our usage of words is not subject to a public check. One's "words" would just be sounds that one could use as he or she pleased.

John Locke–type empiricism and its derivatives such as phenomenalism seem to presuppose we all speak private languages whose terms stand for ideas in the mind. The Wittgenstein argument seems to show that thesis is untenable.

(An *incorrigible* proposition is one that is incapable of being false if you believe it is true.) For that matter, philosophers from before Socrates to the present have searched incessantly for these incorrigible foundations. They have looked everywhere for an unshakable bedrock on which the entire structure of knowledge, especially metaphysical knowledge, might be built. Augustine found the bedrock in revealed truth. Descartes thought he had found it in the certainty of his own existence. Empiricists believed the foundational bedrock of knowledge must somehow or other lie in immediate sensory experience. Kant found the foundation in principles supplied by the mind in the very act of experiencing the world.

But must a belief really rest on *incorrigible* foundations if it is to qualify as knowledge? More fundamentally, must it even rest on *foundations?* In the later part of the twentieth century philosophers questioned whether knowledge requires foundations at all. They questioned the assumption on which much traditional epistemology rested.

Foundationalism holds that a belief qualifies as knowledge only if it logically follows from propositions that are incorrigible (incapable of being false if you believe they are true). For example, take my belief that this before me is a quarter. According to a foundationalist from the empiricist tradition, I *know* that this before me is a quarter only if my belief that it is absolutely follows from the propositions that describe my present sense-data, because these propositions alone are incorrigible. But, the antifoundationalist argues, why not say that my belief that there is a quarter before me *automatically* qualifies as knowledge, unless there is some definite and special reason to think that it is mistaken?

The question of whether knowledge requires foundations is still under wide discussion among epistemologists. It is too early to predict the results of the discussion.

Many of those who attack the foundationalist position have been inclined, more recently, to endorse what is called **naturalized epistemology.** This is the view that traditional epistemological inquiries should be replaced by psychological inquiries into the processes actually involved in the acquisition and revision of beliefs. This view, which in its strongest form amounts to saying that epistemology should be phased out in favor of psychology, is controversial. Nevertheless, recent writing in epistemology has reflected a deep interest in developments in psychology.

Antirepresentationalism

In the first half of the twentieth century, many philosophers (within the analytic tradition, at any rate) *assumed* that the natural sciences give us (or will eventually give us) the correct account of reality. They assumed, in other words, that natural science—and the commonsense beliefs that incorporate science—is the true metaphysics. The task for philosophy, it was thought, was to *certify* scientific knowledge epistemologically. This was to be done, it was supposed, by "reducing" the propositions of science—propositions about physical objects and their atomic constituents—to propositions that refer to sense-data, that is, by analyzing the propositions of science in the language of sensory experience. Eventually, though, as we have seen, philosophers doubted that this grand reduction could be carried out even in principle, and likewise many questioned the idea that knowledge requires foundations anyway.

In epistemology, as we saw, a leading alternative to foundationalism, naturalized epistemology (the scientific study of the processes involved in having knowledge) won adherents. In metaphysics, during the latter part of the twentieth century, an alternative to the view that physical objects are constructs of sense-data became widely held. According to this alternative to phenomenalism, physical objects are **theoretical posits,** entities whose existence we in effect hypothesize to explain our sensory experience. This nonreductionist view of physical objects as posited entities is also, like naturalized epistemology, associated with the work of W. V. O. Quine.

From a commonsense and scientific standpoint, physical objects are independent of the perceiving and knowing mind, independent in the sense that they are what they are regardless of what the mind thinks about them. The thesis that reality consists of such independent objects is known as **realism.** From a realist perspective, there are two epistemological possibilities: (1) we can know this independent reality; (2) we cannot know it: what is actually true may be different from what is thought to be true. The second view is skepticism, and phenomenalism was thought to be the answer to skepticism. But even if true, phenomenalism would refute skepticism only by denying realism; it would refute skepticism, that is to say, only by denying that objects are independent of the mind, or at least independent of our sense-data. The Quinean view of objects as theoretical posits is consistent with realism; however, it is also consistent with skepticism because (the skeptic would say) theoretical posits may not exist in fact.

Now, it would seem that either objects exist outside the mind or they are some sort of constructs of the mind: it would seem that either realism is true or some form of idealism is true. But there is another possibility, according to some philosophers. To understand this third possibility, let's just consider what underlies the realist's conception. What underlies it is the idea that the mind, when it is thinking correctly about the world outside the mind, accurately conceives of this world. Alternatively put, what underlies realism is the idea that true beliefs accurately portray or *represent* reality: what makes them true is the states of affairs to which they "correspond" or that they "mirror" or "depict" or "portray." This view—that beliefs about reality represent reality (either correctly, if they are true, or incorrectly, if they are false)—is called **representationalism.** From the representationalist point of view, a belief counts as knowledge only if it is a true belief, and a belief is true only if it is an accurate representation of the state of affairs that it is about. Representationalism underlay Russell's philosophy, and the *magnum opus* of representationalism was Wittgenstein's *Tractatus Logico-Philosophicus,* commented upon in an earlier box.

But it is possible to question the whole premise of representationalism, and that is exactly what several contemporary philosophers, including, most famously, Richard Rorty, whom we discussed earlier in this chapter, have done. **Antirepresentationalism** takes several forms, but basically it denies that mind or language contains, or is a representation of, reality. According to the "old" picture, the representationalist picture, there is, on one hand, the mind and its beliefs and, on the other, the world or "reality"; and if our beliefs represent reality *as it really is*—that is, as it is "in itself" independent of any perspective or point of view—the beliefs are true. Antirepresentationalists, by contrast, dismiss this picture as unintelligible. They find no significance in the notion that beliefs represent reality (or in the notion that they fail to represent reality, if they are false beliefs); and they find no sense in the idea of the world "as it really is"—that is, as it is independent of this or that perspective or viewpoint. According to antirepresentationalists, truth is not a matter of a belief's corresponding to or accurately representing the "actual" state of affairs that obtains outside the mind. When we describe a belief as true, they hold, we are simply praising that belief as having been proven relative to our standards of rationality. And when we say that some belief is "absolutely true," we just mean that its acceptance is so fully justified, given our standards, that we cannot presently imagine how any further justification could even be possible.

This conception of truth seems to imply that different and perhaps even apparently conflicting beliefs could equally well be true—as long as they are fully justified relative to alternative standards of rationality. Perhaps you, by contrast, would maintain that, although two conflicting beliefs could be *thought* to be true, they could not actually both *be* true. But if you hold this, then it may be because you are a representationalist and think that truth is a matter of a belief's correctly representing reality—reality as it is in itself, independent of any person's or society's perspective. But antirepresentationalists do not understand, or profess not to understand, what this business about a belief's correctly representing the world "as it really is" comes to. They say that nobody can climb outside his or her own perspective, and they say that this talk about the world "as it really is independent of perspective or viewpoint" is just mumbo-jumbo. Antirepresentationalist themes have entered into analytic philosophy through Quine, Hilary Putnam, and other contemporary American analytic philosophers.

Wittgenstein's Turnaround

It is appropriate now to say more about Ludwig Wittgenstein, whom many consider to be the most important analytic philosopher of the twentieth century. Wittgenstein's philosophy divides into two phases. Both had a great influence on his contemporaries, yet the philosophy of the second phase, that of the *Philosophical Investigations* (1953), was largely a rejection of the central ideas of the first, that of the *Tractatus* (1921). This is an unusual but not a unique occurrence in the history of philosophy, for other philosophers have come to reject their earlier positions as well.

In both works, Wittgenstein was concerned with the relationships between language and the world. The *Tractatus* assumes a single, essential relationship; the *Investigations* denies this assumption. In the *Tractatus*, Wittgenstein portrays the function of language as that of describing the world and is concerned with making it clear just how language and thought hook onto reality in the first place.

Well, just how does language hook onto reality? According to Wittgenstein, as we have seen, a proposition (or a thought) *pictures* the fact it represents. It can picture it, he said, because both it and the fact share the same *logical form,* a form that can be exhibited by philosophical analysis. All genuine propositions, he held, are reducible to logically elementary propositions, which, he said, are composed of *names* of absolutely simple objects. A combination of these names (i.e., a proposition) pictures a combination of objects in the world (i.e., a fact). The *Tractatus* is devoted in large measure to explaining and working out the implications of this *picture theory of meaning* across a range of philosophical topics. The result is logical atomism, as explained earlier.

But in the *Investigations,* Wittgenstein cast off completely this picture theory of meaning and the underlying assumption of the *Tractatus* that there is some universal function of language. After all, he noted in the later work, how a picture is *used* determines what it is a picture of—one and the same picture could be a picture of a man holding a guitar, or of how to hold a guitar, or of what a guitar looks like, or of what Bill Jones's fingers look like, and so on. Similarly, what a sentence means is determined by the use to which it is put within a given context or **language game.** Further, said the later Wittgenstein, there is nothing that the various uses of language have in common, and there is certainly no set of ideal elementary propositions to which all other propositions are reducible. In short, according to the later work, the earlier work is completely wrongheaded.

When philosophers ignore the "game" in which language is used, Wittgenstein wrote in the *Investigations*—when they take language "on a holiday" and try to straitjacket it into conformity with some idealized and preconceived notion of what its essence must be—the result is the unnecessary confusion known as a philosophical problem. From this perspective, the history of philosophy is a catalogue of confusions that result from taking language on a holiday.

No better illustration of how taking language on a holiday leads to strange results can perhaps be found than the paradox that lies at the end of Wittgenstein's

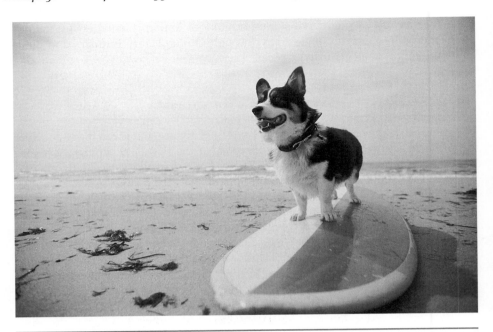

At first Wittgenstein believed that a proposition like "the dog is on the surfboard" pictures a fact much as the photograph pictures that fact. Later he repudiated the "picture theory of meaning."

earlier work, *Tractatus Logico-Philosophicus*. In that work, Wittgenstein had been held captive by a theory of how language links itself to the world, and his discussion of how language links itself to the world was expressed in language. This placed Wittgenstein in the paradoxical situation of having used language to represent how language represents the world. And this, he concluded, could not be done—despite the fact that he had just done it. Language, he said, may be used to represent the world but cannot be used to represent how language represents the world. "What expresses itself in language, we cannot express by means of language."

Thus, Wittgenstein concluded the *Tractatus* with an outrageous paradox: "My propositions serve as elucidations in the following way," he wrote. "Anyone who understands me eventually recognizes them as nonsensical; when he has used them—as steps—to climb up beyond them. (He must, so to speak, throw away the ladder after he has climbed up it.)" The later Wittgenstein just threw away the entire *Tractatus*.

QUINE, DAVIDSON, AND KRIPKE

Outside philosophy departments, **Willard Van Orman Quine** (1908–2000), his student **Donald Davidson** (1917–2003), and **Saul Kripke** (1940–) are not well known. But the three are among the most important recent American philosophers; one doesn't study philosophy at the graduate level in this country without becoming familiar with their work. All made important independent contributions to logic, metaphysics, and the philosophy of language.

Willard Van Orman Quine

Quine's work in logic is rather technical for introductory general texts, but we really must say something about Quine's contributions to philosophy of language. His most famous writings in this arena were the essay "Two Dogmas of Empiricism" (1951) and the book *Word and Object* (1960).

In "Two Dogmas of Empiricism," Quine carefully scrutinized two empiricist ideas: (1) the "analytic/synthetic distinction" and (2) "reductionism."

By **reductionism,** Quine meant the view that *every meaningful statement "reduces" to the experiences that would confirm or disconfirm it*. If you have read Chapter 7, you are familiar with this idea; it is indeed the guiding principle of empiricism. John Locke, remember, held that every idea originates in sense experience; and early twentieth-century empiricist philosophers subscribed to the **translatability thesis,** according to which statements about the world can (in theory) be "translated" into statements about immediate sensory experience. Now, Quine's contrary view was that it is a mistake to suppose that statements *taken in isolation* can be confirmed or disconfirmed. "Our statements about the external world," he wrote, "face the tribunal of sense experience not individually but only as a corporate body." What this means will become clearer shortly.

The second empiricist idea rejected by Quine as a dogma is the idea that *there is a clear boundary between "synthetic" statements and "analytic" statements*. This needs explaining.

For Quine, a true **synthetic** statement is one that holds "contingently," and a true **analytic** statement is one that holds "come what may." For example, take the true synthetic statement, "Barack Obama is married." This is true, but it might have been false. Its truth is contingent, or dependent, on the way the world actually is. By contrast, take the analytic statement, "If Barack Obama is married, he has a spouse." This statement (one would say) must be true. It holds come what may.

But remember that (according to Quine) it doesn't make sense to talk about the confirmation or disconfirmation of *individual* statements. Since (according to Quine) a person's knowledge is an *interlocking system* of beliefs, "no statement is immune to revision" (that's another way of saying that no statement is true come what may) if you are willing to make adjustments elsewhere in your interlocking system of beliefs. For example, you could claim that the earth isn't round if you are willing to subscribe to the view that the evidence that it is round is hallucinatory. You could believe that 2 + 2 is not 4 if you are willing to "make adjustments" in the principles of arithmetic. You could believe that married individuals don't have spouses if you are willing to believe you have been programmed with false memories about what "married" and "spouse" mean.

But this raises the question, Which interlocking system of beliefs, or *ontology*,[1] is the correct one? Quine held that ontologies are neither "correct" nor "incorrect" in any absolute sense. According to him, the scientifically minded person will accept and reject beliefs purely on practical or "pragmatic" grounds. So it isn't

---

[1] Ontology is the branch of metaphysics that seeks to ascertain the most basic categories and entities. For example, many these days think that the most basic entities are things like quarks or strings and the electromagnetic force and so forth. These categories are a part of the "ontology" of physics.

that the physics ontology (quarks, atoms, electromagnetism, and so forth) is "truer" than the Greek-gods ontology; it's just that the former ontology has proved considerably more practical. When it comes to predicting future experience, you get a better result if you believe in quarks and atoms and the laws of physics.

In later essays, including his most famous book, *Word and Object,* Quine went even further. In that book, he held that, not only is it a mistake to regard an ontology as "correct" in any absolute sense, there is no "fact of the matter" as to what objects it even refers to. He thought that any theory, indeed, any language, is subject to **indeterminacy of translation,** meaning (roughly) that alternative incompatible translations are equally compatible with the linguistic behavior of adherents or speakers. He wrote, as well, of the **inscrutability of reference,** meaning (again roughly) that incompatible alternative conceptions of what objects a theory refers to are equally compatible with the totality of physical facts. Quine thus said that he subscribed to "ontological relativity."[2]

Donald Davidson

Davidson is especially well known for having devised a theory of meaning for natural language based on developments in formal logic. Without going into details, which are technical, Davidson wished to develop a theory of meaning for natural languages. (A "natural language" is one that arises naturally for human communication purposes, such as English or Signed English. Formal languages, by contrast, include such things as computer programming languages and symbolic logic.) A theory of meaning for a language, for Davidson, would specify the meaning of every sentence in the language and would account for the fact that, from a finite vocabulary of words, users of the language could understand an infinite number of sentences. Prior to Davidson, the important Polish logician Alfred Tarski had developed a theory of truth for formal languages. Again without going into details, Davidson argued that a Tarskian theory of truth for a formal language could serve as a theory of meaning for a natural language. He thus bridged a gap between developments in formal logic and the concern of philosophers with meaning within natural languages.

At the end of this chapter, we present an excerpt from a nontechnical paper written by Davidson. Descartes, you will recall, tried to discover what follows from the fact that one can't doubt that one thinks. In this paper, Davidson raises the interesting question of how there could even be such a thing as thinking.

Saul Kripke

Kripke made important contributions to logic, but his best-known work is the book *Naming and Necessity* (1972, 1980), a work in the philosophy of language. This little book is really just a transcript of three talks Kripke gave (without notes) at Princeton University. In it, Kripke criticized descriptivism, a theory philosophers

---

[2] In 1968 Quine presented two lectures titled "Ontological Relativity" at Columbia University.

associate with Frege, Russell, and even more recent writers. According to descriptivism, the meaning (or reference) of a proper name is connected to a *description* of the thing. Thus, for example, "Shakespeare" is connected to a description like "the man who wrote Hamlet." Now, Kripke held that a proper name like "Shakespeare" is a *rigid designator,* which designates the same entity in all possible worlds in which the name has a reference. But a description like "the man who wrote Hamlet," he maintained, *isn't* rigid and can designate *different* things in different possible worlds. Therefore, since Shakespeare couldn't have not been Shakespeare, but since Shakespeare might not have written Hamlet or done any of the many things by which he (Shakespeare) is described, "Shakespeare" is not synonymous with descriptions of Shakespeare.

Kripke criticized a subtler version of descriptivism, according to which a description, while not giving a synonym for a name, still determines the name's reference. We won't go into this, however.

Now, according to Kripke, something becomes a name in a given language when somebody names a specific object, for example, when your parents named you Susan Popoffski or whatever. Future uses of "Susan Popoffski," if connected to your original naming by causal chains of designation running through a community of speakers, designate you as well. For example, your parents taught you your name, you met other people and told them your name, you grew up and became famous, and still others learned your name and taught it to still others, and so on. Uses of your name by those in this chain are linked to each other causally; this is referred to as the causal theory of reference, Kripke's alternative to descriptivism.

Who cares? Kripke's refutation of descriptivism was important in the philosophical discussions about the meaning and reference of proper names that had been going on for decades. It was also important because it contradicted the widely held belief of philosophers that *necessary* truths are all *a priori* truths. We'll briefly explain these concepts.

A *necessary truth* is a statement that could not possibly be false—a statement true in all possible worlds. A necessary truth is the opposite of a *contingent truth,* a statement that is true but could have been false—like "Barack Obama is married." An *a priori truth,* on the other hand, is a statement known to be true independently of any experience, like "Squares have four sides." Its opposite is an *a posteriori truth,* a statement that is known to be true through experience. So on the one hand we have the **necessary/contingent** pair, and on the other we have the **a priori/a posteriori** pair. Prior to Kripke, many philosophers ran these two distinctions together by holding that necessary truths are all true a priori and that contingent truths are all true a posteriori. Kripke dissented from this view.

A simple example will explain his thinking, which is very interesting regardless of its place in the history of philosophy. Suppose one and the same thing has two different names, "x" and "y"; and suppose that at first you don't happen to know that "x" and "y" are two distinct names for the very same thing. For example, in the evening you might think you were looking at star x in the eastern sky, and just before dawn you might think you were looking at a different star, star y, in the western sky. Suppose you then discover that "x" and "y" designate the same object. (In fact, supposedly people once thought Hesperus and Phosphorus were the names of two different celestial objects; later, it turned out these were just different names for the same thing, namely, the planet Venus.) Since the names "x" and "y" are rigid designators, when you learned that "x and y are the very same thing," your discovery would count as an a posteriori discovery of a necessary truth. Which means that "necessary" doesn't always accompany "a priori."

An important connected metaphysical topic discussed by Kripke is essentialism, the idea that things have essential properties, properties they cannot not have. Kripke thought that essentialism could be maintained only by distinguishing between a priori truths and necessary truths, as he had done. For example, an essential property of this table is that it is made out of wood. Therefore, it could not possibly have been made out of ice. If it had been made out of ice, it would not be this table, but some other thing. Thus, the statement that this table, if it exists at all, is not made out of ice, is a necessary truth. But it is *not* an a priori truth, because it requires experience to find out that it is made out of wood.

This has repercussions for the mind/body problem, which Kripke addressed as well. Philosophers who subscribed to identity theory, according to which each mind state is identical to some brain state, typically said that the identity is contingent. But according to Kripke, the name of a mental state (e.g., "depression") and the name of a brain process (e.g., "brain activity X") designate things with different essential properties. This means that what they name cannot be equated in the first place.

The identity theorist's reasons for saying that mind state/brain state identity is contingent, Kripke argued, are reasons for saying that they are not identical in the first place.

This all is perhaps somewhat technical, but *Naming and Necessity* is fairly easy to read, and is philosophically very important. "In the philosophy of language," Scott Soames wrote, "*Naming and Necessity* is among the most important works ever. . . . Beyond the philosophy of language, it fundamentally changed the way in which much philosophy is done."[3]

ONTOLOGY

Metaphysics, as you know if you read our first chapter, is the philosophical study of the nature and fundamental features of being. Within analytic philosophy, **ontology** is a branch of metaphysics—the one concerned with what there is. Do physical objects exist? Do facts? Atomic facts? We have touched upon these questions of ontology.

Ontologists also traditionally have been interested in whether and in what sense such things as numbers, sets, points, instants, properties, relations, kinds, propositions, and meanings exist—and here we should add that the pressing question is whether they exist independently of the mind or thought.

---

[3] Soames is the author of (among other things) *Analytical Philosophy: Philosophical Analysis in the Twentieth Century,* currently the definitive comprehensive critical exposition of analytic philosophy.

By the middle of the twentieth century, many analytic philosophers believed that questions about what sorts of things exist were best left up to scientists. The most a metaphysician could do, they held, is to disclose (via philosophical analysis) the ontology presupposed by science or mathematics or psychology or common sense. P. F. Strawson (1919–2006), Michael Dummett (b. 1925), and others cast the task in Kant-like terms, assigning to metaphysics the task of revealing the fundamental "structure" of thought about the world. In *Individuals: An Essay in Descriptive Metaphysics* (1959), Strawson derived what he believed were the basic concepts required by all experience. He held, for example, that all experience requires recognition of reidentifiable particulars as falling under general concepts. His approach in *Individuals* was to try to show that "experience" that did not involve this was unimaginable. As to whether there actually is something out there independent of the mind corresponding to general words or to the names of reidentifiable particulars, Strawson declined to speculate.

But metaphysical theorizing about what exists independent of thought is seductive and difficult to stifle. There seem to be genuine questions of ontology that science simply does not touch. It's not surprising, therefore, that recently there has been an increase in metaphysical discussion of the old-fashioned pre-Kantian variety, in which claims are made as to the actual outside-the-mind ontological status of certain philosophically interesting entities. Here is a list of some of the entities currently subject to ontological debate:

- Selves

- Causal relations and physical laws

- Universals (A universal word is a general word, like *tree* or *round,* that applies to more than one particular thing.)

- Bare particulars (Every particular has properties. But what, exactly, is it that has the properties? A bare particular is a particular thing considered apart from whatever properties it exhibits.)

- Necessity, contingency, impossibility, and possible worlds (The concept of a "possible world" is used to explain possibility, necessity, and contingency.)

- Vagueness (Is vagueness merely a feature of language, or is it also a feature of the actual world? The question turns out to be enormously difficult.)

- Social constructions (A social construction is an artifact of a culture's customs, conventions, mores, and laws; it is not created by nature. "Housewife" and "graduate student," for example, denote social constructions, rather than biological categories. Other categories are more controversial philosophically: are the categories "male," "female," and "transsexual" social constructions? Could it be that *every* category is a social construction? Could it be that *reality* is a social construction?)

- Mereological sums and constituted objects (The **mereological sum** of two or more particulars is the whole consisting of the particulars. Bruder's Ford is a mereological sum of a group of atoms. His Ford also is constituted of automotive parts. It also is made out of steel. What is the relationship between the Ford and these various constituents and parts?)

Meta-Ontology

Not merely are the ontological status of universals and so forth the subjects of philosophical debate. Ontology itself is currently subject to discussion: Can ontological investigation disclose objective truth?

According to **ontological realism** it can; according to **ontological anti-realism** it cannot. Anti-realists include "descriptive metaphysicians" like Strawson, who in effect constrain metaphysics to conceptual exploration. Anti-realists also include those who dismiss metaphysical issues as mostly trivial questions of semantics. There is no consensus as to who is correct.

PHILOSOPHICAL QUESTIONS IN QUANTUM MECHANICS[4]

Quantum mechanics is one of the most successful scientific theories ever produced. It makes numerous bold, precise predictions that have repeatedly been confirmed by experiment. It explains a diverse range of phenomena such as the blueness of the sky, radioactivity, and the structure of the atom. Moreover, it has directly led to the development of a great number of technological marvels: silicon chips, lasers, and MRIs would have never been invented without quantum mechanics. Along with Einstein's theory of relativity, quantum theory forms the foundation of modern physics. But quantum mechanics is not only one of the most successful scientific theories, it is also one of the *weirdest*. It is so weird, and conflicts so much with our commonsense picture of the world and the *classical* physics that preceded it, that the dominant attitude of physicists toward quantum mechanics may be described as "shut up and calculate."[5] In other words, many physicists ignore questions about what quantum mechanics says about the world and focus on solving the equations that allow them to make such accurate predictions and that allow engineers to produce smartphones, dvd players, etc. But philosophers are interested in precisely the question about what quantum mechanics says about the world, especially when it disagrees with the everyday ideas we adopt unreflectively. In this section, we will discuss some of these philosophical questions about quantum mechanics and some of the answers that have been proposed for them.

---

[4] By Zanja Yudell.

[5] Possibly due to David Mermin (http://physicstoday.org/journals/doc/PHTOAD-ft/vol_57/iss_5/10_1.shtml?bypassSSO=1). Note that not all physicists take this attitude to quantum mechanics.

There are so many weird things about quantum mechanics, and so many interesting philosophical questions about it, that we won't possibly be able to consider all of them in this short section. Instead, we will focus on some of the features of quantum mechanics that have come to seem most significant to both philosophers and others who have thought seriously about quantum mechanics.

There is one feature of quantum mechanics in particular that accounts for most of the profound philosophical difficulties associated with the theory. To illustrate this idea, consider a simple system consisting of two boxes and one particle. If we know that there is one particle in the boxes somewhere, we normally think that there are two distinct possiblities: either the particle is in the first box, or it is in the second box. We can call each of these possibilities *states* of the system. So the normal idea is that there are two possible states that this system can take, which we can call Particle in Box 1 and Particle in Box 2. In quantum mechanics, this would be written as "|Particle in Box 1>" and "|Particle in Box 2>." From this point one, we shall follow this notation system as well.

But quantum mechanics says something peculiar about this simple system. If it's possible for it to be in these two states, quantum mechanics also allows it to be in an infinity of other distinct states that are "combinations" of these two states. For example, there's a state that we might want to describe as the particle being 50% |Particle in Box 1> and 50% |Particle in Box 2>.[6] But there's also a state that is 75% |Particle in Box 1> and 25% |Particle in Box 2>, and 10% |Particle in Box 1> and 90% |Particle in Box 2>, etc., for any combination you can think of. Each of these combinations of the two original states is called a **superposition.** The description of superpositions as "combinations" of states is just a loose way of talking about an idea which is very rigorous and clear mathematically, but we will focus on what it means for a system to be in a superposition.

So what does it mean for the system to be in one of these superpositions? That question is one of the most controversial questions about quantum mechanics. Consider the first superposition, which is 50% |Particle in Box 1> and 50% |Particle in Box 2>. One thought is that in such a state there are two particles, one in Box 1 and one in Box 2, with each particle "grayed out" like Marty McFly in *Back to the Future.* Perhaps a system in the state 10% |Particle in Box 1> and 90% |Particle in Box 2> has a much "fainter" particle in Box 1 and the particle in Box 2 is nearly "solid." But this is a misleading way of thinking about the situation: there is only one particle. Indeed, if you were to open up the boxes and look, you would only ever find one particle, either in Box 1 or in Box 2. You would never see the superposition.

So quantum mechanics describes superpositions that are hard to understand and that are never observed when we observe, or *measure*, the system. Making sense of what superpositions are and why they seem to disappear when we make measurements is perhaps the most vexing issue in the philosophy of quantum mechanics and has come to be known as the **measurement problem.**

---

[6] There are actually two such states, although it would be too complicated to get into the difference between these two states.

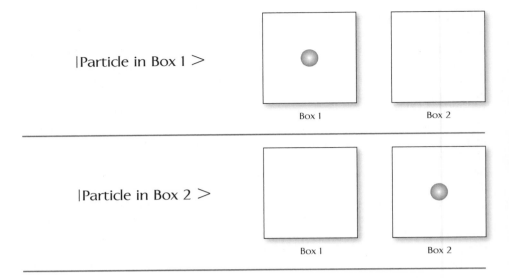

|Particle in Box 1 >

Box 1   Box 2

|Particle in Box 2 >

Box 1   Box 2

By the way, you might wonder why physicists would bother postulating superpositions if they never see them and they cause so much trouble. The short answer, which is all we have room for here, is that they are a necessary feature of the mathematics of quantum mechanics for it to reproduce the empirical results of many, many experiments. You could solve the measurement problem easily by getting rid of superpositions, but then you'd have an **accuracy problem**, since the theory wouldn't make very accurate predictions.

The responses to the measurement problem are called interpretations of quantum mechanics. There are many such interpretations, and they are all weird in various ways. The standard or orthodox interpretation is often called the **Copenhagen interpretation,**[7] and is most commonly accepted by physicists themselves. According to the Copenhagen interpretation, when a system is in the state 50% |Particle in Box 1> and 50% |Particle in Box 2>, there is simply no fact about whether the particle is in Box 1 or in Box 2—it's meaningless to ask which box it's in. However, when someone decides to measure the system by opening up one of the boxes and looking, then the system "chooses" to be in either the state |Particle in Box 1> or the state |Particle in Box 2>. When the system chooses one of the two states, it is said to *collapse* into that state. How the system chooses is a mysterious process governed only by a probabilistic rule. In this case, there is a 50% chance that the particle will be found in Box 1, and a 50% chance that it will be found in Box 2. That means that if you set up a bunch of systems in the original superposition and then opened up the boxes to measure the systems, about half of the time you would find the particle in Box 1 and about half the time you would find the particle in Box 2. If you started with a different superposition, say 10% |Particle in Box 1> and 90% |Particle in Box 2>, then there would be only a

---

[7] There is in fact no single Copenhagen interpretation, but the view described in the text describes what is commonly called the Copenhagen interpretation.

10% chance of finding the particle in Box 1, and a 90% chance of finding the particle in Box 2.

Now, the funny thing about the Copenhagen interpretation is that it attributes a kind of causal power to the act of measurement. When you measure a system and thereby collapse it into one of the two states, you have changed its physical state, just like igniting a stick of dynamite changes its physical state, and this change has real consequences for the future behavior of the system. So it is natural to wonder what exactly a measurement is and what makes it so special that it has this power to have such a significant influence on the world. Many physicists are happy to use Justice Stewart's test for obscenity ("I know it when I see it") to determine what a measurement is, but this standard still leaves it mysterious how such a vaguely described and apparently nonphysical process could have influence on the state of reality. One approach, associated with the physicists John von Neumann and Eugene Wigner, is to embrace the idea that there is something about the very nature of the observer that causes a quantum system to collapse. On this approach, our consciousness, often imagined as a nonphysical substance, has a kind of special power reserved to it that merely physical things like electrons and protons do not. Some have thus taken quantum mechanics to be evidence for mind-body *dualism*, although there are other interpretations of quantum mechanics in which conciousness plays no role in producing collapse. In some popular descriptions of this view, found for example in the movie *What the Bleep Do We Know!?*, conscious observers have the power to directly influence reality and shape it to their will. But this idea is a blatant misunderstanding of quantum mechanics. While it is true on the Copenhagen interpretation that your actions can influence reality, they do it in a fundamentally probabilistic way. You can choose whether or not to look in the boxes, and that will make a difference as to whether the system collapses, but you can't choose to make the particle appear in Box 1.

This fact that probability is a fundamental feature of reality is another notable feature of the Copenhagen interpretation. Prior to the development of quantum mechanics, classical physics had treated probability as an essentially *epistemic* notion (An "epistemic" notion is one that refers to epistemology). It was thought that the fact that a coin flip had a 50% chance of turning up heads merely reflected our ignorance about what was actually a determinate fact—even if we don't know whether the coin will land heads or tails, a powerful enough computer armed with the laws of physics and all the facts about the coin before the flip could predict exactly what would happen. On this classical view, everything that happens in the world is **deterministic**, that is it is completely determined by what went before. But quantum mechanics, as understood by the Copenhagen interpretation, makes the world *indeterministic*. In other words, prior to the flip, there is no fact about whether the coin will land heads or tails. It's completely a matter of chance. This feature of quantum mechanics is a dramatic departure from classical physics, and is the source of Einstein's criticism that "God doesn't play dice with the world." Although indeterminacy was and remains a shocking idea to some, it has also seemed to some philosophers to provide the hope of restoring the possibility of free will. If all physical events are ultimately indeterministic and my actions are physical events, then perhaps my actions can be said to be free and I can be ultimately responsible for my actions.

Unfortunately, it's not as cut and dried as that. Some might say that a random event does not seem any more free than a determined one. If I'm deciding whether to lie or tell the truth and an electron in my brain randomly collapses in a way that leads to my telling the truth, it does not seem as if I am any more responsible for that decision than if the state of my brain had deterministically led to the same result. The debate on this issue is far from settled, but it is clear that quantum indeterminacy does not automatically solve the problem.

Einstein's opposition to quantum indeterminacy is well known, but his most profound challenge to quantum mechanics was his claim that the theory is incomplete. Einstein and his collaborators Boris Podolsky and Nathan Rosen proposed a thought experiment, now known as EPR, that was meant to demonstrate that there must be some physics that quantum mechanics fails to represent. That thought experiment has instead led to a deep insight about quantum mechanics and the world we live in. In one version of the EPR thought experiment, two particles travel in opposite directions from a common source, one going to the left and one going to the right. Once they have traveled a great distance, the lefthand particle enters a device that either puts it in Box 1 or Box 2, and the righthand particle enters a similar device that puts it in Box 3 or Box 4. According to quantum mechanics, the particles can be prepared so that the lefthand particle ends up in a superposition of 50% |lefthand particle in Box 1> + 50% |lefthand particle in Box 2>, and the right hand particle ends up in a superposition of 50% |righthand particle in Box 3> + 50% |righthand particle in Box 4>. But the theory also says that the two particles can be correlated, so that if the lefthand particle ends up in Box 1, then the righthand particle ends up in Box 3, and if the lefthand particle ends up in Box 2, then the righthand particle ends up in Box 4. So the total state can be represented as 50% |lefthand particle in Box 1> |righthand particle in Box 3> + 50% |lefthand particle in Box 2> |righthand particle in Box 4>.

Now according to the Copenhagen interpretation, if you open the boxes on the lefthand side, you will force the superposition to collapse so that the lefthand particle will end up in either Box 1 or Box 2. Let's say it ends up in Box 1. Since the two particles are correlated, that means that if your friend looks in the boxes on the right, she should see the righthand particle in Box 3. If you had seen your particle in Box 2, then your friend would certainly have seen her particle in Box 4. We forgot to mention that you are in a lab on earth, but your friend is in a spaceship circling Alpha Centauri, over four light years away (the experiment took quite a while to set up). So, according to Einstein, when you look in your boxes, there's no way for the collapse of the superposition to affect the boxes all the way over near Alpha Centauri. Instead, he claims, there was no collapse—your particle was already in Box 1 before you looked, and your friend's particle was already in Box 3 before she looks. Since quantum mechanics doesn't say which boxes the particles are in, it's *incomplete.*

A physicist named John Bell turned the tables on Einstein by showing mathematically that if a theory were complete in Einstein's sense, it would have to make empirical predictions that were contrary to the predictions of quantum mechanics. The predictions were then tested (a thought experiment became a real experiment!) by Alain Aspect and others, and the results matched the predictions of quantum mechanics. Einstein's mistake had been to assume that the collapse caused by your observations on earth could not affect what was happening near Alpha Centauri. He did so because he thought that all physical interactions were *local,* which roughly means that they can only affect things nearby. Events on the earth can influence things happening near Alpha Centauri, but it will take over four years for the influences to locally propagate through space to eventually reach Alpha Centauri. Einstein thought that physics was local because his own theory of relativity seems to require locality. But it is now generally accepted that *nonlocality* is an essential feature of quantum mechanics, especially versions like the Copenhagen interpretation that involve collapse. In other words, when you look in the boxes on earth, you are instantaneously causing a physical change near Alpha Centauri. Nonlocality puts quantum mechanics in tension with the theory of relativity, but it also violates our intuitions about nature. If our universe is nonlocal, then events occurring in the distant parts of the universe, beyond what we can ever see, can have an immediate impact on what's happening to us. However, because of quantum indeterminacy, this influence is quite peculiar, and can't be used, for example, for sending signals instantaneously. When we do send a spaceship to Alpha Centauri, it will still take over four years for the news to get back to us that it's safely arrived.

One of the most significant alternatives to the Copenhagen interpretation is called the *many-worlds* or *Everett interpretation.* According to the many-worlds interpretation, superpositions never collapse. Yet when you go to look into the boxes, you will not see a superposition. So what has happened? You have become part of the superposition! More specifically, there is one part of the superposition in which you are seeing the particle in Box 1, and there is another part in which you are seeing the particle in Box 2, and both events are equally real and happening at the same time in the same space. You only ever experience seeing one of the two states, but there's "another you" that's seeing the other state. These two different possibilities are called *branches,* because they are like two branches of a tree that grow from the initial observation. And as each alternate you goes on to observe more superpositions, more branches are created. Each branching event doesn't just create new versions of you, it creates entire new worlds. So now you can see why this view is the many-worlds interpretation—every superposition you observe leads to a new world, every superposition that I observe leads to a new world, and so on for every observer. There will indeed be many, many worlds.

This idea might strike you as even weirder than some of the ideas associated with the Copenhagen interpretation. If so, you might wonder why it is such a popular idea among both physicists and philosophers. It does have some advantages. For one thing, the many-worlds interpretation is deterministic. After the measurement event, only one thing can happen: the particle will be seen in Box 1 *and* it will be seen in Box 2! Moreover, the many-worlds interpretation doesn't make essential use of the concept of measurement, and so doesn't need to get into the messy question of whether consciousness plays a special role in physics. It also may be that the many-worlds interpretation is local, because there is no collapse event to have nonlocal influence. These sorts of advantages might not seem worth it, given that we are forced to believe in a multiplicity of similar worlds all co-existing but invisible to each other. But how are we to compare the costs and benefits of such bizarre pictures of the world?

Indeed, there are many other interpretations of quantum mechanics that we have not yet mentioned, such as Bohmian mechanics, modal interpretations, the Ghirardi-Rimini-Weber theory, and others. Each of these interpretations has its own bizarre consequences that diverge radically from our intuitions about the world. Stepping back a bit, we can see that the legacy of quantum mechanics is that the world is much, much stranger than what we ever could have dreamed—we just don't know which of the many strange ways it could be is the right one.

SELECTION 9.1

The Elimination of Metaphysics*

A. J. Ayer

[*A. J. Ayer was the most famous British exponent of logical positivism. In this selection, Ayer sets forth and elaborates on the verifiability criterion of meaning.*]

The traditional disputes of philosophers are, for the most part, as unwarranted as they are unfruitful. The surest way to end them is to establish beyond question what should be the purpose and method of a philosophical inquiry. And this is by no means so difficult a task as the history of philosophy would lead one to suppose. For if there are any questions which science leaves it to philosophy to answer, a straightforward process of elimination must lead to their discovery.

We may begin by criticizing the metaphysical thesis that philosophy affords us knowledge of a reality transcending the world of science and common sense. Later on, when we come to define metaphysics and account for its existence, we shall find that it is possible to be a metaphysician without believing in a transcendent reality; for we shall see that many metaphysical utterances are due to the commission of logical errors, rather than to a conscious desire on the part of their authors to go beyond the limits of experience. But it is convenient for us to take the case of those who believe that it is possible

to have knowledge of a transcendent reality as a starting-point for our discussion. The arguments which we use to refute them will subsequently be found to apply to the whole of metaphysics.

One way of attacking a metaphysician who claimed to have knowledge of a reality which transcended the phenomenal world would be to inquire from what premises his propositions were deduced. Must he not begin, as other men do, with the evidence of his senses? And if so, what valid process of reasoning can possibly lead him to the conception of a transcendent reality? Surely from empirical premises nothing whatsoever concerning the properties, or even the existence, of anything super-empirical can legitimately be inferred. But this objection would be met by a denial on the part of the metaphysician that his assertions were ultimately based on the evidence of his senses. He would say that he was endowed with a faculty of intellectual intuition which enabled him to know facts that could not be known through sense-experience. And even if it could be shown that he was relying on empirical premises, and that his venture into a nonempirical world was therefore logically unjustified, it would not follow that the assertions which he made concerning this nonempirical world could not be true. For the fact that a conclusion does not follow from its putative premise is not sufficient to show that it is false. Consequently one cannot overthrow a system of transcendent metaphysics merely by

* From A. J. Ayer, *Language, Truth, and Logic,* 2nd ed. (London: Victor Gollancz, 1946). Reprinted by permission of Victor Gollancz, a division of the Orion Publishing Group.

criticizing the way in which it comes into being. What is required is rather a criticism of the nature of the actual statements which comprise it. And this is the line of argument which we shall, in fact, pursue. For we shall maintain that no statement which refers to a "reality" transcending the limits of all possible sense-experience can possibly have any literal significance; from which it must follow that the labors of those who have striven to describe such a reality have all been devoted to the production of nonsense. . . .

. . . Our charge against the metaphysician is not that he attempts to employ the understanding in a field where it cannot profitably venture, but that he produces sentences which fail to conform to the conditions under which alone a sentence can be literally significant. Nor are we ourselves obliged to talk nonsense in order to show that all sentences of a certain type are necessarily devoid of literal significance. We need only formulate the criterion which enables us to test whether a sentence expresses a genuine proposition about a matter of fact, and then point out that the sentences under consideration fail to satisfy it. And this we shall now proceed to do. We shall first of all formulate the criterion in somewhat vague terms, and then give the explanations which are necessary to render it precise.

The criterion which we use to test the genuineness of apparent statements of fact is the criterion of verifiability. We say that a sentence is factually significant to any given person, if, and only if, he knows how to verify the proposition which it purports to express—that is, if he knows what observations would lead him, under certain conditions, to accept the proposition as being true, or reject it as being false. If, on the other hand, the putative proposition is of such a character that the assumption of its truth, or falsehood, is consistent with any assumption whatsoever concerning the nature of his future experience, then, as far as he is concerned, it is, if not a tautology, a mere pseudo-proposition. The sentence expressing it may be emotionally significant to him; but it is not literally significant. And with regard to questions the procedure is the same. We inquire in every case what observations would lead us to answer the question, one way or the other; and, if none can be discovered, we must conclude that the sentence under consideration does not, as far as we are concerned, express a genuine question, however strongly its grammatical appearance may suggest that it does.

As the adoption of this procedure is an essential factor in the argument of this book, it needs to be examined in detail.

In the first place, it is necessary to draw a distinction between practical verifiability, and verifiability in principle. Plainly we all understand, in many cases believe, propositions which we have not in fact taken steps to verify. Many of these are propositions which we could verify if we took enough trouble. But there remain a number of significant propositions, concerning matters of fact, which we could not verify even if we chose; simply because we lack the practical means of placing ourselves in the situation where the relevant observations could be made. A simple and familiar example of such a proposition is the proposition that there are mountains on the farther side of the moon.[1] No rocket has yet been invented which would enable me to go and look at the farther side of the moon, so that I am unable to decide the matter by actual observation. But I do know what observations would decide it for me, if, as is theoretically conceivable, I were once in a position to make them. And therefore I say that the proposition is verifiable in principle, if not in practice, and is accordingly significant. On the other hand, such a metaphysical pseudo-proposition as "the Absolute enters into, but is itself incapable of, evolution and progress,"[2] is not even in principle verifiable. For one cannot conceive of an observation which would enable one to determine whether the Absolute did, or did not, enter into evolution and progress. Of course it is possible that the author of such a remark is using English words in a way in which they are not commonly used by English-speaking people, and that he does, in fact, intend to assert something which could be empirically verified. But until he makes us understand how the proposition that he wishes to express would be verified, he fails to communicate anything to us. And if he admits, as I think the author of the remark in question would have admitted, that his words were not intended to express either a tautology or a proposition which was capable, at least in principle, of being verified, then it follows that he has made an utterance which has no literal significance for himself.

---

[1] This example has been used by Professor Schlick to illustrate the same point.

[2] A remark taken at random from *Appearance and Reality*, by F. H. Bradley.

A further distinction which we must make is the distinction between the "strong" and the "weak" sense of the term "verifiable." A proposition is said to be verifiable, in the strong sense of the term, if, and only if, its truth could be conclusively established in experience. But it is verifiable, in the weak sense, if it is possible for experience to render it probable. In which sense are we using the term when we say that a putative proposition is genuine only if it is verifiable?

It seems to me that if we adopt conclusive verifiability as our criterion of significance, as some positivists have proposed,[3] our argument will prove too much. Consider, for example, the case of general propositions of law—such propositions, namely, as "arsenic is poisonous"; "all men are mortal"; "a body tends to expand when it is heated." It is of the very nature of these propositions that their truth cannot be established with certainty by any finite series of observations. But if it is recognized that such general propositions of law are designed to cover an infinite number of cases, then it must be admitted that they cannot, even in principle, be verified conclusively. And then, if we adopt conclusive verifiability as our criterion of significance, we are logically obliged to treat these general propositions of law in the same fashion as we treat the statements of the metaphysician.

In face of this difficulty, some positivists[4] have adopted the heroic course of saying that these general propositions are indeed pieces of nonsense, albeit an essentially important type of nonsense. But here the introduction of the term "important" is simply an attempt to hedge. It serves only to mark the authors' recognition that their view is somewhat too paradoxical, without in any way removing the paradox. Besides, the difficulty is not confined to the case of general propositions of law, though it is there revealed most plainly. It is hardly less obvious in the case of propositions about the remote past. For it must surely be admitted that, however strong the evidence in favor of historical statements may be, their truth can never become more than highly probable. And to maintain that they also constituted an important, or unimportant, type of nonsense would be unplausible, to say the very least. Indeed, it will be our contention that no proposition, other than a tautology, can possibly be anything more than a probable hypothesis. And if this is correct, the principle that a sentence can be factually significant only if it expresses what is conclusively verifiable is self-stultifying as a criterion of significance. For it leads to the conclusion that it is impossible to make a significant statement of fact at all.

---

[3] E.g., M. Schlick, "Positivismus and Realismus," *Erkenntnis,* Vol. I, 1930. F. Waismann, "Logische Analyse des Warschein-lichkeitsbegriffs," *Erkenntnis,* Vol. I, 1930.

[4] E.g., M. Schlick, "Die Kausalität in der gegenwärtigen Physik," *Naturwissenschaft,* Vol. 19, 1931.

SELECTION 9.2

Identity and Necessity*

Saul Kripke

[*What Kripke writes here relates to the idea that psychological states and processes "are contingently identical to" brain states and processes. Terminology: An identity judgment or statement equates what is designated by one term "X" with what is designated by another term "Y." In other words, it says "X = Y"; for example, "Mark* Twain is Samuel Clemens." *A contingent judgment, if true, theoretically could have been false; that is, it is not true in all possible worlds. For example, "Shakespeare wrote Hamlet," though true, could have been false. To know that an a posteriori judgment is true or false, you have to know more than just the meaning of the words in it.*]

* From Saul Kripke, "Identity and Necessity," in *Identity and Individuation,* edited by Milton K. Munitz. New York: New York University Press, 1971. Reprinted by permission of Saul Kripke.

. . . Let me turn to the case of heat and the motion of molecules. Here surely is a case that is contingent identity! Recent philosophy has emphasized this again and again. So, if it is a case of contingent identity, then let us imagine under what circumstances it would be false. Now, concerning this statement I hold that the circumstances philosophers apparently have in mind as circumstances under which it would have been false are not in fact such circumstances. First, of course, it is argued that "Heat is the motion of molecules" is an *a posteriori* judgement; scientific investigation might have turned out otherwise. As I said before, this shows nothing against the view that it is necessary—at least if I am right. But here, surely, people had very specific circumstances in mind under which, so they thought, the judgement that heat is the motion of molecules would have been false. What were these circumstances? One can distill them out of the fact that we found out empirically that heat is the motion of molecules. How was this? What did we find out first when we found out that heat is the motion of molecules? There is a certain external phenomenon which we can sense by the sense of touch, and it produces a sensation which we call "the sensation of heat." We then discover that the external phenomenon which produces this sensation, which we sense, by means of our sense of touch, is in fact that of molecular agitation in the thing that we touch, a very high degree of molecular agitation. So, it might be thought, to imagine a situation in which heat would not have been the motion of molecules, we need only imagine a situation in which we would have had the very same sensation and it would have been produced by something other than the motion of molecules. Similarly, if we wanted to imagine a situation in which light was not a stream of photons, we could imagine a situation in which we were sensitive to something else in exactly the same way, producing what we call visual experiences, though not through a stream of photons. To make the case stronger, or to look at another side of the coin, we could also consider a situation in which we *are* concerned with the motion of molecules but in which such motion does not give us the sensation of heat. And it might also have happened that we, or, at least, the creatures inhabiting this planet, might have been so constituted that, let us say, an increase in the motion of molecules did not give us this sensation but that, on the contrary, a slowing down of the molecules did give us the very same sensation. This would be a situation, so it might be thought, in which heat would not be the motion of molecules, or, more precisely, in which temperature would not be mean molecular kinetic energy.

But I think it would not be so. Let us think about the situation again. First, let us think about it in the actual world. Imagine right now the world invaded by a number of Martians, who do indeed get the very sensation that we call "the sensation of heat" when they feel some ice which has slow molecular motion, and who do not get a sensation of heat—in fact, maybe just the reverse—when they put their hand near a fire which causes a lot of molecular agitation. Would we say, "Ah, this casts some doubt on heat being the motion of molecules, because there are these other people who don't get the same sensation"? Obviously not, and no one would think so. We would say instead that the Martians somehow feel the very sensation we get when we feel heat when they feel cold and that they do not get a sensation of heat when they feel heat. But now let us think of a counterfactual situation. Suppose the earth had from the very beginning been inhabited by such creatures. First, imagine it inhabited by no creatures at all: then there is no one to feel any sensations of heat. But we would not say that under such circumstances it would necessarily be the case that heat did not exist; we would say that heat might have existed, for example, if there were fires that heated up the air.

Let us suppose the laws of physics were not very different: Fires do heat up the air. Then there would have been heat even though there were no creatures around to feel it. Now let us suppose evolution takes place, and life is created, and there are some creatures around. But they are not like us, they are more like the Martians. Now would we say that heat has suddenly turned to cold, because of the way the creatures of this planet sense it? No, I think we should describe this situation as a situation in which, though the creatures on this planet got our sensation of heat, they did not get it when they were exposed to heat. They got it when they were exposed to cold. And that is something we can surely well imagine. We can imagine it just as we can imagine our planet being invaded by creatures of this sort. Think of it in two steps. First there is a stage where there are no creatures at all, and one can certainly imagine the planet still having both heat and cold, though no one is around to sense it. Then the planet comes through an evolutionary process to be peopled with beings of different neural structure from ourselves. Then these creatures could be such that they were insensitive to heat; they did not feel it in the way we do; but on the other hand, they felt cold in much the same way that we feel heat. But still, heat, would be heat, and cold would be cold. And particularly, then, this goes in no way against saying that in this counterfactual situation heat would still *be* the molecular motion, *be* that which is produced by fires, and so on, just as it would have been if there had been no creatures on the planet at all. Similarly, we could imagine that the planet was inhabited by creatures who got visual sensations when there were sound waves in the air. We should not therefore say, "Under such circumstances, sound would have been light." Instead we should say, "The planet was inhabited by creatures who were in some sense visually sensitive to sound, and maybe even visually sensitive to light." If this is correct, it can still be and will still be a necessary truth that heat is the motion of molecules and that light is a stream of photons.

To state the view succinctly: we use both the terms "heat" and "the motion of molecules" as rigid designators for a certain external phenomenon. Since heat is in fact the motion of molecules, and the designators are rigid, by the argument I have given here, it is going to be *necessary* that heat is the motion of molecules. What gives us the illusion of contingency is the fact we have identified the heat by the contingent fact that there happen to be creatures on this planet—(namely, ourselves) who are sensitive to it in a certain way, that is, who are sensitive to the motion of molecules or to heat—these are one and the same thing. And this is contingent. So we use the description, "that which

causes such and such sensations, or that which we sense in such and such a way," to identify heat. But in using this fact we use a contingent property of heat, just as we use the contingent property of Cicero as having written such and such works to identify him. We then use the terms "heat" in the one case and "Cicero" in the other *rigidly* to designate the objects for which they stand. And of course the term "the motion of molecules" is rigid; it always stands for the motion of molecules, never for any other phenomenon. So, as Bishop Butler said, "everything is what it is and not another thing." Therefore, "Heat is the motion of molecules" will be necessary, not contingent, and one only has the *illusion* of contingency in the way one could have the illusion of contingency in thinking that this table might have been made of ice. We might think one could imagine it, but if we try, we can see on reflection that what we are really imagining is just there being another lectern in this very position here which was in fact made of ice. The fact that we may identify this lectern by being the object we see and touch in such and such a position is something else.

Now how does this relate to the problem of mind and body? It is usually held that this is a contingent identity statement just like "Heat is the motion of molecules." That cannot be. It cannot be a contingent identity statement just like "Heat is the motion of molecules" because, if I am right, "Heat is the motion of molecules" is not a contingent identity statement.

SELECTION 9.3

The Problem of Objectivity*

Donald Davidson

[*Descartes tried to show that knowledge could be derived from the fact that he thinks. Here, Donald Davidson begins discussing how thought or "propositional attitudes" could be possible in the first place.*]

. . . We should be astonished that there is such a thing as thought. . . .

* From Donald Davidson, *Problems of Rationality* (Oxford: Oxford University Press, 2004), pp. 6–11, 12, 15–16. This article first appeared in *Tijdschrift voor Filosofie*, vol. 57 (June 1995). Reprinted by permission of Marcia Cavell, Literary Executor for the Estate of Donald Davidson.

I am not concerned with the scientific explanation of the existence of thought; my interest is in what makes it possible. Let me state the problem a little more carefully. A thought is defined, at least in part, by the fact that it has a content that can be true or false. The most basic form of thought is belief. But one cannot have a belief without understanding that beliefs may be false—their truth is not in general guaranteed by anything in us. Someone who believes there is a dragon in the closet opens the door and sees there is no dragon. He is *surprised;* this is not what he expected. Awareness of the possibility of surprise, the entertainment of expectations—these are essential concomitants of belief.

To recognize the chance that we may be wrong is to recognize that beliefs can be tested—belief is personal, and in this sense subjective; truth is objective. The problem is to account for our having the concept of objectivity—of a truth that is independent of our will and our attitudes. Where can we have acquired such a concept? We cannot occupy a position outside our own minds; there is no vantage point from which to compare our beliefs with what we take our beliefs to be about. Surprise—the frustration of expectation—cannot explain our having the concept of objective truth, because we cannot be surprised, or have an expectation, unless we already command the concept. To be surprised is to recognize the distinction between what we thought and what is the case. To have an expectation is to admit that it may be faulted.

Here is another way—a familiar way—to view the problem. We would never know anything about the world around us if it were not for the stimulation of our sensory organs. (There may be exceptions, but they are not important here.) Why should, or how can, such stimulations generate thoughts of anything beyond? And if beliefs of something beyond were prompted, what conceivable test could there be that such beliefs were true, since the test could only involve more sensory stimulations? (It is as if all we know of the outside world is brought to us by messengers. If we doubt the veracity of what they tell us, how can it help to ask further messengers? If the first messengers are untrustworthy, why should the later ones be any more truthful?) The idea that since we do not will the stimulations of our sensory organs we must suppose they have an external cause is no help, for at what distance must the posited cause lie? Why not at the surface of the skin, or even in the brain? Without an answer to this question, there is no answer to the question what our beliefs are about; and without an answer to this question, it makes no sense to talk of belief—or thought in general.

There are many people, including philosophers, psychologists, and particularly those who admire the amazing cleverness of speechless animals, who identify the ability to discriminate items having a certain property with having a concept—with having the concept of being such an item. But I shall not use the word "concept" in this way. My reason for resisting this usage is that if we were to accept it we would be committed to holding that the simplest

animals have concepts: even an earthworm, which has so little brain that, if cut in two, each part behaves as the undivided whole did, would have the concepts of dry and moist, of the edible and inedible. Indeed, we should have to credit tomato plants or sunflowers with the concepts of day and night.

I should therefore like to reserve the word "concept" for cases where it makes clear sense to speak of a mistake, a mistake not only as seen from an intelligent observer's point of view, but as seen from the creature's point of view. If an earthworm eats poison, it has not in this sense made a mistake—it has not mistaken one thing for another: it has simply done what it was programmed to do. It did not mistakenly classify the poison as edible: the poison simply provided the stimulus that caused it to eat. Even a creature capable of learning to avoid certain foods cannot, for that reason alone, be said to have the concepts of edibility and inedibility. A creature could construct a "map" of its world without having the idea that it was a *map* of anything— that it was a map—and so might be wrong.

To apply a concept is to make a judgment, to classify or characterize an object or event or situation in a certain way, and this requires application of the concept of *truth*, since it is always possible to classify or characterize something wrongly. To have a concept, in the sense I am giving this word, is, then, to be able to entertain propositional contents: a creature has a concept only if it is able to employ that concept in the context of a judgment. It may seem that one could have the concept of, say, a tree, without being able to think that, or wonder whether, something is a tree, or desire that there be a tree. Such conceptualization would, however, amount to no more than being able to discriminate trees—to act in some specific way in the presence of trees—and this, as I said, is not what I would call having a concept. . . .

These mental attributes are, then, equivalent: to have a concept, to entertain propositions, to be able to form judgments, to have command of the concept of truth. If a creature has one of these attributes, it has them all. To accept this thesis is to take the first step toward recognizing the holism—that is, the essential interdependence—of various aspects of the mental.

Let me dwell briefly on the centrality of the concept of truth. It is not possible to grasp or entertain a proposition without knowing what it would be for it to be true; without this knowledge there would be no answer to the question what proposition was being grasped or entertained. . . .

In order to understand a proposition, one must know what its truth conditions are, but one may or may not be concerned with the question whether it is true. I understand what would have to be the case for it to have rained in Perth, Australia, on May 1st, 1912, but I do not care whether or not it did rain there on that date. I neither believe nor disbelieve that it rained in Perth on May 1st, 1912; I don't even wonder about it. The *attitude* I have towards a proposition—of belief, doubt, wonder, hope, or fear—determines how, if at all, I regard its truth. But if I have *any* attitude towards it, even one of total indifference, I must know its truth conditions. Indeed, there is a clear sense in which I know the truth conditions of every proposition I am capable of expressing or considering.

To know the truth conditions of a proposition, one must have the concept of truth. There is no more central concept than that of truth, since having any concept requires that we know what it would be for that concept to apply to something—to apply truly, of course. The same holds for the concept of truth itself. To have the concept of truth is to have the concept of objectivity, the notion of a proposition being true or false independent of one's beliefs or interests. In particular, then, someone who has a belief, who holds some proposition to be true or false, knows that that belief may be true or false. In order to be right or wrong, one must know that it is possible to be right or wrong.

Entertaining any proposition, whatever one's attitude toward the proposition may be, entails believing many other propositions. If you wonder whether you are seeing a black snake, you must have an idea of what a snake is. You must believe things such as: a snake is an animal, it has no feet, it moves with sinuous movement, it is smaller than a mountain. If it is a black snake, then it is a snake and it is black. If it is black, it is not green. Since you wonder what you are seeing, you must know what seeing is: that it requires the use of the eyes, that you can see something without touching it, and so on. I do not wish to give the impression that there is a fixed list of things you must believe in order to wonder whether you are seeing a black snake. The *size* of the list is very large, if not infinite, but membership in the list is indefinite. What is clear is that without many of the sort of beliefs I have mentioned, you cannot entertain the proposition that you are seeing a black snake; you cannot believe or disbelieve that proposition, wish it were false, ask whether it is true, or demand that someone make it false. . . .

We must conclude, I think, that it is not possible for a creature to have a single, isolated, thought. . . .

It follows from what I have said that many of our beliefs must be true. The reason, put briefly if misleadingly, is that a belief owes its character in part to its relations to other, true, beliefs. Suppose most of my beliefs about what I call snakes were false; then my belief that I am seeing what I call a "snake" would not be correctly described as being about a snake. Thus my belief, if it is to be about a snake, whether it is a true belief or a false one, depends on a background of true beliefs, true beliefs about the nature of snakes, of animals, of physical objects of the world. But though many beliefs must therefore be true, most beliefs can be false. This last remark is dangerously ambiguous. It means: with respect to most of our beliefs, any particular one may be false. It does not mean: with respect to the totality of our beliefs, most may be false, for the possibility of a false belief depends on an environment of truths.

SELECTION 9.4

What Is Social Construction?*

Paul A. Boghossian

[*Are the entities postulated by science mere social constructions? Are the beliefs in those things, or the justifications of those beliefs, social constructions? Here philosopher of science Paul A. Boghossian argues they are not.*]

* From Paul Boghossian, "What is Social Construction?" *Times Literary Supplement,* February 23, 2001, p. 6–8. Reprinted by permission of Paul Boghossian.

Socially Constructed Things

Money, citizenship and newspapers are transparent social constructions because they obviously could not have existed without societies. Just as obviously, it would seem, anything that could have—or that did—exist independently of societies could *not* have been socially constructed: dinosaurs, for example, or giraffes, or the elementary particles that are supposed to be the building blocks of all matter and that physicists call "quarks." How could they have been socially constructed if they existed *before* societies did?

Yet when we turn to some of the most prominent texts in the social construction literature, we find an avalanche of claims to the effect that it is precisely such seemingly mind- and society-independent items that are socially constructed. . . .

But it is not easy to make sense of the thought that facts about elementary particles or dinosaurs are a *consequence* of scientific theorizing. How could scientific theorizing have caused it to be true that there were dinosaurs or that there are quarks? Of course, science made it true that we *came to believe* that dinosaurs and quarks exist. Since we believe it, we *act as though* dinosaurs and quarks exist. If we allow ourselves some slightly florid language, we could say that *in our world* dinosaurs and quarks exist, in much the way as we could say that in the world of Shakespeare's *Hamlet,* Ophelia drowns. So, still speaking in this vein, we could say that science made it true that in our world there are dinosaurs and quarks. But all we could coherently mean by this is that science made it true that *we came to believe that* dinosaurs and quarks exist. And that no one disputes. Despite all the evidence in their favor, these beliefs may still be false and the only thing that will make them true is whether, out there, there really were dinosaurs and there really are quarks. Surely, science cannot construct those things; at best, it can discover them. . . .

Socially Constructed Belief

If the preceding considerations are correct, social construction talk does not cogently apply to the *facts* studied by the natural sciences; does it fare any better when applied to the *beliefs* about those facts produced by those sciences?

The issue is not whether science is a social enterprise. Of course, it is. Science is conducted collectively by human beings who come equipped with values, needs, interests and prejudices. And these may influence their behavior in a variety of potentially profound ways: they may determine what questions they show an interest in, what research strategy they place their bets on, what they are willing to fund, and so forth.

The usual view, however, is that none of this matters to the believability of a particular claim produced by science, *if that claim is adequately supported by the factual evidence.* Kepler may have become interested in planetary motion as a result of his religious and occult preoccupations, and for all I know, he may have been strongly invested in getting a certain outcome. But so long as his eventual claim that the planets move in elliptical orbits could be justified by the evidence he presented for it, it does not matter how he came to be interested in the question, nor what prior investment he may have had. The view is now there, with a claim on our attention, and the only way to reject it is to refute the evidence adduced in its favor. It is irrelevant that Kepler would not have engaged in his research had it not been for preoccupations that we do not share or that he may have had extra-evidential motives for hoping for a certain outcome.

To put this point another way, we commonly distinguish between what philosophers of science call the "context of discovery" and what they call the "context of justification." And while it's plausible that social values play a role in the context of discovery, it's not plausible that they play a role in the context of justification. Social constructionists about knowledge deny this; for them it is naïve to suppose that while social values may enter into the one context, they need not enter into the other.

Well, how could social values enter into the context of justification? There are *four* distinct ways of articulating the thought a constructionist may have in mind here; while all four may be found in the literature, they are not always sufficiently distinguished from one other.

To begin with, a constructionist may hold that it is not the factual evidence that does the justifying, but precisely the background social values. And while it may seem incredible that anyone could have seriously thought anything like this, but there are certainly assertions out there that seem to demand just such a reading. . . . However, anyone who really thought that, say, Maxwell's Equations could be *justified* by appeal to Maxwell's, or anyone else's, social or political beliefs would betray a complete incomprehension of the notion of justification. An item of information justifies a given belief by raising the likelihood that it is true. Admittedly, this is not an unproblematic notion. But unless we are to throw it out altogether, it is perfectly clear that one cannot hope to justify the fundamental laws of electromagnetism by appeal to one's political convictions or career interests or anything else of a similar ilk.

If one were absolutely determined to pursue something along these lines, a *slightly* better avenue, and the second of our four options, would be to argue that, although social values do not justify our beliefs, we are not actually moved to belief by things that justify; we are only moved by our social interests.

This view, which is practically orthodoxy among practitioners of what has come to be known as "science studies," has the advantage of not saying something absurd about justification; but it is scarcely any more plausible. On the most charitable reading, it stems from an innocent confusion about what is required by the enterprise of treating scientific knowledge sociologically. . . .

. . . Absent an argument for being skeptical about the very idea of a good reason for a belief—and how could there be such an argument that did not immediately undermine itself?—one of the possible causes for my believing what I do is that I have good evidence for it. Any explanatory framework that insisted on treating not only true and false beliefs symmetrically, but justified and unjustified ones as well, would owe us an explanation for why evidence for belief is being excluded as one of its potential causes. And it would have to do so without undermining its own standing as a view that is being put forward because justified.

This is not, of course, to say that scientific belief must *always* be explained in terms of the compelling evidence assembled for it; the history of science is replete with examples of views—phrenology, for example—for which there never was any good evidence. It is simply to insist that scientific belief is *sometimes* to be explained in terms of compelling evidence and that the history and sociology of science, properly conceived, need have no stake in denying that.

This brings us to a third, milder conception of how social values might be indispensable for the justification of scientific belief. On this view, although evidence can enter into the explanation for why a particular view is believed, it can never be enough to explain it. Any evidence we might possess always *underdetermines* the specific belief that we arrive at on its basis. Something else must close the gap between what we have evidence for and what we actually believe, and that something else is provided by the thinker's background values and interests.

This idea, that the evidence in science always underdetermines the theories that we believe on its basis, has exerted considerable influence in the philosophy of science, even in non-constructionist circles. In its modern form, it originated in the thought of the turn of the century French physicist and philosopher, Pierre Duhem. . . .

Duhem argued that reason alone could never decide which revisions are called for and, hence, that belief revision in science could not be a purely rational matter: something else had to be at work as well. What the social constructionist adds is that this extra element is something social.

This is a clever argument that does not long conceal its difficulties. Is it really true that we could never have more reason to revise one of our theories rather than another in response to recalcitrant experience? Consider Duhem's example of an astronomer peering through his telescope at the heavens and being surprised at what he finds there, perhaps a hitherto undetected star in a galaxy he has been charting. Upon this discovery, according to Duhem, the astronomer may revise his theory of the heavens or he may revise his theory of how the telescope works. And rational principles of belief fixation do not tell him which to do.

The idea, however, that in peering at the heavens through a telescope we are testing our theory of the telescope *just as much* as we are testing our astronomical views is absurd. The theory of the telescope has been established by numerous terrestrial experiments and fits in with an enormous number of other things that we know about lenses, light and mirrors. It is simply not plausible that, in coming across an unexpected observation of the heavens, a rational response might be to revise what we know about telescopes! The point is not that we might *never* have occasion to revise our theory of telescopes; one can certainly imagine circumstances under which that is precisely what would be called for. The point is that not *every* circumstance in which something about telescopes is presupposed is a circumstance in which our theory of telescopes is being tested, and so the conclusion that rational considerations alone cannot decide how to respond to recalcitrant experience is blocked.

Perhaps, however—to come to the fourth and final way in which belief and social values might be intertwined—the correct thought is not that the social must be brought in to fill a *gap* left by the rational, but simply that the rational itself is constitutively social. A good reason for believing something, according to this line of thought, only has that status relative to variable social factors—a sharp separation between the rational and the social is illusory.

This is currently perhaps the single most influential construal of the relation between the rational and the social in constructionist circles. What it amounts to is a relativization of good reasons to variable social circumstance, so that the same item of information may correctly be said to justify a given belief under some social circumstances, in some cultures, but not in others. . . .

But this is an impossible construal of reasons for belief, as Plato understood some time ago (see his *Theatetus*). We cannot coherently think of ourselves as believing and asserting *anything*, if all reasons for belief and assertion are held to be inexorably tied to variable background perspective in the manner being proposed. There are many ways to show this, but perhaps the most telling is this: not even the relativist would be able to adopt such an attitude towards his own view. For, surely, the relativist does not think that a relativism about reasons is justified only relative to his own perspective? If he did, why is he recommending it to us who do not share his perspective?

When we believe something we believe it because we think there are reasons to think it is true, reasons that we think are general enough to get a grip even on people who do not share our perspective. That is why we feel entitled to recommend it to them. It's hard to imagine a way of thinking about belief and assertion that precluded the possibility of that sort of generality. . . .

Conclusion

At its best—as in the work of de Beauvoir and Appiah—social constructionist thought exposes the contingency of those of our social practices that we had wrongly come to regard as inevitable. It does so by relying on the standard canons of good scientific reasoning. It goes astray when it aspires to become either a general metaphysics or a general theory of knowledge. As the former, it quickly degenerates into an impossible form of idealism. As the latter, it assumes its place in a long history of problematic attempts to relativize the notion of rationality. It has nothing new to add to these historically discredited views; if anything, social constructionist versions tend to be murkier and more confused than their traditional counterparts. The difficulty lies in understanding why such generalized applications of social construction have come to tempt so many.

One source of their appeal is no doubt their efficiency. If we can be said to know up front that any item of knowledge only has that status because it gets a nod from contingent social values, then any claim to knowledge can be dispatched if we happen not to share the values on which it allegedly depends. There is no need to get into the often complex details. . . .

The intuitive view is that there is a way things are that is independent of human opinion, and that we are capable of arriving at belief about how things are that is objectively reasonable, binding on anyone capable of appreciating the relevant evidence regardless of their ideological perspective. Difficult as these notions may be, it is a mistake to think that recent philosophy has disclosed any good reasons for rejecting them.

CHECKLIST

To help you review, a checklist of the key philosophers of this chapter can be found online at www.mhhe.com/moore9e.

KEY TERMS AND CONCEPTS

a priori/a
   posteriori 214
accuracy
   problem 219
analysis 194
analytic/synthetic 212
antirepresentationalism
208
Copenhagen
   interpretation 219
foundationalism 206
indeterminism 220
indeterminancy of
   translation 213
inscrutability of
   reference 213
instrumentalism 192
language game 209
logical atomism 202
logical positivism 197
logicism 195

measurement
   problem 218
mereological sum 216
naturalized
   epistemology 206
necessary/
   contingent 214
nihilism 190
ontological
   anti-realism 216
ontological
   realism 216
ontology 215
phenomenalism 204
pragmatism 191
private
   language 205
realism 207
reductionism 212
representationalism
   207

QUESTIONS FOR DISCUSSION AND REVIEW

1. What does philosophical analysis do? In other words, explain what *philosophical analysis is.*

2. "Square circles are nonexistent things." "No squares are circles." Which of these two propositions is simpler philosophically, and why?

3. What is the verifiability criterion of meaning?

4. "The first female president of the United States is unmarried." Is this sentence true or false or neither? Explain why.

5. What does it mean to say there are "atomic" facts?

6. "If X might exist but we have no reason to suppose that it actually does exist, then as metaphysicians we should not concern ourselves with X." Is this true? Why or why not?

7. Apply the principle stated in the preceding question by letting X stand for God, ghosts, and space aliens.

8. Can you know that physical objects exist when no one is perceiving them?

9. Explain the logical positivists' reasons for holding that all metaphysics is meaningless.

10. "At least in part, a thing is what is thought about it within the various contexts in which it is used." What does this mean?

11. The text mentions that the movie *What the Bleep Do We Know!?* incorrectly characterizes the effects of observation on quantum systems. Watch the movie and describe some examples of this mischaracterization. Is there anything else in the movie that disagrees with the text? What claims in the movie agree with the text?

SUGGESTED FURTHER READINGS

Go online to www.mhhe.com/moore9e for a list of suggested further readings.

Part Two
Moral and Political Philosophy

10

Moral Philosophy

Happiness, then, is something final and self-sufficient, and is the end of
action.   —Aristotle

Morality is not properly the doctrine how we should make ourselves happy,
but how we should become worthy of happiness.   —Immanuel Kant

Advice is something you never stop getting, although good, sound advice is
perhaps not too common.

Most advice you get—and give—is of a practical nature: "If you want to live
longer," someone will say, "you should stop smoking." Or: "If I were you, I would
buy life insurance now while you are young."

But advice is not always intended to be merely practical. Sometimes it is moral
advice. Someone—a friend, your minister, a relative—may suggest that you
should do something not because it will be in your own best interest to do it but
because doing it is *morally right*. "You should donate money to a charity," the
person might say. Or: "You should be kind to animals." These suggestions express
moral judgments.

Ethics, or moral philosophy, is the philosophical study of moral judgments—
value judgments about what is virtuous or base, just or unjust, morally right or
wrong, morally good or bad or evil, morally proper or improper. We say *morally*
right and *morally* good and so on because terms like *right* and *good* and *proper* (and
their negative correlates, *wrong* and *bad* and *improper*) can be used in *nonmoral*
value judgments, as when someone speaks of a bad wine or of the right or proper
way to throw a pass.

Many questions can be asked about moral judgments, so ethical philosophers
discuss a wide array of issues. One basic question they ask is, What *is* a moral
judgment? In other words, exactly what does it mean to describe something as

The Good Life

We view philosophy as valuable and applicable to real life. But then, we may be biased because we get paid to philosophize. Nevertheless, here is a case in favor of our view.

As you read about the moral philosophies of Plato, Aristotle, and almost every other thinker covered in Part Two, you might note their concern with the question, *In what does human happiness or well-being or the good life consist?* Maybe this question is not the *central* question of ethics, but it is close to the center. Almost every philosopher we cover in

this part of the book offers an alternative answer to this question. The question is also of considerable practical importance—and worth considering *now*. Ultimately, we all die, and sometimes, unfortunately, people die sooner, sometimes much sooner, than they expected. To get a clear focus on this question, only to learn that it is too late to do anything about it, could be a great tragedy.

Maybe you will find something in this and the next chapter to help you settle on your own definition of the good life.

morally right or wrong, good or evil? What is it to say that one thing ought to be done and another thing ought not be done? Or they might ask, What makes a moral judgment a *moral* judgment? How do moral judgments differ from other value judgments, factual assertions, and pieces of practical advice? What distinguishes reasoning about moral issues from reasoning about other things (from reasoning about the structure of matter, say, or about the qualities of good art)? These are some of the questions ethical philosophers ask.

The most important question of ethics, however, is simply, Which moral judgments are correct? That is, what is good and just and the morally right thing to do? What is the "moral law," anyway? This question is important because the answer to it tells us how we should conduct our affairs. Perhaps it is the most important question not of ethics but of philosophy. Perhaps it is the most important question, period.

A less obvious question of ethics, though logically more fundamental, is whether there is a moral law in the first place. In other words, do moral obligations even exist? Are there really such things as good and bad, right and wrong? And if there are, what is it that makes one thing right and another wrong? That is, what is the ultimate justification of moral standards?

In what follows, we will examine some of these issues and related questions as they have been treated throughout the history of philosophy. However, before we begin, we need to discuss several concepts that have been important throughout the history of moral philosophy.

SKEPTICISM, RELATIVISM, AND SUBJECTIVISM

Many beginning students in philosophy accept one or more of three important ideas about morals. The first, **ethical skepticism,** is the doctrine that moral knowledge is not possible. According to the skeptic, whether there are moral standards is not knowable, or, alternatively, if there are any moral standards, we cannot know what they are.

You should be aware that the beliefs that there is no right or wrong and that "everything is permissible" (which we encountered in the previous chapter) are not skeptical beliefs. A person who makes either of these claims implies that he or she does have moral knowledge.

Another popular idea about ethics is called **descriptive relativism,** according to which the moral standards people subscribe to are different from culture to culture. This idea might seem obviously true, but you must remember that different *practices* do not necessarily entail different *standards.* For example, it might seem that the pro-choice "culture" and the pro-life "culture" obviously have different moral standards, and perhaps they do. On the other hand, they might both accept the standard that it is wrong to kill a living person but just disagree about whether a fetus counts as a living person.

In any case, descriptive relativism is not an ethical doctrine. It says merely that people in different cultures have different beliefs about what is morally right and wrong. It says nothing about what *is* morally right and morally wrong. The idea that what a culture *believes* is morally right or wrong *is* morally right or wrong for people in that culture is known as **cultural relativism,** and it is a popular idea among beginning philosophy students. Many tend to think, for example, that whether or not you should act selfishly is entirely determined by whether or not your culture thinks you should act selfishly. Beginning philosophy students who are cultural relativists sometimes also advocate being accepting toward the practices of other cultures. However, it would be inconsistent for a cultural relativist to advocate being accepting toward another culture's practice if her or his own culture thought that practice was wrong.

Another relativist doctrine is known as **individual relativism,** according to which what is right or wrong is what each individual believes is right or wrong. If you hold this view, then you would have to say that nobody ever acts wrongly, provided he or she is doing what he or she thinks is right. Both individual relativism and cultural relativism are sometimes spoken of as **subjectivist** ethical philosophies, in that what is right or wrong depends entirely on what a person (i.e., a "subject") or a culture (i.e., a group of "subjects") thinks is right or wrong.

EGOISM

Egoism is another popular ethical doctrine, but there are two types of egoism. First, there is **descriptive egoism,** the doctrine that in all conscious action you seek to promote your self-interest above all else. Then there is **prescriptive egoism,** the doctrine that in all conscious action you *ought* to seek your self-interest above all else. The Epicurean ethical philosophy, for example, was a version of prescriptive egoism.

Often, beginning philosophy students accept descriptive egoism as almost self-evidently true. Many also favor prescriptive egoism as an ethical philosophy. Of course we always act to further our own ends! And that is exactly what we *ought* to do, right?

Does acting ethically mean squelching devilish selfish interests in favor of more high-minded objectives? Prescriptive egoism is the idea that you ought to act in your own self-interest.

But some philosophers see a difficulty in accepting both prescriptive and descriptive egoism in that it seems trivial or pointless to tell people they ought to do what you think they are *going to do anyway.* That is like advising someone that she or he has a moral obligation to obey the laws of physics or to remain visible at all times or to occupy space, these philosophers say.

A further comment: If you find yourself subscribing to prescriptive egoism (one ought to seek one's self-interest above all else), as many do, then you should consider this: Does it make sense for you to advocate your own egoistic philosophy? If you ought to seek your own self-interest above all else (as prescriptive egoism says), then should you really go around telling others to seek *their* self-interest above all else? Is telling them that in *your* best interests? Might it not be better for your interests to urge others to promote the *common* good?

HEDONISM

Hedonism is the pursuit of pleasure. Philosophers distinguish between the *descriptive* doctrine known as **psychological hedonism,** according to which the ultimate object of a person's desire *is* always pleasure, and the *ethical* doctrine known as **ethical hedonism,** according to which a person *ought* to seek pleasure over other things. You should remember these doctrines.

The descriptive doctrine may be plausible at first glance, but on closer inspection it appears somewhat doubtful. We do seem to seek things beside pleasure—for example, food, good health, relaxation, rest, rightness in our actions, success, friends, and many other things too. As the British moralist and clergyman Bishop Joseph Butler (1692–1752) observed, we could not seek pleasure at all unless we had desires for something other than pleasure, because pleasure consists in satisfying these desires. And then, too, "the pleasure of virtue," as Irish historian W. E. H. Lecky wrote, "is one which can only be obtained on the express condition of its not being the object sought." In other words, if your motive in acting virtuously is to obtain the pleasure that accompanies virtuous acts, then you are not being virtuous and will not get that pleasure.

As for ethical hedonism, there are two kinds: **egoistic ethical hedonism,** according to which one ought to seek his or her own pleasure over other things, and **universalistic ethical hedonism,** otherwise known as utilitarianism, according to which one ought to seek the greatest pleasure for the greatest number of people over other things.

One difficulty utilitarians face is in explaining why pleasure for others is something one should seek. One common answer is that only by seeking others' pleasure can you experience a full allotment of pleasure for yourself. But this answer seems to assume that one's primary ethical duty is to oneself after all.

THE FIVE MAIN ETHICAL FRAMEWORKS

Moral philosophers these days often regard ethical or moral theories as falling into one of the five following ethical frameworks or perspectives as to what one fundamentally ought to do. We list them in no particular order and mention philosophers who provide good examples of each category, to help you understand those philosophers when you read about them in this chapter.

- First, **divine-command ethics:** What ought I to do? What God ordains, I ought to do. Augustine and Aquinas are good examples.

- Second, **consequentialism:** What ought I to do? Whatever has the most desirable consequences. The Epicureans, Stoics, and utilitarians are good examples.

- Third, **deontological ethics:** What ought I to do? Whatever it is my moral duty to do (in at least some cases, regardless of consequences). Kant is a good example.

- Fourth, **virtue ethics:** What ought I to do? What the virtuous person would do. (For virtue ethics, the primary question is not, What ought I to do? but rather, What kind of person ought I to be?) Plato and Aristotle are good examples.

- Fifth, **relativism:** What ought I to do? What my culture or society thinks I ought to do. None of the philosophers covered in this chapter are relativists (though many students are).

Sometimes *contractarianism* (or *contractualism*) is mentioned as a basic ethical theory. However, more often it is treated as a theory of social justice, the theory that principles of justice are best constructed through negotiations among impartial, informed, and rational agents. We'll discuss this idea in Chapter 11, which deals with political philosophy.

Let's now take a closer look at these five various ethical perspectives as they debuted in the history of moral philosophy.

THE EARLY GREEKS

That moral judgments must be supported by reasons is an idea we owe to the **Sophists,** those professional teachers of fifth-century B.C.E. Greece, and to **Socrates** (c. 470–399 B.C.E.). The Sophists, who attacked the traditional moral values of the Greek aristocracy, demanded rational justification for rules of conduct, as did Socrates. Their demands, together with Socrates' skillful deployment of the dialectical method in moral discussions, mark the beginning of philosophical reasoning about moral issues.

Maybe it was not inevitable that a time would come when someone insisted that moral claims be defended by reasons. When children ask why they should do something their parents think is right, they may be content to receive, and their parents content to give, the simple answer, "Because that is what is done." In some societies, evidently, values are accepted without much question, and demands for justification of moral claims are not issued. In our society it is frequently otherwise, and this is the legacy of the Sophists and Socrates.

It was Socrates especially who championed the use of reason in moral deliberation and with it raised good questions about some still-popular ideas about morality, such as that good is what pleases, that might makes right, and that happiness comes only to the ruthless.

Socrates was also concerned with the meanings of words that signify moral virtues, words like *justice, piety,* and *courage.* Because a moral term can be correctly applied to various specific acts—many different types of deeds count as courageous deeds, for example—Socrates believed that all acts characterized by a given moral term *must have something in common.* He therefore sought to determine (without notable success, we are sorry to report) what the essential commonality is. Socrates' assumption that a virtue has an essential nature, an essence that may be disclosed through rational inquiry, is still made by many philosophers and is central to several famous ethical theories, including Plato's, as you will see shortly.

Socrates also assumed that any sane person who possessed knowledge of the essence of virtue could not fail to act virtuously. He thus believed that ignoble behavior, if not the result of utter insanity, is always the product of ignorance. This is also a view that Plato shared, and it has its adherents today.

Plato

Plato accepted the Socratic idea that all things named by a given term, including any given moral term, share a common essential or "defining" feature. For example, what is common to all actions called heroic, is that they all have a feature or property—heroic-ness—that makes it possible for us to refer to them by the same name. What is common to all brave deeds is that feature that qualifies them all as brave. This essential or defining characteristic Plato referred to as the **Form** of the things in question; and, for various plausible reasons, he regarded this Form as

What do these objects have in common that makes them all chairs? Arms? Legs? Wood? No. What makes them all Chairs is that they share the same Form.

possessing more reality than the particular things that exemplified it. We talked about this in Chapter 3, but let's look into Plato's reasoning again, for this bears closely on Plato's ethics.

For a thing to be a chair, we think you must agree, it must possess that feature that qualifies a thing as a chair. That feature—let's call it *chairness*—is what Plato called the Form. And so, for a thing to qualify as a chair, it must possess chairness. Thus, the Form *chairness* must exist if anything at all is to qualify as a chair. So the Form is more fundamental and "real" than even the chair you are sitting on or any other chair.

Forms, Plato held, are not perceptible to the senses, for what the senses perceive are individual things: particular chairs, particular people, particular brave deeds, and so forth. We do not perceive the Forms through the senses. We cannot see chairness, and we cannot reach out and grasp bravery or humanity. Thus, Forms, he maintained, are known only through reason.

Further, according to Plato, the individual things that we perceive by sense are forever changing. Some things—rocks, for example—change very slowly. Other things, such as people, change a good bit more rapidly. That means that knowledge by sense perception is uncertain and unstable. Not so knowledge of the Forms. Knowledge of the Forms is certain and stable, for the objects known—the Forms—are eternal and unchanging.

Now the various Forms, Plato maintained (and here we will see what all of this has to do with ethics), constitute a *hierarchy* in terms of their inherent value or worth. It is easy enough to understand his point. For example, does not the Form *beauty* (i.e., the essence of beautiful things) seem to you to be inherently of more worth than the Form *wartness* (i.e., the essence of warts)?

At the apex of all Forms, Plato said, is the Form *goodness,* or (as it is often expressed) *the Good,* because it is the Form of highest value. Thus, for Plato, because

a. the Forms define true reality, and because
b. the Form of the Good is the uppermost of all Forms, it follows that
c. individual things are real only insofar as they partake of or exemplify this ultimate Form.

A corollary of (c) is that things are less "real" the less they partake of the Good. Another corollary is that evil is unreal. Make a mental note of the second corollary.

Because the Form of the Good is the source of all value and reality, Plato believed, we must strive to obtain knowledge and understanding of it. Therefore, he maintained, because (remember) Forms can be apprehended only by reason, we should govern ourselves by reason. Similarly, the state should be ruled by intellectuals, he said, but more of this in Chapter 11.

So, to summarize to this point, according to Plato, the true reality of individual things consists in the Forms they exemplify, Forms that are apprehended by reason and not by the senses; and the Form highest in value is the Form of the Good. One should, therefore, strive for knowledge of the Good and be ruled by reason.

But now consider this moral edict that Plato has in effect laid down: "Be governed by reason!" Is this not a little too abstract? Does it not fail to enjoin anything *specific* about what the individual should or should not do?

Plato would have answered "no" to both questions. The human soul, he said (a couple of thousand years before Freud proposed his analogous theory of the id, the ego, and the superego), has three different elements: an element consisting of raw appetites, an element consisting of drives (like anger and ambition), and an intellectual element (i.e., an element of thought or reason). For each of these elements, there is an excellence or virtue that obtains when reason is in charge of that element, as is the case when you govern yourself by reason. When our *appetites* are ruled by reason, we exhibit the virtue of *temperance;* when our *drives* are governed by reason, we exhibit *courage;* and when the *intellect* itself is governed by reason, we exhibit *wisdom.*

Thus, Plato held, the well-governed person, the person ruled by reason, exhibits the four cardinal virtues of temperance, courage, wisdom, and "justice." How did justice get in the list? Justice is the virtue that obtains when all elements of the soul function as they should in obedience to reason.

Given Plato's understanding of the soul, the principle "Be governed by reason," which follows from the theory of Forms, dictates that you be temperate, courageous, wise, and just. And what, in turn, these dictates mean more specifically was

Plato and Divine-Command Ethics

Plato examined the idea that what is morally right and good is determined by divine command, that is, by the edict or decree of God—a popular idea today in Western (and other) societies—and the result of that examination was a question: Is something right or good because the gods (or God) decree that it is, or is it decreed by the gods (or God) as right or good because it is right or good? (If the question interests you, you might wish to read Plato's very short dialogue *Euthyphro*.)

Some critics of "divine-command" theories of ethics argue that Plato's question puts the adherents of these theories in an awkward position. If you say that God decrees something because it *is* good, then you seem to imply that God is not the ultimate authority or the ultimate source of goodness: you seem to imply that there is something beyond God that makes good things good things. But if you say that something is good because God decrees it, you seem to imply that God's decrees are arbitrary; he could just as well have decreed that the thing was not good.

In short, the question implies—so it is argued—either that God's moral prescriptions are arbitrary or that God is not the ultimate source of goodness.

much discussed by Plato, though we will not go into the details. Further, he said, only by being virtuous—that is, by possessing these four virtues—can you have a well-ordered soul and thus have the psychological well-being that is true happiness. In this way Plato connected virtue with happiness, a connection we still acknowledge by saying, "Virtue is its own reward."

But is a well-ordered or just or virtuous soul really required for happiness? Plato did not merely assert that it is and expect us to close our eyes and blindly swallow the assertion. He knew as well as anyone that exactly the opposite seems to be true: that the people who seem to be the best off often seem to be very unscrupulous. So Plato examined the matter rather carefully, especially in the *Republic*. In that dialogue, Plato has various characters explain and defend the view that the life of the person who cleverly and subtly promotes his own ends at the expense of other people is preferable to the life of the virtuous person. Plato (in the person of his Socrates character) does think that this view is mistaken and attempts (at considerable length) to explain what is wrong with it—this attempt actually is the main theme of the *Republic*. Whether he succeeds you may wish to consider for yourself at some point. In any case, a more powerful defense of being *unjust* and *unvirtuous* than the one Plato sets forth (and tries to refute) in the *Republic* has never been devised.

Now you may agree with Plato's conclusion, that the virtuous course of action is the one most apt to produce your own well-being, because you believe that God will reward you in an afterlife if you are virtuous here and now and punish you if you are not. Notice, though, what you are assuming if you accept this belief, namely, that virtuous activity does *not* promote its own reward (i.e., happiness) in *this* life. Plato, though, believed that your well-being in *this* life is best promoted by virtuous activity. (See the box "Plato and Divine-Command Ethics.")

The Go-for-It Philosophy of Aristippus

At about the time Plato lived in Athens, another Greek, Aristippus (435–366 B.C.E.), who lived in Cyrene, espoused an ethical doctrine quite different from Plato's. Aristippus said our lives should always be dedicated to the acquisition of as many pleasures, preferably as intense as possible, as we can possibly obtain. Even when intense pleasures lead to subsequent pain, they should still be sought, he said, for a life without pleasure or pain would be unredeemingly boring. Pleasures are best obtained, according to Aristippus, when one takes control of a situation and other people and uses them to one's own advantage.

Perhaps you know people who agree with Aristippus.

Cyrenaicism, which is the name of this hedonistic (pleasure-seeking) philosophy, was the historical antecedent of Epicureanism. As you can see from the text, Epicurus's pleasure-oriented philosophy is considerably more moderate than Aristippus'. Epicurus recommended avoiding intense pleasure as producing too much pain and disappointment over the long run.

We will conclude by mentioning that Plato was interested in such popular views (popular both then and now and perhaps forevermore) as that *goodness is the same thing as pleasure,* that *self-control is not the best way to get happiness,* and that *it is better to exploit others than to be exploited by them.* He found, when he considered these ideas carefully, that they are mistaken. So if you are tempted to agree with any of these ideas, we recommend that you read the *Republic* and another famous Platonic dialogue, the *Gorgias,* before arranging your affairs in the belief that they are true. You should also read the box "The Go-for-It Philosophy of Aristippus." We present a brief excerpt from the *Gorgias* at the end of the chapter.

Aesara, the Lucanian

A strong echo of Platonic ethical themes may be found in the work of **Aesara** [ai-SAH-ruh], a Greek philosopher from Lucania (in southern Italy), who probably lived around 350 B.C.E. Only a fragment of her original work survives. Aesara has been mentioned only rarely in textbooks in philosophy, perhaps because of the scanty remains of her work, perhaps owing to other reasons. But she is interesting and worth reading.

Like Plato, Aesara was concerned with the nature of human well-being, or the good life. And like Plato, she saw the key to this to be the well-ordered or virtuous or "just" soul—the balanced and harmoniously functioning psyche. Also like Plato, she saw that the well-functioning state replicates the balance and order that exists in the well-functioning soul.

Aesara's analysis of the human psyche or soul was very similar to Plato's. She thought the soul has three parts: the mind, spiritedness, and desire. The *mind* analyzes ideas and reaches decisions. *Spiritedness* is the part of the soul that gives a person the ability to carry out decisions; we might call it the *will.* The element of *desire* contains moral emotions such as love.

It is worth noting that the role of women in ancient Greek society was to stay at home and raise virtuous, rational offspring, the male versions of whom would run the world of government and the marketplace—the world outside the home. As a woman, Aesara was keenly aware that men, even men philosophers, sometimes tended to think that justice applied only to the world outside the home. Are two different approaches to moral philosophy needed, one for inside the home and another for dealings with people outside the family and for public institutions? We will encounter this question again in the twentieth century, but it seems clear that Aesara's answer would be "no." All morally significant decisions, whether regarding our families or the state, should reflect the appropriate proportions of reason, will power, and such positive affective emotions as love.

Only a fragment of Aesara's original work remains. Even though Aesara's influence on the history of philosophy was less than that of, say, Plato or Aristotle, we remain convinced of the value of including Aesara's thoughts here. A more elegant statement than Aesara's cannot be found for two ancient Greek ideas—the idea that from the well-ordered soul, the soul characterized by the harmonious functioning and proper proportioning of its elements, springs virtue, and the idea that the human soul is the model for society. "Human nature," she said, "provides the standard for law and justice for both the home and the city." If you understand the nature of the soul, you understand how society and social justice ought to be.

Aristotle

The ultimate source of all value for Plato was the Form of the Good, an entity that is distinct from the particular things that populate the natural world, the world we perceive through our senses. This Platonic idea, that all value is grounded in a *nonnatural* source, is an element of Plato's philosophy that is found in many ethical systems and is quite recognizable in Christian ethics. But not every ethical system postulates a nonnatural source of value.

Those systems that do not are called *naturalistic ethical systems*. According to **ethical naturalism,** moral judgments are really judgments of fact about the natural world. Thus, **Aristotle,** for instance, who was the first great ethical naturalist, believed that the good for us is defined by our natural objective.

Now, what would you say is our principal or highest objective by nature? According to Aristotle, it is the attainment of happiness, for it is that alone that we seek for its own sake. And because the attainment of happiness is naturally our highest objective, it follows that happiness is our highest good.

In what does happiness, our highest good, consist? According to Aristotle, to answer we must consider the human being's function. To discover what goodness is for an ax or a chisel or anything whatsoever, we must consider its function, what it actually does. And when we consider what the human animal does, as a *human* animal, we see that, most essentially, it (a) lives and (b) reasons.

Thus, happiness consists of two things, Aristotle concluded: *enjoyment (pleasure)* and the *exercise and development of the capacity to reason.* It consists in part of enjoyment because the human being, as a living thing, has biological needs and impulses the satisfaction of which is pleasurable. And it consists in part of developing and exercising the capacity to reason, because only the human being, as distinct from other living things, has that capacity. Because this capacity differentiates humans from other living things, its exercise was stressed by Aristotle as the most important component of happiness. Pleasure alone does not constitute happiness, he insisted.

The exercise of our unique and distinctive capacity to reason was termed by Aristotle *virtue*—thus Aristotle's famous phrase that happiness is activity in accordance with virtue. There are two different kinds of virtues. To exercise actively our reasoning abilities, as when we study nature or cogitate about something, is to be *intellectually* virtuous. But we also exercise our rational capacity by moderating our impulses and appetites, and when we do this, we were said by Aristotle to be *morally* virtuous.

The largest part of Aristotle's major ethical work, the *Nicomachean Ethics*, is devoted to analysis of specific moral virtues, which Aristotle held to be the **mean between extremes** (e.g., courage is the mean between fearing everything and fearing nothing). He emphasized as well that virtue is a matter of *habit:* just as an ax that is only occasionally sharp does not fulfill its function well, the human who exercises his rational capacities only occasionally does not fulfill his function, that is, is not virtuous.

Aristotle also had the important insight that a person's pleasures reveal his true moral character. "He who faces danger with pleasure, or, at any rate, without pain, is courageous," he observed, "but he to whom this is painful is a coward." Of course, we might object that he who is willing to face danger *despite* the pain it brings him is the most courageous, but this is a quibble.

Another distinction made by Aristotle is that between instrumental ends and intrinsic ends. An **instrumental end** is an act performed as a means to other ends. An **intrinsic end** is an act performed for its own sake.

For example, when we, Bruder and Moore, sat down to write this book, our end was to finish it. But that end was merely instrumental to another end—to provide our readers with a better understanding of philosophy.

But now notice that the last goal, the goal of providing our readers with a better understanding of philosophy, is instrumental to a further end, namely, an enlightened society.

Notice, too, that when your teacher grades you and the other students in the class, that act is instrumental to your learning, and that end also is instrumental to an enlightened society.

As a matter of fact, all the activities in the university are aimed at producing an enlightened society. For example, your teacher may recently have received a promotion. Promotions are instrumental to effective teaching in your university, and effective teaching also is instrumental to an enlightened society.

But notice that that end, an enlightened society, is merely instrumental to another end, at least according to Aristotle. For why even have an enlightened society? An enlightened society is good, Aristotle would say, because in such a society people will be able to fulfill their natural function as human beings. And therefore, he would say, when we understand what the natural function of people is, then we finally will know what is intrinsically good, good for its own sake. Then we will know what the "Good of Man" is.

So to sum up the main points, Aristotle's ethics were basically naturalistic: human good is defined by human nature. Plato's were nonnaturalistic: goodness in all its manifestations is defined by the Form of the Good. Despite these differences, Aristotle and Plato would doubtless have agreed to a great extent in their praise and condemnation of the activities of other people. Aristotle, too, deemed the cardinal moral virtues to be courage, temperance, justice, and wisdom, and both he and Plato advocated the intellectual life.

Notice, too, that Plato and Aristotle both conceived of ethics as focusing on good *character traits* of individuals—virtues—rather than on a set of *rules for actions* (such as "treat others as you would have others treat you"). In the last quarter of the twentieth century (as we shall see in Chapter 12), there was considerable interest among Anglo-American philosophers in this type of ethical theory, which is known as *virtue ethics*. From the point of view of virtue ethics, the fundamental ethical question is not so much, What ought one do? but rather, What kind of person ought one to be?

Despite these similarities, it must be kept in mind that the ultimate source of all moral value—that is, the Good—was for Plato a nonnatural "Form," whereas Aristotle sought to define the good for humans in terms of what the human organism in fact naturally seeks, namely, happiness.

Ever since Aristotle's time, ethical systems often fall into one of two categories: those that find the supreme moral good as something that *transcends* nature and thus follow the lead of Plato, and those that follow Aristotle by grounding morality in human nature.

EPICUREANISM AND STOICISM

In the Greek and Roman periods following Aristotle, there were four main "schools" of philosophy: the Epicureans, the Stoics, the Skeptics, and the Neoplatonists. The Neoplatonists and the Skeptics were discussed in Part One.

The Skeptics denied the possibility of any knowledge, and this denial included moral knowledge. They said that no judgments can be established and that it does not matter if the judgments are factual judgments or value judgments (a value judgment assigns a value to something). Accordingly, they advocated tolerance toward others, detachment from the concerns of others, and caution in your own actions. Whether the Skeptics were *consistent* in advocating toleration, detachment, and caution while maintaining that no moral judgment can be established, you might consider for yourself.

Epicureanism and Stoicism, which mainly concern us in this chapter, were both naturalistic ethical philosophies, and both had a lasting effect on philosophy and ethics. To this day, "taking things philosophically" means responding to disappointments as a Stoic would, and the word *epicure* has its own place in the everyday English found outside the philosophy classroom.

Epicureanism

Epicureanism, the theory that personal pleasure is the highest good, began with **Epicurus** [ep-uh-KYUR-us] (341–270 B.C.E.), flourished in the second and first centuries B.C.E., spread to Rome, and survived as a school until almost the third century C.E. Though few today would call themselves Epicureans, there is no question that many people still subscribe to some of the central tenets of this philosophy. You may do so yourself. We do.

According to Epicurus, it is natural for us to seek a pleasant life above all other things; it follows, he reasoned (as perhaps you will, too), that we ought to seek a pleasant life above all other things. In this sense, Epicurus was a naturalist in ethics.

The pleasant life, Epicurus said, comes to you when your desires are satisfied. And there are three kinds of desires, he maintained:

- Those that are *natural and must be satisfied* for one to have a pleasant life (such as the desire for food and shelter)
- Those that, *though natural, need not necessarily be satisfied* for a pleasant life (including, for example, the desire for sexual gratification)
- Those that are *neither natural nor necessary* to satisfy (such as the desire for wealth or fame)

The pleasant life is best achieved, Epicurus believed, by neglecting the third kind of desire and satisfying only desires of the first kind, although desires of the second kind may also be satisfied, he said, when doing so does not lead to discomfort or pain. It is *never* prudent to try to satisfy unnecessary/unnatural desires, he said, for in the long run trying to do so will produce disappointment, dissatisfaction, discomfort, or poor health. There is, surely, much that is reasonable in this philosophy, even though many people spend a good bit of time and energy trying to satisfy precisely those desires that, according to Epicurus, are both unnecessary and unnatural.

As is evident, Epicurus favored the *pleasant life* over momentary pleasures and attached great importance to the avoidance of pain as the prime ingredient in the pleasant life. It is one of the ironies of philosophy that the word *epicure* is often used to denote a fastidious person excessively fond of refined tastes—a snob. Epicurus was certainly not an epicure in this sense, for he recommended a life of relaxation, repose, and moderation, as well as avoidance of the pleasures of the flesh and passions. He would not have been fond of expensive champagne or caviar.

The Stoics

If Epicurus was not exactly an epicure (at least in one meaning of the word), were the Stoics stoical? A stoic is a person who maintains a calm indifference to pain and suffering, and yes, the Stoics were stoical.

The school was founded by **Zeno** (c. 335–c. 263 B.C.E.; not the same Zeno mentioned in Chapter 2), who met his students on the *stoa* (Greek for "porch"). **Stoicism** spread to Rome and survived as a school until almost the

Athletes often subscribe to the idea that physical improvement requires stoical acceptance of physical discomfort. No pain, no gain.

third century C.E. Its most famous adherents, other than Zeno, were **Epictetus** [ep-ik-TEET-us] (c. 55–c. 135 C.E.), the Roman statesman Cicero (106–43 B.C.E.), and Marcus Aurelius (121–180 C.E.), the Roman emperor.

Like the Epicureans, the Stoics believed that it is only natural for a person to seek a pleasant life and that therefore a person ought to seek such a life. But the Stoics were much influenced by the Cynics (see the box "Diogenes the Cynic"), who went *out of their way* to find hardship. The Stoics saw that the Cynics, by actively pursuing hardship, acquired the ability to remain untroubled by the pains and disappointments of life. The Stoics thought there was some sense in this. It occurred to them that untroubledness or serenity is a desirable state indeed.

The Stoics, however, more than the Cynics, had a *metaphysical justification* for their ethics. All that occurs, the Stoics believed, occurs in accordance with natural law, which they equated with reason. **Natural law,** they said, is the vital force that activates or (as we might say) energizes all things. It follows that

1. Whatever happens is the inevitable outcome of the logic of the universe.
2. Whatever happens, happens with a reason and therefore is for the best.

So, according to the Stoic philosophy, you can do nothing to alter the course of events, because they have been fixed by the law of nature. Do not struggle against the inevitable, the Stoics said. Instead, understand that what is happening is for the best, and accept it.

Diogenes the Cynic

According to the **Cynics,** who were fiercely individualistic, the wise person avoids even the most basic comforts and seeks total self-reliance by reducing all wants to a minimum and by forgoing any convenience or benefit offered by society. The most famous Cynic, the fourth-century B.C.E. philosopher **Diogenes** [dy-AH-juh-neez], is said to have dressed in rags and lived in an empty tub and even to have thrown out his drinking cup when he observed a child drinking from his hands. Alexander the Great, who admired Diogenes, is said to have made his way to the latter and announced that he would fill Diogenes' greatest need. Diogenes replied that he had a great need for Alexander to stop blocking his sunlight.

Diogenes is also reported to have masturbated in public while observing that it was too bad that hunger could not be relieved in similar fashion merely by rubbing your stomach. His point in part was simply to flout conventions, but it was apparently also to contrast sexual needs with the need for food.

According to another story, Diogenes visited the home of a wealthy man. The man asked Diogenes to avoid spitting on the floor or furnishings because the home was expensively appointed. Diogenes responded by spitting in the man's face and commented that it was the only worthless thing in the room.

Whether these stories are true or not, the indifference to material things that they portray was appreciated by the Stoics. Yet even though the Stoics saw the advantages to scaling back needs in the manner of the Cynics, they were not nearly so flamboyant in what they said and did. The Cynics were often willing to do or say something just to shock people.

Incidentally, as the word is most commonly used today, a cynic is one who sneers at sincerity, helpfulness, and other virtuous activity as inspired by ulterior motives. It is clear how the word acquired this meaning, given the contempt the Cynics had for traditional institutions and practices.

If you are wise, according to the Stoics, you will approach life as an actor approaches his or her part. You will realize that you have no control over the plot or assignment of roles, and therefore you will distance yourself psychologically from all that happens to the character you play. Does the character you play grow ill in the play? Well, you will *act* the part to the best of your ability, but you certainly will not permit yourself to suffer. Do your friends die in the play? Do you die? It is all for the best because it is dictated by the plot.

Now, perhaps you are thinking, Well, if I cannot control what happens to me, then how on earth can I control my attitude about what happens? If what happens is inevitable, then what happens to my attitudes is inevitable, too, right? Nevertheless, this was the Stoics' doctrine: *You can control your attitude. Remain uninvolved emotionally in your fate, and your life will be untroubled.*

The Stoic philosophy also had a political ethic according to which the Stoic had a duty to serve other people and respect their inherent worth as equals under natural law. So the Stoics thought that, although you should seek the untroubled life for yourself, your ethical concerns are not limited to your own welfare. Whether this social component of Stoicism is consistent with a philosophy of emotional noninvolvement, acceptance of the natural order, and seeking tranquility for yourself may be questioned, of course. In fact, whether a philosophy of self-interest is compatible with concern for the common good is one of the most important questions of ethics, and you know quite well that this is a live issue even today.

Let's summarize this section: According to the Epicureans, one's ultimate ethical objective is to lead the pleasant life through moderate living. According to the Stoics, the objective is to obtain the serene or untroubled life through acceptance of the rational or natural order of things while remembering that one is obligated to be of service to one's fellow creatures. Stoicism in particular had an impact on Christian thought, primarily through the philosophy of St. Augustine, to whom we shall turn next.

One of the selections at the end of this chapter is from Epictetus, among the most famous of Stoics. Epictetus also is unusual among philosophers in that he was sold as a slave when a child but was given an education and later freed, thereafter becoming an influential teacher of philosophy. As you might expect from what we have said about Stoicism and Epicureanism, the two philosophies are very similar (even though Epictetus thought he was recommending a way of life quite different from that of the Epicureans).

CHRISTIANIZING ETHICS

Let us next turn to the way the Christian religion shaped the ancient idea of ethics and to the figure most responsible for that transformation.

St. Augustine

St. Augustine (354–430 C.E.) is one of the towering figures of Christian philosophy. It is he who first gave Christianity philosophical weight and substance.

Augustine found philosophical justification for Christianity in the metaphysics of Plato, as reinterpreted by the Neoplatonist Plotinus (205–270 C.E.). Christianity rests on the belief in a transcendent God, and with the assistance of Platonic metaphysics, St. Augustine was able to make philosophically intelligible to himself the concept of a *transcendent realm,* a realm of being beyond the spatiotemporal universe that contains (or is) the source of all that is real and good. He also saw in Platonic and Neoplatonic doctrines the solution to the *problem of evil.* This problem can be expressed in a very simple question: How could evil have arisen in a world created by a perfectly good God?

One solution to this problem that Augustine considered was that evil is the result of a creative force other than God, a *force of darkness,* so to speak. But isn't there supposed to be just one and only one Creator? That is what Augustine believed, so this solution was not acceptable.

For Plato, remember, the Form of the Good was the source of all reality, and from this principle it follows that all that is real is good. Thus, given Plato's principle, evil *is not real.* St. Augustine found this approach to the problem of evil entirely satisfactory. Because evil is not something, it was not created by God.

This theory of evil is plausible enough as long as you are thinking of certain "physical" evils, such as blindness or droughts (though others, such as pain, seem as real as can be). Blindness, after all, is the absence of sight, and droughts are the absence of water.

Unfortunately, however, the absence theory does not plausibly explain *moral* evil, the evil that is the wrongdoing of men and women. How did Augustine account for moral evil? His explanation of moral evil was a variation of another idea of Plato's, the idea that a person never knowingly does wrong, that evil actions are the result of ignorance of the good, of misdirected education, so to say. But Augustine added a new twist to this idea. Moral evil, he said, is not exactly a case of misdirected *education* but, instead, a case of misdirected *love*. This brings us to the heart of Augustine's ethics.

For Augustine, as for the Stoics, a natural law governs all morality, and human behavior must conform to it. But for Augustine this was not an impersonal rational principle that shapes the destiny of the cosmos. The Augustinian natural law is, rather, the eternal law of God as it is written in the heart of man and woman and is apprehended by them in their conscience; and the eternal law is the "reason and will of God."

Thus, the ultimate source of all that is good, for Augustine, was God, and God alone is intrinsically good. Our overriding moral imperative is therefore to love God. The individual virtues are simply different aspects of the love of God.

Augustine did not mean that you must love *only* God. He meant that, although there is nothing wrong with loving things other than God, you must not love them as if they were good in and of themselves, for *only God is intrinsically good*. To love things other than God as if they were inherently good—for example, to love money or success as if these things were good in and of themselves—is *disordered* love: it is to turn away from God, and moral evil consists in just this disordered love.

Now, do not let any of this make you think that Augustine was unconcerned with happiness, for as a matter of fact he did indeed think we should seek happiness. But happiness, he argued, consists in having all you want and wanting no evil. This may seem to be an odd notion at first, but when you think about it, it is by no means absurd. In any event, the only conceivable way to have all you want and to want no evil, Augustine thought, is to make God the supreme object of your love.

So, for Augustine, moral evil arises when man or woman turns away from God. Thus, *God* is not the creator of moral evil; it is *we* who create evil. But does it not then follow that *we* can create good? No, for God, remember, is the source of all that is good. We can do good only *through* God, Augustine said.

In sum, Augustine borrowed a theme from Plato by maintaining that physical evil can always be explained as the absence of something, and his concept of moral evil as arising from misdirected love can be viewed as a variation of Plato's idea of moral evil as ignorance of the good. In this way, Augustine thought he had solved the problem of evil without doing damage to principles of Christian faith.

One other aspect of Augustine's moral philosophy must be emphasized. According to Augustine, our highest good, or virtue, consists in loving and having God. By contrast, sin is distorted or misdirected or disordered love. So virtue and sin, according to Augustine, are *conditions of the soul*. What counted, for Augustine, was living out of love for God; doing supposedly good deeds was of secondary importance. When it comes to appraising a person's moral worth, therefore, what matters is not the person's accomplishments but, rather, the *state of mind* from which the person acts. We shall see that this idea—that a person's intent is what matters morally—came to play an important role in moral philosophy.

St. Hildegard of Bingen

Augustine was the last of the great late ancient philosophers. Between the sixth century and the eleventh, Europe went through the Dark Ages, as we discussed in Chapter 5. **Hildegard** (1098–1179) was a light at the end of the tunnel. Her ethical writings typify the beginning of a period of religious mysticism that never came to a complete end: religious mysticism just went out of fashion with the onslaught of rationalism that began with Descartes (see Chapter 6). Mysticism, we perhaps should mention, is belief in (or experience of) a form of higher, spiritual, mystical realm often found in trances or dreams.

Hildegard was unquestionably an important figure in the history of philosophy (see the Profile). It is true that she and other religious mystical philosophers are usually called "theologians," but what they had to say is important for both ethics and moral epistemology. They provided theories of the nature of moral knowledge.

For mystical philosophers, mystical experience provides as certain a form of knowledge as pure rational introspection ever could. Their mystical experiences often take the form of visions and sometimes take the form of ideas, thoughts, and even whole books that seemingly are dictated directly by some divine source during these experiences. We are not going to assess the validity of such claims here; we are just going to reproduce and talk about their contents.

In one of her books, Hildegard listed thirty-five vices and their opposite virtues. This kind of list of opposites is a traditional format for talking about virtue and vice and dates back to Pythagoras. One vice, *Immoderation* (lack of moderate desires), is opposed to the virtue *Discretion* (keeping things within appropriate bounds). Hildegard described Immoderation in the following allegory:

> This one is just like a wolf. She is furiously cunning, in hot pursuit of all evils, without distinction. With flexed legs, she crouches, looking in all directions, in such a way that she would devour anything she could snatch. She has a tendency to anything low-grade, following the worst habits of her peculiar mind. She considers every empty, worthless thing.

Now, before you jump to conclusions about this medieval Benedictine nun, before you dismiss her views on virtue and vice as narrow and constricted, take a look at her accounts of human sexuality. In these excerpts from her philosophy of medicine in *Causa et Curae* (*Causes and Cures*), she gave the following accounts of what she considered to be healthy male and female sexuality:

> There are some men showing much virility, and they have strong and solid brains. The wind also which is in their loins has two tents to its command, in which it blows as if into a chimney. And these tents surround the stem of all manly powers, and are helpers to it, just like small buildings placed next to a tower which they defend. Therefore, there are two, surrounding the stem, and they strengthen and direct it so that the more brave and allied, they would attract the wind and release it again, just like two bellows which blow into a fire. When likewise they erect the stem in its manliness, they hold it bravely and thus at a later time the stem blossoms into a fruit.

PROFILE: St. Hildegard of Bingen (1098–1179)

Hildegard was born at the end of the eleventh century in the Rhine River valley in Germany. She was the tenth child and was therefore "tithed" to God; at age seven or eight, she was sent to live with a group of women in a hermitage that eventually became the Benedictine convent of Disibodenberg. Hildegard learned Latin and studied the Bible, and she read the philosophical works of early Church fathers, including St. Jerome and St. Augustine.

Even as a child, Hildegard experienced mystical visions. By the time Hildegard had been head of the convent at Disibodenberg for three years, God commanded her, during one of these visions, to begin writing them down and to teach others their content. This put Hildegard in a difficult position because women were considered by the Church as well as by society to have no religious, theological, or philosophical authority. But the Bishop of Mainz (Germany) was impressed by her writings and convinced Pope Eugene III to consider them. The pope was convinced that the visions were genuine messages from God and had part of Hildegard's messages read to the bishops, who had come from all over Europe to attend a conference called the Synod of Trier during the winter of 1147–1148.

Hildegard and her little convent were now better known than the adjoining monastery. As Hildegard's fame spread, more and more women flocked to her convent. When the monks at the monastery refused to give the nuns the additional living quarters and library space they needed, Hildegard moved the convent. The monks, who controlled the dowries of the nuns, tried to retain the money and valuables. But Hildegard had some power now and effectively convinced the bishops that the monks were obligated to turn the sizable dowries over to her. These funds and artifacts were needed to finance the construction of the new convent at Bingen and to provide support for her nuns. She was a formidable champion for the education of women, which at that time meant establishing convents (she founded two) where ancient copies of philosophical and religious texts were hand-copied by nuns who had been taught to read Latin.

Hildegard was a prolific writer. She wrote books on natural science and on medicine (she is credited with developing the theory that disease can be transmitted by dirty water—resulting in the construction of massive sewage systems in Germany), wrote music (recently released on CD!), and wrote lengthy works of religious philosophy that she had lavishly illustrated with replications of the visions upon which they were based.

She was a prodigiously influential thinker and traveled and "preached" the meaning of her visions throughout Germany. She was regularly consulted by a succession of four popes, and her many correspondents included two emperors, a king, and two queens. Hildegard lived to a ripe old age despite a lifetime of recurrent illnesses and the hardships of extended preaching tours.

And:

> Pleasure in a woman is compared to the sun which caressingly, gently, and continuously fills the earth with its heat, so that it can bear fruits, since if it would heat the earth more harshly in its constancy, it would hurt the fruits more than it would produce them. And so pleasure in a woman caressingly and gently, but nevertheless continuously, would have heat so that she can conceive and produce fruit. For when pleasure surges forth in a woman, it is lighter in her than it is in a man.

Clearly, sexual pleasure was not on this nun's list of vices.

Heloise and Abelard

An important thinker who lived at the same time as Hildegard was the French abbess **Heloise** [HEL-oh-eez] (1098–1164). Heloise, like Hildegard, was concerned with virtue and vice, although Heloise was especially concerned with a specific virtue.

For Heloise, philosophy was life. If you believed in the truth of a theory of morality, you lived according to its principles. End of story. Heloise's writings on moral philosophy are found in her *Problemata* (Problems) and *Epistolae* (Letters), written when Heloise was in her thirties and all addressed to **Peter Abelard** (1079–1144), another major figure in the history of ethical philosophy and the most important logician of his time. The famous love story of Abelard and Heloise is explained in the box "The Truth about Heloise and Abelard."

The ethics of Heloise has two primary components. The first component, adapted from the Roman Stoic philosopher Cicero, places high value on the virtue *Disinterested Love*. True love for another, whether or not sexual, is completely unselfish and asks nothing, Heloise believed. The lover loves the beloved for who the beloved is. A true lover supports the beloved in achieving his goals and realizing his highest moral potential. In an ideal loving relationship, the beloved has reciprocal feelings for the lover. He loves her for herself, for who she is. He aspires to help her realize her highest moral potential and the fulfillment of her goals. He has no selfish desires.

The other major component of Heloise's moral philosophy concerns the **morality of intent,** which she derived basically from Abelard's own teachings. Think back to the Augustinian theory: it is not *what you do* that matters but rather the *state of mind* with which you do it (virtue is essentially a matter of having a mind that is disposed to do right). This theory was accepted throughout the Dark Ages and into the Middle Ages. The one who explored this theory most carefully prior to St. Thomas Aquinas was Abelard.

Abelard drew a distinction between moral defects or imperfections and other defects or imperfections of the mind, such as being stupid or having a bad memory. Moral defects dispose you to do what you should not do—or not do what you should do. He also drew a distinction between moral defects and sin. Sin is "contempt of God"—failing to do or renounce what we should.

Armed with these distinctions, Abelard argued that sin does not consist in *acting* on evil desires. In fact, it does not even consist in *having* evil desires. Sin consists instead in *consenting* to act on evil desires. Further, a wrongful act—an act that ought not be done, such as killing someone—can be committed without an evil will, in which case, although the act is wrong, the person who acts is not morally reprehensible.

Thus, Abelard's position was that virtue consists not in having no evil desires but in not consenting to act on them. And "the evil will itself, when restrained, though it may not be quenched, procures the palmwreath for those who resist it."

Heloise, too, accepted this theory: "In a wicked deed, rectitude of action depends not on the effect of the thing but on the affections of the agent, not on what is done but with what dispositions it is done."

This conception of ethics certainly played an important role in the relationship between Abelard and Heloise. Heloise argued that, by voluntarily marrying Abelard, she would have been the cause of Abelard's being barred from final

The Truth about Heloise and Abelard

Heloise (1098–1164) was a French philosopher and poet who received an early education at the Benedictine convent of Argenteuil. By the time she was sixteen years old, she was known as the most learned woman in France. Heloise's uncle Fulbert, who was her guardian and also a canon at Notre Dame, hired an unordained cleric named Pierre Abelard (1079–1144) to teach Heloise philosophy.

The traditional literature tends to describe Heloise and Abelard's relationship as one of the great love affairs of all time, right up there with Romeo and Juliet. Now, that is true to a certain extent. Heloise certainly fell in love with her philosophy teacher—but she refused to have sex with him.

Not a modern-day Heloise and Abelard, we hope.

Abelard acknowledged that Heloise verbally refused to have sex and physically fought him off. In his words, "I frequently forced your consent (for after all you were the weaker) by threats and blows." Or, as we might say today if he were brought up on charges: on some occasions he beat her and raped her, and on other occasions he threatened to beat her again if she did not stop resisting.

Heloise became pregnant. Abelard offered to marry her. Heloise refused. As usual, Abelard would not take no for an answer. As her due date came near, he took her to his sister's farm in the country, where she gave birth. They named their son Astrolabe (after an astronomical instrument). Abelard convinced Heloise to marry him so that their son would not be a bastard. You see, illegitimate children could not be baptized back then, so if Heloise had not married Abelard, she would have been condemning their son to an eternity in limbo.

Now, saving your baby from eternal limbo might well be enough to make you marry someone who, incidentally, had already become an important medieval philosopher. But it is important, if you are going to understand Heloise's moral philosophy, to know about the other sordid details of their personal life. (Unfortunately, there are more.)

When the happy couple returned to Paris (leaving the baby at the farm), they lied to Uncle Fulbert about having gotten married. If the story got out that Abelard was married, Heloise knew, he would not be permitted to continue studying for the priesthood. The Cathedral School of Notre Dame, where Abelard taught, was turning into the University of Paris. It would be the first institution of higher learning in France (the second in Europe) to accept students who were not studying to be priests.

Heloise thought it would be a waste of Abelard's talents for him to miss out on this new experiment in education: a university. Worse, Heloise would feel responsible for keeping Abelard from fulfilling his ambitions.

Fulbert, though, was no fool. He figured things out and announced that Abelard had gotten married. Heloise tried to protect Abelard by denying the marriage, so Uncle Fulbert started mistreating Heloise (who was living at his house). To make it appear as if Heloise were not lying, Abelard ordered her to return to the convent and become a nun, which she did. At this point, Uncle Fulbert, who evidently was not given to halfway measures, hired thugs to castrate Abelard. (Heloise, who was in Argenteuil at the convent, did not hear about this for years.) But now that having sex with Heloise was permanently out of the question, Abelard sought final ordination as a priest. He set up a convent called the Paraclete and made Heloise its abbess. For decades, she never knew why.

ordination to the priesthood. She did not want to be morally responsible for that outcome. She felt he forced and tricked her into marrying him and that this was a consequence of her pregnancy, for which she was not morally responsible. Abelard's *Historica Calamitatum* (*Story of My Calamities*), as well as Heloise's letters to Abelard, insists that she never agreed to have sex with him: he beat and raped her. She would not accept moral responsibility for the pregnancy because she had no evil intent to seduce him.

But because they actually were married, Abelard could order Heloise to enter a convent. After she did so, Abelard had almost no contact with her. Heloise did not understand why Abelard ignored her letters nor why he ignored the physical and spiritual welfare of her nuns. Decades later, she read his book and learned about his castration. She put two and two together.

Heloise might have loved Abelard in this ideal, disinterested type of love, but it was a one-way street. Although she loved him for himself and expressed that love by helping him achieve his goals (priesthood and a job as a philosopher at the emerging university), his love for her was predominantly sexual. After he was no longer able to have sex, she realized, Abelard had made her head of her own convent. Heloise had obeyed Abelard (who was both her husband and her religious superior), running the convent and teaching the nuns. All those years, Heloise had lived according to the moral theory she thought Abelard shared, loving him unselfishly, for himself.

St. Thomas Aquinas

Augustine fashioned a philosophical framework for Christian thought that was essentially Platonic. He found many Platonic and Neoplatonic themes that could be given a Christian interpretation and thus is sometimes said to have Christianized Plato. Eight centuries later, **St. Thomas Aquinas** [uh-QUINE-nuss] (1225–1274), in a somewhat different sense, Christianized the philosophy of Aristotle. Aquinas's task was perhaps the more difficult of the two, for the philosophy of Aristotle, with its this-worldly approach to things, was less congenial to a Christian interpretation. Thus, it is customary to speak of Aquinas as having *reconciled* Aristotelianism with Christianity. In Aquinas's ethical philosophy, this amounted by and large to accepting both Christianity and the philosophy of Aristotle wherever that could be done without absurdity.

Aristotle said that the good for each kind of thing is defined with reference to the function or the nature of that kind of thing and is in fact the goal or purpose of that kind of thing. In the case of humans, goodness is happiness. Aquinas agreed. The natural (moral) law, which is God's eternal law as it is applied to humans on earth, is apprehended by us in the dictates of our conscience and practical reasoning, which guide us to our natural goal, happiness on earth.

But there is also, according to Aquinas, an eternal, atemporal good—namely, happiness everlasting. The law that directs us to that end is God's divine law, which the Creator reveals to us through his grace.

Thus, the natural law of Aquinas is the law of reason, which leads us to our natural end insofar as we follow it. The **divine law** is God's gift to us, revealed through his grace. Therefore, according to Aquinas, there are two sets of virtues:

the "higher" virtues of faith, love, and hope; and the natural virtues, such as forti-
tude and prudence, which are achieved when the will, directed by the intellect,
moderates our natural drives, impulses, and inclinations. And Aquinas, like Aristotle,
thought of the virtues as matters of character or habit—in Aquinas's view, the
habit of acting according to the provisions of natural law.

Although Aquinas's ethics are thus a type of virtue-ethics, he did treat the
moral goodness of actions. When evaluating an act, and only voluntary acts are
subject to moral evaluation, we must consider not only what was done but also
why it was done and the circumstances under which it was done.

Now, suppose someone does something, or refrains from doing it, because the
person's conscience tells him or her that this would be the morally proper thing to
do or refrain from doing. And suppose, further, that in this case the individual's
conscience is mistaken. Yes, an erring conscience is possible, according to Aquinas,
despite the fact that it is through conscience that we become aware of natural law.
In such a case, if the person acts as he or she honestly thinks is morally right, and
the mistake in thinking is due to involuntary ignorance on the person's part, the
person has not really sinned, according to Aquinas.

Aquinas's ethical system is detailed and systematic, and it is difficult to convey
this in this brief summary. Aquinas treated highly general and abstract principles
such as the ultimate objective of human existence, the nature of goodness, and
the sources of action and also applied these principles to specific and concrete
moral questions.

HOBBES AND HUME

You have seen that the naturalism found in Aristotle's ethics and the nonnaturalistic ethics of Plato, with its conception of a transcendental source of ultimate value,
flowed in separate streams through the philosophy of the centuries until the time
of Aquinas. If it is not quite true to say that Aquinas channeled the waters from
each of these two streams into a common bed, it may at least be said that he con-
trived to have them flow side by side, though in separate channels.

But the next philosopher we wish to discuss, **Thomas Hobbes** (1588–1679),
drew exclusively from the Aristotelian channel. This is not surprising, for Hobbes
was one of the first philosophers of the modern period in philosophy, a period
marked by the emergence of experimental science, in which once again nature
itself was an object of study, just as it had been for Aristotle. (You should be aware,
nevertheless, that Hobbes, reacting to the Aristotelianism of his Oxford tutors, had
harsh things to say about Aristotle.)

Hobbes

Hobbes's metaphysics was a relentless materialism. All that exists, he said, are
material things in motion. Immaterial substance does not exist. There is no such
thing as the nonphysical soul. Thoughts, emotions, feelings—all are motions of the

Hobbes and the Beggar

The story is told of Hobbes that he was asked by a clergyman why he was giving alms to a beggar.

"Is it because Jesus has commanded you to do so?" the latter asked.

"No," came Hobbes's answer.

"Then why?"

"The reason I help the man," said Hobbes, "is that by doing so I end my discomfort at seeing his discomfort."

One moral that might be drawn from the story is that even the most altruistic and benevolent actions can be given an egoistic interpretation. Why did Hobbes help the beggar? To relieve his own discomfort. Why do saints devote their lives to relieving the suffering of others? Because it brings them pleasure to do so. Why did the soldier sacrifice his life to save his comrades? To end the distress he felt at thinking of his friends' dying—or maybe even because it pleased him to think of others praising him after his demise.

In short, because those who act to relieve their own discomfort or to bring pleasure to themselves are acting for their own self-interest, all of these seemingly altruistic actions can be interpreted egoistically.

Are you convinced?

Well, if you are, you should know that many philosophers are uncomfortable with this egoistic analysis of altruistic behavior. After all (they argue), it brings the saint pleasure to help others only if the saint is genuinely motivated to help others, right? Thus, if egoism is equated with the doctrine that we are never motivated to help others, it is false. If it is equated with the doctrine that we only act as we are motivated to act, it is true, but not particularly interesting.

matter within the brain, caused by moving things outside the brain. Even our reasoning and volition are purely physical processes.

As for values, according to Hobbes the words *good* and *evil* simply denote that which a person desires or hates. And Hobbes, like Aristotle, the Epicureans, the Stoics, and Aquinas, believed that one has a natural "end" or objective toward which all activity is directed. Hobbes specified this object of desire as the preservation of one's life. One seeks personal survival above all other things, he held. Hobbes also said that one has a "natural right" to use all means necessary to defend oneself or otherwise ensure one's survival.

Thus, Hobbes was a descriptive egoist, in the sense we explained earlier in this chapter. That is, he believed that, in all conscious action, one seeks to promote one's self-interest (for Hobbes this meant seeking survival) above all else. A story is reported in the box "Hobbes and the Beggar" that Hobbes was asked by a clergyman why he was giving alms to a beggar; Hobbes reportedly said he did so to end his own discomfort at seeing the beggar's discomfort. Beginning students in philosophy often are tempted to give a similar "selfish" analysis of even the most apparently unselfish actions; a difficulty in that idea is explained in the box.

Was Hobbes also a prescriptive egoist? That is, did he also think that one *ought* to seek to promote one's self-interest above all else? In general, Hobbes did not attempt to determine how people ought to behave in some absolute sense; he seems intent on describing how they ought to behave *if* they want best to secure their natural objective. A question he left for subsequent philosophers, and one that has not been resolved to this day, is this: If the universe is material, can there really *be* absolute values? Do good and evil, justice and injustice, exist in some *absolute* sense, or must they be regarded, as Hobbes so regarded them, as expressions of desires or the products of human agreements?

Hobbes's major work, *Leviathan,* is a classic in moral and political philosophy and encompasses as well metaphysics, epistemology, ethics, and psychology. It secured for Hobbes a prime-time place in all histories of Western thought.

Hume

Hobbes maintained that the idea of incorporeal or immaterial substance was a contradiction in terms, but he denied being an atheist. Nevertheless, he certainly did not rest his ethics on the authority of the Church. And although most of the major philosophers of the modern period shrank from Hobbes's extreme materialism, they, too—most of them—sought to discover the basic principles of morality elsewhere than in scripture. Some, such as Locke, though believing that these principles are decreed by God, held, like Hobbes, that they are discoverable—and provable—by reason.

But in the eighteenth century, **David Hume** (1711–1776) argued with some force that moral principles are neither divine edicts nor discoverable by reason. Hume's general position regarding God, as we shall see in Part Three, was that the order in the universe does offer some slight evidence that the universe has or had a creative force remotely analogous to human intelligence. But we certainly cannot affirm anything about the moral qualities of the creator, he held; and we cannot derive guidelines for our own actions from speculating about his (its) nature. Christianity Hume regarded as superstition.

Value Judgments Are Based on Emotion, Not Reason

Hume held likewise that moral judgments are not the "offspring of reason." Scrutinize an act of murder as closely as you can, he said. Do you find anything in the *facts of the case* that reveal the act is morally wrong? The *facts,* he said, are simply that one person has terminated the life of another in a certain way at a particular time and place. Reasoning can disclose how long it took for death to occur, whether the victim suffered great pain, what the motives of the killer were, as well as the answers to many other factual questions such as these. But it will not show the *moral wrongfulness* of the act. The judgment that an act is immoral, Hume maintained, comes not from reason but from *emotion.* Perhaps this idea has occurred to you as well. For an example, see the box "Cold-Blooded Murder."

It is the same, Hume believed, with all value judgments. Is the judgment that a portrait is beautiful founded on reason? Of course not. Reason can disclose the chemical composition of the paints and canvas, the monetary value of the work, and many similar factual things. But whether the portrait is beautiful is an issue that cannot be settled by reason.

Thus, for Hume, moral judgments, and all value judgments, were based on emotion. Actions that we find morally praiseworthy or blameworthy create within us feelings of pleasure or displeasure, respectively. Now, obviously, these feelings are

Cold-Blooded Murder

A fundamental principle of Hume's philosophy was that moral judgments are not the offspring of reason.

A consideration that might favor Hume's thesis is that we tend to think of particularly heinous deeds—execution-style murders, for example—as "cold-blooded" and "heartless," not as "irrational."

This is an indication that we view the murderer as lacking in *feeling* rather than as deficient in *reason*.

Is it hard to believe that an absolutely brilliant mind could commit murder? We think not. But is it hard to believe that someone with normal sensibilities could commit murder? We think that it is. These considerations favor Hume's principle.

different in kind from aesthetic pleasures and pleasures of the palate. Humans clearly have a capacity for moral pleasure as well as for other types of pleasure: we are *morally sensitive creatures*. Behavior that pleases our moral sensibilities elicits our approval and is deemed good, right, just, virtuous, and noble. Behavior that offends our moral sense is deemed bad, wrong, unjust, base, and ignoble.

Benevolence

But just what is it about behavior that elicits our moral approval? *What do virtuous, good, right, and noble acts have in common?* Hume's answer was that the type of act we deem morally praiseworthy is one taken by an agent *out of concern for others*. The act that pleases our moral sensibilities is one that reflects a *benevolent character* on the part of the agent, he said. By "agent," philosophers mean the person who did the act.

Why does benevolence bring pleasure to us when we witness, read about, or contemplate it? A cynical answer is that we imagine ourselves benefiting from the benevolent activity, and imagining this is pleasant. Do you get a warm glow when you read about someone coming to the aid of a fellow person? Well, according to the cynical view, that is because you picture yourself on the receiving end of the exchange.

But this cynical theory is unnecessarily complex, said Hume. The reason you get that pleasant feeling when you read about or see someone helping someone else is that you *sympathize* with others. It just plainly upsets a normal person to see others suffering, and it pleases a normal person to see others happy. True, there are people who suffer from the emotional equivalent of color blindness and lack the capacity to sympathize with others. But these people are not the norm. The normal human being is a sympathetic creature, maintained Hume.

This aspect of Hume's moral philosophy may well have some significance for us today. On one hand, we tend to believe that you should care for others but, on the other hand, that you must also certainly look out for yourself. And we are inclined to think that there is a problem in this because self-concern and other-concern seem mutually exclusive. But if Hume was correct, they are not. Looking out for your own interests includes doing what brings you pleasure. And if Hume was correct, caring for others will bring you an important kind of pleasure. Indeed, if Hume was correct, when you praise an action as good, it is precisely because it brings you this kind of pleasure.

It is important to notice, finally, the emphasis Hume placed on character. As we said, according to Hume, the act that pleases our moral sensibilities is one that reflects a benevolent *character* on the part of the agent. Hume believed that when we morally praise (or condemn) someone, it is the person's character we praise (or condemn) primarily: his or her actions we find praiseworthy (or condemnatory) mainly as an indication of character. This idea—that we apply moral attributes primarily to a person's character and secondarily to the person's actions—is common in the virtue-ethics tradition of Plato, Aristotle, and Aquinas. In this respect, Hume is part of that tradition.

Can There Be Ethics after Hume?

"Morality," Hume said, "is more properly felt than judged of." Ethical standards are not fixed by reason, he held; further, even if there is a God, he maintained, it is impossible for us to gain moral guidance from him.

Loosely speaking, therefore, ethics after Hume seems generally to have had these options. First, it might seek to establish that, despite Hume, morality *can* be grounded on reason or God. As we shall see next, this was the option taken by Kant, who favored reason as the ultimate ground of morality. Second, ethics might try to find objective sources of moral standards other than reason and God. This is what the utilitarians tried to do, as we shall see shortly. Third, it might try to determine how one should conduct one's affairs given the absence of objective moral standards. This is a primary concern of contemporary existentialists, as we saw in Chapter 8. Fourth, ethics might abandon the search for moral standards altogether and concentrate instead on such factual questions as, What do people believe is good and right? What does it mean to say that something is good or right? How do moral judgments differ from other kinds of judgments? What leads us to praise certain actions as moral and condemn others as immoral? These are some of the issues that captured the attention of many twentieth-century philosophers, such as G. E. Moore, whom we will encounter in Chapter 12.

KANT

Immanuel Kant (1724–1804) disagreed entirely with Hume's discounting of the possibility that reason can settle whether an act is morally right. In Kant's opinion, reason and reason alone can settle this. Kant's argument, paraphrased and distilled, went like this:

1. *Scientific inquiry can never reveal to us principles that we know hold without exception.* Scientific inquiry is based on experience, and in the final analysis experience can show only how things have been to this point, not how they must be. For example, science reveals to us physical "laws" that hold true of the universe as it is now, but it cannot provide absolutely conclusive

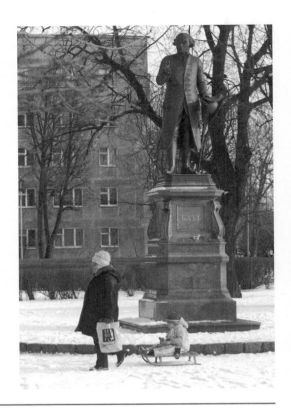

A scene from Königsburg today. The home of Immanuel Kant.

guarantees that these laws will forever hold true. (If you have difficulty understanding this point, rereading the section on Kant in Chapter 7 will help.)

2. *Moral principles, however, hold without exception.* For example, if it is wrong to torture helpless animals, then it would be wrong for anyone, at any time, to do so.

Thus, from these two premises—that moral principles hold without exception and that scientific investigations cannot reveal what holds without exception—it follows that

3. *Moral principles cannot be revealed through scientific investigation.* Because Kant believed that any principle that holds without exception is knowable only through reason, he maintained that *reason alone can ascertain principles of morality.*

The Supreme Principle of Morality

Further, according to Kant, because a moral rule is something that holds without exception—that is, holds universally—you should act only on principles that could hold universally. For example, if you think you must cheat to pass an exam, then the principle on which you would act (if you were to cheat) would be this: *To obtain a passing grade, it is acceptable to cheat.* But now consider: If this principle were a universal law, then a passing grade would be meaningless, right? And in that case the principle itself would be meaningless. In short, the principle logically could not hold universally, and (this comes to the same thing) it would be irrational for anyone to want it to hold universally.

Now, if it would be irrational for you to want the principle on which you act to be a universal law, then that principle is morally improper, and the act should not be done. Thus, for Kant, the supreme prescription of morality, which he called the supreme **categorical imperative,** was *to act always in such a way that you could, rationally, will the principle on which you act to be a universal law.* In Kant's words, "Act only on that maxim whereby you can at the same time will that it should become a universal law."

Because, in Kant's view, a universal law would in effect be a sort of law of nature, he offered a second formulation of the categorical imperative: "Act as if the maxim of your action were to become by your will a Universal Law of Nature."

Why You Should Do What You Should Do

Moral principles, Kant observed, may always be expressed in the imperative form: Do not steal! Be kind to others! Further, because moral imperatives must hold without exception, they are different from **hypothetical imperatives,** which state, in effect, that one ought to do something *if* such-and-such an end is desired.

For example, the imperatives "If you wish to be healthy, then live moderately!" and "If you wish to secure your own survival, then surrender your rights to a sovereign power!" are both hypothetical imperatives. Neither is a **moral imperative,** for a moral imperative holds unconditionally, or *categorically.* This means that a moral imperative commands obedience for the sake of no other end than its own rightness.

Thus, for Kant, what I should do, I should do *because it is right.* Doing something for any other purpose—for the sake of happiness or the welfare of humankind, for example—is not to act morally. It is to act under the command of a hypothetical imperative, which is not unconditional, as a moral imperative must be. According to Kant, you should do your moral duty simply because it is your moral duty. You should be aware that duty-based ethical systems, like Kant's, are known as deontological ethical systems.

Furthermore, according to Kant, it's not the *effects or consequences* of your act that determine whether your act is good, for these are not totally within your control. What is within your control is the *intent* with which you act. Thus, what determines whether your act is good or bad is the intent with which it is undertaken. He wrote, "Nothing can possibly be conceived in the world, or even out of it, which can be called good, without qualification, except a good will."

And because a morally good will is one that acts solely for the sake of doing what is right, it follows, in Kant's opinion, that *there is no moral worth* in, say, helping others because you are sympathetic or inclined to do so. Moral worth lies only in helping others for the sake of doing the right thing.

Because to violate the supreme principle of morality, the supreme categorical imperative, is to be irrational, rationality may be said to be the source of all value. Hence, the rational will alone was deemed inherently good by Kant. Accordingly, Kant offered yet another formulation of the supreme categorical imperative: *Treat rational beings (i.e., humans) in every instance as ends and never just as means!*

That this is an alternative formulation of the same principle may be seen in the fact that, if you were to violate the categorical imperative and do something that you could not rationally will to be a law for all, then in effect you would be treating the interests of others as subordinate to your own; that is, you would be treating others as means and not as ends. Kant, it is often said (for obvious reasons), was the first philosopher to provide a *rational basis* for the golden rule found in many religions: Do unto others as you would have them do unto you.

Did Kant provide a viable response to Hume's idea that reason cannot determine whether an act is morally right? You decide.

THE UTILITARIANS

Kant, we have seen, may well have offered a sound refutation of Hume's idea that moral principles are not determined by reason. It is therefore perhaps strange that two of the most celebrated ethical philosophers of the nineteenth century, the Englishmen **Jeremy Bentham** (1748–1832) and **John Stuart Mill** (1806–1873), largely ignored the rationalistic ethics of Kant, Bentham perhaps more so than Mill. Bentham and Mill did not, however, ignore Hume. Instead, they developed further Hume's idea that traits and actions that are virtuous promote the welfare of people, the "general happiness."

Bentham and Mill were utilitarians, which means they believed that *the rightness of an action is identical with the happiness it produces as its consequence.* What is new or exciting about this? Didn't Aristotle and the Epicureans and Augustine and Aquinas also advocate pursuing happiness? The difference is that, according to those earlier philosophers, it is *your own happiness* that you should strive for.

By contrast, the utilitarians said that the morally best act is the one that produces the greatest amount of happiness *with everyone considered.* But this is ambiguous: should we aim at increasing the *average* happiness or the *total* happiness—even if this would reduce the happiness per person? Usually the utilitarians are interpreted as favoring increasing the average happiness. In any case, they believed that, when you are trying to produce happiness, it is not just your own happiness you should aim for but rather the happiness of people in general.

It is common to attribute to the utilitarians the view that the right act is the one that produces "the greatest happiness for the greatest number." That phrase—the greatest happiness for the greatest number—is unfortunate, because it tells us to maximize two different things. (Just try to plot the greatest happiness for the greatest number as a single line on a graph, with happiness as one variable and number as a second variable!) You can say, "The more people who have a given amount of happiness, the better," and you can say, "The more happiness a given number of people have, the better." But it is not clear what you could mean by saying, "The more happiness the greater number of people have, the better." We will interpret the utilitarians as favoring the view that the more happiness a given number of people have, the better (i.e., the higher the average happiness, the better). And again, according to this philosophy, your own happiness is *not* more important morally than that of others.

Notice, too, that for the utilitarians it was the *consequences* of an act that determined its rightness, a position that contrasts strongly with Kant's idea that the moral worth of an act depends on the *will* or *motive* with which it is taken.

Bentham

Bentham, the earlier of the two utilitarians, equated happiness with pleasure. "Nature," he wrote, "has placed mankind under the governance of two sovereign masters, *pain* and *pleasure*. It is for them alone to point out what we ought to do, as well as determine what we shall do."

The words *ought, right, good,* and the like have meaning only when defined in terms of *pleasure*, Bentham said. This fact is evident, he argued, in that all other intelligible moral standards either must be interpreted in terms of the pleasure standard or are simply disguised versions of the pleasure standard in the first place.

For example, suppose you maintain that the right act is the one that is preferred by God. Well, said Bentham, unless we know God's preferences—that is, unless we know what, exactly, pleases God—what you maintain is pretty meaningless, is it not? And the only way "to know what is His pleasure," he said, is by "observing what is our own pleasure and pronouncing it to be His."

Or consider the theory that a moral obligation to obey the law stems from a "social contract" among members of society. That theory, said Bentham, is unnecessarily complicated. For when we have a moral obligation to obey the law, he said, that obligation is more simply explained by the fact that obedience to the law would result in more pleasure for more people than disobedience would.

Bentham believed that the pain and pleasure an act produces can be evaluated solely with reference to *quantitative* criteria. Which of two or more courses of action you should take should be determined by considering the probable consequences of each possible act with respect to the certainty, intensity, duration, immediacy, and extent (the number of persons affected) of the pleasure or pain it produces, and with respect to the other kinds of sensations it is likely to have as a result over the long run. This "calculus" of pleasure, as it is often called, represents a distinctive feature of Bentham's ethics. Bentham believed that, by using these criteria, one could and should calculate which of alternative courses of action would produce the greatest amount of pleasure and which, therefore, ought morally to be taken.

Through all of this you should be asking: But why ought I seek the *general* happiness and not give higher priority to my own? Bentham's answer was that your own happiness *coincides* with the general happiness: what brings pleasure to you and what brings pleasure to others fortunately go together.

You may wish to consider whether this answer is fully satisfactory.

PROFILE: Jeremy Bentham (1748–1832)

You will find it easy to identify with Jeremy Bentham—if, that is, you studied Latin when you were four, started college when you were twelve, graduated by age fifteen, and finished law school and were admitted to the bar all while you were still a teenager.

Yes, Bentham was a sharp youth. When he was fifteen, he went to hear Sir William Blackstone, the famous English jurist. Bentham said that he instantly spotted errors in Blackstone's reasoning, especially on natural rights. Bentham came to believe that the whole notion of natural rights, including that found in the American Declaration of Independence, was just "nonsense on stilts." In 1776 he published his first book, *Fragment on Government*, a critique of Blackstone.

For David Hume and Hume's *Treatise on Human Nature,* however, Bentham had more respect, and he claimed that the work made the scales fall from his eyes about ethics. Bentham's own ethical philosophy reflects the great influence of Hume.

Though qualified to do so, Bentham never actually practiced law. He was much more interested in legal and social reform and wrote daily commentaries on English law and society. He advocated a simplified and codified legal system and worked for prison and education reform and extension of voting rights. Bentham also published numerous pamphlets on such abuses as jury packing and extortionate legal fees, and his followers, the "Benthamites," were an effective political force that endured after his death.

Bentham was in the habit of not finishing books that he started to write, and the only major philosophical treatise that he published himself is the *Introduction to the Principles of Morals and Legislation* (1789). The title states exactly Bentham's main concern in life: applying sound principles of morality to the law.

If you want to know what Bentham looked like, do not stop with a picture. Bentham's embalmed body, complete with a wax head and dressed just as he liked to, is there for you to see at University College, London.

Mill

John Stuart Mill, who claimed to have discovered in Bentham's ethical theory what he needed to give purpose to his own life, was also concerned with providing a philosophical justification for the utilitarian doctrine that it is the *general* happiness that one should aim to promote. The justification, according to Mill, lies in the fact that a moral principle by its very nature singles out no one for preferential treatment. Thus, Mill wrote, "as between his own happiness and that of others," the utilitarian is required "to be as strictly impartial as a disinterested and benevolent spectator." Compare Mill's justification with that of Bentham. Mill's justification is sounder, is it not?

Probably the most important difference between Mill and Bentham is that Mill believed that some pleasures are *inherently better* than others and are to be preferred even over a greater amount of pleasure of an inferior grade.

That some pleasures are better than others can be seen, Mill argued, in the fact that few people would be willing to trade places with an animal or even with a more ignorant person than themselves, even if the exchange guaranteed their having the fullest measure of an animal's or an ignoramus's pleasure. Here is what he meant. Would you trade places with a pig or a lunkhead? Would you do it even if you knew that as a pig or a lunkhead you would have more pig or lunkhead pleasures than you now have pleasure as an intelligent human being?

The cartoon points up the foolishness of the notion that we can seek pleasure *by itself*. Such a search has no direction. What we seek is food, shelter, companionship, sex, and so forth—we do not, strictly speaking, seek pleasure per se. And if you tried to seek pleasure, you would not know how to go about finding it. Your seeking must always be for something, such as food, that is not *itself* pleasure.

Thus, for Mill, in determining the pleasure for which we should strive, we must consider the *quality* of the pleasure as well as the quantity. Choose the pleasure of the highest quality.

Now, this is all very well, but what settles which of two pleasures is of higher quality? Mill's answer was quite simple: Of two pleasures, if there is one to which most who have experienced both give a decided preference, that is the more desirable pleasure.

Notice what this answer seems to entail. It seems to entail that the pleasures preferred by the *intellectual* will be found to be of superior quality, for nonintellectuals "only know their own side of the question. The other party to the comparison knows both sides," said Mill.

According to Mill, then, it is not simply the quantity of pleasure an act produces that determines its moral worth; the quality of the pleasure produced must also be taken into account. Mill is thus said to have recognized implicitly (though not in so many words) a factor other than pleasure by which the moral worth of actions should be compared: the factor of quality. In other words, he is said to have proposed, in effect, a standard of moral worth other than pleasure, a standard of "quality" by means of which pleasure itself is to be evaluated. So he sometimes is said not to be a "pure" utilitarian, if a utilitarian is one who believes that the pleasure an act produces is the only standard of good.

It is not unusual, therefore, to find philosophers who think of Bentham's philosophy as more consistently utilitarian than Mill's, though everyone refers to both Mill and Bentham as "the" utilitarians.

There is one other, sort of fuzzy, difference between Bentham and Mill. Bentham's utilitarianism is what today is called **act utilitarianism:** the rightness of an *act* is determined by its effect on the general happiness. Mill also subscribed to act utilitarianism in some passages, but in other places he seems to have advocated what is called **rule utilitarianism.** According to this version of utilitarianism, we are to evaluate the moral correctness of an action not with reference to its impact on the general happiness but rather with respect to the impact on the general happiness of the *rule* or principle the action exemplifies.

Take this case, for example: Suppose that by murdering us you would increase the general happiness (maybe unknown to anyone, we harbor some awful contagious disease). Act utilitarianism would say that you should murder us. But a rule utilitarian, as Mill in some places seems to be, would say that if society accepted murder as a rule of conduct, ultimately the general happiness would be diminished, so you should not murder us. Rule utilitarianism is, in a way, much more Kantian than is act utilitarianism.

FRIEDRICH NIETZSCHE

Another important nineteenth-century philosopher, one who believed that all previous moral philosophy was tedious and soporific and who had no use at all for the utilitarians, was **Friedrich Nietzsche** (1844–1900). In Nietzsche's view, moralities are social institutions, and basically there are just two moralities: master morality and slave morality, the morality of the masses. Slave morality—for Nietzsche,

The paradox of hedonism. The British moralist Henry Sidgwick (1838–1900) noted the curious fact, which he called the *paradox of hedonism,* that the desire for pleasure, if too predominant, defeats its own aim. (Sidgwick also observed that "the pleasures of thought and study can only be enjoyed in the highest degree by those who have an ardour of curiosity which carries the mind temporarily away from self and its sensations.")

epitomized by Christian ethics—emphasizes such virtues as compassion, humility, patience, warmheartedness, and turning the other cheek. These "virtues" glorify weakness. Master morality, by contrast, is the morality of noble individuals, who are egoistic, hard, intolerant, but bound by a code of honor to their peers. Noble individuals define harm entirely in terms of what is harmful to themselves and despise altruism and humility.

According to Nietzsche, the enhancement of the species is always the result of aristocratic societies, which, he held, are the ultimate justification of human social existence. The primal life force, for Nietzsche, is the will-to-power, whose essence is the overpowering and suppression of what is alien and weaker and which finds its highest expression in the noble man, or *Übermensch* ("Superman" in German). The principle by which the *Übermensch* lives is "There is no god or human over me." He is the source of ethical truth.

Nietzsche followed the ancient Greek philosopher Heraclitus (Chapter 2) in holding that life is quintessentially strife or warfare. It is only within the dark eye of battle that human energies are truly stretched and fruit-bearing actions become possible. Battles make heroes, he thought; peace renders us weak and ineffectual. One of Nietzsche's most famous proverbs was, "What doesn't kill us makes us stronger."

The ultimate battle, Nietzsche thought, takes place within the human frame and is the battle between two forces, the Apollonian and the Dionysian. The Greek god Apollo represents the force of measure, order, and harmony. The Greek god Dionysius (or Bacchus in the Roman world) represents the counterforce of excess, destruction, and creative power, the ecstatic rush and rave of the original, formless will. In the human soul, these two forces contest each other for ascendancy. While both are necessary if one is to be fully and creatively alive, the creative Dionysian force has been lost almost entirely in the slave mentality, with its emphasis on humility, meekness, mediocrity, and the denial of life.

The selection from Nietzsche at the end of the chapter conveys many of these themes clearly and will make it obvious why attempts often are made to censor Nietzsche from schools and libraries.

SELECTION 10.1

Gorgias*

Plato

[*You may know someone—or may be someone—who thinks that one should fully indulge one's appetites, or that pleasure, whatever its nature, is the key to happiness. In this excerpt from the Dialogue* Gorgias, *Plato has the character Callicles advancing this view and Socrates rebutting it.*]

---

* From *Socratic Dialogues*, translated and edited by W. D. Woodhead (Edinburgh: Thomas Nelson & Sons, 1953).

Socrates: . . . You say we should not curb our appetites, if we are to be what we should be, but should allow them the fullest possible growth and procure satisfaction for them from whatever source, and this, you say, is virtue.

Callicles: That is what I say. . . .

S: Consider whether you would say this of each type of life, the temperate and the undisciplined.

Imagine that each of the two men has several jars, in the one case in sound condition and filled, one with wine, another with honey, another with milk, and many others with a variety of liquids, but that the sources of these liquids are scanty and hard to come by, procured only with much hard labor. Imagine then that the one after filling his vessels does not trouble himself to draw in further supplies but as far as the jars are concerned is free from worry; in the case of the other man the sources, as in the first instance are procurable but difficult to come by, but his vessels are perforated and unsound and he is ever compelled to spend day and night in replenishing them, if he is not to suffer the greatest agony. If this is the character of each of the lives, do you still insist that the life of the uncontrolled man is happier than that of the orderly? Do I or do I not persuade you with this image that the disciplined life is better than the intemperate?

C: You do not, Socrates. The man who has filled his vessels can no **longer** find any pleasure, but this is what I just now described as living the life of a stone. Once the vessels are filled, there is neither pleasure nor pain any more. But a life of pleasure demands the largest possible influx.

S: Then if there is a big influx, must there not also be a great outflow, and must not the holes for the outflow be large?

C: Certainly.

S: It is the life of a plover you mean, not that of a corpse or a stone. And now tell me. You are thinking of some such thing as being hungry and, when hungry, eating?

C: I am.

S: And being thirsty and, when thirsty, drinking?

C: Yes, and experiencing all the other appetites and being able to satisfy them and living happily in the enjoyment of them.

S: Good, my worthy friend, just continue as you began, and mind you do not falter through shame. And I too, it seems, must throw all shame aside. First of all then, tell me whether one who suffers from the itch and longs to scratch himself, if he can scratch himself to his heart's content and continue scratching all his life, can be said to live happily. . . .

C: Well then, I say that even one who scratches himself would live pleasantly.

S: And if pleasantly, happily?

C: Certainly.

S: If it was only his head that he wanted to scratch—or can I push the question further? Think what you will answer, Callicles, if anyone should ask all the questions that naturally follow. And as a climax of all such cases, the life of a catamite—is not that shocking and shameful and miserable? Will you dare to say that such people are happy, if they have what they desire in abundance?

C: Are you not ashamed, Socrates, to drag our discussion into such topics?

S: Is it I who do this, my noble friend, or the man who says so unequivocally that pleasure, whatever its nature, is the key to happiness, and does not distinguish between pleasures good and evil? But enlighten me further as to whether you say that the pleasant and the good are identical, or that there are some pleasures which are not good.

C: To avoid inconsistency if I say they are different, I assert that they are the same. . . .

S: Tell me, do you not think that those who fare well experience the opposite of those who fare ill?

C: I do.

S: Then if these things are opposites, the same must hold true of them as of health and sickness. A man cannot be both in health and sick at the same time, nor be rid of both conditions at the same time.

C: How do you mean?

S: Take, for example, any part of the body separately and consider it. A man perhaps has trouble with his eyes, which is called ophthalmia.

C: Of course.

S: Then his eyes are not at the same time sound.

C: By no means.

S: And what of when he is rid of ophthalmia? Does he then get rid of the health of his eyes, and is he finally quit of both conditions?

C: Certainly not.

S: For that would be miraculous and irrational, would it not?

C: Very much so.

S: But, I suppose, he acquires and gets rid of each in turn.

C: I agree.

S: And is it not the same with strength and weakness?

C: Yes.

S: And swiftness and slowness?

C: Certainly.

S: And good things and happiness, and their opposites, evils and wretchedness—does he possess and get rid of each of these in turn?

C: Assuredly, I think.

S: Then if we discover certain things which a man possesses and gets rid of simultaneously, it is obvious that these cannot be the good and the evil. Do we agree on this? Do not answer until you have considered it carefully.

C: I am in the most complete possible accord.

S: Back then to our previous admissions. Did you say hunger was pleasant or painful? Actual hunger, I mean.

C: Painful, but to satisfy hunger by eating is pleasant.

S: I understand. But hunger itself at least is painful, is it not?

C: I agree.

S: And thirst too?

C: Most certainly.

S: Am I to ask any further then, or do you admit that every deficiency and desire is painful?

C: I admit it; you need not ask.

S: Very well then, but to drink when thirsty you say is pleasant?

C: I do.

S: Now in this statement the word 'thirsty' implies pain, I presume.

C: Yes.

S: And drinking is a satisfaction of the deficiency and a pleasure?

C: Yes.

S: Then you say that in drinking there is pleasure?

C: Certainly.

S: When one is thirsty?

C: I agree.

S: That is, when in pain?

C: Yes.

S: Then do you realize the result—that you say a man enjoys pleasure simultaneously with pain, when you say that he drinks when thirsty? Does not this happen at the same time and the same place, whether in body or soul? For I fancy it makes no difference. Is this so or not?

C: It is.

S: Yes, but you say also that when one is faring well it is impossible for him at the same time to fare ill.

C: I do.

S: But you have agreed it is possible to experience pleasure at the same time as pain.

C: Apparently.

S: Then pleasure is not the same as faring well, nor pain as faring ill, and so the pleasant is different from the good.

C: I do not understand what your quibbles mean, Socrates.

S: You understand, Callicles, but you are playing coy. But push on a little further, that you may realize how cunning you are, you who admonish me. Does not each one of us cease at the same time from thirsting and from his pleasure in drinking?

C: I do not know what you mean.

S: Do not behave so, Callicles, but answer for our sakes too, that the arguments may be concluded.

C: But Socrates is always the same, Gorgias. He asks these trivial and useless questions and then refutes.

S: What difference does that make to you? In any case you do not have to pay the price, Callicles, but suffer Socrates to cross-examine you as he will.

C: Well then, ask these petty little questions, since Gorgias so wishes.

S: You are lucky, Callicles, in having been initiated in the Great Mysteries before the Little; I did not think it was permitted. Answer then from where you left off, whether thirst and the pleasure of drinking do not cease for each of us at the same time.

C: I agree.

S: And does not one cease from hunger and other desires, and from pleasures at the same time?

C: That is so.

S: Does he not then cease from pains and pleasures at the same time?

C: Yes.

S: Yes, but he does not cease from experiencing the good and the ill simultaneously, as you yourself agreed. Do you not agree now?

C: I do. What of it?

S: Only this, that the good is not the same as the pleasant, my friend, nor the evil as the painful. For we cease from the one pair at the same time, but not from the other, because they are distinct. How then could the pleasant be the same as the good, or the painful as the evil? Let us look at it in a different way, if you like, for I think that even here you do not agree. But just consider. Do you not call good people by that name because of the presence in them of things good, just as you call beautiful those in whom beauty is present?

SELECTION 10.2

The Nicomachean Ethics*

Aristotle

[*This is an excerpt from one of the classics of Western philosophy. In it, Aristotle provides a "rough outline" of the good.*]

Let us again return to the good we are seeking, and ask what it can be. It seems different in different actions and arts; it is different in medicine, in strategy, and in the other arts likewise. What then is the good of each? Surely that for whose sake everything

else is done. In medicine this is health, in strategy victory, in architecture a house, in any other sphere something else, and in every action and pursuit the end; for it is for the sake of this that all men do whatever else they do. Therefore, if there is an end for all that we do, this will be the good achievable by action, and if there are more than one, these will be the goods achievable by action.

So the argument has by a different course reached the same point; but we must try to state this even more clearly. Since there are evidently more than one end, and we choose some of these (e.g. wealth, flutes, and in general instruments) for the sake of something else, clearly not all ends are final ends; but the chief good is evidently something final.

* The author's footnotes have been deleted. From "Ethica Nicomachea," translated by W. D. Ross, from *The Works of Aristotle,* translated into English under the editorship of W. D. Ross, Vol. IX (Oxford: Oxford University Press, 1925). By permission of Oxford University Press.

Therefore, if there is only one final end, this will be what we are seeking, and if there are more than one, the most final of these will be what we are seeking. Now we call that which is in itself worthy of pursuit more final than that which is worthy of pursuit for the sake of something else, and that which is never desirable for the sake of something else more final than the things that are desirable both in themselves and for the sake of that other thing, and therefore we call final without qualification that which is always desirable in itself and never for the sake of something else.

Now such a thing happiness, above all else, is held to be; for this we choose always for itself and never for the sake of something else, but honour, pleasure, reason, and every virtue we choose indeed for themselves (for if nothing resulted from them we should still choose each of them), but we choose them also for the sake of happiness, judging that by means of them we shall be happy. Happiness, on the other hand, no one chooses for the sake of these, nor, in general, for anything other than itself.

From the point of view of self-sufficiency the same result seems to follow; for the final good is thought to be self-sufficient. Now by self-sufficient we do not mean that which is sufficient for a man by himself, for one who lives a solitary life, but also for parents, children, wife, and in general for his friends and fellow citizens, since man is born for citizenship. But some limit must be set to this; for if we extend our requirement to ancestors and descendants and friends' friends we are in for an infinite series. Let us examine this question, however, on another occasion; the self-sufficient we now define as that which when isolated makes life desirable and lacking in nothing; and such we think happiness to be; and further we think it most desirable of all things, without being counted as one good thing among others—if it were so counted it would clearly be made more desirable by the addition of even the least of goods; for that which is added becomes an excess of goods, and of goods the greater is always more desirable. Happiness, then, is something final and self-sufficient, and is the end of action.

Presumably, however, to say that happiness is the chief good seems a platitude, and a clearer account of what it is is still desired. This might perhaps be given, if we could first ascertain the function of man. For just as for a flute-player, a sculptor, or any artist, and, in general, for all things that have a function or activity, the good and the 'well' is thought to reside in the function, so would it seem to be for man, if he has a function. Have the carpenter, then, and the tanner certain functions or activities, and has man none? Is he born without a function? Or as eye, hand, foot, and in general each of the parts evidently has a function, may one lay it down that man similarly has a function apart from all these? What then can this be? Life seems to be common even to plants, but we are seeking what is peculiar to man. Let us exclude, therefore, the life of nutrition and growth. Next there would be a life of perception, but *it* also seems to be common even to the horse, the ox, and every animal. There remains, then, an active life of the element that has a rational principle; of this, one part has such a principle in the sense of being obedient to one, the other in the sense of possessing one and exercising thought. And, as 'life of the rational element' also has two meanings, we must state that life in the sense of activity is what we mean; for this seems to be the more proper sense of the term. Now if the function of man is an activity of soul which follows or implies a rational principle, and if we say 'a so-and-so' and 'a good so-and-so' have a function which is the same in kind, e.g. a lyre-player and a good lyre-player, and so without qualification in all cases, eminence in respect of goodness being added to the name of the function (for the function of a lyre-player is to play the lyre, and that of a good lyre-player is to do so well): if this is the case, [and we state the function of man to be a certain kind of life, and this to be an activity or actions of the soul implying a rational principle, and the function of a good man to be the good and noble performance of these, and if any action is well performed when it is performed in accordance with the appropriate excellence: if this is the case,] human good turns out to be activity of soul in accordance with virtue, and if there are more than one virtue, in accordance with the best and most complete.

But we must add 'in a complete life.' For one swallow does not make a summer, nor does one day; and so too one day, or a short time, does not make a man blessed and happy.

Let this serve as an outline of the good; for we must presumably first sketch it roughly, and then later fill in the details.

SELECTION 10.3
Epicurus to Menoeceus*

Epicurus

[*Epicurus, like Callicles in the first selection, advocates living a life devoted to acquiring pleasure. But when you read this selection, you will see that Epicurus's concept of pleasure is much more sophisticated than Callicles'.*]

The things which I [unceasingly] commend to you, these do and practice, considering them to be the first principles of the good life. . . .

Become accustomed to the belief that death is nothing to us. For all good and evil consists in sensation, but death is deprivation of sensation. And therefore a right understanding that death is nothing to us makes the mortality of life enjoyable, not because it adds to it an infinite span of time, but because it takes away the craving for immortality. For there is nothing terrible in life for the man who has truly comprehended that there is nothing terrible in not living. . . . Death, the most terrifying of ills, is nothing to us, since so long as we exist, death is not with us; but when death comes, then we do not exist. It does not then concern either the living or the dead, since for the former, it is not, and the latter are no more. . . .

We must then bear in mind that the future is neither ours, nor yet wholly not ours, so that we may not altogether expect it as sure to come, nor abandon hope of it, as if it will certainly not come.

We must consider that of desires some are natural, others vain, and of the natural some are necessary and others merely natural; and of the necessary some are necessary for happiness, others for the repose of the body, and others for very life. The right understanding of these facts enables us to refer all choices and avoidances to the health of the body and the soul's freedom from disturbance, since this is the aim of the life of blessedness. For it is to obtain this end that we always act, namely, to avoid pain and fear. And when this is once secured for us, all the tempest of the soul is dispersed, since the living crea-

ture has not to wander as though in search of something that is missing, and to look for some other thing by which he can fulfill the good of the soul and the good of the body. For it is then that we have need of pleasure, when we feel pain owing to the absence of pleasure; but when we do not feel pain, we no longer need pleasure. And for this cause we call pleasure the beginning and end of the blessed life. For we recognize pleasure as the first good innate in us, and from pleasure we begin every act of choice and avoidance, and to pleasure we return again, using the feeling as the standard by which we judge every good.

And since pleasure is the first good and natural to us, for this very reason we do not choose every pleasure, but sometimes we pass over many pleasures, when greater discomfort accrues to us as the result of them: and similarly we think many pains better than pleasures, since a greater pleasure comes to us when we have endured pains for a long time. Every pleasure then because of its natural kinship to us is good, yet not every pleasure is to be chosen: even as every pain also is an evil, yet not all are always of a nature to be avoided. Yet by a scale of comparison and by the consideration of advantages and disadvantages we must form our judgment on all these matters. For the good on certain occasions we treat as bad, and conversely the bad as good.

And again independence of desire we think a great good—not that we may at all times enjoy but a few things, but that, if we do not possess many, we may enjoy the few in the genuine persuasion that those have the sweetest pleasure in luxury who least need it, and that all that is natural is easy to be obtained, but that which is superfluous is hard. And so plain savours bring us a pleasure equal to a luxurious diet, when all the pain due to want is removed; and bread and water produce the highest pleasure, when one who needs them puts them to his lips. To grow accustomed therefore to simple and not luxurious diet gives us health to the full, and makes a man alert for the needful employments of life, and when after long intervals we approach luxuries disposes us better towards them, and fits us to be fearless of fortune.

---

* From *Epicurus: The Extant Remains*, translated by Cyril Bailey (Oxford: Clarendon Press, 1926). By permission of Oxford University Press.

When, therefore, we maintain that pleasure is the end, we do not mean the pleasures of profligates and those that consist in sensuality, as is supposed by some who are either ignorant or disagree with us or do not understand, but freedom from pain in the body and from trouble in the mind. For it is not continuous drinkings and revellings, nor the satisfaction of lusts, nor the enjoyment of fish and other luxuries of the wealthy table, which produce a pleasant life, but sober reasoning, searching out the motives for all choice and avoidance, and banishing mere opinions, to which are due the greatest disturbance of the spirit.

Of all this the beginning and the greatest good is prudence. Wherefore prudence is a more precious thing even than philosophy: for from prudence are sprung all the other virtues; and it teaches us that it is not possible to live pleasantly without living prudently and honourably and justly, not, again, to live a life of prudence, honour and justice without living pleasantly. For the virtues are by nature bound up with the pleasant life, and the pleasant life is inseparable from them. For indeed who, think you, is a better man than he who holds reverent opinions concerning the gods, and is at all times free from fear of death, and has reasoned out the end ordained by nature?

SELECTION 10.4

The Encheiridion★

Epictetus

[*Epictetus, like Epicurus and Callicles, advocates a life of pleasure. Epictetus advises us to get straight on what things are under our control and what things aren't. What happens isn't under our control, but our attitudes are. Therefore, the key to happiness is, when something bad happens, to take a stoical attitude.*]

1. Some things are under our control, while others are not under our control. Under our control are conception, choice, desire, aversion, and, in a word, everything that is our own doing; not under our control are our body, our property, reputation, office, and in a word, everything that is not our own doing. Furthermore, things under our control are by nature free, unhindered, and unimpeded; while the things not under our control are weak, servile, subject to hindrance, and not our own. Remember, therefore, that if what is naturally slavish you think to be free, and what is not your own to be your own, you will be hampered, will grieve, will be in turmoil,

and will blame both gods and men; while if you think only what is your own to be your own, and what is not your own to be, as it really is, not your own, then no one will ever be able to exert compulsion upon you, no one will hinder you, you will blame no one, will find fault with no one, will do absolutely nothing against your will, you will have no personal enemy, no one will harm you, for neither is there any harm that can touch you. . . .

Make it, therefore, your study at the very outset to say to every harsh external impression, "You are an external impression and not at all what you appear to be." After that examine it and test it by these rules which you have, the first and most important of which is this: Whether the impression has to do with the things which are under our control, or with those which are not under our control; and, if it has to do with some one of the things not under our control, have ready to hand the answer, "It is nothing to me."

2. Remember that the promise of desire is the attainment of what you desire, that of aversion is not to fall into what is avoided, and that he who fails in his desire is unfortunate, while he who falls into what he would avoid experiences misfortune. If, then, you avoid only what is unnatural among those things which are under your control, you will fall into none of the things which you avoid; but if you

★ Reprinted by permission of the publishers and the Trustees of the Loeb Classical Library from *Epictetus: Volume II,* Loeb Classical Library Volume 218, translated by W. A. Oldfather, Cambridge, Mass.: Harvard University Press, Copyright 1928 by the President and Fellows of Harvard College. The Loeb Classical Library® is a registered trademark of the President and Fellows of Harvard College.

try to avoid disease, or death, or poverty, you will experience misfortune. Withdraw, therefore, your aversion from all the matters that are not under our control, and transfer it to what is unnatural among those which are under our control. But for the time being remove utterly your desire; for if you desire some one of the things that are not under our control you are bound to be unfortunate; and, at the same time, not one of the things that are under our control, which it would be excellent for you to desire, is within your grasp. But employ only choice and refusal, and these too but lightly, and with reservations, and without straining. . . .

5. It is not the things themselves that disturb men, but their judgments about these things. For example, death is nothing dreadful, or else Socrates too would have thought so, but the judgment that death is dreadful, this is the dreadful thing. When, therefore, we are hindered, or disturbed, or grieved, let us never blame anyone but ourselves, that means, our own judgments. It is the part of an uneducated person to blame others where he himself fares ill; to blame himself is the part of one whose education has begun; to blame neither another nor his own self is the part of one whose education is already complete. . . .

8. Do not seek to have everything that happens happen as you wish, but wish for everything to happen as it actually does happen, and your life will be serene. . . .

11. Never say about anything, "I have lost it," but only "I have given it back." Is your child dead? It has been given back. Is your wife dead? She has been given back. "I have had my farm taken away." Very well, this too has been given back. "Yet it was a rascal who took it away." But what concern is it of yours by whose instrumentality the Giver called for its return? So long as He gives it to you, take care of it as of a thing that is not your own, as travellers treat their inn. . . .

15. Remember that you ought to behave in life as you would at a banquet. As something is being passed around it comes to you; stretch out your hand and take a portion of it politely. It passes on; do not detain it. Or it has not come to you yet; do not project your desire to meet it, but wait until it comes in front of you. So act toward children, so toward a wife, so toward office, so toward wealth; and

then some day you will be worthy of the banquets of the gods. But if you do not take these things even when they are set before you, but despise them, then you will not only share the banquet of the gods, but share also their rule. . . .

16. When you see someone weeping in sorrow, either because a child has gone on a journey, or because he has lost his property, beware that you be not carried away by the impression that the man is in the midst of external ills, but straightway keep before you this thought: "It is not what has happened that distresses this man (for it does not distress another), but his judgment about it." Do not, however, hesitate to sympathize with him so far as words go, and, if occasion offers, even to groan with him; but be careful not to groan also in the centre of your being.

17. Remember that you are an actor in a play, the character of which is determined by the Playwright; if He wishes the play to be short, it is short; if long, it is long; if He wishes you to play the part of a beggar, remember to act even this role adroitly; and so if your role be that of a cripple, an official, or a layman. For this is your business, to play admirably the role assigned you; but the selection of that role is Another's. . . .

20. Bear in mind that it is not the man who reviles or strikes you that insults you, but it is your judgment that these men are insulting you. Therefore, when someone irritates you, be assured that it is your own opinion which has irritated you. And so make it your first endeavour not to be carried away by the external impression; for if once you gain time and delay, you will more easily become master of yourself.

21. Keep before your eyes by day death and exile, and everything that seems terrible, but most of all death; and then you will never have any abject thought, nor will you yearn for anything beyond measure. . . .

33. Lay down for yourself, at the outset, a certain stamp and type of character for yourself, which you are to maintain whether you are by yourself or are meeting with people. And be silent for the most part, or else make only the most necessary remarks, and express these in few words. But rarely, and when occasion requires you to talk, talk indeed, but about no ordinary topics. Do not talk about gladiators, or

horse-races, or athletes, or things to eat or drink—topics that arise on all occasions; but above all, do not talk about people, either blaming, or praising, or comparing them. If, then, you can, by your own conversation bring over that of your companions to what is seemly. But if you happen to be left alone in the presence of aliens, keep silence.

Do not laugh much, nor at many things, nor boisterously.

Refuse, if you can, to take an oath at all, but if that is impossible, refuse as far as circumstances allow. . . .

In things that pertain to the body take only as much as your bare need requires, I mean such things as food, drink, clothing, shelter, and household slaves; but cut down everything which is for outward show or luxury.

In your sex-life preserve purity, as far as you can, before marriage, and if you indulge, take only those privileges which are lawful. However, do not make yourself offensive, or censorious, to those who do indulge, and do not make frequent mention of the fact that you do not yourself indulge.

If someone brings you word that So-and-so is speaking ill of you, do not defend yourself against what has been said; but answer: "Yes, indeed, for he did not know the rest of the faults that attach to me; if he had, these would not have been the only ones he mentioned." . . .

41. It is a mark of an ungifted man to spend a great deal of time in what concerns his body, as in much exercise, much eating, much drinking, much evacuating of the bowels, much copulating. But these things are to be done in passing; and let your whole attention be devoted to the mind. . . .

44. The following statements constitute a non-sequitur: "I am richer than you are, therefore I am superior to you"; or, "I am more eloquent than you are, therefore I am superior to you." But the following conclusions are better: "I am richer than you are, therefore my property is superior to yours"; or "I am more eloquent than you are, therefore my elocution is superior to yours." But you are neither property nor elocution. . . .

46. On no occasion call yourself a philosopher, and do not, for the most part, talk among laymen about your philosophic principles, but do what follows from your own principles.

SELECTION 10.5

Foundations of the Metaphysics of Morals*

Immanuel Kant

[*In the first paragraph Kant states the "categorical imperative," the supreme principle of morality. He then illustrates the principle by examining four concrete and specific examples.*]

There is, therefore, only one categorical imperative. It is: Act only according to that maxim by which you can at the same time will that it should become a universal law.

* From Beck, Lewis White, *Immanuel Kant: Foundations of the Metaphysics of Morals,* 2nd Edition, © 1990. Reprinted by permission of Pearson Education, Inc., Upper Saddle River, NJ.

Now if all imperatives of duty can be derived from this one imperative as a principle, we can at least show what we understand by the concept of duty and what it means, even though it remains undecided whether that which is called duty is an empty concept or not.

The universality of law according to which effects are produced constitutes what is properly called nature in the most general sense (as to form), i.e., the existence of things so far as it is determined by universal laws. [By analogy], then, the universal imperative of duty can be expressed as follows: Act as though the maxim of your action were by your will to become a universal law of nature.

We shall now enumerate some duties, adopting the usual division of them into duties to ourselves and to others and into perfect and imperfect duties.[1]

1. A man who is reduced to despair by a series of evils feels a weariness with life but is still in possession of his reason . . . sufficiently to ask whether it would not be contrary to his duty to himself to take his own life. Now he asks whether the maxim of his action could become a universal law of nature. His maxim, however, is: For love of myself, I make it my principle to shorten my life when by a longer duration it threatens more evil than satisfaction. But it is questionable whether this principle of self-love could become a universal law of nature. One immediately sees a contradiction in a system of nature whose law would be to destroy life by the feeling whose special office is to impel the improvement of life. In this case it would not exist as nature; hence that maxim cannot obtain as a law of nature, and thus it wholly contradicts the supreme principle of all duty.

2. Another man finds himself forced by need to borrow money. He well knows that he will not be able to repay it, but he also sees that nothing will be loaned him if he does not firmly promise to repay it at a certain time. He desires to make such a promise, but he has enough conscience to ask himself whether it is not improper and opposed to duty to relieve his distress in such a way. Now, assuming he does decide to do so, the maxim of his action would be as follows: When I believe myself to be in need of money, I will borrow money and promise to repay it, although I know I shall never do so. Now this principle of self-love or of his own benefit may very well be compatible with his whole future welfare, but the question is whether it is right. He changes the pretension of self-love into a universal law and then puts the question: How would it be if my maxim became a universal law? He immediately sees that it could never hold as a universal law of nature and be consistent with itself; rather, it must necessarily contradict itself. For the universality of a law which says that anyone who believes himself to be in need

could promise what he pleased with the intention of not fulfilling it would make the promise itself and the end to be accomplished by it impossible; no one would believe what was promised to him but would only laugh at any such assertion as vain pretense.

3. A third finds in himself a talent which could, by means of some cultivation, make him in many respects a useful . . . man. But he finds himself in comfortable circumstances and prefers indulgence in pleasure to troubling himself with broadening and improving his fortunate natural gifts. Now, however, let him ask whether his maxim of neglecting his gifts, besides agreeing with his propensity to idle amusement, agrees also with what is called duty. He sees that a system of nature could indeed exist in accordance with such a law, even though man (like the inhabitants of the South Sea Islands) should let his talents rust and resolve to devote his life merely to idleness, indulgence, and propagation—in a word, to pleasure. But he cannot possibly will that this should become a universal law of nature or that it should be implanted in us by a natural instinct. For, as a rational being, he necessarily wills that all his faculties should be developed, inasmuch as they are given to him for all sorts of possible purposes.

4. A fourth man, for whom things are going well, sees that others (whom he could help) have to struggle with great hardships, and he asks, "What concern of mine is it? Let each one be as happy as heaven wills, or as he can make himself; I will not take anything from him or even envy him; but to his welfare or to his assistance in time of need I have no desire to contribute." If such a way of thinking were a universal law of nature, certainly the human race could exist, and without doubt even better than in a state where everyone talks of sympathy and good will, or even exerts himself occasionally to practice them while, on the other hand, he cheats when he can and betrays or otherwise violates the rights of man. Now although it is possible that a universal law of nature according to that maxim could exist, it is nevertheless impossible to will that such a principle should hold everywhere as a law of nature. For a will which resolved this would conflict with itself, since instances can often arise in which he would need the love and sympathy of others, and in which he would have robbed himself, by such a law of nature springing from his own will, of all hope of the aid he desires.

The foregoing are a few of the many actual duties, or at least of duties we hold to be actual, whose

---

[1] It must be noted here that I reserve the division of duties for a future *Metaphysics of Morals* and that the division here stands as only an arbitrary one (chosen in order to arrange my examples). For the rest, by a perfect duty I here understand a duty which permits no exception in the interest of inclination; thus I have not merely outer but also inner perfect duties. This runs contrary to the usage adopted in the schools, but I am not disposed to defend it here because it is all one to my purpose whether this is conceded or not.

derivation from the one stated principle is clear. We must be able to will that . . . a maxim of our action become a universal law; this is the canon of the moral estimation of our action generally. Some actions are of such a nature that their maxim cannot even be *thought* as a universal law of nature without contradiction, far from it being possible that one could will that it should be such. In others this internal impossibility is not found, though it is still impossible to *will* that their maxim should be raised to the universality of a law of nature, because such a will would contradict itself. We easily see that the former maxim conflicts with the stricter or narrower (imprescriptible) duty, the latter with broader (meritorious) duty. Thus all duties, so far as the kind of obligation (not the object of their action) is concerned, have been completely exhibited by these examples in their dependence on the one principle.

SELECTION 10.6
Utilitarianism

John Stuart Mill

[*Here, John Stuart Mill states in plain English what utilitarianism is and corrects popular misconceptions of it.*]

What Utilitarianism Is

. . . The creed which accepts as the foundation of morals "utility" or the "greatest happiness principle" holds that actions are right in proportion as they tend to promote happiness; wrong as they tend to produce the reverse of happiness. By happiness is intended pleasure and the absence of pain; by unhappiness, pain and the privation of pleasure. To give a clear view of the moral standard set up by the theory, much more requires to be said; in particular, what things it includes in the ideas of pain and pleasure, and to what extent this is left an open question. But these supplementary explanations do not affect the theory of life on which this theory of morality is grounded—namely, that pleasure and freedom from pain are the only things desirable as ends; and that all desirable things (which are as numerous in the utilitarian as in any other scheme) are desirable either for pleasure inherent in themselves or as means to the promotion of pleasure and the prevention of pain.

Now such a theory of life excites in many minds, and among them in some of the most estimable in feeling and purpose, inveterate dislike. To suppose that life has (as they express it) no higher end than pleasure—no better and nobler object of desire and pursuit—they designate as utterly mean and groveling,

as a doctrine worthy only of swine, to whom the followers of Epicurus were, at a very early period, contemptuously likened; and modern holders of the doctrine are occasionally made the subject of equally polite comparisons by its German, French, and English assailants.

When thus attacked, the Epicureans have always answered that it is not they, but their accusers, who represent human nature in a degrading light, since the accusation supposes human beings to be capable of no pleasures except those of which swine are capable. . . . It is quite compatible with the principle of utility to recognize the fact that some kinds of pleasure are more desirable and more valuable than others. It would be absurd that, while in estimating all other things quality is considered as well as quantity, the estimation of pleasure should be supposed to depend on quantity alone.

If I am asked what I mean by difference of quality in pleasures, or what makes one pleasure more valuable than another, merely as a pleasure, except its being greater in amount, there is but one possible answer. Of two pleasures, if there be one to which all or almost all of who have experience of both give a decided preference, irrespective of any feeling of moral obligation to prefer it, that is the more desirable pleasure. If one of the two is, by those who are competently acquainted with both, placed so far above the other that they prefer it, even though knowing it to be attended with a greater amount of discontent, and would not resign it for any quantity of the other pleasure which their nature is capable of, we are justified in ascribing to the preferred enjoyment a

From *Utilitarianism*, reprinted from *Fraser's Magazine*, 7th ed, (London: Longmans, Green, and Company, 1879).

superiority in quality so far outweighing quantity as to render it, in comparison, of small amount.

Now it is an unquestionable fact that those who are equally acquainted with and equally capable of appreciating and enjoying both do give a most marked preference to the manner of existence which employs their higher faculties. Few human creatures would consent to be changed into any of the lower animals for a promise of the fullest allowance of a beast's pleasures; no intelligent human being would consent to be a fool, no instructed person would be an ignoramus, no person of feeling and conscience would be selfish and base, even though they should be persuaded that the fool, the dunce, or the rascal is better satisfied with his lot than they are with theirs. They would not resign what they possess more than he for the most complete satisfaction of all the desires which they have in common with him. If they ever fancy they would, it is only in cases of unhappiness so extreme that to escape from it they would exchange their lot for almost any other, however undesirable in their own eyes. A being of higher faculties requires more to make him happy, is capable probably of more acute suffering, and certainly accessible to it at more points, than one of an inferior type; but in spite of these liabilities, he can never really wish to sink into what he feels to be a lower grade of existence. . . . It is indisputable that the being whose capacities of enjoyment are low has the greatest chance of having them fully satisfied; and a highly endowed being will always feel that any happiness which he can look for, as the world is constituted, is imperfect. But he can learn to bear its imperfections, if they are at all bearable; and they will not make him envy the being who is indeed unconscious of the imperfections, but only because he feels not at all the good which those imperfections qualify. It is better to be a human being dissatisfied than a pig satisfied; better to be Socrates dissatisfied than a fool satisfied. And if the fool, or the pig, are of a different opinion, it is because they only know their own side of the question. The other party to the comparison knows both sides.

It may be objected that many who are capable of the higher pleasures occasionally, under the influence of temptation, postpone them to the lower. But this is quite compatible with a full appreciation of the intrinsic superiority of the higher. Men often, from infirmity of character, make their election for the nearer good, though they know it to be the less valuable; and this is no less when the choice is between two bodily pleasures than when it is between bodily and mental. They pursue sensual indulgences to the injury of health, though perfectly aware that health is the greater good. It may be further objected that many who begin with youthful enthusiasm for everything noble, as they advance in years, sink into indolence and selfishness. But I do not believe that those who undergo this very common change voluntarily choose the lower description of pleasures in preference to the higher. I believe that, before they devote themselves exclusively to the one, they have already become incapable of the other. Capacity for the nobler feelings is in most natures a very tender plant, easily killed, not only by hostile influences, but by mere want of sustenance; and in the majority of young persons it speedily dies away if the occupations to which their position in life has devoted them, and the society into which it has thrown them, are not favorable to keeping that higher capacity in exercise. Men lose their high aspirations as they lose their intellectual tastes, because they have not the time or opportunity for indulging them; and they addict themselves to inferior pleasures, not because they deliberately prefer them, but because they are either the only ones to which they have access or the only ones which they are any longer capable of enjoying. It may be questioned whether anyone who has remained equally susceptible to both classes of pleasures ever knowingly and calmly preferred the lower, though many, in all ages, have broken down in an ineffectual attempt to combine both.

From this verdict of the only competent judges, I apprehend there can be no appeal. On a question which is the best worth having of two pleasures, or which of two modes of existence is the most grateful to the feelings, apart from its moral attributes and from its consequences, the judgment of those who are qualified by knowledge of both, or, if they differ, that of the majority among them, must be admitted as final. And there needs to be the less hesitation to accept this judgment respecting the quality of pleasures, since there is no other tribunal to be referred to even on the question of quantity. What means are there of determining which is the acutest of two pains, or the intensest of two pleasurable sensations, except the general suffrage of those who are familiar with both? Neither pains nor pleasures are homogeneous, and pain is always heterogeneous with pleasure. What is there to decide whether a particular pleasure is worth purchasing at the cost of a particular pain, except the feelings and judgment of the experienced? When, therefore, those feelings and judgment declare the pleasures derived from the higher faculties to be preferable *in kind,* apart from the question of intensity, to those of which the animal nature, disjoined from the higher faculties, is susceptible, they are entitled on this subject to the same regard.

I have dwelt on this point as being a necessary part of a perfectly just conception of utility or happiness considered as the directive rule of human conduct. But it is by no means an indispensable condition to the acceptance of the utilitarian standard; for that standard is not the agent's own greatest happiness, but the greatest amount of happiness altogether; and if it may possibly be doubted whether a noble character is always the happier for its nobleness, there can be no doubt that it makes other people happier, and that the world in general is immensely a gainer by it. Utilitarianism, therefore, could only attain its end by the general cultivation of nobleness of character, even if each individual were only benefited by the nobleness of others, and his own, so far as happiness is concerned, were a sheer deduction from the benefit. But the bare enunciation of such an absurdity as this last renders refutation superfluous.

According to the greatest happiness principle, as above explained, the ultimate end, with reference to and for the sake of which all other things are desirable—whether we are considering our own good or that of other people—is an existence exempt as far as possible from pain, and as rich as possible in enjoyments, both in point of quantity and quality; the test of quality and the rule for measuring it against quantity being the preference felt by those who, in their opportunities of experience, to which must be added their habits of self-consciousness and self-observation, are best furnished with the means of comparison. This, being according to the utilitarian opinion the end of human action, is necessarily also the standard of morality, which may accordingly be defined "the rules and precepts for human conduct," by the observance of which an existence such as has been described might be, to the greatest extent possible, secured to all mankind; and not to them only, but, so far as the nature of things admits, to the whole sentient creation.

. . . The utilitarian morality does recognize in human beings the power of sacrificing their own greatest good for the good of others. It only refuses to admit that the sacrifice itself is a good. A sacrifice which does not increase or tend to increase the sum total of happiness, it considers as wasted. The only self-renunciation which it applauds is devotion to the happiness, or to some of the means of happiness, of others, either of mankind collectively or of individuals within the limits imposed by the collective interests of mankind.

I must again repeat what the assailants of utilitarianism seldom have the justice to acknowledge, that the happiness which forms the utilitarian standard of what is right in conduct is not the agent's own happiness but that of all concerned. As between his own happiness and that of others, utilitarianism requires him to be as strictly impartial as a disinterested and benevolent spectator. In the golden rule of Jesus of Nazareth, we read the complete spirit of the ethics of utility. "To do as you would be done by," and "to love your neighbor as yourself," constitute the ideal perfection of utilitarian morality.

SELECTION 10.7

Beyond Good and Evil*

Friedrich Nietzsche

[*This passage contains a succinct, orderly, and easy-to-read statement by Friedrich Nietzsche of his conception of morality and the two types of morality (master morality and slave morality).*]

Every enhancement of the type "man" has so far been the work of an aristocratic society—and it will be so again and again—a society that believes in the long ladder of an order of rank and differences in value between man and man, and that needs slavery in some sense or other. . . . Let us admit to ourselves, without trying to be considerate, how every higher culture on earth so far has *begun*. Human beings whose nature was still natural, barbarians in every terrible sense of the word, men of prey who were still in possession of unbroken strength of will and lust for power, hurled themselves upon weaker, more civilized, more peaceful races, perhaps traders or cattle raisers, or upon mellow old cultures whose last vitality was even then flaring up in splendid fireworks of spirit and corruption. In the beginning, the noble caste was always the barbarian caste: their predominance did not lie mainly in physical strength or in strength of the soul—they were more whole human beings (which also means, at every level, "more whole beasts").

. . . The essential characteristic of a good and healthy aristocracy, however, is that it experiences itself *not* as a function (whether of the monarchy or the commonwealth) but as their *meaning* and highest justification—that it therefore accepts with a good conscience the sacrifice of untold human beings who, *for its sake,* must be reduced and lowered to incomplete human beings, to slaves, to instruments. Their fundamental faith simply has to be that society must *not* exist for society's sake but only as the foundation and scaffolding on which a choice type of being is able to raise itself to its higher task and to a higher state of *being*—comparable to those sun-seeking vines of Java—they called *Sipo Matador*—that so long and so often enclasp an oak tree with their tendrils until eventually, high above it but supported by it, they can unfold their crowns in the open light and display their happiness.

Refraining mutually from injury, violence, and exploitation and placing one's will on a par with that of someone else—this may become, in a certain rough sense, good manners among individuals if the appropriate conditions are present (namely, if these men are actually similar in strength and value standards and belong together in *one* body). But as soon as this principle is extended, and possibly even accepted as the *fundamental principle of society,* it immediately proves to be what it really is—a will to the *denial* of life, a principle of disintegration and decay.

Here we must beware of superficiality and get to the bottom of the matter, resisting all sentimental weakness: life itself is *essentially* appropriation, injury, overpowering of what is alien and weaker; suppression, hardness, imposition of one's own forms, incorporation and at least, at its mildest, exploitation—but why should one always use those words in which a slanderous intent has been imprinted for ages?

Even the body within which individuals treat each other as equals, as suggested before—and this happens in every healthy aristocracy—if it is a living and not a dying body, has to do to other bodies what the individuals within it refrain from doing to each other: it will have to be an incarnate will to power, it will strive to grow, spread, seize, become predominant—not from any morality or immorality but because it is *living* and because life simply *is* will to power. But there is no point on which the ordinary consciousness of Europeans resists instruction as on this: everywhere people are now raving, even under scientific disguises, about coming conditions of society in which "the exploitative aspect" will be removed—which sounds to me as if they promised to invent a way of life that would dispense with all organic functions. "Exploitation" does not belong to a corrupt or imperfect and primitive society: it belongs to the *essence* of what lives, as a basic organic function; it is a consequence of the will to power, which is after all the will of life. . . .

Wandering through the many subtler and coarser moralities which have so far been prevalent on earth, or still are prevalent, I found that certain features recurred regularly together and were closely associated—until I finally discovered two basic types and one basic difference.

There are *master morality* and *slave morality*—I add immediately that in all the higher and more mixed cultures there also appear attempts at mediation between these two moralities, and yet more often the interpenetration and mutual misunderstanding of both, and at times they occur directly alongside each other—even in the same human being, with a *single* soul. The moral discrimination of values has originated either among a ruling group whose consciousness of its difference from the ruled group was accompanied by delight—or among the ruled, the slaves and dependents of every degree.

In the first case, when the ruling group determines what is "good," the exalted, proud states of the soul are experienced as conferring distinction and determining the order of rank. The noble human being separates from himself those in whom the opposite of such exalted, proud states finds expression: he despises them. It should be noted immediately that in this first type of morality the opposition of "good" and *"bad"* means approximately the same as "noble" and "contemptible."

(The opposition of "good" and "*evil*" has a different origin.) One feels contempt for the cowardly, the anxious, the petty, those intent on narrow utility; also for the suspicious with their unfree glances, those who humble themselves, the doglike people who allow themselves to be maltreated, the begging flatterers, above all the liars; it is part of the fundamental faith of all aristocrats that the common people lie. "We truthful ones"—thus the nobility of ancient Greece referred to itself.

It is obvious that moral designations were everywhere first applied to *human beings* and only later, derivatively, to actions. Therefore it is a gross mistake when historians of morality start from such questions as: why was the compassionate act praised? The noble type of man experiences *itself* as determining values; it does not need approval; it judges, "what is harmful to me is harmful in itself"; it knows itself to be that which first accords honor to things; it is *value-creating*. Everything it knows as part of itself it honors: such a morality is self-glorification. In the foreground there is the feeling of fullness, of power that seeks to overflow, the happiness of high tension, the consciousness of wealth that would give and bestow: the noble human being, too, helps the unfortunate, but not, or almost not, from pity, but prompted more by an urge begotten by excess of power. The noble human being honors himself as one who is powerful, also as one who has power over himself, who knows how to speak and be silent, who delights in being severe and hard with himself and respects all severity and hardness. . . . Noble and courageous human beings who think that way are furthest removed from that morality which finds the distinction of morality precisely in pity, or in acting for others . . . faith in oneself, pride in oneself, a fundamental hostility and irony against "selflessness" belong just as definitely to noble morality as does a slight disdain and caution regarding compassionate feelings and a "warm heart." . . .

A morality of the ruling group, however, is most alien and embarrassing to the present taste in the severity of its principle that one has duties only to one's peers; that against beings of a lower rank, against everything alien, one may behave as one pleases or "as the heart desires," and in any case "beyond good and evil." . . .

It is different with the second type of morality, *slave morality.* Suppose the violated, oppressed, suffering, unfree, who are uncertain of themselves and weary, moralize: what will their moral valuations have in common? Probably, a pessimistic suspicion about the whole condition of man will find expression, perhaps a condemnation of man along with his condition. The slave's eye is not favorable to the virtues of the powerful: he is skeptical and suspicious, *subtly* suspicious, of all the "good" that is honored there—he would like to persuade himself that even their happiness is not genuine. Conversely, those qualities are brought out and flooded with light which serve to ease existence for those who suffer: here pity, the complaisant and obliging hand, the warm heart, patience, industry, humility, and friendliness are honored—for these are the most useful qualities and almost the only means for enduring the pressure of existence. Slave morality is essentially a morality of utility.

Here is the place for the origin of that famous opposition of "good" and "evil": into evil one's feelings project power and dangerousness, a certain terribleness, subtlety, and strength that does not permit contempt to develop. According to slave morality, those who are "evil" thus inspire fear; according to master morality it is precisely those who are "good" that inspire, and wish to inspire, fear, while the "bad" are felt to be contemptible.

The opposition reaches its climax when, as a logical consequence of slave morality, a touch of disdain is associated also with the "good" of this morality—this may be slight and benevolent—because the good human being has to be *undangerous* in the slaves' way of thinking: he is good-natured, easy to deceive, a little stupid perhaps, *un bonhomme* [a "good person"]. Wherever slave morality becomes preponderant, language tends to bring the words "good" and "stupid" closer together.

One last fundamental difference: the longing for *freedom,* the instinct for happiness and the subtleties of the feeling of freedom belong just as necessarily to slave morality and morals as art and enthusiastic reverence and devotion are the regular symptom of an aristocratic way of thinking and evaluating. . . .

A *species* comes to be, a type becomes fixed and strong, through the long fight with essentially constant *unfavorable* conditions. Conversely, we know from the experience of breeders that species accorded superabundant nourishment and quite generally extra protection and care soon tend most strongly toward variations of the type and become rich in marvels and monstrosities (including monstrous vices).

Now look for once at an aristocratic commonwealth—say, an ancient Greek *polis,* or Venice—as an arrangement, whether voluntary or involuntary, for breeding: human beings are together there who are dependent on themselves and want their species to prevail, most often because they *have to* prevail or run the terrible risk of being exterminated. Here that boon, that excess, and that protection which favor variations are lacking; the species needs itself as a species, as something that can prevail and make itself durable by virtue of its very hardness, uniformity, and simplicity of form, in a constant fight with its neighbors or with the oppressed who are rebellious or threaten rebellion. Manifold experience teaches them to which qualities above all they owe the fact that, despite all gods and men, they are still there, that they have always triumphed: these qualities they call virtues, these virtues alone they cultivate. They do this with hardness, indeed they want hardness; ever aristocratic morality is intolerant—in the education of youth, in their arrangements for women, in their marriage customs, in the relations of old and young, in their penal laws (which take into account deviants only)—they consider intolerance itself a virtue, calling it "justice."

In this way a type with few but very strong traits, a species of severe, warlike, prudently taciturn men, closemouthed and closely linked (and as such possessed of the subtlest feeling for the charms and nuances of association), is fixed beyond the changing generations; the continual fight against ever constant *unfavorable* conditions is, as mentioned previously, the cause that fixes and hardens a type.

Eventually, however, a day arrives when conditions become more fortunate and the tremendous tension decreases; perhaps there are no longer any enemies among one's neighbors, and the means of life, even for the enjoyment of life, are superabundant. At one stroke the bond and constraint of the old discipline are torn: it no longer seems necessary, a condition of existence—if it persisted it would only be a form of *luxury,* an archaizing *taste.* Variation, whether as deviation (to something higher, subtler, rarer) or as degeneration and monstrosity, suddenly appears on the scene in the greatest abundance and magnificence; the individual dares to be individual and different.

At these turning points of history we behold beside one another, and often mutually involved and entangled, a splendid, manifold, junglelike growth and upward striving, a kind of *tropical* tempo in the competition to grow, and a tremendous ruin and self-ruination, as the savage egoisms that have turned, almost exploded, against one another wrestle "for sun and light" and can no longer derive any limit, restraint, or consideration from their previous morality. It was this morality itself that dammed up such enormous strength and bent the bow in such a threatening manner; now it is "outlived." The dangerous and uncanny point has been reached where the greater, more manifold, more comprehensive life transcends and *lives beyond* the old morality; the "individual" appears, obliged to give himself laws and to develop his own arts and wiles for self-preservation, self-enhancement, self-redemption.

All sorts of new what-fors and wherewithals; no shared formulas any longer; misunderstanding allied with disrespect; decay, corruption, and the highest desires gruesomely entangled; the genius of the race overflowing from all cornucopias of good and bad; a calamitous simultaneity of spring and fall, full of new charms and veils that characterize young, still unexhausted, still unwearied corruption. Again danger is there, the mother of morals, great danger, this time transposed into the individual, into the neighbor and friend, into the alley [*sic*], into one's own child, into one's own heart, into the most personal and secret recesses of wish and will: what may the moral philosophers emerging in this age have to preach now?

These acute observers and loiterers discover that the end is approaching fast, that everything around them is corrupted and corrupts, that nothing will stand the day after tomorrow, except *one* type of man, the incurably *mediocre.* The mediocre alone have a chance of continuing their type and propagating—they are the men of the future, the only survivors: "Be like them! Become mediocre!" is now the only morality that still makes sense, that still gets a hearing.

But this morality of mediocrity is hard to preach: after all, it may never admit what it is and what it wants. It must speak of measure and dignity and duty and neighbor love—it will find it difficult *to conceal its irony.*

CHECKLIST

To help you review, a checklist of the key philosophers of this chapter can be found online at www.mhhe.com/moore9e.

KEY TERMS AND CONCEPTS

act utilitarianism 268
categorical
   imperative 263
consequentialism 238
cultural relativism 236
Cynicism 249
Cyrenaicism 243
deontological
   ethics 238
descriptive egoism 236
descriptive
   relativism 236
divine law 256
divine-command
   ethics 238
egoistic ethical
   hedonism 238
egoism 236
Epicureanism 247
ethical hedonism 237
ethical naturalism 244
ethical
   skepticism 235
ethics 234
Form 239
hedonism 237

hypothetical
   imperative 263
individual
   relativism 236
instrumental versus
   intrinsic ends 245
mean between
   extremes 245
moral
   imperative 263
morality of intent 254
natural law 248
paradox of
   hedonism 268
prescriptive
   egoism 236
psychological
   hedonism 237
relativism 238
rule utilitarianism 268
Stoicism 247
subjectivism 236
universalistic ethical
   hedonism 238
virtue ethics 238

QUESTIONS FOR DISCUSSION AND REVIEW

1. "What is right is what you yourself believe is right." Critically evaluate this statement.

2. What is the connection between virtue and happiness in the philosophy of Plato?

3. In what does happiness consist, according to Aristotle? When can we be said to be virtuous?

4. What is the connection between habit and moral character, for Aristotle?

5. Compare and contrast the ethical philosophies of Epicureanism and Stoicism. Which do you think is the superior philosophy, and why?

6. Is it a sound policy to reduce all wants to a minimum and to achieve utter self-reliance by avoiding all the comforts of society?

7. Can you control your attitude if you cannot control your fate?

8. Explain Augustine's solution to the problem of evil, and determine whether it is sound.

9. Do we seek personal survival above all other things?

10. Do we always act selfishly? Explain.

11. Can reasoning disclose the moral wrongfulness of an act of murder?

12. Is it abnormal not to have sympathy for others? Are selfish people really admired in today's society?

13. Suppose you stole something that did not belong to you. Could you rationally will the principle on which you acted to be a universal law? Explain.

14. Explain the difference between a hypothetical imperative and a categorical imperative.

15. Which is it: Does the nature of an act or its consequences determine whether it is good, or is it the intent with which the act has been undertaken? Or is it something else altogether?

16. What does it mean to say that rational beings should be treated as ends and not as means? Give an example of treating another as a means.

17. Is your own happiness more important morally than that of others? ("It is to me" does not count as an answer.)

18. Was Bentham correct in saying that *ought, right, good,* and the like have meaning only when defined in terms of pleasure?

19. Is it true that the ultimate object of a person's desire is always pleasure? Explain.

20. Was Mill correct in saying that some pleasures are inherently better than others?

21. How does Mill propose to establish which of two pleasures is qualitatively better? Can you think of a better way of establishing this?

22. Leslie, who is in the Peace Corps, volunteers to aid starving Ethiopians. She travels to Ethiopia and, risking her own health and safety, works herself nearly to exhaustion for two years, caring for as many people as she can. Meanwhile, her father, Harold, dashes off a huge check for the Ethiopian relief fund. In fact, his check helps more people than Leslie's actions do. But, morally speaking, is Harold more praiseworthy than Leslie? What would Bentham say? Mill? You?

23. What does Nietzsche mean when he says life is the will to power?

24. "There cannot be moral values if there is no God." Critically evaluate this assertion.

SUGGESTED FURTHER READINGS

Go online to www.mhhe.com/moore9e for a list of suggested further readings.

11

Political Philosophy

Man, when perfected, is the best of all animals, but, when separated
from law and justice, he is the worst of all. . . . Justice is the bond of men
in states.   —Aristotle

That one human being will desire to render the person and property
of another subservient to his pleasures, notwithstanding the pain
or loss of pleasure which it may occasion to that individual, is the
foundation of government.   —James Mill[1]

While the state exists there is no freedom. Where there is freedom, there
will be no state.   —Vladimir I. Lenin

Ethics is the philosophical study of moral judgments. But many moral judgments are at the same time political judgments.

Should goods be distributed equally? Or should they be distributed according
to need? Or perhaps according to merit, or according to contribution to production, or to existing ownership, or to something else?

Is it justifiable for a government to restrict the liberty of its citizens and, if so,
in what measure?

When, if ever, is fine or imprisonment legitimate? And what is the purpose of
fine and imprisonment: punishment? deterrence? rehabilitation?

Are there natural rights that all governments must respect? What form of
political society or state is best? Should there even be a state?

---

[1] James Mill (1773–1836) was a Scottish philosopher, historian, and economist and the father of John
Stuart Mill, about whom you will read in this chapter.

The answers to these questions are moral judgments of a political variety. Political philosophy considers such issues and the concepts that are involved in them.

More generally, **political philosophy** seeks to find the best form of political existence. It is concerned with determining the state's right to exist, its ethically legitimate functions and scope, and its proper organization. Political philosophy also seeks to describe and understand the nature of political relationships and political authority, though scholars whose inquiries are focused within the purely descriptive branch of political philosophy now usually call themselves political scientists.

PLATO AND ARISTOTLE

Let's start with Plato and Aristotle because they were the first to try to build a political philosophy from the ground up.

Plato

According to **Plato's** *Republic,* the human soul has three different elements, one consisting of raw appetites, another consisting of drives (such as anger and ambition), and a third consisting of thought or intellect. In the virtuous or just person, each of these three elements fulfills its own unique function and does so under the governance of reason. Likewise, according to Plato, in the ideal or just state there are also three elements, each of which fulfills its unique function and does so in accordance with the dictates of reason.

The lowest element in the soul—the appetitive element—corresponds in the well-ordered state to the class of *craftsmen.* The soul's drive element corresponds in the state to the class of *police-soldiers,* who are auxiliaries to the *governing class.* This last class, in the well-ordered state, corresponds to the intellectual, rational element of the soul.

The governing class, according to Plato, comprises a select few highly educated and profoundly rational individuals, including women so qualified. An individual becomes a member of a class by birth, but he or she will move to a higher or lower class according to aptitude.

In the healthy state, said Plato, as in the well-ordered soul, the rational element is in control. Thus, for Plato, the ideal state is a class-structured aristocracy ruled by **philosopher-kings.**

Unlike the craftsmen, the ruling elite and their auxiliaries, who jointly are the guardians of society, have neither private property nor even private families: property, wives, and children are all possessions held in common. Reproduction among the guardians is arranged always to improve the bloodline of their posterity in intelligence, courage, and other qualities apt for leadership. The guardians not only must be trained appropriately for soldiering but also must be given a rigorous intellectual education that, for the few whose unique abilities allow it, prepares them for advanced work in mathematics and dialectic (that is, the Socratic method; see

Chapter 3). These few, at age fifty and after many years of public service, advance to membership in the ruling aristocracy and to leadership of the state. Such was Plato's vision of the ideal political structure.

It is important to be aware that, from Plato's perspective, the state, like the person, is a *living organism* whose well-being must be sought by its subjects. Although he assumed that the healthy state is best for the individuals in it, Plato also believed that the health or well-being of the state is *desirable for its own sake*. And just as a person's health or well-being requires the proper functioning and coordination of the elements of the soul under the overarching rule of reason, the state's health or well-being lies in the proper functioning and coordination of its elements under the rule of the reasoning elite. The ideal state, according to Plato, is well ordered in this way, and its being well ordered in this way is something that is intrinsically desirable.

In Book VIII of the *Republic,* Plato identified five forms of government. The preferred form, of course, is an **aristocracy,** governed by rational philosopher-kings. According to Plato, however, even if this ideal state could be achieved, it would in time degenerate into a **timocracy,** in which the ruling class is motivated by love of honor rather than by love for the common good. A timocracy in turn gives way to a **plutocracy,** which is rule by men who primarily desire riches. Under a plutocracy, society becomes divided between two classes, the rich and the poor, Plato thought. Nevertheless, this form of government, Plato said, is preferable to the next degeneration, **democracy,** which results because "a society cannot hold wealth in honor and at the same time establish self-control in its citizens." (Perhaps we will eventually see whether Plato is correct that a society that honors wealth cannot maintain self-control.) With Plato's democracy, people's impulses are unrestrained, and the result is lack of order and direction. "Mobocracy" is what we would call Plato's "democracy" today. **Tyranny,** the last form of government in Plato's classification, results when the democratic mob submits itself to a strongman, each person selfishly figuring to gain from the tyrant's rule and believing that the tyrant will end democracy's evil. In fact, Plato thought, the tyrant will acquire absolute power and enslave his subjects. Further, he, the tyrant, will himself become a slave to his wretched craving for power and self-indulgence. Plato was not always an optimist.

Aristotle

Aristotle, too, regarded the state as an organism, as a living being that exists for some end, for some purpose. That purpose, he believed, is to promote the good life for humans. (The good life, for Aristotle, was one that gives you the highest human good—happiness.) Thus, Aristotle offered a standard of evaluation of the state different from Plato's. For Aristotle, a state was good only to the degree to which it enables its citizens themselves to achieve the good life, whereas for Plato a state was good to the extent that it is well ordered.

Aristotle, who had studied the constitutions, or basic political structures, of numerous Greek city-states and other states, was a practical thinker. He insisted that the form of the ideal state depends on, and can change with, circumstances. Unlike Plato, Aristotle did not set forth a recipe for the ideal state. A state, he said,

Aristotle, the Political Scientist

Aristotle was a keen observer of the world around him, including the political world. But he wasn't merely a describer of political systems. Aristotle did enunciate principles in terms of which various forms of government can be *evaluated*. Also, when he listed *monarchy, aristocracy,* and *polity* as proper forms of government and *tyranny, oligarchy,* and *democracy* as their corresponding improper forms,

he was not merely describing these forms, as a modern-day political scientist might, but was also evaluating them, as a political philosopher will do.

Nor was Aristotle a historian of political systems. (You would have no inkling, from reading Aristotle's *Politics,* that the Greek city state system of government went out of existence forever during his lifetime!)

can be ruled properly by one person; but it can also be ruled properly by a few people or by many. When a state is properly ruled by one person, he said, it is a **monarchy;** improper rule by one is *tyranny.* Proper rule by the few is *aristocracy;* improper rule, **oligarchy.** Proper rule by the many is a **polity,** and improper rule by them is a *democracy.* Good forms of government tend to degenerate into bad, he thought, as Plato also did. Aristocracies become oligarchies, monarchies become tyrannies, polities become democracies. (Also see the box "Aristotle, the Political Scientist.")

Though Aristotle thought that states may be good or bad irrespective of their form, he observed that political societies always have three classes: a lower class of laborers and peasants; a middle class of craftsmen, farmers, and merchants; and an upper class of aristocrats. He further observed that political power rests in one or another of these social classes or is shared by them variously, irrespective of the form of the state.

Aristotle, like Plato, was no egalitarian. (An **egalitarian** believes that all humans are equal in their social, political, and economic rights and privileges.) But even though Plato's ideal state has no slaves, Aristotle held that some people are by nature suited for slavery, whereas others by nature are suited for freedom. Even freemen are not equals, Aristotle held. Those who, like laborers, do not have the aptitude (or time) to participate in governance should not be citizens. But, he said, beware: the desires of lesser men for equality are the "springs and fountains" of revolution and are to be so recognized by a properly functioning government, which takes precautions to avoid revolt.

NATURAL LAW THEORY AND CONTRACTARIAN THEORY

Aristotle was an ethical naturalist (see Chapter 10). For answers to questions about what *ought* to be the case, he looked around him (i.e., he turned to "nature") to see what *is* the case. To determine what the purpose of the state ought to be, he considered what the purpose of existing states actually is. Ought all people to be equal in freedom? In citizenship? Aristotle's answers to these and other questions of political ethics were grounded on what he observed. In this instance, the apparent natural inequality of people he perceived prompted him to answer negatively.

Because of his naturalism, Aristotle is sometimes viewed as the source of **natural law political theory.** According to this theory, questions of political ethics are to be answered by reference to the so-called natural law, which alone supposedly determines what is right and wrong, good and bad, just and unjust, proper and improper.

As you saw in Chapter 10, however, the first relatively clear concept of natural law per se is probably found not in Aristotle's writings but later, in Stoic philosophy, in which the natural law is conceived as an impersonal principle of reason that governs the cosmos. But the Stoics were not primarily political philosophers. So it is to the celebrated Roman statesman Cicero (106–43 B.C.E.) that we turn for the classic expression of the Stoic concept of natural law as applied to political philosophy. "True law," wrote Cicero,

> is right reason in agreement with Nature; it is of universal application, unchanging and everlasting. . . . There will not be different laws at Rome and at Athens; or different laws now and in the future, but one eternal and unchangeable law will be valid for all nations and all times.

In other words, Cicero is proposing that there is only one valid law, the natural law of reason, which holds eternally and universally. This was a bold idea, and to a certain extent we still accept it today.

Augustine and Aquinas

In the thought of **Augustine** (354–430) and **Aquinas** (c. 1225–1274), the natural law as conceived by the Stoics, which according to Cicero was the only valid basis for human law, was *Christianized.* Natural law was conceived by these Church philosophers to be the eternal moral law of *God* as humans apprehend it through the dictates of their conscience and reason.

With Augustine and Aquinas, two vital questions were raised: the relationship of secular law to the natural law of God and, correspondingly, the relationship of state to church. According to both thinkers, the laws of the state must be just, which meant, for them, that the laws of the state must accord with God's natural law. If secular laws do not accord, they held, they are not truly laws, and there is no legitimate state. For Augustine, the purpose of the state was to take "the power to do hurt" from the wicked; for Aquinas, it was to attend to the common good (which, for Aquinas, meant much more than merely curbing human sinfulness). For both, the Church provides for a person's spiritual needs, and, though the state does have rights and duties within its own sphere, it is subordinate to the Church, just as its laws are subordinate to natural law.

Perhaps Aquinas's most distinctive contribution to political philosophy was his discussion of law. Aquinas distinguished among four kinds of law. Most fundamental is **eternal law,** which is, in effect, the divine reason of God that rules over all things at all times. Then there is **divine law,** which is God's gift to man, apprehended by us through revelation rather than through conscience or reason, and which directs us to our *supernatural* goal, eternal happiness. **Natural law** is God's eternal law as it applies to man on earth; in effect, it is the fundamental principles of morality as apprehended by us in our conscience and practical reasoning. Natural law directs us to our *natural* goal, happiness on earth. Finally, **human law** is the laws and statutes of society that are derived from man's understanding of natural law. A rule or decree of a ruler or government must answer to a higher authority, said Aquinas; it must conform to natural law. Any rule or statute that does not, he said, should not be obeyed: "We ought to obey God rather than men." Aquinas's conception of law, especially of natural law and human law, bears widely on our own conceptions.

Hobbes

Whereas Augustine, Aquinas, and other Christian thinkers conceived of the natural law as the moral law of God, **Thomas Hobbes** (1588–1679), whose ethical principles were discussed in Chapter 10, construed the natural law as neither the law of God nor moral law. In fact, Hobbes's conception of natural law amounted to discarding the older religious concept.

Hobbes did not speak of the natural law in the singular, as did the classical and Church philosophers, but of natural *laws* in the plural. These, for Hobbes, were simply rational principles of prudent action, prescriptions for best preserving your own life. According to Hobbes, who was a naturalist and in this respect resembled Aristotle, there is no higher authority beyond nature that passes judgment on the morality or immorality of human deeds. You obey the laws of nature insofar as you act rationally, and insofar as you do not, you do not live long.

Hobbes's first law of nature was *to seek peace as far as you have any hope of obtaining it, and when you cannot obtain it, to use any means you can to defend yourself.* As you can see, this "law" is indeed simply a prescription of rational self-interest.

It is easy to understand why Hobbes regarded this as the first law of nature. From Hobbes's perspective, the question of how best to prolong one's life was a pressing issue for most people. Historians emphasize the importance of the Scientific Revolution in the seventeenth century, which included the discoveries of Gilbert, Kepler, Galileo, Harvey, Boyle, Huygens, Newton, and others. The seventeenth century, in fact, reads like a *Who's Who* of scientific discoverers. But most seventeenth-century Europeans, plain folk and ruling aristocrats alike, had never even heard of these discoveries, and even if they had, they would have considered them uninteresting and irrelevant. That is because the seventeenth century was a century of political chaos and brutal warfare both in England and on the Continent. The Thirty Years' War, an ugly spectacle, happened during this century, and most Europeans were somewhat preoccupied with the safety of their skins. For most of them, the question of personal survival was of more than academic interest.

Hobbes's second law was *to be content, for the sake of peace and self-preservation, provided others are also content, with only so much liberty "against other men" as you would allow other men against yourself.* And the third law was *"that men perform the covenants they have made."* (A covenant is an agreement or contract, a compact.)

But nobody, Hobbes said, is so stupid as to live up to an agreement that turns out not to be in her or his own best interest. So, if you want people to live by their agreements, you have to make sure that they will suffer if they try to break them.

This means you have to have some third power to enforce them. "Without the terror of some power to cause them to be observed," Hobbes wrote, covenants are only words.

In light of these considerations, Hobbes concluded, if you apply the three "laws of nature" listed here to real-life situations, what they mean is this: For their own welfare, people should transfer both their collective strength and their right to use whatever is necessary to defend themselves to a sovereign power that will use the acquired power to *compel* all citizens to honor their commitments to one another and to live together peacefully. This is the best road to peace and security, according to Hobbes. Without this central power to make them honor their agreements and keep them in line, people live in a "state of nature," a state of unbridled war of each against all, a state of chaos, mistrust, deception, meanness, and violence in which each person stops at nothing to gain the upper hand, and life is "solitary, poor, nasty, brutish, and short."

The central **sovereign power** to which people will transfer their power and rights, if they are smart enough to see that it is in their own self-interest to do so, was called by Hobbes the **Leviathan.** (A leviathan is a sea monster often symbolizing evil in the Old Testament and Christian literature.) When people transfer their power and rights to the Leviathan, they in effect create a **social contract.** It is this contract that delivers people from the evils of the natural state to civil society and a state of peace.

The social contract is thus an agreement between individuals who, for the sake of peace, are willing to make this absolutely unconditional and irrevocable transfer of right and power to the sovereign, or Leviathan.

According to Hobbes, only when people have contracted among themselves and created the Leviathan is there *law* or *justice,* and Hobbes was speaking of civil laws, not natural laws. *Justice* and *injustice* Hobbes defined as the keeping and the breaking of covenants. Because covenants and laws are meaningless unless there is a Leviathan to enforce them, law and justice can exist only under a Leviathan.

Now, the original social covenant, or contract, that creates the Leviathan is not a contract between the Leviathan and its subjects, Hobbes stressed. It is a contract

Power Politics: Niccolò Machiavelli

One of the most famous political treatises of all time, Machiavelli's *The Prince* (1532), explains how a prince best may gain and maintain power and is often regarded as the foundational treatise of modern political science.

Niccolò Machiavelli [mock-yah-VEL-ee] (1469–1527) did not mince words. He stated frankly that, in the actions of princes, the ends justify the means, and that princes who wished to survive had to learn how *not* to be good and how to be feared as well as loved. If the prince has to choose between the two, being feared or being loved, Machiavelli added, it is much safer for him to be feared. *The Prince* was a shocker when it was written and is still a shocker today. It established Machiavelli's reputation as a cold-blooded advocate of power politics.

Machiavelli, however, though he recognized the importance of power in politics and had but little belief in the intelligence or rationality of the common run of men, made a distinction between the virtuous leader and the villainous or ignoble one, finding little to admire in the latter type.

Further, his more expansive earlier political work, *Discourses on Livy* (1531), reveals his preference for free republics over monarchies as better means of securing liberty, order, stability, and the interests of all, though he thought that, under the prevailing circumstances, the only way to secure order was to establish an absolute power that could curb the excesses of the ambitious and avaricious.

In the Roman republic, people had been more devoted to liberty than in his time, he thought, and in general they had been stronger in character and less prone to become prey to evil-minded men. Why had people changed? Christianity, he perceived, in emphasizing humility, meekness, and contempt for worldly objects, had made men feeble and needy of the absolute rule of a prince.

---

among the subjects themselves. There is not and cannot be any covenant *between* the Leviathan and its subjects. Here is why: because the Leviathan holds all the power, it would be free to break any pledge, promise, agreement, commitment, contract, or covenant that it made. And that means that a covenant between the Leviathan and its subjects would be unenforceable and hence would be empty words.

Therefore, because logically there cannot be any covenant between the Leviathan and its subjects, and because justice is defined by Hobbes as the keeping of a covenant, it is *impossible* for the Hobbesian sovereign or Leviathan to act unjustly toward its subjects. Likewise, the Leviathan's laws—and the Leviathan's laws are the only laws, for they alone can be enforced—cannot be unjust. The Leviathan, according to Hobbes, has the right to lay down any laws it can enforce (although, as you will see shortly, it cannot require us to take our own lives), and we are not only physically but also morally obliged to obey them, for only through its laws are we kept from anarchy.

That no covenant exists between the Leviathan and its subjects means that the Leviathan has no legal or moral obligation to them. That it has no legal or moral obligation to its subjects means that they are *gambling* when they agree among themselves unconditionally to transfer all power and rights to it; they are gambling that life under its rule (conditions of "peace") will be better than it would be under the conditions of anarchy that otherwise would obtain. Perhaps a rational sovereign is likely to see that it is not in his own self-interest to destroy or abuse his subjects, but there is always a chance that he will not.

Hobbes, obviously, thought the gamble a wise one. Were people to live without a common power, he wrote, a power "to keep them all in awe," their innate viciousness

PROFILE: Thomas Hobbes (1588–1679)

Scientific discovery, geometry, and the violence of civil war and anarchy—these were the major influences on Hobbes's philosophy.

A graduate of Oxford, Hobbes became a tutor in the influential Cavendish family, in which role he was able to meet many of the important intellectual figures of his day, including Galileo and Bacon. Through his acquaintance with the work of these and other early scientists, it occurred to him that everything that happens does so as the result of physical matter in motion. This perception became the basis of his entire philosophy, including his metaphysics and political thought.

Amazingly, it was not until his early forties that Hobbes chanced on a copy of Euclid's *Elements*. This work influenced him to think that all knowledge could be derived deductively from axioms based on observation. Consequently, he devised a comprehensive plan, which he never fully completed, to apply the Euclidean deductive method to all questions of physical nature, human nature, and the nature of society.

Hobbes's political philosophy, however, has earned him his greatest fame. The basic themes of his political writings—that man is by nature violent, self-serving, and at war with all other men, and that for their own defense against their natural predaciousness, people must submit to a strong power capable of enforcing peace—are clear reflections of the political turbulence of his times. During Hobbes's lifetime, the Thirty Years' War on the European continent struck down half the population, and in England a state of anarchy followed the Civil War and the rule of Oliver Cromwell. Moreover, the plague ravaged England no fewer than four times during Hobbes's long life. Hobbes was no stranger to death, destruction, chaos, and the willingness of men to sacrifice others for their own ends.

would preclude development of any commerce, industry, or culture, and there would be "no knowledge on the face of the earth; no account of time; no arts; no letters; no society." There would be only, he wrote, "continual fear, and danger of violent death." In Hobbes's view, given the alternatives of anarchy and dictatorship (the Leviathan)— and these are the only alternatives—the most reasonable choice is dictatorship, even though it does involve the risk of despotism.

Hobbes did make the political establishment of the Leviathan subject to certain minimal safeguards for its subjects. If the Leviathan fails to provide security to its subjects, they may transfer their allegiance to another sovereign. Further, because no one has the right to take his own life, this right is not among those transferred to the Leviathan at the time of the social contract of its subjects. Therefore, the Leviathan cannot rightfully compel a subject to take his or her own life.

Critics of Hobbes, not surprisingly, scoff at such "safeguards." As a practical matter, the Leviathan, having been given the collective power of its subjects, is able to do whatever it pleases with its subjects. As John Locke said, with Hobbes you trade the chance of being ravaged by a thousand men acting independently for the chance of suffering the same fate at the hands of one person who has a thousand men at his command.

One other important concept in Hobbes's political philosophy needs to be mentioned here: Hobbes used the phrase *natural right* and asserted that, when peace cannot be obtained, we have a natural right to use all means to defend ourselves. Today we think of a natural right as something that it would be immoral for others to deprive us of. For example, when we say that a person has a natural right to life, we mean that it would be wrong for others to deprive the person of life. For Hobbes the emphasis was slightly different. He meant that, when peace cannot be obtained, we suffer no moral restrictions whatsoever and that, if necessary for survival, each person can use any method he or she wants—including depriving another of his or her life. For Hobbes, one's natural right to life does not prohibit any activity.

We have spent some time here on Hobbes. This is because Hobbes, in basing the creation and power of the Leviathan on a social contract, was the first philosopher to enunciate systematically the concept that the state, and with it justice, is created through an agreement or "contract" among the people whom the state comprises. This is, of course, a familiar notion to Americans because the United States Constitution, about which more will be said later, is the social contract that brought this country into existence.

So Hobbes really did more than reject the principle of natural law as representing God's will and its corollary that the laws of the state and the state itself derive their legitimacy from their harmony with this divine natural law. According to Hobbes, the legitimacy of the state and its laws derives from an initial consent of those governed (though keep in mind that this consent is "required" by those principles of practical reason that Hobbes referred to as natural laws). With Hobbes began an important tradition in Western political philosophy, so-called **contractualism.** Contractualism is the idea that the legitimacy of the state and/or the principles of sound justice derive their legitimacy from a societal agreement or social contract. *Contractarianism* is often used as a synonym. You will encounter other contractarian theories besides Hobbes's as we proceed, beginning with the philosophy of John Locke.

TWO OTHER CONTRACTARIAN THEORISTS

Two other contractarian theorists from the modern period, John Locke and Jean-Jacques Rousseau, were very important to the history of political philosophy. Both influenced American political thought, especially Locke, the earlier of the two.

John Locke

Hobbes lived much of his life during a time of rather unpleasant turmoil, and he quite reasonably thought that civil peace should be a primary objective for people. **John Locke** (1632–1704), who was born some forty or so years later, responded in his writing to a threat other than that of anarchy and chaos—namely, the threat posed by a Roman Catholic monarch in Anglican England. To avoid getting lost in the maze known as English history, let's just say that this Catholic monarch, James II, was a blunderer of the first rank who not only suspended laws against fellow Catholics but also did his best to populate higher offices with them. In response, English aristocrats invited the Dutch head of state, the Protestant

PROFILE: John Locke (1632–1704)

Locke, like Hobbes, was educated at Oxford. Though he became a lecturer there, he turned to the study of medicine, and as the physician, friend, and advisor of Lord Ashley (who later was the Earl of Shaftesbury and Lord Chancellor of the Realm), Locke became an influential man of state.

When Shaftesbury, who was involved in a plot to overthrow King Charles II, was forced to leave England, Locke found himself suspected of disloyalty by the king and went into exile in Holland in 1683. Five years later, when Prince William and Princess Mary of Orange were called to the throne in the Glorious Revolution, Locke returned to England as part of the entourage of the future Queen Mary.

Locke's two most important works, *Two Treatises of Government* and *An Essay Concerning Human*

Understanding, were published in 1690, by which time Locke already was a famous philosopher and a respected political advisor. In his last years, he withdrew from political affairs and devoted himself to religious contemplation and study of the Epistles of St. Paul.

His contributions to epistemology and political theory were of major and lasting significance, and he is recognized as an articulate advocate of natural rights and religious freedom, as well as a strong opponent of the divine right of kings.

Locke's *Two Treatises of Government* were published anonymously. During his life, rumors correctly reported that Locke was the author of these works, but Locke always denied this.

William of Orange, to take the throne (which, of course, he was happy to do). When William landed in England, James was forced to flee to France, and in 1688 the throne was offered jointly to William and his wife, Mary, who, incidentally, was James's daughter.

This switch was known as the Glorious Revolution, and its relationship to Locke's writings was this: Locke wished to define a right to resistance within a theoretical framework that would not at the same time undermine the state's power to govern effectively. Although Locke wrote his *Two Treatises of Government* before the Glorious Revolution, he published them in 1690, and they were regarded as the philosophical justification of the Glorious Revolution.

Locke's treatises, and especially the *Second Treatise of Government*, are essentially an outline of the aims and purposes of the state. They have affected democratic theory at least as much as anything else that has ever been written. At the time of the American Revolution, Locke's political thought was well known to American political leaders and had become considerably incorporated in American popular political thought as well. It had a marked impact on the contents and wording of the Declaration of Independence, the Constitution, and the Bill of Rights and has had a continued substantial impact on American political thought and political institutions to this day. All Americans are directly or indirectly influenced by John Locke.

Locke, unlike Hobbes, believed there is a natural moral law that is more than a set of practical principles for survival. According to Locke, we are all made by God and are his "property." It logically follows that we are obliged to preserve ourselves

Catharine Trotter Cockburn and John Locke

Catharine Trotter Cockburn (1679–1749) was an Englishwoman who, with no apparent formal education, learned French, Latin, and Greek and read philosophy. Until very recently, her philosophical writings went unexamined by scholars. We mention her here in connection with Locke.

Trotter was an immensely successful playwright before she turned to writing philosophy. London's Drury Lane is the predecessor of New York's Broadway. When Trotter was a teenager, her first play, *Agnes de Castro*, was produced at Drury Lane. It was so popular that she was immediately able to get hundreds of subscribers to pay money in advance to support the writing of her next play. (The list of her subscribers reads like a *Who's Who* of England.) When she was twenty-one, she had three blockbuster plays on Drury Lane at the same time.

Edward Stillingfleet, the Bishop of Wooster, was a subscriber to Trotter's plays. He was, in addition, a major critic of Locke's *Essay Concerning Human Understanding*, especially of its consequences for morality and religion. He thought that Locke's views challenged the authority of divine revelations on the nature of morality, and he wrote several highly publicized (and unbelievably long) letters condemning Locke. An individual named Thomas Burnet of the Charterhouse anonymously published three sets of "Remarks" in support of Bishop Stillingfleet's criticism of Locke. Everyone ducked these broadsides, even Locke. Nobody would say a word against the powerful Bishop of Wooster.

Then Catharine Trotter anonymously published *A Defence of Mr. Locke's Essay of Human Understanding, Wherein Its Principles, with Reference to Morality, Revealed Religion, and the Immortality of the Soul, Are Considered and Justified: In Answer to Some Remarks on That Essay.* She published her defense of Locke anonymously because she was afraid that a defense of Locke by a woman would further inflame Bishop Stillingfleet. (How could a woman claim any religious or moral authority to give an opinion?) However, within six months, Catharine Trotter was identified as the author of the *Defence*, and her plays all closed, in an apparent blacklisting. Locke sought her out and gave her some books and a large sum of money in gratitude.

Leibniz (see Chapter 6) was working on his own critique of Locke but put off finishing it until he could read Trotter's *Defence*. Several years after publishing *Defence*, Catharine Trotter married a clergyman named Cockburn [KO-burn] and continued to publish philosophical pamphlets defending Locke's philosophy from his religious critics until shortly before her death.

and, as far as possible, the rest of humankind. Accordingly, except for the sake of just punishment, no person may take away or impair another's "life, liberty, health, limbs or goods," or anything on which these various items may depend.

That no person may destroy or impair another's life, liberty, or property requires, according to Locke, that each person has inalienable **natural rights** and duties. They are inalienable and natural in that their existence is entailed by the fact that we are God's creations. This conception of natural rights is more in accord with contemporary popular views than is the conception of Hobbes, discussed earlier.

Locke was considerably less gloomy than Hobbes in his opinion of people and was not nearly so pessimistic about what they might do to one another in the absence of civil society (i.e., in a hypothetical "state of nature"). Nevertheless, he thought it plainly advantageous to individuals to contract among themselves to

According to Locke, your property is what you mix your labor with (subject to certain provisos mentioned in the text). But here is a problem: Just *what* is the astronaut mixing his labor with? The entire planet? Or just with what he has walked on? Or maybe just with the sign and the ground in which it is pounded? Also, *whose* labor is involved here, only the astronaut's?

establish a state to govern them, because the state, chiefly through its laws, offers the means to protect the right to property and to ensure "the peace, safety, and public good of the people."

Thus Locke, like Hobbes, held that the state is created and acquires its legitimacy by an agreement or social compact on the part of its citizens and subjects. For both philosophers the purpose of the social compact is to ensure the "public good," but for Locke the purpose is also to protect natural rights. For Hobbes, each subject *gives up* his rights to the Leviathan in exchange for, or rather in hopes of obtaining, peace and security. For Locke, the subject *entrusts* his rights to the state for safeguarding.

For Locke, then, the legitimacy of the state and its governing of its citizens rests on their prior consent to the state's existence, authority, and power. Without that prior consent, it is a violation of a person's natural rights for the state to exercise political power over him. Because men are "by nature all free, equal and independent," he wrote, "no one can be . . . subjected to the political power of another without his consent."

It is plain, however, that most people in most states have never explicitly given their consent to be governed by the state. Do you recall ever having given such consent? Therefore, can it not be argued that existing states, by having laws and punishing lawbreakers, in effect violate the natural rights of their citizens?

Locke resolves this problem by maintaining that, if we accept any of the advantages of citizenship—if, for instance, we own property or rely on the police or travel on a public highway—then we have given **tacit consent** to the state to make and enforce laws, and we are obliged to obey these laws. In this way, Locke can maintain that states do not violate the natural rights of citizens (and others subject to their authority) by exercise of governmental authority over them, even though these individuals have never explicitly expressed their consent to that authority.

Locke and the Right to Property   That people have a natural right to property, Locke regarded as evident. Because all people are created by God and thus (as explained earlier) have a right to their body (their "limbs"), it follows, Locke reasoned, that they have a right to their body's labor and thus to whatever things they "mix their labor with." That is, they have a right to those things, provided that the things do not already belong to or are not needed to sustain someone else, and provided that they do not exceed in amount what can be used before spoiling. Because money is durable, a person may "heap up as much of it" as he can, said Locke.

Locke's theory of property implies that *although all people equally have a right to property, they do not all have a right to equal property*, because how much property a person lawfully has will depend on his ingenuity and industriousness. This distinction is important because it can go some way toward justifying an unequal distribution of wealth.

Separation of Power   When people agree to unite themselves in a state, Locke said, they consent to entrust to it the power to make and enforce laws and punish transgressors, and they consent to submit to the will of the majority. The majority must decide for itself what form of government is best—that is, whether it (the majority) will run the government itself or will delegate its ruling power to a select few, or even to one, or will adopt yet some other arrangement. The body to which the power is delegated (or the majority itself, if the power is not delegated to anyone) is the *legislative*, or lawmaking, branch of the government.

Lawmaking is the central function of government, in Locke's opinion, for it is only through law that people are assured of equal, fair, and impartial treatment and are protected from the arbitrary exercise of power by the government.

But, Locke thought, the persons who make the laws should not themselves execute them, and so, he said, the government should have an *executive* branch as well. Further, in addition to the legislative and executive branches of government, there must be, he believed, a *federative* branch with the power to make war and peace. Though Locke believed it essential that there be a judiciary to settle disputes and fix the degree of punishment for lawbreakers, the idea that the judiciary should be a separate branch of government was not Locke's but that of the influential French jurist Montesquieu [MAHN-tes-kyu] (1689–1755).

Locke's political theory also contrasts sharply with Hobbes's in that, for Hobbes, political power is *surrendered* to an *executive authority*, whereas for Locke, political power is *delegated* to the *legislature*. Also, as we have seen, Locke, unlike Hobbes, called for a division of governmental authority.

Because, according to Locke, the power of the government is entrusted to it by the people of the state, the government is the *servant* of the people. Whenever, in the view of the people, the government acts contrarily to that trust, the people may dismiss their servant. In other words, when this violation of trust is perceived to have happened, rebellion is justified.

It is plain, then, that several basic concepts of the American democratic form of government are found in the political theory of John Locke. These include the ideas that people have natural rights that the government cannot infringe on, that the government is the servant of the people and its power is entrusted to it by them, that law rather than force is the basis of the government, that the will of the people is determined by majority vote, and that the government should be divided into separate branches.

Jean-Jacques Rousseau

According to Hobbes and Locke, people are better off in the properly constituted state than they are or were in the "state of nature." Quite a different point of view was expressed by **Jean-Jacques Rousseau** [roo-SO] (1712–1778), at least in his early political writings.

In the state of nature, in which there was neither state nor civilization, people were essentially innocent, good, happy, and healthy, maintained Rousseau in his *Discourse on the Origin and Foundation of the Inequality among Men* (1754). Further, in the state of nature, he said, people enjoyed perfect freedom. But with the advent of private property, this all changed. "The first man who, having enclosed a piece of ground, bethought himself of saying *This is mine,* and found people simple enough to believe him, was the real founder of civil society," which brought with it the destruction of natural liberty and which, "for the advantage of a few ambitious individuals, subjected all mankind to perpetual labor, slavery and wretchedness."

To put this in some sort of perspective, Rousseau wrote this indictment of civilization in 1754. This was sixty-seven years after Newton had published his *Principia.* It was two years after Benjamin Franklin, with key and kite, had proved that lightning is electricity. Thirty years earlier, Fahrenheit had devised his thermometer. Bach had been dead four years, and it had been twenty-three years since he had completed the Brandenburg Concertos, a masterpiece of mathematical reasoning expressed in music. This, in short, was the eighteenth century, the Enlightenment, the age of light, the Age of Reason. Civilization was *stuffed* with benefits. Philosophers were (as always) critical, but *this* critical? Civilization a step backward? Rousseau was regarded as insane.

But Rousseau later came to think that in the proper society people would surrender their individual liberty for a different and more important *collective*

They're forcing him to be free.

According to Rousseau, when you force a person to accept the general will, you are forcing him to be free.

PROFILE: Jean-Jacques Rousseau (1712–1778)

He [Rousseau] is surely the blackest and most atrocious villain, beyond comparison, that now exists in the world; and I am heartily ashamed of anything I ever wrote in his favor.   —David Hume

Rousseau—philosopher, novelist, and composer—loved many women and eventually became paranoid to the point of madness. He was born a watchmaker's son in Geneva. In his early teens he was apprenticed to an engraver but ran away from his master. When he was about sixteen, he met Baroness Louise de Warens, who became his patroness and later his lover. With her he spent most of his time until he was thirty, attempting through wide reading to remedy the deficiencies in his education. In 1742 he went to Paris by himself to make his fortune, which he failed to do, with a new system of musical notation he had invented. There he became a close associate of several important literary figures of the time, including, most significantly, Denis Diderot (editor of the *Encyclopédie*, the crowning jewel of eighteenth-century rationalism). There he also met Thérèse Le Vasseur, an almost illiterate servant girl, who became his common-law wife.

In 1749 Rousseau won first prize in a contest sponsored by the Academy of Dijon for his essay on the question, Has the progress of the sciences and art contributed to the corruption or to the improvement of human conduct? His answer, startling to the sensibilities of the French Enlightenment, was an attack on the corrupting effects of civilization and instantly made him famous. A second essay, *Discourse on the Origin and Foundation of Inequality among Men* (1754), which again portrayed the evils brought to man by civilization, was also highly controversial. Voltaire, to whom Rousseau had sent a copy of the work, thanked him for his "new book against the human race."

At this time Rousseau, disillusioned with Paris, went briefly to Geneva to regain his Genevan citizenship, but he soon returned to Paris and retired to the estate of yet another woman, Madame d'Épinay. Always emotional, temperamental, suspicious, and unable to maintain constant friendships, he suspected his friends—Diderot, Mme. d'Épinay, and others—of conspiring to ruin him. He departed and became the guest of the Duc de Luxembourg, at whose chateau he finished the novel *La Nouvelle Heloise* (1761), written under the influence of his love for (yes!) the sister-in-law of Mme. d'Épinay.

The Social Contract and his treatise on education, *Émile*, both published the following year, were so offensive to ecclesiastic authorities that Rousseau had to leave Paris. He fled to Neuchâtel and then to Bern. Finally, in 1766 he found a haven with David Hume in England. But after a year, Rousseau, who by this time had become deeply paranoid, quarreled with Hume, who he thought was plotting against him. In fact, Hume had been trying to procure a royal pension for Rousseau. (Hume's last opinion of Rousseau is stated at the beginning of this Profile.) Rousseau now returned to France and eventually to Paris, even though he was in danger of arrest. He was left undisturbed, however, and spent his last years copying music, wandering about reading his *Confessions* out loud, and insulting the curious throngs who came to look at him.

Still, few philosophers have had as much impact as Rousseau on political philosophy, politics, education, or literature.

liberty. Through a social compact, a people may agree, in effect, to unite into a collective whole called "the state" or "the sovereign," and through the state or sovereign enact laws reflective of the *general will*. An important point to be aware of here is that, for Rousseau, the state or sovereign is *an entity in its own right*, a "moral person" (as Rousseau says), a nonbiological organism that has its own life and its own *will*. Rousseau's concept of the **general will**—that is, the will of a politically united people, the will of the state—is his most important contribution to political philosophy.

If you have difficulty conceiving of a state as a person or an organic entity, remember that Plato also viewed the state as an organism. Or think of a football team, which can easily be regarded as something "over and beyond" the individual players that make it up, or of a corporation, which the law regards as a person.

The general will, according to Rousseau, defines what is to be the common good and thus determines what is right and wrong and should and should not be done. And the state or sovereign (i.e., the people as a collective agent) expresses this general will by passing laws.

Further, the general will, the will of the people taken collectively, represents the *true* will of each person. Thus, insofar as the individual's actions coincide with the common will, he is acting as he "really" wants to act—and to act as you really want to act is to be free, said Rousseau. Compelling a person to accept the general will by obeying the laws of the state is *forcing him to be free,* Rousseau wrote in a famous passage. So we may lose individual or "natural" liberty when we unite to form a collective whole, but we gain this new type of "civil" liberty, "the freedom to obey a law which we prescribe for ourselves." Thus, Rousseau wrote, "it is to law alone that men owe justice and [civil] liberty."

The question arises, of course: Just how do we know what the general will is? Rousseau's answer: If we, the citizens, are enlightened and are not allowed to influence one another, then a majority vote determines what the general will is.

> The general will is found by counting votes. When, therefore, the opinion which is contrary to my own prevails, this proves neither more nor less than that I was mistaken, and that what I thought to be the general will was not so.

Rousseau, however, distinguished between the "will of all" and the general will. The former, Rousseau wrote,

> is indeed but a sum of private wills: but remove from these same wills the pluses and minuses that cancel each other, and then the general will remains as the sum of the differences.

According to Rousseau, it makes no sense to think of either delegating or dividing the general will. Therefore, he calculated, in the state there cannot validly be a division of powers (in contrast to what Locke thought), and though we may commission some person or persons to administer or enforce the law, these individuals act only as our deputies, not as our representatives.

Rousseau maintained that the citizens of the state have the right at any time to terminate the social contract. He also held that they have the right at any time to depose the officials of the state. The implication of the right of the citizenry to terminate the social contract at any time and of their right to remove officials of the state at any time is that the citizenry have a right of revolution and a right to resume anarchy at any time. Thus, Rousseau is thought to have provided a philosophical justification for anarchy and revolution.

Did Rousseau also unwittingly establish a philosophical basis for totalitarianism? Some think that is the case because he said that "the articles of the social contract [reduce] to this single point: the total alienation of each person, and all his rights, to the whole community." If the community is regarded not just as the sum total of its members but as an entity somehow over and above the individuals in it, an entity with its own life and will that can itself do no wrong and must always be obeyed, then Rousseau's words do have an ominous ring and invoke concepts that are incorporated wholesale in the philosophy of fascism. (Hitler's claim that the Führer instinctively knows the desires of the Volk [German for "the people"] and is therefore due absolute obedience is an appeal to the general will.) Also ominous is what Rousseau wrote near the end of *The Social Contract* (1762):

> If any one, after he has publicly subscribed to these dogmas [which dispose a person to love his duties and be a good citizen], shall conduct himself as if he did not believe them, he is to be punished by death.

U.S. CONSTITUTIONAL THEORY—APPLIED PHILOSOPHY

U.S. constitutional political philosophy incorporates several important philosophical concepts and ideas. As we have seen, before the U.S. Constitution was written, philosophers had theorized about a social compact as the foundation of the state. But there had been only a few instances of written constitutions, and these were of no lasting importance. England was the only great power that had ever had a constitution, which lasted only a few months during Oliver Cromwell's rule. Thus, the first significant experience with written constitutions was the U.S. Constitution.

The main trend in U.S. political thought has been embodied in the development of theory pertaining to the Constitution. The trend relates essentially to natural law and natural rights and to the incorporation in the federal and state constitutions of a social contract to establish or control a political state. The Constitution is a continuing experiment in applied philosophy.

Natural Law and Rights in the Declaration of Independence

In 1776, the Declaration of Independence proclaimed the doctrines of natural, or divine, law and of natural, or God-given, rights. The Declaration asserted that there are "Laws of Nature and of Nature's God," and the framers appealed "to the Supreme Judge of the World for the rectitude of our intentions." The Declaration also asserted that it is "self-evident" that

> all men are created equal, that they are endowed by their Creator with certain unalienable rights, that amongst these are Life, Liberty and the pursuit of happiness.

The framers also stated that "it is the Right of the People to alter or abolish" any form of government whenever that form of government becomes destructive of "its ends to secure" the unalienable rights with which men are endowed by their Creator.

In proclaiming the existence of natural or divine law and of natural or God-given rights, the Declaration incorporated what had become widespread political theory in the colonies by the time of the American Revolution, a theory prevalent among those who opposed the British king and parliament. This political theory

The Jefferson Memorial. Thomas Jefferson was the main author of The Declaration of Independence.

was rooted in (1) familiarity with the writings of European political theorists, particularly the British ones, and (2) in the colonies, the constant preaching of the clergy, who had been dominant in civil and political as well as religious matters, that the moral code reflected divine law and should determine civil rights.

As for the philosophically vexing question of who should say what natural or divine law ordains and what God-given rights are in particular, by the time of the Declaration it was no longer generally conceded that this power belonged primarily to the clergy. Instead, it was recognized that the power lies ultimately in the people and mediately in the legislative branch of government, subject, some people thought, to judicial review. The last provision, that the power of the legislative branch is subject to judicial review, is now almost universally accepted, as we shall see.

Natural Law and Rights in the U.S. Constitution

The original Constitution was directed toward establishing law and order and not toward guaranteeing natural rights. There is no explicit reference to divine law or God-given rights in the original. Before the adoption of the Bill of Rights (the first ten amendments to the Constitution), the Constitution refers to natural law or divine rights only implicitly and only in its preamble, in stating its purpose to "establish Justice, insure domestic tranquility, provide for the common defense, promote the General Welfare, and secure the Blessings of Liberty." However, it is plausible to say that these purposes are those of natural law and that the "Blessings of Liberty" include natural rights. In addition, the Bill of Rights arguably limits the federal government in ways dictated by natural law and arguably guarantees rights in ways dictated by the existence of natural rights. Without question, the rights explicit and implicit in the preamble and in the Bill of Rights were regarded by the framers of the Constitution and by the American people in general as the unalienable rights to which the Declaration of Independence alluded.

In ***Marbury v. Madison,*** decided by the Supreme Court in 1803 under Chief Justice John Marshall, and in Supreme Court cases in its wake, it became firmly established that, under the Constitution, the Supreme Court has the power to declare void federal and state laws that violate it. Thus, it is for the Supreme Court to determine the extent to which what may be called natural law and rights are incorporated in the Constitution.

Under Section 1 of the Fourteenth Amendment, ratified July 9, 1869, most of the limitation on government and guarantees of rights contained in the Bill of Rights became applicable to the states as well as to the federal government. The relationship of the authority of the states to the authority of the federal government has always been a central issue in American constitutional philosophy.

The Right to Privacy

What specific rights are explicit and implicit in the Bill of Rights and other clauses of the Constitution is not crystal clear. For example, the Constitution does not mention a right to vote, a right to refuse medical treatment, a right to travel freely, or a right to have children. One issue concerning which there is much current discussion is whether the Constitution protects a right to privacy. The question is especially controversial because, in its landmark decision in ***Roe v. Wade,*** the Supreme Court upheld a woman's right to abortion as included within the right to privacy. A right to privacy arguably also would cover a right to engage in various forms of sexual intimacies; whether there is such a constitutional right therefore is questioned by those who would proscribe sexual practices they regard as immoral. Differences on the issue tend to fall along partisan lines, with Democrats generally believing that such a right is implied in the Constitution and Republicans generally believing that it is not. In 1987, President Ronald Reagan's nominee to the Supreme Court, Robert H. Bork, was rejected by the U.S. Senate mainly because of his views on the question of whether there is a constitutional right to privacy. Subsequent nominees have all been questioned carefully about their views on the subject.

In 2003, in ***Lawrence v. Texas,*** the Court ruled that a Texas law prohibiting homosexual sodomy was unconstitutional. Significantly, the majority opinion was based not on a right to privacy but on the grounds that the antisodomy law was a violation of rights "implicit in ordered liberty." The case perhaps represented a shift in the Court's thinking toward an emphasis on constitutional guarantees of liberty rather than privacy. Many constitutional scholars view *Lawrence v. Texas* as a landmark decision for a variety of different reasons, including its potential impact on statutes prohibiting certain types of sexual practices.

CLASSIC LIBERALISM AND MARXISM

We turn now to the nineteenth century, the century ushered in by Romanticism in art, music, and literature; by grandiose metaphysical speculations in philosophy; and (to mention something non-European for a change) by the accession of Muhammad Ali (the pasha of Egypt, not the boxer). It was the century that saw spreading industrialization and nationalism, Darwin and Freud, the Suez Canal, civil war in America, the emergence of Italy and Germany as states, and the invention of photography and the automobile. The two major political philosophies were liberalism and Marxism. They still are, for the most part, despite the demise of Soviet communism. (See the box "Marxism and Liberalism Compared" later in this chapter.) Marxism, of course, is the socialist philosophy of Karl Marx (1818–1883). **Liberalism** (from the Latin word for "liberty") is the philosophy well expressed by John Stuart Mill (1806–1873)—who will be discussed shortly— in his treatise *On Liberty:* "The sole end for which mankind are warranted, individually or collectively, in interfering with the liberty of action of any of their number, is . . . to prevent harm to others. His own good, either physical or moral, is not a sufficient warrant."

Adam Smith

The most important classical liberal economic theorist was **Adam Smith** (1723–1790), a contemporary of David Hume. The principle of Smith's economic theory is that, in a laissez-faire economy (one in which the government remains on the sidelines), each individual, in seeking her or his own gain, is led "by an invisible hand" to promote the common good, though doing so is not her or his intention. As an exponent of the benefits for everyone of **capitalism** (a system of private ownership of property and the means of production and distribution) and a **free-market economy** (in which individuals may pursue their own economic interests without governmental restrictions on their freedom), Smith advocated positions that resemble those of many contemporary American conservatives. His *An Inquiry into the Nature and Causes of the Wealth of Nations* (1776) has become a classic among American political conservatives.

Utilitarianism and Natural Rights

Utilitarianism, as you may recall from the preceding chapter, is the theory that the rightness of an act derives from the happiness or pleasure it produces as its consequences. You may also recall the name **Jeremy Bentham** (1748–1832), the famous utilitarian. Here we mention him for his view that talk about natural rights is so much nonsense. And, indeed, utilitarian philosophy in general does not easily accommodate a belief in natural rights. Why? Well, consider a possible natural right—for example, the right to keep what you have honestly earned. If taking from you what you have honestly earned and distributing it to people who are poorer than you are increases the sum total of happiness, utilitarianism apparently requires that we do this, despite your "natural right." Utilitarianism seems to require violating any so-called natural right if doing so increases happiness.

Utilitarians often attempt to accommodate our intuitions about natural rights by maintaining that in civilized society more happiness results when what are called natural rights are respected than when they are not. They say that natural rights should be regarded as secondary rules of conduct that must be obeyed for the sake of the general happiness. However, in viewing natural rights as a system of moral rules that promote general happiness, utilitarians do not always explain why such rules should not be overridden when doing so better promotes the general happiness.

Harriet Taylor

Like many women philosophers, **Harriet Taylor** (1807–1858) has been known to the public primarily through her association with a male philosopher; in Taylor's case the male philosopher was John Stuart Mill (coming up next). Taylor and Mill shared a long personal and professional intimacy, and each shaped and influenced the ideas of the other. However, Taylor was a published author of poetry before she even met Mill in 1831. Recently, a draft of an essay on toleration of nonconformity was discovered in Taylor's handwriting; it appears to have been written in 1832. She was a regular contributor of poetry, book reviews, and a literary piece to the radical, utilitarian, and feminist journal *The Monthly Repository*. Later, Mill, too, became a regular contributor, and eventually Taylor and Mill began writing together. However, their writings were published under Mill's name, partly because a man's name gave the work more legitimacy within a sexist culture but also because Taylor's husband was unhappy with the idea of his wife's gaining notoriety. Nevertheless, from the evidence of their manuscripts and their personal correspondence, it is possible to piece together an idea of which works were primarily Taylor's and which were Mill's; she was a profound thinker in her own right.

Taylor was interested both in sweeping transformations of society and in specific legal reforms. One of her greatest concerns was the tendency of English society to stifle individuality, originality, and radical political and religious views. English society, in her opinion, was intolerant of opinions that failed to conform to the mainstream. She considered the intolerance of nonconformity to be morally wrong and ultimately dangerous to human progress. Taylor's essay on such intolerance is a stirring statement of the theory that "the opinion of society—majority opinion—is the root of all intolerance." Her defense of minority viewpoints and individuality predated by twenty-seven years Mill's famous treatise *On Liberty* (see the excerpt from this work at the end of the chapter).

John Stuart Mill

Like Locke and Rousseau, **John Stuart Mill** (1806–1873) was much concerned with liberty. Mill, you will recall from the previous chapter, was a utilitarian. He

PROFILE: John Stuart Mill (1806–1873)

Many years ago, one of the authors came across a table of projected IQ scores for various historic "geniuses" in a psychology text. (Who knows how the scores were calculated?) At the top of the list, with some incredible score, was John Stuart Mill.

Mill began reading Greek at three and Latin at eight; by adolescence he had completed an extensive study of Greek and Latin literature as well as history, mathematics, and logic. Mill's education was administered by his father, who subjected young John to a rigorous regimen.

At fifteen Mill settled on his lifelong objective, to work for social and political reform, and it is as a reformer and an ethical and political philosopher that he is most remembered. Mill championed individual rights and personal freedom and advocated emancipation of women and proportional representation. His most famous work, *On Liberty* (1859), is thought by many to be the definitive defense of freedom of thought and discussion.

In ethics Mill was a utilitarian, concerning which we have much to say in Chapter 10. He published *Utilitarianism* in 1863.

Mill's interests also ranged over a broad variety of topics in epistemology, metaphysics, and logic. His *System of Logic* (1843), which was actually read at the time by the person in the street, represented an empiricist approach to logic, abstraction, psychology, sociology, and morality. Mill's *methods of induction* are still standard fare in university courses in beginning logic.

When Mill was twenty-five, he met Harriet Taylor, a merchant's wife, and this was the beginning of one of the most celebrated love affairs of all time. Twenty years later, and three years after her husband died, Mrs. Taylor married Mill, on whose thought she had a profound influence. *On Liberty* was perhaps jointly written with her and, in any case, was dedicated to her.

Harriet Taylor died in 1858. Mill spent his remaining years in Avignon, France, where she had died, to be near her grave.

Mill's *Autobiography*, widely read, appeared in the year of his death. Mill still is the most celebrated English philosopher of his century.

believed that happiness not only is good but also is *the* good, the ultimate end of all action and desire. "Actions are right in proportion as they tend to promote happiness, wrong as they tend to produce the reverse of happiness," he wrote. But remember that utilitarians are not egoists, and Mill believed that it is not one's own happiness that one should seek but instead the greatest amount of happiness altogether—that is, the general happiness.

Unlike Rousseau, Mill did not view a community, a society, a people, or a state as an organic entity separate and distinct from the sum of the people in it. When Mill said that one should seek the general happiness, he was not referring to the happiness of the community as some kind of organic whole. For Mill, the general happiness was just the total happiness of the individuals in the group.

Now, Mill, following Bentham and Hume and like Rousseau, rejected Locke's theory that people have God-given natural rights. But he maintained that the general happiness requires that all individuals enjoy personal liberty to the fullest extent consistent with the liberties of others. "The only part of the conduct of anyone, for which he is amenable to society, is that which concerns others. In the part which merely concerns himself, his independence is . . . absolute." Mill regarded personal liberty, including freedom of thought and speech, as essential to the general happiness. It is essential, he argued, because truth and the development of the individual's character and abilities are essential to the general happiness, and only

This idea comes straight from J. S. Mill, who observed that "no instructed person" would consent to become an ignoramus even if he were persuaded that as an ignoramus he would be happier than he presently is. Plato had a similar thing in mind when he said that a person who had found knowledge would rather be the slave of the poorest master than be ignorant.

if there is personal liberty can truth be ascertained and each individual's capacities developed. It therefore follows that an individual should enjoy unrestrained personal liberty up to the point where his or her activities may harm others.

Of course, it is difficult to identify *when* an action may be said to harm others. Liberalism places the burden of proof on the person who claims that harm to others will be done. That the burden must be so placed is Mill's position.

The best form of government, according to Mill, is that which, among all realistic and practical alternatives, produces the greatest benefit. The form of government best suited to do this, he maintained, is representative democracy. But Mill was especially sensitive to the threat to liberty posed in democracies by the tyranny of public opinion as well as by the suppression by the majority of minority points of view. For this reason he emphasized the importance of safeguards such as proportional representation, universal suffrage, and enforcement of education by the state.

Now, promoting the general happiness would seem sometimes to justify (if not explicitly to require) restrictions on personal liberty. Zoning ordinances, antitrust laws, and motorcycle helmet laws, to take modern examples, are, arguably, restrictions of this sort. Mill recognized the dilemma that potentially confronts anyone who wishes both to promote the general happiness and to protect personal liberty. His general position is this: The government should not do anything that could be done more effectively by private individuals themselves; and even if something could be done more effectively by the government, if the government's doing it would deprive individuals of an opportunity for development or education, the government should not do it. In short, Mill was opposed to enlarging the power of the government unnecessarily.

Georg Wilhelm Friedrich Hegel

Georg Wilhelm Friedrich Hegel (1770–1831), whose metaphysics we considered in Chapter 7, offered a social political theory as part of his metaphysics. When you read about Karl Marx in the next section, you will see parallels with Hegel, though stripped of the metaphysical trappings.

Hegel believed that "the human is nothing other than the series of his acts." But our acts, he said, are driven by desires. What is your deepest desire? According to Hegel, the deepest human desire is for *universal recognition,* and it alone provides true and lasting satisfaction. However, since this desire is the universal condition of the species, humans are in continuous "life and death fights" with each other, he reasoned. Each person wants to override, negate, and destroy all others. Do you disagree? For Hegel, if you do not enter into this fight, then you are not truly a human being. You could think of Hegel as basing human action on the idea from Heraclitus (Chapter 2), that war is the father of all.

The victor in war, he said, is lord and master. What makes the master victorious is a willingness to go all the way in battle. He would rather die than submit and be dominated. The master is a fighter who demands to be recognized by others, namely, those whom he has defeated: his slaves. The master's keenest pleasure consists in knowing that his slaves recognize his superiority—though he is not averse to the physical goods that his slaves produce for him.

However, there are limitations in being a lord and master. First is the frustration of not being recognized by equals but only by inferior slaves. Second is the master's static, nonevolving status. The master cannot grow and will eventually be outstripped by the very slaves he now owns and exploits. Let us consider how this happens.

The slave, according to Hegel, *begins* in a subordinate position—because of his unwillingness to fight to the death for recognition. Facing the possibility of death and experiencing the dread of ultimate nothingness, the slave opted for subservience rather than annihilation. As a result, he works for the master's ends and not his own. His life is in service to another. His master is free; he is not. He, the slave, is an object for the master's use and pleasure.

Nevertheless, his suffering, alienation, and coerced work eventually provide the slave with an intuition of his ideal or free self—and an intuition, as well, of the means eventually to achieve it. Consider the issue closely: The master attained freedom and domination by overcoming the instinct to live. The slave gradually, through his work and the accompanying thoughts of self-regard that arise out of it, comes to an idea that he likewise can come to dominate Nature. But the slave's form of domination is creative; it modifies and shapes Nature to thought and ideals, giving rise to a *science* of the natural world.

So the work and service of the slave lead to a transformation of Nature through science. Likewise, work and servitude transform and ultimately free the slave to a higher self. He gradually achieves self-regard based on his accomplishment of transforming Nature; to put it in Hegelian terminology, he becomes the incarnation or embodiment of the Absolute Idea and the realization of Absolute Knowledge. The ultimate result is that the slave has weapons not only to overcome the fear of death but also to escape the yoke of the master. Moreover, through this struggle, the slave provides the changes that determine the evolution of history. This fact provides the slave with an ultimate prestige as well as with freedom and autonomy. The slave is a slave no more but has risen above the master and Nature alike.

Now, this process that the slave undergoes to become free is a hard and enduring struggle. Furthermore, not all labor is freeing, Hegel believed. The all-important labor lies in *Bildung,* or self-building education. This shapes and humanizes the slave, bringing him ever closer to his own idea of selfhood. At the same time, it shapes and transforms the world, bringing it closer to its ideal realization. This dual process yields the "world historical individual," one who shapes the course of history. For Hegel, history is determined by historical individuals who understand instinctively what must be done and have the drive to do it. Their work *is* the progress of the world.

The struggle between master and slave has many stages, according to Hegel. One important stage is Christian ideology, in which the slave ceases to struggle for freedom. Instead, he commits to absolute slavehood under an absolute master. He equates freedom and happiness with the Hereafter, which he thinks begins with death. Consequently, he finds no reason to fight for freedom, and self-denial is considered a virtue. For Hegel, this phase of history expresses the ultimate domination of the slave's fear of death. He believed that freedom and self-realization occur only by surmounting this absolute enslavement to death.

The final stage of human development occurs in the demise of the master–slave dialectic. This happens when we accept our finitude and learn to live in this world as autonomous and free individuals. The key is to overcome fear of death. Through work and *Bildung,* as explained earlier, the individual is gradually formed and becomes self-conscious; he leaves the static, empty, boring stage of sheer being and becomes a particular, progressive, conscious realization of the Universal or Absolute Idea. This stage of human development represents for Hegel the actualization of the idea of the god-man. This god-man is immanent, present reality as Absolute Self-Consciousness. Here Hegel is following Spinoza's equation of Nature and God (*Natura sive deus*). Hegel claimed that, after Spinoza, all philosophy would be Spinozism.

Hegel saw this final development of the human spirit in Napoleon, or, to put it more precisely, he saw it in the person of Napoleon as infused with Hegelian self-consciousness. The idea of a transcendental god having evolved into an immanent Universal existing in the world was, for Hegel, the Ideal State realized in history. Only in such a state can a person find ultimate satisfaction and total autonomy. Only in such a state can true individuality be achieved as a unique synthesis of Particularity and Universality. The evolution to this Ideal State involves not only human consciousness of the Absolute Idea but also its concrete realization in history.

Marxism

The utilitarians pursued social and political reform. **Karl Marx** (1818–1883) went even further. Marx wanted not merely to reform society but to transform it.

Marx, who is famous for (among other things) his remark that philosophers have tried only to understand the world, whereas the real point is to change it, did not regard his work as philosophy. This must be kept in mind in the following

PROFILE: Karl Marx (1818–1883)

When one of the authors was in high school, his civics teacher, Mr. Benson, listed the most important figures in history as (alphabetically) Einstein, Freud, Jesus, and Marx. His Western bias notwithstanding, Mr. Benson was certainly right about the preeminence of these four, especially Jesus and Marx. Of course, the followers of Marx probably outnumber even the followers of Jesus (and by a good margin). Some people, moreover, regard themselves as both Marxists and Christians.

Marx was the son of a Jewish lawyer who converted to Lutheranism despite having descended from generations of rabbis; Marx was thus raised as a Protestant. He studied at German universities in Bonn, Berlin, and Jena, first in law and then in philosophy. His PhD at Jena (received when he was only twenty-three) was based on a completely ordinary dissertation on Democritus and Epicurus.

While in Berlin, Marx had come under the sway of Hegelianism (see Chapter 7) and a group of radical Hegelians. But later, strongly influenced by the philosophy of Ludwig Feuerbach, he rejected idealism for materialism and his own theory of history as the outworking of economic factors.

Marx's radical views prevented him from occupying an academic post. In 1842 he became editor of a Cologne newspaper that during his tenure became much too radical for the authorities and was suppressed. The twenty-five-year-old Marx then went to Paris, where he mingled with many famous radicals and established another radical periodical. In Paris he also met his future collaborator, Friedrich Engels.

In about a year Marx was expelled from Paris, and from 1845 to 1848 he lived in Brussels. While there, he helped form a workers' union that, together with other similar groups, became known as the Communist League. It was for this organization that he and Engels wrote their famous and stirring *Communist Manifesto* (1848). Marx spent a brief period again in Paris and then in Cologne, participating in both the French and the German revolutions of 1848. He was, however, expelled once again from both countries. In 1849 he went to London and stayed there for the rest of his life.

In London, Marx required financial help from Engels, for just as some are addicted to gambling, Marx was addicted to reading and writing, and these activities did not produce much of an income. Despite Engels's help and the small amount of money he received for articles he wrote for the New York *Tribune,* he lived in poverty, illness, and—when his children and wife died one by one—immense sadness.

During this period Marx wrote the *Critique of Political Economy* (1859) and, more important, the work destined to become the primary document of international communism, *Capital* (vol. 1, 1867; vols. 2 and 3, edited by Engels, 1885 and 1894). In 1864 he helped create the International Working-men's Association (the so-called First International), which he later led. A famous clash between Marx and the anarchist Mikhail Bakunin, however, led to its dissolution within about ten years (for more on anarchism, see the section by that title later in this chapter). Marx died of pleurisy in London when he was sixty-five.

discussion of Marx's thought. Marx offered a description and analysis of the human social and political condition, but he did not himself present this understanding as the absolute and final truth.

The Means of Production versus Productive Relations   For Marx the ideal society has no economic classes, no wages, no money, no private property, and no exploitation. Each person will not only be provided a fully adequate material existence but will also be given the opportunity to develop freely and completely all physical and mental faculties. The alienation (estrangement) of the individual from the surrounding world will be minimal.

Furthermore, according to Marx, this type of society will ultimately arise as the result of the historical process. Here is why.

Humans, Marx believed, are social animals with physical needs, needs that are satisfied when we develop the means to satisfy them. These means of producing the satisfaction of needs are called the **means** or **forces of production.** The utilization of any one set of means of production leads to fresh needs and therefore to further means of production. For example, the invention of iron tools (a new means of production) for the cultivation of needed crops leads to still a newer need—for iron—and therewith to the means for satisfying this newer need.

Thus, human history consists of successive stages of development of various means of production.

Furthermore, the utilization of any given means of production, whether it is a simple iron tool or a complex machine, necessarily involves certain social relationships, especially those involving property. These social relationships (or, as we might say, institutions or practices) are called the **productive relations.** Thus, the social relationships (the productive relations) depend on the stage of evolution of the forces of production.

The forces of production at a given stage, however, develop to the point where they come into conflict with the existing social relationships, which are then destroyed and replaced by new social relationships. For example, the need at the end of the Middle Ages to supply the new markets in the Far East and the colonies in the New World required new methods of manufacture and commerce, which brought with their development societal changes incompatible with the feudal social structure of the Middle Ages.

The new social relationships then endure until new needs arise and a new stage is reached in the evolution of the forces of production.

This **dialectical process** repeats itself over and over again and is the history of people, economics, and society. To put this another way, *history is the result of productive activity in interplay with social relationships.* According to Marx, this interplay accounts not only for all socioeconomic–political situations but also for morality, law, religion, and, to a greater or lesser extent, even philosophy and art.

Class Struggle   As already stated, according to Marx the critical social relationships involve property. With the advent of private property, society became divided into two classes: those with property and those without.

Hostility between the two classes was, and is, inevitable, Marx said. Those with property, of course, are the dominant class, and government and morality are always the instruments of the dominant class. When the forces of production create conflict with the existing social relationships, **class struggle** becomes acute, revolution results, and a new dominant class seizes control of the organs of state and imposes its ethic. This dialectical process repeats itself until private property and the division of society into opposed classes disappears.

Capitalism and Its Consequences   In modern capitalist societies, what has happened, according to Marx, is that the means of production are primarily concentrated

Marxism and Liberalism Compared

"Classical" liberalism and "orthodox" Marxism both drew from the Enlightenment (eighteenth-century) belief that the natural order produces perfection. Both looked forward to a future of ever-increasing human freedom and happiness and placed great faith in human goodness.

To highlight some of the similarities and differences between these philosophies, here is a list of ten doctrines that many orthodox Marxists accept, together with comments on how a group of classical liberals might respond to them. (Note that we said "classical" liberals. Contemporary so-called liberals share some but not all the values of classical liberals, and contemporary so-called conservatives do so as well. You will read more about contemporary usage of the term *liberal* in Chapter 12.)

1. *Ideally, society should provide for human beings as much happiness, liberty, opportunity for self-development, and dignity as possible.*

Liberals would agree to this claim, and who would not? Utilitarian liberals, however, would emphasize the importance of happiness over the other three values or would regard the others as part of happiness.

2. *The only society that can provide these ends is a socialized society—that is, one in which both ownership and production are socialized.*

Many nineteenth-century (and contemporary) liberals would not have denied that their ultimate ethical objectives could be achieved within a socialist society, but most would have denied that socialism *alone* could accommodate these objectives. Most also thought that these objectives are more likely to be achieved within a constitutionally based representative democracy with a market economy.

3. *In nonsocialist societies, the function of the state is to serve and protect the interests of the powerful.*

Liberals maintained that in nonsocialist societies it is possible for the state to serve and protect the interests and rights of all its subjects, both strong and weak, even though few states, if any, were thought effectively to have done so.

4. *A group's interests can be protected only through exercise of its power.*

A common liberal response is that a group's interests can be and are best protected through *law*. Marxists would say in rejoinder that, ever since Locke, the "rule of law" has been slanted toward protecting property and the propertied class.

5. *Human essence is defined historically, and economic factors largely determine history.*

Liberals also emphasized the importance of economics to social history and evolution but stressed that certain fundamental human characteristics (e.g., having rights, desiring pleasure) are unalterable by history.

6. *The value of a commodity is determined by the amount of labor required for its production.*

Liberals regarded this thesis as an oversimplification and maintained that many factors affect the value of a commodity.

7. *Capitalist societies necessarily are exploitative of a laboring class.*

Private ownership, many liberals believed (and still do), is not inherently or necessarily exploitative, though individual capitalists may exploit their workers. Exploitation, they say, may be eliminated through appropriately formulated laws, and a society in which a great unevenness in the distribution of wealth exists may nevertheless permit equal freedom and opportunity for all.

8. *A capitalist state cannot be reformed, for two reasons: (a) It is inherently exploitative. (b) True reforms are not in the interest of the ruling class, which therefore will not permit them. Because such a state cannot be reformed, it must be replaced.*

Liberals thought (and still think) that, through reform, many states, including most capitalist states, can gradually be improved. They did not deny the appropriateness of revolutionary overthrow of dictatorships. Contemporary Marxists insist that liberal reforms in the United States are made possible through exploitation of third world nations.

9. *The redistribution of goods through welfare, taxation, and similar means is mere tokenism serving only to pacify the exploited classes in order to protect the exploiting class from uprising and revolt.*

(continued)

Marxism and Liberalism Compared *(continued)*

Liberals thought (and still think) that measures like these, if they benefit the less well off, are required by principles of fairness, justice, or utilitarian considerations.

10. *The philosophy of liberalism, with all its talk of fairness and justice, is merely an attempt to rationalize and legitimize capitalist oppression.*

Liberals regard this as an *argumentum ad hominem* (an attack on them rather than a refutation of their position). Liberal claims must be evaluated on their own merits, they say.

---

in large factories and workshops in which a group of individual workers cooperatively produces a product. They collectively "mix their labor with the product," as Locke would say. But the product they mix their labor with is not owned by them. Rather, it is appropriated by the owners of the factories, who thus in effect also own the workers. Out of this circumstance comes the fundamental conflict of capitalist society: *production is socialized, but ownership is not.*

Furthermore, Marx argued, capitalists obviously must sell what their workers produce for more than they pay the workers to make it. The laborers thus produce goods that are worth more than their wages. This exploitation of the workers is inevitable as long as the conflict between socialized means of production and nonsocialized ownership continues. It is a necessary part of the capitalist system and is not a result of wickedness or inhumanity on the part of the capitalist.

There are two further unavoidable consequences of continuing capitalism, in Marx's opinion. First, the longer the capitalist system continues, the smaller and wealthier the possessing class becomes. This is simply the result of the fact that the surplus value of products—that is, the value of a product less its "true" cost, which is the cost of the labor put into it—continues to accrue to the capitalists. Further, as smaller capitalists cannot compete, and as a result fail in their enterprise and sink into the ranks of the workers, society's wealth becomes increasingly concentrated: fewer and fewer people control more and more of it.

Alienation   The second consequence of continued capitalism, according to Marx, is the increasing **alienation** of the workers. The more wealth the workers produce, the poorer they become, relatively speaking, for it is not they who retain this wealth. So the result of increased productivity for the workers is, paradoxically (but inevitably), their *devaluation* in their own eyes and in fact. They have become mere commodities.

In addition, because workers produce through their labor what belongs to others, neither the workers' labor nor the products they make are their own. Both labor and products are as alien things that dominate them. Thus, workers feel at home with themselves only during their leisure time and in eating, drinking, and having sex. Workers' presence at work is not voluntary but imposed and, whenever possible, avoided. Because they have put their lives into what belongs to others, workers are abject, debased, physically exhausted, and overcome with malaise.

Golden Domes of the Kremlin Palace.

And because the relation of people to themselves is first realized and expressed in the relationship between each person and another, workers are alienated from their fellows.

Capitalism Is Self-Liquidating   The situation Marx described is, in his view, self-liquidating. The capitalist system of property ownership is incompatible with the socialized conditions of production and ultimately destined to failure. Inevitable overproduction will result in economic crises, a falling rate of profit, and increased exploitation of the working class, which will increasingly become conscious of itself and its own intolerable condition, the inadequacy of capitalism, and the inevitability of history. The revolution of the **proletariat** (working class), leading to a dictatorship of the proletariat, will follow. In this instance, however, the overturning of the existing social order will eventually result in the classless society just described, for property, as well as the means of production, will have become socialized. The disappearance of classes will mark the end of class struggle and also, therefore, the end of political power because the sole function of political power is the suppression of one class at the expense of another.

Marxism and Communism

By the end of the nineteenth century, most European socialist parties were committed to Marxism, but a split developed between the **revolutionists,** those who believed (as for the most part had Marx) that a violent revolution was necessary to set in place the collective ownership of the means of production and distribution of goods, and the **revisionists** or **evolutionary socialists,** those who thought that these ends could be achieved through peaceful (and piecemeal) reform.

Although evolutionary socialism became strong in Great Britain and survives in the socialist parties of many nations to the present day, the revolutionists gained ascendancy in the Second International, the successor to Marx's International Workingmen's Association, or the First International (though the "revolutionists" were not particularly revolutionary). Under the leadership of Lenin, the revolutionist Bolsheviks came to control the Russian Social Democratic Labor Party and seized control of Russia itself in the Revolution of 1917, becoming in 1918 the Communist Party of the USSR.

Although the Russian Communists withdrew from the Second International and founded the Third International or Comintern in 1919 to gain leadership of the world socialist movement, most European Socialist parties disassociated themselves from the Communists. The term **Communism,** with a capital *C,* today still denotes the Marxist-Leninist ideology of the parties founded under the banner of the Comintern and is to be distinguished from lowercase-*c* **communism,** which denotes any form of society in which property or other important goods are held in common by the community.

Anarchism

Anarchists deny that the state is necessary for peace, justice, equality, the optimum development of human capacities, or, indeed, for any other worthwhile pursuit. In the nineteenth century, **anarchism** was the main philosophical alternative to liberalism and Marxism.

Pierre Joseph Proudhon [prew-DOHn] (1809–1865), the so-called father of anarchism, was among the first in modern times to call himself an anarchist. Proudhon believed that all authoritarian political institutions hinder human development and should be replaced by social organizations founded on the free and voluntary agreement of individuals, organizations in which no person has power over another. The existence of private property, he argued, creates social inequalities and injustice and gives rise to government; both it and government should be eliminated, though not through violent means. Communists were much influenced by Proudhon's attack on the idea of private property.

The famous Russian anarchist Communists Mikhail Bakunin [ba-KOO-nin] (1814–1876) and Prince Piotr Kropotkin [krah-POT-kin] (1842–1921) both emphasized the intrinsic goodness of the individual and viewed law and government as the instruments of the privileged classes and the true source of human corruption (both Bakunin and Kropotkin were aristocrats, incidentally). Kropotkin, much influenced by Charles Darwin, held that humans have a biologically grounded propensity to cooperate that will hold society together even in the absence of government. Bakunin—who, unlike Proudhon and Kropotkin, advocated the violent overthrow of all government—was active in the Communist First International. A clash between Marx and Bakunin, and more generally between

Marxist Communists and anarchist Communists concerning the necessity of a transitional dictatorship of the proletariat, led to the demise of that organization.

The slogan "From each according to his means, to each according to his needs" came from the anarchist Communists.

SELECTION 11.1

Crito*

Plato

[*In this dialogue, Plato portrayed "Socrates" in prison the day before his execution. Socrates' friend Crito has come to help Socrates escape, but Socrates refuses. In this excerpt, Socrates explains why it is wrong for him to try to escape: because doing so would violate an implicit agreement with the state.*]

Socrates: Then consider the matter in this way— imagine I am about to escape, and the Laws and the State come and interrogate me: "Tell us, Socrates," they say, "what are you doing? Are you going to overturn us—the Laws and the State, as far as you are able? Do you imagine that a State can continue and not be overthrown, in which the decisions of Law have no power, but are set aside and overthrown by individuals?"

What will be our answer, Crito, to these and similar words? Anyone, and especially a clever orator, will have a good deal to say about the evil of setting aside the Law which requires a sentence to be carried out. We might reply, "Yes, but the State has injured us and given an unjust sentence." Suppose I say that?

Crito: Very good, Socrates.

S: "And was that our agreement with you?" the Law would say, "Or were you to abide by the sentence of the State?" And if I were surprised at their saying this, the Law would probably add: "Answer, Socrates, instead of opening your eyes: you are in the habit of asking and answering questions. Tell us what complaint you have against us which justifies you in attempting to destroy us and the State? In the first place did we not bring you into existence? Your father married your mother by our aid and conceived you. Say whether you have any objection against those of us who regulate marriage?" None, I should reply. "Or against those of us who regulate the system of care and education of children in which you were trained? Were not the Laws, who have the charge of this, right in commanding your father to train you in the arts and exercise?" Yes, I should reply.

"Well then, since you were brought into the world, nurtured and educated by us, can you deny in the first place that you are our child and slave, as your fathers were before you? And if this is true you are not on equal terms with us. Nor can you think you have a right to do to us what we are doing to you. Would you have any right to strike or do any other evil to a father or to your master, if you had one, when you have been struck or received some other evil at his hands? And because we think it is right to destroy you, do you think that you have any right to destroy us in return, and your country so far as you are able? And will you, O expounder of virtue, say you are justified in this? Has a philosopher like you failed to discover your country is more to be valued and higher and holier by

---

* From Christopher Biffle, *A Guided Tour of Five Works by Plato*, 3rd ed., Mountain View, CA: Mayfield, 2001, pp. 66–69. Based on the nineteenth-century translation by Benjamin Jowett. Copyright © 2001 by The McGraw-Hill Companies, Inc. Reprinted by permission of The McGraw-Hill Companies, Inc.

far than mother and father or any ancestor, and more regarded in the eyes of the gods and of men of understanding? It should be soothed and gently and reverently entreated when angry, even more than a father, and if not persuaded, it should be obeyed. And when we are punished by the State, whether with imprisonment or whipping, the punishment is to be endured in silence. If the State leads us to wounds or death in battle, we follow as is right; no one can yield or leave his rank, but whether in battle or in a court of law, or in any other place, he must do what his city and his country order him. Or, he must change their view of what is just. If he may do no violence to his father or mother, much less may he do violence to his country," What answer shall we make to this, Crito? Do the Laws speak truly, or do they not?

C: I think that they do.

S: Then the Laws will say: "Consider, Socrates, if this is true, that in your present attempt you are going to do us wrong. For, after having brought you into the world, nurtured and educated you, and given you and every other citizen a share in every good we had to give, we further give the right to every Athenian, if he does not like us when he has come of age and has seen the ways of the city, he may go wherever else he pleases and take his goods with him. None of us Laws will forbid or interfere with him. Any of you who does not like us and the city, and who wants to go to a colony or to any other city, may go where he likes, and take his possessions with him. But he who has experience of the way we order justice and administer the State, and still remains, has entered into an implied contract to do as we command him. He who disobeys us is, as we maintain, triply wrong; first, because in disobeying us he is disobeying his parents; second, because we are the authors of his education; third, because he has made an agreement with us that he will duly obey our commands. He neither obeys them nor convinces us our commands are wrong. We do not rudely impose our commands but give each person the alternative of obeying or convincing us. That is

what we offer and he does neither. These are the sort of accusations to which, as we were saying, Socrates, you will be exposed if you do as you were intending; you, above all other Athenians."

Suppose I ask, why is this? They will justly answer that I above all other men have acknowledged the agreement.

"There is clear proof," they will say, "Socrates, that we and the city were not displeasing to you. Of all Athenians you have been the most constant resident in the city, which, as you never leave, you appear to love. You never went out of the city either to see the games, except once when you went to the Isthmus, or to any other place unless you were on military service; nor did you travel as other men do. Nor had you any curiosity to know other States or their Laws: Your affections did not go beyond us and our State; we were your special favorites and you agreed in our government of you. This is the State in which you conceived your children, which is a proof of your satisfaction. Moreover, you might, if you wished, have fixed the penalty at banishment in the course of the trial—the State which refuses to let you go now would have let you go then. You pretended you preferred death to exile and that you were not grieved at death. And now you have forgotten these fine sentiments and pay no respect to us, the Laws, whom you destroy. You are doing what only a miserable slave would do, running away and turning your back upon the agreements which you made as a citizen. First of all, answer this very question: Are we right in saying you agreed to be governed according to us in deed, and not in word only? Is that true or not?"

How shall we answer that, Crito? Must we not agree?

C: We must, Socrates.

S: Then will the Laws say: "You, Socrates, are breaking the agreements which you made with us at your leisure, not in any haste or under any compulsion or deception, but having had 70 years to think of them, during which time you were at liberty to leave the city, if we were not to your liking or if our covenants appeared to you to be unfair. You might have gone either to Lacedaemon or Crete, which you often praise for their good government, or to some other Hellenic or foreign state. You, above all other Athenians, seemed to be so fond of the State and of us, her Laws, that you never left her. The lame, the blind, the maimed were not more stationary in the State than you were. Now you run away and forsake your agreements. Not, Socrates, if you will take our advice; do not make yourself ridiculous by escaping out of the city.

"Just consider, if you do evil in this way, what good will you do either yourself or your friends? That your friends will be driven into exile and lose their citizenship, or will lose their property, is reasonably certain. You yourself, if you fly to one of the neighboring cities, like Thebes or Megara, both of which are well-governed cities, will come to them as an enemy, Socrates. Their government will be against you and all patriotic citizens will cast suspicious eye upon you as a destroyer of the Laws. You will confirm in the minds of the judges the justice of their own condemnation of you. For he who is a corruptor of the Laws is more than likely to be corruptor of the young. Will you then flee from well-ordered cities and virtuous men? Is existence worth having on these terms? Or will you go to these cities without shame and talk to them, Socrates? And what will you say to them? Will you say what you say here about virtue, justice, institutions, and laws being the best things among men. Would that be decent of you? Surely not.

"If you go away from well-governed states to Crito's friends in Thessaly, where there is a great disorder and immorality, they will be charmed to have the tale of your escape from prison, set off with ludicrous particulars of the manner in which you were wrapped in a goatskin or some other disguise and metamorphosed as the fashion of runaways is— that is very likely. But will there be no one to remind you in your old age you violated the most sacred laws from a miserable desire of a little more life? Perhaps not, if you keep them in a good temper. But if they are angry you will hear many degrading things; you will live, but how? As the flatterer of all men and the servant of all men. And doing what? Eating

and drinking in Thessaly, having gone abroad in order that you may get a dinner. Where will your fine sentiments about justice and virtue be then? Say that you wish to live for the sake of your children, that you may bring them up and educate them—will you take them into Thessaly and deprive them of Athenian citizenship? Is that the benefit which you would confer upon them? Or are you under the impression that they will be better cared for and educated here if you are still alive, although absent from them because your friends will take care of them? Do you think if you are an inhabitant of Thessaly they will take care of them, and if you are an inhabitant of the other world they will not take care of them? No, if they who call themselves friends are truly friends, they surely will.

"Listen, then, Socrates, to us who have brought you up. Think not of life and children first, and of justice afterwards, but of justice first, that you may be justified before the rulers of the other world. For neither will you nor your children be happier or holier in this life, or happier in another, if you do as Crito bids. Now you depart in innocence, a sufferer and not a doer of evil; a victim, not of the Laws, but of men. But if you escape, returning evil for evil and injury for injury, breaking the agreements which you have made with us, and wronging those whom you ought least to wrong, that is to say, yourself, your friends, your country, and us, we shall be angry with you while you live. Our brethren, the Laws in the other world, will receive you as an enemy because they will know you have done your best to destroy us. Listen, then, to us and not to Crito."

This is the voice which I seem to hear murmuring in my ears, like the sound of a divine flute in the ears of the mystic. That voice, I say, is humming in my ears and prevents me from hearing any other. I know anything more which you may say will be useless. Yet speak, if you have anything to say.

C: I have nothing to say, Socrates.

S: Then let me follow what seems to be the will of the god.

SELECTION 11.2

Republic*

Plato

[*Here Plato, through "Socrates" (who is the first speaker), explained the relation between the male and the female guardians of society, as well as other features of the ideal state.*]

Socrates: . . . It looks as though our rulers will have to make considerable of falsehood and deception for the benefit of those they rule. And we heared that all such falsehoods are useful as a form of drug.

Glaucon: And we were right.

S: Well, it seems we were right, especially where marriages and the producing of children are concerned.

G: How so?

S: It follows from our previous agreements, first, that the best men must have sex with the best women as frequently as possible, while the opposite is true of the most inferior men and women, and, second, that if our herd is to be of the highest possible quality, the former's offspring must be reared but not the latter's. And this must all be brought about without being noticed by anyone except the rulers, so that our herd of guardians remains as free from dissension as possible.

G: That's absolutely right.

S: Therefore certain festivals and sacrifices will be established by law at which we'll bring the brides and grooms together, and we'll direct our poets to compose appropriate hymns for the marriages that take place. We'll leave the number of marriages for the rulers to decide, but their

aim will be to keep the number of males as stable as they can, taking into account war, disease, and similar factors, so that the city will, as far as possible, become neither too big nor too small.

G: That's right.

S: Then there'll have to be some sophisticated lotteries introduced, so that at each marriage the inferior people we mentioned will blame luck rather than the rulers when they aren't chosen.

G: There will.

S: And among other prizes and rewards the young men who are good in war or other things must be given permission to have sex with the women more often, since this will also be a good pretext for having them father as many of the children as possible.

G: That's right.

S: And then, as the children are born, they'll be taken over by the officials appointed for the purpose, who may be either men or women or both, since our offices are open to both sexes.

G: Yes.

S: I think they'll take the children of good parents to the nurses in change of the rearing pen situated in a separate part of the city, but the children of inferior parents, or any child of the others that is born defective, they'll hide in a secret and unknown place, as is appropriate.

G: It is, if indeed the guardian breed is to remain pure.

S: And won't the nurses also see to it that the mothers are brought to the rearing pen when their breasts have milk, taking every precaution to insure that no mother knows her own child and providing wet nurses if the mother's milk is insufficient? And won't they take care that the mothers suckle the children for only a reasonable amount of time and that the care of sleepless children and all other such troublesome duties are taken over by the wet nurses and other attendants?

G: You're making it very easy for the wives of the guardians to have children.

S: And that's only proper. So let's take up the next thing we proposed. We said that the children's parents should be in their prime.

G: True.

S: Do you share the view that a woman's prime lasts about twenty years and a man's about thirty?

G: Which years are those?

S: A woman is to bear children for the city from the age of twenty to the age of forty, a man from the time that he passes his peak as a runner until he reaches fifty-five. . . .

S: However, I think that when women and men have passed the age of having children, we'll leave them free to have sex with whomever they wish, with these exceptions: For a man—his daughter, his mother, his daughter's children, and his mother's ancestors; for a woman—her son and his descendants, her father and his ancestors. Having received these instructions, they should be very careful not to let a single fetus see the light of day, but if one is conceived and forces its way to the light, they must deal with it in the knowledge that no nurture is available for it.

G: That's certainly sensible. But how will they recognize their fathers and daughters and the others you mentioned?

S: They have no way of knowing. But a man will call all the children born in the tenth or seventh month after he became a bridegroom his sons, if they're male, and his daughters, if they're female, and they'll call him father. He'll call their children his grandchildren, and they'll call the group to which he belongs grandfathers and grandmothers. And those who were born at the same time as their mothers and fathers were having children they'll call their brothers and sisters. Thus, as we were saying, the relevant groups will avoid sexual relations with each other. But the law will allow brothers and sisters to have sex with one

another if the lottery works out that way and the Pythia[1] approves.

G: That's absolutely right.

S: This, then, Glaucon, is how the guardians of your city have their wives and children in common. We must now confirm that this arrangement is both consistent with the rest of the constitution and by far the best. Or how else are we to proceed?

G: In just that way.

S: Then isn't the first step towards agreement to ask ourselves what we say is the greatest good in designing the city—the good at which the legislator aims in making the laws—and what is the greatest evil? And isn't the next step to examine whether the system we've just described fits into the tracks of the good and not into those of the bad?

G: Absolutely.

S: Is there any greater evil we can mention for a city than that which tears it apart and makes it many instead of one? Or any greater good than that which binds it together and makes it one?

G: There isn't.

S: And when, as far as possible, all the citizens rejoice and are pained by the same successes and failures, doesn't this sharing of pleasures and pains bind the city together?

G: It most certainly does.

S: But when some suffer greatly, while others rejoice greatly, at the same things happening to the city or its people, doesn't this privatization of pleasures and pains dissolve the city?

G: Of course.

S: And isn't that what happens whenever such words as "mine" and "not mine" aren't used in unison? And similarly with "someone else's"?

G: Precisely.

S: Then, is the best-governed city the one in which most people say "mine" and "not mine" about the same things in the same way?

---

[1] The priestess of Apollo at Delphi.

G: It is indeed. . . .

S: Therefore, in our city more than in any other, they'll speak in unison the words we mentioned a moment ago. When any one of them is doing well or badly, they'll say that "mine" is doing well or that "mine" is doing badly.

G: That's absolutely true.

S: Now, didn't we say that the having and expressing of this conviction is closely followed by the having of pleasures and pains in common?

G: Yes, and we were right.

S: Then won't our citizens, more than any others, have the same thing in common, the one they call "mine"? And, having that in common, won't they, more than any others, have common pleasures and pains?

G: Of course.

S: And, in addition to the other institutions, the cause of this is the having of wives and children in common by the guardians?

G: That more than anything else is the cause.

S: But we agreed that the having of pains and pleasures in common is the greatest good for a city, and we characterized a well-governed city in terms of the body's reaction to pain or pleasure in any one of its parts.

G: And we were right to agree.

S: Then, the cause of the greatest good for our city has been shown to be the having of wives and children in common by the auxiliaries.

G: It has.

S: And, of course, this is consistent with what we said before, for we said somewhere that, if they're going to be guardians, they mustn't have private houses, property, or possessions, but must receive their upkeep from the other citizens as a wage for their guardianship and enjoy it in common.

G: That's right.

S: Then isn't it true, just as I claimed, that what we are saying now, taken together with what we said before, makes even better guardians out of them and prevents them from tearing the city apart by not calling the same thing "mine"? If different people apply the term to different things, one would drag into his own house whatever he could separate from the others, and another would drag things into a different house to a different wife and children, and this would make for private pleasures and pains at private things. But our people, on the other hand, will think of the same things as their own, aim at the same goal, and, as far as possible, feel pleasure and pain in unison.

G: Precisely.

S: And what about lawsuits and mutual accusations? Won't they pretty well disappear from among them, because they have everything in common except their own bodies? Hence they'll be spared all the dissension that arises between people because of the possession of money, children, and families.

G: They'll necessarily be spared it.

S: Nor could any lawsuits for insult or injury justly occur among them, for we'll declare that it's a fine and just thing for people to defend themselves against others of the same age, since this will compel them to stay in good physical shape.

G: That's right. . . .

S: Then, in all cases, won't the laws induce men to live at peace with one another?

G: Very much so.

S: And if there's no discord among the guardians, there's no danger that the rest of the city will break into civil war, either with them or among themselves.

G: Certainly not.

S: I hesitate to mention, since they're so unseemly, the pettiest of the evils, the guardians would therefore escape: The poor man's flattery of the rich, the perplexities and sufferings involved in bringing up children and in making the money necessary to feed the household, getting into debt, paying it off, and in some way or other providing enough money to hand over to their wives and household slaves to manage. All of the various troubles men endure in these matters are obvious, ignoble, and not worth discussing.

G: They're obvious even to the blind.

S: They'll be free of all these, and they'll live a life more blessedly happy than that of the victors in the Olympian games.

G: How?

S: The Olympian victors are considered happy on account of only a small part of what is available to our guardians, for the guardians' victory is even greater, and their upkeep from public funds more complete. The victory they gain is the preservation of the whole city, and the crown of victory that they and their children receive is their upkeep and all the necessities of life. They receive rewards from their own city while they live, and at their death they're given a worthy burial.

G: Those are very good things.

S: Do you remember that, earlier in our discussion, someone—I forget who—shocked us by saying that we hadn't made our guardians happy, that it was possible for them to have everything that belongs to the citizens, yet they had nothing? We said, I think, that if this happened to come up at some point, we'd look into it then, but that our concern at the time was to make our guardians true guardians and the city the happiest we could, rather than looking to any one group within it and molding it for happiness.

G: I remember.

S: Well, then, if the life of our auxiliaries is apparently much finer and better than that of Olympian victors, is there any need to compare it to the lives of cobblers, farmers, or other craftsmen?

G: Not in my opinion.

S: Then it's surely right to repeat here what I said then: If a guardian seeks happiness in such a way that he's no longer a guardian and isn't satisfied with a life that's moderate, stable, and—as we say—best, but a silly, adolescent idea of happiness seizes him and incites him to use his power to take everything in the city for himself, he'll come to know the true wisdom of Hesiod's[2] saying that somehow "the half is worth more than the whole."

[2] Hesiod was an early Greek poet who is thought to have lived around 700 B.C.E.—Ed.

G: If he takes my advice, he'll keep to his own lifestyle. . . .

S: Then doesn't it remain for us to determine whether it's possible to bring about this association among human beings, as it is among animals, and to say just how it might be done?

G: You took the words right out of my mouth.

S: As far as war is concerned, I think it's clear how they will wage it.

G: How so?

S: Men and women will campaign together. They'll take the sturdy children with them, so that, like the children of other craftsmen, they can see what they'll have to do when they grow up. But in addition to observing, they can serve and assist in everything to do with the war and help their mothers and fathers. Haven't you noticed in the other crafts how the children of potters, for example, assist and observe for a long time before actually making any pots?

G: I have indeed.

S: And should these craftsmen take more care in training their children by appropriate experience and observation than the guardians?

G: Of course not; that would be completely ridiculous.

S: Besides, every animal fights better in the presence of its young.

G: That's so. But, Socrates, there's a considerable danger that in a defeat—and such things are likely to happen in a war—they'll lose their children's lives as well as their own, making it impossible for the rest of the city to recover.

S: What you say is true. But do you think that the first thing we should provide for is the avoidance of all danger?

G: Not at all.

S: Well, then, if people will probably have to face some danger, shouldn't it be the sort that will make them better if they come through it successfully?

G: Obviously.

S: And do you think that whether or not men who are going to be warriors observe warfare when they're still boys makes such a small difference that it isn't worth the danger of having them do it?

G: No, it does make a difference to what you're talking about.

S: On the assumption, then, that the children are to be observers of war, if we can contrive some way to keep them secure, everything will be fine, won't it?

G: Yes.

SELECTION 11.3

Leviathan*

Thomas Hobbes

[*This is one of the most widely read passages in the history of political philosophy, in which Hobbes explained why people in the state of nature are always in a condition of war and puts forth the only way this condition can be avoided.*]

Of the Natural Condition of Mankind As Concerning Their Felicity and Misery

Nature has made men so equal, in the faculties of the body, and mind; as that though there be found one man sometimes manifestly stronger in body, or of quicker mind than another; yet when all is reckoned together, the difference between man, and man, is not so considerable, as that one man can thereupon claim to himself any benefit, to which another may not pretend, as well as he. For as to the strength of body, the weakest has strength enough to kill the strongest, either by secret machination, or by confederacy with others, that are in the same danger with himself.

And as to the faculties of the mind . . . I find yet a greater equality amongst men, than that of strength. . . . That which may perhaps make such equality incredible, is but a vain conceit of one's own wisdom, which almost all men think they have in a greater degree, than the vulgar; that is, than all men but themselves, and a few others, whom by fame, or for concurring with themselves, they approve. For such is the nature of men, that

howsoever they may acknowledge many others to be more witty, or more eloquent or more learned; yet they will hardly believe there be many so wise as themselves; for they set their own wit at hand, and other men's at a distance. But this proves rather that men are in that point equal, than unequal. For there is not ordinarily a greater sign of the equal distribution of any thing, than that every man is contented with his share.

From this equality of ability, arises equality of hope in the attaining of our ends. And therefore if any two men desire the same thing, which nevertheless they cannot both enjoy, they become enemies; and in the way to their end, which is principally their own conservation, and sometimes their delectation only, endeavour to destroy, or subdue one another. And from hence it comes to pass, that where an invader has no more to fear, than another man's single power; if one plant, sow, build, or possess a convenient seat, others may probably be expected to come prepared with forces united, to dispossess, and deprive him, not only of the fruit of his labour, but also of his life, or liberty. And the invader again is in the like danger of another.

And from this diffidence of one another, there is no way for any man to secure himself, so reasonable, as anticipation; that is, by force, or wiles, to master the persons of all men he can, so long, till he see no other power great enough to endanger him: and this is no more than his own conservation requires, and is generally allowed. . . .

Again, men have no pleasure, but on the contrary a great deal of grief, in keeping company where

---

* Edited slightly for the modern reader.

there is no power able to over-awe them all. For every man looks that his companion should value him, at the same rate he sets upon himself: and upon all signs of contempt, or undervaluing, naturally endeavours, as far as he dares, (which amongst them that have no common power to keep them in quiet, is far enough to make them destroy each other), to extort a greater value from his condemners, by damage; and from others, by the example.

So that in the nature of man, we find three principal causes of quarrel. First, competition; secondly, diffidence; thirdly, glory.

The first, makes men invade for gain; the second, for safety; and the third for reputation. The first use violence, to make themselves masters of other men's persons, wives, children, and cattle; the second, to defend them; the third for trifles, as a word, a smile, a different opinion, and any other sign of undervalue, either direct in their persons, or by reflection in their kindred, their friends, their nation, their profession, or their name.

Hereby it is manifest, that during the time men live without a common power to keep them all in awe, they are in that condition which is called war; and such a war, as is of every man, against every man. For WAR, consists not in battle only, or the act of fighting; but in a tract of time, wherein the will to contend by battle is sufficiently known: and therefore the notion of *time,* is to be considered in the nature of war; as it is the nature of weather. For as the nature of foul weather, lies not in a shower or two of rain; but in an inclination thereto of many days together; so the nature of war, consists not in actual fighting; but in the known disposition thereto, during all the time there is no assurance to the contrary. All other time is PEACE.

Whatsoever therefore is consequent to a time of war, where every man is enemy to every man; the same is consequent to the time, wherein men live without other security, than what their own strength, and their own invention shall furnish them withal. In such condition, there is no place for industry; because the fruit thereof is uncertain: and consequently no culture of the earth; no navigation, nor use of the commodities that may be imported by sea; no commodious building; no instruments of moving, and removing, such things as require much force; no knowledge of the face of the earth; no account of time; no arts; no letters, no society; and which is worst of all, continual fear, and danger of

violent death; and the life of man, solitary, poor, nasty, brutish, and short. . . .

To this war of every man, against every man, this also is consequent; that nothing can be unjust. The notions of right and wrong, justice and injustice have there no place. Where there is no common power, there is no law: where no law, no injustice. Force, and fraud, are in war the two cardinal virtues. Justice and injustice are none of the faculties neither of the body, nor mind. If they were, they might be in a man that were alone in the world, as well as his senses, and passions. They are qualities that relate to men in society, not in solitude. It is consequent also to the same condition, that there be no propriety, no dominion, no *mine* and *thine* distinct; but only that to be every man's, that he can get; and for so long, as he can keep it. And thus much for the ill condition, which man by mere nature is actually placed in; though with a possibility to come out of it, consisting partly in the passions, partly in his reason.

The passions that incline men to peace, are fear of death, desire of such things as are necessary to commodious living; and a hope by their industry to obtain them. And reason suggests convenient articles of peace, upon which men may be drawn to agreement. These articles, are they, which otherwise are called the Laws of Nature: whereof I shall speak more particularly, in the two following chapters. . . .

Of the First and Second Natural Laws, and of Contracts

. . . And because the condition of man (as has been declared in the preceding chapter) is a condition of war of everyone against everyone; in which case everyone is governed by his own reason; and there is nothing he can make use of, that may not be a help to him, in preserving his life against his enemies; it follows that in such a condition every man has a right to everything; even to one another's body. And therefore, as long as this natural right of man to everything endures, there can be no security to any man (how strong or wise he is) of living out the time which nature ordinarily allows men to live. And consequently it is a precept or general rule of reason, *that every man ought to endeavor peace, as far as he has hope of obtaining it; and when he cannot obtain it he may seek and use all helps and advantages of war.* The first branch of which rule contains the first and fundamental law of nature; which is *to seek peace and follow it.* The second, the sum of the Right of Nature; which is, *by all means we can, to defend ourselves.*

From this fundamental law of nature, by which men are commanded to endeavor peace, is derived this second law; *that a man be willing, when others are also, as far as for peace, and defense of himself he shall think it necessary, to lay down this right to all things; and be contented with so much liberty against other men, as he would allow other men against himself.* For as long as every man holds this right of doing anything he likes; so long are all men in the condition of war. But if other men will not lay down their right, as well as he; then there is not reason for anyone to divest himself of his: For that would be to expose himself to prey (which no man is bound to) rather than to dispose himself to peace. . . .

The mutual transferring of right, is that which men call CONTRACT. . . .

Of the Causes, Generation, and Definition of a Commonwealth

The final cause, end, or design of men (who naturally love liberty and dominion over others) in the introduction of that restraint upon themselves (in which we see them live in commonwealths) is the foresight of their own preservation and of a more contented life; that is to say, of getting themselves out from that miserable condition of war, which is necessarily consequent (as has been shown) to the natural passions of men, when there is no visible power to keep them in awe, and tie them by fear of punishment to the performance of their covenants, and observation of those laws of nature set down in the fourteenth and fifteenth chapters.

For the laws of nature (as justice, equity, modesty, mercy, and, in sum, doing to others as we would be done to) of themselves, without the terror of some power to cause them to be observed, are contrary to our natural passions, that carry us to partiality, pride, revenge, and the like. And covenants, without the sword, are but words, and of no strength to secure a man at all. Therefore notwithstanding the laws of nature (which everyone has then kept, when he has the will to keep them, when he can do it safely) if there be no power erected, or not great enough for our security; every man will, and may lawfully rely on his own strength and art, for caution against all other men. . . .

The only way to erect such a common power as may be able to defend them from the invasion of foreigners and the injuries of one another and thereby to secure them in such a way as that by their own industry, and by the fruits of the earth, they may nourish themselves and live contentedly; is to confer all their power and strength upon one man or upon one assembly of men, that may reduce all their wills, by plurality of voices, unto one will: which is as much as to say, to appoint one man or assembly of men to bear their person. . . .

This is more than consent or concord; it is a real unity of them all in one and the same person, made by covenant of every man with every man, in such manner as if every man should say to every man, I authorize and give up my right of governing myself to this man or to this assembly of men, on this condition that you give up the right to him and authorize all his actions in like manner. This done, the multitude so united in one person, is called a COMMONWEALTH, in Latin, *Civitas*. This is the generation of that great LEVIATHAN, or rather (to speak more reverently) of that mortal God to which we owe under the immortal God our peace and defense. For by this authority, given him by every particular man in the commonwealth, he has the use of so much power and strength conferred on him, by terror thereof, he is enabled to form the wills of them all, to peace at home, and mutual aid against their enemies abroad. And in him consists the essence of the commonwealth; which (to define it) is *one person, of whose acts a great multitude by mutual covenants one with another have made themselves every one the author, to the end he may use the strength and means of them all, as he shall think expedient, for their peace and common defense.*

And he that carries this person, is called SOVEREIGN, and said to have sovereign power; and everyone besides, his SUBJECT.

The attaining to this sovereign power, is by two ways. One, by natural force; as when a man makes his children submit themselves and their children to his government, as being able to destroy them if they refuse; or by war subdues his enemies to his will, giving them their lives on that condition. The other is when men agree amongst themselves, to submit to some man, or assembly of men, voluntarily on confidence to be protected by him against all others. This latter may be called a political commonwealth, or commonwealth by institution; and the former a commonwealth by acquisition.

SELECTION 11.4

On Liberty

John Stuart Mill

[*The first two sentences of this famous passage state clearly what Mill intended to accomplish in his essay.*]

Chapter 1. Introductory

The object of this Essay is to assert one very simple principle, as entitled to govern absolutely the dealings of society with the individual in the way of compulsion and control, whether the means used be physical force in the form of legal penalties or the moral coercion of public opinion. That principle is, that the sole end for which mankind are warranted, individually or collectively, in interfering with the liberty of action of any of their number, is self-protection. That the only purpose for which power can be rightfully exercised over any member of a civilized community, against his will, is to prevent harm to others. His own good, either physical or moral, is not a sufficient warrant. He cannot rightfully be compelled to do or forbear because it will be better for him to do so, because it will make him happier, because, in the opinions of others, to do so would be wise, or even right. There are good reasons for remonstrating with him, or reasoning with him, or persuading him, or entreating him, but not for compelling him, or visiting him with any evil, in case he do otherwise. To justify that, the conduct from which it is desired to deter him must be calculated to produce evil to some one else. The only part of the conduct of any one, for which he is amenable to society, is that which concerns others. In the part which merely concerns himself, his independence is, of right, absolute. Over himself, over his own body and mind, the individual is sovereign. . . .

It is proper to state that I forgo any advantage which could be derived to my argument from the idea of abstract right, as a thing independent of utility. I regard utility as the ultimate appeal on all ethical questions; but it must be utility in the largest sense, grounded on the permanent interests of man as a progressive being. Those interests, I contend, authorize the subjection of individual spontaneity to external control, only in respect to those actions of each, which concern the interest of other people. If any one does an act hurtful to others, there is a prima facie case for punishing him, by law, or, where legal penalties are not safely applicable, by general disapprobation. There are also many positive acts for the benefit of others, which he may rightfully be compelled to perform; such as, to give evidence in a court of justice; to bear his fair share in the common defence, or in any other joint work necessary to the interest of the society of which he enjoys the protection; and to perform certain acts of individual beneficence, such as saving a fellow creature's life, or interposing to protect the defenceless against ill-usage, things which whenever it is obviously a man's duty to do, he may rightfully be made responsible to society for not doing. A person may cause evil to others not only by his actions but by his inaction, and in either case he is justly accountable to them for the injury. The latter case, it is true, requires a much more cautious exercise of compulsion than the former. To make any one answerable for doing evil to others, is the rule; to make him answerable for not preventing evil, is comparatively speaking, the exception. . . .

But there is a sphere of action in which society, as distinguished from the individual, has, if any, only an indirect interest; comprehending all that portion of a person's life and conduct which affects only himself, or, if it also affects others, only with their free, voluntary, and undeceived consent and participation. When I say only himself, I mean directly, and in the first instance: for whatever affects himself, may affect others *through* himself; and the objection which may be grounded on this contingency, will receive consideration in the sequel. This, then, is the appropriate region of human liberty. It comprises, first, the inward domain of consciousness, demanding liberty of conscience, in the most comprehensive sense; liberty of thought and feeling; absolute freedom of opinion and sentiment on all subjects, practical or speculative, scientific, moral, or theological. The liberty of expressing and publishing opinions may seem to fall under a different principle, since it belongs to that part of the conduct of an individual which concerns other people; but, being almost of as much importance as the liberty of thought itself, and resting in great part on the same reasons, is practically inseparable from it. Secondly, the principle requires liberty of tastes and pursuits; of framing the plan of our life to suit our own character; of doing as we like, subject to such consequences as may follow; without impediment from our fellow-creatures, so long as what we do does not harm them, even though they should think our conduct foolish, perverse, or wrong. Thirdly, from this liberty of each individual, follows the liberty, within the same limits, of combination among individuals; freedom to unite, for any purpose not

involving harm to others: the persons combining being supposed to be of full age, and not forced or deceived.

No society in which these liberties are not, on the whole, respected, is free, whatever may be its form of government; and none is completely free in which they do not exist absolute and unqualified. The only freedom which deserves the name, is that of pursuing our own good in our own way, so long as we do not attempt to deprive others of theirs, or impede their efforts to obtain it. Each is the proper guardian of his own health, whether bodily, or mental and spiritual. Mankind are greater gainers by suffering each other to live as seems good to themselves, than by compelling each to live as seems good to the rest.

SELECTION 11.5

Communist Manifesto*

Karl Marx and Friedrich Engels

[*Marx and Engels's* Communist Manifesto *is one of the most famous political documents of all time. This selection includes the most important aspects of the Marxist analysis of economic history. The bourgeoisie, as you know, is the middle class, which in Marxist theory is in opposition to the proletariat, the class of industrial wage-earners, who earn their living by selling their labor.*]

1. Bourgeois and Proletarians

The history of all hitherto existing society is the history of class struggles.

Freeman and slave, patrician and plebeian, lord and serf, guild-master and journeyman, in a word, oppressor and oppressed, stood in constant opposition to one another, carried on an uninterrupted, now hidden, now open fight, a fight that each time ended either in a revolutionary reconstitution of society at large or in the common ruin of the contending classes.

In the earlier epochs of history we find almost everywhere a complicated arrangement of society into various orders, a manifold gradation of social rank. In ancient Rome we have patricians, knights, plebeians, slaves; in the Middle Ages, feudal lords, vassals, guild-masters, journeymen, apprentices, serfs; in almost all of these classes, again, subordinate gradations.

The modern bourgeois society that has sprouted from the ruins of feudal society has not done away with class antagonisms. It has but established new classes, new conditions of oppression, new forms of struggle in place of the old ones.

Our epoch, the epoch of the bourgeoisie, possesses, however, this distinctive feature: it has simplified the class antagonisms. Society as a whole is splitting up more and more into two great hostile camps, into two great classes directly facing each other: Bourgeoisie and Proletariat.

From the serfs of the Middle Ages sprang the chartered burghers of the earliest towns. From these burgesses the first elements of the bourgeoisie were developed.

The discovery of America, the rounding of the Cape, opened up fresh ground for the rising

---

* The authors' footnotes have been omitted.

Bourgeoisie. The East Indian and Chinese markets, the colonization of America, trade with the colonies, the increase in the means of exchange and in commodities generally, gave to commerce, to navigation, to industry, an impulse never before known, and thereby, to the revolutionary element in the tottering feudal society, a rapid development.

The feudal system of industry, under which industrial production was monopolized by closed guilds, now no longer sufficed for the growing wants of the new markets. The manufacturing system took its place. The guildmasters were pushed on one side by the manufacturing middle class; division of labor between the different corporate guilds vanished in the face of division of labor in each single workshop.

Meantime the markets kept ever growing, the demand ever rising. Even manufacture no longer sufficed. Thereupon, steam and machinery revolutionized industrial production. The place of manufacture was taken by the giant, Modern Industry, the place of the industrial middle class by industrial millionaires—the leaders of whole industrial armies, the modern bourgeois. . . .

The need of a constantly expanding market for its products chases the bourgeoisie over the whole surface of the globe. It must nestle everywhere, settle everywhere, establish connections everywhere.

In place of the old wants, satisfied by the production of the country, we find new wants, requiring for their satisfaction the products of distant lands and climes. In place of the old local and national seclusion and self-sufficiency, we have intercourse in every direction, universal interdependence of nations. . . .

The bourgeoisie, by the rapid improvement of all instruments of production, by the immensely facilitated means of communication, draws all, even the most barbarian, nations into civilization. The cheap prices of its commodities are the heavy artillery with which it batters down all Chinese walls, with which it forces the barbarians' intensely obstinate hatred of foreigners to capitulate. It compels all nations, on pain of extinction, to adopt the bourgeois mode of production; it compels them to introduce what it calls civilization into their midst, i.e., to become bourgeois themselves. In a word, it creates a world after its own image.

The bourgeoisie has subjected the country to the rule of the towns. It has created enormous cities, has greatly increased the urban population as compared with the rural, and has thus rescued a considerable part of the population from the idiocy of rural life. Just as it has made the country dependent on the towns, so it has made barbarian and semi-barbarian countries dependent on the civilized ones, nations of peasants on nations of bourgeois, the East on the West.

The bourgeoisie keeps doing away more and more with the scattered state of the population, of the means of production, and of property. It has agglomerated population, centralized means of production, and has concentrated property in a few hands. The necessary consequence of this was political centralization. . . .

The bourgeoisie during its rule of scarce one hundred years has created more massive and more colossal productive forces than have all preceding generations together. Subjection of nature's forces to man, machinery, application of chemistry to industry and agriculture, steam navigation, railways, electric telegraphs, clearing of whole continents for cultivation, canalization of rivers, whole populations conjured out of the ground—what earlier century had even a presentiment that such productive forces slumbered in the lap of social labor?

We see then: the means of production and of exchange, on the foundation of which the bourgeoisie built itself up, were generated in feudal society. At a certain stage in the development of these means of production and of exchange, the conditions under which feudal society produced and exchanged, the feudal organization of agriculture and manufacturing industry, in a word, the feudal relations of property became no longer compatible with the already developed productive forces; they became so many fetters. They had to be burst asunder; they were burst asunder.

Into their place stepped free competition, accompanied by a social and political constitution adapted to it and by the economic and political sway of the bourgeois class.

A similar movement is going on before our own eyes. Modern bourgeois society with its relations of production, of exchange and of property, a society that has conjured up such gigantic means of production and of exchange, is like the sorcerer who is no longer able to control the powers of the nether world whom he has called up by his spells. For many a decade past the history of industry and commerce is but the history of the revolt of modern productive forces against modern conditions of production, against the property relations that are the conditions for the existence of the bourgeoisie and of its rule. It is enough to mention the commercial crises that by their periodical return put on trial, each time more threateningly, the existence of the entire bourgeois society. In these crises a great part not only of the existing products, but also of the previously created productive forces, are periodically destroyed. In these crises there breaks out an epidemic that in all earlier epochs would have seemed an absurdity—the epidemic of overproduction. Society suddenly finds itself put back into a state of momentary barbarism; it appears as if a famine, a universal war of devastation had cut off the supply of every means of subsistence; industry and commerce seem to be destroyed; and why? Because there is too much civilization, too much means of subsistence, too much industry, too much commerce. The productive forces at the disposal of society no longer tend to further the development of the conditions of bourgeois property; on

the contrary, they have become too powerful for these conditions, by which they are fettered, and as soon as they overcome these fetters, they bring disorder into the whole of bourgeois society, endanger the existence of bourgeois property. The conditions of bourgeois society are too narrow to comprise the wealth created by them. And how does the bourgeoisie get over these crises? On the one hand by enforced destruction of a mass of productive forces; on the other, by the conquest of new markets and by the more thorough exploitation of the old ones. That is to say, by paving the way for more extensive and more destructive crises and by diminishing the means whereby crises are prevented.

The weapons with which the bourgeoisie felled feudalism to the ground are now turned against the bourgeoisie itself.

But not only has the bourgeoisie forged the weapons that bring death to itself; it has also called into existence the men who are to wield those weapons—the modern working class, the proletarians.

CHECKLIST

To help you review, a checklist of the key philosophers of this chapter can be found online at www.mhhe.com/moore9e.

KEY TERMS AND CONCEPTS

QUESTIONS FOR DISCUSSION AND REVIEW

1. According to Plato, the ideal state consists of three classes. What are they, what are their functions, and how is class membership determined?

2. Evaluate Aristotle's idea that people who do not have the aptitude or time to participate in governance should not be citizens.

3. Explain the four types of law distinguished by Aquinas.

4. In the absence of civil authority, would anyone live up to an agreement that

turned out not to be in his or her own best interest?

5. Which is better, in your view, dictatorship or anarchy? Why?

6. What is Locke's argument for saying that each person has inalienable natural rights?

7. "All people equally have a right to property, but they do not all have a right to equal property." What does this mean? Do you agree?

8. Explain Locke's concept of private property. Is this a realistic concept?

9. Can you think of any justification for the principle that people have natural rights other than that proposed by Locke?

10. Do people have a natural right to privacy? Explain.

11. "The only part of the conduct of anyone, for which he is amenable to society, is that which concerns others. In the part which merely concerns himself, his independence is absolute." Do you agree? Why or why not?

12. What, for utilitarians, are "natural rights"?

13. What did Taylor think was so important about toleration? In what ways did she think English society was intolerant?

14. Would Rousseau have agreed with Socrates' explanation to Crito (Selection 11.1) about why he should not try to escape from prison? Why or why not?

SUGGESTED FURTHER READINGS

Go online to www.mhhe.com/moore9e for a list of suggested further readings.

12

Recent Moral and Political Philosophy

The moral order is just as much a part of the fundamental nature of the universe as is the spatial or numerical structure expressed in the axioms of geometry or arithmetic.　—W. D. Ross

Hamlet: There is nothing either good or bad, but thinking makes it so.　—William Shakespeare

Contemporary ethical theory begins with **G. E. Moore** (1873–1958). Moore opened up new issues for consideration and altered the focus of ethical discussion. Much of twentieth-century analytic ethics, at least until recently, treated issues that were raised by Moore or by philosophers responding either to him or to other respondents. Although analytic ethical philosophers discussed many questions that were not directly (or indirectly) considered by Moore, even these questions were raised along tributaries that can be traced back to the main waterway Moore opened. Some people regret the influence Moore had on ethics. You will have to draw your own conclusions.

G. E. MOORE

Moore believed that the task of the ethical philosopher is to conduct a "general inquiry into what is good." This seems reasonably straightforward, down to earth, and useful. If you know what good or goodness is, and if you know what things are

Contemporary moral philosophy began with
G. E. Moore.

good, then you also know what proper conduct is, right? This, at any rate, is what
Moore maintained, because he believed that the morally right act is the one that
produces the greatest amount of good.

Now, good, or goodness, which is the same thing, is a *noncomplex* and *non-natural* property of good things, Moore argued. Goodness is noncomplex in that it
cannot be broken down or "analyzed" into simpler constituents. It is not at all like
the property of being alive, for example. A thing's being alive consists in many
simpler things, like having a beating heart and a functioning brain (at least for
humans and other animals). But a thing's being *good* is rather more like a person's
being in pain, at least with respect to the question of complexity. Pain is pain, and
that is that. Pain cannot be broken down into simpler constituent parts. (How we
come to have pain can be explained, but that is a different matter.) Good, too, is
simple, according to Moore: it is a property that cannot be further analyzed or
broken down into simpler constituent parts. Thus, good is also *indefinable*, he said;
at least you cannot come up with a definition of good that states its constituent
parts (because there are none). Good is good, and that is that.

Good is also a nonnatural property, Moore stated. This is what he meant.
Suppose that you pronounce that something is good. Is that equivalent to saying
that it is a certain size or shape or color or that it is pleasant or that it is worth a lot
of money? Of course not. Size, shape, color, pleasantness, and monetary value are
all natural properties: they are a part of nature, construed broadly. They can be
perceived. But good is not equivalent to these or any other natural properties, or
so said Moore. Take something you regard as good, like an act of generosity, for
instance. Now list all the natural properties (that is, all the properties that can be

apprehended by sense) of this act. Do you find goodness on the list? Not at all. What you find are items such as the duration, location, causes, and consequences of the generous act. The goodness of the act is not identical with any of these items. It is something quite different from the act's natural properties.

That goodness does not equate with any natural property is easily seen, Moore argued, in a passage that became one of the most famous in all of twentieth-century ethics. Think of any natural property, for instance, pleasantness. Now, it is certainly reasonable to ask if pleasantness is good. But if pleasantness were *equivalent* to good, then asking, Is pleasantness good? would be the same as asking, Is good good? and that is *not* a reasonable question. Because it is legitimate and intelligible to ask of any natural property whether that property is good, it follows that good is not equivalent to any natural property. You can see that Moore did not agree with the utilitarians, who equated the goodness of an act with the pleasure it produced as a consequence.

Moore wanted especially to know which "good" things we can really hope to obtain. His answer: personal affection and aesthetic enjoyments. He wrote: "Personal affection and aesthetic enjoyments include by far the greatest good with which we are acquainted." Note how different this answer is from any that would have been proposed by the other philosophers we have discussed.

But the remarkable thing is that it was not Moore's opinion about what things are good that interested other philosophers. Rather, it was his "metaethical" opinions that were most discussed. If you are new to philosophy, you may never have heard of metaethics, and so we must digress for a moment from Moore to explain.

NORMATIVE ETHICS AND METAETHICS

Let's go back to the concept of a moral value judgment, or, more succinctly, the concept of a **moral judgment,** a judgment that states or implies that something is good or bad, right or wrong, a judgment like "You should be more generous," or "It was wrong for the president not to speak out more vigorously for minorities when she had the chance to do so," or "Act so as to promote the greatest happiness." Making and defending (or criticizing) moral judgments is the business of **normative ethics.** It's called "normative" because, when you make or defend (or criticize) a moral judgment, you are appealing to a moral standard, or norm.

Many people assume that moral philosophy is concerned primarily with supplying moral judgments; in other words, many people assume that moral philosophy is normative. And, indeed, prior to Moore, moral philosophy was mainly normative. However, a moral philosopher need not be concerned only (or even at all) with *making* moral judgments. Instead, he or she may be concerned with such issues as how moral value judgments are verified or validated, or what sort of thing is goodness, or how goodness and rightness are related, or what sort of thing is a moral judgment. Notice that questions of this sort do not require a moral judgment as an answer. The attempt to find answers to questions of this sort, in other words, the attempt to understand the sources, criteria, meaning, verification, or validation of moral value judgments—rather than to make moral judgments—is known as **metaethics.**

It was Moore's metaethical views, not his normative claims about what actually is good, that provoked the most discussion in the professional philosophical literature. Most important, Moore had held that goodness is a simple, nonnatural, and indefinable property. Is this **antinaturalism** doctrine correct, as Moore had argued? Much contemporary analytic ethical philosophy, which has grown out of the issues raised by Moore and by those who in turn responded to Moore, has been concerned with this and related metaethical issues. Now, frankly, many people outside moral philosophy find this state of affairs just awful. Philosophers, they say, should propose theories about what people (and societies and governments) should do and about what things are good. They should recommend courses of action, offer ethical counseling, and take a stand on the issues of the day. In short, they should make moral judgments. But—until fairly recently—contemporary analytic moral philosophers haven't regarded the making of moral judgments as an important aspect of their professional work in philosophy. Further, contemporary analytic moral philosophers interested in metaethics regard their work as quite important, even if to others it may seem boring or even trivial. Take Moore's anti-naturalist position, that goodness is a simple, nonnatural, and indefinable property. If this metaethical position is correct, then all who equate goodness with a natural property, as many have done for more than twenty centuries, have based their values on a mistake.

EMOTIVISM AND BEYOND

The utilitarians defined the rightness of an action in terms of the happiness it produces as a consequence. This view implies that moral judgments are a type of *factual judgment,* a judgment about how much happiness an action produces.

Moore denied that the rightness of an act or the goodness of an end can be defined in terms of happiness or any other natural property or thing. But he did agree with the utilitarians that moral judgments are a type of factual judgment. To say that an end is good or that an act is right, for Moore, is to state a fact. It is to attribute a property to the thing in question, a "nonnatural" property. Whether a certain type of act possesses the property of goodness is a question of fact, even though the fact is nonempirical.

A radically different view of moral judgments was set forth by the emotivists, a group of analytic philosophers who had read Moore and disagreed with him.

The **emotivists** maintained that *moral judgments have no factual meaning whatsoever.* Such judgments, according to the emotivists, *are not even genuine propositions.* In their view, the judgment "It is right to keep your promises" is neither true nor false: the utterance is not really a proposition at all.

Thus, according to the emotivists, there is no question about what we are saying if, for example, we state, "Abortion is wrong." Because we are not really asserting a genuine proposition, we are not really *saying* anything at all. The only interesting question, they thought, is what we *are doing* when we saying something like "Abortion is wrong."

And what we are doing, they said, is *expressing our distaste* for abortion and also, sometimes, *encouraging others to feel the same way*. Thus, C. L. Stevenson (1908–1979), an influential emotivist, maintained that an ethical judgment like "Abortion is wrong" is a linguistic act by which the speaker expresses her or his attitude toward abortion and seeks to influence the attitude, and in turn the conduct, of the listener.

Emotivism had strong adherents within analytic philosophy, but it seemed to many other analytic philosophers that the emotivist analysis of ethical judgments was not essentially correct. The contemporary British linguistic philosopher R. M. Hare (1919–2002) said that the function of moral discourse is not to express or influence attitudes but rather to *guide conduct*.

A moral judgment, according to Hare, is a kind of **prescriptive judgment** that is "universalizable": when I make a moral judgment such as "You ought to give Smith back the book you borrowed," I am prescribing a course of conduct, and my prescription is general and exceptionless (i.e., I believe that anyone else in the same or relevantly similar situation ought to conduct himself or herself similarly).

That emotivism misrepresents, or indeed trivializes, moral discourse is now fairly widely accepted by contemporary philosophers.

Despite their differences, Moore and the emotivists all agreed that descriptive statements and value judgments are logically distinct. If you say that (1) I did not do what I promised you I would do, you are making a purely descriptive statement. If you say that (2) I did not do what I ought to have done, you are making a value judgment. Most of the philosophers of the first half of the twentieth century accepted Hume's opinion that "you cannot deduce an 'ought' from an 'is'" and held that it is a mistake to think that any moral value judgment is logically entailed by any descriptive statement. This mistake was called the **naturalist fallacy.** Thus, for example, it would be committing the naturalist fallacy to suppose that (2) is logically deducible from (1).

But is the naturalist fallacy really a fallacy? The issue is important because, if you hold that moral evaluations are logically independent of descriptive premises, it would then seem that you could commend morally any state of affairs you pleased—and would not logically have to accept as evidence for a moral evaluation the empirical evidence that most people accept as evidence. Eventually, philosophers began to consider this issue carefully. Among the first to do so were Oxford University's Phillipa Foot (1920–2010) and University of California at Berkeley's John Searle (1932–), and now many philosophers do not accept the idea that moral evaluations are logically independent of the descriptive premises on which, in everyday conversation, they are often based. Instead, they maintain there are empirical criteria for ascribing moral predicates to actions, people, and states of affairs.

Now, these two related developments—the rejection of emotivism and the emerging idea that there are empirical criteria for moral evaluations—are important. Here is why. If it is assumed that moral judgments are just expressions of taste

Environmental Philosophy

Frequently, philosophy departments offer courses in environmental ethics, one of the three main areas of **applied ethics.** The other two are business ethics and biomedical ethics. There is an extensive literature in environmental ethics, but, generally, discussion seems to fall under these two headings:

1. What, if any, are the root *philosophical* causes of ecological crises? Some see ecological problems as primarily due to *shallow* factors including near-sightedness, ignorance, and greed. Others seek a more basic explanation of ecological maladies, and discussion seems to have focused on three possible candidates. Some, the deep ecologists, think the fundamental explanation of ecological crises is anthropocentrism, the view that humans are the central value of the universe. Others, known as ecofeminists, think the root problem is patriarchalism, or the oppression and exploitation of women—and nature—as subservient to men. Still others, the social ecologists, think the fundamental causes are deep-seated authoritarian social structures based on domination and exploitation by privileged groups. Although there is considerable controversy among these groups, other environmental philosophers view their distinctions as irrelevant to such pressing problems as overconsumption and militarization.

2. What entities have moral standing and intrinsic values? For example, do nonhuman animals have rights or interests? Do plants? Do species? Do biotic communities, ecosystems, wilderness, or the planetary biosphere? And, closely related, what properties or characteristics must a thing have to have moral standing? For example, must it be able to experience sensation? Or must it just be alive? Must it simply have an end or goal or good of its own?

Writings on animal rights constitute a large literature in their own right, independent of environmental ethics.

and are logically independent of any empirical facts about the world, then why bother discussing concrete moral issues? Given these assumptions, there would seem to be little room for reasoned deliberation in ethical matters. Consequently, as these assumptions were called into question, there was a renewal of interest in concrete ethical issues by moral philosophers. Much discussed in recent years, for example, have been issues of sexual morality, affirmative action, biomedical ethics, business ethics, and treatment of the environment. For an example, see the box "Environmental Philosophy."

But now a word of caution: that there has been a recent widespread and apparently growing interest in concrete moral questions should not lead you to conclude that metaethics is dead. It is probably true, as we move forward in the twenty-first century, that many professors of ethics focus their courses on concrete moral dilemmas such as abortion, equal rights, pornography, and so on. Nevertheless, several issues in metaethics are currently in controversy. Included are these:

- What makes a principle a *moral* principle? Can moral principles be about just anything? Or do they have some essential type of content?

- A *morally obligatory act* is one you ought to do, other things being equal. A *supererogatory act* is one that is morally commendable but beyond the call of duty. Is this a legitimate distinction? Can traditional philosophical theories of ethics accommodate this distinction, if it is legitimate?

- Is ethical truth relative to the ethical beliefs of a society or culture? That is, is ethical relativism true?
- How should one understand the question, Why should I be moral? Is it a legitimate question?
- Is there a necessary connection between believing that something is morally obligatory and being motivated to choose to do it? (So-called *internalists* assert that there is such a connection; *externalists* deny that there is.)
- What gives a being moral standing?
- Do some beings have a higher moral standing than others?
- How are moral judgments about institutions and other collectives to be understood? Groups are sometimes said to be morally responsible for their actions. Is this responsibility something over and above the responsibility of the individuals in the group?
- Is there a moral difference between doing something that you know will have certain undesirable consequences and doing it with the intention of producing those consequences?

However a good example of moral philosophy that is *not* a piece of metaethics is included among the readings at the end of the chapter, the piece by James Rachels (1941–2003). In the article, Rachels discusses whether it is true that letting people die of starvation is as bad as killing them (the idea that the two are equally bad is known as the **Equivalence Thesis**). Although Rachels does not try to prove that the two are equally bad, he does try to show that letting people die is considerably worse than we usually think it is.

Further, at the same time that emotivism and antinaturalism were being examined, an independent development in political philosophy occurred, one that has also had a terrific impact on current moral philosophy. This development stems from the work of John Rawls, who, as we shall see shortly, set forth a contractarian theory of distributive justice—a theory for determining the appropriate distribution of the benefits and burdens of social cooperation. As a result of Rawls's work, there has been widespread discussion of the soundness of contractarianism itself and considerable interest in applying contractarian principles toward the resolution of specific moral issues. Therefore, Rawls's work also served to reinforce the current interest in "real-life" moral issues.

JOHN RAWLS, A CONTEMPORARY LIBERAL

Perhaps the single most influential publication in moral philosophy in the twentieth century was *A Theory of Justice* (1971), by Harvard professor **John Rawls** (1921–2002). The work heralded a renewed concern in philosophy with justice; further, virtually every philosophical writer on justice subsequent to the publication of this work identified his or her position with reference to it. One recent commentator, Professor Charles Larmore of the University of Chicago, has said that

Rawls was one of the three most important philosophers of the twentieth century, the other two being Wittgenstein (Chapter 9) and Heidegger (Chapter 8).

Rawls wrote from within the liberal tradition, but he had grown dissatisfied with the utilitarianism on which liberalism was often based. He was also dissatisfied with attempts merely to circumscribe utilitarianism with ad hoc "self-evident" principles about our duties. Rawls said that in writing *A Theory of Justice* he wanted to "carry to a higher order of abstraction the traditional doctrine of the social contract." The result was a lengthy and systematic attempt to establish, interpret, and illuminate the fundamental principles of justice; to apply them to various central issues in social ethics; to use them for appraising social, political, and economic institutions; and to examine their implications for duty and obligation. We focus our discussion on the principles themselves.

The Fundamental Requirements of the Just Society

According to Rawls, because society is typically characterized by a conflict as well as an identity of interests, it must have a set of principles for assigning basic rights and duties and for determining the appropriate distribution of the benefits and burdens of social cooperation. These are the *principles of distributive or social justice.* They specify the kinds of social cooperation that can be entered into and the forms of government that can be established. (It is here that Rawls's theory of justice intersects with traditional philosophical questions about the ethically legitimate functions and organization of the state.) For Rawls, a society (or a state) is not well

John Rawls.

ordered unless (1) its members know and accept the same principles of social justice and (2) the basic social institutions generally satisfy and are generally known to satisfy these principles.

If a society is to be well ordered, its members must determine by rational reflection what are to be their principles of justice, said Rawls. If the principles selected are to be reasonable and justifiable, they must be selected through a procedure that is *fair*. (Rawls's book is an elaboration on a 1958 paper he wrote titled "Justice As Fairness.")

The Veil of Ignorance and the Original Position

Now, if the selection of principles of justice is to be fair, the possibility of bias operating in their selection must be removed, correct? Ideally, therefore, in our selection of the principles, none of us should have insider's knowledge. We should all be ignorant of one another's—and our own—wealth, status, abilities, intelligence, inclinations, aspirations, and even beliefs about goodness.

Of course, no group of people ever were or could be in such a state of ignorance. Therefore, said Rawls, we must select the principles as if we were behind a **veil of ignorance.** This is to ensure that nobody is advantaged or disadvantaged in the choice of principles by her or his own unique circumstances.

If from behind a veil of ignorance we were to deliberate on what principles of justice we would adopt, we would be in what Rawls called the **original position** (or sometimes the *initial situation*). Like Locke and Rousseau's state of nature, the original position is an entirely hypothetical condition. (As noted, people never were and never could be in such a condition of ignorance.) Rawls's concepts of a veil of ignorance and an original position are intended "simply to make vivid to ourselves the restrictions that it seems reasonable to impose on arguments for principles of justice, and therefore on these principles themselves." Determining our principles of justice by imagining ourselves in the original position simply ensures that we do not tailor our conception of justice to our own case.

In short, according to Rawls, the basic principles of justice are those to which we will agree if we are thinking rationally and in our own self-interest and if we eliminate irrelevant considerations. Because the basic principles of justice are those to which we will agree, Rawls's theory of justice is said to be a *contractarian* theory, as were the theories of Hobbes, Locke, and Rousseau.

The Two Principles of Social Justice

The principles we would select in the original position, if we are thinking rationally and attending to our own self-interest, are two, Rawls said.

The first, which takes precedence over the second when questions of priority arise, requires that *each person has an equal right to "the most extensive basic liberty compatible with a similar liberty for others."*

The second requires that *social and economic inequalities be arranged "so that they are both (a) reasonably expected to be to everyone's advantage and (b) attached to positions and offices open to all."*

These two principles, wrote Rawls, are a special case of a more general conception of justice to the effect that *all social goods (e.g., liberty, opportunity, income) are to be distributed equally unless an unequal distribution is to everyone's advantage.*

We are led to this concept, Rawls wrote, when we decide to find a concept of justice that "nullifies the accidents of natural endowment and the contingencies of social circumstances as counters in quest for political and economic advantage."

It follows from these principles, of course, that an unequal distribution of the various assets of society—wealth, for instance—*can be just,* as long as these inequalities are to everyone's benefit. (For example, it may be to everyone's benefit that physicians are paid more than, say, concrete workers.)

It also follows from the priority of the first principle over the second that, contrary to what utilitarian theory seems to require, someone's personal liberty *cannot* be sacrificed for the sake of the common good. Does the pleasure of owning slaves bring more happiness to the slave owners than it brings unhappiness to the slaves? If so, then the total happiness of society may be greater with slavery than without it. Thus, slavery would be to the common good, and utilitarianism would require that it should be instituted. Of course, utilitarians may maintain that slavery or other restrictions of liberties will *as a matter of fact* diminish the sum total of happiness in a society and for this reason cannot be condoned, but they must nevertheless admit that, *as a matter of principle,* violations of liberty would be justified for the sake of the happiness of the many. According to Rawls's principles, such violations for the sake of the general happiness are not justified.

The Rights of Individuals

Although Rawls did not explicitly discuss the "rights" of individuals as a major topic, his theory obviously can be interpreted as securing such rights (see, for example, Rex Martin's 1985 book, *Rawls and Rights*). Many have believed that, without God, talk of rights is pretty much nonsense; Rawls does not discuss God, and it seems plain that he does not need to do so to speak meaningfully of a person's rights. According to Rawls, a just society guarantees persons the right to pursue their own ends so long as they do not interfere with the right of others to pursue their own ends. It is not acceptable to restrict this "right" for some supposed higher good. Rawls, in effect, attempts to derive social ethics from a basis in rational self-interest rather than from God, natural law, human nature, utility, or other ground.

Why Should I Accept Rawls's Provisions?

If Rawls's theory is correct, he has spelled out in plain language the fundamental requirements of the just society. Furthermore, if his theory is correct, these are the requirements that self-interested but rational people would, on reflection, accept. This means that Rawls's theory provides a strong answer to the person who asks of any provision entailed by one or the other of the two principles just stated, "Why should *I* accept this provision?"

Self-Respect

The most important good, according to John Rawls, is self-respect.

Self-respect? Yes.

Self-respect, says Rawls, has two aspects: first, a conviction that one's plans and aspirations are worthwhile, and second, confidence in one's ability to accomplish these objectives.

Without self-respect, therefore, our plans have little or no value to us, and we cannot continue in our endeavors if we are plagued by self-doubt. Thus, self-respect is essential for any activity at all. When we lack it, it seems pointless to do anything, and even if some activity did seem to have a point, we would lack the will to do it. "All desire and activity become empty and vain, and we sink into apathy and cynicism."

Let's say, for example, that you want to know what is wrong with enslaving another person. The answer is that the wrongfulness of slavery logically follows from the two principles of social justice. But why *should you agree* to those principles? The answer is that you *would* agree to them. Why? Because they are the principles that would be selected by self-interested but rational people playing on a level playing field—one, that is, on which no one has an unfair advantage. They are the principles that would be selected by self-interested but rational people if the procedure through which they were selected was unbiased by anyone having insider's knowledge of his or her or anyone else's unique circumstances. They are, in short, the principles that self-interested but rational people would select if the procedure by which they were selected was a *fair* one. So, then, the reason you *should* accept that slavery is wrongful is because you *would* accept the principles from which the wrongfulness of slavery logically follows.

Few philosophical works by analytic philosophers have received such widespread attention and acclaim outside the circles of professional philosophers as has Rawls's *A Theory of Justice*. Though uncompromisingly analytical, it deals with current issues of undeniable importance and interest and does so in light of recent work in economics and the social sciences. The book has been reviewed not merely in philosophical journals but also in the professional literature of other disciplines and very widely in the popular press and in magazines of opinion and social commentary. It has been the focal point of numerous conferences, many of them interdisciplinary.

In a later work, *Political Liberalism* (1993), Rawls considered more carefully how his conception of justice as fairness can be endorsed by the diverse array of incompatible religious and philosophical doctrines that exist over time in a modern democratic society like ours. To answer this question, he found that he must characterize justice more narrowly than he did earlier, as a freestanding *political conception* rather than as a *comprehensive value system* (like Christianity) that governs all aspects of one's life, both public and private. Political justice becomes the focus of an overlapping consensus of comprehensive value systems and thus can still be embraced by all in a pluralistic democratic society. This change in Rawls's theory marked a change in Rawls's own theoretical understanding of justice as fairness. As a practical matter, though, the two principles of justice mentioned earlier still constitute the best conception of political cooperation required for stability in a democratic regime, in Rawls's view.

ROBERT NOZICK'S LIBERTARIANISM

If any other book by an analytic philosopher attracted as much attention as *A Theory of Justice*, it was *Anarchy, State, and Utopia*, published three years later (1974) by **Robert Nozick** [NO-zik] (1938–2002). By this time (thanks largely to Rawls), it was not unusual to find analytic philosophers speaking to "big" issues, and Nozick certainly did that.

The reaction to *Anarchy, State, and Utopia* was more mixed than that to Rawls's book, and, though many reviewers acclaimed it enthusiastically, others condemned it, often vehemently. These negative reactions are easily understandable in view of Nozick's vigorous espousal of principles of political philosophy that are not very popular with many contemporary liberal political theorists.

The basic question asked in *Anarchy, State, and Utopia* is, simply: Should there even be a political state and, if so, why? Nozick's answer was worked out in elaborate detail through the course of his book, but it consisted essentially of three claims:

1. A minimal state, limited to the narrow functions of protection against force, theft, fraud, breach of contracts, and so on, is justified.
2. Any more extensive state will violate persons' rights not to be forced to do certain things and is unjustified.
3. The minimal state is inspiring as well as right.

To each of these three claims, Nozick devoted one part of his book. The first two parts are the most important.

A Minimal State Is Justified

The first claim, that a minimal state is justified, will seem so obvious to many as hardly to require lengthy argument. The basic idea accepted by political theorists in the liberal political tradition, from John Locke through Mill and up to and including Rawls, is that the political state—as compared with a state of anarchy or "the state of nature"—"advances the good of those taking part of it" (to quote Rawls). But does it?

If, as Nozick believed, "individuals have rights, and there are things no person or group may do to them (without violating their rights)," then it may well be true, as anarchists believe, that "any state necessarily violates people's moral rights and hence is intrinsically immoral." In the first part of his book, Nozick considered carefully whether this anarchist belief is true. His conclusion was that it is not. To establish this conclusion, he attempted to show that a minimal state can arise by the mechanism of an "invisible hand" (see the box "Invisible-Hand Explanations") from a hypothetical state of nature without violating any natural rights. As intuitively plausible as Nozick's conclusion is on its face, his defense of it is controversial, and the issue turns out to be difficult.

Invisible-Hand Explanations

Often an action intended for a certain purpose generates unforeseen indirect consequences. According to Adam Smith, people, in intending only their own gain, are "led by an invisible hand to promote an end" that was not part of their intention, namely, the general good.

Nozick, after Adam Smith, called an **invisible-hand explanation** one that explains the seemingly direct result of what someone has intended or desired to happen as not being brought about by such intentions or desires at all.

For example, it *looks* as if the state is the result of people's desire to live under a common government, and this is indeed what Locke—and many philosophers, political scientists, economists, and others—thought. But Nozick attempted to provide an invisible-hand explanation of the state as the by-product of certain *other* propensities and desires that people would have within a state of nature. Nozick's explanation was intended to show how a minimal state can arise without violating people's rights.

Another famous invisible-hand explanation presents the institution of money as the outcome of people's propensity to exchange their goods for something they perceive to be more generally desired than what they have. Another describes the characteristics and traits of organisms as the result of natural selection rather than God's wishes.

Only the "Night-Watchman" State Does Not Violate Rights

The main claim advanced by Nozick in the second part of his book, and by far the most controversial claim of the work as a whole, is that any state more powerful or extensive than the minimal **night-watchman state** that protects its citizens from force and fraud and like things impinges on the individual's natural rights to his or her holdings and therefore is not legitimate or justifiable. It is further a corollary to this claim that concepts of justice that mandate the distribution of assets in accordance with a formula (e.g., "to each according to his_____") or in accordance with a goal or objective (e.g., to promote the general happiness) always require *re*distributing the goods of society and thus require taking from some individuals the goods that are rightfully theirs. Such concepts of justice are therefore illegitimate, according to Nozick.

Nozick's own concept of justice rested on an idea that comes naturally to many people (at least until they imagine themselves in Rawls's "initial situation" behind a "veil of ignorance" about their own assets and abilities). The idea is that *what is yours is yours:* redistributing your income or goods against your wishes for the sake of the general happiness or to achieve any other objective is unjust. Nozick defended this idea. *A person is entitled to what he or she has rightfully acquired, and justice consists in each person's retaining control over his or her rightful acquisitions.* This is Nozick's **entitlement concept of social justice.**

Nozick did not clarify or attempt to defend his entitlement concept of social justice to the extent some critics would like (he basically accepted a refined version of Locke's theory of property acquisition, according to which, you will remember, what is yours is what you mix your labor with). Instead, he mainly sought to show that alternative conceptions of social justice, conceptions that ignore what a person is entitled to by virtue of rightful acquisition, are defective. According to Nozick, social justice, that is, justice in the distribution of goods, is not achieved by redistributing these goods to achieve some objective but rather by permitting them to remain in the hands of those who have legitimately acquired them:

> Your being forced to contribute to another's welfare violates your rights, whereas someone else's not providing you with things you need greatly, including things essential to the protection of your rights, does not *itself* violate your rights, even though it avoids making it more difficult for someone else to violate them.

According to Nozick's view of social justice, taking from the rich without compensation and giving to the poor is never just (assuming the rich did not become rich through force or fraud, etc.). This would also be Locke's view. According to the strict utilitarian view, by contrast, doing so *is* just if it is to the greater good of the aggregate of people (as would be the case, for example, if through progressive taxation you removed from a rich person's income an amount that he or she would miss but little and used it to prevent ten people from starving). Finally, according to Rawls's view of justice, taking from the rich and giving to the poor is just if it is to the greater good of the aggregate, *provided* it does not compromise anyone's liberty (which, in the case just envisioned, it arguably would not).

The Rights of Individuals

In the opening sentence of his book, Nozick asserted that individuals have rights, and indeed his entire argument rested on that supposition, especially those many aspects that pertain to property rights. Unfortunately, Nozick's theoretical justification of the supposition was very obscure: it had something to do, evidently, with a presumed inviolability of individuals that prohibits their being used as means to ends and perhaps also with the necessary conditions for allowing them to give meaning to their lives. If Nozick didn't make his thought entirely clear in this area, he did set forth very plainly the implications for social theory, as he saw them, of assuming that natural rights exist. In addition, his work contained many interesting and provocative side discussions, including critical discussions of Marx's theory of exploitation.

COMMUNITARIAN RESPONSES TO RAWLS

According to Rawls, in a just society individuals are guaranteed the right to pursue their own ends to the extent that they do not interfere with the right of others to pursue their own ends. Compromising this basic right to individual liberty for the sake of any so-called higher good is not acceptable in the Rawlsian view, and any such "good" is not really a good thing at all. You could say that, for Rawls, the right to personal liberty is more basic or fundamental than goodness. This is a view widely held by liberals.

Animals and Morality

One interesting side discussion in Nozick's *Anarchy, State, and Utopia* concerns the moral status of animals.

Animals are not mere objects, Nozick said: the same moral constraints apply to what one may do to animals as to what one may do to people. Even a modern utilitarian, who holds that the pleasure, happiness, pain, and suffering that an action produces determine its moral worth, must count animals in moral calculations to the extent they have the capacities for these feelings, Nozick suggested.

Furthermore, he argued, utilitarianism is not adequate as a moral theory concerning animals (or humans) to begin with. In his view, neither humans nor animals may be used or sacrificed against their will for the benefit of others; that is, neither may be treated as means (to use Kant's terminology) but only as ends. Nozick's argument for this view was not a negative argument that challenges a reader to find an acceptable ethical principle that would prohibit the killing, hurting, sacrificing, or eating of humans for the sake of other ends that would not equally pertain to animals. Can you think of one?

Here is a good place to mention that the question of animal rights has been widely discussed by contemporary philosophers—and the animal rights movement of recent years, which frequently makes headlines, has received strong theoretical support from several of them. Others do not think that animals have rights in the same sense in which humans have them, and they are not philosophically opposed to medical experimentation involving animals or to eating them. (As far as we know, Nozick was not an activist in the animal rights movement.)

However, some recent critics of Rawls say there exists a common good whose attainment has priority over individual liberty. Some of these critics are known as **communitarians,** for they hold that this common good is defined by one's society or "community." Important communitarian critics of Rawls include Michael Sandel (*Liberalism and the Limits of Justice*, 1982), Michael Walzer (*Spheres of Justice*, 1983, and *Thick and Thin*, 1994), and Alasdair MacIntyre (most widely known work: *After Virtue*, 1984).

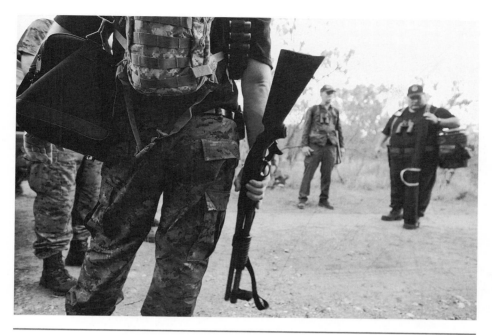

Modern-day members of militias complain about the government usurping the rights of its citizens (especially the right to bear arms). With whom would they sympathize more, Nozick or Rawls?

Sandel believed that the community is an intersubjective or collective self because self-understanding comprehends more than just an individual human being: it comprehends one's family or tribe or class or nation or people—in short, one's community, with its shared ends and common vocabulary and mutual understandings. The Rawlsian principle of equal liberty is subordinate to the good of this social organism, for Sandel.

Walzer (also famous for his theorizing on just and unjust wars—see the box "War!") contrasted "thick" or particularist moral argument, which is internal to and framed within a specific political association or "culture," with "thin" moral argument, which is abstract and general and philosophical. Political philosophers, according to Walzer, seek an abstract, universal (thin) point of view and are concerned with the appropriate structure of political association in general. But any full account of how social goods ought to be distributed, he said, will be thick; it "will be idiomatic in its language, particularist in its cultural reference, and historically detailed." For Walzer, a society is just if its way of life is faithful to the shared understanding of its members. There "are no eternal or universal principles" that can replace a "local account" of justice. All such principles are abstractions and simplifications that nevertheless still reflect particular cultural viewpoints. (Notice how Walzer's political philosophy echoes some of the relativistic themes discussed in current epistemology and metaphysics—see Chapter 9.)

War!

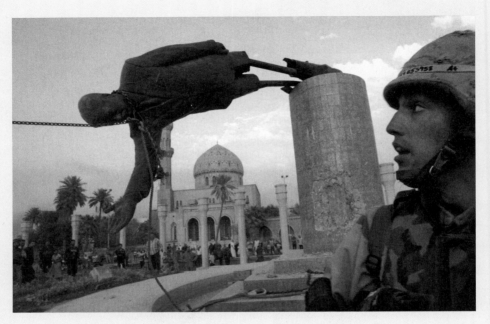

The philosophical literature on war—its legality, morality, causes, and significance—is pretty expansive, and we simply do not have space to go there, except briefly.

One important ethical issue pertains to the justness of war: when is a war just, and when is a war fought justly? The classical theory of the justness of a war comes from Augustine and especially Aquinas. Augustine said that just wars are those that avenge injuries: a state should be punished if it fails to right a wrong done by its citizens. Aquinas held that there are three conditions for a just war: (1) the ruler leading the war must have the authority to do so, (2) a just cause is required, and (3) right intention is required: those making the war must intend to achieve good and avoid evil.

A landmark discussion of justness in war was the 1977 book *Just and Unjust Wars* by Michael Walzer. Walzer covered many important issues that were later widely talked about in connection with the U.S. invasion of Iraq in 2003: preventive war and preemptive war, noncombatant immunity versus military necessity, terrorism, the right to neutrality, war crimes, and nuclear deterrence. Here we will say a few words about Walzer's view on when a war is just, as an example of philosophical discussion of the subject.

Walzer held that states have rights, including the right to political sovereignty, territorial integrity, and self-determination. He did not just throw this thesis out as a talk-radio host might but attempted to derive the rights of states from the rights of individual people, arguing that states' rights are simply the collective form of individual rights. States, like people, have duties to one another (as well as to their citizens) and can commit and suffer crimes (just as people can). Any use of military force by one state against another constitutes criminal aggression and justifies forceful resistance. However, the use of military force by one state on another can be justified only as a response to aggression and (except for a few unusual cases) not for any other end. For Walzer, democratic governments are not the only ones that have a right to political sovereignty; undemocratic and even tyrannical governments may have such a right as well. "Though states are founded for the sake of life and liberty," he wrote, "they cannot be challenged in the name of life and liberty by any other states."

These same themes were discussed, of course, when the United States went to war with Iraq in 2003. They will be discussed again, of that you can be sure.

ALASDAIR MACINTYRE AND VIRTUE ETHICS

Alasdair MacIntyre's (1929–) famous book *After Virtue* (2nd ed., 1984) was the major impetus behind a relatively recent surge in interest by philosophers in **virtue ethics.**

Prior to MacIntyre, the theories most influential in contemporary moral philosophy were those from the utilitarians and from Kant. Moral philosophy (excluding metaethics) usually took the form of rules or principles of conduct: *act so as to promote the most happiness possible; social and economic inequalities should be arranged so that they are to everyone's advantage;* and so forth. But after MacIntyre, there's been much interest in the virtues, those beneficial traits of character—courage, compassion, generosity, truthfulness, justness, and the like—that enable individuals to flourish as human beings. The idea is that traits of character are in many ways morally more fundamental than rules for action. A cowardly act, for example, seems less commendable than a courageous one, even if the cowardly act happens to have better consequences. Whether acts count as moral or immoral seems to depend less on their consequences or on the intent of the person acting and more on the type of character they reflect. Other philosophers in the virtue ethics tradition include Plato, Aristotle, Aquinas, Nietzsche, and (in certain respects) Hume.

In *After Virtue* MacIntyre wrote, "There is no way to possess the virtues except as part of a tradition in which we inherit them and our understanding of them from a series of predecessors." The first in this series of predecessors, according to MacIntyre, were the "heroic societies" typified in Homer's *Iliad*. Here, "every individual has a given role and status within a well-defined and highly determinate system of roles and statuses." Consequently, moral duties are known and understood, and affairs lack ethical ambiguity.

MacIntyre went on to trace the evolution of ethical thought through the Sophists, Plato, Aristotle, the Stoics, the Middle Ages, and the Enlightenment, right up to Nietzsche. For MacIntyre, it is from Aristotle and the Aristotelian tradition that we have the most to learn. Among other lessons, MacIntyre accepted Aristotle's view that human nature cannot be specified merely by stating the average human's characteristics; instead, we must conceive of human nature in terms of its potentialities. Virtues, from this perspective, are traits that promote human flourishing and thus naturally produce pleasure.

For MacIntyre, Nietzsche represents the ultimate alternative to Aristotle. For with Nietzsche, the person must "raze to the ground the structures of inherited moral belief and argument." Nietzsche or Aristotle? For MacIntyre the choice is clear.

In addition to these themes, MacIntyre emphasized the "concept of a self whose unity resides in the unity of a narrative which links birth to life to death as narrative beginning to middle to end." That is, according to MacIntyre, the only way to make sense of decisions and actions is in their context in the person's story in which they happen. An action viewed in and of itself, independent of its place in the story that is this person's life, is unintelligible. This does not mean that your life can follow just any old story line. Your life story must be the search for attainment of your potential as human; that is, it must be the search for your excellence or good. The virtues, MacIntyre wrote, sustain us in a relevant kind of quest for the good.

However, each person's own quest for her or his own good or excellence must be undertaken from within that person's moral tradition. "The notion of escaping . . . into a realm of entirely universal maxims which belong to man as such, whether in its eighteenth-century Kantian form or in the presentation of some modern analytical moral philosophies, is an illusion."

How do we find the good? MacIntyre distinguished between the excellences or goods that are internal to a practice and those that are external to it. For example, a good internal to the practice of medicine is patients' health; an external good is wealth. To attain a good internal to a practice, you must operate within a certain social context, abiding by the rules of the practice, which have arisen through the history of the practice. A virtue, for MacIntyre, may be analyzed as a quality required to attain a good internal to a practice. Unless some of the practitioners are virtuous, the practice will decay. Entire moral traditions are also subject to degeneration unless they have their virtuous practitioners.

Further, to understand the human good, we can begin with the goods internal to human practices, noting how they are ordered in comparison with each other. For example, the good internal to one practice, medicine, let's say, stands at a higher level than the good internal to another practice, playing football, perhaps. As we try to rank goods and to order our own affairs accordingly, we come to have a clearer understanding of the human good and ourselves.

Putting this complex understanding of virtue together, MacIntyre concluded:

> The virtues find their point and purpose not only in sustaining the relationships necessary if the goods internal to practices are to be achieved and not only in sustaining the form of an individual life in which that individual may seek out his or her good as the good of his or her whole life, but also in sustaining those traditions which provide both practices and individual lives with their necessary historical context.

MARTHA NUSSBAUM

To the general public, few if any contemporary professional philosophers are better known than **Martha Nussbaum** (1947–   ), currently of the University of Chicago, who has written and spoken widely on issues interesting to the general public. However, if one had to identify three areas of scholarship with which Nussbaum is associated in the minds of professional philosophers, they would perhaps be

- Virtue theory and Greek ethics (*The Fragility of Goodness: Luck and Ethics in Greek Tragedy and Philosophy*, 1986)

- International social justice, particularly regarding women's opportunities and human development (especially the work she did with Nobel Prize–winning economist Amartya Sen)

- The role of emotions in decision making (*Upheavals of Thought: The Intelligence of Emotions*, 2001; *Hiding from Humanity: Disgust, Shame, and the Law,* 2004)

A more recent book, *Frontiers of Justice: Disability, Nationality, Species Membership* (2005), is (among other things) a treatise on how John Rawls's contract theory

Martha Nussbaum.

of social justice can be improved to take care of three unfinished pieces of business: doing justice to people with physical and mental disabilities, extending justice to the people of all nations, and extending justice beyond the realm of the human to nonhuman animals. In contrast to the contractarian approach of Rawls, Nussbaum set forth a contrasting "capabilities approach," which emerged in her earlier collaboration with economist Amartya Sen. The theory of Rawls, she wrote, offers a fair and impartial procedure to generate a just outcome, and "just" means whatever follows from decisions made in the "original situation" from behind the "veil of ignorance." By contrast, according to the **capabilities approach** favored by Nussbaum, all nations and governments should provide for the core ingredients of human dignity such as (for example) the ability to live a life of normal length in good health and with the freedom to move about safe from violent assault, to be able to exercise one's mental, physical, imaginative, and creative powers, and to be able to laugh and play and enjoy recreational opportunities. The Nussbaum capabilities approach thus focused on specific desirable *outcomes* rather than on a specific just procedure that may (or may not) yield such outcomes. It is also cross-cultural and universal and "is under no pressure to hypothesize that the parties to the social compact are 'free, equal, and independent.'" Most importantly, for Nussbaum, the capabilities approach denies that social justice must secure mutual advantage, a key desideratum of contract theories. It is likely, she wrote, that "the arrangements we need to make to give justice to developing nations, and to people with severe impairments within our own nation, will be very expensive and will not be justifiable as mutually advantageous in the narrow economic sense of advantage. That is too bad."[1] Her concept that creatures have a natural good and are entitled to pursue it is distinctly Aristotelian.

HERBERT MARCUSE, A RECENT MARXIST

The thought of Karl Marx has been interpreted, expanded, and amended by his many followers, conspicuously so, of course, by the Communist Party. Today, Marxism, like Christianity (as philosopher and social historian Sidney Hook said), is a family of doctrines continually being renewed and revised. It is more appropriate to treat the details of the further evolution of Marxist thought in a text on political history than in this summary overview of political philosophy. Still, because Marxism has been very important in contemporary political philosophy, we shall describe briefly the views of a contemporary Marxist.

In the late 1960s, the most famous philosopher in the United States was **Herbert Marcuse** [mar-KOO-zeh] (1898–1979). This was the era of tumultuous social and political unrest, the era of the New Left, Vietnam War protest, "people power," militant black and feminist disaffection, hippies, acid, four-letter words, and Woodstock. Marcuse was in. (See the box "Marcuse in Southern California.")

Marcuse's reputation on the street arose from his book *One-Dimensional Man* (1964), a Marxist-oriented appraisal of contemporary industrial society. For the New Left, the book was a clear statement of deficiencies in American society.

As we have seen, it is a Marxist doctrine (or, at any rate, a doctrine of orthodox Marxists) that a disenfranchised working class is the inevitable instrument of social change. But according to Marcuse, the working class has been *integrated* into advanced capitalist society. Indeed, it has been integrated so well that it "can actually be characterized as a pillar of the establishment," he said. This integration has been effected, he believed, through the overwhelming efficiency of technology in improving the standard of living. Because today's workers share so largely in the comforts of consumer society, they are far less critical of the status quo than if they had been indoctrinated through propaganda or even brainwashed.

In fact, Marcuse said, today's workers do not merely share these comforts, they actually "*recognize themselves* in their commodities." "They find their soul in their automobile, hi-fi set, split-level home, kitchen equipment." Their needs have been determined by what are, in effect, new forms of social control, such as advertising, consumerism, the mass media, and the entertainment industry, all of which produce and enforce conformity in what people desire, think, and do.

Thus, according to Marcuse, in the West, with its advanced capitalist societies, the workers have lost their individual autonomy, their capacity to choose and act

---

[1] *Frontiers of Justice*, pp. 89–90.

Offstage music at Woodstock, 1969.

for themselves, to refuse and to dissent and to create. Yes, needs are satisfied, but the price the workers pay for satisfaction of need is loss of ability to think for themselves. Further, the perceived needs that are satisfied, in Marcuse's opinion, are *false* needs, needs stimulated artificially by producers to sell new products, needs whose satisfaction promotes insane wastefulness and does not lead to true fulfillment of the individual or release from domination.

Marcuse emphasized that the integration of the working class into the advanced capitalist society by the satisfaction of false needs created by advertising, television, movies, music, and other forms of consumerism does not mean that society has become classless. Despite the fact that their "needs" are satisfied, members of the working class are still slaves, in effect, because they remain mere instruments of production that capitalists use for their own purposes. Further, he wrote in *One-Dimensional Man,*

> if the worker and his boss enjoy the same television program and visit the same resorts, if the typist is as attractively made up as the daughter of her employer . . . if they all read the same newspaper, then this assimilation indicates not the disappearance of classes, but the extent to which the needs and satisfactions that serve the preservation of the Establishment are shared by the underlying population.

Thus, the working class in advanced capitalist societies, according to Marcuse, has been transformed from a force for radical change into a force for conservatism and the status quo.

Marcuse in Southern California

What may sometimes be the penalty for advocating an unpopular political philosophy is illustrated by the treatment Herbert Marcuse received during his stay in Southern California in the late 1960s.

Marcuse left Germany after Hitler's rise to power and became a U.S. citizen in 1940. He obtained work with the Office of Strategic Services and the State Department and thereafter held positions at Harvard, Columbia, and Brandeis. Later, in 1965, he accepted a postretirement appointment at the University of California, San Diego, where he was a quiet but popular professor. Although he had acquired by then a worldwide reputation among leftists and radicals for his social criticism, in San Diego he was not widely known beyond the campus.

In 1968, however, it was reported in the national media that Marcuse had invited "Red Rudi" Dutschke, a notorious West German student radical, to visit him in San Diego. After this, the local populace quickly informed itself about Marcuse. The outcry against any possible Dutschke visit and against the perceived radicalism of Marcuse in that conservative naval community was vigorous and strident. In thundering editorials, the *San Diego Union* denounced Marcuse and called for his ouster. Thirty-two American Legion posts in San Diego County demanded termination of his contract and offered the regents of the University of California the money to buy it out. Marcuse began receiving death threats and hate mail, and his student followers armed themselves with guns to protect him.

When his appointment neared its end in 1969, the question of reappointment arose and attracted nationwide attention. With the strong support of the faculty but in the face of strenuous opposition from the *Union*, the Legion, and other powerful groups, university chancellor John McGill decided to offer Marcuse a one-year contract of reappointment. When the regents of the University of California met to discuss McGill's decision, they had to do so under the protection of the San Francisco Police Department's Tactical Force. Though a substantial number strongly dissented, the majority supported McGill. Marcuse was reappointed.

By the expiration of the reappointment contract, Marcuse had passed the age of mandatory retirement. Nevertheless, he was permitted to keep his office and to teach informally.

The neutralizing of possible sources of radical social change through the integration of the working class into a one-dimensional society is visible everywhere to Marcuse. In the political sphere, the one-dimensionalization of society is apparent in the unification of labor and capital against communism in a "welfare and warfare state," in which the cold war and the arms race unite all against the Communist threat while simultaneously stimulating the economy through the production of weapons.

Likewise, he said, a one-dimensional quality pervades contemporary art, language, philosophy, science, and all of contemporary culture. Thus, for example, art has lost its power to criticize, challenge, and transcend society and has been integrated as mere entertainment mass-produced in paperbacks, records, and television shows. As such, art now serves to promote conformity in thought, aspiration, and deed. The same is true of philosophy and science, he believed. The elite classes can tolerate free speech simply because such conformity of thought in art, philosophy, science, and politics is present.

Thus, as Marcuse saw it, advanced capitalist society has managed to assimilate and integrate into itself the forces that oppose it and to "defeat or refute all protest in the name of the historical prospects of freedom from toil and domination." Still, at the very end of *One-Dimensional Man*, Marcuse acknowledged that there is a slim chance of revolutionary change at the hands of a substratum of the outcasts of society, such as persecuted ethnic minorities and the unemployed and unemployable.

In his later thought, moreover, Marcuse perceived a weakening of the integration of the working classes into society and a growing awareness on the part of workers, students, and the middle class that consumer prosperity has been purchased at too high a price and that a society without war, exploitation, repression, poverty, or waste is possible. The revolution that will produce this society, Marcuse said—and only through revolution can it be created, he maintained—will be born not of privation but of "disgust at the waste and excess of the so-called consumer society."

THE OBJECTIVISM OF AYN RAND

What book has most inflenced Americans? If you guessed *The Bible*, you'd be right, at least according to a survey by the Book-of-the-Month Club and the Library of Congress. How about second place? That honor belongs to Ayn Rand's novel, *Atlas Shrugged*, published in 1957.

Ayn Rand (1905–1982), born Alissa Rosenbaum, graduated from the University of Petrograd (Leningrad) in 1924, moved to the United States the following year, and eventually became a Hollywood screenwriter. Lately there has been a resurgence of interest in her thought; Paul Ryan, the 2012 vice-presidential candidate for the Republican Party, claimed that reading Rand is what led him to a career in public service and thought that "there is no better place to find the moral case for capitalism and individualism than through Ayn Rand's writings and works." At the other end of the political spectrum, *Reader Supported News*, on August 13, 2012, referred to Rand as "a lunatic whose books are a big driver in the long-term right-wing campaign to delude millions of people into believing that there's no such thing as society."

Let's see what the fuss is about.

Rand's best-known works, in addition to *Atlas Shrugged*, are *The Fountainhead* (1943), *We the Living* (1936), and *Anthem* (1938). *The Fountainhead* was published only after twelve rejections, but it eventually became a best seller, selling over 6.5 million copies worldwide. Altogether, her book sales passed the 25 million mark by 2008 and continue to sell briskly.

We the Living, Rand's first novel, is about the struggle for freedom in Soviet Russia. The book's heroine becomes the mistress of a high-ranking Communist Party member in order to raise money for her lover's medical treatment, but eventually is shot when she tries to escape the country after denouncing Communism. After many rejections, a major publishing company finally bought the book's rights and published it, but it didn't sell. Rand made only $100 in royalties.

Anthem is a brief dystopian novel (a dystopia is the opposite of a utopia) that takes place in the future at a time when the world has returned to the dark

Rewritten by Anne D'Arcy.

ages: collectivism rules, individuality is forbidden, and even speaking words that reflect self, such as "ego," "I," "Me", or "Myself" is punishable by death. A desire to learn is considered a transgression against the collective society; people are educated only for what they need to do for the job they are assigned by the Council responsible for such decisions. The protagonist, Equality 7-2521 (yes, that is his name), is different, however. He longs to study math and science and eventually secretly re-invents the light bulb, which he mistakenly believes will be accepted by the Council as a gift to the collective. Instead, he is imprisoned and tortured for having dared to be an individual. He escapes with his secret lover, they change their names, and they begin to create a brave new world together. At the end of the novel, Equality 7-2521 announces, "My happiness is not the means to any end. It is the end. It is its own purpose. Neither am I the means to any other end others may wish to accomplish. I am not a tool for their use. I am not a servant of their needs."

The Fountainhead is the saga of Roark, an architect who takes on the collectivists who surround him in order to preserve the integrity of his work. The novel begins with Roark's expulsion from architecture school for refusing to follow traditional designs. He finds it difficult to get work for the same reason; he refuses to alter his ideas and must take a job as a manual laborer as a result. Roark displays the characteristics Rand most admired: intelligence, reason, and individual achievement. Other characters in the novel are archetypes of the opposite: bland, unimaginative, and slaves to collectivism. The novel builds up to Roark's successful design of a temple, but when another character adds a silly ornament to it at the last minute, destroying Roark's sense of the purity of his design, Roark dynamites the building. At the trial that follows, he defends his action in an eloquent speech that reflects Rand's basic philosophy of reason as the most important value, along with the individual mind as opposed to collective thought. Roark is acquitted and goes on to successfully rebuild, having triumphed as an individual. In 1949, a film version of *The Fountainhead* was released, starring Patricia Neal and Gary Cooper.

Atlas Shrugged, Rand's most important book, took fourteen years to write. It's the story of John Galt, a physicist and inventor who organizes a strike to protest taxation and other forms of exploitation. It is not about labor unions, however. In the words of one of the characters, "We are on strike against the dogma that the pursuit of one's happiness is evil." Another character says, "Money rests on the axiom that every man is the owner of his mind and his effort." And another says, "I have made my money by my own effort, in free exchange . . . I refuse to apologize for my success." Of course these ideas were controversial then, just as they are now. The reviews were very hostile, yet the sales continued to rise. Controversy sells.

After these successes, Rand turned to nonfiction writing and public speaking. Her philosophy, called Objectivism, captured the enthusiastic attention of many young followers and still does. She developed the ideas of ethical egoism, laissez-faire capitalism, and individual rights, applying them to social issues. Rand's claim was that everyone needs a philosophy, which is necessary to living thoughtfully and well, and that this philosophy must also contribute to an environment that is accepting of living a life of knowledge and achievement. Social change must begin with an individual's moral rebellion; ideals are communicated via rational discussion. She talked about "the murder of the human soul by the collectivist culture,"

U.S. Representative Paul Ryan of Wisconsin, and nominee of the Republican Party for U.S. vice president in 2012. Mr. Ryan has said that he was inspired by Ayn Rand's writings.

but Rand didn't mean what religious believers mean by the word "soul" since she was a staunch atheist. Instead, she meant that the right philosophy is needed for the rebirth of the human spirit [soul] and the rebuilding of society.

Rand considered Aristotle the greatest of all philosophers, regarding him as a realist who established ethics on an objective understanding of human behavior rooted in knowable principles. Unlike Aristotle, however, she thought that certainty in morality was possible. Rand was also influenced by Nietzsche, and she followed his contempt for the ignorance of most humans. Nietzsche scorned having pity on people who don't think for themselves, who have no will of their own, and Rand thought there was no worse injustice than giving to the undeserving. She had Kira, her protagonist in *We the Living* (1936), say: "What are your masses but millions of dull, shriveled, helpless souls that have no thoughts of their own, no dreams of their own, no will of their own, who eat and sleep and chew helplessly the words that others have put into their brains? . . . I loathe most of them." Like Nietzsche, she thought of pity as a dangerous weakness that, historically, has allowed the weak, the ignorant, and the undeserving to become parasites on the strong and productive. She spoke of the "sanction of the victim," the unwitting assent of the man of ability (the victim) to concede the false premise that his inferiors have the moral right to the product of his labor. In truth, she thought, progress is to be made only by the brilliant few who affirm life and pleasure, who think for themselves, and who are the creative artists of life. These are the heroic, larger-than-life figures who change the world for the better.

Still following Nietzsche, Rand saw human fulfillment as the struggle of the individual to improve, to become something higher. She believed that rights are vested in the individual, never in the group. The state exists to protect individual rights, to the exclusion of almost all else. The government certainly must not provide undeserved bonuses to the mediocre, mindless, and meaningless masses. However, she added to this concept the idea that the maximally fulfilled life involves productivity and money-making. She embraced a form of laissez-faire capitalism so pure that it alienated her from conservatives and libertarians, whom she eventually came to despise. She spoke of an ideal society based on a "utopia of greed" in which the government would be so noninterventional as to be invisible. In this utopia, the ideas and actions of the brilliant would provide the basis for the just state according to her moral principles. Essentially, for Rand, morality meant creating something and then making money from it. She considered inheritance, fraud, or any other kind of nonproductivity as looting. The dollar symbolized the victory of the creative mind over the state, over religion, and over the unthinking masses. "Money," Rand insisted, "is the barometer of society's virtue." "Run for your life from any man who tells you that money is evil. That sentence is the leper's bell of an approaching looter." "Wealth is the product of man's capacity to think."

Rand lived her philosophy of Objectivism, so she used some words in a way that may be perplexing at first. The word "value" is one she used frequently. She described everything in terms of material worth. Even when her husband died, and she went into a depression, she would only say, "I have lost my top value."

Rand described her philosophy in essence as the concept of man as a heroic being, with his own happiness the moral purpose of his life, with productive achievement as his noblest activity, and reason as his only absolute. Asked if she could explain Objectivism while standing on one foot, Rand offered the following: Metaphysics: Objective Reality; Epistemology: Reason; Ethics: Self-interest; Politics: Capitalism. According to the Ayn Rand Institute, these essentials of Objectivism can be summarized as follows.

Metaphysics: Reality, the external world, exists outside man's consciousness and is independent of any observer's knowledge, beliefs, feelings, desires, or fears. Facts are facts, and the task of man's consciousness is to perceive reality, not to create or invent it. Objectivism rejects belief in the supernatural.

Epistemology: Man's reason can identify and integrate the material his senses provide. Reason is the only means of acquiring knowledge. Objectivism rejects any form of mysticism, any acceptance of faith or feeling as a means of knowledge, and it rejects the claim that certainty is impossible.

Human nature: Reason is man's basic means of survival, but the exercise of reason depends on each individual's choice. What people refer to as their "soul" or "spirit" is actually their consciousness, and what they call "free will" is the mind's freedom to think or not. This freedom of choice determines one's life or character. Objectivism thus rejects any form of determinism, such as God, fate, economic conditions, upbringing, genetic factors, and any belief that one is a victim of circumstances beyond his control.

Ethics: Reason is man's only proper guide to action and judge of values, and rationality is man's basic virtue. So the standard of ethics is that man is an end in himself, not a means to the ends of others; he must live for his own sake, neither sacrificing himself to others nor sacrificing others to himself. He must work for his rational self-interest. The achievement of his own happiness is the highest moral purpose of his life. Altruism is soundly rejected by Objectivism.

Politics: The basic social principle is that no man has the right to seek values from others by means of physical force except in self-defense. Men must work with each other as traders, giving value for value, by free mutual consent. The only social system that meets this definition is laissez-faire capitalism, a system based on the recognition of individual rights. The government's only function is to protect those individual rights from those who initiate the use of physical force. Objectivism thus rejects any form of collectivism, such as socialism or fascism, and also rejects the current notion that the government should regulate the economy and redistribute wealth.

Aesthetics: Rand described art as "a selective re-creation of reality according to the artist's metaphysical value-judgments." Her own approach to art (her novels) was that of a Romantic Realist who presents men as the ideal but places her characters in the here and now. Her goal was artistic, not didactic, she claimed. She wanted only to present the ideal man who serves his own ends and does not allow himself to be a means to any further end.

Rand's philosophy and her feisty, strong-minded critiques created many enemies while she was alive that survive her death. Objectivism is not often taught in university courses, not because Rand is controversial, but primarily because her personal knowledge of philosophy was limited. Even so she commented derisively on other philosophers' work and failed miserably in the area of analytical philosophy. In other words, she was never a real student of philosophy. Some philosophers find faulty reasoning and logical loopholes in her writings, believers are offended by her blatant atheism, environmentalists oppose her self-centered views, and many feminists are outraged at her stances relating to women.

Rand believed that environmentalists present a grave danger to society because their goal is to worship nature at the expense of technological development. In the name of preserving nature, she said, environmentalists have made development an evil word, inhibiting technological progress. They see nature as having intrinsic value when, in fact, their approach destroys human values.

Rand's belief that men are superior to women and that women should not hold the highest office of the land, the presidency, offends most thinking people, not just feminists. Nevertheless, there is academic interest in Rand's ideas. The Ayn Rand Institute sponsors an annual essay contest for students, offering 600 prizes and $100,000 in prize money each year, and The Ayn Rand Society is a professional society affiliated with the American Philosophical Association. Its members are scholars at various colleges and universities, and its aim is to foster academic study of Rand's philosophical thought and writings. There are feminist rereadings of Ayn Rand that view her philosophy of individualism as a contribution to a humane feminist ethic, and Rand's female characters have been viewed by some as the archetype of a female epic heroine. Her female characters can be interpreted as expressing authentic sexual freedom and power that challenges the status quo.

In short, the jury is still out on Ayn Rand's Objectivism.

"ISMs"

Liberalism, communism, socialism, capitalism, fascism, conservatism—these ill-defined terms are sometimes thought to denote mutually exclusive alternative forms of government. Actually, they do not stand for parallel alternatives at all. We shall conclude this chapter with a brief scan of some of these "isms."

Classical **liberalism** emphasized the rationality and goodness of humans, individual freedom, representative government, individual property rights, social progress through political reform, and laissez-faire economics, which, by the way, is the view that the government should not interfere in economic affairs beyond the minimum necessary to maintain peace and property rights. A guiding principle of liberalism was eloquently articulated by Mill: the sole end for which people are warranted in interfering with an individual's liberty is never the individual's own good but rather to prevent harm to others.

Contemporary liberals also subscribe to these assorted concepts, except they are not so wedded to the laissez-faire idea. They are willing to put up with (or even ask for) government involvement in economic affairs when such involvement is perceived to promote equality of opportunity or to protect people from exploitation or discrimination or to protect the environment, or is done even merely to raise the overall quality of life. Thus, contemporary liberals tend to support social welfare programs paid for through taxation, as well as civil rights, women's rights, gay rights, affirmative action, and environmentalism. But contemporary liberals tend to oppose militarism, imperialism, exploitation of third world countries, censorship, governmental support of religion, and anti-immigration crusades. American liberals are inclined to interpret the Bill of Rights very, well, liberally.

Conservatism was originally a reaction to the social and political upheaval of the French Revolution. Conservatives, as the word suggests, desire to conserve past social and political traditions and practices as representing the wisdom of a society's experience and are opposed to widespread social reform or experimentalism. Even so, Edmund Burke (1729–1797), the most eloquent and influential conservative writer of the eighteenth century, if not of all time, advocated many liberal and reform causes. Burke considered "society" as a contract among the dead, the living, and those to be born, and each social contract of each state but a clause in the great primeval contract of eternal society.

Contemporary American conservatism is in large measure a defense of private enterprise, laissez-faire economic policies, and a narrow or literal interpretation of the Bill of Rights. Conservatives are reluctant to enlist the power of government, especially its power to tax, to remedy social ills. Critics (liberals, mostly) charge that conservatives give mere lip service to the importance of individual liberty and consider it of lesser importance than a free-market economy. Conservatives respond that individual liberty is best protected by limiting the scope of government, especially in economic matters, and by dispersing its power. In emphasizing both personal freedom and free-market economics and in distrusting centralized power, modern conservatism is similar to nineteenth-century laissez-faire liberalism.

Communists (with a capital *C*), as explained in Chapter 11, accept the social, political, and economic ideology of the Communist Party, including the idea that the dictatorship of the proletariat will come about only through revolution; **communism** (lowercase *c*) is simply a form of economic organization in which the primary goods (usually the means of production and distribution) are held in common by a community. The definitions of **socialism** and communism are essentially the same, and Communists, of course, are advocates of communism.

Capitalism is an economic system in which ownership of the means of production and distribution is maintained primarily by private individuals and corporations. Capitalism, therefore, is an opposite to socialism and communism.

Fascism is the totalitarian political philosophy espoused by the Mussolini government of Italy prior to and during World War II, which emphasized the absolute primacy of the state and leadership by an elite who embody the will and intelligence of the people. Adolph Hitler and the National Socialists (Nazis) of Germany embraced elements of fascism; today the term *fascist* is used loosely to denounce any totalitarian regime.

Finally, another important political "ism" is **democratic socialism,** a term that denotes a popular political structure (especially in Western Europe) that many Americans have not heard of. Under democratic socialism, there are a democratically elected executive and legislature, and there is no state ownership of business, though it permits considerable government intervention in the business sector. Yet this type of system provides guarantees of individual rights and freedom as well as a social safety net for the poor, the old, and the sick, as in Communist political arrangements.

SELECTION 12.1

Killing and Starving to Death*

James Rachels

[Is it as bad, morally, to let a person die as it is to kill him or her? Many say "no." In this selection, James Rachels challenged this view. The "Equivalence Thesis" is the idea that letting people die is as bad as killing them.]

* From *Philosophy*, vol. 54, no. 208 (April 1979). © The Royal Institute of Philosophy 1979. Reprinted with the permission of Cambridge University Press.

Although we do not know exactly how many people die each year of malnutrition or related health problems, the number is very high, in the millions. By giving money to support famine relief efforts, each of us could save at least some of them. By not giving, we let them die.

Some philosophers have argued that letting people die is not as bad as killing them, because in general our "positive duty" to give aid is weaker than our "negative duty" not to do harm. I maintain the opposite: letting die is just as bad as killing. At first this may seem wildly implausible. When reminded that people are dying of starvation while we spend money on trivial things, we may feel a bit guilty, but certainly we do not feel like murderers. Philippa Foot writes:

> Most of us allow people to die of starvation in India and Africa, and there is surely something wrong with us that we do; it would be nonsense, however, to pretend that it is only in law that we make a distinction between allowing people in the underdeveloped countries to die of starvation and sending them poisoned food. There is worked into our moral system a distinction between what we owe people in the form of aid and what we owe them in the way of noninterference.

No doubt this would be correct if it were intended only as a description of what most people believe. Whether this feature of "our moral system" is rationally defensible is, however, another matter. I shall argue that we are wrong to take comfort in the fact that we *only* let these people die, because our duty not to let them die is equally as strong as our duty not to kill them, which, of course, is very strong indeed.

Obviously, the Equivalence Thesis is not morally neutral, as philosophical claims about ethics often are. It is a radical idea that, if true, would mean that some of our "intuitions" (our prereflective beliefs about what is right and wrong in particular cases) are mistaken and must be rejected. Neither is the view I oppose morally neutral. The idea that killing is worse than letting die is a relatively conservative thesis that would allow those same intuitions to be preserved. However, the Equivalence Thesis should not be dismissed merely because it does not conform to all our prereflective intuitions. Rather than being perceptions of the truth, our "intuitions" might sometimes signify nothing more than our prejudices or selfishness or cultural conditioning. . . . In what follows I shall argue that many of our intuitions concerning killing and letting die *are* mistaken, and should not be trusted.

I

We think that killing is worse than letting die, not because we overestimate how bad it is to kill, but because we underestimate how bad it is to let die. The following chain of reasoning is intended to show that letting people in foreign countries die of starvation is very much worse than we commonly assume.

Suppose there were a starving child in the room where you are now—hollow-eyed, belly bloated, and so on—and you have a sandwich at your elbow that you don't need. Of course you would be horrified; you would stop reading and give her the sandwich or, better, take her to a hospital. And you would not think this an act of supererogation; you would not expect any special praise for it, and you would expect criticism if you did not do it. Imagine what you would think of someone who simply ignored the child and continued reading, allowing her to die of starvation. Let us call the person who would do this Jack Palance, after the very nice man who plays such vile characters in movies. Jack Palance indifferently watches the starving child die; he cannot be bothered even to hand her the sandwich. There is ample reason for judging him very harshly; without putting too fine a point on it, he shows himself to be a moral monster.

When we allow people in faraway countries to die of starvation, we may think, as Mrs. Foot puts it, that "there is surely something wrong with us." But we most emphatically do not consider ourselves moral monsters. We think this, in spite of the striking similarity between Jack Palance's behavior and our own. He could easily save the child; he does not, and the child dies. We could easily save some of those starving people; we do not, and they die. If we are not monsters, there must be some important difference between him and us. But what is it?

One obvious difference between Jack Palance's position and ours is that the person he lets die is in the same room with him, while the people we let die are mostly far away. Yet the spatial location of the dying people hardly seems a relevant consideration. It is absurd to suppose that being located at a certain map coordinate entitles one to treatment that one would not merit if situated at a different longitude or latitude. Of course, if a dying person's location meant that we *could not* help, that would excuse us. But, since there are efficient famine relief agencies willing to carry our aid to the faraway countries, this excuse is not available. It would be almost as easy for us to send these agencies the price of the sandwich as for Palance to hand the sandwich to the child.

The location of the starving people does make a difference, psychologically, in how we feel. If there were a starving child in the same room with us, we could not avoid realizing, in a vivid and disturbing way, how it is suffering and that it is about to die. Faced with this realization our consciences probably would not allow us to ignore the child. But if the dying are far away, it is easy to think of them only abstractly, or to put them out of our thoughts altogether. This might explain why our conduct would be different if we were in Jack Palance's position, even though, from a moral point of view, the location of the dying is not relevant.

There are other differences between Jack Palance and us, which may seem important, having to do with the sheer numbers of people, both affluent and starving, that surround us. In our fictitious example Jack Palance is one person, confronted by the need of one other person. This makes his position relatively simple. In the real world our position is more complicated, in two ways: first, in that there are millions of people who need feeding, and none of us has the resources to care for all of them; and second, in that for any starving person we *could* help there are millions of other affluent people who could help as easily as we.

On the first point, not much needs to be said. We may feel, in a vague sort of way, that we are not monsters because no one of us could possibly save *all* the starving people—there are just too many of them, and none of us has the resources. This is fair enough, but all that follows is that, individually, none of us is responsible for saving everyone. We may still be responsible for saving someone, or as many as we can. This is so obvious that it hardly bears mentioning, yet it is easy to lose sight of, and philosophers have actually lost sight of it. In his article "Saving Life and Taking Life," Richard Trammell says that one morally important difference between killing and letting die is "dischargeability." By this he means that, while each of us can discharge completely a duty not to kill anyone, no one among us can discharge completely a duty to save everyone who needs it. Again, fair enough: but all that follows is that since we are only bound to save those we can, the class of people we have an obligation to save is much smaller than the class of people we have an obligation not to kill. It does *not* follow that our duty with respect to those we can save is any less stringent. Suppose Jack Palance were to say: "I needn't give this starving child the sandwich because, after all, I can't save everyone in the world who needs it." If this excuse will not work for him, neither will it work for us with respect to the children we could save in India or Africa.

The second point about numbers was that, for any starving person we *could* help, there are millions of other affluent people who could help as easily as we. Some are in an even better position to help since they are richer. But by and large these people

are doing nothing. This also helps explain why we do not feel especially guilty for letting people starve. How guilty we feel about something depends, to some extent, on how we compare with those around us. If we were surrounded by people who regularly sacrificed to feed the starving and we did not, we would probably feel ashamed. But because our neighbors do not do any better than we, we are not so ashamed.

But again, this does not imply that we should not feel more guilty or ashamed than we do. A psychological explanation of our feelings is not a moral justification of our conduct. Suppose Jack Palance were only one of twenty people who watched the child die; would that decrease his guilt? Curiously, I think many people assume it would. Many people seem to feel that if twenty people do nothing to prevent a tragedy, each of them is only one-twentieth as guilty as he would have been if he had watched the tragedy alone. It is as though there is only a fixed amount of guilt, which divides. I suggest, rather, that guilt multiplies, so that each passive viewer is fully guilty, if he could have prevented the tragedy but did not. Jack Palance watching the girl die alone would be a moral monster; but if he calls in a group of his friends to watch with him, he does not diminish his guilt by dividing it among them. Instead, they are all moral monsters. Once the point is made explicit, it seems obvious.

The fact that most other affluent people do nothing to relieve hunger may very well have implications for one's own obligations. But the implication may be that one's own obligations *increase* rather than decrease. Suppose Palance and a friend were faced with two starving children, so that, if each did his "fair share," Palance would only have to feed one of them. But the friend will do nothing. Because he is well-off, Palance could feed both of them. Should he not? What if he fed one and then watched the other die, announcing that he has done *his* duty and that the one who died was his friend's responsibility? This shows the fallacy of supposing that one's duty is only to do one's fair share, where this is determined by what would be sufficient *if* everyone else did likewise.

To summarize: Jack Palance, who refuses to hand a sandwich to a starving child, is a moral monster. But we feel intuitively that we are not so monstrous, even though we also let starving children die when we could feed them almost as easily. If this intuition is correct, there must be some important difference between him and us. But when we examine the most obvious differences between his conduct and ours—the location of the dying, the differences in numbers—we find no real basis for judging ourselves less harshly than we judge him. Perhaps there are some other grounds on which we might distinguish our moral position, with respect to actual starving people, from Jack Palance's position with respect to the child in my story. But I cannot think of what they might be. Therefore, I conclude that if he is a monster, then so are we—or at least, so are we after our *rationalizations* and thoughtlessness have been exposed. . . .

The preceding is not intended to prove that letting people die of starvation is as bad as killing them. But it does provide strong evidence that letting die is much worse than we normally assume, and so that letting die is much *closer* to killing than we normally assume. These reflections also go some way towards showing just how fragile and unreliable our intuitions are in this area. They suggest that, if we want to discover the truth, we are better off looking at arguments that do not rely on unexamined intuitions.

SELECTION 12.2

A Theory of Justice*

John Rawls

[*Here, Rawls explained his conception of justice as fairness, the original position, the veil of ignorance, and the two basic principles of social justice.*]

My aim is to present a conception of justice which generalizes and carries to a higher level of abstraction the familiar theory of the social contract as found, say, in Locke, Rousseau, and Kant. In order to do this we are not to think of the original contract as one to enter a particular society or to set up a particular form of government. Rather, the guiding idea is that the principles of justice for the basic structure of society are the object of the original agreement. They are the principles that free and rational persons concerned to further their own interests would accept in an initial position of equality as defining the fundamental terms of their association. These principles are to regulate all further agreements; they specify the kinds of social cooperation that can be entered into and the forms of government that can be established. This way of regarding the principles of justice I shall call justice as fairness.

Thus we are to imagine that those who engage in social cooperation choose together, in one joint act, the principles which are to assign basic rights and duties and to determine the division of social benefits. Men are to decide in advance how they are to regulate their claims against one another and what is to be the foundation charter of their society. Just as each person must decide by rational reflection what constitutes his good, that is, the system of ends which it is rational for him to pursue, so a group of persons must decide once and for all what is to count among them as just and unjust. The choice which rational men would make in this hypothetical situation of equal liberty, assuming for the present that this choice problem has a solution, determines the principles of justice.

In justice as fairness the original position of equality corresponds to the state of nature in the traditional theory of the social contract. This original position is not, of course, thought of as an actual historical state of affairs, much less as a primitive condition of culture. It is understood as a purely hypothetical situation characterized so as to lead to a certain conception of justice. Among the essential features of this situation is that no one knows his place in society, his class position or social status, nor does any one know his fortune in the distribution of natural assets and abilities, his intelligence, strength, and the like. I shall even assume that the parties do not know their conceptions of the good or their special psychological propensities. The principles of justice are chosen behind a veil of ignorance. This ensures that no one is advantaged or

---

* Rawls's footnotes have been omitted. Reprinted by permission of the publisher from *A Theory of Justice* by John Rawls, pp. 11–14, Cambridge, Mass.: The Belknap Press of Harvard University Press. Copyright © 1971, 1999 by the President and Fellows of Harvard College.

disadvantaged in the choice of principles by the outcome of natural chance or the contingency of social circumstances. Since all are similarly situated and no one is able to design principles to favor his particular condition, the principles of justice are the result of a fair agreement or bargain. For given the circumstances of the original position, the symmetry of everyone's relations to each other, this initial situation is fair between individuals as moral persons, that is, as rational beings with their own ends and capable, I shall assume, of a sense of justice. The original position is, one might say, the appropriate initial status quo, and thus the fundamental agreements reached in it are fair. . . .

Justice as fairness begins, as I have said, with one of the most general of all choices which persons might make together, namely, with the choice of the first principles of a conception of justice which is to regulate all subsequent criticism and reform of institutions. Then, having chosen a conception of justice, we can suppose that they are to choose a constitution and a legislature to enact laws, and so on, all in accordance with the principles of justice initially agreed upon. Our social situation is just if it is such that by this sequence of hypothetical agreements we would have contracted into the general system of rules which defines it. . . .

I shall maintain . . . that the persons in the initial situation would choose two rather different principles: the first requires equality in the assignment of basic rights and duties, while the second holds that social and economic inequalities, for example inequalities of wealth and authority, are just only if they result in compensating benefits for everyone, and in particular for the least advantaged members of society. These principles rule out justifying institutions on the grounds that the hardships of some are offset by a greater good in the aggregate. It may be expedient but it is not just that some should have less in order that others may prosper. But there is no injustice in the greater benefits earned by a few provided that the situation of persons not so fortunate is thereby improved. The intuitive idea is that since everyone's well-being depends upon a scheme of cooperation without which no one could have a satisfactory life, the division of advantages should be such as to draw forth the willing cooperation of everyone taking part in it, including those less well situated. Yet this can be expected only if reasonable terms are proposed. The two principles mentioned seem to be a fair agreement on the basis of which those better endowed, or more fortunate in their social position, neither of which we can be said to deserve, could expect the willing cooperation of others when some workable scheme is a necessary condition of the welfare of all. Once we decide to look for a conception of justice that nullifies the accidents of natural endowment and the contingencies of social circumstance as counters in quest for political and economic advantage, we are led to these principles. They express the result of leaving aside those aspects of the social world that seem arbitrary from a moral point of view.

SELECTION 12.3

Anarchy, State, and Utopia*

Robert Nozick

[*If the members of your society voluntarily limit their liberty for their mutual advantage, then are you obliged to limit your liberty if you benefit from the arrangement? Nozick said "no."*]

A principle, suggested by Herbert Hart, which (following John Rawls) we shall call the *principle of fairness*, would be of service here if it were adequate. This principle holds that when a number of persons engage in a just, mutually advantageous, cooperative venture according to rules and thus restrain their liberty in ways necessary to yield advantages for all, those who have submitted to these restrictions have a right to similar acquiescence on the part of those who have benefited from their submission. Acceptance of benefits (even when this is not a giving of express or tacit undertaking to cooperate) is enough, according to this principle, to bind one. . . .

The principle of fairness, as we stated it following Hart and Rawls, is objectionable and unacceptable. Suppose some of the people in your neighborhood (there are 364 other adults) have found a public address system and decide to institute a system of public entertainment. They post a list of names, one for each day, yours among them. On his assigned day (one can easily switch days) a person is to run the public address system, play records over it, give news bulletins, tell amusing stories he has heard, and so on. After 138 days on which each person has done his part, your day arrives. Are you obligated to take your turn? You *have* benefited from it, occasionally opening your window to listen, enjoying some music or chuckling at someone's funny story. The other people *have* put themselves out. But must you answer the call when it is your turn to do so? As it stands, surely not. Though you benefit from the arrangement, you may know all along that 364 days of entertainment supplied by others will not be worth your giving up *one* day. You would rather not have any of it and not give up a day than have it all and spend one of your days at it. Given these preferences, how can it be that you are required to participate when your scheduled time comes? . . .

At the very least one wants to build into the principle of fairness the condition that the benefits to a person from the actions of the others are greater than the costs to him of doing his share. . . .

If the principle of fairness were modified so as to contain this very strong condition, it still would be objectionable. The benefits might only barely be worth the costs to you of doing your share, yet others might benefit from *this* institution much more than you do; they all treasure listening to the public broadcasts. As the person least benefited by the practice, are you obligated to do an equal amount for it? . . .

On the face of it, enforcing the principle of fairness is objectionable. You may not decide to give me something, for example a book, and then grab money from me to pay for it, even if I have nothing better to spend the money on. You have, if anything, even less reason to demand payment if your activity that gives me the book also benefits you; suppose that your best way of getting exercise is by throwing books into people's houses, or that some other activity of yours thrusts books into people's houses as an unavoidable side effect. Nor are things changed if your inability to collect money or payments for the books which unavoidably spill over into others' houses makes it inadvisable or too expensive for you to carry on the activity with this side effect. One cannot, whatever one's purposes, just act so as to give people benefits and then demand (or seize) payment. Nor can a group of persons do this. If you may not charge and collect for benefits you bestow without prior agreement, you certainly may not do so for benefits whose bestowal costs you nothing, and most certainly people need not repay you for costless-to-provide benefits which yet *others* provided them. So the fact that we partially are "social products" in that we benefit from current patterns and forms created by the multitudinous actions of a long string of long-forgotten people, forms which include institutions, ways of doing things, and language (whose social nature may involve our current use depending upon Wittgensteinian matching of the speech of others), does not create in us a general floating debt which the current society can collect and use as it will.

Perhaps a modified principle of fairness can be stated which would be free from these and similar difficulties. What seems certain is that any such principle, if possible, would be so complex and involuted that one could not combine it with a special principle legitimating *enforcement* within a state of nature of the obligations that have arisen under it. Hence, even if the principle could be formulated so that it was no longer open to objection, it would not serve to obviate the need for other persons' *consenting* to cooperate and limit their own activities.

SELECTION 12.4

Frontiers of Justice*

Martha Nussbaum

[*From Martha Nussbaum's Introduction to a recent book.*]

Theories of social justice should be abstract. They should, that is, have a generality and theoretical power that enables them to reach beyond the political conflicts of their time, even if they have their origins in such conflicts. Even political justification requires such abstraction: for we cannot justify a political theory unless we can show that it can be stable over time, receiving citizens' support for more than narrowly self-protective or instrumental reasons. And we cannot show that it can be stable without standing back from immediate events.

On the other hand, theories of social justice must also be responsive to the world and its most urgent problems, and must be open to changes in their formulations and even in their structures in response to a new problem or to an old one that has been culpably ignored.

Most theories of justice in the Western tradition, for example, have been culpably inattentive to women's demands for equality and to the many obstacles that stood, and stand, in the way of that equality. Their abstraction, though in some ways valuable, concealed a failure to confront one of the world's most serious problems. Attending adequately to the problem of gender justice has large theoretical consequences, since it involves acknowledging that the family is a political institution, not part of a "private sphere" immune from justice. Correcting the oversight of previous theories is therefore not a matter of simply applying the same old theories to a new problem; it is a matter of getting the theoretical structure right.

Today there are three unsolved problems of social justice whose neglect in existing theories seems particularly problematic. (No doubt there are still other such problems, which as yet we do not see.) First,

there is the problem of doing justice to people with physical and mental impairments. These people are people, but they have not as yet been included, in existing societies, as citizens on a basis of equality with other citizens. The problem of extending education, health care, political rights and liberties, and equal citizenship more generally to such people seems to be a problem of justice, and an urgent one. Because solving this problem requires a new way of thinking about who the citizen is and a new analysis of the purpose of social cooperation (one not focused on mutual advantage), and because it also requires emphasizing the importance of care as a social primary good, it seems likely that facing it well will require not simply a new application of the old theories, but a reshaping of theoretical structures themselves.

Second is the urgent problem of extending justice to all world citizens, showing theoretically how we might realize a world that is just as a whole, in which accidents of birth and national origin do not warp people's life chances pervasively and from the start. Because all the major Western theories of social justice begin from the nation-state as their basic unit, it is likely that new theoretical structures will also be required to think well about this problem.

Finally, we need to face the issues of justice involved in our treatment of nonhuman animals. That animals suffer pain and indignity at the hands of humans has often been conceded to be an ethical issue; it has more rarely been acknowledged to be an issue of social justice. If we do so acknowledge it (and readers of this book will have to judge for themselves whether the case for so doing has been well made), it is clear, once again, that this new problem will require theoretical change. Images of social cooperation and reciprocity that require rationality in all the parties, for example, will need to be reexamined and new images of a different type of cooperation forged.

There are many approaches to social justice in the Western tradition. One of the strongest and most enduring has been the idea of the social contract, in which rational people get together, for mutual advantage, deciding to leave the state of nature and to govern themselves by law. Such theories have had enormous influence historically, and have recently been developed with great philosophical depth in the distinguished work of John Rawls. Such theories are probably the strongest theories of justice we have. At any rate, Rawls has powerfully made the case that they do better than the various forms of Utilitarianism in articulating, probing, and organizing our considered judgments about justice. . . .

I begin from the conviction that these three problems are indeed serious unsolved problems of justice. I argue that the classical theory of the social contract cannot solve these problems, even when put in its best form. It is for this reason that I focus throughout the book on Rawls, who to my mind expresses the classical idea of the social contract in its strongest form and makes the strongest case for its superiority to other theories. If Rawls's distinguished theory has serious shortcomings in these three areas, as I hope to show, *a fortiori* other, less developed or less appealing forms of the contract doctrine are likely to have such problems. I hope to show that the type of difficulty we shall encounter cannot be handled by merely applying the old theoretical structure to the new case; it is built into the theoretical structure itself, in such a way as to lead us to search for a different type of theoretical structure, albeit one in which major elements in Rawls's theory will survive and provide valuable guidance.

These problems are not simply problems in academic philosophy. Doctrines of the social contract have deep and broad influence in our political life. Images of who we are and why we get together shape our thinking about what political principles we should favor and who should be involved in their framing.

The common idea that some citizens "pay their own way" and others do not, that some are parasitic and others "normally productive," are the offshoots, in the popular imagination, of the idea of society as a scheme of cooperation for mutual advantage. We could challenge those images in practical politics without identifying their source. It is actually quite helpful, however, to go to the root of the problem, so to speak: for then we see much more clearly why we got into such a difficulty and what we must change if we wish to advance. Thus, although this book engages with philosophical ideas in detail and with attention to the complexities and nuances of the theories in question, it is also intended as an essay in practical philosophy, which may guide us back to some richer ideas of social cooperation (old as well as new) that do not involve such difficulties. . . .

My project here is both critical and constructive. For I shall argue that, with respect to all three of the problems under consideration, the version of the "capabilities approach" that I have long been developing, suggests promising insights, and insights superior to those suggested, for those particular problems, by the social contract tradition. (As we shall see, I also hold that my approach converges in large measure with a different type of contractarianism, one based purely on Kantian ethical ideas without the idea of mutual advantage.) My previous account of the capabilities approach in *Women and Human Development* outlined the view, spoke about issues of method and justification, and discussed in detail its treatment of two particularly difficult problems, the problem of religion and the problem of the family. It also commended the approach as superior to preference-based Utilitarianism, in a detailed confrontation with that theory.

CHECKLIST

To help you review, a checklist of the key philosophers of this chapter can be found online at www.mhhe.com/moore9e.

KEY TERMS AND CONCEPTS

QUESTIONS FOR DISCUSSION AND REVIEW

1. Are moral value judgments merely expression of taste? Explain.

2. Is it worse morally to send starving people poisoned food than to let them starve to death? Why?

3. Explain the differences among liberalism, communism, socialism, capitalism, fascism, and conservatism.

4. Do you agree that the principles of justice stated by Rawls are those to which we will agree if we are thinking rationally and in our own self-interest and are not influenced by irrelevant considerations? Explain.

5. Can an unequal distribution of the various assets of society be just? Explain.

6. Would it be right and proper to legalize human slavery if that resulted in an increase in the overall happiness of society? Why or why not?

7. Can you think of an ethical principle that would prohibit the killing, hurting, sacrificing, or eating of humans for the sake of other ends that would not equally pertain to animals?

8. Is self-respect the most important good, as Rawls says?

9. Which do you think is more important, the common good or individual freedom? Why?

10. Are our needs determined by advertising, consumerism, the mass media, and the entertainment industry?

SUGGESTED FURTHER READINGS

Go online to www.mhhe.com/moore9e for a list of suggested further readings.

Part Three
Philosophy of Religion: Reason and Faith

13

Philosophy and Belief in God

It is morally necessary to assume the existence of God.   —Immanuel Kant

God is dead.   —Friedrich Nietzsche

What is the difference between a theologian and a philosopher of religion? Let's back up about four steps and get a running start at the question. If you subscribe to a religion, and the opinion polls say you most likely do, then you also accept certain purely philosophical doctrines. For example, if you believe in a nonmaterial God, then you believe that not all that exists is material, and that means you accept a metaphysics of immaterialism. If you believe you should love your neighbor because God said you should, then you are taking sides in the debate among ethical philosophers concerning ethical naturalism. You have committed yourself to a stand against naturalism.

Your religious beliefs commit you as well to certain epistemological principles. A lot of people who make no claim to have seen, felt, tasted, smelled, or heard God still say they know God exists. So they must maintain that humans can have knowledge not gained through sense experience. To maintain this is to take sides in an important epistemological issue, as you know from Part One.

These and many other metaphysical, ethical, and epistemological points of view and principles are assumed by, and incorporated in, religion, and it is the business of the philosophy of religion to understand and rationally evaluate them.

Of course, *theology* also seeks clear understanding and rational evaluation of the doctrines and principles found in religion, including those that are metaphysical, ethical, and epistemological. But, for the most part, theologians start from premises and assumptions that are themselves religious tenets. The philosopher of religion, in contrast, does not make religious assumptions in trying to understand and evaluate religious beliefs.

The Black Cat

An old saying goes that the difference between a metaphysician and a theologian is this: The metaphysician looks in a dark room for a black cat that is not there. The theologian looks in the same place for the same thing.

And finds it.

The religions of the world differ in their tenets, of course. Therefore, a philosopher of religion usually focuses on the beliefs of a specific religion or religious tradition, and in fact it is the beliefs of the Judaeo-Christian religious tradition that have received the most discussion by Western philosophers. Philosophers of religion may focus on the beliefs of a specific religion, but they will not proceed in their inquiries from the *assumption* that these beliefs are true, even though they may in fact accept them as a personal matter.

What are some of the metaphysical, ethical, and epistemological beliefs of the Judaeo-Christian tradition that philosophers have sought to understand and evaluate? Many of these beliefs have to do with *God:* that he exists, that he is good, that he created the universe and is the source of all that is real, that he is a personal deity, that he is a transcendent deity, and so forth. Many have to do with *humans:* that humans were created in the image of God, that they have free will, that they can have knowledge of God's will, that the human soul is immortal, and so on. Other beliefs have to do with *features of the universe:* for example, that there are miracles, that there is supernatural reality, that there is pain and suffering (a fact thought to require reconciliation with the belief in a good and all-powerful God). And still others have to do with *language:* that religious language is intelligible and meaningful, that religious utterances are (or are not) factual assertions or are (or are not) metaphorical or analogical, that terminology used in descriptions of God means the same (or does not mean the same) as when it is used in descriptions of other things.

This is a long list of issues. To simplify things, we will concentrate here only on the philosophical consideration of the Christian belief in the existence of God. Let's begin with two Christian greats, St. Anselm and St. Aquinas.

TWO CHRISTIAN GREATS

Other chapters have begun with discussions of ancient Greek philosophers, and we could have begun this chapter, too, with the ancient Greeks. Many modern religious beliefs contain ideas that were discussed by, and in some cases originated with, the Greeks. But we have narrowed the focus here to the philosophical consideration of the Judaeo-Christian belief in God's existence, and it is appropriate to begin with the man who was abbot of Bec and, later, archbishop of Canterbury.

Anselm

St. Anselm (c. 1033–1109) was among the first to evaluate the belief in the Christian God from a purely philosophical perspective, that is, from a perspective that does not make religious assumptions from the outset. Nonetheless, Anselm never entertained the slightest doubt that God exists. Further, he made no distinction between philosophy and theology, and he thought it impossible for anyone to reason about God or God's existence without already believing in him.

Still, Anselm was willing to evaluate *on its own merit and independently of religious assumptions* the idea that God does *not* exist.

The Ontological Argument   This idea, that God does not exist, is attributed in Psalms 14:1 to the "fool," and Anselm thought it plain that anyone who would deny God's existence is *logically* mistaken and is indeed an utter fool. Anselm reasoned that the fool is in a self-contradictory position. The fool, Anselm thought, is in the position of saying *that he can conceive of a being greater than the greatest being conceivable.* This may sound like a new species of doubletalk, so we must consider Anselm's reasoning carefully. You may find it helpful to read the box "*Reductio Proofs*" before we begin.

Anselm began with the premise that by *God* is meant "the greatest being conceivable," or, in Anselm's exact words, "a being than which nothing greater can be conceived."

Now, the fool who denies that God exists at least understands what he denies, said Anselm charitably. Thus, God at least exists in the fool's understanding. But, Anselm noted, a being that exists both in the understanding and outside in reality is greater than a being that exists only in the understanding. (That is why people prefer real houses and cars and clothes and vacations to those they just think about.)

But this means, Anselm said, that the fool's position is absurd. For his position is that God exists only in the understanding but not in reality. So the fool's position, according to Anselm, is that "the very being, than which nothing greater can be conceived, is one, than which a greater can be conceived." And yes, this silliness is something like doubletalk, but Anselm's point is that the denial of God's existence leads to this silliness. Hence, God exists: to think otherwise is to be reduced to self-contradiction and mumbo-jumbo.

This line of argument, according to which it follows from the very concept of God that God exists, is known as the **ontological argument.** It represents Anselm's most important contribution to the philosophy of religion. If Anselm's argument is valid, if Anselm did establish that it is self-contradictory to deny that God exists and hence established that God does exist, then he did so without invoking any religious premises or making any religious presuppositions. True, he made, in effect, an assumption about the concept of God, but even a non-Christian or an atheist, he thought, must concede that what is meant by *God* is "the greatest being conceivable." Thus, if the argument is valid, even those who are not moved by faith or are otherwise religious must accept its conclusion. Anselm, in effect, argued that the proposition "God exists" is *self-evident* and can no more be denied than can the proposition "A square has four sides," and anyone who thinks otherwise is either a fool or just does not grasp the concept of God.

Reductio Proofs

If a claim logically entails something that is absurd, nonsensical, or just plain false, you reject the claim, correct?

For example, if the claim that the butler killed Colonel Mustard in the kitchen means that the butler was in two different places at the same time (because it is known that he was in the library at the time of the murder), then you reject the claim that the butler killed Colonel Mustard in the kitchen.

This type of proof of a claim's denial is known as *reductio ad absurdum:* by demonstrating that a claim reduces to an absurdity or just to something false, you prove the denial of the claim. By showing that claim *C* entails falsehood *F*, you prove *not-C*.

Reductios, as they are called, are encountered frequently in philosophy and in real life. Anselm's ontological argument is a **reductio proof.** Here the claim, *C*, is that

God does not exist.

This claim, argued Anselm, entails the falsehood, *F*, that

the very being than which nothing greater can be conceived is one than which a greater can be conceived.

The conclusion of the argument is thus *not-C*, that

God does exist.

Anselm gave another version of the ontological argument that goes like this: Because God is that than which nothing greater can be conceived, God's nonexistence is inconceivable. For anyone whose nonexistence *is* conceivable is not as great as anyone whose nonexistence is *not* conceivable, and thus is not God.

Are you convinced? Many are not. Many regard the ontological argument in any version as a cute little play on words that proves absolutely nothing.

Gaunilo's Objection   One who found the argument unconvincing was a Benedictine monk from the Abbey of Marmontier, a contemporary of Anselm whose name was **Gaunilo** [GO-nee-low]. One of Gaunilo's objections was to the first version of the argument, which, he argued, could be used to prove ridiculous things. For example, Gaunilo said, consider the most perfect island. Because it would be more perfect for an island to exist both in reality and in the understanding, the most perfect island must exist in reality, if Anselm's line of reasoning is sound. For if this island did not exist in reality, then (according to Anselm's reasoning) any island that did exist in reality would be more perfect than it—that is, would be more perfect than the most perfect island, which is impossible. In other words, Gaunilo used Anselm's reasoning to demonstrate the necessary existence of the most perfect island, implying that any pattern of reasoning that can be used to reach such an idiotic conclusion must obviously be defective.

Anselm, however, believed that his reasoning applied only to God: because God is that than which a greater cannot be conceived, God's nonexistence is inconceivable; whereas, by contrast, the nonexistence of islands and all other things is conceivable.

As you will see in the selection from Anselm at the end of the chapter, which contains the first version of his ontological argument, Anselm was able to express his thought with elegant simplicity. Please accept our invitation to figure out what, if anything, is wrong with his reasoning.

Do not be confused when Anselm says that God is "something than which nothing greater can be thought." He just means, in plain English, "God is the being with the following characteristic: when you try to think of a greater or higher being, you cannot do it."

Aquinas

About a century and a half after Anselm died, **St. Thomas Aquinas** (c. 1225–1274), whom we have discussed in earlier chapters, interpreted Aristotelian philosophy from a Christian perspective. Aristotle, as we have had occasion to mention, emphasized the importance to philosophy of direct observation of nature. In keeping with his empiricist, Aristotelian leanings, Aquinas regarded the ontological argument as invalid. You cannot prove that God exists, he said, merely by considering the word *God,* as the ontological argument in effect supposes. For that strategy to work, you would have to presume to know God's essence. The proposition "God exists," he said, unlike "A square has four sides," is not self-evident to us mere mortals. Although you can prove God's existence in several ways, he asserted, you cannot do it just by examining the concept of God. You have to consider what it is about nature that makes it manifest that it requires God as its original cause.

The ways in which the existence of God can be proved are in fact five, according to Aquinas. Although Aquinas's theological and philosophical writings fill many volumes and cover a vast range of topics, he is most famous for his **Five Ways** (but some philosophers—discussed later—do not regard Aquinas's proofs of God as his best philosophy). It would be surprising if you were not already familiar with one or another of Aquinas's Five Ways in some version. In any case, they are included as a reading selection at the end of the chapter.

The First Way   The first way to prove that God exists, according to Aquinas, is to consider the fact that natural things are in motion. As we look around the world and survey moving things, it becomes clear that they did not put themselves into motion. But if every moving thing were moved by another moving thing, then there would be no **first mover;** if no first mover existed, there would be no other mover, and nothing would be in motion. Because things are in motion, a first mover must therefore exist that is moved by no other, and this, of course, is God.

We should note here that Aquinas is usually understood as meaning something quite broad by *motion*—something more like "change in general "—and as including under the concept of movement the coming into, and passing out of, existence. Thus, when he said that things do not put themselves into motion, do not suppose that he thought that you cannot get up out of your chair and walk across the room. He meant that things do not just bring themselves into existence.

The Second Way   Aquinas's second way of proving God's existence was very similar to the first. In the world of sensible things, nothing causes itself. But if everything were caused by something else, then there would be no first cause, and if no first cause existed, there would be no first effect. In fact, there would be no

PROFILE: St. Thomas Aquinas (c. 1225–1274)

Aquinas, the son of a count of Aquino in Italy, studied for many years with Albertus Magnus ("Albert the Great"). Albertus, who had the unusual idea that Christian thinkers should be knowledgeable about philosophy and science, wished to make all of Aristotle's writings available in Latin. His fondness for Aristotle was a strong influence on his pupil, Aquinas.

Aquinas eventually received his doctorate from the University of Paris in his late twenties and soon acquired a substantial reputation as a scholar. For ten years in his thirties and early forties, he was a professor for the Papal Court and lectured in and around Rome.

Now, the thirteenth century was a time of considerable intellectual controversy between the Platonists and the Aristotelians. Some theologians believed that the teachings of Aristotle could not be harmonized with Christian doctrines. This belief was in part a reaction to Averroës (1126–1198), a brilliant Arabian philosopher, and his followers, whose philosophy was built entirely around the ideas of Aristotle. The Averroist philosophy conflicted with Church doctrine on creation and personal immortality, making Aristotle odious to some Christian theologians.

But Aquinas was no Averroist and defended his own version of Aristotle with inexorable logic. He returned to Paris in 1268 and became involved in a famous struggle with the Averroists, which he won. Although some factions within the Church voiced strong opposition to his philosophy, opposition that lasted for many years after his death, slowly but surely Aquinas's thinking became the dominant system of Christian thought. He was canonized (officially declared a saint) in 1323.

Aquinas was a stout fellow, slow and deliberate in manner. He was thus nicknamed the Dumb Ox. But he was a brilliant and forceful thinker, and his writings fill many volumes and cover a vast array of theological and philosophical topics. His most famous works are the *Summa Contra Gentiles* (1258–1260) and the *Summa Theologica* (1267–1273), a systematic theology grounded on philosophical principles. He was, in addition, a most humane and charitable man.

In 1879, Pope Leo XIII declared Aquinas's system to be the official Catholic philosophy.

second, third, or fourth effect either: if no first cause existed, there would be no effects, period. So we must admit a first cause, to wit, God. (This is a good time to read the box on the next page, "The Big Bang.")

Note that Aquinas did not say anything in either of the first two proofs about things being moved or caused by *earlier* motions or causes. The various motions and causes he is talking about are simultaneous. His argument is not the common one, that things must be caused by something earlier, which must be caused by something earlier, and so on, and that because this chain of causes cannot go back infinitely, there must be a first cause, God. In Aquinas's opinion, there is no philosophical reason that the chain of causes could not go back infinitely. But there cannot be an infinite series of *simultaneous* causes or movers, he thought.

The Third Way   Aquinas's third way is easily the most complicated of the Five Ways. Many consider it his finest proof, though Aquinas himself seemed to prefer the first.

Many paraphrasings of the third proof are not faithful to what Aquinas actually said, which is essentially this: In nature some things are such that it is possible for them not to exist. Indeed, everything you can lay your hands on belongs to this "need-not-exist" category; whatever it is, despite the fact that it does exist, it need

The Big Bang

The view now accepted by most scientists is that the universe is an explosion, known as the **Big Bang**. Unlike other explosions, the Big Bang does not expand outward into space, like a dynamite or bomb explosion, nor does it have a duration in external time, as do all other explosions, because all space and all time are located within it. The beginning of the Big Bang is the beginning of space and time and of matter and energy, and it is, in fact, the beginning of our expanding universe.

The most prevalent view among the qualified experts who have an opinion on the matter is that it is impossible to know what transpired in the Big Bang before 10^{-43} seconds after zero time, when the Big Bang began. But for various reasons that we need not go into here, most of these experts do apparently believe that there was a zero time, that the universe did have an absolute beginning, that there was a first physical event.

Now, either the first physical event, assuming that such a thing did take place, is explainable, or it is not. On one hand, it is difficult to believe that the first physical event has no explanation, for that amounts to saying that the entire universe, with its incredible size and complexity, was just a chance occurrence, a piece of good luck. But on the other hand, if the first physical event is explicable, then it would seem that the explanation must refer to some sort of nonphysical phenomenon, which certainly could be called "God."

Thus, the Big Bang theory, if true—and there seems to be much reason for supposing that it is true—may require philosophers to make a hard choice between an unexplainable universe and one explainable only by reference to something nonphysical.

not have existed. Now, that which need not exist, said Aquinas, at some time did not exist. Therefore, if everything belongs to this category, then at one time nothing existed, and then it would have been impossible for anything to have begun to exist—and thus even now nothing would exist. Thus, Aquinas reasoned, not everything is such that it need not exist: "There must exist something the existence of which is *necessary*."

This is not quite the end of the third proof, however, for Aquinas believed that he had not yet ruled out the possibility that the necessity of this necessary being might be caused by another necessary being, whose necessity might be caused by another, and so on and so on. So, he asserted, "It is impossible to go on to infinity in necessary things which have their necessity caused by another." Conclusion: There must be some necessary being that has its own necessity, and this is God.

We said the third way was complicated.

The Fourth and Fifth Ways   Aquinas's fourth way to prove God was to consider the fact that all natural things possess degrees of goodness, truth, nobility, and all other perfections. Therefore, there must be that which is the source of these perfections, namely, pure goodness and truth, and so on, and this is what we call God.

And the fifth way or proof of God's existence was predicated on the observation that natural things act for an end or purpose. That is, they function in accordance with a plan or design. Accordingly, an intelligent being exists by which things are directed toward their end, and this intelligent being is God.

Aquinas's first three proofs of God's existence are versions of what today is called the **cosmological argument.** The cosmological argument is actually not

Our galaxy has maybe 2 billion Earth-like planets, and there are at least 80 billion galaxies in the observable universe. Do the math. That's a lot of opportunities for life to take hold.

one argument but a type of argument. Proponents of arguments of this type think that the existence of *contingent* things, things that could possibly not have existed, points to the existence of a noncontingent or *necessary* being, God, as their ultimate cause, creator, ground, energizer, or source of being. Note the difference between the cosmological argument and ontological arguments, which endeavor to establish the existence of God just by considering his nature or analyzing the concept of God, as we saw attempted by Anselm.

Aquinas's fourth proof, which cites the existence of goodness or good things, is called the **moral argument.** Here again, the term does not refer to just one argument but rather to a type of argument, and, as we will see, some of the "versions" of the moral argument resemble one another only vaguely.

Arguments like Aquinas's fifth proof, according to which the apparent purposefulness or orderliness of the universe or its parts or structure points to the existence of a divine designer, are called **arguments from design,** or **teleological arguments.**

Let's summarize all of this. Between them, Anselm and Aquinas introduced what have turned out to be the four principal arguments for God's existence. These are

- the ontological argument
- the cosmological argument

- the teleological or design argument
- the moral argument

Notice that none of these four arguments rests on any religious assumptions. They should therefore require the assent of every nonreligious person, if they are sound.

To a certain extent, the history of the philosophy of religion is a continuing discussion of various versions and aspects of these four arguments. Therefore, understanding each type of argument provides you with a good grasp of the basics of the philosophy of religion.

Now, before we leave Aquinas, we should call your attention to the fact that the distinction we drew at the beginning of this chapter between theology and the philosophy of religion is pretty much the same as the distinction Aquinas drew between theology and philosophy.

According to Aquinas, if your thinking proceeds from principles that are revealed to you in religion and that you accept on religious faith, then your thinking is theological, though he did not often use the word *theology*. If your reasoning proceeds from what is evident in sensory experience, then your thinking is philosophical.

According to Aquinas, some theological truths, truths of revelation, are such that philosophy could never discover them. For example, philosophy cannot establish that the universe had a beginning and is not eternal. And not everything discovered by philosophy is important for salvation. But philosophy and theology, although separate disciplines, are not incompatible; in fact, they complement each other, he thought (in contrast to some other Christian thinkers who thought that philosophy could lead to religious errors).

From the standpoint of theology, that God exists is a given, a truth that you start out knowing. From the standpoint of philosophy, that God exists is not a given but may be inferred from your experience.

Thus, Aquinas's proofs of God's existence are philosophical proofs. They do not depend for their soundness on any religious principles.

MYSTICISM

Quite a different approach to God may be found in the writings of the anchoress **Julian of Norwich** (1342–1414?), one of the great mystics of all time.

Anchoress? That is a person who had the great fortune to be anchored for life to a church. You will find more information on this in the nearby Profile on Julian.

Why do you believe in God, if you do? Perhaps at some point you had a "mystical experience"—you experienced God directly; God *came* to you. If you have had this type of experience, you may be unable to offer a justification or argument for your belief, and your inability to do so may not bother you in the slightest. If you have had a mystical experience of God, this whole business of debating the strengths and weaknesses of arguments about God may strike you as just so much mental exercise.

It is, however, one thing to say, "God came to me" and quite another to explain why this mystical experience is a reliable form of knowledge. Before we go

PROFILE: The Anchoress, Julian of Norwich (1342–1414?)

Her name was Julian, but sometimes she is called Juliana. She lived in the English cathedral city of Norwich during a nasty time in history. The Hundred Years' War, the Great Schism in the Church, the ruthless suppression of the Peasant's Revolt in Norwich, and the condemnation of John Wycliffe for heresy made the mid-fourteenth century a rough time for Norwich. The fact that the Black Plague hit Norwich when Julian was six, again when she was nineteen, and again when she was twenty-seven did not exactly make Norwich a fun place to live.

Julian became an anchoress. It was the custom at that time to "anchor" someone to a church. Anchoring was a kind of permanent grounding of a scholarly nun or priest (it was an honor, not a punishment). The lucky person, someone known for saintly behavior and devotion to theology, was walled up alive in a small cell within the outer wall of the church. Food, books, and other items would be passed through a window, and occasionally the anchoress would be allowed to talk through the window to important clergy and nobility. She spent her life there, and when she died, she was entombed in a crypt in the church.

Julian wrote two versions (one short and one long) of her *Booke of Showings* (revelations). The short version is a partial description of a series of visions she had in 1373 when she was seriously ill. She became an anchoress soon after that experience. That left her lots of time for study, thought, and religious discussion. Many theologians and philosophers visited her to discuss the "showings" she described in the short version. She spent the next twenty years revising the manuscript, including fuller details and much analysis of what she thought the revelations meant.

Back then, women were not supposed to claim to have any religious or philosophical authority (or any other kind of authority, for that matter). To avoid criticism for having the crust to act as if she knew something, a woman writer typically began her text with a "humility formula." Here is Julian's as she wrote it:

Botte god for bede that ze schulde saye or take it so that I am a techere, for I meene nouzt soo, no I mente nevere so; for I am a womann, leued, febille and freylle.

Some of Julian's words had special religious and philosophical meanings that her readers would have understood. What she was saying was: "God says do not you act like I am a teacher. I do not mean to claim to be, and I never meant so. For I am a woman, ordinary ('lewd'), morally weak ('feeble'), and likely to fall from virtue ('frail')." Having disclaimed any authority, Julian went on to write seven hundred pages of philosophy.

Julian's interests were in the nature and certainty of religious knowledge. She held that there were three sources of religious knowledge: natural reason, teachings of religious leaders, and visions given by God. As God gives visions to whomever God chooses, and God loves everyone, in theory everyone is a candidate for mystical revelations. Julian of Norwich lived during the Crusades, when heretics were claiming that the Catholic religion was based on false ideas. How can someone tell true religious claims from false ones? Might God make revelations to ordinary people? Julian and many other mystics, including Hildegard of Bingen, St. John of the Cross, and his teacher St. Teresa of Avila (all of whom are known as philosophers), thought so. To claim that only religious leaders have a direct line to God suggests that God has limited ability to communicate. Julian called God "Christ, Our Mother" and "God, our Father." In her mind, God was both male and female, mother and father. God made us and nurtures us through the hard times.

any further, let's be clear. We are not talking about *hunches*—as in when you have a hunch that something good or bad will happen, and it does. We are talking about serious beliefs people hold on the basis of this peculiar form of experience, beliefs like "God is real" or "Jesus has touched me."

In a very rich mystical experience, one that comes with all the accessories, the mystic is often unconscious, appears to be delirious, or seems to be having what today is sometimes called an out-of-body experience. The mystic may be dreaming, awake, or in a trance. He or she may see visions or hear voices. Commonly, those who have such experiences report being told things by God. Sometimes they are told to write down what they experience or to teach others. Before the development of rationalism in the seventeenth century, back before philosophers mostly believed that reason was the premier tool for acquiring knowledge, mystical experiences like this were given more credence. Today, there is something of a tendency, at least among sophisticates, to discount such experiences as malfunctions in brain chemistry or temporal lobe disturbances or the like.

Julian of Norwich was a mystic, but she also *analyzed* her mystical experiences, or "showings," as she called them. Her analysis focused on the nature of personal religious and moral knowledge as well as on whether it is possible to know God. She denied that there is any meaningful difference in the validity of mystical revelations made directly to one's soul and knowledge derived through reason. She

Basilica of Saint Peter, Vatican City, Rome, Italy.

held, indeed, that it is mistaken to divorce reason from experience, especially from mystical experience.

Julian also emphasized the importance of the "not showns"—what logically should have been part of the vision but was missing. She believed God intended her to use insight, instinct, and reason to figure out what was not being communicated directly and to piece together the missing parts of the puzzle.

In Julian's view, God lives in us and we in God; we are one with God and are nurtured and fed knowledge of God and of ourselves by our divine parent. Thus, she believed we could know God only partly through revelation; further knowledge comes through loving God. In addition, she maintained we could come to love God by loving our own souls.

Thomas Aquinas (who had recently been made a saint) had analyzed visions as the language God uses to convey God's meaning. Julian went beyond analysis to attempt to make the experiences of visionaries relevant to others. She believed that ordinary people could learn from visionaries and find comfort and reason to hope in their visions. Hope, we can imagine, must have been a valuable commodity in mid-fourteenth-century England, faced with seemingly endless outbreaks of plague, war, and religious disputation.

SEVENTEENTH-CENTURY PERSPECTIVES

For our purposes here, we can now pass lightly over some three hundred years from the Middle Ages through the Renaissance to the seventeenth century. This is not to suggest that the time was unimportant for the history of religion. Europe had seen a mixture not only of enlightenment and religious revolution but also of reaction and intolerance; it had brought forth not only printed books and open discussion but also gunpowder and the stake. Luther had challenged the very foundations of Catholic doctrine, and Protestantism had spread throughout Europe. In England, Henry VIII had forced creation of the Anglican Church so that he could marry young Anne Boleyn and then, through a liberal use of execution, secured a loyal following. A new disorder had been rung in by the time of Descartes' birth, and before his death modern science was offering its own challenge to the established orthodoxy.

But all of this, though of great significance to the history of religion, was only indirectly important to the history of the philosophy of religion. The main point for our purposes is that the seventeenth century was the age of scientific discovery amid intellectual uncertainty and political and religious instability, an age in which past authorities, institutions, and truths were questioned and often rejected or discarded.

Descartes

The next figure with whom you should be familiar in the philosophy of religion is **René Descartes** (1596–1650). Descartes, longing for an unshakable intellectual footing, made it his primary business to devise what he thought was a new method for attaining certainty in his turbulent age. When he employed his new method, however, it revealed to him the certain existence of God.

As we saw in Chapter 6, Descartes' method was to challenge every belief, no matter how plausible it seemed, to ascertain which of his beliefs, if any, were absolutely unassailable. Employing this method, Descartes found that he could not doubt his existence as a thing that thinks: *cogito, ergo sum* (I think, therefore I am). He also found that he could not doubt the existence of God, for basically three reasons. These three reasons are Descartes' proofs of God.

Descartes' First Proof   Having established as absolutely certain his own existence as a thinking thing, Descartes found within his mind the idea of God, the idea of an infinite and perfect being. Further, he reasoned, because there must be a cause for his idea, and because there must be as much reality or perfection in the cause of an idea as there is in the content of the idea, and because he himself therefore certainly could not be the cause of the idea, it follows, he concluded, that God exists.

Let's call this Descartes' first proof. It is a simple proof, although Descartes made it seem somewhat complicated because he had to explain *why* his idea of God could not have arisen from a source other than God, and, of course, it is difficult to do this.

As you can see, Descartes' first proof was sort of a combination ontological–cosmological argument. It was ontological in that the mere idea of God was held by Descartes to entail that God exists. It was cosmological in that the existence of some contingent thing—Descartes' idea of God—was considered by Descartes to require God as its ultimate cause.

Descartes' Second Proof   Descartes had two other proofs of God's existence. His second proof was only subtly different from the first and is basically this:

1. I exist as a thing that has an idea of God.
2. Everything that exists has a cause that brought it into existence and that sustains it in existence.
3. The only thing adequate to cause and sustain me, a thing that has an idea of God, is God.
4. Therefore, God exists.

In this second proof, God was invoked by Descartes as the cause of *Descartes,* a being that had the idea of God; whereas in the first proof, God was invoked by Descartes as the cause of Descartes' *idea* of God. In the second proof, Descartes also utilized the important notion that a thing needs a cause to *conserve* or *sustain* it in existence. You will encounter this idea again.

Descartes' Third Proof   In contrast with the first two, Descartes' third proof was a straightforward and streamlined version of the ontological argument:

1. My conception of God is the conception of a being that possesses all perfections.
2. Existence is a perfection.

According to Descartes, when you think it through, you see that you couldn't have an idea of God unless God existed.

3. Therefore, I cannot conceive of God as not existing.
4. Therefore, God exists.

Now, assuming that this argument successfully gets you to conclusion (3), how about that move from (3) to (4)? Descartes had no difficulty with that move and said simply, "From the fact that I cannot conceive God without existence, it follows that existence is inseparable from Him, and hence that He really exists." He also offered what he thought was a parallel argument to support the move, and it was to this effect: Just as the fact that you cannot conceive of a triangle whose angles do not equal 180° means that a triangle must have angles that equal 180°, the fact that you cannot conceive of God as not existing means that God must exist.

Descartes' three proofs may be novel, but certain objections instantly spring to mind. A common criticism made of the first two proofs is that it seems possible to devise plausible alternative explanations for one's having an idea of God, explanations other than that given by Descartes. Descartes himself anticipated this objection and endeavored to show why the most likely alternative explanations fail.

The third proof—Descartes' version of the ontological argument—is more difficult to criticize, but about one hundred fifty years later, Immanuel Kant formulated what became the classic refutation of ontological arguments. More about this when we turn to Kant.

A different sort of objection to Descartes' proofs is that, given Descartes' method—according to which he vowed not to accept any claim that is in the least bit doubtable—Descartes should not have accepted without question either the principle that he and his ideas must be caused or the principle that there must be as much perfection and reality in the cause as in the effect. Although Descartes regarded his proofs of God as providing certainty, they seem to rest on principles that many people would think of as less than certain. Yet Descartes seemed to accept these principles without hesitation.

Nevertheless, Descartes' proofs are important in the history of our subject, for they raise the important question—at least the first two proofs raise this question—just how *does* a person come to have the idea of an *infinite* being?

Leibniz

You may recall the name of Gottfried Wilhelm, Baron von Leibniz, or at least the "Leibniz" part, from our discussion in Chapter 6. **Leibniz** (1646–1716) was one of the Continental rationalists of the seventeenth century (Descartes and Spinoza were the other two). He is remembered for developing calculus independently of Newton and for his metaphysical doctrine of **monads**—the individual nonphysical units of activity that, he said, are the ultimate constituents of reality. Remember also that the Leibnizian metaphysical system is, or so Leibniz believed, derivable logically from a few basic principles, including, perhaps most famously, the principle of sufficient reason.

Leibniz and the Principle of Sufficient Reason   The **principle of sufficient reason** was used by Leibniz as a proof of God. According to this principle, there is a sufficient reason why things are exactly as they are and are not otherwise. To see how the proof works, consider any occurrence whatsoever, say, the leaves falling from the trees in autumn. According to the principle in question, there must be a sufficient reason for that occurrence. Now, a *partial* reason for any occurrence is that something else happened, or is happening, that caused or is causing the occurrence—in our example, the days turning cold. But that happening is only a *partial* reason for the occurrence in question because it, too, requires a sufficient reason for happening. Why did the days turn cold?

So it is plain, thought Leibniz, that as long as you seek the sufficient reason for an occurrence from within the sequence of happenings or events, you never get the complete, final, sufficient reason for the occurrence. You only get to some other event, and that itself needs a reason for having happened. (The days turned cold because of a shift southward in the jet stream. The jet stream shifted southward because of a reduction in solar radiation. The solar radiation was reduced because of changes in the earth's orientation relative to the sun. And so forth.) So, unless there is something *outside* the series of events, some reason for the *entire series itself,* there is no sufficient reason for *any* occurrence.

Therefore, reasoned Leibniz, because there is a sufficient reason for every occurrence, it follows that there is something outside the series of events that is its own sufficient reason. And this "something outside," of course, is God. Further, because God is a sufficient reason for God's own existence, God is a *necessary* being, argued Leibniz.

In this way, then, the principle of sufficient reason, coupled with the fact that something has occurred or is occurring, leads straightaway to a necessary being, God—at least according to Leibniz.

This proof is yet another cosmological argument, and it is very much like Aquinas's third way. In fact, there is a tendency in the literature to interpret Aquinas's third way in this Leibnizian mode. Further, Leibniz's "argument from sufficient reason" is thought by many contemporary philosophers to be the soundest cosmological argument and the soundest proof of God of any type ever put forward. As you will see directly when we turn to David Hume, however, not everyone has been impressed with the argument.

Later, we will mention that Kant thought that the cosmological argument depended on the ontological argument. Kant thought this, apparently, because Leibniz's version ends up seeming to prove the existence of a necessary being, and it is the concept of God as a necessary being that is the foundation of the ontological argument. But it does seem doubtful that Leibniz's argument *depends* on the ontological argument or in any way *assumes* the existence of a necessary being. Instead, the argument seems to *prove* the existence of a necessary being.

Leibniz thought other proofs of God were sound, including an amended version of Descartes' ontological argument and a couple of others that rest on Leibniz's metaphysics. Leibniz, however, is most noted for the cosmological argument we have explained here.

Leibniz and the Problem of Evil   Unfortunately, pain and suffering are undeniably real. Cancer, natural disasters, war, poverty, racism, murder, animal cruelty—the list of causes is almost endless. How can it be said that the Creator is good, when little animals freeze to death or are incinerated in forest fires, when innocent men are tortured or beheaded by their fellow men, or when innocent women and children burn to death in atomic bomb attacks. Yes, much of the problem is due to evil in man; but the question then arises, Why would a good Creator create men who are evil? After all, He knew in advance, when He created people, that some of them would do such things.

This is the Problem of Evil, perhaps first posed by Epicurus, though not in these exact words. Obviously, if you believe that God is good and the all-knowing, all-powerful Creator of All, you need to confront this problem. **Theodicy** was Leibniz's word for an argument in defense of God's goodness despite the existence of evil, though the first to wrestle with this problem in a detailed way was St. Augustine (354–430 C.E.). Augustine's line of defense is widely accepted even today and includes the following elements:

- Human evil results when humans use their free will to turn away from God.

- Evil is the privation, or lack of good, that results from this turning away.

- Because a lack of something is not something, this evil is not something God created.

- Human sin is canceled out in the end by divine retribution.

- Our view of the world is limited and finite, meaning that we are not in a position to judge its overall goodness.

Now, Leibniz, remember, subscribed to the principle of sufficient reason, which logically entails (he thought) that God exists. It also requires that this must be the most perfect of all possible worlds, for otherwise God would not have chosen this world for existence. So Leibniz owed his readers an explanation of how evil got into the picture.

Leibniz's explanation, briefly, was that, for God to create things other than himself, the created things logically must be limited and imperfect. Thus, to the extent that creation is imperfect, it is not wholly good, and thus it is "evil."

If you are real, God, why did you let the Democrats win the election?

This, of course, is a variation of the Problem of Evil (discussed in the text in the section on Leibniz) from a Republican's viewpoint.

Further, Leibniz argued, you have to look at the entire painting. You cannot pronounce it bad if you look at this or that small part, for if you do that, all you will see is a confused mass of colors. Likewise, you have to look at the world from a global perspective and not focus on this or that unpleasant aspect of it.

Not everyone, of course, has found this explanation of evil satisfactory. The optimism expressed in Leibniz's dictum that this is the best of all possible worlds was skewered with dripping sarcasm by Voltaire (1694–1778) in his famous novel *Candide*. Leibniz was of the opinion that one must look at evil from a global perspective, from which unfortunate events might be perceived as part of a larger fabric that, taken as a whole, is a perfect creation. This notion, in Voltaire's opinion, is meaningless from the standpoint of the individual who suffers a dreadful misfortune, and Voltaire had no difficulty in ridiculing it. If you look at the events of the world with a sober eye, Voltaire suggested, you will see anything but a just, harmonious, and ordered place. What you are more likely to see is injustice, strife, and rampant disorder.

"When death crowns the ills of suffering man, what a fine consolation to be eaten by worms," he wrote. You get the idea.

EIGHTEENTH- AND NINETEENTH-CENTURY PERSPECTIVES

Recall now Aquinas's fifth way, a version of the teleological argument, which also often is called the argument from design. The basic idea of this type of proof of God's existence is that the world and its components act for a purpose and thus exhibit design; therefore, the world was created by an intelligent designer. One of the most famous criticisms of the design argument was made by the British empiricist David Hume.

Hume

David Hume (1711–1776) was born some sixty years after Descartes died, during a period of European history that saw the clear emergence of two rivals, science and religion. Between Descartes' *Meditations* and Hume's writings on religion, science had made strong advances, especially in 1687 with the publication of Sir Isaac Newton's *Principia Mathematica*. Although Newton himself did not question God's existence, his system seemed to confirm scientifically what Hobbes earlier had concluded philosophically (see Chapter 6) and what Descartes seemed most to fear: that the universe is an aggregate of matter in motion that has no need of, and leaves no room for, God. Hume's case-hardened doubts about religion could make blood pressures soar, but by the time Hume put them in print, they were by no means considered capital offenses.

Hume's empiricist epistemological principles (if valid) in fact rule out the possibility of any meaningful ontological argument. But this is complicated business and need not detain us, because it is Hume's harsh criticisms of the cosmological and especially the teleological arguments that have been most influential in the philosophy of religion. The most important criticism of the ontological argument comes from Kant, anyway. (Hume's thinking on the subject of miracles has also been influential; we discuss it in the box "Miracles.")

Hume and the Argument from Design   Hume stated the teleological argument (that is, the argument from design) and then went on to criticize it severely. Here is his fair and balanced statement of the argument:

> Look round the world; contemplate the whole and every part of it: you will find it to be nothing but one great machine, subdivided into an infinite number of lesser machines, which again admit of subdivisions, to a degree beyond what human senses and faculties can trace and explain. All these various machines, and even their most minute parts, are adjusted to each other with an accuracy, which ravishes into admiration all men, who have ever contemplated them. The curious adapting of means to ends, throughout all nature, resembles exactly, though it

---

Miracles

Some Christians regard miracles as evidence of divine action. Hume, however, was highly skeptical of reports of miracles.

A miracle, he reasoned, is a violation of a natural law, such as that water flows downhill or that fire consumes wood. Thus, before it is reasonable to accept a report of a miracle as true, the evidence that supports the report must be even stronger than that which has established the natural law.

Because the evidence that a natural law holds is the uniform experience of humankind, it is almost inconceivable that any report of a miracle could be true. Therefore, before it would be reasonable to accept such a report, it would have to be a miracle in its own right for the report to be false. In fact, the report's being false would have to be a *greater* miracle than the miracle it reports.

"No testimony," wrote Hume, "is sufficient to establish a miracle, unless the testimony be of such a kind, that its falsehood would be more miraculous than the fact that it endeavors to establish."

much exceeds, the productions of human contrivance; of human design, thought, wisdom, and intelligence. Since therefore the effects resemble each other, we are led to infer, by all the rules of analogy, that the causes also resemble; and that the Author of Nature is somewhat similar to the mind of men; though possessed of much larger faculties, proportioned to the grandeur of the work, which he has executed. By this argument a posteriori, and by this argument alone, we do prove at once the existence of a Deity, and his similarity to human mind and intelligence.

Now note that in this proof of God, as stated by Hume, the reasoning is from an *effect* (the "world," i.e., the universe) and its parts to its *cause* (God). Further, this is an **argument by analogy,** in which the effect (the world or universe) is likened to a human contrivance, the cause is likened to a human creator, and the mechanism of creation is likened to human thought and intelligence. Hume's criticisms of the proof are mainly related to (1) the appropriateness of these analogies, and (2) the legitimacy of this particular instance of effect-to-cause reasoning.

Hume began his criticism by noticing that, in an effect-to-cause proof, we cannot attribute to the supposed cause any qualities over and beyond those required for the effect. For example, is the world absolutely perfect? Is it free from every error, mistake, or incoherence? No? Then you cannot say that its cause is absolutely perfect either. Does the world reflect infinite wisdom and intelligence? Hume's own opinion was that, at best, the world reflects these qualities to *some degree;* and, therefore, though we perhaps can infer that the cause has these qualities to a similar degree, we are unauthorized to attribute to it these qualities in a higher degree, and we certainly are not authorized to attribute to it these qualities in an *infinite* degree.

We also are not authorized to attribute to it other qualities, such as pure goodness or infinite power. The existence of evil and misery, in Hume's opinion, certainly does *not* indicate that the cause of the world is pure goodness coupled with infinite power. His point was not that the existence of pain and misery necessarily means that the creator of the world is *not* good or omnipotent. Rather, his point was just that, given the existence of evil and misery in the world, we cannot legitimately try to prove that the creator is all-good and all-powerful *by looking at the world.* To do that is to attribute something other to the cause than is found in the effect.

Hume also questioned whether we even *know* how perfect or good the world is. Given the limitations of our position, given that we have no basis for a comparison, can we be sure that the world does not contain great faults? Are we entitled to say that the world deserves considerable praise? If an ignorant chucklehead pronounces the only poem he has ever heard to be artistically flawless, does his opinion count for much?

Further, he noted, in the design proof of God, a cause is inferred from a single effect, namely, the world. But, Hume asked, is it legitimate to infer a cause from a *single* effect? If I learn (to take a modern illustration of the point) that a certain weird kind of sound is caused by a new type of electronic instrument, then when I hear that kind of sound again, I can infer that it was caused by a similar instrument. But if it is the first time I hear the sound, I cannot say much at all about its cause, save perhaps that it was not made by a trombone or guitar. In other words, if we have experience of only a single instance of the effect, as seems to be the case with the world, then it is not clear "that we could form any conjecture or inference at all concerning its cause."

Of course, we have had experience with the building of machines and ships and houses and so forth. But can the world really be compared to any of these? Can we pretend to show much similarity between a house and the universe? To speak of the origin of *worlds,* wrote Hume, "It is not sufficient, surely, that we have seen ships and cities arise from human art and contrivance."

Hume laid a great deal of emphasis on the limitedness of our viewpoint. We, who are but a part of the universe, use our intelligence and thought to build cities and machines. And so we suppose there must be a divine creator who used thought and intelligence to create the universe. But we and our creations are but a tiny aspect of the universe, and human thought and intelligence are just one of hundreds of known principles of activity. Is it legitimate, Hume asked, for us to suppose that the mechanism by which one small aspect of the universe rearranges little bits of wood and steel and dirt is the same mechanism by which *the entire universe* was originally created?

Further, even if we can liken the creation of the world to the building of a house or boat, there is this further problem, said Hume: If we survey a ship, we would be tempted to attribute a great deal of ingenuity to its builder, when in fact its builder may be a beef-brained clod who only copied an art that was perfected over the ages by hundreds of people working through a series of trials, mistakes, corrections, and gradual improvements. Can we be sure the world was not the result of a similar process of trial and error and even intermittent bungling, involving a multitude of lesser "creators"?

For that matter, Hume asked, is it even proper to liken the world to a ship or watch or machine or other human artifact? Is not the world arguably as much like a living organism as a machine? And are not living organisms produced by processes radically different from those by which human artifacts are made?

This, then, is the substance of Hume's complaints about the design argument. Given what seemed to him to be its several difficulties, Hume's own conclusion was just this: There is an apparent order in the universe, and this apparent order provides some slight evidence of a cause or causes bearing some remote analogy to human intelligence. But that is all the evidence warrants, Hume thought.

Hume and the Cosmological Argument

A cosmological argument, in the version Hume examined, says that anything that exists must have a cause (or reason or explanation) that is different from itself. But because the series of causes cannot go to infinity, there must be a first uncaused cause, God. A variation of the basic argument allows that the causal series can go to infinity but still stands in need of an uncaused cause that causes the whole infinite series. In either case, the uncaused cause cannot *not* exist. Thus, the uncaused cause is a **necessary being.**

Hume's objections to these lines of argument were that, *first,* as far as we can make out, the universe may itself be "the necessarily existent being"; *second,* if you maintain that everything has a prior cause, it is *contradictory* also to maintain that there was a first cause; and *third,* if I explain the cause of each member of a series of things, there is no further need for an explanation of the *series itself* as if it were some *further* thing.

A Verbal Dispute?

Hume also had the startling idea that the dispute between theists and atheists might be only a verbal dispute. This was his reasoning:

Hume suggested that atheists and true believers are not all that different in their views.

Theists say that the universe was created by the divine will. But they concede that there is a great and immeasurable difference between the creative activity of the divine mind and mere human thought and its creative activity.

But what do atheists say? They concede that there is some original or fundamental principle of order in the universe, but they insist that this principle can bear only some remote analogy to everyday creative and generative processes or to human intelligence.

Thus, atheist and theist are very close to saying the same thing!

The main difference between them seems to lie only in this, Hume said: The theist is most impressed by the necessity of there being or having been a fundamental principle of order and generation in the universe, whereas the atheist is most impressed by how wildly different such a principle must be from any creative activity with which we are familiar. But then the more pious the theist, the more he will emphasize the difference between divine intelligence and human intelligence; the more he will insist that the workings of God are incomprehensible to mere mortals. The more pious the theist, in short, the more he will be like the atheist!

Kant

This brings us to **Immanuel Kant** (1724–1804), whose contribution to the philosophy of religion equals in importance his work in epistemology and ethics. Kant invented one of the most famous moral arguments for God's existence. But Kant's criticisms of traditional proofs of God have seemed to many commentators to be more cogent than his proof, and in any case they are among the most important criticisms in the literature.

According to Kant, there are only three (traditional) ways of proving God's existence, and none of them works.

What Is Wrong with the Ontological Proof?

First is the ontological argument. Remember that, according to Anselm's version of the argument, God is the greatest being conceivable. Hence, if you suppose that God does not exist, you are supposing that the greatest being conceivable is not the greatest being conceivable, and that is nonsense. According to Descartes' version, God possesses all perfections, and because existence is a perfection, God exists.

Now, we are sure you will agree there is something very sneaky about the ontological argument, in any version. It seems intuitively wrong, somehow; yet it is difficult to pin down exactly what the problem is.

Kant provided a criticism that has withstood the test of time, though in recent years there have been challenges to it. What is wrong with the argument, Kant said, is that it assumes that *existence is a* predicate, *that is, a characteristic or an attribute*. Because Anselm assumed that existence is a characteristic, he could argue that a being that lacked existence lacked an important characteristic and thus could not be the greatest being conceivable. Because Descartes assumed that existence is a characteristic, he could argue that God, who by definition possesses all perfections, necessarily possesses the characteristic of existence.

But existence, said Kant, is not a characteristic at all. Rather, it is a *precondition* of having characteristics. Is there any difference between a warm day and an *existing* warm day? If you state that the potato salad is salty, do you further characterize the salad if you state that it is salty *and exists?* If you tell the mechanic that your tire is flat, do you further enlighten him if you add that the tire also *exists?* The answer to all such questions, in Kant's view, is obviously "no." To say of something that it exists is not to characterize it: existence is not a predicate.

So, to apply this lesson first to Descartes: Existence is *not* a perfection or any other kind of characteristic. Certainly, *if* there *is* a being that possesses all perfections,

Our cars are all mechanically sound, come with a six-month written guarantee, and exist.

USED CARS

Kant argued that existence is not a characteristic and that you do not enlarge a description of a thing to say that it exists. Of course, you may wish to assert that something—God, say, or ghosts—exists, but that sort of assertion is not really a description, Kant would maintain.

then God exists, for existence is a precondition of something's having any perfections at all. But this fact does not mean that God actually exists.

And to apply this lesson to Anselm: Existence is not a characteristic, and so it is not one that belongs to greatness. Certainly, *if* the greatest being conceivable exists, then God exists, because God by definition is that being, and something cannot possess any aspect of greatness without existing. But that fact does not mean that such a being exists.

What Is Wrong with the Cosmological and Teleological Proofs?

The second way of proving God's existence, according to Kant, is the cosmological argument, which, he asserted, reduces to this: If something exists, an absolutely necessary being must likewise exist. I, at least, exist. Therefore, an absolutely necessary being exists.

This is certainly a simple and streamlined version of the cosmological argument compared with the arguments set forth by Aquinas, Descartes, Leibniz, and Hume. Unfortunately, Kant, who generally did not try to make things easy for his reader, made up for this unusual lapse into simplicity and clarity by submitting the argument to several pages of exceedingly subtle and confusing analysis.

Kant's basic criticisms of the cosmological argument, however, were two: First, the argument really rests on the ontological argument. His explanation of why and how this is so is notoriously obscure and probably unsound; let's just let it go. Second, and more important anyway, the argument employs a principle (that everything contingent has a cause) that has significance only in the *experienced* world. The argument then uses that principle, Kant maintained, to arrive at a conclusion that goes beyond experience. (Kant, as we tried to make clear in Chapter 7, believed that causality is a concept applicable only to things-as-experienced. Why Kant held this position is too complicated to repeat here, but his case against the cosmological argument rests on his being correct about causality, which some people are inclined to doubt.)

The third and final way of trying to prove God's existence, according to Kant, is the teleological argument, the argument that cites the purposiveness and harmonious adaptation of nature as proof of the divine designer. Kant's main criticism was that at best the argument proves only the existence of an *architect* who *works* with the matter of the world, and not a creator. A similar line of thinking was found in Hume, as we saw.

Belief in God Rationally Justified

Despite Kant's criticisms of the three traditional proofs for God's existence, Kant believed in God. Further, amazingly to some, he thought this belief is rationally justified for any moral agent. Here, as almost always, his thinking is complicated, but what he had in mind was this:

Although we do not have theoretical or metaphysical knowledge of God, although we cannot prove or demonstrate that God exists, we must view the world *as if* it were created by God. Why? Because, Kant said, only if we assume the existence of God can we believe that virtue will be rewarded with happiness. Virtue, Kant held, is worthiness to be happy and is the supreme good. But without believing in God, the virtuous individual cannot be certain that the happiness of which he is worthy will in fact be his or that, in general, a person's happiness will be proportionate to his moral worth.

Thus, in Kant's opinion, God's existence cannot be proved but can and must rationally be assumed by a moral agent. That God exists, Kant said, is a postulate of *practical* reason. This particular argument for assuming that God exists is another version of the moral argument that we first encountered with Aquinas.

Kierkegaard

It is interesting to contrast Kant's philosophy with that of the Danish philosopher **Søren Kierkegaard** (1813–1855), who was born a little before Kant died. Neither philosopher thought you could rationally prove God exists. But the similarity between the two ends there.

For Kierkegaard, "to exist" is to be engaged in time and history. Because God is an eternal and immutable being, "existence" does not even apply to God. But God as Christ existed, for Kierkegaard. Christ, however, is a paradox that the human intellect cannot comprehend, for in Christ the immutable became changing, the eternal became temporal, and what is beyond history became historical.

In short, Kierkegaard thought that God is beyond the grasp of reason and that the idea that God came to us as a man in the person of Jesus is intellectually absurd. Yet, at the same time, Kierkegaard's primary mission was to show what it is to be a Christian, and he himself was totally committed to Christianity. How can this be?

First, the notion that we can sit back and weigh objectively the evidence about God's existence pro and contra, that we can conduct an impartial investigation of the issue and arrive at the "truth," was totally rejected by Kierkegaard. He would not have bothered reading this chapter.

In fact, Kierkegaard mocked the whole idea of objective truth as giving meaning to life. Truth, he said, is subjective. Truth lies not in *what* you believe, but in *how you live*. Truth is passionate commitment. For example, think of a person who worships the "true" God but does so merely as a matter of routine, without passion or commitment. Compare this person with one who worships a mere idol but does so with the infinite commitment of his soul. In fact, said Kierkegaard, "The one prays in truth to God though he worships an idol; the other prays falsely to the true God, and hence worships in fact an idol."

Second, Kierkegaard rejected completely the Aristotelian idea that the essential attribute of humans is their capacity to reason. For Kierkegaard, the most important attribute of man was not thought but *will*. Man is a being that *makes choices*.

But if truth is not objective, then there are no external principles or criteria that are objectively valid and against which one might judge one's choices. How, then, are we to choose, if there are no objective, rational criteria, and we have only our own judgment to rely on? This problem—the problem of knowing how and what to choose in the absence of objective truth—became, after Kierkegaard, the central problem of existentialism.

Kierkegaard's answer was that we must commit ourselves totally to God. Salvation can be had only through a **leap of faith,** through a nonintellectual, passionate, "infinite" commitment to Christianity. "Faith constitutes a sphere all by itself, and every misunderstanding of Christianity may at once be recognized by its transforming it into a doctrine, transferring it to the sphere of the intellectual."

God's Foreknowledge and Free Will

God supposedly knows everything. So whatever you did, he knew before you did it that you would do it. Did you sleep late this morning? God knew that you would.

And that means that you could not have *not* slept late this morning, because God knew that you would sleep late. And if you could not have not slept late, then in what sense did you sleep late of your own free will? See the problem? It seems that the view that God knows everything conflicts with the idea that you have free will.

This problem is sometimes dismissed by beginning philosophy students as "merely verbal" or as "easily solved." If this is true, it will come as news to the heavyweight philosophers and theologians who have grappled with it, including Paul, Augustine, Luther, Calvin, and others. It is because they saw the logical implications of crediting God with omniscience (all-knowingness) that Calvinists (followers of the great sixteenth-century Protestant theologian John Calvin), for example, believed that God must preordain who will be saved and who will be damned.

What Kierkegaard said must not be confused with what earlier Christian thinkers had maintained. Earlier Christian thinkers had said that faith precedes understanding and had held that you must have faith in God before rational thought about him can begin. But thinkers such as Augustine and Anselm had still looked for, and had fully expected there to be, rational grounds for confirming what they already accepted by faith. Kierkegaard, in contrast, thought that no such rational grounds exist: God is an intellectual absurdity.

Further, he held that rational grounds for believing in God, if there were any, would actually be *incompatible* with having faith. "If I wish to preserve myself in faith I must constantly be intent upon holding fast to the *objective uncertainty* [of God]," he said. The objective uncertainty of God, for Kierkegaard, is thus essential to a true faith in him. Only if there is objective uncertainty, he wrote, can "[I] remain out upon the deep, over seventy thousand fathoms of water, still preserving my faith."

Nietzsche

"God is dead," said Nietzsche. By this infamous remark, **Friedrich Nietzsche** (1844–1900) did not mean that God once existed and now no longer does. He meant that all people with an ounce of intelligence would now perceive that there is no intelligent plan to the universe or rational order in it: they would now understand that there is no reason why things happen one way and not another and that the harmony and order we imagine to exist in the universe is merely pasted on by the human mind.

Nietzsche, however, would have regarded very few people as having this required ounce of intelligence, and he in fact had a way of denigrating everyone in sight. For the mass of people, Nietzsche thought, God certainly is not dead. But these people, in Nietzsche's opinion, are pathetic wretches governed by a worldview inculcated by religion, science, and philosophy, a worldview that in Nietzsche's opinion makes them feeble losers who are motivated mainly by

Religion: Illusion with a Future

Religion, according to the founder of psychoanalysis, Sigmund Freud (1856–1939), is an exercise in mass delusion and serves mainly to keep people in a state of psychological infantilism. Religion is wish-fulfillment; it offers up the "figure of an enormously exalted father" who reassures us as our own fathers did. The infallible and omnipotent father in heaven assures us that there is meaning and purpose in life and that all will be well in the end. However, although religion enables us to retain our status as children throughout our lives, it is a dangerous illusion. Religion intimidates intelligence with its demands for unconditional submission to inscrutable laws and keeps us from distinguishing between fact and wishful thinking. It does this even when philosophers and theologians try to salvage the illusion by redefining God as an "impersonal, shadowy and abstract principle."

Sometimes belief in religion is fostered by the psychological feeling of the oneness of everything. Such "oceanic feelings," according to Freud, are just a recurrence of the limitless narcissism typical of early childhood. Freud thought human beings would be happier if they retained a modicum of reality in their thinking and cultivated their own gardens, as Voltaire had suggested.

resentment. They view the world as a rational, law-governed place and adhere to a slave morality that praises the man who serves his fellow creatures with meekness and self-sacrifice.

In Nietzsche's opinion, the negative morality of these pitiful slaves—the mass of humankind, ordinary people—must be reevaluated and replaced by life-affirming values. The new morality will be based on the development of a new kind of human being, whom Nietzsche calls the *Übermensch* ("overman" or "superman"). Such a one not only accepts life in all its facets, including all its pain, but also makes living into an art. Among the forerunners of the overman, Nietzsche cited Alexander the Great and Napoleon.

Nietzsche's thesis that there is no God and its apparent corollary, that there are no absolute and necessary criteria of right and wrong, were accepted by such twentieth-century existentialist philosophers as Albert Camus and Jean-Paul Sartre. For these thinkers, the fundamental problem of philosophy is how to live one's life, given the absence of absolutely valid standards by which to evaluate one's choices and decisions.

Nietzsche, Kierkegaard, and some existentialists would all have agreed that the various rational discussions about God's existence to which this chapter is devoted are impotent and meaningless. (However, for an interesting alternative view, you might like to read the box "Religion: Illusion with a Future," which discusses the views of Sigmund Freud.)

James

William James (1842–1910) published his first major work, *The Will to Believe and Other Essays*, in 1897. By the year 1900, there was a marked increase in agnosticism and antagonism between the religious view of the world as a divinely created paradise planned for the sake of human spiritual growth and the supposedly scientific

PROFILE: William James (1842–1910)

Few philosophers have been better writers than William James, whose catchy phrases gave life and succulence to even the driest philosophical subjects. James had a knack for words, and he was able to state complex ideas with easy elegance. This might be expected because James was the older brother of Henry James, the great American novelist.

The James children were raised by their wealthy and eccentric theologian father in an intellectually stimulating atmosphere that promoted their mental development. The Jameses benefited from diverse educational experiences in several schools both in America and in Europe and were largely free to pursue their own interests and develop their own capacities. They became refined and cosmopolitan.

William James had wide-ranging interests. Though fascinated with science, he decided, at age eighteen, to try to become a painter. But he was also wise enough to see very soon that his artistic urge exceeded his ability.

So James went off to Harvard and studied science. Then he entered the college's medical school, though he did not intend to practice medicine, and in his late twenties he received his medical degree. A few years later, he joined the Harvard faculty as a lecturer on anatomy and physiology and continued to teach at Harvard until 1907. From 1880 on, he was a member of the Harvard Department of Philosophy and Psychology. You should not think that James got interested in philosophy all of a sudden. He had always been fond of the subject and tended to give a philosophical interpretation to scientific questions.

James suffered from emotional crises until he was able to resolve the question of free will and to answer the compelling arguments for determinism. Around 1870, in the ideas of the French philosopher Charles Renouvier, he found philosophical justification for believing in free will, and with it, apparently, the cure to his episodes of emotional paralysis.

In 1890, James published his famous *Principles of Psychology*, thought by many to be his major work. Equally important from a purely philosophical standpoint is his *The Will to Believe and Other Essays in Popular Philosophy* (1897). In this work is James's solution to the problem of free will, in the essay "The Dilemma of Determinism." Other important works include *The Varieties of Religious Experience* (1902), *Pragmatism* (1907), *A Pluralistic Universe* (1909), *The Meaning of Truth* (1909), *Some Problems in Philosophy* (1911), and *Essays in Radical Empiricism* (1912).

William James was perhaps the most famous American intellectual of his time. Yet today some philosophers think of him as a lightweight—a popularizer of philosophical issues who failed to make a substantial contribution to technical philosophy (whatever that is). He is thought to bear the same relation to Hume or Kant, say, that Tchaikovsky bears to Mozart or Bach, the philosophical equivalent of the composer who only cranks out pretty melodies. But this is all a mistake. The discerning reader will find in James a great depth of insight.

view of the cosmos as a blind churning of material particles in accordance with physical laws. Over the past two hundred years, the blind-churning view had become more and more congenial to Western intellectuals. Around mid-century, Darwin had explained how the origin of species need not be divine, and Karl Marx had pronounced religion to be the opiate of the people. Hume and Kant did not force philosophers to question the old proofs of God, the times did. Before the end of the century, Friedrich Nietzsche could proclaim that God was dead.

But God was not, and is not, dead for everyone. In fact, for very many, the question of God's existence was at the time, and still is (1) a *live* issue and furthermore (2) a *momentous* one. For William James it was both. It was also, according to James, (3) *forced*, which means you cannot suspend judgment in the matter. For James, to profess agnosticism and to pretend to suspend judgment is in fact "backing the field against the religious hypothesis" (that is, deciding against God).

James argued for deciding the issue of God's existence in favor of God. He began his argument, not a simple one, by noting that "*our nonintellectual nature does influence our convictions.*" Indeed, usually our convictions are *determined* by our nonintellectual or "passional" nature, rather than by reason, he maintained. Sometimes we even deliberately will what we believe, James held.

Having argued that our nonintellectual nature influences our opinions, James next distinguished between the *two commandments* of rational thinkers. These are

1. to believe the truth
2. to avoid errors

Some individuals, James noted, favor (2) over (1): they would rather avoid errors than find the truth. "Better go without belief forever than believe a falsehood" is the creed dictated to them by their passional nature: better dead than misled. But favoring (2) over (1) is not James's creed. There are worse things than falling into error, he said. In some cases, he argued, it is best to regard "the chase for truth as paramount, and the avoidance of error as secondary."

It is this way in religious matters, he said. When it comes to religion it is better to yield to the hope that all of it may be true than to give way to the fear of being in error. If you permit the fear of error to rule you and say to yourself, "Avoid error at any cost!" then you will withhold assent to religious beliefs. Doing so will, of course, *protect* you from being in error—if the religious beliefs are incorrect. But if you withhold your assent to religious beliefs, then you will also *lose the benefits* that come from accepting those beliefs. And it is worse, James thought, to lose the benefits than to gain the protection from erring.

Further, if the religious beliefs are *true* but the evidence for them is insufficient, then the policy "Avoid error at any cost!" effectively cuts you off from an opportunity to make friends with God. Thus, in James's opinion, the policy "Avoid error at all cost!"—when applied to religion—is a policy that keeps you from accepting certain propositions even if those propositions are really true, and that means that it is an irrational policy.

James stressed that he was *not* saying that you should believe what, as he put it, "you know ain't true." His strategy applies, he said, only to *momentous* and *living* issues that cannot be resolved by the intellect itself. It applies only to issues like God's existence.

Applying the same strategy to the question of whether we have free will, James focused not directly on the question itself but rather on the outcomes that attend acceptance of the alternative viewpoints. Acceptance of determinism is unsatisfactory, James believed, because it entails never regretting what happens (what happened had to happen, according to determinism, so it is illogical to feel that it should not have happened). Thus, acceptance of determinism is inconsistent with the practices of moral beings, who perceive themselves as making genuine choices that can affect the world for better or for worse.

TWENTIETH-CENTURY PERSPECTIVES

James's reasoning elicited much criticism. Skeptics and believers both took issue with it. Skeptics thought James had elevated wishful thinking to the status of proof, and believers questioned James's implicit assumption that God's existence cannot be established. Still others said that belief grounded in James's way was not the uncompromising and unqualified faith in God demanded by religion. From their perspective, James's belief in God amounted to a gamble akin to **Pascal's wager** (see the box on the next page) rather than to true religious acceptance of God.

James in any event takes us into the twentieth and twenty-first centuries, and we shall now consider more recent discussions of God's existence. The first is something like an argument that God does not exist, but in actuality it is an argument that the whole issue is pretty meaningless to begin with.

God and Logical Positivism

In the late 1920s, a group of philosophers, mathematicians, and scientists led by Moritz Schlick, a philosopher at the University of Vienna, set forth a group of ideas known as **logical positivism.** A central tenet of this **Vienna Circle** and of logical positivism, as we saw in Chapter 9, is the **verifiability principle,** according to which the factual meaning of a proposition is the experience you must have to know it is true. What does it mean to say, "The sprinkler is on"? Well, to find out whether that proposition is true, you would have to look out the window or go out into the yard or otherwise do some checking. The experience required to do the checking is what the proposition means, according to the verifiability principle.

What this principle entails is that a pronouncement that is not verifiable has no factual meaning. Take the remark "The sprinkler stopped working due to fate." What kind of checking would you do to see whether this was true? There is no experience a person might have that would verify this remark. Therefore, it is factually meaningless, the logical positivists would say.

Of course, some propositions are true by virtue of what their words mean: for example, "You are older than everyone who is younger than you." Such *analytic propositions,* as they are called, are rendered true by definition rather than by experience, according to the logical positivists. But the proposition "The sprinkler stopped working due to fate" is not like that. It is not an analytic proposition, so it has to be verifiable in experience if it is to have factual meaning. And because it is not, it does not.

So, according to the logical positivists, the many philosophical assertions from metaphysics, epistemology, and ethics that are neither analytic nor verifiable are factually meaningless. These assertions may perhaps express emotional sentiments, but they are neither true nor false. Rudolph Carnap (1891–1970), one of the most famous members of the Vienna Circle, even declared, "We reject *all* philosophical questions, whether of Metaphysics, Ethics or Epistemology."

Today, few philosophers would call themselves logical positivists, for reasons mentioned in Chapter 9. But most philosophers would still maintain that *empirical* or *factual* propositions must in *some* sense and to *some* extent be verifiable by experience.

Pascal's Wager

The French mathematician and philosopher Blaise Pascal (1623–1662) is famous, among other reasons, for his wager–argument for God. Either God exists or he does not. By believing that he exists, you lose nothing if he does not, and you gain a lot, namely, happiness and eternal life, if he does. So believing that God exists is a prudent wager; you will not lose anything, and you might gain much.

James denied that he was offering a version of Pascal's wager in his argument for the existence of God. You may wish to consider whether his denial is warranted.

So what, then, about assertions such as "God exists" or "God loves us"? These look like factual propositions. But are they in any sense verifiable? A reading by Antony Flew at the end of the chapter addresses the issue from a positivist perspective, according to which the utterances "God exists" and "God does not exist" are both meaningless.

In recent years Professor Flew abandoned his "atheistic" position. His recent book *There Is a God,* published in 2007 and written with Roy Abraham Varghese, is what Flew called his last will and testament. In it he proclaimed, "I now believe there is a God!" His major reasons? God provides the best explanation of how the laws of nature came to be, how life originated from nonlife, and how the universe came into existence.

Unfortunately, controversy exists as to how much of the book represents Flew's own thinking and how much represents the opinion of his coauthor. The arguments presented in the book stand or fall on their own merits, however.[1]

Mary Daly: The Unfolding of God

An entirely different line of thinking about God is evident in what contemporary feminist scholar **Mary Daly** (1928–2010) said on the subject in *Beyond God the Father* (1973).

The biblical and popular image of God as a *great father in heaven,* Daly wrote, a father who rewards and punishes according to his mysterious and seemingly arbitrary will, arose in patriarchal societies. Furthermore, according to Daly, the image serves patriarchal society by making mechanisms for the oppression of women seem right and fitting. "If God in 'his' heaven is a father ruling 'his' people, then it is in the 'nature' of things and according to divine plan and the order of the universe that society be male-dominated." Given the biblical and popular image of God, "the husband dominating his wife represents God himself." "If God is male, then the male is God."

This image of God as Lord and Father, which has been sustained "by the usual processes of producing plausibility such as preaching and religious indoctrination," perpetuates the artificial polarization of human qualities into the traditional sexual stereotypes, Daly maintained. This image of the person in authority and the popular

---

[1] For supposed evidence that Flew was in a state of mental decline when he wrote the book, see http://www.nytimes.com/2007/11/04/magazine/04Flew-t.html?_r=1.

Is this your image of God? Mary Daly thinks it probably is NOT, and she thinks that fact is important.

understanding of "his" role continually renew the eternal masculine stereotypes. They also nourish and justify domination and manipulation both toward persons and toward the environment. They perpetuate the eternal female stereotypes of emotionalism, passivity, self-abnegation, and the like.

Of course, a defender of the traditional image of God will probably protest that God is popularly conceived also as love. But, according to Mary Daly, the concept of God as love is split with the image of the "vengeful God who represents his chosen people." This split has perpetuated a double standard of behavior. God, she wrote, is like Vito Corleone of *The Godfather,* a "marriage of tenderness and violence blended in the patriarchal ideal." Given this image, worshipers feel justified in being intolerant. Thus, we should not be surprised by the numerous examples of fanatical believers who cruelly persecute "those outside the sacred circle." Nor should we be surprised when those who are anointed by society—scientists and leaders, for example—are given the blessings of priests for inventing and using napalm and the like to perpetrate atrocities.

Now, when Daly's view is compacted as it is here, it may perhaps seem like an angry and exaggerated diatribe. But Daly countered that it would surely be unrealistic *not* to believe that the instruments for symbolism and communication, which include the whole theological tradition in world religions, have been formulated by males under the conditions of patriarchy. It is therefore "inherent in these symbolic and linguistic structures that they serve the purposes of patriarchal social arrangements." If further proof is needed, one need merely consider (she said) the blatant misogynism of religious "authorities" from Augustine to Aquinas, Luther, Knox, and Barth, which has "simply been ignored or dismissed as trivial."

The problem, then, Daly said, is how to transform "the collective imagination so that this distortion of the human aspiration to transcendence loses its credibility." The

God Is Coming, and She Is Furious

So says the bumper sticker.

Most people who believe in God think of God as, in some sense or another, a male.

But in what sense is God a male? Certainly not in the sense that he possesses male genetic or anatomic features. And it seems doubtful that the qualities we attribute to him are uniquely male. For example, God, it is said, is knowing, loving, caring. But these are not uniquely male characteristics.

Even the qualities associated with God when he is viewed as like an earthly ruler are not uniquely male qualities. Queens, too, can be beneficent, just, powerful, and wise rulers. And the concept of God as the creator of the heavens and earth—that concept seems to call to mind nonhuman properties as much as anything else.

So our custom of speaking of God in the masculine voice is largely honorific. We honor God by speaking and thinking of him as a male: God is the best there is; therefore, God is not female or neuter.

But honoring God by referring to him as "he" implies we think there is something inferior about not being a male. If God is defined as male, everything outside maleness is automatically inferior. For this reason, various feminist philosophers have been more than casually interested in the question, Why is God thought to be a male?—and in the possible harmful social consequences of our internalized ideas about **God's gender.**

---

question is how to "cut away the Supreme Phallus": "God"—the word, the image—must be *castrated*. Why, indeed, Daly wrote, must "God" even be a *noun?* Why not a verb—the "most active and dynamic verb of all," the "Verb of Verbs," the verb infinitely more personal than a mere static noun, the verb that conveys that God is "Be-ing"? "God," as an intransitive verb, she wrote, would not be conceived as an object—which implies limitation—for God as Be-ing is contrasted only with nonbeing.

But the confrontation with "the structured evil of patriarchy" must go beyond mere tinkering with the language used to talk about God, she said. To stop at that level, she wrote, would be to trivialize the "deep problem of human becoming in women."

And just what *is* the "deep problem of becoming"? It is a striving toward psychic wholeness, toward self-realization, toward self-transcendence—becoming who we really are. This becoming of women requires existential courage, Daly wrote, to confront the experience of *nothingness*. It is a "radical confrontation" with nothingness. We are all threatened by nonbeing, she wrote, and the only solution is self-actualization—not denial of self. An example of such denial of self provided by Daly is the woman who "singlemindedly accepts the role of housewife." This individual "may to some extent avoid the experience of nothingness, but she also avoids a fuller participation in being which would be her only real security." "Submerged in such a role, she cannot achieve a breakthrough to creativity." The women's revolution must, therefore, ultimately be religious. It must reach "outward and inward toward the God beyond and beneath the gods who have stolen our identity."

According to Daly, three false "demons dressed as God" especially need expurgation: the God of "explanation," who legitimizes suffering as due to God's will; God the Judge, whose chief activity lies in issuing after-death rewards and promises compensation for women's subjugation in this life; and, closely related, God the Judge of Sin, who maintains "false consciences and self-destructive guilt feelings." This last god enforces the rules of the patriarchal game (and is most blatant in arch-conservative religions, Daly wrote).

Does this seem angry? From Daly's perspective, women are dealing with "demonic power relationships" and "structured evil"; therefore, rage is *required* as a positive creative force. Anger, she wrote, "can trigger and sustain movement from the experience of nothingness to recognition of participation in being." According to Daly,

> When women take positive steps to move out of patriarchal space and time, there is a surge of new life. I would analyze this as participation in God the Verb who cannot be broken down simply into past, present, and future time, since God is form-destroying, form-creating, transforming power that makes all things new.

Intelligent Design or Evolution?

The publication in 1859 of Charles Darwin's *On the Origin of Species by Means of Natural Selection; or, the Preservation of Favoured Races in the Struggle for Life* (usually referred to as *On the Origin of Species*) provoked responses from within Catholicism and conservative Protestantism. Pope Pius IX declared evolution a heresy in 1870 (though in 1996, in a message to the Pontifical Academy of Sciences, Pope John Paul II observed that, while the occurrence of evolution is more than a theory, "theories of evolution which, in accordance with the philosophies inspiring them, consider the mind as emerging from the forces of living matter . . . are incompatible with the truth about man"). In 1874 Princeton theologian Charles Hodge, a Presbyterian, asked, "What is Darwinism?" and answered, "It is atheism."

Historian George Marsden, writing in 1984, found that, twenty years after the publication of *On the Origin of Species*, Bible-believing American Protestant scientists and even conservative theologians did not make opposition to all forms of evolution a necessary test of faith. But reconciliationist positions began to lose favor in the evangelical community after the Scopes "monkey trial," July 10–21, 1925, in Dayton, Tennessee.

Many fundamentalists retreated to a Christian subculture. Bible schools flourished, and many taught human origins from a perspective dubbed "creation-science."

Contemporary defenders include John D. Morris of the Institute for Creation Research (ICR) in El Cajon, California, who wrote in a 1992 newsletter article that evolution "embraces strict naturalism, an anti-God philosophy, and results in a denial of the major doctrines of Scripture. . . . If no supernatural agency has been at work throughout history, then creation is dead. But if evolutionists even allow a spark of supernatural design in history, then evolution is dead, for evolution necessarily relies on solely natural processes."

In the 1990s, three controversial books were published, spearheading the intelligent design movement. **Intelligent design** is the idea that a complete explanation of the universe requires positing an intelligent designer. The three books were: *Darwin on Trial* (first published in 1991) by Phillip E. Johnson (a graduate of Harvard University who has taught law at University of California, Berkeley, for more than three decades); *Darwin's Black Box: The Biochemical Challenge to Evolution* (1996) by Lehigh University biochemist Michael J. Behe; and *Intelligent Design: The Bridge between Science and Theology* (1999) by William A. Dembski, holder of a doctorate in mathematics from the University of Chicago and a doctorate in philosophy from the University of Illinois at Chicago, whose more technical treatment of the subject had been published by Cambridge University Press the year before.

Johnson, Behe, and Dembski, leaders of the intelligent design movement, rejected the "young earth" position of ICR in favor of a more academically engaged critique of Darwinian foundations. In an essay published in the *New York Times* in 1996, Behe wrote that the theory of evolution founders in explaining cellular development. "Many cellular systems are what I term 'irreducibly complex.' That means the system needs several components before it can work properly. An everyday example of irreducible complexity is a mousetrap, built of several pieces (platform, hammer, spring and so on). Such a system probably cannot be put together in a Darwinian manner, gradually improving its function. You can't catch a mouse with just the platform and then catch a few more by adding the spring. All the pieces have to be in place before you catch any mice."

For Dembski, irreducible complexity is a specific case of a more general understanding of how to detect intelligent, as opposed to mere natural, causes: "Whenever we infer design, we must establish three things: *contingency, complexity* and *specification.* Contingency ensures that the object in question is not the result of an automatic and therefore unintelligent process that had no choice in its production. Complexity ensures that the object is not so simple that it can readily be explained by chance. Finally, specification ensures that the object exhibits the type of pattern characteristic of intelligence."

Evolutionary biologist Richard Dawkins, in *The Blind Watchmaker* (1986) and other works, responded that any appearance of purpose in biological systems is merely the result of time and chance. "To 'tame' chance means to break down the very improbable into less improbable small components arranged in series. No matter how improbable it is that an X could have arisen from a Y in a single step, it is always possible to conceive of a series of infinitesimally graded intermediates between them. However improbable a large-scale change may be, smaller changes are less improbable."

Johnson focused on a critique of evolutionism's materialist assumptions, what he called "methodological naturalism." The chemical or physical laws of nature, he wrote, "produce simple repetitive order, and chance produces meaningless disorder. When combined, law and chance work against each other to prevent the emergence of a meaningful sequence. In all human experience, only intelligent agency can write an encyclopedia or computer program." Dawkins's blind watchmaker (natural selection and mutation) cannot, Johnson insisted, create complex *new* genetic information. Johnson also presented a version of the claim that materialism is self-refuting. (The argument was popularized by the British writer C. S. Lewis and adopted by the American analytic philosopher Alvin Plantinga.) Johnson asked sarcastically, "If unthinking matter causes the thoughts the materialists *don't* like, then what causes the thoughts they *do* like?" This takes us back to the problem of explanation. The materialist must explain human reason, and indeed the existence of anything at all, in terms of "unthinking matter." If, for Dawkins, the appearance of purpose in evolution is merely an illusion, then what is the status of purposive human reason? If that, too, is an illusion, then there is no good reason to accept the argument. If it is not illusion, how can Dawkins explain the rise of genuine purpose or meaning from a purposeless flow of cause and effect?

In recent years, proponents of intelligent design and creationism have won and lost battles to make inroads in public education. Most notably, in 1999, the Kansas Board of Education, reflecting the views of its conservative majority, wrote new state science standards that ushered creationism back into mainstream debate. The board mandated the teaching of so-called microevolution (changes within species) as illustrative of the working of natural selection. But the teaching of macroevolution (the origin of new organs or species) was made optional at the district level. In the revised document, science was no longer defined as human activity that seeks natural explanations but as one that seeks logical explanations.

Two years later, however, in 2001, after an election that changed its composition, the Kansas school board reversed its earlier course. Evolution was reinstated "as a broad, unifying theoretical framework in biology." But then elections in 2002 and 2004 changed the board again, and it again became more conservative. In 2005, the board approved science standards declaring that basic Darwinian theory is challenged by fossil evidence and molecular biology and rewrote the definition of science so that it was no longer limited to the search for natural explanations. The vote was regarded as a victory for advocates of intelligent design. But in the summer of 2006, when five of the ten seats on the board were up for election in the state's primary election, the conservatives who had approved the standards again lost control of the Board of Education.

In another famous school board case, in October 2004 the board of the Dover (Pennsylvania) Area School District, about twenty-five miles from Philadelphia, became the first in the nation to require high school science teachers to teach the concept of intelligent design as an alternative to the theory of evolution. The next month, however, voters in the district ousted the eight school board members who were up for reelection. And right after that, in December, eleven parents filed a lawsuit challenging the policy. U.S. District Judge John Jones, an appointee of President George W. Bush (who backed the teaching of intelligent design), ruled that teaching intelligent design would violate the constitutional separation of church and state. Intelligent design, Jones held, is an untestable hypothesis grounded in religion and has no place in the science classroom. He described the school board's decision as "breathtaking inanity" and those on the board who supported it as an "ill-informed faction."

In 2009, the Texas Board of Education made changes in the language in the state's curriculum that are thought to make it harder for creationism to be taught in Texas public schools.

God, the Fine-Tuner

In a recent book, Martin Rees, the Royal Astronomer of England, identified six numbers that are a "recipe for the universe." N, for example, represents the strength of the forces that hold atoms together divided by the force of gravity between them. This and the other five numbers have an unusual property: they are precisely tuned for our universe to be. If any of them were the teensiest bit different, the universe could not have existed and observers would not be here to talk about them.[2]

---

[2] Martin Rees, *Just Six Numbers* (New York, Basic Books, 2000), pp. 1–4. See also John Leslie's *Universes* (New York: Routledge, 1989), Chapters 2 and 3.

On the face of it, it might seem unlikely that such remarkable fine-tuning could happen simply by chance. It is as if the six fundamental control knobs of the universe were set exactly right for stars, life, and observers to evolve. The knobs seem to have been set for our eventual arrival. The best explanation of this fine-tuning, according to some philosophers and scientists, is that the universe was created by a cosmic intelligence.

At the end of this chapter is an excerpt from Richard Dawkins's book, *The God Delusion,* in which Dawkins considers this fine-tuning argument.

Who Needs Reasons for Believing in God?

For a belief to be rational, must we have supporting evidence for its truth? Maybe not, if the belief is a **basic belief,** a belief that is not inferred from evidence or from other beliefs but rather itself provides the rational foundation from which other beliefs are derived. For example, it seems rational to believe that there is an external world, that the past existed, and that other people have minds. Yet do we believe these things on the basis of evidence? On the contrary (it might be argued), we accept these beliefs just straight out and without evidence. Further, it is because we accept these things that we can even talk of evidence and rational inference in the first place. For example, unless we assume there was a past, the "evidence" we have that the car *now* has a flat because it ran over a nail does not make any sense— because without a past, there was no past for the car to have done anything.

Contemporary analytic philosopher **Alvin Plantinga** [PLAN-tin-guh] (1932–) has argued that the theist may accept the belief in God as a "basic belief," a belief that it is rational to hold without supporting evidence and that is foundational for the entire system of the theist's beliefs. Rationally speaking, the theist has the right, Plantinga suggests, to *start from* belief in God. The belief need not be an *end product* of justification and inference.

Interested? An easy-to-read essay by Plantinga titled "Advice to Christian Philosophers" may be found in the journal *Faith and Philosophy,* vol. 1, no. 3 (July 1984), pp. 253–271.

SELECTION 13.1
Proslogion★

St. Anselm

[*This passage is St. Anselm's famous ontological argument.*]

★ From *Problems in Philosophical Inquiry,* 1st edition, by Julius R. Weinberg and Keith E. Yandell. Copyright © 1971. Reprinted with permission of Wadsworth, a division of Thomson Learning: www.thomsonrights.com. Fax 800 730-2215.

Lord, who gives understanding to faith give to me as much as you deem suitable, that I may understand that You are as we believe You to be, and that You are what we believe You to be. Now we believe that You are something than which nothing greater can be thought. But perhaps there is no such nature since "the fool hath said in his heart: There is no

God"? But surely this very same fool, when he hears what I say: "something than which nothing greater can be thought," understands what he hears, and what he understands is in his mind, even if he does not understand that it exists. For it is one thing for a thing to be in the mind, but something else to understand that a thing exists. For when a painter pre-thinks what is about to be made, he has it in mind but he does not yet understand that it exists because he has not yet made it. But when he has already painted it, he both has it in his mind and also understands that it exists because he has already made it. Hence, even the fool is convinced that something exists in the mind than which nothing greater can be thought, because when he hears this he understands and whatever is understood is in the mind. But surely that than which a greater cannot be thought cannot exist merely in the mind. For if it exists merely in the mind, it can be thought to exist also in reality which is greater. So if that than which a greater cannot be thought exists merely in the mind, that very same thing than which a greater cannot be thought is something than which a greater can be thought. But surely this cannot be. Hence, without doubt, something than which a greater cannot be thought exists both in the mind and in reality.

Indeed, it exists so truly that it cannot be thought not to be. For something can be thought to exist which cannot be thought not to exist, which is greater than what can be thought not to exist. So, if that than which a greater cannot be thought can be thought not to exist, that very thing than which a greater cannot be thought, is not that than which a greater cannot be thought; which is impossible. So there exists so truly something than which a greater cannot be thought that it cannot be thought not to exist.

You are that very thing, Lord our God.

SELECTION 13.2
Summa Theologica★   *St. Thomas Aquinas*

[*Aquinas's five proofs of God's existence are set forth here in his Five Ways.*]

The existence of God can be proved in five ways.

The first and more manifest way is the argument from motion. It is certain, and evident to our senses, that in the world some things are in motion. Now whatever is moved is moved by another, for nothing can be moved except it is in potentiality to that towards which it is moved; whereas a thing moves inasmuch as it is in act. For motion is nothing else than the reduction of something from potentiality to actuality. But nothing can be reduced from potentiality to actuality, except by something in a state of actuality. Thus that which is actually hot, as fire, makes wood, which is potentially hot, to be actually hot, and thereby moves and changes it. Now it is not possible that the same thing should be at once in actuality and potentiality in the same respect, but only in different respects. For what is actually hot cannot simultaneously be potentially hot; but it is simultaneously potentially cold. It is therefore impossible that in the same respect and in the same way a thing should be both mover and moved, *i.e.,* that it should move itself. Therefore, whatever is moved must be moved by another. If that by which it is moved be itself moved, then this also must needs be moved by another, and that by another again. But this cannot go on to infinity, because then there would be no first mover, and, consequently, no other mover, seeing that subsequent movers move only inasmuch as they are moved by the first mover; as the staff moves only because it is moved by the hand. Therefore it is necessary to arrive at a first mover, moved by no other; and this everyone understands to be God.

The second way is from the nature of efficient cause. In the world of sensible things we find there is an order of efficient causes. There is no case known (neither is it, indeed, possible) in which a thing is found to be the efficient cause of itself; for so it would be prior to itself which is impossible. Now in efficient

---

★ From *Basic Writings of Saint Thomas Aquinas*, ed. Anton C. Pegis, Vol. 1. Copyright © 1945 by Random House, Inc. Copyright renewed 1973 by Random House, Inc. First Hackett Publishing Company edition 1997. Reprinted by permission of Hackett Publishing Company, Inc. All rights reserved.

causes it is not possible to go on to infinity, because in all efficient causes following in order, the first is the cause of the intermediate cause, and the intermediate is the cause of the ultimate cause, whether the intermediate cause be several, or one only. Now to take away the cause is to take away the effect. Therefore, if there be no first cause among efficient causes, there will be no ultimate, nor any intermediate, cause. But if in efficient causes it is possible to go on to infinity, there will be no first efficient cause, neither will there be an ultimate effect, nor any intermediate efficient causes; all of which is plainly false. Therefore it is necessary to admit a first efficient cause, to which everyone gives the name of God.

The third way is taken from possibility and necessity, and runs thus. We find in nature things that are possible to be and not to be, since they are found to be generated, and to be corrupted, and consequently, it is possible for them to be and not to be. But it is impossible for these always to exist, for that which can not-be at some time is not. Therefore, if everything can not-be, then at one time there was nothing in existence. Now if this were true, even now there would be nothing in existence, because that which does not exist begins to exist only through something already existing. Therefore, if at one time nothing was in existence, it would have been impossible for anything to have begun to exist; and thus even now nothing would be in existence—which is absurd. Therefore, not all beings are merely possible, but there must exist something the existence of which is necessary. But every necessary thing either has its necessity caused by another, or not. Now it is impossible to go on to infinity in necessary things which have their necessity caused by another, as has been already proved

in regard to efficient causes. Therefore we cannot but admit the existence of some being having of itself its own necessity, and not receiving it from another, but rather causing in others their necessity. This all men speak of as God.

The fourth way is taken from the gradation to be found in things. Among beings there are some more and some less good, true, noble, and the like. But *more* and *less* are predicated of different things according as they resemble in their different ways something which is the maximum, as a thing is said to be hotter according as it more nearly resembles that which is hottest; so that there is something which is truest, something best, something noblest, and consequently, something which is most being, for those things that are greatest in truth are greatest in being. . . . Now the maximum in any genus is the cause of all in that genus, as fire, which is the maximum of heat, is the cause of all hot things, as is said in the same book. Therefore there must also be something which is to all beings the cause of their being, goodness, and every other perfection; and this we call God.

The fifth way is taken from the governance of the world. We see that things which lack knowledge, such as natural bodies, act for an end, and this is evident from their acting always, or nearly always, in the same way, so as to obtain the best result. Hence it is plain that they achieve their end, not fortuitously, but designedly. Now whatever lacks knowledge cannot move towards an end, unless it be directed by some being endowed with knowledge and intelligence; as the arrow is directed by the archer. Therefore some intelligent being exists by whom all natural things are directed to their end; and this being we call God.

SELECTION 13.3

Monadology*

G. W. Leibniz

[Leibniz explained the principle of sufficient reason and then used the principle to prove that God exists.]

* From G. W. Leibniz, *Philosophical Texts*, translated by Richard Francks and R.S. Woolhouse, with introduction and notes by R. S. Woolhouse (Oxford: Oxford University Press, 1998), pp. 272–273. By permission of Oxford University Press.

. . . 31. Our reasonings are founded on two great *principles: the principle of contradiction,* in virtue of which we judge to be false anything that involves contradiction, and as true whatever is opposed or contradictory to what is false. . . .

32. And that *of sufficient reason,* in virtue of which we hold that no fact could ever be true or

existent, no statement correct, unless there were a sufficient reason why it was thus and not otherwise—even though those reasons will usually not be knowable by us. . . .

33. There are also two kinds of *truth*: those of *reasoning*, and those of *fact*. Truths of reasoning are necessary, and their opposite is impossible; those of fact are contingent, and their opposite is possible. When a truth is necessary, the reason for it can be founded by analysis, by resolving it into simpler ideas and truths until we arrive at the basic ones. . . .

34. Thus mathematicians use analysis to reduce speculative *theorems* and practical *canons* to *definitions, axioms*, and *postulates*.

35. And finally there are the simple ideas, which cannot be given a definition; and there are axioms and postulates—in a word, *basic principles*, which can never be proved, but which also have no need of proof: these are *identical propositions*, the opposite of which contains an explicit contradiction.

36. But a *sufficient reason* must also be found for *contingent truths*, or *truths of fact*—for the series of things which fills the universe of created things, that is. Here the resolution into particular reasons could be continued endlessly, because of the immense variety of things in nature, and because of the infinite divisibility of bodies. There are an infinite number of shapes and of motions, present and past, which play a part in the efficient cause of my present writing; and there are an infinite number of tiny inclinations and dispositions of my soul, present and past, which play a part in its final cause. . . .

37. But since all this detail only involves other prior and more detailed contingencies, each one of which also stands in need of a similar analysis in order to give an explanation of it, we are no further forward: the sufficient or final reason must lie outside the succession or *series* in this detailed specification of contingencies, however infinite it may be.

38. And that is why the final reason for things must be in a necessary substance, in which the detailed specification of changes is contained only eminently, as in their source; and that is what we call *God*. . . .

39. Now, since this substance is a sufficient reason for all this detail, which is interconnected throughout, *there is only one God, and that God is enough*.

40. We can also see that this supreme substance, which is unique, universal, and necessary (because there is nothing outside it which is independent of it, and it is a straightforward consequence of possible being), must be incapable of limits, and must contain fully as much reality as is possible.

41. From which it follows that God is absolutely perfect, since *perfection* is nothing but the total amount of positive reality taken in the precise sense, leaving aside the limitations or boundaries of things that have them. And there, in something which has no boundaries—in God, that is—perfection is absolutely infinite. . . .

42. It also follows that created things have their perfections from the influence of God, but that they have their imperfections from their own natures, which are necessarily bounded. For that is what distinguishes them from God. . . . This original imperfection of created things is shown by the natural inertia of bodies. . . .

SELECTION 13.4

The Gay Science*

Friedrich Nietzsche

[*Nietzsche said, "God is dead." Here he elaborates.*]

The Meaning of Our Cheerfulness

The greatest recent event—that "God is dead," that the belief in the Christian god has become unbelievable—is already beginning to cast its first shadows over Europe. For the few at least, whose eye—the *suspicion* in whose eyes is strong and subtle enough for this spectacle, some sun seems to have set and some ancient and profound trust has been turned into doubt; to them our old world must appear daily more like evening, more mistrustful, stranger, "older." But in the main one may say: The event itself is far too great, too distant, too remote from the multitude's capacity for comprehension even for the tidings of it to be thought of as having *arrived* as yet. Much less may one suppose that many people know as yet *what* this event really means—and how much must collapse now that this faith has been undermined because it was built upon this faith, propped by it, grown into it; for example, the whole of our European morality. This long plenitude and sequence of breakdown, destruction, ruin, and cataclysm that is now impending—who could guess enough of it today to be compelled to play the teacher and advance proclaimer of this monstrous logic of terror, the prophet of a gloom and an eclipse of the sun whose like has probably never yet occurred on earth?

Even we born guessers of riddles who are, as it were, waiting on the mountains, posted between today and tomorrow, stretched in the contradiction between today and tomorrow, we firstlings and premature births of the coming century, to whom the shadows that must soon envelop Europe really *should* have appeared by now—why is it that even we look forward to the approaching gloom without any real sense of involvement and above all without any worry and fear for *ourselves?* Are we perhaps still too much under the impression of the *initial consequences* of this event—and these initial consequences, the consequences for *ourselves,* are quite the opposite of what one might perhaps expect: They are not at all sad and gloomy but rather like a new and scarcely describable kind of light, happiness, relief, exhilaration, encouragement, dawn.

Indeed, we philosophers and "free spirits" feel, when we hear the news that "the old god is dead," as if a new dawn shone on us; our heart overflows with gratitude, amazement, premonitions, expectation. At long last the horizon appears free to us again, even if it should not be bright; at long last our ships may venture out again, venture out to face any danger; all the daring of the lover of knowledge is permitted again; the sea, *our sea,* lies open again; perhaps there has never yet been such an "open sea."

SELECTION 13.5

Theology and Falsification*

Antony Flew

[*In this famous selection, British philosopher Antony Flew challenged those who believe in God to specify what they would accept as evidence that God does not exist or does not love us. Why should a believer try to do this? Flew explained why. In recent years, Flew had expressed more sympathy toward deism.*]

Let us begin with a parable. It is a parable developed from a tale told by John Wisdom in his haunting and revelatory article "Gods." Once upon a time two explorers came upon a clearing in the jungle. In the clearing were growing many flowers and many weeds. One explorer says, "Some gardener must tend this plot." The other disagrees, "There is no gardener." So they pitch their tents and set a watch. No gardener is ever seen. "But perhaps he is an invisible gardener." So they set up a barbed-wire fence. They electrify it. They patrol with bloodhounds. (For they remember how H. G. Wells's "invisible man" could be both smelt and touched though he could not be seen.) But no shrieks ever suggest that some intruder has received a shock. No movements of the wire ever betray an invisible climber. The bloodhounds never give cry. Yet still the Believer is not convinced. "But there is a gardener, invisible, intangible, insensible to electric shocks, a gardener who has no scent and makes no sound, a gardener who comes secretly to look after the garden which he loves." At last the

Sceptic despairs, "But what remains of your original assertion? Just how does what you call an invisible, intangible, eternally elusive gardener differ from an imaginary gardener or even from no gardener at all?"

In this parable we can see how what starts as an assertion, that something exists or that there is some analogy between certain complexes of phenomena, may be reduced step by step to an altogether different status, to an expression perhaps of a "picture preference." The Sceptic says there is no gardener. The Believer says there is a gardener (but invisible, etc.). One man talks about sexual behavior. Another man prefers to talk of Aphrodite (but knows that there is not really a superhuman person additional to, and somehow responsible for, all sexual phenomena). The process of qualification may be checked at any point before the original assertion is completely withdrawn and something of that first assertion will remain (Tautology). Mr. Wells's invisible man could not, admittedly, be seen, but in all other respects he was a man like the rest of us. But though the process of qualification may be, and of course usually is, checked in time, it is not always judiciously so halted. Someone may dissipate his assertion completely without noticing that he has done so. A fine brash hypothesis may thus be killed by inches, the death by a thousand qualifications.

And in this, it seems to me, lies the peculiar danger, the endemic evil, of theological utterance. Take such utterances as "God has a plan," "God created the world," "God loves us as a father loves his children." They look at first sight very much like assertions, vast cosmological assertions. Of course, this is no sure sign that they either are, or are intended to be, assertions. But let us confine ourselves to the cases where those who utter such sentences intend them to express assertions. (Merely remarking parenthetically that those who intend or interpret such utterances as crypto-commands, expressions of wishes, disguised ejaculations, concealed ethics, or as anything else but assertions, are unlikely to succeed in making them either properly orthodox or practically effective.)

Now to assert that such and such is the case is necessarily equivalent to denying that such and such is not the case. Suppose then that we are in doubt as to what someone who gives vent to an utterance is asserting, or suppose that, more radically, we are sceptical as to whether he is really asserting anything at all, one way of trying to understand (or perhaps it will be to expose) his utterance is to attempt to find what he would regard as counting against, or as being incompatible with, its truth. For if the utterance is indeed an assertion, it will necessarily be equivalent to a denial of the negation of that assertion. And anything which would count against the assertion, or which would induce the speaker to withdraw it and to admit that it had been mistaken, must be part of (or the whole of) the meaning of the negation of that assertion. And to know the meaning of the negation of an assertion is, as near as makes no matter, to know the meaning of that assertion. And if there is nothing which a putative assertion denies then there is nothing which it asserts either: and so it is not really an assertion. When the Sceptic in the parable asked the Believer, "Just how does what you call an invisible, intangible, eternally elusive gardener differ from an imaginary gardener or even from no gardener at all?" he was suggesting that the Believer's earlier statement had been so eroded by qualification that it was no longer an assertion at all.

Now it often seems to people who are not religious as if there was no conceivable event or series of events the occurrence of which would be admitted by sophisticated religious people to be a sufficient reason for conceding "There wasn't a God after all" or "God does not really love us then." Someone tells us that God loves us as a father loves his children. We are reassured. But then we see a child dying of inoperable cancer of the throat. His earthly father is driven frantic in his efforts to help, but his Heavenly Father reveals no obvious sign of concern. Some qualification is made—God's love is "not a merely human love" or it is "an inscrutable love," perhaps—and we realize that such sufferings are quite compatible with the truth of the assertion that "God loves us as a father (but, of course . . .)." We are reassured again. But then perhaps we ask: what is this assurance of God's (appropriately qualified) love worth, what is this apparent guarantee really a guarantee against? Just what would have to happen not merely (morally and wrongly) to tempt but also (logically and rightly) to entitle us to say "God does not love us" or even "God does not exist?" I therefore put to the succeeding symposiasts the simple central question: "What would have to occur or to have occurred to constitute for you a disproof of the love of, or of the existence of, God?"

SELECTION 13.6

After the Death of God the Father★   *Mary Daly*

[*How is "God" an instrument of oppression? How do religious texts dehumanize women? Mary Daly offered her arguments in* Beyond God the Father, *from which this brief passage is excerpted.*]

The biblical and popular image of God as a great patriarch in heaven, rewarding and punishing according to his mysterious and seemingly arbitrary will, has dominated the imagination of millions over thousands of years. The symbol of the Father God, spawned in the human imagination and sustained as plausible by patriarchy, has in turn rendered service to this type of society by making its mechanisms for the oppression of women appear right and fitting. If God in "his" heaven is a father ruling "his" people, then it is in the "nature" of things and according to divine plan and the order of the universe that society be male-dominated.

Within this context a mystification of roles takes place: the husband dominating his wife represents God "himself." The images and values of a given society have been projected into the realm of dogmas and "Articles of Faith," and these in turn justify the social structures which have given rise to them and which sustain their plausibility. The belief system becomes hardened and objectified, seeming to have an unchangeable independent existence and validity of its own. It resists social change that would rob it of its plausibility. Despite the vicious circle, however, change can occur in society, and ideologies can die, though they die hard.

As the women's movement begins to have its effect upon the fabric of society, transforming it from patriarchy into something that never existed before—into a diarchal situation that is radically new—it can become the greatest single challenge to the major religions of the world, Western and Eastern. Beliefs and values that have held sway for thousands of years will be questioned as never before. This

revolution may well be also the greatest single hope for survival of spiritual consciousness on this planet. . . .

Beyond the Inadequate God

The various theologies that hypostatize transcendence, that is, those which in one way or another objectify "God" as *a being,* thereby attempt in a self-contradictory way to envisage transcendent reality as finite. "God" then functions to legitimate the existing social, economic, and political status quo, in which women and other victimized groups are subordinate.

"God" can be used oppressively against women in a number of ways. First, it occurs in an overt manner when theologians proclaim women's subordination to be God's will. This of course has been done throughout the centuries, and residues remain in varying degrees of subtlety and explicitness in the writings of twentieth-century thinkers such as Barth, Bonhoeffer, Reinhold Niebuhr, and Teilhard de Chardin.

Second, even in the absence of such explicitly oppressive justification, the phenomenon is present when one-sex symbolism for God and for the human relationship to God is used. The following passage illustrates the point:

> To believe that God is Father is to become aware of oneself not as a stranger, not as an outsider or an alienated person, but as a son who belongs or a person appointed to a marvelous destiny, which he shares with the whole community. To believe that God is Father means to be able to say "we" in regard to all men.

A woman whose consciousness has been aroused can say that such language makes her aware of herself as a stranger, as an outsider, as an alienated person, not as a daughter who belongs or who is appointed to a marvelous destiny. She cannot belong to *this* without assenting to her own lobotomy.

Third, even when the basic assumptions of God-language appear to be nonsexist, and when language is somewhat purified of fixation upon maleness, it is damaging and implicitly compatible with sexism if it encourages detachment from the reality of the human struggle against oppression in its concrete manifestations. That is, the lack of explicit relevance of intellection to the fact of oppression in its precise forms, such as sexual hierarchy, is itself oppressive. This is the case when theologians write long treatises on creative hope, political theology, or revolution without any specific acknowledgment of or application to the problem of sexism or other specific forms of injustice. Such irrelevance is conspicuous in the major works of "theologians of hope" such as Moltmann, Pannenberg, and Metz. This is not to say that the vision of creative eschatology is completely irrelevant, but that it lacks specific grounding in the concrete experiences of the oppressed. The theorizing then has a quality of unreality. Perhaps an obvious reason for this is that the theologians themselves have not shared in the experience of oppression and therefore write from the privileged distance of those who have at best a "knowledge about" the subject. . . .

Women's Liberation and Revelatory Courage

I have already indicated that it would be unrealistic to dismiss the fact that the symbolic and linguistic instruments for communication—which include essentially the whole theological tradition in world religions—have been formulated by males under the conditions of patriarchy. It is therefore inherent in these symbolic and linguistic structures that they serve the purposes of patriarchal social arrangements. Even the usual and accepted means of theological dissent have been restricted in such a way that only some questions have been allowed to arise. Many questions that are of burning importance to women now simply have not occurred in the past (and to a large extent in the present) to those with "credentials" to do theology. Others may have been voiced timidly but quickly squelched as stupid, irrelevant, or naïve. Therefore, attempts by women theologians now merely to "up-date" or to reform theology within acceptable patterns of question-asking are not likely to get very far.

Moreover, within the context of the prevailing social climate it has been possible for scholars to be aware of the most crudely dehumanizing texts concerning women in the writings of religious "authorities" and theologians—from Augustine to Aquinas, to Luther, to Knox, to Barth—and at the same time to treat their unverified opinions on far more imponderable matters with utmost reverence and respect. That is, the blatant misogynism of these men has not been the occasion of a serious credibility gap even for those who have disagreed on this "point." It has simply been ignored or dismissed as trivial. By contrast, in the emerging consciousness of women this context is beginning to be perceived in its full significance and as deeply relevant to the worldview in which such "authorities" have seen other seemingly unrelated subjects, such as the problem of God. Hence the present awakening of the hitherto powerless sex demands an explosion of creative imagination that can withstand the disapproval of orthodoxy and overreach the boundaries cherished by conventional minds.

SELECTION 13.7

The God Delusion*

Richard Dawkins

[*British science expositor Richard Dawkins here considers the "Anthropic Principle," according to which, because observers of the universe exist, the universe had to be such as to permit their eventual emergence.*]

* From *The God Delusion* by Richard Dawkins, New York, Houghton Mifflin Company, 2006, 169–180.

The Anthropic Principle: Cosmological Version

We live not only on a friendly planet but also in a friendly universe. It follows from the fact of our existence that the laws of physics must be friendly enough to allow life to arise. It is no accident that when we look at the night sky we see stars, for stars are a necessary prerequisite for the existence of most of the chemical elements, and without chemistry there could be no life. Physicists have calculated that, if the laws and constants of physics had been even slightly different, the universe would have developed in such a way that life would have been impossible. Different physicists put it in different ways, but the conclusion is always much the same.[1] Martin Rees, in *Just Six Numbers,* lists six fundamental constants, which are believed to hold all around the universe. Each of these six numbers is finely tuned in the sense that, if it were slightly different, the universe would be comprehensively different and presumably unfriendly to life.[2] . . .

I won't go through the rest of Rees's six numbers. The bottom line for each of them is the same. The actual number sits in a Goldilocks band of values outside which life would not have been possible. How should we respond to this? Yet again, we have the theist's answer on the one hand, and the anthropic answer on the other. The theist says that God, when setting up the universe, tuned the fundamental constants of the universe so that each one lay in its Goldilocks zone for the production of life. It is as though God had six knobs that he could twiddle, and he carefully tuned each knob to its Goldilocks value. As ever, the theist's answer is deeply unsatisfying, because it leaves the existence of God unexplained. A God capable of calculating the Goldilocks values for the six numbers would have to be at least as improbable as the finely tuned combination of numbers itself, and that's very improbable indeed. This is exactly the premise of the whole discussion we are having. It follows that the theist's answer has utterly failed to make any headway towards solving the problem at hand. I see no alternative but to dismiss it, while at the same time marvelling at the number of people who can't see

the problem and seem genuinely satisfied by the 'Divine Knob-Twiddler' argument. . . .

Hard-nosed physicists say that the six knobs were never free to vary in the first place. When we finally reach the long-hoped-for Theory of Everything, we shall see that the six key numbers depend upon each other, or on something else as yet unknown, in ways that we today cannot imagine. The six numbers may turn out to be no freer to vary than is the ratio of a circle's circumference to its diameter. It will turn out that there is only one way for a universe to be. Far from God being needed to twiddle six knobs, there are no knobs to twiddle.

Other physicists (Martin Rees himself would be an example) find this unsatisfying, and I think I agree with them. It is indeed perfectly plausible that there is only one way for a universe to be. But why did that one way have to be such a set-up for our eventual evolution? Why did it have to be the kind of universe which seems almost as if, in the words of the theoretical physicist Freeman Dyson, it 'must have known we were coming'? The philosopher John Leslie uses the analogy of a man sentenced to death by firing squad. It is just possible that all ten men of the firing squad will miss their victim. With hindsight, the survivor who finds himself in a position to reflect upon his luck can cheerfully say, 'Well, obviously they all missed, or I wouldn't be here thinking about it.' But he could still, forgivably, wonder why they all missed, and toy with the hypothesis that they were bribed, or drunk.

This objection can be answered by the suggestion, which Martin Rees himself supports, that there are many universes, co-existing like bubbles of foam, in a 'multiverse' (or 'megaverse,' as Leonard Susskind prefers to call it).[3] The laws and constants of any one universe, such as our observable universe, are by-laws. The multiverse as a whole has a plethora of alternative sets of by-laws. The anthropic principle kicks in to explain that we have to be in one of those universes (presumably a minority) whose by-laws happened to be propitious to our eventual evolution and hence contemplation of the problem. . . .

It is tempting to think (and many have succumbed) that to postulate a plethora of universes is a profligate luxury which should not be allowed. If

---

[1] The physicist Victor Stenger (in e.g. *God, the Failed Hypothesis*) dissents from this consensus, and is unpersuaded that the physical laws and constants are particularly friendly to life. Nevertheless, I shall bend over backwards to accept the 'friendly universe' consensus, in order to show that, in any case, it cannot be used to support theism.

[2] I say 'presumably,' partly because we don't know how different alien forms of life might be, and partly because it is possible that we make a mistake if we consider only the consequences of changing one constant at a time. Could there be other *combinations* of values of the six numbers which would turn out to be friendly to life, in ways that we do not discover if we consider them only one at a time? Nevertheless, I shall proceed, for simplicity, as though we really do have a big problem to explain in the apparent fine-tuning of the fundamental constants.

---

[3] Susskind (2006) gives a splendid advocacy of the anthropic principle in the megaverse. He says the idea is hated by most physicists. I can't understand why. I think it is beautiful—perhaps because my consciousness has been raised by Darwin.

we are going to permit the extravagance of a multiverse, so the argument runs, we might as well be hung for a sheep as a lamb and allow a God. Aren't they both equally uparsimonious ad hoc hypotheses, and equally unsatisfactory? People who think that have not had their consciousness raised by natural selection. The key difference between the genuinely extravagant God hypothesis and the apparently extravagant multiverse hypothesis is one of statistical improbability. The multiverse, for all that it is extravagant, is simple. God, or any intelligent, decision-taking, calculating agent, would have to be highly improbable in the very same statistical sense as the entities he is supposed to explain. The multiverse may seem extravagant in sheer *number* of universes. But if each one of those universes is simple in its fundamental laws, we are still not postulating anything highly improbable. The very opposite has to be said of any kind of intelligence.

Some physicists are known to be religious (Russell Stannard and the Reverend John Polkinghorne are the two British examples I have mentioned). Predictably, they seize upon the improbability of the physical constants all being tuned in their more or less narrow Goldilocks zones, and suggest that there must be a cosmic intelligence who deliberately did the tuning. I have already dismissed all such suggestions as raising bigger problems than they solve. But what attempts have theists made to reply? How do they cope with the argument that any God capable of designing a universe, carefully and foresightfully tuned to lead to our evolution, must be a supremely complex and improbable entity who needs an even bigger explanation than the one he is supposed to provide?

The theologian Richard Swinburne, as we have learned to expect, thinks he has an answer to this problem, and he expounds it in his book *Is There a God?* He begins by showing that his heart is in the right place by convincingly demonstrating why we should always prefer the simplest hypothesis that fits the facts. Science explains complex things in terms of the interactions of simpler things, ultimately the interactions of fundamental particles. I (and I dare say you) think it a beautifully simple idea that all things are made of fundamental particles which, although exceedingly numerous, are drawn from a small, finite set of *types* of particle. If we are sceptical, it is likely to be because we think the idea too simple. But for Swinburne it is not simple at all, quite the reverse.

Given that the number of particles of any one type, say electrons, is large, Swinburne thinks it too much of a coincidence that so many should have the same properties. One electron, he could stomach. But billions and billions of electrons, *all with the same properties,* that is what really excites his incredulity. For him it would be simpler, more natural, less demanding of explanation, if all electrons were different from each other. Worse, no one electron should naturally retain its properties for more than an instant at a time; each should change capriciously, haphazardly and fleetingly from moment to moment. That is Swinburne's view of the simple, native state of affairs. Anything more uniform (what you or I would call more simple) requires a special explanation. 'It is only because electrons and bits of copper and all other material objects have the same powers in the twentieth century as they did in the nineteenth century that things are as they are now.'

Enter God. God comes to the rescue by deliberately and continuously sustaining the properties of all those billions of electrons and bits of copper, and neutralizing their otherwise ingrained inclination to wild and erratic fluctuation. That is why when you've seen one electron you've seen them all; that is why bits of copper all behave like bits of copper, and that is why each electron and each bit of copper stays the same as itself from microsecond to microsecond and from century to century. It is because God constantly keeps a finger on each and every particle, curbing its reckless excesses and whipping it into line with its colleagues to keep them all the same.

But how can Swinburne possibly maintain that this hypothesis of God simultaneously keeping a gazillion fingers on wayward electrons is a *simple* hypothesis? It is, of course, precisely the opposite of simple. Swinburne pulls off the trick to his own satisfaction by a breathtaking piece of intellectual *chutzpah.* He asserts, without justification, that God is only a *single* substance. What brilliant economy of explanatory causes, compared with all those gigazillions of independent electrons all just happening to be the same! . . .

. . . What could be simpler than that?

Well, actually, almost everything. A God capable of continuously monitoring and controlling the individual status of every particle in the universe *cannot* be simple. His existence is going to need a mammoth explanation in its own right. Worse (from the point of view of simplicity), other corners of God's giant consciousness are simultaneously preoccupied with the doings and emotions and prayers of every single human being—and whatever intelligent aliens there might be on other planets in this and 100 billion other galaxies. He even, according to Swinburne, has to decide continuously *not* to intervene miraculously to save us when we get cancer. That would never do, for, 'If God answered most prayers for a relative to recover from cancer, then cancer would no longer be a problem for humans to solve.' And *then* what would we find to do with our time?

Not all theologians go as far as Swinburne. Nevertheless, the remarkable suggestion that the God Hypothesis is *simple* can be found in other modern theological writings. Keith Ward, then Regius Professor of Divinity at Oxford, was very clear on the matter in his 1996 book *God, Chance and Necessity:*

> As a matter of fact, the theist would claim that God is a very elegant, economical and fruitful explanation for the existence of the universe. It is economical because it attributes the existence and nature of absolutely everything in the universe to just one being, an ultimate cause which assigns a reason for the existence of everything, including itself. It is elegant because from one key idea—the idea of the most perfect possible being—the whole nature of God and the existence of the universe can be intelligibly explicated.

Like Swinburne, Ward mistakes what it means to explain something, and he also seems not to understand what it means to say of something that it is simple. I am not clear whether Ward really thinks God is simple, or whether the above passage represented a temporary 'for the sake of argument' exercise. Sir John Polkinghorne, in *Science and Christian Belief,* quotes Ward's earlier criticism of the thought of Thomas Aquinas: 'Its basic error is in supposing that God is logically simple—simple not just in the sense that his being is indivisible, but in the much stronger sense that what is true of any part of God is true of the whole. It is quite coherent, however, to suppose that God, while indivisible, is internally complex.' Ward gets it right here. Indeed, the biologist Julian Huxley, in 1912, defined complexity in terms of 'heterogeneity of parts,' by which he meant a particular kind of functional indivisibility.

Elsewhere, Ward gives evidence of the difficulty the theological mind has in grasping where the complexity of life comes from. He quotes another theologian-scientist, the biochemist Arthur Peacocke (the third member of my trio of British religious scientists), as postulating the existence in living matter of a 'propensity for increased complexity.' Ward characterizes this as 'some inherent weighting of evolutionary change which favours complexity.' He goes on to suggest that such a bias 'might be some weighting of the mutational process, to ensure that more complex mutations occurred.' Ward is sceptical of this, as well he should be. The evolutionary drive towards complexity comes, in those lineages where it comes at all, not from any inherent propensity for increased complexity, and not from biased mutation. It comes from natural selection: the process which, as far as we know, is the only process ultimately capable of generating complexity out of simplicity. The theory of natural selection is genuinely simple. So is the origin from which it starts. That which it explains, on the other hand, is complex almost beyond telling: more complex than anything we can imagine, save a God capable of designing it.

CHECKLIST

To help you review, a checklist of the key philosophers of this chapter can be found online at www.mhhe.com/moore9e.

KEY TERMS AND CONCEPTS

QUESTIONS FOR DISCUSSION AND REVIEW

1. Explain in your own words Anselm's two ontological proofs of God.

2. Critically evaluate Leibniz's solution to the problem of evil.

3. In your own words, summarize Hume's criticisms of the teleological argument. Are these criticisms sound? Why or why not?

4. Explain Hume's reasoning for remaining skeptical of reports of miracles. Is this reasoning sound?

5. Hume maintained that, if you explain the cause of each event in a series by reference to earlier events in the series, there is no sense in then trying to find a single cause for the entire series of events. Is this right? What does it have to do with the question of God's existence?

6. Does the world/universe—or something in it—give evidence of divine design? Explain.

7. Does the theory of evolution undermine the design argument?

8. Explain James's argument for God. Is it a version of Pascal's wager? Is it sound? Why?

9. Which is "better," to doubt everything that is less than certain or highly probable, or to believe falsehoods?

10. "It is impossible for normal people to believe that free will does not exist. Therefore, it does exist." Evaluate this remark.

11. "He died because God called on him." "The sprinkler stopped working due to fate." Are these claims equally meaningless? Explain. Is the claim "God exists" verifiable or falsifiable? Are any (other) claims made about God verifiable?

12. Assuming there is scientific evidence that the universe had an absolute beginning, does that evidence also prove the existence of God? Explain.

13. Can you logically believe both that God knows everything and that there is free will? Explain the difficulty.

14. "Even assuming that the existence of God explains why there is a world, what explains why there is a God?" Does this question contain a valid criticism of the cosmological proof of God?

15. Would universal acceptance of atheism be morally disastrous for society?

SUGGESTED FURTHER READINGS

Go online to www.mhhe.com/moore9e for a list of suggested further readings.

Part Four
Other Voices

14

Feminist Philosophy*

Feminism is an entire world view or *Gestalt*, not just a laundry list of "women's issues."   —Charlotte Bunch

Girls and boys develop different relational capacities and senses of self as a result of growing up in a family in which women mother.   —Nancy Chodorow

As nature [during the Scientific Revolution] came to seem more like a woman whom it is appropriate to rape and torture than like a nurturing mother; did rape and torture come to seem a more natural relation of men to women?   —Sandra Harding

What is **feminist philosophy?** Feminist philosophy as an academic discipline did not emerge until the seventies in the United States, Europe, and Australia. But this doesn't mean there were no feminist philosophers until then—far from it! There have been women philosophers since the eighteenth century, and they have made significant contributions to feminist philosophy today.

An important thing to remember as we explore this chapter is that there is really no such thing as feminism; instead, there are feminisms. This is because feminism has developed out of different issues and goals in different countries, cultures, and circumstances. Feminists do not always agree on what the agenda should be, but what they do all share is a deep commitment that women and men should be treated equally. Beyond that, complexities have evolved.

As feminist theory has mushroomed in the field of women's studies, new interdisciplinary bases have formed, and each of these contributes to the proliferation of feminisms. Similarly, *feminist philosophy* must now be considered a loose term for the

---

* Revised and updated by Anne D'Arcy.

many varieties of feminist philosophical discourse: liberal, Marxist/socialist, radical/anarchical, ecological, phenomenological, postmodern, and postfeminist.

Traditional philosophy has developed around some major categories of questions and issues—metaphysical concerns about the nature of reality; epistemological concerns of truth and knowledge; ethical concerns of morality and the good; political concerns of rights and responsibilities—so we can see that philosophy as an intellectual discipline has provided us with the grounding to understand ordinary life as we live it. It has historically presented itself as a neutral, disinterested set of discourses, and therein lies the problem as feminist philosophers view it. Traditional philosophy is viewed by feminists as a masculine body of theoretical concepts through its sexism, its underlying patriarchal constructs, and its social misogyny (misogyny is hatred of women): it is a phallocentric (male-centered) strategy. Traditional philosophy, feminist thinkers claim, has tended to define women in negative ways, to misrepresent them, and to render them subservient or even invisible.

Feminist philosophy has evolved in response to these perceived systematic injustices and to demands that the fundamental questions of philosophy be reconceived before they can be reconsidered. Feminist philosophy is thus both a reconstruction of traditional philosophy and a revisionist approach to those philosophical claims that are seen to misrepresent women. The challenge of feminist philosophy is to transform the ideas of traditional philosophy by producing new ideas that include women and women's issues and ideas.

Feminist thought in general is often divided into categories known as first wave, second wave, postfeminism, and third wave. Note that these distinctions do have approximate timelines, but the borders are somewhat merged because feminists do not all agree to be categorized and have independent ideas that may carry over from one wave to another. As Marilyn Frye pointed out, "Thought is universal, but philosophy is local—temporally, culturally, and historically specific."

THE FIRST WAVE

One of the grandmothers of feminist thought was **Mary Wollstonecraft** (1759–1797). She was a precursor of the first-wave feminist movement, which did not begin in any organized way until the 1850s and lasted to the early part of the twentieth century. Some scholars regard her as the founder of what is now the feminist movement. Wollstonecraft was particularly interested in the education of women, opposing Rousseau's view that women's role was to please men and be useful to them in various solicitous ways. Wollstonecraft argued that educating women to be the ornaments and playthings of men would have negative consequences for society in the long run as well as for the women themselves. She argued that women are as capable as men of the "masculine" virtues of wisdom and rationality if they are permitted to cultivate them. She published several important pamphlets and books, including what has now become a classic of feminist thought, *A Vindication of the Rights of Woman*.

Mary Wollstonecraft.

Anna Doyle Wheeler (1765–1833) was another major contributor to pre-first-wave thought. An Irish self-educated philosopher and an avid utilitarian, Wheeler published numerous articles before collaborating with utopian/reformist philosopher **William Thompson** (1775–1833). Together they published "The Appeal of One Half of the Human Race, Women, against the Pretensions of the Other Half, Men, to Restrain Them in Political, and Thence in Civil and Domestic, Slavery." In this essay Wheeler and Thompson argued that denying rights to women is not consistent with the utilitarian principle of the greatest happiness of the greatest number. It was a stirring defense of equal rights for women. Another important utilitarian was **Harriet Taylor** (1807–1858), who was a vociferous proponent of women's suffrage and was among the first to assert that differences between men and women that are not biological are socially constructed.

The first wave of feminist thought worked toward obtaining voting rights for women, abolition, and temperance causes; it saw some dramatic results, including changes in the right to vote and property rights for women. But larger social problems remained: women were still educated differently, still viewed primarily as ornamental and nurturing, still paid less, and still valued differently than men.

THE SECOND WAVE

The personal is political.   —Carol Hanisch (1970)

The term *second wave* refers to the swell of feminist activism in the United States, Britain, and Europe from the late 1960s through the late 1980s. To some degree, second-wave theory still exists, and some second-wave theorists continue to write, so there is not a firm chronological boundary between the waves. That philosophy has traditionally been a male occupation is indisputable. What is more odious, proclaimed second-wave feminists, is the way some philosophers, particularly Plato, Aristotle, Rousseau, and Kant, have denigrated women.

Simone de Beauvoir.

Philosopher and novelist **Simone de Beauvoir** [bow-VWAHR] (1908–1986) recognized the problem. Earlier feminists were primarily English and American, steeped in the traditions of empiricism and utilitarianism. Beauvoir came from the Continental traditions of existentialism and phenomenology. Her approach focused less on the public world of laws, rights, and education, and more on the cultural mechanisms of oppression, which placed women in the role of **Other** to man's **Self.** She developed this notion of women's otherness in her book *The Second Sex*, which undertook a sweeping analysis of all the ideas and forces that conspired to keep women in a subordinate position relative to men. Despite the vitriolic response from her French contemporaries, *The Second Sex* had far-reaching ramifications for other feminist philosophers. Not only had Beauvoir answered the question "What is a woman?" with her famous statement "One is not born, but rather becomes, a woman," but she had successfully created a bridge between philosophical concepts and the social constructs that create them. Feminist thinkers who followed now had a broad platform from which to go in the various directions the second wave has produced.

The word **patriarchy** was coined early in the second wave to represent the set of institutions that legitimized universal male power. *The Second Sex* had opened the door to radical feminist perspectives that explored the existence of patriarchal constructs in everything from politics to the economy to rape, pornography, prostitution, and marriage. Even heterosexuality was seen as a patriarchal dictate.

The sixties, seventies, and early eighties saw an explosion of feminist theory. Here is a *short list* (!) of representative writings by American and Continental women about women from a feminist standpoint in this era. Just scanning this list will give you an excellent sense of some of the concerns of the period: Betty Friedan's *The Feminist Mystique* (1963); Robin Morgan's *Sisterhood Is Powerful* (1970); Kate Millett's *Sexual Politics* (1970); Shulamith Firestone's *The Dialectic of Sex* (1970); Germaine Greer's *The Female Eunuch* (1971); Ti-Grace Atkinson's *Amazon Odyssey* (1974); Charlotte Bunch's *Lesbianism and the Women's Movement* (1975); Andrea Dworkin's *Pornography: Men Possessing Women* (1979); Susan Brownmiller's *Against Our Will: Men, Women, and Rape* (1975); Eva Figes's *Patriarchal Attitudes* (1970); Mary Daly's *Gyn/Ecology: The Metaethics of Radical Feminism* (1978); Adrienne Rich's *Of Woman Born* (1976) and her "Compulsory

Heterosexuality and Lesbian Existence" (1980); Monique Wittig's *Les guérillières* (1971) and her *Lesbian Body* (1975); Barbara Smith's *Home Girls: A Black Feminist Anthology* (1983); Juliet Mitchell's *Psychoanalysis and Feminism* (1975); Gloria Steinem's numerous essays on difference; Joyce Trebilcot's "Two Forms of Androgynism" (1977); Marilyn Frye's "Sexism" (1983); Carol Gilligan's *In a Different Voice* (1982); Nancy Chodorow's *The Reproduction of Mothering* (1978); Nel Noddings's *Caring: A Feminine Approach to Ethics and Moral Education* (1984); Sara Ruddick's "Maternal Thinking" (1986); Alison Jaggar's *Feminist Politics and Human Nature* (1983); Susan Griffin's *Women and Nature* (1980) and her *Pornography and Silence: Culture's Revenge against Nature* (1981); Christine Delphy's *Close to Home: A Materialist Analysis of Women's Oppression* (1984), Hélène Cixous's *La Jeune Nee* [The Newly Born Woman] (1975); Zillah Eisenstein's *Capitalist Patriarchy and the Case for Socialist Feminism* (1979) and her *The Radical Future of Liberal Feminism* (1981); Ann Ferguson's "Androgyny as an Ideal for Human Development" (1977); H. Eisenstein and A. Jorden (eds.), *The Future of Difference* (1980); Jane Gallop's *Feminism and Psychoanalysis: The Daughter's Seduction* (1982); Sandra Harding and M. Hintikka (eds.), *Discovering Reality: Feminist Perspectives on Epistemology, Methodology, and Philosophy of Science* (1983); Luce Irigaray's *Speculum de l'autre femme* [*Speculum of the Other Woman*] (1974) and her *This Sex Which Is Not One* (trans. 1981); Julia Kristeva's *Desire in Language* (trans. 1980) and her "Women's Time" (trans. 1981); Sarah Lucia Hoagland's *Lesbian Ethics* (1988); Diana Fuss, *Essentially Speaking* (1989); Patricia Hill Collins's *Black Feminist Thought: Knowledge, Consciousness, and the Politics of Empowerment* (1990); bell hooks's *Ain't I a Woman? Black Women and Feminism* (1981); Angela Davis's *Women, Race and Class* (1981); Alice Walker's *In Search of Our Mothers' Gardens: Womanist Prose* (1983); Cherrie Moraga and Gloria Anzaldua's *This Bridge Called My Back: Writings of Radical Women of Color* (1979).

What this list of titles reflects is an interesting phenomenon: women at the grassroots level and women in academia began to push for revolutionary changes in the ways men and women have traditionally interacted in terms of power and authority. Further, the mushrooming of theory began to take shape in ways that can be categorized into different approaches, such as liberal, Marxist/socialist, and radical. Special-interest women's theory emerged: lesbian feminism, black feminism, feminist men, and, beginning around 1990, cyberfeminism and ecofeminism. Feminist theory had now arrived in full force and was being integrated into our ordinary lives as well as into academic scholarship. When there are so many feminist perspectives and voices and interest groups, there will inevitably be conflict. As you can readily see from the list, feminists do not speak in one voice; they do not agree as to which issues should be given priority, nor do they always find common ground in their various agendas.

Liberal feminism was the earliest form of feminist theory. There are numerous feminist positions within this category, but what they all share is a belief in autonomy and equality for women. The central claim of liberal feminists is that all humans deserve freedom of choice and equality of opportunity. Toward this end, liberal feminists operate in the public sphere, working to change restrictive laws and eliminating barriers to women's advancement in the workplace. Feminist philosophers identifying as liberal feminists examine the ideals that underlie the political inequalities and analyze strategies that can effect change. Critics of liberal feminism argue that liberal feminism is a white, middle-class, Western women's movement that doesn't adequately address the needs of minority and non-Western women.

Radical feminism identifies patriarchy as the root cause of women's subordination in the global sphere, focusing on women's reproduction, women's sexuality, and the feminine ideal. Radical feminists argue that drastic steps must be taken to change social attitudes that foster rape, violence, and general contempt for women by reducing women to their sexuality. Accordingly, they target cultural phenomena such as advertising, pornography, and music that treat women as sexual objects. Like the other feminist theoretical positions, radical feminism has many forms. Radical feminists are interested in women's experience rather than any specific form of social justice. But this is problematic for critics of radical feminism, because identifying women by their "female nature" is considered an essentialist position in that it claims that all women have a universal nature in common. Mary Daly and some of the French feminist philosophers fall under the umbrella of radical feminism, focusing on epistemology and female forms of writing.

Lesbian feminism views the social norm of heterosexuality as a form of oppression. For a time, lesbianism was regarded as the politically correct identity for all feminists, heterosexual or not. Lesbian feminists argue that lesbians are doubly oppressed—first as women, and second as women who reject men as sexual partners. Lesbian feminism has its roots in the lesbian community at large, but it is also informed by feminist ethics. Not only does it critique traditional gender roles, but it also challenges the dominant tradition of moral philosophy by pointing out that lesbian morality is the morality of a community, not isolated individuals' moral choices.

Socialist feminism combines Marxist and radical feminist perspectives. Following Marxist principles, socialist feminists regard the bearing and raising of children as forms of productive activity. They strive to equate these activities that reflect women's experience with "male" work production activities. Socialist feminists agree with radical feminists that there is a need to correct women's oppression in their everyday lives, but they disagree with radical feminists in their view that women's oppression is not caused solely by male dominance. Nevertheless, no one position defines socialist feminists. What they do agree on is that the differences between men and women that are based on economic divisions of labor should be reconstructed.

Black feminism is an American phenomenon. Like lesbian feminists, black feminist theorists claim a dual oppression—both gender and race. In addition, class issues intersect with race and gender. Black feminists do not identify with the label "women's experience" of oppression, because their experience is situated in the struggles created not only by gender but also by race and class. Black theorists ascribe subjectivity to black feminists who are working to educate others about their unique experience. This is in opposition to traditional epistemology, which presents knowledge as objective and universal. Black feminism is also known as "womanism," a term coined by Alice Walker, a key figure in black feminist thought along with Patricia Hills Collins, Angela Davis, Audre Lorde, and bell hooks.

Second-wave feminists have made progress in many arenas. Shelters for battered women and their children, public education on abuse and rape, contraception, legalization of abortion, women's studies programs, childcare services in the workplace, and a host of sexual harassment policies are examples of the products of their activism and publications.

THE THIRD WAVE

The pleasurable is political as well.   —Terri Senft

It is not that the second wave ended and the third wave replaced it. The 1990s and early 2000s brought new activists and theorists, but there are second-wavers who continue to write and champion their causes, and there are independent feminist philosophers who don't identify with either second or third wave. So, although third-wave feminism is generally thought to have begun between 1983 and the early 1990s out of disappointment with the lack of gains made in the second wave, particularly regarding violence against women and sexual harassment, it is even more difficult to categorize third-wave activists than second-wave theorists. In addition, third-wave thought rejects what it views as the second wave's essentialism—that is, a female identity that represents all women. Other third-wavers want to reinstate the values of the second wave, which they feel have been disintegrating and need renewed attention.

Beyond this, third-wave feminism is a challenge to describe because it contains so many strands of theory, some of which are in conflict. Some of these are **queer theory, ecofeminism, postcolonial theory, postmodernism,** and cultural critique, especially as it relates to sexuality. The movement often calls itself "sex-positive." For example, it is pro-pornography, which is diametrically opposed to second-wave thought. Members of this movement support transsexuals, who were rejected by second-wavers as merely surgically altered men, and they reject the binary distinctions of male and female. Leslie Heywood and Jennifer Drake, in their collection called *Third Wave Agenda: Being Feminist, Doing Feminism* (1997), defined the third wave as "a movement that contains elements of second wave critique of beauty culture, sexual abuse, and power structures while it also acknowledges and makes use of the pleasure, danger, and defining power of those structures." This is as close to a definition as you are likely to find for third-wave feminism.

Despite what may appear to be their limited list of political concerns, third-wavers have not settled on an agenda that represents them. Another complication is that some third-wave thinkers and activists do not want to be labeled as feminist at all! Third-wave thinkers believe that women should think for themselves as individuals, that feminism is a personal perspective that changes with each woman who practices it. Despite some tension between second- and third-wavers, whether the third is an extension of the second wave or an entirely new wave of thought is a matter of opinion rather than definition.

In general, third-wave thinkers are young women (and men) under the age of thirty-five for whom feminism was an established heritage. Those who identify as third wave see themselves as redefining feminist issues and goals and have different, broader perspectives about such second-wave givens as oppression and pornography. They assert that each individual's freedom of choice defines or redefines the issues that were very much at the core of the second-wave feminist agenda. Equity feminism, global human rights, and gender issues are part of their concerns, and popular culture—music, film, the media—are areas that third-wavers penetrate and appropriate for themselves. Bell hooks, who was prominent in the second wave and continues to lecture about the intersections of "white supremacist capitalist patriarchy," has transitioned as a third-wave icon because of her preoccupation with popular culture. The "Riot grrl" punk movement, "kawaii (cutie punk)" in Japanese culture, and the hip-hop "nasty girl" movements are third-wave phenomena, as are some elements of queer theory, the DIY ethic, art projects, transgender politics, women-of-color issues, and postcolonial theory, all of which add up to a unique collection of strands of feminist thought that cannot be categorized as a coherent new feminist theory.

The Third Wave Foundation, Code Pink, and the Feminist Majority Leadership Alliance are third-wave activist organizations that reflect interest in the areas of race, class, and sexuality, but third-wavers do not believe it is necessary to join an organization to contribute to issues of concern to women.

Cyberculture has made it easy for third-wavers to connect and communicate. 'Zines and blogs abound. Examples of third-wave print publications are *Bitch* and *Bust*. Some of the third-wave texts worth consulting are Rebecca Walker's *To Be Real: Telling the Truth and Changing the Face of Feminism* (1995) (Rebecca Walker is Alice Walker's daughter); Jennifer Baumgardner and Amy Richards, *ManifestA: Young Women, Feminism, and the Future* (2000); Stacy Gillis, Gillian Howie, and Rebecca Munford, *Third Wave Feminism: A Critical Exploration* (2007); Eve Ensler, *The Vagina Monologues* (2001); Leslie Heywood and Jennifer Drake, *Third Wave Agenda: Being Feminist, Doing Feminism* (1997); Astrid Henry, *Not My Mother's Sister: Generational Conflict and Third-Wave Feminism* (2004).

Postfeminism is another nebulous category that defies specifics because it contains so many conflicting elements, most of which have little to do with feminist philosophy. Some feminists assert that postfeminism is a reactionary movement whose purpose is to disrupt fixed definitions and descriptions of women's issues, goals, and theory. Postfeminists argue that all authoritative models of gender must be deconstructed and reevaluated. Some postfeminists believe that feminists have already met their goals and need to move past struggle and resistance. Another group regards postfeminism as primarily British and American third-wavers with their liberal assortment of goals and issues previously. This group is focused on activism, not theory.

And yet another group of feminists, represented by Naomi Wolf (1962–), discuss what Wolf calls "victim feminism" and call for replacing it with "power feminism"; Rene Denfeld (1967–) doesn't oppose feminism per se, but she sees feminism as needing a major overhaul in ideology as well as activism. Katie Roiphe (1968–) and Natasha Walter (1967–) want a sharp shift in feminist objectives. Roiphe particularly targets women's studies, which she sees as precluding any point of view that disagrees with feminism and feminist activism and as creating a

Deodorants are sometimes packaged differently for men and women.

culture of fear among women. Walter's views are similar to Wolf's: she sees second-wave feminism as having achieved certain goals and says it is time now to recognize that, although there is still work to be done, for the most part, women can achieve what they need as individuals.

All of these postfeminists view second-wave values as lacking in appeal to younger feminists. They are sometimes regarded as antifeminist or as part of a conservative group that dismisses the feminist agenda as no longer relevant because women have already made the progress they set out to make. This group sees feminism as being no longer viable or necessary. The extremist element of the postfeminist movement could be regarded as represented by Rush Limbaugh, who has coined the term *feminazi* to describe unspecified feminists whose agendas he disagrees with.

It should be apparent by now that nothing about feminist theory is static and predictable. There are as many forms of feminism as there are feminists, and that isn't likely to change anytime soon.

FEMINIST MORAL THEORY

Moral theory is another area that has been recently reconceptualized by feminist perspectives. **Carol Gilligan,** a psychologist who worked with Lawrence Kohlberg on his research on the moral development of people, observed that women seemed not to score as highly as men on Kohlberg's moral development scale. Was this a failure in moral development on the part of women? Gilligan noticed that the research on *children's* moral development was actually research on *boys'* moral development; the original studies had been done in boys' schools and universities and then were just assumed to fit the case of little girls and young women. Little girls who did not fit the mold set by the research on little boys were judged to be inadequate or defective just because they were not like little boys.

Gilligan did her own research and concluded, in her famous book *In a Different Voice* (1982), that women develop differently from men and that their moral intuitions and perspectives are different as well. The reason this fact had not been recognized is that men and women speak different languages they assume are the same, "using similar words to encode disparate experiences of self and social relationships. Because these languages share an overlapping moral vocabulary, they contain a propensity for systematic mistranslation, creating misunderstandings which impede communication and limit the potential for cooperation and care in relationships."

Gilligan found that, when we look at the way women reason about moral dilemmas, we find they put more emphasis on care and on preserving personal relationships: *issues of abstract justice and rights are secondary in their moral deliberation.* Girls place more weight than boys do on knowing the context of a moral dilemma before rendering judgment. Thus, *context* and *care for others* are central features in women's moral reasoning.

Much of Gilligan's research was grounded in the insights of psychoanalyst **Nancy Chodorow** [CHO-duh-row]. Chodorow argued that our contemporary child-rearing practices foster a strong need for connectedness in little girls and for separation and autonomy in little boys. Because mothers are the first people children get attached to and identify with, girls and boys must then go through substantially different processes in establishing their gender identities: the girls can continue to perceive themselves as continuous with their mothers, but the boys must make a shift to adopt the male gender identity.

Little girls and little boys thus learn very different lessons about how to relate to the world and others in it. Girls develop their sense of themselves as women by means of *personal identification* with their mothers. According to Chodorow, personal identification consists in "diffuse identification with someone else's general personality, behavioral traits, values, and attitudes." Boys, however, develop their identities by means of *positional identification:* "Positional identification consists, by contrast, in identification with specific aspects of another's role." In other words, boys learn that to be a man means to be away at work, whereas girls learn that to be a woman means to be just like mommy in her personality, values, and so forth.

Chodorow argued that this split in gender development has resulted in a great deal of grief for the culture: boys wind up not just isolated and separate but positively **misogynous** because of their efforts to establish themselves as "not-mother." Girls, in contrast, often suffer because they do not extricate themselves sufficiently from others in their milieu and wind up unable to distinguish their own needs from those of others; hence, they are more easily subject to exploitation. Chodorow concluded that these problems could be diminished if men and women took equal responsibility for child rearing and work outside the home, thereby allowing both boys and girls to participate in both positional and personal identification.

Presumably, little girls would become more autonomous, and little boys would become more "connected" and less misogynous.

Another important theorist, **Nel Noddings,** in *Caring, a Feminine Approach to Ethics and Moral Education* (1984), described an ethics of caring as arising out of the memory of natural caring, in which the one caring responds to the one cared for out of love and natural inclination. An **ethics of caring** is not a set of principles or maxims but a way of responding to people and situations.

The ethics of caring was contrasted by Gilligan and Noddings with the abstract ethics of rights, justice, fairness, rules, and blind impartiality. Noddings noted that, in the ethics of rights and justice, one's thought, in considering a moral situation, "moves immediately to abstraction where thinking can take place clearly and logically in isolation from the complicating factors of particular persons, places, and circumstances," whereas within an ethics of caring, one's thought "moves to concretization where its feelings can be modified by the introduction of facts, the feeling of others, and personal histories." Noddings, unlike Gilligan, thought the ethics of caring preferable to an ethics of rights; Gilligan did not make this claim of superiority.

Another writer who has picked up on these themes and worked toward developing a moral theory in response to them is **Sara Ruddick.** In her 1986 essay, "Maternal Thinking," Ruddick discussed the concerns and perspectives of mothers in some patriarchal cultures and then considered how these concerns and perspectives can structure our moral responses to the world. Ruddick called this approach to the world **maternal thinking.**

Ruddick described the social reality of motherhood as expressed in the heterosexual nuclear family of white, middle-class, capitalist America. She invited women from other traditions to reflect on the ways in which their experiences of mothering and being mothered are both similar to and different from her own experiences. Mothers must preserve their children, foster their children's development, and shape them into people who are acceptable to the next generation. Mothers are typically held responsible for these three things, though they do not have anywhere near complete control over their children's environment. In response to the very real fragility of children, who can be killed or disabled in accidents, suffer through long, painful illnesses, or simply fail to thrive in an often hostile world, mothers can develop a metaphysical attitude called "holding." Ruddick said it is "an attitude elicited by the work of 'world-*protection,* world-*preservation,* world-*repair* . . . the invisible weaving of a frayed and threadbare family life.'" Since mothers recognize that they love very fragile beings, maternal thinking sees humility and resilient cheerfulness as virtues. Humility in this sense is the knowledge that one has sharp limits on what can be done to protect and preserve fragile beings in a harsh world. The resilient cheerfulness is the refusal to sink into melancholy about one's own limitations. Ruddick distinguished this cheerfulness from "cheery denial"; the good humor she had in mind is not the simple refusal to see the world as it is. Rather, it is the much harder task of seeing the pain in the world but refusing to be paralyzed and overcome by it.

Ruddick suggested we might employ these virtues in dealing with the world at large, not merely with our own children. A morality that extends the metaphor of maternal thinking would be less self-centered and less prone to hyperindividualism than other paradigms of morality. It is important to note, too, that Ruddick believes that "maternal practice" is something anyone can do, regardless of gender. Men who adopt this attitude toward the world and toward others are maternal thinkers even though they are not biological mothers. Ruddick is not guilty of biological determinism here.

Feminist ethics is not an undifferentiated monolith speaking forth in single loud acclaim for an ethics of caring and in denigration of an ethics of rights and justice. Some feminist ethicists have noted that a care-centered ethic has perhaps not been freely chosen by women but, rather, has arisen to serve the needs of patriarchal society. Men, it might be said, would hardly object to being surrounded by caring attendants. Other feminist moral and political philosophers, including one we discuss next, have emphasized the utility of an ethics of rights and justice as a foundation for social institutions where the competing claims of persons who do not know each other must be balanced. We have seen how Harriet Taylor operated within this framework to advance the cause of women in the nineteenth century.

SEXISM AND LANGUAGE

Language has contributed to women's lower social status in quite varied ways. Many terms that are supposed to be gender neutral are not; *man*, for example, is supposed to serve double duty, referring both to humanity as a whole and to male human beings. Similarly, *he* is the pronoun used both when we know that the person being referred to is male and when we do not know the gender of the individual. This is not logical; either there should be one pronoun to refer to everybody, or there should be three pronouns: male, female, and as-yet-undetermined. Feminist theorists have argued that by making words like *man* and *he* serve both as gender-specific and gender-neutral terms, the net effect is to "erase" women from our conversational landscape. The actual psychology of human beings is such that when we hear *he*, we think "male," even if that was not the speaker's intention. Philosopher Janice Moulton gave a good example of this tendency to hear *man* and *he* as male even when the original use of the term was gender-neutral. She asked us to consider the familiar syllogism:

1. All men are mortal.
2. Socrates is a man.
3. Therefore, Socrates is mortal.

Now substitute the name Sophia for Socrates. Clearly, the "man" in the first line is supposed to be gender neutral; it is supposed to mean "all members of the human species." Yet when the name Sophia is substituted, the second term of the syllogism seems glaringly false. Thus, Moulton argued, to say we have two meanings for *man*, one gender neutral and one gender specific, and we can always keep them clear and separate really does not hold water. Though we might like to believe there are two clearly differentiated uses of *man* and *he*, in practice we hardly make that distinction at all. This point is all the clearer when we realize that generations of logic teachers have taught that syllogism without ever noticing that it is invalid, since the "man" in the first term and the "man" in the second term have different extensions and intentions.

Sometimes the causality seems to flow the other way. Many historians and anthropologists have noted that anything associated with women tends to get devalued over time. Occupations associated with women tend to pay less and have lower status than those associated with men. This holds true across cultures even when the occupation is objectively the same; for instance, in cultures where the women build the homes, that occupation is looked down on, but in our own culture being a contractor is a perfectly respectable thing to do and often is quite well paid.

The same phenomenon holds true of language. Words associated with women come to have lower status and can even degenerate into insults. Many slang expressions and metaphors are evidence of this. These metaphors and slang expressions are taken to be evidence of underlying cultural attitudes toward women. Sometimes words start out with perfectly legitimate, nonderogatory literal meanings and, through their association with women, come to have derogatory and insulting slang meanings. Consider the words *queen, dame, madam, mistress, hussy* (which originally meant *housewife*), and *spinster*. None of the male equivalents of those words have suffered the same kind of devaluation. Through slang, women also get unflatteringly allied to animals, as in *vixen, bitch, pussy, biddy,* and *cow*. And finally, the words we use to describe sexual intercourse are often extremely violent—and the violence is metaphorically directed toward the women, not the men. The word *fuck* has *strike* as its etymological ancestor; *ream* and *drill* do not require any arcane linguistic background to understand. The language use and the attitudes are thought to influence one another; hence, if we make an effort not to use such violent metaphors, perhaps the attitudes of violence will decrease a little as well. But, for the present, it seems painfully clear that our language at least partly reflects certain hostile dispositions.

Stephanie Ross, for example, in her 1981 article "How Words Hurt: Attitude, Metaphor, and Oppression," argued that *screw* is a usefully representative metaphor that tells us more than we wanted to know about certain cultural attitudes toward women: "A screw is hard and sharp; wood by contrast is soft and yielding; force is applied to make a screw penetrate wood; a screw can be unscrewed and reused but wood—wherever a screw has been embedded in it—is destroyed forever." Ross argued that, if we acknowledge that the metaphors we use convey cultural attitudes, then we can see that the attitude toward sex is that women are permanently harmed by intercourse. Furthermore, there is an odd mechanical connotation in the word *screw*. It suggests that intercourse is something alienated from ordinary human flesh and behavior. It is an interesting exercise to list all the common slang terms for sexual intercourse and try to analyze all the meanings and connotations associated with the metaphors.

One expression that students use routinely without examining the underlying sexist connotation is *you guys,* used to refer to any group composed of men, men and women, and even all women. In her article "Sexist Language Matters" and in an informal essay titled "Goodbye, You Guys," Sherryl Kleinman argued that if women really had equal status with men they wouldn't be included in the clearly masculine term *you guys*. Her argument is especially powerful when she asks men to consider how they would feel about being called "you gals." Think about the points Kleinman makes if you're tempted to dismiss use of the term as "so common that it doesn't matter" or as not containing any intention to denigrate women when you use it. Sexist language matters.

FEMINIST EPISTEMOLOGY

Many feminist writers have argued that traditional epistemology is a limited theoretical approach to human knowing. Mainstream epistemology has tended toward assuming that ideal knowers are disembodied, purely rational, fully informed, and completely objective entities. Although most philosophers admit that no human being ever approximates this ideal knower, since real people have bodies, personal histories, points of view, and so forth, most philosophers are reluctant to let go of that ideal.

Feminist epistemologists have made several challenges. First, they argue, it is troubling that the ideal *knower* resembles the ideal *male,* since men are supposedly more rational, objective, and unemotional. Feminists suggest that this conveniently excludes the knowledge claims of women right off the bat. Lorraine Code, one of today's leading feminist epistemologists, points out that, for feminists, "the questions continually arise: Whose science—or whose knowledge—has been proved? Why has its veneration led Western societies to discount other findings, suppress other forms of experience, deny epistemic status to female . . . wisdom?"

Let us take one example of the way scientific knowledge can be biased. Lila Leibowitz cited a case in which E. O. Wilson, the sociobiologist, argued that mouse lemurs are "essentially solitary" except for certain periods in the mating cycle. It turns out that female mouse lemurs nest together; it is the males who are "essentially solitary," and this behavior is generalized over the entire species. "Dominant" males are those who manage to breed. But why should we suppose them to be dominant just for that simple reason? Perhaps those males are merely the ones the females like best, for some reason known only to the female lemurs. This "evidence" of dominant behavior is then quickly overgeneralized to provide support for Wilson's view that almost all males of almost all species are dominant over females. Scientists are not idealized objective observers. As the Wilson example shows, they import their own prejudices and biases into their observations and theories. Feminist epistemologists ask that this fact about all human beings—male and female—be acknowledged. They point out that knowledge is never gathered in a vacuum. People look for answers to specific questions, even—perhaps especially—in science. Knowledge gathering is always done to serve human purposes, and those purposes shape the kind of knowledge that is gathered.

This is not to say that feminist epistemologists want to denigrate or discount rationality or objectivity. But many are concerned that the rational/emotional, objective/subjective dichotomies are false and misleading. Most emotions are structured by rationality. Suppose, for example, you come across a friend who is obviously extremely angry. You might ask, "What's wrong? What are you angry about?" If the answer is, "Light blue shirts are back in style!" you would probably ask a few more questions, since this seems too insignificant to be intensely angry about. Was your friend traumatized by light blue shirts as a child? Was he or she forced to wear them every day? If the answer is, "No, I just hate light blue shirts!" you might plausibly conclude that your friend is a little weird. Only emotions based on plausible reasons make sense to most of us. It is not true that people generally have emotional responses "for no reason at all"; if they do, they are often considered mentally unstable. Reason and emotion are more interconnected than that. Feminist epistemologists generally emphasize that knowledge gathering is a human project and must be identified as such. Reason, emotion, social class, gender, and other factors play a role in what we can know. Any ideal that rules out the "human factor" in its characterization of knowledge is bound to be wrong and will unjustly privilege the group claiming that true knowledge is only obtainable by people who are just like them and have only their social characteristics.

In the reading selections at the end of this chapter, you will find one by **Sandra Harding,** a feminist philosopher of science, who believes that the epistemologies of scientists and philosophers of science are revealed by the metaphors they use; in the selection, she examines some of the apparently misogynous (women-hating) metaphors used by scientists and philosophers at the beginning of the Scientific Revolution.

FRENCH FEMINIST PHILOSOPHY AND PSYCHOANALYTICAL THEORY

French feminist philosophy deserves a section of its own. France has produced many distinguished philosophers—Descartes, Sartre, Camus, Lacan, Foucault, and Derrida, among many others—and some of the finest minds have formulated French thought. In French society, philosophy plays an integral role, affecting not only culture, psychology, and politics, but art, literature, and drama as well. French feminism has evolved out of these rich philosophical roots quite differently from the way U.S. feminism has developed, and it is considerably more complex to come to understand.

In France, students take, on the average, two courses in philosophy and logic in order to graduate from the lycée (high school). U.S. students might get their first introduction to critical thinking in college in an English department, not in a philosophy department, so they might never learn about formal logic or philosophy at all. But in France, even students who do not go on to higher education have learned logic and have a solid background in the work of key philosophers. As a result, politics and philosophy are more connected in France than in the United States. French politicians may have more trouble getting away with glittering generalities and other forms of fallacious reasoning—it would be instantly recognized!

In the 1980s, a few Francophile feminist critics in the United States began to take notice of what the French feminist philosophers were doing. Alice Jardine,

Toril Moi, and Jane Gallop were primarily responsible for the introduction of French psychoanalytical theory into American academia, but few others could follow their lead because they lacked facility in the French language, and very few of the French texts were published in English until the late eighties. By the time the texts were generally available, many were a decade old. The French theorists by then had gone on to other topics and genres. Most of the American scholars who attempted to read the French feminist philosophers were not up to the intellectual challenge because they did not share the intellectual and social histories. Consequently, the three feminist philosophers we will discuss in this chapter were often dismissed or misunderstood.

In general, French feminist philosophy is a feminism based on psychoanalytic theory, concerned with the unconscious and with gendered subjectivity. In other words, the major voices in French feminist thought have all examined the "I" in some form, sometimes looking at agency, sometimes at the way the subject is produced, sometimes at linguistics as it contributes to the formation of the subject, sometimes at literary/textual expressions, and sometimes at psycholinguistics, which is the language of the unconscious. French feminist philosophy draws heavily on the ideas of Freud, Lacan, and Derrida, so we must examine aspects of their theory in order to understand the way French feminist philosophy has evolved.

Sigmund Freud (1859–1939) developed two pillars of psychoanalysis, the Oedipus complex and the castration complex. Simply put, the Oedipus complex is the notion that the male child desires to possess the mother and kill the father as a rival. The castration complex involves the male child's fear of being castrated by the father. A correlate is the theory that the female child experiences penis envy when she discovers that male children have penises and she doesn't.

Jacques Lacan (1901–1981) took Freud's consciousness studies to a new depth. Rejecting parts of Freud's work, Lacan placed it instead in the context of semiotics, linguistics, and literature. This puts him in direct conflict with philosophers who assume a rational, unified consciousness. Lacan's subject is split between consciousness and unconsciousness, the latter being the absence of identity. According to Lacan, both subjectivity and sexuality are functions of the symbolic as produced by language, and both consciousness and unconsciousness are structured like a language. His theory developed the relationship between the acquisition of language and the development of the self.

Lacan's work is very difficult for laypersons to understand. To simplify, he saw masculinity and femininity as a result of the child's development of an identity, that is, the *meaning* of sexual difference, not the anatomical differences themselves. Thus, sexual difference becomes a part of language, thought, and culture.

In his discussion of the pre-oedipal stage, where there is no separation between the self of the child and its mother, there is no Other. It is not until the child enters the "symbolic order" of the patriarchal culture that the child perceives the phallus as the symbol of the father, and then the self splits into self and other. This phenomenon also results in the birth of the unconscious, which Lacan regarded as repressed desire.

Lacan theorized that there is never an end to desire. Because the stage of merged identity with the mother has ceased, the person is doomed to eternal fragmentation, and all of life is a seeking for that lost unity. Three French feminist philosophers in particular—Hélène Cixous, Luce Irigaray, and Julia Kristeva—had built on Lacan's theory. They theorized about Lacan's discussions of the relationship of gender to repressed desire, resulting in a model for both social relations and, on an abstract level, textual relations. Meaning, they said, is created out of this intersection between the two.

These three French theorists acknowledged the existence of a female self (subject) who is still and always Other. They extrapolated from Lacan's theory of psycholinguistics as it relates to the language of the unconscious. In this language, there is no grammar or syntax, nor are there words. Instead, the communications are in terms of gaps, silences, interruptions, moments between decisions, and other nonverbal transactions. However, it is very important to note that all three of these French feminist philosophers disputed Lacan's (and Freud's) "Law of the Father" in various ways unique to each.

Another important influence in French feminist philosophy was **Jacques Derrida** (1930–2004). Like Lacan, Derrida focused on unseen discourse, one that is different from conscious discourse. For Derrida, a text always contains its own subversions, elements that are not reducible. These may be as simple as punctuation, indications of pauses, missing expressions, or they may be as complex as sophisticated literary devices, figurative representations, remarks that deflect, divert, or expose undercurrents—in other words, a textual unconscious.

Derrida delighted in targeting figures such as Plato, Aristotle, Rousseau, Mill, Hegel, Heidegger, Nietzsche, Freud, and others because theirs were the central texts that must be deconstructed in order to reveal other forms of subjectivity. What Lacan did to subject-as-consciousness, Derrida did to texts, setting up the text as its own Other, different from itself. Derridean thought is about constructing binary oppositions so that they play off each other, and this is a key tactic in feminist philosophy as well.

Derrida was not posing a theory, however. Instead he was using a process. His "theory" of "deconstruction" is really a progression of close readings of philosophical/literary texts, which become destabilized in the process of using metaphors, images, phrases, and other linguistic devices that keep the main text from staying whole and unfragmented. Just as Lacan insisted that both the conscious and the unconscious are always present, Derrida insisted that both the text and its subtext (its hidden meaning) are always present, always already there. When the subtext is expressed, paradoxes come into focus, excesses and holes in the text are exposed, and the text thus exceeds its own borders, becoming fluid and subject to multiple interpretations. Whatever spills over the edges of the text displaces subjectivity, so the subject changes shape and form and is no longer a stable symbol of power and authority. A deconstructed text is potentially endless because each deferral creates another set of relationships. In this process, the text deconstructs itself.

What takes place between the two poles (binary oppositions) is a combination of sameness and difference, a kind of "play"—a free radical, a kind of endless escape from anything stable and unitary. Derrida called this space "différance," which does not translate into our word "difference." It is, instead, as just described, a free space where all sorts of things can take place without being pinned down to a specific meaning.

This open circle of reinscription is of paramount interest to the three feminist philosophers under discussion here. Each in her own way created a "feminine" writing (*écriture féminine*) that dissolves the traditional invisible line between author and text. Each used highly experimental literary forms. And each, in her way, created a new language from the roots provided by Lacan and Derrida.

Luce Irigaray

A discourse may poison, surround, encircle, imprison or liberate, heal, nourish, fertilize. —Luce Irigaray, *Speaking Is Never Neutral*

Luce Irigaray [e-RIG-uh-ray] (1930–   ), born in Belgium, is a philosopher and psychoanalyst trained in linguistics. Some readers find it disconcerting that she doesn't ascribe boundaries to philosophy or use systematic reasoning. She moves with ease across disciplines in ways that most academics find overwhelming. Irigaray focuses on sexual difference, which is a concern of psychoanalysis; the historical roots of language, which is a linguistic concern; and the realities of women's lives, which is a sociopolitical concern; and she also has ethical concerns. So what she is really doing, as British feminist philosopher Margaret Whitford pointed out, is rethinking the whole social contract. In this process, even the sex of the philosopher comes under scrutiny.

Because Irigaray uses associative thinking in her discourse, her texts are difficult to follow. She requires the reader to stretch, to project herself, and to identify in imaginative ways. For Irigaray, the entrance into écriture féminine (literally, "women's writing") includes all the facets of woman—her roles, interactions, places in history, places in the pre-oedipal stage—the changing plurality that is woman. Irigaray recognizes all the aspects of feminism in philosophical discourse and the ways those are multiplying, and she is doing something creative about it.

Irigaray's argument centers on female desire. Male and female desire/language are fundamentally alien to each other, Irigaray claims. The patriarchal order of the **phallus** as linear, rational, and symbolic cannot comprehend feminine expressions of desire/language. There is no space for the feminine in the traditional masculinist order of discourse or in the masculine structure of desire. So Irigaray looks at what could be described as cultural representations, both in texts and in psychoanalysis. She focuses in particular on texts that reflect the repression of the feminine.

Irigaray is critical of Freudian theory because it describes women as dependent and secondary, but she uses Freudian theory as a representional system by inverting it. If woman is not one, for example, then she is *more than one*. In her *Speculum of the Other Woman,* she problematizes the representational system, rejecting the maternal function of woman in particular. Woman is more than her capacity for motherhood, and a woman's individual identity must be reconceptualized in order to free her of Freud's legacy for her.

The feminine Irigaray envisions is not related to women's anatomical nature. Instead, she focuses on women's experienced reality, a re-visioning of Lacan, which also short-circuits Freud's model. She thus deconstructs both. She frees woman to be her own source to produce meaning so that woman has her own identity apart from what is traditionally assigned to her as culturally produced identity.

The language of Irigaray's texts is elliptical, poetic, rhythmic, ambiguous, playful, and often mocking in tone. Her imagery expresses both a multiplicity and an excess of female sexuality. She carves her way through patriarchal constructs of sexuality and textuality, making space for the female voice/body. She does this by describing the options, by seizing Lacan's mirror and stepping through it, like Alice in the looking-glass, building metaphors and smashing binary polarizations along the way.

On the other side of the looking-glass, Irigaray's vision of woman is a speaking subject. The purpose of crossing through the mirror is the process itself, the process of "jamming the theoretical machinery." Once that machinery has been silenced, then woman can speak.

For readers not trained in psychoanalysis, Irigaray is difficult to follow. It is helpful to understand that in psychoanalytic technique, words are not important in the ways they are in traditional masculinist discourse. In the unconscious, there are no words, only moving, fluid, half-formed associations. The way to understand these movements is not through words, which create meanings that are fixed in ways that movement is not, but to express them in new ways that suggest meanings in the plural and do not define in closed ways.

Critics of Irigaray accuse her of **essentialism,** of focusing on the essential female qualities of embodiment. This is in part because some of these scholars keep trying to get to the bottom of her theory, stripping away the trappings, and fail to understand that Irigaray's whole process must be understood, not just the bottom line. The process *is* the bottom line, and not to see this distorts her theory. Looking for analytical connections and rational progressions in Irigaray's work is a mistake that cannot describe what she has created: ways to reconstruct the female body through metaphors and symbols. Whereas her earlier works (*Speculum of the Other Woman* and *This Sex Which Is Not One*) focused on the history of philosophy as seen through embodiment, her later works focus on woman's capacity to define herself.

Irigaray moves the divine into her discussion of the feminine by linking God, language, and woman in the process of "becoming." There is always the movement, never a static condition. Her notion of "Divine Women" is difficult for those raised in traditional Christian belief structures to comprehend. She discusses salvation and grace, but only as forms of escapism. God becomes a metaphor for being that is situated in space and time yet has the capacity for autonomous identity, a metaphor to describe becoming. Reappropriating the divine as female is part of the struggle to reclaim autonomy for women. Her work in the area of religion must be understood as part of her larger project, that of creating an ideal for women to work toward. By constructing a new divine in one's own image, Irigaray is moving her project to the ultimate realm of exchange, the infinite.

Julia Kristeva (1941–   )

Woman is here to shake up, to disturb, to deflate masculine values, and not to espouse them. Her role is to maintain difference by pointing to them, by giving them life, by putting them into play against one another.   —Julia Kristeva, *Polylogues*

Born in Bulgaria, **Julia Kristeva** [krisst-EH-vuh] moved to France in 1966 to continue her education and to escape Stalinist communism. A brilliant young woman, she was appointed professor of linguistics studies in 1974. She has been contributing ever since to the theories of language, poetics, psychoanalysis, political philosophy, and literature. In each field, she practices a radical critique of what she calls the "signifying practice." Although she resists being counted as a feminist and is often rejected by feminists as antifeminist, Kristeva has nevertheless contributed significantly to feminist theories of discourse.

Early on, Kristeva studied women in China out of her conviction that Marxist principles could rescue women from inequality. But when she saw the actual conditions under which Chinese women lived, she became disenchanted with Marxist politics and switched from political writing to psychoanalysis. She became convinced that she could make more difference in the status of women by treating one patient at a time. Her writing is dense and difficult, partly because her field is linguistics and partly because she believes that all writing should be in the traditional structure of discourse, the only discourse there is. Feminist critics of her work do not always realize that her view of language is centered on the speaking subject and that she is committed to a more complex analysis than many theorists take the pains to follow. She requires that we go deeper, where language is more than naming and communication, where it becomes a device for the production of subjectivity.

Even though Kristeva uses Lacanian terms, her work is original and revolutionary. For example, in *Revolution in Poetic Language,* she reworks Lacan's separation of the preconscious and symbolic orders into what she calls the **semiotic** (i.e., dealing with sign and symbol systems) and the symbolic, looking closely at what takes place between the two orders. Expanding the Lacanian model of the mirror stage, she argues that the female semiotic has been devalued, that both the prelinguistic level and the symbolic are present in the subject. She argues further that the reason feminine signification has been marginalized is precisely because it threatens the traditionally masculinist symbolic discourse. And, contrary to Freud and Lacan, in her view every child can choose to identify with either parent after the mirror stage.

Kristeva focuses on the maternal semiotic as disruptive to the rational, unified, speaking subject, challenging the symbolic order. The core of her work is in the area of what she calls "subject-in-process," which is another way of describing the subject as unstable. This concept of the self links her linguistic theory and her psychoanalytical theory to her social concerns. Closely related is her work in the maternal semiotic. Only if both the unstable subject and the maternal semiotic could be under the control of the symbolic would the masculinist speaking subject be victorious. Because this cannot occur, given the nature of semiotic discourse and the unstable subject, the symbolic is always subverted or at risk.

In "Women's Time," Kristeva differentiates between the time of the symbolic order as linear, sequential, and goal oriented, and the semiotic order, which contains another kind of time. In this essay, she emphasizes the multiple nature of women's expressions in order to open up sexual difference.

Kristeva's writing is startlingly effective when she breaks out of a style that at first seems suspiciously patterned after masculinist discourse. In "Stabat Mater," which is about motherhood and the cult of the Virgin Mary as mother of all, she begins with a typically masculinist analysis, then intersperses feminine text about the birth of her own son; the result is a complete splitting of the discourse. The feminine text of the piece is open, a literal and figurative birthing. The effect is a visual delight and a stirring commentary on both the paradox she is describing in the texts and on masculine-feminine discourse in general. More than this: she creates her own intertextual reading of herself. "Stabat Mater" does not behave as a text "should." It looks different, and it acts differently; it winds and jumps on the page. Juxtaposed as the two texts are, they are nevertheless parallel, feminine and masculine texts complementing, rather than opposing, one another. The essay successfully transgresses the line between literature and theory, between the abstract and the personal, and between the semiotic and the symbolic.

In her later work Kristeva shows a preoccupation with the divine. Although she doesn't believe in an actual divinity, she sees religion as a feminine discourse, a place where love and ethics meet. For her, theology is a kind of constructed fantasy invented to ward off the reality of death, a way to blind ourselves to the ultimate truth of death as nothingness. She sees religion as a language that maintains the tension between our psychological needs and our personal cognition of reality. So she uses religious discourse to mediate a healing space between spirit and flesh, the symbolic and the semiotic, self and other, while not buying into it as ultimate truth. She asserts that we need the rituals of religion, which are an expression of the semiotic. She views religion as a healing art form if it is divested of its harsh and punitive doctrines. Claiming religion as the feminine semiotic, she opens it to imaginative spaces that heal the psyche and permit language to expand.

Finally, Kristeva's most recent work consists of a number of mystery novels in which she deals with "radical evil," which she explains as "the desire for death," and various other themes such as motherhood, historical projects, and psychic pain. These are detective action novels with the usual violence and serial killers, to be sure, but they are also mysteries for the intelligent reader to ponder. Here is theory in practice: she has freed herself to make her own way with ease in any environment, in both intellectual and ordinary life.

Hélène Cixous (1937–   )

I don't write. Life becomes text starting out from my body. I am already text.   —Hélène Cixous

Hélène Cixous [aay-LAYN seek-soo] was born in Algeria, and her early education was there. She described herself as "triply marginalized" as an Algerian colonial, female, and a Jew. As a Jew, she was not permitted to attend regular school, but she nevertheless learned French, Arabic, Hebrew, German, Spanish, and English. Later, in order to study the work of Clarice Lispector in the original, she also learned Portuguese. In 1955 her family emigrated to France, where at the age of 21 she became the youngest student to pass l'agrégation in English. Earlier, Simone de Beauvoir had been the youngest ever to pass it in French. In 1958 she published her 900-page doctoral thesis, and in 1969 she won the *Prix Médicis*, a prestigious literary award, for *Dedans,* an autobiographical novel about her oedipal attachment to her father.

Cixous worked with Jacques Lacan for two years before accepting a chair position at the radical left-wing French institution that was to become the scene of the famous 1968 student upheavals and the subsequent intellectual revolution. She went on to create the first doctoral program in women's studies in Europe. Today she continues to supervise the program as it has evolved and gives international lectures. Despite this heavy schedule of responsibilities, she continues to produce, in her seventies, a text nearly every year.

Jacques Derrida, who was Cixous's longtime mentor and friend until his death in 2004, once said of Hélène Cixous that her entire body of work is "nearly untranslatable." This is because even in the original French her texts use subtle displacements and because they spill over into multiple disciplines. Her work is philosophy, poetry, fiction, literary criticism, autobiography, commentary, and psychoanalytical theory, often all at the same time. In contrast, most U.S. feminist thinkers are educated in and publish in only one primary discipline unless they are consciously interdisciplinary.

In spite of her focus on women's writing and female embodiment as a metaphor for women's writing in her texts, *feminist* is not a word she has been willing to agree to as a label for her perspective, largely because feminism has evolved in different ways in Europe and the United States. In more recent years, however, her work is quite clearly feminist. While her work is political, it is political in a textual sense; she recognizes that social structures are inherent in language, so she writes at the limits of language in a style called écriture féminine (ay-cree-tur fem-in-ee) to mitigate the damage done by "masculinist" structures in philosophical writing.

Another reason Cixous is difficult for American scholars to understand is that even after all these years, only part of her hundreds of essays and novels have been translated into English. And the focus of her work doesn't fit into American feminists' agenda. Many find her work essentialist or utopian because she doesn't write about domestic violence, child care, abortion, pornography, or poverty, the mainstay feminist activist issues. This is not to say that she avoids sociopolitical conflicts between the sexes, but she does it from a plane that is less familiar to U.S. scholars—from the unconscious, from the ambiguous feminine language that originates there.

Cixous's many themes are reworked continually in subsequent texts in the way that Derrida's sentences are restatements: the circles of thought expand and become ever more inclusive. Some of these themes are the author and the writing process, the reading-writing relationship, the reader-writer relationship, philosophical questions, psychoanalytical concerns (especially those related to identity and other self-other relations), birth, death, endings, love lost/found, the prehistory of art, internal landscapes, embodiment, autobiography, the maternal/paternal (especially the absent father), the revisioning of motherhood, the reweaving of myths, arriving/departing, the metaphors of exile, the stretching of the concept of the gift/exchange/spending . . . the list is dizzying, but under Cixous's pen these topics take on life and breath, interact with each other, and move from text to text, transforming themselves as the shapes of concepts appear, shift, and disappear.

Themes not only repeat but are refined and presented through new characters, through multidimensional selves of indeterminate gender, each struggling in a different challenge of relation. It would be tempting to say that all these themes spring from the basic category of self and other, but this would be doing Cixous's work a disservice. The word *category* is not in the Cixousian vocabulary; her themes defy boundaries. Her texts "escape" all limitations in the way that Derrida's conversations contain endless deferrals. Methods of discussing Cixous's work always fall short of the intricate, elusive richness that is always present in her texts.

Cixous's novels do not have traditional beginnings, middles, and endings. All of her texts are "open," which is to say that even when considering philosophical questions, looking closely at Hegel, Kierkegaard, Heidegger, Nietzsche, Deleuze, and Derrida, her writings are not on a conceptual level. Her goal is to read texts, including philosophical texts, and to displace those that are "masculine" to find the feminine elements. She wants to efface the Western ideal that privileges concepts, truth, presence, mastery, and patriarchal law, so she examines dialectical structures that dominate the formation of subjectivity. She opposes absolute knowledge. Thus even her philosophical discussions are rooted in autobiographical fiction as her work interrogates and subverts the linguistic representations of women society has assigned them. The subversion is always done in creative ways that are both serious and playful, and is always, in one way or another, related to women's subjectivity.

Cixous's work can be recognized in four phases. Her early work was literary criticism focusing on Joyce, Gide, Shakespeare, Woolf, Kafka, and Jeffers. These writings were in traditional academic prose. The second phase is the Freud/Lacan period. Her first and only volume of short stories dealt with various facets of identity, the unconscious, and dream work. Her third period was the discovery of Clarice Lispector, a Brazilian writer whom she described as her "unhoped-for other." This period was a flurry of books and essays on the feminine element in Lispector's work.

The fourth phase is her work in theater. The "other" in her plays is often whole races of people as she engages with historical representations. Her plays, which contribute to social change more than her other genres, deal with humanity's global pain and injustice. But even though these phases can be traced chronologically, they do not represent distinct areas. She continues to write autobiographical fiction, and it continues to cross over the boundaries of genre. There are no real beginnings or endings in the study of Cixous, any more than there are beginnings or endings in her novels. All of her texts—not just the plays—are performative, in the sense that they show rather than tell. They draw the reader into regions that are both familiar and alien, comforting and threatening, intellectually stimulating and emotionally challenging. This is how she opens up spaces in her texts to create expanded meaning out of ambiguous realms and entices the reader to learn to read and write in a new language.

Irigaray, Kristeva, and Cixous all use a form of *écriture féminine,* which doesn't translate into "feminine writing" in the sense in which Americans use the word *feminine.* The French word *feminine* doesn't have the connotations of sly, pretentious, coy, and manipulative that it has in English. Instead, it is a language that is in the process of continued evolution, that uses metaphor to cross the boundaries between theory and other forms of discourse.

Each writer who uses *écriture féminine* has her own style of it. Cixous's is a libidinal form of discourse that includes encounter with other, embodiment, moments of epiphany, and experiences of passion that disrupt the socialized binary structure of consciousness. In this way, she is able to transcend the limits that conventional methods of understanding difference impose on language and social relations. Perhaps the most important thing to remember about Cixous is that she does not conceive of the body as a biological universal or as a referential independent of texts. The whole focus of her work is to demonstrate that language doesn't exist outside the body.

"Laugh of the Medusa"   The myth of the Medusa is an ancient one. Medusa was a beautiful young woman whom the goddess Athena turned into a monster with hair made of live snakes because Medusa had sex with Poseidon. Subsequently, any man who looked at Medusa would be turned into stone. Perseus later killed Medusa and presented Athena with her head, which still retained the power to turn men into stone. Freud gave this myth a psychosexual interpretation. He identified Medusa's decapitated head with men's terror of castration: decapitation equals castration. Medusa's paralyzing effect on men was interpreted by Freud as the erect penis, and the snakes that are Medusa's hair were all penises. For Freud, this combination of erection and terror represented the two ways men feel about women—they desire women, and they fear women as different, mysterious, and dangerous. Medusa was both alive and capable of causing men's desire, and dead, causing men to fear that they would be dead as well if they consummated their desire. Man, who considers himself whole, may have his identity altered by the woman/monster.

So, on one hand, man desires to possess woman, and on the other, he fears being subsumed into woman by the sex act. Freud argued that men's dread of women is based on their difference, which man finds incomprehensible and therefore terrifying. He fears being weakened or overcome by her feminine qualities. Woman becomes castrating woman. The menacing Medusa's many penises, however, according to Freud, metaphorically reassure the man that his own penis will not be lost.

In "Laugh of the Medusa," an early Cixous's text that has become a classic of feminist literature, the feminine body is not a body at all; it is embodied textual movement, a metaphor. Once the body is understood as text, this piece becomes easier to understand. Cixous moved back and forth from the literal level to the metaphoric level when she wrote of woman. The same is true when she wrote of the "feminine." Yes, she was talking about femaleness and female bodies, but she was simultaneously using it as a metaphor for linguistic representation. Cixous transformed Freud's "dark continent" as women's writing, which is alien to men. Medusa is not to be feared, Cixous argued: she is approachable and even has a sense of humor. Women must show men their "sexts" (sex + text), the new women's writing in which there is space for difference, and there is no Lacanian "lack." Like all of her writing, Cixous's "Laugh of the Medusa" first defined the oppressive structures that frame our cultural lives, then deconstructed and reconstructed them in ways that free women to write themselves.

JUDITH BUTLER: GENDER, SEX, AND PERFORMATIVITY

It goes without saying that all feminist philosophers work on issues of gender and sexuality. One, in particular, however, deserves special mention for her enormously wide-ranging examinations of the intricacies of these studies: Judith Butler (1956–). She's an American **poststructuralist** philosopher who has made impressive contributions not only to the field of Western feminist philosophy but also to political philosophy, Jewish philosophy, ethics, literary theory, sexuality studies, psychoanalytic theory, and queer theory. She has done work in the areas of loss, mourning, race, war, censorship, and ethical violence, and has formulated a theory of responsibility. She has been awarded many honors, awards, and fellowships for her research. She has a long list of books, lectures, and publications dating from 1987 to the present. She is currently a professor at the University of California, Berkeley, and is a visiting professor at Columbia University.

Her work is dizzyingly dense and complex, however, and she is not without critics for this very reason. She weaves threads of other philosophers' thoughts and her own ideas into an impressive socio-philosophical discussion of the ways gender and sex intersect and offers a possible solution for the problems she identifies, a word she coined: **performativity.**

Butler's basic question focuses on identity and subjectivity, specifically, the widespread belief that gendered behaviors are natural, but this is an oversimplification of her radical, complex exploration of identity within language, conventions, and institutions. In her first book, which was written as her doctoral dissertation, *Subjects of Desire: Hegelian Reflections in Twentieth-Century France* (1987), she tries to understand how gender came to be regarded as naturally occurring rather than a choice. She traces the process by which we become "subjects," but by subjects, she doesn't mean an individual; rather, she describes a linguistic structure that is always in a process that doesn't complete itself. In other words, the subject is always "becoming." A person becomes gendered as soon as s/he is named; Butler says a "boundary" is set at that time. An important aspect of this view is that if identity is a social construction, then there must be ways to change, challenge, and reconstruct it, and in her books she is always searching for these ways. She distinguishes as part of the problem the thin line between a subjectivity that holds power and one that acts in subversive ways to prevent power from being the standard by which identity is constructed. She is always asking in one way or another, what power is, and how power can be subverted.

A complication of Butler's already complex interrogations is that her various texts are in dialogue with each other, and she doesn't answer any of the questions she poses. There is no linear, rational progression of ideas to examine, which can be exasperating and confusing for the reader. Instead, her theories move in circles, intersecting, crossing over, and never reach a final outcome. This mode of inquiry draws on the Hegelian notion of the dialectic: a thesis is proposed, then it is negated by its antithesis and resolved into a synthesis, which provides the starting point for the next round of the process. Butler isn't looking for absolute knowledge, however, as Hegel was; she is only examining ideas in an open-ended process. This is understandably frustrating for the reader who has been conditioned to look for "the bottom line."

There are also contradictions in Butler's theories, which she openly admits and takes pains to revise and improve. Why doesn't she resolve her discussions, you may well ask? It's because the point of her explorations is that the subject is always, endlessly in process. Butler's "subject" is not the stable entity that others have described, and feminist philosophy in general has now begun to support that idea as well. Both women as a category and women as bodies created by society's constructions of them figure prominently in Butler's and now in other feminist philosophers' thought. This is one of her major contributions.

Her views of identity/the subject as always becoming is exemplified by the way she writes. She claims that in order to understand the formulation of the subject, one must understand the specific historical and argumentative contexts in which the subject is in process. This is similar to what Hegel did in his *Phenomenology of Spirit,* and in her *Subjects of Desire,* Butler points this out: " . . . if we question the presumptions . . . that the prose asks us to, we will experience the incessant movement of the sentence that constitutes its meaning." To benefit best from Butler, we need to do the same, allow ourselves to be caught up in her ruminations and let her take us where she goes, rather than trying to make immediate sense of a particular idea. This is the challenge of reading Butler.

While Hegel (Georg Wilhelm Friedrich Hegel, 1770–1831) was Butler's first influence, there have been many others since her first publication, *Subjects of Desire.* Michel Foucault's (1926–1984) work in the constructions of sex and sexuality in different cultures and contexts and Jacques Derrida's (1930–2004) theory of language that describes meaning as an event with no beginning or end, rather than a fixed idea, are both strong influences. The difference between Hegel and Derrida is a significant one in terms of Butler's project: Hegel's Spirit does eventually reach absolute knowledge, whereas Derrida's linguistic journeys and searches are always circular and never-ending: words only acquire meaning in relation to other words. Butler has also found Continental philosophers, particularly Simone de Beauvoir (1909–1986), Jean Paul Sartre (1905–1980), Julia Kristeva (1941–), and Monique Wittig (1935–2003), rich in ideas she expands on. Marxists, psychoanalysts, and anthropologists also contribute to her thought. She interrogates Friedrich Nietzsche (1844–1900), Sigmund Freud (1859–1939), Jacques Lacan (1901–1981), and Pierre Bourdieu (1930–2002). What's interesting about all these important thinkers in Butler's work is that she doesn't identify with any one particular theoretical approach or any particular scholar. She mixes and matches, uses a range of theoretical approaches, borrowing and sometimes appropriating, in ways that are unusually provocative.

In *Gender Trouble* (1990), Butler's most well-known book, gender was described as something we "do." It's a sequence of actions that are always occurring. Both gender and sex (sexed identity, not sexual intercourse) underwent Butler's scrutiny in this regard: they are what Butler calls "performative," i.e., in process, in movement, verbs as opposed to nouns. This is probably her most difficult idea to grasp, and her explications take place over several books and many articles. Butler claims that there is no body that is not always already gendered, that bodies, both male and female, are gendered from the beginning of their social existence. Gender is more than a process, however; it's a particular kind of process within its social framework.

Her most important contribution to feminist theory arose in this book: she challenged the idea that "woman" is a unitary category, that gender is something one has.

In *Bodies That Matter: On the Discursive Limits of Sex* (1993), she continued the discussion. If there is no subject that pre-exists subjectivity, no agent doing the acting, then how can there be a performance? A performance needs at least one performer, does it not? This is only confusing if it is not understood that she wasn't claiming that gender IS a performance. She was talking about performativity, which is quite different.

By performativity, Butler means authoritative speech acts that create what they say, producing the effects they are describing. They bring to life the concepts they specify, all of which are within societal norms and customs. Examples would be "I pronounce you," "I baptize you," and "I own this." By repeating the phrases, the acts become even more powerful and entrenched. Butler sees gender as an act as well, something that has been practiced, repeated, and rehearsed as part of a social script. When we perform these actions, we strengthen the script and make it part of social convention.

Butler doesn't regard gender identity as two categories, male and female, and she asserts that gender, sex, and sexuality are not voluntary choices in our society. She proposes breaking the connections between sex and gender as well so that gender can be "flexible and freefloating." Butler goes ever deeper as she explores these ideas in her various texts. She recounts a cartoon that illustrates a nurse handing a mother her newborn daughter, saying, "It's a lesbian!" This is what Butler would call a "performative" exclamation. The baby is now clearly labeled within the dominant norms of culture. Her sex/gender have been cited.

Gender is an act, then, that creates "masculine" or "feminine" persons, but since these gender identities are constructed by language, then clearly there is no gender identity that exists prior to the naming. There is no subject, no "I" outside this linguistic convention that constructs masculine and feminine. According to Butler, there is no body that exists outside of gendered discourse. Bodies can't be separated from the acts of discourse that have created them. The concept of performativity rescues the categories from being unitary and distinct. We "do" heterosexuality; we "do" homosexuality.

Perhaps the clearest expression of Butler's project appears in her "Performative Acts and Gender Constitution: An Essay in Phenomenology and Feminist Theory" (1990): "gender cannot be understood as a role which either expresses or disguises an interior 'self,' whether that 'self' is conceived as sexed or not. As performance which is performative, gender is an 'act,' broadly construed, which constructs the social fiction of its own psychological interiority." The key words here are "social fiction." The nature of gender identity is an artificial construct, an illusion created by our performances. There is no stable subjectivity that exists prior to the performed gender. "Because gender is not a fact," says Butler, "the various acts of gender create the idea of gender, and without these acts, there would be no gender at all".

The same is true, according to Butler, of the concept of sex. Feminists have considered sex to be the biological identity of male and female and gender to be the historical result of social conventions that determine separate behaviors. But

Butler challenges this concept as well, arguing that sex is also a cultural norm, a process. So "sex," in Butler's view, is also a fiction even though it is a focus of culture. Just as gender is a linguistic construction, so is sex, says Butler. It is an artificial norm, and it is subject to change. Both gender and sex, then, are a performance; it's not about who we are, but rather, it is about what we do. Further, we all do gender performance. But we can decide to change the form of that performance. We can initiate "gender trouble" by causing subversive confusion, by choosing to do a different performance. This is Butler's prescription for how we can work to change gender norms and the traditional binary construction of masculine and feminine.

These ideas of identity as flexible and free and the concept of gender as performance create the foundations of **queer theory,** and indeed, Butler is considered a queer theorist par excellence. Queer theory resists definition, but it can be understood as a variety of theories that disrupt whatever is a cultural "norm." In *Queer Theory: An Introduction,* Annamarie Jagose writes that queer theory's "debunking of stable sexes, genders and sexualities develops out of a specifically lesbian and gay reworking of the post-structuralist figuring of identity as a constellation of multiple and unstable positions." Queer theory doesn't advocate the changing of identities; instead, it encourages the dramatization of the supposedly stable relations between sex and gender. Interestingly, queer theory doesn't repudiate all binary contrasts, only those that are stable constructs. The emphasis is on shifting boundaries, unstable identities that change so that heterosexuality as a fixed social construct is challenged. Queer theory creates a deeply philosophical argument for disrupting sexual difference.

In *Giving an Account of Oneself* (2005), Butler took the many strands of her inquiry about selfhood to a startling place in the field of ethics. Clearly, she claimed, one can only be responsible for one's acts if one has self-knowledge. If you think about this before going on, isn't the accepted definition of insanity the state of a person who is NOT responsible for his/her acts because s/he didn't know if what s/he was doing was right or wrong? Butler asserted that if any concept of responsibility demands the self's complete transparency to itself, and if that self is a social construction, one constructed by discourse, then there are limits to what the self can know of itself. A truly responsible self knows the limits of its knowing. And this brings us back around to the social world that has brought us into selfhood in the first place, a social world we can't know completely because we are a part of it.

What is the point, you may ask, of Butler's huge body of work? What is she trying to prove? Why is she so fiercely searching out all the intricacies of gender and sex? Toward what end? The answer is that she is trying to rescue the rights of people whose identities don't conform to the norm of heterosexuality—gays, lesbians, bisexuals, transsexuals, transvestites—and anyone who doesn't fit into these categories but is not a heterosexual. Her work has opened up all sorts of debates and explorations into identity and identity politics, language, subjectivity, gender and sex, feminist theory, queer theory, and philosophy. Posing such difficult questions that transcend so many fields and disciplines and affect the ways we think about what we tend to take for granted is Butler's continuing project.

SELECTION 14. 1

A Vindication of
the Rights of Woman

Mary Wollstonecraft

[*In the following selection, Wollstonecraft defended the view that society should abandon the practice of enculturating women to weakness and servility.*]

I love man as my fellow; but this sceptre, real, or usurped, extends not to me, unless the reason of man. In fact, the conduct of an accountable being must be regulated by the operations of its own reason; or on what foundation rests the throne of God?

It appears to me necessary to dwell on these obvious truths, because females have been insulated, as it were; and, while they have been stripped of the virtues that should clothe humanity, they have been decked with artificial graces that enable them to exercise a short-lived tyranny. Love, in their bosoms, taking the place of every nobler passion, their sole ambition is to be fair, to raise emotion instead of inspiring respect; and this ignoble desire, like the servility in absolute monarchies, destroys all strength of character. Liberty is the mother of virtue, and if women be, by their very constitution, slaves, and not allowed to breathe the sharp invigorating air of freedom, they must ever languish like exotics, and be reckoned beautiful flaws in nature. . . .

But should it be proved that woman is naturally weaker than man, whence does it follow that it is natural for her to labour to become still weaker than nature intended her to be? Arguments of this cast are an insult to common sense, and savour of passion. The *divine right* of husbands, like the divine right of kings, may, it is to be hoped, in this enlightened age, be contested without danger, and though conviction may not silence many boisterous disputants, yet, when any prevailing prejudice is attacked, the wife will consider, and leave the narrow-minded to rail with thoughtless vehemence at innovation.

It is time to effect a revolution in female manners—time to restore to them their lost dignity—and make them, as a part of the human species, labour by reforming themselves to reform the world. It is time to separate unchangeable morals from local manners.

SELECTION 14.2

The Second Sex*

Simone de Beauvoir

[*This extract is from Beauvoir's 1949 classic,* The Second Sex.]

If her functioning as a female is not enough to define woman, if we decline also to explain her through "the eternal feminine," and if nevertheless we admit, provisionally, that women do exist, then we must face the question: what is a woman?

---

* From THE SECOND SEX by Simone de Beauvoir, translated by Parshley. A new translation by Sheila Malovany-Chevallier and Constance Borde will be published by Jonathan Cape 2009. Reprinted by permission of The Random House Group Ltd.

To state the question is, to me, to suggest, at once, a preliminary answer. The fact that I ask it is in itself significant. A man would never set out to write a book on the peculiar situation of the human male. But if I wish to define myself, I must first of all say: "I am a woman"; on this truth must be based all further discussion. A man never begins by presenting himself as an individual of a certain sex; it goes without saying that he is a man. The terms *masculine* and *feminine* are used symmetrically only as a matter of form, as on legal papers. In actuality the relation of the two sexes is not quite like that of two electrical poles, for man represents both the positive and the neutral, as is indicated by the common use of *man* to designate human beings in general; whereas woman represents only the negative, defined by limiting criteria, without reciprocity. In the midst of an abstract discussion it is vexing to hear a man say: "You think thus and so because you are a woman"; but I know that my only defence is to reply: "I think thus and so because it is true," thereby removing my subjective self from the argument. It would be out of the question to reply: "And you think the contrary because you are a man," for it is understood that the fact of being a man is no peculiarity. A man is in the right in being a man; it is the woman who is in the wrong. It amounts to this: just as for the ancients there was an absolute vertical with reference to which the oblique was defined, so there is an absolute human type, the masculine. Woman has ovaries, a uterus: these peculiarities imprison her in her subjectivity, circumscribe her within the limits of her own nature. It is often said that she thinks with her glands. Man superbly ignores the fact that his anatomy also includes glands, such as the testicles, and that they secrete hormones. He thinks of his body as a direct and normal connection with the world, which he believes he apprehends objectively, whereas he regards the body of woman as a hindrance, a prison, weighed down by everything peculiar to it. "The female is a female by virtue of a certain *lack* of qualities," said Aristotle; "we should regard the female nature as afflicted with a natural defectiveness." And St Thomas for his part pronounced woman to be an "imperfect man," an "incidental" being. This is symbolized in Genesis where Eve is depicted as made from what Bossuet called "a supernumerary bone" of Adam.

Thus humanity is male and man defines woman not in herself but as relative to him; she is not regarded as an autonomous being. Michelet writes: "Woman, the relative being. . . ." And Benda is most positive in his *Rapport d'Uriel:* "The body of man makes sense in itself quite apart from that of woman, whereas the latter seems wanting in significance by itself. . . . Man can think of himself without woman. She cannot think of herself without man." And she is simply what man decrees; thus she is called "the sex," by which is meant that she appears essentially to the male as a sexual being. For him she is sex—absolute sex, no less. She is defined and differentiated with reference to man and not he with reference to her; she is the incidental, the inessential as opposed to the essential. He is the Subject, he is the Absolute—she is the Other.

The category of the *Other* is as primordial as consciousness itself. In the most primitive societies, in the most ancient mythologies, one finds the expression of a duality—that of the Self and the Other. This duality was not originally attached to the division of the sexes; it was not dependent upon any empirical facts. It is revealed in such works as that of Granet on Chinese thought and those of Dumézil on the East Indies and Rome. The feminine element was at first no more involved in such pairs as Varuna–Mitra, Uranus–Zeus, Sun–Moon, and Day–Night than it was in the contrasts between Good and Evil, lucky and unlucky auspices, right and left, God and Lucifer. Otherness is a fundamental category of human thought.

Thus it is that no group ever sets itself up as the One without at once setting up the Other over against itself. If three travellers chance to occupy the same compartment, that is enough to make vaguely hostile "others" out of all the rest of the passengers on the train. In small-town eyes all persons not belonging to the village are "strangers" and suspect; to the native of a country all who inhabit other countries are "foreigners"; Jews are "different" for the anti-Semite, Negroes are "inferior" for American racists, aborigines are "natives" for colonists, proletarians are the "lower class" for the privileged. . . .

. . . One is not born, but rather becomes, a woman. No biological, psychological, or economic fate determines the figure that the human female presents in society; it is civilization as a whole that produces this creature, intermediate between male and eunuch, which is described as feminine. Only the intervention of someone else can establish an individual as an *Other*. . . .

. . . New relations of flesh and sentiment of which we have no conception will arise between the sexes; already, indeed, there have appeared between men and women friendships, rivalries, complicities, comradeships—chaste or sensual—which past centuries could not have conceived. To mention one point, nothing could seem more debatable than the opinion that dooms the new world to uniformity and hence to boredom. I fail to see that this present world is free from boredom or that liberty ever creates uniformity.

To begin with, there will always be certain differences between man and woman; her eroticism, and therefore her sexual world, have a special form of their own and therefore cannot fail to engender a sensuality, a sensitivity, of a special nature. This means that her relations to her own body, to that of the male, to the child, will never be identical with those the male bears to his own body, to that of the female, and to the child; those who make much of "equality in difference" could not with good grace refuse to grant me the possible existence of differences in equality. Then again, it is institutions that create uniformity. Young and pretty, the slaves of the harem are always the same in the sultan's embrace; Christianity gave eroticism its savour of sin and legend when it endowed the human female with a soul; if society restores her sovereign individuality to woman, it will not thereby destroy the power of love's embrace to move the heart.

It is nonsense to assert that revelry, vice, ecstasy, passion, would become impossible if man and woman were equal in concrete matters; the contradictions that put the flesh in opposition to the spirit, the instant to time, the swoon of immanence to the challenge of transcendence, the absolute of pleasure to the nothingness of forgetting, will never be resolved; in sexuality will always be materialized the tension, the anguish, the joy, the frustration, and the triumph of existence. To emancipate woman is to refuse to confine her to the relations she bears to man, not to deny them to her; let her have her independent existence and she will continue none the less to exist for him *also:* mutually recognizing each

other as subject, each will yet remain for the other an *other.* The reciprocity of their relations will not do away with the miracles—desire, possession, love, dream, adventure—worked by the division of human beings into two separate categories; and the words that move us—giving, conquering, uniting—will not lose their meaning. On the contrary, when we abolish the slavery of half of humanity, together with the whole system of hypocrisy that it implies, then the "division" of humanity will reveal its genuine significance and the human couple will find its true form. "The direct, natural, necessary relation of human creatures is the *relation of man to woman,*" Marx has said. "The nature of this relation determines to what point man himself is to be considered as a *generic being,* as mankind; the relation of man to woman is the most natural relation of human being to human being. By it is shown, therefore, to what point the *natural* behaviour of man has become *human* or to what point the *human* being has become his *natural* being, to what point his *human nature* has become his *nature.*"

The case could not be better stated. It is for man to establish the reign of liberty in the midst of the world of the given. To gain the supreme victory, it is necessary, for one thing, that by and through their natural differentiation men and women unequivocally affirm their brotherhood.

SELECTION 14.3

The Reproduction of Mothering:
Psychoanalysis and the Sociology of Gender*

Nancy Chodorow

[*Chodorow argues that gender identity is socially constructed differently for women and men because women are the primary family caretakers. This inequality can be corrected by a fundamental reorganization of parenting.*]

This book is a contribution to the feminist effort. It analyzes the reproduction of mothering as a central and constituting element in the social organization and reproduction of gender. In what follows, I

* REPRODUCTION OF MOTHERING: PSYCHOANALYSIS AND THE SOCIOLOGY OF GENDER (PAPER) by Nancy Chodorow. Copyright 1978 by University of California Press-Books. Reproduced with permission of University of California Press via Copyright Clearance Center.

argue that the contemporary reproduction of mothering occurs through social structurally induced psychological processes. It is neither a product of biology nor of intentional role-training. I draw on the psychoanalytic account of female and male personality development to demonstrate that women's mothering reproduces itself cyclically. Women, as mothers, produce daughters with mothering capacities and the desire to mother. These capacities and needs are built into and grow out of the mother–daughter relationship itself. By contrast, women as mothers (and men as non-mothers) produce sons whose nurturant capacities and needs have been systematically curtailed and repressed. This prepares men for their less effective later family role, and for primary participation in the impersonal extrafamilial world of work and public life. The sexual and familial division of labor in which women mother and are more involved in interpersonal, affective relationships than men produces in daughters and sons a division of psychological capacities which leads them to reproduce this sexual and familial division of labor.

I attempt to provide a theoretical account of what has unquestionably been true—that women have had primary responsibility for child care in families and outside of them; that women by and large want to mother, and get gratification from their mothering; and finally, that, with all the conflicts and contradictions, women have succeeded at mothering. . . .

Post-Oedipal Gender Personality: A Recapitulation

Children of both sexes are originally matrisexual, though, as many accounts suggest, they have different kinds of relationships to their mother and later their father. Girls, for many overdetermined reasons, do develop penis envy and may repress knowledge of their vagina because they cannot otherwise win their heterosexual mother; because of exhibitionistic desires; because the penis symbolizes independence from the (internalized) powerful mother; as a defense against fantasies of acting on sexual desires for their father and anxiety at the possible consequence of this; because they have received either conscious or unconscious communication from their parents that penises (or being male) are better, or sensed maternal conflict about the mother's own genitals; and because the penis symbolizes the social privileges of their father and men. The only psychoanalytic account of the origin of penis envy that seems inconceivable is Freud's original claim that a girl "makes her judgment and her decision in a flash"—that as soon as she learns about genitals different from hers, she wants a penis. Yet there is little to suggest either that penis envy completely permeates women's lives, or that the envy, jealousy, vanity, and pettiness that supposedly result from penis envy are characteristic of women. Similarly, most contemporary analysts agree that passivity, masochism, and narcissism are psychological defenses found in both women and men, and have the same object-relational origins in each, in the early mother–infant relationship. To the extent that these are (or were) more characteristically women's solutions to anxiety or guilt, this is not because of female biology but because the particular generating mother–child pattern is more characteristic of women's than men's early experience.

The oedipus complex, according to the psychoanalytic paradigm, is a time of major developmental differentiation in personality and of a relative fixing of personality structure for girls and boys. For the traditional psychoanalyst, the major developmental outcomes of the oedipus complex are erotic heterosexuality and superego formation, masculinity and femininity. Even within this traditional account, however, with its teleological formulation of conscious parental and social goals arising from their own assumptions about appropriate gender roles, and unconscious goals arising from unconscious parental attitudes to gender and sexuality and their own oedipal stance, it is clear that what is being negotiated and what needs explaining is different for boys and girls as a result of the asymmetrical structure of parenting. For boys, gender identifications are more the issue; for girls, psychosexual development. Because both are originally involved with their mother, the attainment of heterosexuality—achieved with the feminine change of object—is the major traditional oedipal goal for girls. For boys the major goal is the achievement of personal masculine identification with their father and sense of secure masculine self, achieved through superego formation and disparagement of women. Superego formation and further identification with their mother also happen for girls, and giving up the original attachment to their mother is also an issue for boys. Yet the ways these happen, the conflicts and defenses involved, and typical gender differences between them are not elaborated in the psychoanalytic account. (These differences include varying forms of superego operation; differences in what identification with the parent of the same gender means, differences in what doubt about femininity and doubt about masculinity consist in; the particular ways in which each does and does not give up the mother as a love object; and implications for asymmetries in modes of libidinal relationship and heterosexual love.)

My account suggests that these gender-related issues may be influenced during the period of the oedipus complex, but they are not its only focus or outcome. The negotiation of these issues occurs in the context of broader object-relational and ego processes. These broader processes have equal influence on psychic structure formation, and psychic life and relational modes in men and women.

They account for differing modes of identification and orientation to heterosexual objects, for the more asymmetrical oedipal issues psychoanalysts describe. These outcomes, like more traditional oedipal outcomes, arise from the asymmetrical organization of parenting, with the mother's role as primary parent and the father's typically greater remoteness and his investment in socialization especially in areas concerned with gender-typing.

The oedipal period is a nodal time of the creation of psychic reality in a child and of important internalizations of objects in relation to the ego. The main importance of the oedipus complex, I argue, is not primarily in the development of gender identity and socially appropriate heterosexual genitality, but in the constitution of different forms of "relational potential" in people of different genders. The oedipus complex is the form in which the internal interpersonal world will later be imposed on and help to create the external. Post-oedipal (and, in the girl, postpubertal) personality is the relatively stable foundation upon which other forms of relational development will build.

A girl continues a preoedipal relationship to her mother for a long time. Freud is concerned that it takes the girl so long to develop an oedipal attachment to her father and the "feminine" sexual modes that go with this attachment. The stress is on the girl's attachment as *pre*oedipal rather than on the attachment itself.

It is important to stress the other side of this process. Mothers tend to experience their daughters as more like, and continuous with, themselves. Correspondingly, girls tend to remain part of the dyadic primary mother–child relationship itself. This means that a girl continues to experience herself as involved in issues of merging and separation, and in an attachment characterized by primary identification and the fusion of identification and object choice. By contrast, mothers experience their sons as a male opposite. Boys are more likely to have been pushed out of the preoedipal relationship, and to have had to curtail their primary love and sense of empathic tie with their mother. A boy has engaged, and been required to engage, in a more emphatic individuation and a more defensive firming of experienced ego boundaries. Issues of differentiation have become intertwined with sexual issues. This does not mean that women have "weaker" ego boundaries than men or are more prone to psychosis. Disturbances in the early relation to a caretaker have

equally profound effects on each, but these effects differ according to gender. The earliest mode of individuation, the primary construction of the ego and its inner object-world, the earliest conflicts and the earliest unconscious definitions of self, the earliest threats to individuation, and the earliest anxieties which call up defenses all differ for boys and girls because of differences in the character of the early mother–child relationship for each.

Girls emerge from this period with a basis for "empathy" built into their primary definition of self in a way that boys do not. Girls emerge with a stronger basis for experiencing another's needs or feelings as one's own (or of thinking that one is so experiencing another's needs and feelings). Furthermore, girls do not define themselves in terms of the denial of preoedipal relational modes to the same extent as do boys. Therefore, regression to these modes tends not to feel as much a basic threat to their ego. From very early, then, because they are parented by a person of the same gender (a person who has already internalized a set of unconscious meanings, fantasies, and self-images about this gender and brings to her experience her own internalized early relationship to her own mother), girls come to experience themselves as less differentiated than boys, as more continuous with and related to the external object-world and as differently oriented to their inner object-world as well. . . .

. . . Women's mothering, then, produces asymmetries in the relational experiences of girls and boys as they grow up, which account for crucial differences in feminine and masculine personality, and the relational capacities and modes which these entail. Women and men grow up with personalities affected by different boundary experiences and differently constructed and experienced inner object-worlds, and are preoccupied with different relational issues. Feminine personality comes to be based less on repression of inner objects, and fixed and firm splits in the ego and more on retention and continuity of external relationships. From the retention of preoedipal attachments to their mother, growing girls come to define and experience themselves as continuous with others; their experience of self contains more flexible or permeable ego boundaries. Boys come to define themselves as more separate and distinct, with a greater sense of rigid ego boundaries and differentiation. The basic feminine sense of self is connected to the world, the basic masculine sense of self is separate.

SELECTION 14.4

Woman's Place in Man's Life Cycle★

Carol Gilligan

[*In this essay Gilligan argues that a woman's moral development is related to her psychological development, which is altered by the conflicting responsibilities of her role as nurturer. This results in a contextual mode of thinking that frames moral decisions.*]

"It is obvious," Virginia Woolf said, "that the values of women differ very often from the values which have been made by the other sex." . . . Yet, she adds, it is the masculine values that prevail. As a result, women come to question the "normality" of their feelings and to alter their judgments in deference to the opinion of others. In the nineteenth-century novels written by women, Woolf sees at work "a mind slightly pulled from the straight, altering its clear vision in the anger and confusion of deference to external authority." . . . The same deference that Woolf identifies in nineteenth-century fiction can be seen as well in the judgments of twentieth-century women. Women's reluctance to make moral judgments, the difficulty they experience in finding or speaking publicly in their own voice, emerge repeatedly in the form of qualification and self-doubt, in intimations of a divided judgment, a public and private assessment which are fundamentally at odds. . . .

Yet the deference and confusion that Woolf criticizes in women derive from the values she sees as their strength. Women's deference is rooted not only in their social circumstances but also in the substance of their moral concern. Sensitivity to the needs of others and the assumption of responsibility for taking care lead women to attend to voices other than their own and to include in their judgment other points of view. Women's moral weakness, manifest in an apparent diffusion and confusion of judgment, is thus inseparable from women's moral strength, an overriding concern with relationships and responsibilities. The reluctance to judge can

itself be indicative of the same care and concern for others that infuses the psychology of women's development and is responsible for what is characteristically seen as problematic in its nature.

Thus women not only define themselves in a context of human relationship but also judge themselves in terms of their ability to care. Woman's place in man's life cycle has been that of nurturer, caretaker, and helpmate, the weaver of those networks of relationships on which she in turn relies. While women have thus taken care of men, however, men have in their theories of psychological development tended either to assume or devalue that care. The focus on individuation and individual achievement that has dominated the description of child and adolescent development has recently been extended to the depiction of adult development as well. Levinson in his study, *The Seasons of a Man's Life*, . . . elaborates a view of adult development in which relationships are portrayed as a means to an end of individual achievement and success. In the critical relationships of early adulthood, the "Mentor" and the "Special Woman" are defined by the role they play in facilitating the man's realization of his "Dream." Along similar lines Vaillant, . . . in his study of men, considers altruism a defense, characteristic of mature ego functioning and associated with successful "adaptation to life," but conceived as derivative rather than primary in contrast to Chodorow's analysis, in which empathy is considered "built-in" to the woman's primary definition of self.

The discovery now being celebrated by men in mid-life of the importance of intimacy, relationships, and care is something that women have known from the beginning. However, because that knowledge has been considered "intuitive" or "instinctive," a function of anatomy coupled with destiny, psychologists have neglected to describe its development. In my research, I have found that women's moral development centers on the elaboration of that knowledge. Women's moral development thus delineates a critical line of psychological development whose importance for both sexes becomes apparent in the intergenerational framework of a life-cycle perspective. While the subject of moral development provides the final illustration of the reiterative pattern in the observation and assessment of sex differences in the literature on human development, it also indicates more particularly why the nature and significance of women's development has for so long been obscured and considered shrouded in mystery. . . .

. . . Research on moral judgment has shown that when the categories of women's thinking are examined in detail . . . the outline of a moral conception different from that described by Freud, Piaget, or Kohlberg begins to emerge and to inform a different description of moral development. In this conception, the moral problem is seen to arise from conflicting responsibilities rather than from competing rights and to require for its resolution a mode of thinking that is contextual and inductive rather than formal and abstract.

This conception of morality as fundamentally concerned with the capacity for understanding and care also develops through a structural progression of increasing differentiation and integration. This progression witnesses the shift from an egocentric through a societal to the universal moral perspective that Kohlberg described in his research on men, but it does so in different terms. The shift in women's judgment from an egocentric to a conventional to a principled ethical understanding is articulated through their use of a distinct moral language, in which the terms "selfishness" and "responsibility" define the moral problem as one of care. Moral development then consists of the progressive reconstruction of this understanding toward a more adequate conception of care.

SELECTION 14.5

Conclusion: Epistemological Questions*

Sandra Harding

[*Harding explains major theories of feminist science and attempts to examine concerns of gender-loyalty and scientific objectivity.*]

A second set of epistemological issues has arisen between the feminist empiricists and standpoint theorists, on the one hand, and the feminist critics of Enlightenment assumptions—the feminist postmodernists—on the other hand. The empiricists and standpoint theorists are both attempting to ground accounts of the social world which are less partial and distorted than the prevailing ones. In this sense, they are attempting to produce a feminist science—one that better reflects the world around us than the incomplete and distorting accounts provided by traditional social science. This science would not substitute one gender-loyalty for the others, but, instead, advance the objectivity of science. The feminist postmodernists raise questions about this epistemological project. Can there be a feminist science, or is any *science* doomed to replicate undesirable—and perhaps even androcentric—ways of being in the world?

There appear to be two at least somewhat distinct origins of skepticism about the kind of epistemological project in which both the feminist empiricists and the standpoint theorists are engaged. One emerges from feminists who participate in the agendas of such otherwise disparate discourses as those of semiotics, deconstruction, and psychoanalysis. The other has appeared in the writings of women of color.

The discourses mentioned are all deeply skeptical of universalizing claims for reason, science, language, progress, and the subject/self. Thus both of the feminist epistemological strategies we examined are legitimate targets of such skepticism, since they assume that through reason, observation, and progressive politics, the more authentic "self" produced by feminist struggles can tell "one true story" about "the world": there can be a kind of feminist author of a new "master story," a narrative about social life which feminist inquiry will produce. The critics respond, but "perhaps 'reality' can have 'a' structure only from the falsely universalizing perspective of the master. That is, only to the extent that one person or group can dominate the whole, can 'reality' appear to be governed by one set of rules or be constituted by one privileged set of social relations."

This kind of criticism points to the way science constructs the fiction of the human mind as a glassy mirror which can reflect a world that is out there and ready-made for reflecting. In contrast, we can detect ("in reality"?) that at any moment in history there are many "subjugated knowledges" that conflict with, and are never reflected in, the dominant stories a culture tells about social life. Moreover, some argue that women are a primary location of these subjugated knowledges—in fact, that the female subject is a "site of differences." From this perspective, there can never be *a* feminist science, sociology, anthropology, or epistemology, but only many stories that different women tell about the different knowledge they have.

A second source of criticism of a unitary feminist perspective implied by the two epistemological strategies emerges from women of color. For instance, Bell Hooks insists that what makes feminism possible is not that women share certain kinds of experiences, for women's experiences of patriarchal oppression differ by race, class, and culture. Instead, feminism names the fact that women can federate around their common resistance to all the different forms of male domination. Thus there could not be "a" feminist standpoint as the generator of true stories about social life. There could, presumably, only be feminist oppositions, and criticisms of false stories. There could not be feminist science, because feminism's opposition to domination stories locates feminism in an antagonistic position towards any attempts to do science—androcentric or not. These strains of postmodernism are richer and more complex than these few paragraphs can reveal. But one can already sense the troubles they create for other feminist epistemologies.

Should feminists be willing to give up the political benefits which can accrue from believing that we are producing a new, less biased, more accurate, social science? Social scientists might well want to respond to the postmodernist critics that we do need to federate our feminisms in opposition to all of the ways in which domination is enacted and institutionalized. But it is premature for women to be willing to give up what they have never had. Should women—no matter what their race, class, or culture—find it reasonable to give up the desire to know and understand the world from the standpoint of their experiences *for the first time?* As several feminist literary critics have suggested, perhaps only those who have had access to the benefits of the Enlightenment can "give up" those benefits.

There are good reasons to find valuable the tension between these two epistemological positions. We need to think critically about the fundamental impulses of knowledge-seeking, and especially of science, even as we transform them to feminists' (plural!) ends.

One can easily see that the new feminist analyses unsettle traditional assumptions about knowledge as they challenge familiar beliefs about women, men, and social life. How could it have been otherwise when our ways of knowing are such an important part of our ways of participating in the social world?

SELECTION 14.6

The Laugh of the Medusa*

Hélène Cixous

[*In this essay Cixous is arguing on two levels—the metaphorical and the literal—about the nature of women's sexuality and the need for women to write themselves.*]

I shall speak about women's writing: about *what it will do.* Woman must write her self: must write

* From Helene Cixous, "The Laugh of the Medusa," in E. Abel and E.K. Abel (eds) *The Signs Reader: Women, Gender and Scholarship.* Copyright © 1993, The University of Chicago Press. Reprinted by permission of the University of Chicago Press.

about women and bring women to writing, from which they have been driven away as violently as from their bodies—for the same reasons, by the same law, with the same fatal goal. Woman must put herself into the text—as into the world and into history—by her own movement.

The future must no longer be determined by the past. I do not deny that the effects of the past are still with us. But I refuse to strengthen them by repeating them, to confer upon them an irremovability the equivalent of destiny, to confuse the biological and the cultural. Anticipation is imperative.

Since these reflections are taking shape in an area just on the point of being discovered, they necessarily bear the mark of our time—a time during which the new breaks away from the old, and, more precisely, the (feminine) new from the old (*la nouvelle de l'ancient.*) Thus, as there are no grounds for establishing a discourse, but rather an arid millennial ground to break, what I say has at least two sides and two aims: to break up, to destroy; and to foresee the unforeseeable, to project.

I write this as a woman, toward women. When I say "woman," I'm speaking of woman in her inevitable struggle against conventional man; and of a universal woman subject who must bring women to their senses and to their meaning in history. But first it must be said that in spite of the enormity of the repression that has kept them in the "dark"—that dark which people have been trying to make them accept as their attribute—there is, at this time, no general woman, no one typical woman. What they have *in common* I will say. But what strikes me is the infinite richness of their individual constitutions: you can't talk about *a* female sexuality, uniform, homogeneous, classifiable into codes—any more than you can talk about one unconscious resembling another. Women's imaginary is inexhaustible, like music, painting, writing: their stream of phantasms is incredible.

I have been amazed more than once by a description a woman gave me of a world all her own which she had been secretly haunting since early childhood. A world of searching, the elaboration of a knowledge, on the basis of a systematic experimentation with the bodily functions, a passionate and precise interrogation of her erotogeneity. This practice, extraordinarily rich and inventive, in particular as concerns masturbation, is prolonged or accompanied by a production of forms, a veritable aesthetic activity, each stage of rapture inscribing a resonant vision, a composition, something beautiful. Beauty will no longer be forbidden.

I wished that that woman would write and proclaim this unique empire so that other women, other unacknowledged sovereigns, might exclaim: I, too, overflow; my desires have invented new desires, my body knows unheard-of songs. Time and again I, too, have felt so full of luminous torrents that I could burst—burst with

forms much more beautiful than those which are put up in frames and sold for a stinking fortune. And I, too, said nothing, showed nothing; I didn't open my mouth, I didn't repaint my half of the world, I was ashamed. I was afraid, and I swallowed my shame and my fear. I said to myself: You are mad! What's the meaning of these waves, these floods, these outbursts? Where is the ebullient, infinite woman who, immersed as she was in her naiveté, kept in the dark about herself, led into self-disdain by the great arm of parental-conjugal phallocentrism, hasn't been ashamed of her strength? Who, surprised and horrified by the fantastic tumult of her drives (for she was made to believe that a well-adjusted normal woman has a . . . divine composure), hasn't accused herself of being a monster? Who, feeling a funny desire stirring inside her (to sing, to write, to dare to speak, in short, to bring out something new), hasn't thought she was sick? Well, her shameful sickness is that she resists death, that she makes trouble.

And why don't you write? Write! Writing is for you, you are for you; your body is yours, take it. I know why you haven't written. (And why I didn't write before the age of twenty-seven.) Because writing is at once too high, too great for you, it's reserved for the great—that is, for "great men"; and it's "silly." Besides, you've written a little, but in secret. And it wasn't good, because it was in secret, and because you punished yourself for writing, because you didn't go all the way; or because you wrote, irresistibly, as when we would masturbate in secret, not to go further, but to attenuate the tension a bit, just enough to take the edge off. And then as soon as we come, we go and make ourselves feel guilty—so as to be forgiven; or to forget, to bury it until the next time.

Write, let no one hold you back, let nothing stop you: not man; not the imbecilic capitalist machinery, in which publishing houses are the crafty, obsequious relayers of imperatives handed down by an economy that works against us and off our backs; and not *yourself*. Smug-faced readers, managing editors, and big bosses don't like the true texts of women—female-sexed texts. That kind scares them.

I write woman: woman must write woman. And man, man. So only an oblique consideration will be found here of man; it's up to him to say where his masculinity and femininity are at: this will concern us once men have opened their eyes and seen themselves clearly.[1]

Now women return from afar, from always: from "without," from the heath where witches are kept alive; from below, from beyond "culture"; from their childhood which men have been trying desperately to make them forget, condemning it to "eternal rest." The little girls and their "ill-mannered" bodies immured, well-preserved, intact unto themselves, in the mirror. Frigidified. But are they ever seething underneath! What an effort it takes—there's no end to it—for the sex cops to bar their threatening return. Such a display of forces on both sides that the struggle has for centuries been immobilized in the trembling equilibrium of a deadlock. . . .

. . . It is by writing, from and toward women, and by taking up the challenge of speech which has been governed by the phallus, that women will confirm women in a place other than which is reserved in and by the symbolic, that is, in a place other than silence. Women should break out of the snare of silence. They shouldn't be conned into accepting a domain which is the margin or the harem.

Listen to a woman speak at a public gathering (if she hasn't painfully lost her wind). She doesn't "speak," she throws her trembling body forward; she lets go of herself, she flies; all of her passes into her voice, and it's with her body that she vitally supports the "logic" of her speech. Her flesh speaks true. She lays herself bare. In fact, she physically materializes what she's thinking; she signifies it with her body. In a certain way she *inscribes* what she's saying, because she doesn't deny her drives the intractable and impassioned part they have in speaking. Her speech, even when "theoretical" or political, is never simple or linear or "objectified," generalized: she draws her story into history.

There is not that scission, that division made by the common man between the logic of oral speech and the logic of the text, bound as he is by his antiquated relation—servile, calculating—to mastery. From which proceeds the niggardly lip serice which engages only the tiniest part of the body, plus the mask.

In women's speech, as in their writing, that element which never stops resonating, which, once we've been permeated by it, profoundly and imperceptibly touched by it, retains the power of moving us—that element is the song: first music from the first voice of love which is alive in every women. Why this privileged relationship with the voice? Because no woman stockpiles as many defenses for countering the drives as does a man. You don't build walls around yourself, you don't forgo pleasure as "wisely" as he. Even if phallic mystification has generally contaminated good relationships, a woman is never far from "mother" (I mean outside her role functions: the "mother" as nonname and as source of goods). There is always within her at least a little of that good mother's milk. She writes in white ink.

Woman for women—There always remains in woman that force which produces/is produced by the other—in particular, the other woman. *In* her, matrix, cradler; herself giver as her mother and child; she is her own sister-daughter. You might object, "What about she who is the hysterical offspring of a bad mother?" Everything will be changed once woman gives woman to the other woman. There is hidden and always ready in woman the source; the locus for the other. The mother, too, is a metaphor. It is necessary and sufficient that the best of herself be given to woman by another woman for her to be able to love herself and return in love the body that was "born" to her. . . .

. . . It is impossible to *define* a feminine practice of writing, and this is an impossibility that will remain, for this practice can never be theorized, enclosed, coded—which doesn't mean that it doesn't exist. But it will always surpass the discourse that regulates the phallocentric system; it does and will take place in areas other than those subordinated to philosophico-theoretical domination. It will be conceived of only by subjects who are breakers of automatisms, by peripheral figures that no authority can ever subjugate. . . .

---

[1] Men still have everything to say about their sexuality, and everything to write. For what they have said so far, for the most part, stems from the opposition activity/passivity, from the power relation between a fantasized obligatory virility meant to invade, to colonize, and the consequential phantasm of woman as a "dark continent" to penetrate and to "pacify." (We know what "pacify" means in terms of scotomizing the other and misrecognizing the self.) Conquering her, they've made haste to depart from her borders, to get out of sight, out of body. The way man has of getting out of himself and into her whom he takes not for the other but for his own, deprives him, he knows, of his own bodily territory. One can understand how man, confusing himself with his penis and rushing in for the attack, might feel resentment and fear of being "taken" by the woman, of being lost in her, absorbed, or alone.

. . . To this self-effacing, merger-type bisexuality, which would conjure away castration (the writer who puts up his sign: "bisexual written here, come and see," when the odds are good that it's neither one nor the other), I oppose the *other bisexuality* on which every subject not enclosed in the false theater of phallocentric representationalism has founded his/her erotic universe. Bisexuality: that is, each one's location in self (*repérage en soi*) of the presence—variously manifest and insistent according to each person, male or female—of both sexes, nonexclusion either of the difference or of one sex, and, from this "self-permission," multiplication of the effects of the inscription of desire, over all parts of my body and the other body.

Now it happens that at present, for historico-cultural reasons, it is women who are opening up to and benefiting from this vatic bisexuality which doesn't annual differences but stirs them up, pursues them, increases their number. In a certain way, "woman is bisexual"; man—it's a secret to no one—being poised to keep glorious phallic monosexuality in view. By virtue of affirming the primacy of the phallus and of bringing it into play, phallocratic ideology has claimed more than one victim. As a woman, I've been clouded over by the great shadow of the scepter and been told: idolize it, that which you cannot brandish. But at the same time, man has been handed that grotesque and scarcely enviable destiny (just imagine) of being reduced to a single idol with clay balls. And consumed, as Freud and his followers note, by a fear of being a woman! For, if psychoanalysis was constituted from woman, to repress femininity (and not so successful a repression at that—men have made it clear), its account of masculine sexuality is now hardly refutable; as with all the "human" sciences, it reproduces the masculine view, of which it is one of the effects. . . .

. . . Let the priests tremble, we're going to show them our sexts! Too bad for them if they fall apart upon discovering that women aren't men, or that the mother doesn't have one. But isn't this fear convenient for them? Wouldn't the worst be, isn't the worst, in truth, that women aren't castrated, that they have only to stop listening to the Sirens (for the Sirens were men) for history to change its meaning? You only have to look at the Medusa straight on to see her. And she's not deadly. She's beautiful and she's laughing. . . .

. . . This doesn't mean that she's an undifferentiated magma, but that she doesn't lord it over her body or her desire. Though masculine sexuality gravitates around the penis, engendering that centralized body (in political anatomy) under the dictatorship of its parts, woman does not bring about the same regionalization which serves the couple head/genitals and which is inscribed only within boundaries. Her libido is cosmic, just as her unconscious is world-wide. Her writing can only keep going, without ever inscribing or discerning contours, daring to make these vertiginous crossings of the other(s) ephemeral and passionate sojourns in him, her, them, whom she inhabits long enough to look at from the point closest to their unconscious from the moment they awaken, to love them at the point closest to their drives; and then further, impregnated through and through with these brief, identificatory embraces, she goes and passes into infinity. She alone dares and wishes to know from within, where she, the outcast, has never ceased to hear the resonance of fore-language. She lets the other language speak—the language of 1,000 tongues which knows neither enclosure nor death. To life she refuses nothing. Her language does not contain, it carries; it does not hold back, it makes possible. When id is ambiguously uttered—the wonder of being several—she doesn't defend herself against these unknown women whom she's surprised at becoming, but derives pleasure from this gift of alterability. I am spacious, singing flesh, on which is grafted no one knows which I, more or less human, but alive because of transformation.

SELECTION 14.7

Goodbye, You Guys★
[Professor of Sociology University of North Carolina, Durham.]

Sherryl Kleinman

I hear it everywhere. I press the button on the answering machine and a friend's voice says, "Hope you guys are doing well." I sit down with a friend at a restaurant, and the server asks, "What would you guys like to drink?" A student in my gender class looks out over a group of thirty-five women and five men and says, "You guys, I have an announcement."

Not that long ago women were being told that "he" and "mankind" included us—but we were skeptical. Feminists—women and men—argued that language matters, that words are the tools of thought, and that erasing women through terms like "mankind" made it easier to treat women as less than persons. Remember the uproar when women asserted our existence by demanding "she or he" and "humankind"? But feminists persisted and our language changed. *Postal carrier, first-year student, chairperson,* and *firefighter* slowly made their way onto paper and into speech. Many people began to see that it's a problem when the so-called generic person has a man's face.

So when did "you guys" sneak by and then sneak in? I suspect it entered the scene around the time that official titles like "chairman" were being challenged. You can push the provost to change *freshman* to *first-year student* or complain to publishers about their use of *congressman* in text books. But you can't go to court to make your friends stop using "you guys."

Some women tell me that "you guys" is different from "mankind." It's informal. It makes everyone feel included. It's an equalizer. As one woman put it, "It's friendly. It's not like calling us sluts or bitches."

That's what worries me. Too many of us believe "you guys" is benign. But imagine a world—as Douglas Hofstadter did in his 1986 satire on sexist language—where people used generics based on race rather than gender. In that world, people would use "freshwhite," "chairwhite," and yes, "you whiteys." Substituting "white" for "man" makes it easy to see why using "man" for all human beings is wrong.

Perhaps some women believe that being "one of the guys" will protect them from the hazards of being women. "You guys" provides the guise of inclusion in the dominant group. But if women really had equal status with men, we wouldn't have to disappear into their term. After all, can you think of one, just one, instance when a female term has been used to describe a group of women and men? Can you even imagine that happening?

I'm not saying that those of us who use "you guys" have bad intentions. But let's consider the consequences. Think about the messages we get about the value of women—hundreds of times a day, every day—when we hear it. So let's recognize (as feminists did with "mankind") that a friendly-sounding phrase like "you guys" can do damage.

I think about my colleague's five-year-old daughter who ran out of the room crying when she heard the teacher say, "What do you guys think?" She thought the teacher didn't care about what she thought. The teacher told her that of course she was included. Her tears stopped, but what was the lesson? She learned that her opinion as a girl counts only when she's a guy. She learned, as most of us have, that men set the standard.

I think about my friend's six-year-old son who refused to believe that the female firefighter who came to his school to talk to the class—dressed in uniform—actually fought fires. The firefighter repeatedly referred to herself as a "fireman." Despite the protests of the teacher and the firefighter, the boy would not be convinced. "A fireman can't be a woman," he said. His mother, who is fastidious in her use of nonsexist language, had a tough time doing damage control.

Several months ago I was complaining, as usual, about the "you guys" problem. "What we need is a card that explains why we don't want to be called 'guys'!"

★ From Sherryl Kleinman, "Goodbye, 'You Guys,'" Feminista (www.feminista.com" www.feminista.com). January 2001. Reprinted by permission. In this article she rejects on the significance of the fact that it is widely thought to be acceptable to refer to a group of women as "you guys", but not to a group of men as "you gals."

Smita Varia, a veteran of my gender course, said, "Let's write one."

And so we did. Smita enlisted T. Christian Helms, another former student, to design a graphic for the card. . . . We hope you'll agree that the card doesn't scold people. Give it to friends and ask them to think about it. Leave it with a big tip after you've been "you guysed" during a meal. The card explains the problem and offers alternatives. You can also access the layout of the card from our website: http://www.youall.freeservers.com.

It's impossible to legislate against "you guys," so I'm calling for no less than an anti-you-guys movement. Does that sound silly? If so, maybe it's because many of us secretly believe that guys are better. And the guys know they're better, too. If you don't believe me, saunter up to a group of them and offer a friendly, "Hey, gals, how're you doing?" Let me know what happens.

CHECKLIST

To help you review, a checklist of the key philosophers of this chapter can be found online at www.mhhe.com/moore9e.

KEY TERMS AND CONCEPTS

black feminism,   427
ecofeminism,   428
écriture féminine,   443
essentialism,   440
ethics of caring,   432
feminist
   philosophy,   422
French feminist
   philosophy,   436
lesbian feminism,   427
liberal feminism,   426
maternal thinking,   432
metaethics,   441
misogynous,   431

patriarchy,   425
performativity,   446
phallus,   439
postcolonial
   theory,   428
poststructuralism   446
postfeminism,   429
postmodernism,   428
queer theory,   428
radical feminism,   427
Self/Other,   425
semiotic,   441
socialist
   feminism,   427

QUESTIONS FOR DISCUSSION AND REVIEW

1. Define feminist philosophy.

2. What were the results of first-wave efforts?

3. Explain Beauvoir's theory of Self and Other as it relates to women and men.

4. What was Beauvoir's major contribution to what we now call feminist philosophy?

5. What are the major differences between second- and third-wave feminism?

6. What is radical about "radical feminism"?

7. According to Ruddick, how does "maternal thinking" affect moral reasoning?

8. Summarize Kleinman's reasoning in her argument that the term *you guys* should not be used to include women.

9. How does postfeminism relate to second- and third-wave goals?

10. What are the main differences between U.S. and French feminist philosophy?

11. What is Derrida's contribution to French feminist philosophy?

12. What is *écriture féminine?*

13. What are the main reasons American scholars have found Cixous's work so difficult?

14. In which ways have you personally benefited or suffered from our sexist society?

15. Think back to your early childhood. What were some of the ways you were programmed to behave in masculine or feminine ways? Think about gifts you received, games you played, toys you played with, clothing and colors you were encouraged to choose. How did these contribute to your sense of yourself as male or female?

16. Which one idea in this chapter has influenced your thinking most? Explain.

17. What does Judith Butler mean by performativity? How is it different from performance?

18. Explain Butler's theory of subjectivity in simple terms.

19. How does Butler's work contribute to queer theory?

20. Why doesn't Butler write in a straightforward way instead of the circular kinds of reasoning that make it difficult to read her work?

SUGGESTED FURTHER READINGS

Go online to www.mhhe.com/moore9e for a list of suggested further readings.

15

Eastern Influences

The tree that brushes the heavens grew from the tiniest sprout. The most elegant pagoda, nine stories high, rose from a small pile of earth. The journey of a thousand miles began with but a single step.   —Lao Tzu

Asia is the world's largest continent and contains a third of earth's solid surface. It has as many inhabitants as all other continents combined. Its ancient civilizations—China, India, Japan, Korea, Vietnam, and others—are reinventing themselves economically, culturally, and politically. China, India, and North Korea now have nuclear weapons. The future belongs to Asia. Is there a point to studying Eastern thinkers? Can they possibly say anything to us? The answer seems obvious.

But familiarizing ourselves with Eastern philosophy is important not merely to understand emerging global powers but also to know ourselves. As the German poet Hölderlin observed, we never understand our home until we leave it. The philosophies of other civilizations provide new vantage points from which to view our own thought. They offer a different perspective, one from which we may reconsider and reevaluate what is important to us in our own thinking. Additionally, they are a potential source of fresh ideas and new concepts.

For many of the Westerners who have studied it, the philosophy of ancient Eastern thinkers has offered secure guidance to the full and contented life.

In this chapter, we consider Hinduism and Buddhism in India; Taoism, Confucianism, and Ch'an Buddhism in China; and Zen Buddhism and the samurai tradition in Japan. No effort is made to present the history of these important traditions or to trace their evolution over the centuries. Our intent is merely to introduce these philosophies and their most important thinkers. For a brief overview of Islamic philosophy, see the box on page 470.

Eastern philosophy and Eastern religions are closely intertwined. Both Confucianism and Taoism took on the trappings of religion, with priests, rituals, and moral codes. Some forms of Taoism also were influenced by Chinese popular religions and superstitions. Today in Taiwan, for example, there are six levels of Taoism, including two kinds of Taoist priests, the red and the black. Only the highest level reflects the Taoist philosophy in its purest form, free from religious and superstitious add-ons.

Buddhism in China was influenced not only by Confucianism and Taoism but by popular religions as well. In India, a similar interaction took place among ancient Buddhism and various religious belief systems and practices.

HINDUISM

India, now a country of more than a billion people, more than three times the population of the United States, is also one of the oldest civilizations; remains have been found that date as far back as 50,000 B.C.E. Today, India is roughly 82 percent Hindu, 11 percent Muslim, 2 percent Sikh, about 2 percent Christian, and about 1 percent Buddhist; it has even smaller percentages of Jainists, Zoroastrians, and Jews. Islam swept into India starting in 1001, and the harshness of Islamic rulers established an antagonism between Muslims and Hindus that still exists.

The European conquest of India began in 1510, when the Portuguese seized Goa (today popular with Europeans for its beaches). The English arrived in 1612 in the form of the East India Company; initially, a power struggle among European countries vying to defend and extend their economic interests led to the stationing of troops in India by England, France, and other countries. Eventually, however, England annexed the entire country, and, as a colony of England, India became known as "the jewel in the crown." Unfortunately, the British systematically stripped India of its wealth. Some three hundred years later, in 1947, through the nonviolent resistance and disobedience of Mohandas Gandhi and his followers and the Muslim League, India was given back independence.

One element of Indian culture that is worth mentioning here is the caste system. The *Vedas,* the ancient Hindu religious texts, divided society into four classes or castes. Because the gods determined one's caste, one was meant to stay there. The highest caste were the Brahmins, the priests and teachers; next-highest were the Kshatriyas, the rulers and warriors; then came the Vaishyas, the merchants; and then the Shudras, the farmers and laborers. The largest group of all is below all of the castes. These people are known as the Parjanyas or Antyajas, or Untouchables. They are the outcasts; members of society above them were not allowed to touch them or even to enter their shadows lest they become unclean and in need of ablution. (Untouchability was abolished by the Indian constitution in 1917.)

The long history of Indian philosophy has given rise to two main schools of thought, Hinduism and Buddhism. Hinduism, for example, contains both monism and dualism. Both also have had a long list of great thinkers, such as Nagarjuna (on the foundations of Buddhism). But this text must limit itself to a brief sketch of these traditional movements. **Hinduism,** from the Urdu word for India, *Hind,* is the Western term for the religious beliefs and practices of the majority of the Indian people.

The origins of Hinduism stretch back into the unknown past. Unlike other religions, it had no founder, and there is no single religious body to judge orthodoxy. In fact, Hinduism does not even contain a unified set of doctrines—or, to the extent it does, they are given diversified interpretations. All of this makes it difficult to talk about Hinduism in a limited space. Speaking of Hinduism as a single belief system is something like speaking of philosophy in the same way. It is best to view it as a spiritual attitude that gives rise to a wide range of religious and philosophical beliefs and practices. These range from the worship of village and forest deities, which often take zoomorphic forms, to complex metaphysical theories.

Common to all forms of Hinduism, however, is acceptance of the authority of the Vedic scriptures as the basis for understanding the true hidden nature of things. The **Vedas** are the most ancient religious texts of Hinduism—indeed, they are the oldest religious texts in an Indo-European language. The *Vedas* were the literature of the Aryans, who invaded northwest India around 1500 B.C.E. Many, if not most, Hindu writings are commentaries on the Vedic scriptures.

In terms of popular religion, three contemporary movements might be mentioned. *Saivism* worships Siva as the supreme being and source of the universe; *Saktism* worships Sakti, the female part of the universe and the wife of Siva. *Vaisnavism* worships the personal god **Vishnu.** Buddha, according to orthodox Hindus, was an incarnation (*avatar*) of Vishnu.

The basis of Hindu philosophy is the belief that reality is absolutely one, that there is only one ultimate reality-being-consciousness (see the box "Ommmmm"). Six classical philosophical schools or traditions, however, interpret this reality variously: these six insights, as they are called, are *Nyāya, Vaiśesika, Sāmkhya, Yoga, Mīmāmsā,* and *Vedānta.* All are designed to lead the searcher to a knowledge of the Absolute and the liberation of the soul. Vedanta is tradition based on the *Upanishads* and is the best known in the West (*Vedanta* means "the end of the Veda").

Philosophically, the most important Vedic scripture is the last book, the **Upanishads.** The *Upanishads,* which date from about the eighth to the fifth centuries B.C.E., are the inspiration for the six systems of philosophy just mentioned. The *Upanishads* are best known for the theories of **brahman** (the ultimate cosmic principle or reality), **atman** (the inner self), and the identification of *brahman* with *atman.* There are four great sayings (*mahavakya*) of the *Upanishads,* which are all ways of saying that *brahman* and *atman* are one:

1. Consciousness is *brahman.*
2. That art thou.
3. The self is *brahman.*
4. I am *brahman.*

Brahman is considered the ultimate reality or principle and the source and sustainer of all things, including people and gods. It is absolute and eternal spirit—the supreme consciousness, the One, the One-and-only-One. A lower manifestation of

Ommmmm

During the 1960s, Indian philosophy, or what passed for it, became popular in the American youth culture, thanks in part to the Beatles' interest in it and in the music of the Indian sitar master Ravi Shankar. In San Francisco and New York and Madison, Wisconsin, it was common to see hippies chanting "*Ommmmm, ommmmm, ommmmm*" in an effort to induce a mystical state of higher consciousness.

What is "*ommm*"? It is the sound of the letters *A*, *U*, and *M*, which are the symbols in Hindu writings for the three ordinary states of consciousness: waking experience, dreaming sleep, and deep sleep. There is in addition, according to Hinduism, a fourth state (in Vedanta philosophy, *moksa*), one of higher awareness, which is described in the *Mandukya Upanishad* as "the coming to peaceful rest of all differentiated existence." *Yoga* is the general term for the spiritual disciplines in Hinduism and Buddhism that aim at attainment of this higher state. It is also the name of one of the six orthodox systems of Hindu philosophy (see text).

brahman—namely, *brahma*—may be thought of as an individual deity or personal god, but *brahman* itself is without attributes or qualities. This absolute remains the hidden, unknown, ultimate mystery.

Atman is the self, the soul, the principle of individual life. Ultimately, however, the individual must come to a realization, through meditation and contemplation, that *brahman* and *atman* are the same thing—*brahman-atman*. With the realization of this absolute oneness of all things comes recognition of the relative nonreality of the world and of the individual ego. The identification of *brahman* and *atman* is sometimes spoken of by commentators as a pantheism, but it goes beyond the claim that all things are God. In Hinduism, the gods are parts or symbolic personifications of the absolute principle, *brahman*.

Further, the identification of *brahman* and *atman* has been subject to various interpretations over the centuries. It has been looked on as both transcendent and immanent. Samkara, who is thought to have lived between 788 and 820 C.E. and who gave the most rigorous interpretation of the *Upanishads,* was a pure monist who thought that all things are one—only the ultimate principle exists, and all else is an illusion. But another way of looking at the ultimate principle or reality was introduced by Rāmānuja (b. 1027 C.E.). He believed in the ultimate principle, but he also believed that souls are real and that the world is not merely an illusion. For a time, at least, the souls and the world must be separate from the ultimate principle to be of service to it, he held.

Yet a third way of interpreting the underlying ultimate reality is represented by the outright dualism of Madhva (1199–1278), who believed that, although the ultimate principle is the cause of the world, the soul still has a separate and independent existence of its own. You can see that Hindu philosophy in fact admits a variety of viewpoints.

The metaphysical question as to what constitutes the ultimate reality is not the only philosophical concern within Hinduism. There is also the issue of the human being's relation to that ultimate principle. Human life is a journey. Humans, though basically good, are caught up in a cycle of desire and suffering that is the direct result of ignorance and ego. In short, they are miserable. The desires that torment them are many and diverse, including sensual lusts and the desire for existence. The end result is *samsara,* the cycle of being born, dying, and being reborn. The human being often goes through a series of rebirths in various forms until he or she can escape the treadmill.

That which keeps an individual imprisoned by the transmigratory cycle is **karma,** which means "action" or "deed" in Pali. It refers to the chain of causes and necessary consequences in the world of human actions. Every action inevitably has its effect, and traces of these effects can last over several lifetimes. A good action brings joy; a bad action brings sorrow. And the consequences of actions build up over a lifetime and through multiple lifetimes. It is these residues that will help determine the quality of the next **reincarnation.** Despite the fact that humans create their own limitations through their choices of actions and motives, they nonetheless have the power to continue to choose or to resist falling victim to selfish desires. Building up good karma and reducing bad karma may eventually lead a person to escape the bondage of karma altogether by surrender to God and the liberation of enlightenment.

It is the renunciation of desires and the giving up of possessions and worldly attachments that can lead to **nirvana,** or permanent liberation from the cycle of birth, death, and rebirth. *Nirvana* is the Sanskrit word for "extinction," and it means the merging of the individual, transitory existence into the ultimate reality, namely, brahman. This is a condition of bliss at the highest state of transcendent consciousness. As part of brahman, we watch *lila,* or the entire history of the world and of our lives.

Human life, then, is a journey wherein we try to control both the mind and the senses and become God-oriented in the hope of experiencing total fulfillment in oneness with God. This means going from the state of everyday, ordinary consciousness to the blissful contemplation of the divine being itself. The human being seeks God by eliminating the shadow between the two, that is, the illusion of duality and separation.

Much of the wisdom of Hinduism in all times lies in its sages. This certainly holds true for the twentieth century, whose wise men include Rabīndranāth Tagore (1861–1941), Sri Aurobindo Ghose (1872–1950), and Mohandas K. Gandhi (1869–1948) (see Chapter 16). Tagore won the Nobel Prize in 1913 for his poetry, in which he expressed the human quest for freedom and the divine. Aurobindo, who was educated in the West, sought political freedom for India. After being accused of terrorism and violence, he withdrew from political life altogether and developed a theory of spiritual evolution according to which the individual through self-effort can rise to ever-higher states of spiritual consciousness.

Gandhi, of course, is known everywhere for his use of nonviolence to help attain political freedom for India and for striving to instill a sense of self-respect in all human beings (he called the lowest caste, the Untouchables, the children of God). Through the example of his simple life and teachings, Gandhi tried to make the traditional values of Hinduism available to all.

BUDDHISM

Buddhism arose in India in the person of a prince, **Siddhartha Gautama** [sid-HAR-tuh, GO-tuh-muh], later known as **Buddha** [BOO-duh] (c. 563–c. 483 B.C.E.), "the Enlightened One." Originally, Buddhism essentially was a philosophical response to what might be called the problem of suffering—and suffering is here to be understood in the broad sense as including not merely outright pain and misery but also sorrow, disappointment, frustration, discontent, disaffection, pessimism, and the sense of unfulfillment that so often grows with the passing of the years.

Buddha

When he was twenty-nine, Siddhartha, tortured by the suffering he saw around him, abandoned a life of luxury as well as a wife and son to discover why it is that suffering exists and what its cure must be. After six years of wandering and meditation, he found enlightenment.

Buddha's answer to the problem of suffering was contained in his doctrine of the **Four Noble Truths:** (1) There is suffering; (2) suffering has specific and identifiable causes; (3) suffering can be ended; (4) the way to end suffering is through enlightened living as expressed in the Eightfold Path.

According to Buddha, suffering is in part the result of the transience and hence uncertainty of the world: indeed, all human problems are rooted in the fact of change and the uncertainty, anxiety, and fear that it causes. Suffering is also in part the result of karma. Karma, as we have seen, is the doctrine that one's point of departure in this life is determined by one's decisions and deeds in past lives and that decisions and deeds in this life determine one's beginning points in future incarnations. *Karma,* to repeat, means "action" or "deed." The intention of an action determines whether the action is morally good or bad. The effect of an action leaves a trace that extends over several lifetimes, thereby helping to determine the quality of the reincarnation.

But the most immediate causes of human suffering, according to Buddha, are ignorance, which closes the door to enlightenment, and selfish craving, which enslaves an individual to desires and passions. The individual who is ruled by desires cannot possibly be happy in an ever-changing, uncertain world, especially because what happens is so much beyond one's control. For even when life goes as is hoped for, there is no guarantee that it will continue that way, and inevitably anxiety and fear overwhelm temporary satisfaction.

According to Buddha, through meditation and self-abnegation, selfish craving can be stilled and ignorance overcome. The result of doing so is a cessation of suffering in nirvana, a permanent state of supreme enlightenment and serenity that brings the continuing cycle of reincarnation to an end for the individual.

But Buddha held that attainment of nirvana requires more than merely letting go of selfish desires. It requires understanding that what are ordinarily thought of as one's body and one's consciousness are not real, are not the true Self. This

PROFILE: Siddhartha Gautama Buddha (563–483 B.C.E.)

Siddhartha Gautama, the Buddha, was born in northeastern India. His father was a wealthy king or clan chieftain, Suddhodana by name; through his mother, Maya, he was related to the Shakya tribe of Nepal. The family enjoyed a luxurious lifestyle, and his father sought to keep Siddhartha sheltered from the dust and trouble of the outside world. The young Siddhartha was athletic, handsome, and highly intelligent. He was married at the age of sixteen to Yasodhara, who eventually gave birth to a son, Rahula.

One day on a visit to the city of Kapilavastu, Siddhartha became deeply disturbed by the sight of suffering in its various guises. First, he encountered an old man whose body showed the ravages of the years. Next, he saw a man in the throes of a virulent disease. Finally, he passed a funeral with its corpse and attendant mourners, meeting the problem of death on one hand and anguish on the other. His last experience of that eventful day was to behold a monk deep in meditation. All of these sights had a profound effect on Siddhartha, and the problem of suffering became the central focus of his thoughts. At the age of twenty-nine, he slipped away from his family during the night and entered the forest to seek a solution to the conundrum of suffering, shaving his head and taking on the raiments of poverty.

Early on in his quest, Siddhartha studied under at least two Hindu ascetics. From them he learned a form

Two gigantic statues of Buddha (the larger shown here) in the Bamiyan Valley, Afghanistan, were blown up by the Taliban in 2001. The Taliban, an Islamist movement, ruled much of Afghanistan from 1996 to 2001.

of yoga as well as the arts of breathing and motionless meditation. Later, Siddhartha joined a small band of ascetics who begged for a living. Like them, Siddhartha performed many acts of self-abnegation and self-renunciation. He grew extremely thin from excessive fasting and one day fell unconscious from his attempts to control his senses. When he awoke, he was fed milk and gruel. From that moment, it was clear to Siddhartha that ascetic practices, in and of themselves, do not lead to enlightenment.

Siddhartha dwelt in the forest for about six years. Thereafter he is thought to have sought a *middle way* between sensual indulgence and ascetic self-denial, striving for enlightenment through concentrating his mind in deep meditation. Siddhartha achieved enlightenment one day while meditating under a fig tree near the present-day town of Gaya in northeastern India. He continued to meditate for seven days. Henceforth this tree was known as the *bodhi* tree—the tree of enlightenment.

For almost fifty years Siddhartha, now the Buddha or Enlightened One, went about teaching the way of dealing with suffering. He founded a group or order, to which his wife and son ultimately belonged. Before he died, his philosophy had already found a large following. For Western readers, perhaps the most affecting account of the life of Buddha is presented by Hermann Hesse in his novel *Siddhartha*.

understanding, this totally nonegoistic perspective, is itself freedom from egoistic thoughts and desires and brings with it as well freedom from all fear and anxiety. By rejecting the fetters of egoistic craving, the individual overcomes the false self and achieves "the unsurpassed state of security . . . and utter peace" that is nirvana.

The way to the cessation of suffering is the **Eightfold Path.** In effect, the Eightfold Path sets forth the means of proper living:

1. *Right View,* which implies having adequate knowledge about those things that make human life sick and unwholesome—ignorance, selfish craving and grasping, and so on.

Islamic Philosophy

Muslim philosophy arose around the eighth century, a time when Western Europe was experiencing its Middle Ages. From the beginning, it took into account theological considerations such as the person of Mohammed, the Quran, and the schools of theology, but these were not the only sources of influence. Neoplatonism and Aristotle played important roles in shaping both the problems faced and their proposed solutions. Many translations from the Greek were made during the ninth century.

Among the concerns of the early Islamic philosophers were the nature of God (Allah), the hierarchy of creation, the nature of human beings, and their place within the universe, as well as the relationship between theology and philosophy. **Al-Kindi** [el-KIN-dee] (d. after 870) developed the idea of God as an absolute and transcendent being, which was in accord with certain Muslim ideas of the time. His definition of God took elements from both Aristotle and the Neoplatonists. He developed a cosmology based on the Neoplatonist idea of emanation, where everything evolves out of God and in some way participates in God. Al-Kindi also added the Muslim notion that God created the first being out of nothing by force of will.

Al-Fārābī [el-fuh-RAHB-ee] (875–950) further elaborated on the notion of God in terms of Plotinus's notion of the One and also the notion that everything emanates out of the One. He added Aristotle's notion of God as the first cause of everything. Al-Fārābī looked to the prophet-philosopher to gain the philosophical illumination that would be of profound meaning to his society.

Avicenna [av-uh-SEN-uh] (Abū ʿAli ibn-Sīnā, 980–1037) produced the medieval system of thought best known in the West. He envisioned God as a Necessary Being who emanated the contingent, temporal world out of himself. Everything was dependent on God, and the ultimate goal of human activity was a prophetic mind that attains an intuitive knowledge of God and his creation. For Avicenna, there was a parallelism between philosophy and theology. During this time, philosophy, and especially the mystical identification of a thinker with God, were occasionally considered a threat to Muslim orthodoxy. For example, **Al-Ghazālī** [el-guh-ZAHL-ee] (1058–1111) in his *Incoherence of the Philosophers* attacked Avicenna. Among other things, he criticized Avicenna's notion of the eternity of the world as well as the lower status given to

2. *Right Aim,* which requires overcoming selfish passions and desires by an effort of will and thus having no resentment, envy, or reason to harm another person.

3. *Right Speech,* which means refraining from lies, deceptions, harmful gossip, idle chatter or speculation about others, and so on.

4. *Right Action,* which means not responding to improper desires and cravings, including those that are sexual, and above all not taking a human life. Right Action also includes doing good deeds (described by Buddha as the "treasure" of the wise).

5. *Right Living,* which requires obtaining one's livelihood through proper means and living one's life free from selfish cravings and graspings.

6. *Right Effort,* which means struggling against immoral and corrupt conditions.

7. *Right Mindfulness,* which is the source of Right Effort. Right Mindfulness implies having a duty to attain enlightenment and to understand the nature and effects of selfish craving. The right-minded person, according to Buddha, has no sense of attachment toward body, feelings, perceptions, activities, and thought, and naturally controls all covetous longings and desires. Right Mindfulness likewise means to develop the noble principles of life, especially the six just listed. It develops a pure mind and a clear memory,

the religious law as a mere symbol of higher truths to be accessed through intuition.

The antagonism between mystical philosophy and Muslim orthodoxy represents an ongoing problem. **Averroës** [ah-VAIR-oh-eez] (1126–1198), for example, was interpreted as holding a theory of two separate truths, the truth of religion and the truth of philosophy. Averroës, who taught the idea of eternal creation, was trying to extricate Aristotle's thought from both Neoplatonic and Islamic derivations.

Perhaps what is most intriguing to modern-day Western thought is the development of Sufism. **Sufism** represents a mystical, theosophical, and ascetic strain of Muslim belief that seeks union with God (Allah). **Sadr al-Dīn als Shīrazī** (1571–1640), later known as Mulla Sadrā, sought a monistic return to the First Principle of Being. Sufism, perhaps to a greater degree than orthodox Islamic belief, was influenced by the mystical tendencies of Neoplatonism and gnosticism. There was a seeking after a direct communion with the Absolute Being, who likewise represented Absolute Beauty. Through ascetic practices and concentrated inwardness, a human being might experience a sudden illumination and a sense of ecstatic union with God (Allah). This intuition might reveal to the person his utter nothingness, on one hand, as well as his pantheistic immanence in God, on the other. It is hardly surprising that a number of Sufis during the medieval period were executed for the blasphemy of identifying themselves with God. This ongoing difficulty was to some degree mollified by Al-Ghazālī, who brought Sufism closer to orthodox Muslim belief by playing down the pantheistic elements of Sufism.

There have been four main periods of Sufism: the first period (c. 750–1050), the second period (c. 1050–1450), the modern period (c. 1450–1850), and the contemporary period (1850 to the present). There are about one hundred Sufi orders in the world today, with several million adherents. The movement has produced a number of great mystical poets; **Kabir** [kuh-BEER] (1435–1518) from Benares, India, is one of the best known in the West thanks to Robert Bly's translations. The Sufi literature, Sufi poetry, and the whirling dervishes have continued to influence the West's own contemporary pantheistic and mystical traditions.

which are necessary if our every action, no matter how seemingly trivial, is to be imbued with mindfulness. It brings all human activities under conscious control and thoughtfulness.

8. *Right Contemplation,* which is the ultimate concentration of mind, integrates the aforementioned principles in dealing with all aspects of life. It is the liberating consciousness that frees the mind from the bonds of our cravings, inclinations, and desires. Any personal consciousness is replaced by an "invisible, infinite, all-penetrating consciousness" that brings lasting peace. It is pure cognition, free from any selfishness. Buddha emphasizes that this way is achieved slowly. Deliverance is attained step by step, by constant effort in building an unshakable concentration. Right concentration is uninterrupted, blissful thoughtfulness that purifies deeds, words, and thoughts.

As you can see, the first two stages of the Eightfold Path have to do with the initial mental outlook of the individual, the next four specify appropriate behavior, and the last two pertain to the higher mental and spiritual qualities involved in a total disattachment from self.

Two additional concepts traditionally believed to have been introduced by Gautama Buddha became important for later Buddhism. The first concept Gautama

Buddhism and the West

The parallel concern of Buddhists and Stoics (see Chapter 10) with the problem of suffering is intriguing, but it is difficult to say whether there was any reciprocal influence between Buddhism and the philosophies of ancient Greece and Rome. The first major modern Western philosopher to be influenced in a significant way by Buddhist thought was Arthur Schopenhauer (1788–1860). Schopenhauer believed that human life is basically not rational and that humans are driven by blind and insatiable will. Only by overcoming one's ego and desires can a state of calm bliss be achieved, according to Schopenhauer.

After Schopenhauer, Buddhist and other Asian ideas have increasingly come to the West, mostly via Indian and Japanese gurus, monks, and martial artists. Many of these ideas are now entering the mainstream of popular culture.

Buddha identifies in his *Sayings* as "clinging to existence" (*upadana*). This clinging is an extreme form of egoistic craving or desire and must be "destroyed" if the human being is ever to reach a state of peace and imperturbability. This clinging can take different forms—a clinging to the body and its worldly pleasure, a clinging to views, a clinging to rules and rituals, and a clinging to ego beliefs. It is necessary to cultivate nonclinging or nonattachment but in such a way that there is not clinging to nonclinging.

The other important concept is silence (*moneyya*). Gautama Buddha sat and meditated under the bodhi tree to reach enlightenment. Such enlightenment requires going beyond the verbiage and logics of discursive reasoning. In the *Sayings*, Gautama Buddha is thought to have spoken of three kinds of silence: the silence of body, the silence of mind, and the silence of word. Only the person who is silent in all three ways can be said to be free of taint. Silent meditation becomes a critical way to enlightenment in later developments of Buddhism.

Buddha believed that he had found the cause of suffering in the world and a way of escaping it as well. He set forth a strategy for eliminating unnecessary fear and specified a way of living that is calming for the person but that also allows the person to be of service to others. Buddha did not believe in a divine creator or in divine salvation; thus, in his thinking, the problem of suffering is one that humans must cope with themselves.

The Indian monk Bodhidharma purportedly brought Buddhism to China about 520 C.E. There it gradually mixed with Taoism, Confucianism, and other influences and underwent a rather marked transformation (see the box "Buddhism and the West").

TAOISM

Chinese philosophy, like Indian philosophy, goes back to the prehistoric past. China's history is dominated by dynasties that at first did not extend over the entire country. Shang, the first dynasty, lasted from the seventeenth century to the eleventh century B.C.E.—enduring, you might notice, more than twice as long as the United States of America. But by the fifth century B.C.E., China had fallen into many single warring states—a period when war became "professionalized" and thus more destructive than when it was a seasonal sport of feudal lords in golden chariots. It was during this period and in response to the situation that the two great indigenous philosophical systems in China were born, **Taoism** [DOW-ism] and Confucianism [kun-FYOO-shin-ism].

Confucianism stemmed, of course, from Confucius (551–479 B.C.E.); the beginnings of Taoism are more obscure although even older. (The word *Tao* has a number of meanings but is usually translated as "the Way" in the West.) Two of the early Taoist figures were **Lao Tzu** [LAO-tsuh] (c. sixth century B.C.E.) and his chief follower, Chuang Tzu [CHWANG-tsuh] (c. fourth century B.C.E.). The dialectic between Confucianism and Taoism suffused much of Chinese history and life, from architecture and clothing styles to politics and economic strategies.

Later, during the Han dynasty (206 B.C.E.–220 A.D.), China became a centrally controlled state run by bureaucrats, which it has remained to this day, although this unity was often broken along the way. During this time, the great third religion of China, Buddhism, was introduced from India. In China, Buddhism quickly took on a unique character, in large part due to its synthesis with elements of Taoism. It was not long before the ultimate reality in Chinese Buddhism, the *Buddha dharma*, was being identified with the *Tao*.

Lao Tzu

In an oft-reported meeting between Confucius and Lao Tzu, Confucius expressed his admiration for the depth of Lao Tzu's thought. Lao Tzu, in turn, is said to have expressed doubts about the heroes of the past whom Confucius had chosen as models of behavior. Lao Tzu also tried to convince Confucius of the hopelessness of the latter's attempts to improve society by direct action.

This little story nicely illustrates an essential difference between Confucius and Lao Tzu and between Confucianism and Taoism. Confucius sought to become an advisor to a ruler and directly to change society for the better, using heroes of the past as models. Lao Tzu's vision of things and strategies for change are very different. Within the Taoist tradition, one strain of thought even uses Lao Tzu's ideas as a means cunningly to obtain and retain power (the military and political strategies of Sun Tzu might be mentioned as an example).

Lao Tzu's view of humankind is like that of the Greek philosopher Socrates in at least one respect. Both thought that even the wisest of humans is still ignorant. Both held that to act on that ignorance under the pretense that it is knowledge is folly that leads not to progress and betterment within the individual and society but to the opposite effect. It is especially here that Taoists like Lao Tzu and Chuang Tzu found Confucius wanting. They thought that he sought to impose solutions without knowledge or understanding.

According to Lao Tzu, what is needed is not interference with the world but rather humble understanding of the way it functions, namely, understanding of the Tao. Humans cannot force change on the world without injuring themselves. All

PROFILE: Lao Tzu (c. 6th Century B.C.E.)

Almost nothing is known of Lao Tzu's life, because he spent it trying to remain unknown and nameless. He is thought to have been born in the early sixth century B.C.E. and to have worked in the archives at Loyang (present-day Hunan province). Confucius is thought to have visited the older man during one of his journeys. These quotations reveal some of Lao Tzu's insights on the **Tao,** or **Way.**

> The Tao that can be told of is not
>   the eternal Tao;
> The name that can be named is not the eternal
>   name.
> The Nameless is the origin of Heaven and
>   Earth.
>
> Can you understand all and penetrate all with-
>   out taking any action?
> To produce and to rear them,
> To produce, but not to take possession of them,
> To act, but not to rely on one's own ability,
> To lead them, but not to
>   master them—

> This is called profound and secret
>   virtue.
> Reversion is the action of Tao.
> Weakness is the function of Tao.
> All things in the world come from
>   being.
> And being comes from non-being.
>
> Tao produced the One.
> The One produced the two.
> The two produced the three.
> And the three produced the ten
>   thousand things.
>
> To know that you do not know is the best.
>
> To pretend to know when you do not know
>   is a disease.
>
> The sage desires to have no desire . . . and
>   returns to what the multitude has missed
>   (Tao).
> Thus he supports all things in their natural
>   state, but does not take any action.
>
> A good traveler leaves no track or trace.

arbitrary interventions using models of the past simply lead to further disorder. The sage, he maintained, is the one who knows enough to do nothing: instead of intervening, he simply follows the patterns of the universe, of the ineffable Tao that gives order and substance to all things.

Now, the Tao, for Lao Tzu, is one, natural, and eternal (see the box "The Tao, Logos, and God"). It gives rise to the expansive forces (**yang**) in the universe, and it gives rise to the contractive forces (**yin**). The Tao is like an empty bowl that holds and yields the vital energy (*ch'i*) in all things. It is also the *means* by which things come to be, take shape, and reach fulfillment. In contrast to Confucius, who believed that the Tao can be improved on (note Confucius's remark that "it is man that can make the Way great"), Lao Tzu believed that the Tao cannot be improved on, for it *is* the natural order of things.

According to Lao Tzu, the wise person, the sage, cultivates tranquility and equilibrium in his life in order to recognize the Tao. He comes to recognize that the enduring foundation of life is peace, not strife. The harshest storm, the sage understands, can last only a short while. He frees himself of selfish desires and turns his attention to the deep-rooted Tao, where all is one, and by doing so, he acquires the secrets of both the quiet and the long-lasting life.

The Tao, Logos, and God

Ancient Chinese and Western philosophy show a striking similarity in their identification of the first principle (beginning) of all being and truth. In ancient Chinese philosophy, this first principle is the eternal Tao, the source of all necessity, meaning, order, and existence, the Way the universe functions. Yet the Tao itself, according to Taoism, remains hidden, its nature ineffable. Any attempt to define the Tao or even to describe it in words must fail. According to Lao Tzu, it is the sign of the truly wise man that he will not even try to name it. He only seeks to submit to it and follow it humbly.

In ancient Greek philosophy, a like notion was posited as the root of all things. Heraclitus (c. 540–c. 480 B.C.E.) named it *logos* and regarded it as the source of all order, lawfulness, and justice. There is no consensus on how *logos* should be translated into English, and dictionaries provide many different meanings for the term, including "reason," "proportion," "word," and others.

Logos, as Heraclitus saw it, is almost entirely unknown by earthly mortals—in part because nature loves to hide. Humans, Heraclitus thought, see the world in terms of opposites and as full of strife. But the deeper reality is the *logos,* the unity of opposites in which all is one. Seeing this deeper reality is reserved only for the gods and for those few humans who can escape conventional modes of understanding, according to Heraclitus.

The concept of God as it evolved in traditional Christian philosophy is a variation of Heraclitus's notion of *logos* as developed by Plato and Aristotle and reinterpreted by St. Augustine, St. Thomas Aquinas, and others. In fact, the "Word" that was "in the beginning" in the book of John was *logos* in the Greek text. (John's contribution to the Bible may not have been originally composed in Greek, of course.)

By following the Tao, Lao Tzu held, the behavior of the sage is natural and free, for he harbors no unfit desires and no unnatural expectations. He simply does what is appropriate in the present circumstances. Like water, he accepts the lowest places with contentment and without resistance. He deems valuable what others consider worthless and have discarded. And, because he is selfless, he seeks to care for all things and to benefit them rather than use them for his own ends.

The sage's way, maintained Lao Tzu, is modest, slow, and cautious (see the box "Lao Tzu on Virtuous Activity"). Again like water, the sage is **soft and supple** rather than hard, and (like water), while appearing to do nothing, he achieves lasting effects. To others, the results seem mysteriously produced, for they are produced without apparent effort. The sage is merely following the flow and letting events unfold at their proper time and in their own way. Further, in doing so, he seeks to remain hidden, and he takes no credit for what is achieved, for he seeks neither possession nor domination. This absence of selfish desire is his secret virtue.

Lao Tzu believed that all enduring change is brought about by weakness, not by strength; by submission, not by intervention. Like an infant, the sage conserves his vital force and progresses gradually day by day. His strength lies in his softness and flexibility. As he lives in accord with the Tao, he is preserved from harm.

Lao Tzu extended his philosophy of nonstriving to the political sphere (see the box "Lao Tzu on Government"). He recognized the disadvantages of coercion: the use of force brings retaliation, and mutual hostility quickly escalates, to the detriment of both sides. As coercion and the use of force arise from greed, he advocated a political strategy of nonacquisitiveness, in which weapons are regarded as instruments of

Lao Tzu on Virtuous Activity

Good words shall gain you honor in the market-place, but good deeds shall gain you friends among men.

There is no guilt greater than
   to sanction unbridled
   ambition.
No calamity greater than to
   be dissatisfied with one's
   own lot.
No fault greater than to wish
   continually of receiving.

With the faithful I would keep faith; with the un-faithful I would also keep faith, in order that they may become faithful.

The ability to perceive the significance of the small things of the world is the secret of clear-sightedness; the guarding of what is soft and vulnerable is the secret of strength.

The superior man hoards nothing. The more he uses for the benefit of others, the more he possesses himself. The more he gives to his fellow men, the more he has of his own.

The superior man is skillful in dealing with men, and so does not cast away anyone from his doorway.

The superior man prizes three things. The first is gentleness, the second is frugality, the third is humility. By being gentle he can be bold; by being frugal he can be liberal, and by being humble he becomes a leader among men.

The superior man anticipates tasks that are difficult while they are still easy, and does things that would become great while they are small. Therefore, the superior man, while he never does what is great, is able on that account to accomplish the greatest of things.

The superior man diminishes his actions and diminishes them again until he arrives at doing nothing on purpose.

   Having arrived at this point of non-action, there is nothing that he does not do.

He who keeps his mouth open and spends his breath in the continual promotion of his affairs will never, in all his life, experience safety.

destruction and wars are to be fought only when absolutely necessary and then only with regret.

The wise ruler, Lao Tzu believed, understands that violence is a last resort and knows that it can often be avoided by anticipation, by reconciling potential enemies and resolving difficulties when they first arise. It is because such a ruler side-steps problems by anticipation that his success is unfathomable to others. And because he recognizes that there is no safety in the use of force, he remains calm and unhurried in dealing with any problems that cannot be avoided. His preference is to yield rather than to attack. Gentleness brings him eventual victory with apparently no effort. His strategy is "not to advance an inch but rather to retreat a foot." Slowly he wins over the enemy without the use of weapons. And the gain is lasting because it is achieved without the destructiveness of war and therefore without the long memories of resentment.

To achieve peace and stability, the sage ruler has no wish to dominate or exploit others, Lao Tzu believed. Rather, the wise ruler encourages openness and broad-mindedness. Cognizant of the sometimes violent ways of the world, he is cautious and reserved. The very essence of his method lies in not requiting injury with injury, a practice that leads only into the endless cycle of revenge. He responds to injury with kindness. He remains faithful even to the unfaithful. In this

Lao Tzu on Government

It is the way of Heaven to take from those who have too much and give to those who have too little. But the way of man is not so. He takes away from those who have too little, to add to his own superabundance.

He who assists the ruler with Tao does not dominate the world with force.
The use of force usually brings requital.
Wherever armies are stationed, briers and thorns grow . . .
Whatever is contrary to Tao will soon perish.

Weapons are the instruments of evil, not the instruments of a good ruler.
When he uses them unavoidably, he regards calm restraint as the best principle. Even when he is victorious, he does not regard it as praiseworthy.
For to praise victory is to delight in the slaughter of men.

Tao invariably takes no action, and yet there is nothing left undone.

If kings and barons can keep it, all things will transform spontaneously.
If, after transformation, they should desire to be active,
I would restrain them with simplicity, which has no name.
Simplicity, which has no name, is free of desires.
Being free of desires, it is tranquil.
And the world will be at peace of its own accord.

Violent and fierce people do not die a natural death.
I shall make this the father [basis or starting point] of my teaching.

Govern the state with correctness.
Operate the army with surprise tactics.
Administer the empire by engaging in no activity.

way, he gradually and effortlessly turns people from that lower nature that tends to dominate in times of war and strife, away from aggressive ambition to thoughtfulness and the search for modest goals.

A kingdom, according to Lao Tzu, cannot be preserved by force or cunning. Further, he said, too much government only means confusion. Too many laws create disorder rather than prevent it. Too much activity upsets the balance within a state, just as it does in the life of the individual. The wise ruler does only what is absolutely necessary; because his heart is calm and nonacquisitive, his subjects are not excited to hysteria by either fear or avarice. The state achieves a stability in which all things come to completion in accordance with the Way.

In sum, according to Lao Tzu, the way of life recommended by the Tao is one of simplicity, tranquility, weakness, unselfishness, patience, and, above all, nonstriving or nonaction—allowing the world to follow its natural course. For Lao Tzu, this way of life is its own reward. Lao Tzu was concerned with this world, the world of living people; he was concerned with the human condition and not with otherworldly or supernatural subjects.

You may well think Lao Tzu's philosophy naive or idealistic. Lao Tzu was only too aware that a path of quiet nonstriving was one that few, if any, had chosen or would choose to tread. He made it quite clear that he did not expect rule by force to die out soon or quickly to be replaced by a policy of noninterference. He only drew up what he thought would be a superior way of living for any who might wish to consider his opinion in the matter.

Sun Tzu

Perhaps the oldest treatise on military strategy and methods is *The Art of War,* presumably written somewhere around 512 B.C.E. by **Sun Tzu** [SWUN-tsuh] (544–496 B.C.E.), a Chinese mercenary. According to traditional accounts, an ancient Chinese king had the good sense to hire Sun Tzu to command his forces, with the result that his kingdom became the most powerful of his period. Supposedly, ever since that time great military generals such as Napoleon and Mao Tse-tung have carefully studied *The Art of War.* Some people attribute the success of the comparatively under-armed forces of North Vietnam to their generals' following of Sun Tzu's prescriptions. Sun Tzu's philosophy reportedly is widely employed outside the military arena by those anxious to attain power or success or otherwise to advance their agendas. Luis Felipe "Big Phil" Scolari, who coached the 2002 World Cup–winning Brazilian soccer team, is said to have applied Sun Tzu to the soccer field. The film *Wall Street* (starring Michael Douglas) satirically suggested that Sun Tzu was (or is) being used by savvy corporation CEOs, and some say that the philosophy driving China, an economic juggernaut to whom the United States is billions of dollars in debt, comes not so much from Karl Marx as from Sun Tzu.

An important principle of *The Art of War* is that warfare should not be taken lightly, because it can mean the physical or financial ruin of a state as well as the death or enslavement of its inhabitants. Therefore, Sun Tzu said, all elements of a conflict must be studied carefully and all possible consequences anticipated. Merely by lasting too long, a war can ruin a country, even if the country "wins" militarily.

Another principle of Sun Tzu is that knowledge is everything. Winning requires not merely knowing one's opponent but also being realistic about oneself. Understanding only one of these options means winning only half the time; knowing neither means losing always. History provides confirmation of Sun Tzu's prediction of disaster for nations that overestimate their own abilities and underestimate their opponents'. Germany's invasion of the Soviet Union in World War II is an obvious example. Two recent Clint Eastwood films, *Flags of Our Fathers* and *Letters from Iwo Jima,* although primarily concerned with heroism, duty, and honor, show what happens when a fighting force is blinded by fanaticism.

Sun Tzu also prescribed using force only as a last resort. In fact, he rarely used the word *force* (*li*). This seems to contrast with the military strategy of von Clausewitz,[1] for whom domination is to be achieved both by force and political cunning. An oft-quoted saying in the Clausewitzian tradition is, "God is on the side of the big battalions."[2] For Sun Tzu, it was better to win before force was used and even better never to be in a position to have to use it. Battles must be won beforehand; and if violence does break out, destruction should be kept to a minimum.

---

[1] Carl Philipp Gottfried von Clausewitz (1780–1831) was a Prussian general and a military theorist. He is known for his treatise *On War.*

[2] A remark attributed to Count Roger de Bussy-Rabutin (a French writer famous for his memoirs, 1618–1693) and repeated in various forms by Voltaire, Frederick the Great, Bismarck, George Bernard Shaw, Stalin, and many others.

Sun Tzu also did not accept the idea that an enemy must be crushed utterly.[3] Decimating the enemy or the enemy's property will lead to endless hatred and an increased possibility of retaliation. Force should be used only as a last resort and with regret, he counseled.

Still, according to Sun Tzu, the enemy must taste bitterness (to quote an old Chinese proverb). But the ability to use sheer force must be tempered by keen psychological insight. One must change the opponent's mind-set from one of confidence and security to one of doubt, indecision, and fear. The decisive turning points in war are those in which these states have come to dominate the mind of the opponent.

According to Sun Tzu, decisive victories are almost always best achieved through surprise. Surprise, in turn, requires deception. Strategy in war involves mastering what today would be called mind games. To outmaneuver one's opponent, one must understand the opponent's intentions, tactics, psychology, preparation, and determination, while keeping him or her ignorant as to one's own hand. The one who is invisible will win the contest. Unpredictability is an excellent overall strategy; it induces fear and undermines determination.

Sun Tzu also thought that timing is of the essence and must be derived from analyzing the situation itself, not from wishful thinking. Patience in war is a key virtue: one must wait until exactly the right moment and then act decisively. Thus, flexibility and speed of action are also important.

According to Sun-Tzu, the strategy of war must be all-encompassing, in that war does not really begin at some fixed point nor end with the signing of a treaty. War is not limited to the battlefield, and it is not just for the generals, because it encompasses politics, economics, and societal relations as well. A wise leader, according to Sun Tzu, studies both peace and war and is especially sensitive to the long-term consequences of battle. The end of battle is not the end of war.

With this great emphasis on planning, knowledge, and psychology, it is not surprising that Sun Tzu believed that a country's thinkers are as important as its military advisers. Deep thinking across a range of variables beyond the military decide a nation's destiny, he thought.

Chuang Tzu

Chuang Tzu [CHWANG-tsuh] (c. fourth century B.C.E.), the most important Taoist next to Lao Tzu, perceived that many people live their lives as "slaves of power and riches." Chained by ambition and greed, they are unable to rest and are in constant friction with the world around them. They often feel trapped and do not know how to change their situation. They seem blind to what is happening and why it is happening. Their lives are driven and hectic, and they are in constant warfare with an indifferent world, a world that does not acquiesce to their desires.

But the world has its own wisdom, Chuang Tzu believed, as did Lao Tzu before him, and things come to fruition only at their proper time. Nature cannot

---

[3] The main thought behind Stanley Bing's 2004 satire, *Sun Tzu Was a Sissy*.

PROFILE: Chuang Tzu (c. 4th Century B.C.E.)

Chuang Tzu was born in the fourth century B.C.E. in the kingdom of Meng, which borders present-day Shantung. He had a wife, was poor, and worked for an office connected with the city of Tsi Yuan. Little else is known about him except that he enjoyed differing with the followers of Confucius. He was not interested in holding public office, because doing so, he feared, might disturb his peace of mind. A few of his insights emerge in these quotations:

The mind of a perfect man is like a mirror. It grasps nothing. It expects nothing. It reflects but does not hold. Therefore, the perfect man can act without effort.

Proof that a man is holding fast to the beginning lies in the fact of his fearlessness.

The still mind discovers the beautiful patterns in the universe.

Flow with whatever may happen and let your mind be free: Stay centered by accepting whatever you are doing. This is the ultimate.

Only the intelligent know how to identify all things as one. Therefore he does not use [his own judgment] but abides in the common [principle]. The common means the useful and the useful means identification. Identification means being at ease with oneself. When one is at ease with himself, one is near Tao. This is to let [nature] take its own course.

Heaven and earth are one attribute; the ten thousand things [infinite things] are one horse.

When "this" or "that" have no opposites, there is the very axis of Tao.

He who knows the activities of Nature lives according to Nature. . . . How do we know that what I call Nature is not really man and what I call man is not really Nature?

Your master happened to come because it was his time, and he happened to leave because things follow along. If you are content with the time and willing to follow along, then grief and joy have no way to enter in.

be forced or hurried, because nature, Chuang Tzu believed, unfolds according to the Tao: a tree's fruit must be picked only when it is ripe, not before and not after. If people choose to impose their will on the world, the result is strife, disquietude, and disruption.

Chuang Tzu also believed, as did Lao Tzu, that there is no need for people to force things for the sake of ambition or in the pursuit of profit or, indeed, for any other objective. Because it is the Tao, and not the person, that determines what is possible and what will happen, the wise individual accepts the course of events as it unfolds, with neither hope nor regret, for the Tao brings all things to fulfillment in due time (see the box "Cook Ting"). Thus, for Chuang Tzu, as for Lao Tzu, the secret of the sage—the key to freedom from fear and stress—is simply to follow the Way of things, responding to them appropriately and dwelling in nonaction. The sage is a mirror: he seeks to be utterly clear about what is before him, but he has no wish to change things.

As was true for Lao Tzu, Chuang Tzu applied his principles to statecraft, though he placed somewhat less emphasis on political affairs than did Lao Tzu. The sage ruler, Chuang Tzu believed, first gains knowledge of himself and of his subjects—gains knowledge of his and their nature and destiny—then effortlessly

Cook Ting

Chuang Tzu gave this story of Cook Ting as an illustration of the secret of the sage—to follow the Way of things, responding to them appropriately and never with force.

Cook Ting was cutting up an ox for Lord Wen-hui. At every touch of his hand, every heave of his shoulder, every move of his feet, every thrust of his knee—zip! zoop! He slithered the knife along with a zing, and all was in perfect rhythm, as though he were performing the dance of the Mulberry Grove or keeping time to the Ching-shou music.

"Ah, this is marvelous!" said Lord Wen-hui. "Imagine skill reaching such heights!"

Cook Ting laid down his knife and replied, "What I care about is the Way, which goes beyond skill. When I first began cutting up oxen, all I could see was the ox itself. After three years I no longer saw the whole ox. And now—now I go at it by spirit and don't look with my eyes. Perception and understanding have come to a stop and spirit moves where it wants. I go along with the natural makeup, strike in the big hollows, guide the knife through the big openings, and follow things as they are. So I never touch the smallest ligament or tendon, much less a main joint.

"A good cook changes his knife once a year—because he cuts. A mediocre cook changes his knife once a month—because he hacks. I've had this knife of mine for nineteen years and I've cut up thousands of oxen with it, and yet the blade is as good as though it had just come from the grindstone. There are spaces between the joints, and the blade of the knife has really no thickness. If you insert what has no thickness into such spaces, then there's plenty of room—more than enough for the blade to play about it. That's why after nineteen years the blade of my knife is still as good as when it first came from the grindstone.

"However, whenever I come to a complicated place, I size up the difficulties, tell myself to watch out and be careful, keep my eyes on what I'm doing, work very slowly, and move the knife with the greatest subtlety, until—flop! the whole thing comes apart like a clod of earth crumbling to the ground. I stand there holding the knife and look all around me, completely satisfied and reluctant to move on, and then I wipe off the knife and put it away."

"Excellent!" said Lord Wen-hui. "I have heard the words of Cook Ting and learned how to care for life!"

Cook Ting does not wear himself out by trying to force things. This would mean unnecessary friction. Like water, he seeks the empty places. When things become knotted, he only slows down and proceeds carefully. Even then, there is no need for friction or confrontation. Cook Ting's task is done by following rather than disturbing the order of things. By anticipating problems, he solves them before they become major. Total satisfaction is his reward.

"goes along with what is right for things." He permits nothing to disturb either his own inner harmony or the harmony within the state. Like a tiger trainer who anticipates the wildness of his charges, he knows how to deal with the violence of others before it arises, thus minimizing the need for force. In his fearless adherence to the Way, he remains free from selfish designs and preset goals. Because he puts forth no special effort, his success is unfathomable to others (see the box "Chuang Tzu on Virtuous Activity"). This philosophy is, of course, quite similar to that espoused by Lao Tzu. (And Chuang Tzu, like Lao Tzu before him, was quite aware that rulership in accordance with these principles would be a rare occurrence.)

Chuang Tzu's philosophy is also distinctive for the emphasis he placed on the danger of usefulness. Useful trees, like fruit and nut trees, he explained, are constantly cut back, kept small, and soon stripped of their fruit. Only "useless"

Chuang Tzu on Virtuous Activity

Chuang Tzu was fishing in the river Phu when the king of Khu sent two high officers to him with the message, "I wish to trouble you with the charge of all within my territories."

Chuang Tzu kept holding his rod without looking around and said, "I have heard that in Khu there is a magnificent tortoise shell, the wearer of which died three thousand years ago, and which the king keeps in his ancestral temple. Was it better for the tortoise to die and leave its shell to be thus honored? Or would it have been better for it to live and drag its tail after it over the mud?"

The two officers replied, "It would have been better for it to live and drag its tail through the mud."

"Go your way," said Chuang Tzu. "I will keep on dragging my tail after me through the mud."

Public spirited, and with nothing of the partisan; easy and compliant, without any selfish tendencies; following in the wake of others, without a double mind; not easily distracted because of any anxious thoughts; not scheming in the exercise of one's wisdom; not choosing between parties, but going along with all—all such courses are the path to true enlightenment.

Vacuity, tranquility, mellowness, quietness, and taking no action are the roots of all things. . . . These are the virtue of rulers and emperors when they manage things above.

If one assumes office with them [scholars] to pacify the world, his achievements will be great . . . and the empire will become unified. In tranquility he becomes a sage, and in activity he becomes a king. He takes no action and is honored. He is simple and plain and none in the world can compete with him in excellence. For such a one understands this virtue of Heaven and Earth. He is called the great foundation and the great source of all being and is in harmony with nature. One who is in accord with the world is in harmony with men. To be in harmony with men means human happiness, and to be in harmony with Nature means the happiness of Nature.

---

trees live out their full term of life unhindered and unsavaged—but then it is only these useless trees that are able to provide shade and beauty. Likewise, Chuang Tzu reasoned, the sage avoids becoming too useful, if he is to fulfill his destiny. These and other nuggets of Chuang Tzu's philosophy are set forth in nearby boxes.

CONFUCIANISM

Three great systems of thought dominate Chinese civilization: **Confucianism,** Taoism, and Buddhism. The predominant system is the one founded by **Confucius** [kun-FYOO-shus] (551–479 B.C.E.). Confucian political philosophy has dominated Chinese life in a way unequaled by any similar philosophy in the West.

Confucius

Confucius loved learning, and by age fifteen he had committed his life to a diligent study of the ancient wise men. In addition, he sought a better way and order of doing things. Learning and knowledge, Confucius believed, must be practical.

They must transform life for the better. The result of his own learning was a system of moral, political, and social precepts bound together by what is best called a philosophy of nature and by a faith in the perfectibility of the human character. The switch in Chinese thought from concern for the deity to concern for human effort and excellence began hundreds of years before Confucius was born. Nonetheless, it was Confucius who made humanity (*jen*) a cornerstone of Chinese philosophy. "The measure of man," he said, "is man." The nature and duties of the human being must be studied diligently and cultivated, he insisted, and humanity is to be loved.

To help others, Confucius said, one must first establish one's own humane character, which is done by imitating models of superior men from the past. Once the individual has a character that contains nothing contrary to humanity, he can rely on his humanity in all his actions. Through humanistic thinking and acting, according to Confucius, the superior man makes the Way (Tao) great.

That the human person is perfectible was a central tenet of Confucius's thinking. The human person, Confucius believed, is not always good but can become better. Betterment, he thought, comes through learning and service to others. No one begins with wisdom, but with diligence and determined study, wisdom can be acquired. And once acquired, wisdom becomes an instrument for perfecting oneself, the family, and society. Even nature itself, Confucius believed, cannot resist the power of wisdom: "It is man that can make the Way great," he said, "and not the Way that can make man great."

The Way, as here mentioned by Confucius, is a key concept in his philosophy. For Confucius, as for the Taoists, the Way, or Tao, is basically the path taken by natural events. Confucius uses the word *Way* or *Tao* often and in different senses. There is a way of the good man, a way of music, a way of proper government, and a cosmological way. Confucius even speaks of "my *tao*." Although interpreters are not in total agreement about this, it would seem that the Tao, for Confucius, is not a fixed and eternal transcendental principle that stands outside and above events and determines them. Rather, it is affected in no small part by human thought and human action. One can study the practices of the wise ancients to learn how to make the Way great in one's own time. Essentially, this means knowing how best to regulate your life. Confucius set forth ideals of human behavior based on his understanding of the Way.

For Confucius, everything "thrives according to its nature." One way in which heaven works, he thought, is through the principle of the **Mean,** which provides a standard of measure for all things. Human behavior should avoid extremes and seek moderation. In the philosophy of Confucius, when things function in accordance with this principle of the Mean, they stand in a relationship of mutual dependence. In other words, the principle essentially requires reciprocal cooperation among things—between people and between people and nature. And when the principle is followed, things flourish and nourish one another without conflict or injury.

Confucius formulated this principle of reciprocity in a general way as it applied to human affairs by saying, "Do not do to others what you would not want them to do to you." Likewise, according to Confucius, "A virtuous man wishing to establish himself seeks also to establish others, and wishing to enlighten himself,

PROFILE: Confucius (551–479 B.C.E.)

Confucius, or, in Chinese, K'ung Fu Tzu (K'ung the Great Master), was born "without rank in humble circumstances" in the small Chinese kingdom of Lu. Information about his life is scanty and is derived chiefly from the **Analects,** a collection of his sayings assembled by his disciples. Because of his father's death, he had to work at an early age to help support his mother. He was largely self-taught, and his hunger for learning was insatiable. With the exception of a brief period in which he served as prime minister of Lu, he did not have many opportunities to put his principles about statecraft into practice.

Confucius's ideas have influenced Chinese and Asian ways of life like those of no other philosopher, although their impact has varied from period to period. From the third century to the seventh, Confucianism was eclipsed by other philosophies, but under the T'ang dynasty (618–907) it became the state religion. Neoconfucianism (which incorporated a more developed metaphysics along with Taoist and Buddhist principles) emerged during the Sung dynasty (960–1279) and was the predominant stream of Chinese philosophy until its decline in the twentieth century, which was especially rapid after the Communist revolution in 1949. This was, in part, a consequence of the difference between Chinese communism and the more traditional worldviews. But it was also a side effect of the change in the system of state civil service examinations, which had formerly been based on the Chinese classic texts, including Confucius.

seeks also to enlighten others." Just as nature is built on a principle of reciprocal cooperation rather than strife, so reciprocal cooperation must reign in human affairs, he believed.

Confucius limited his investigation and concern to this changing world: his philosophy was this-worldly and not other-worldly. When he was asked about serving the spirits of the dead, he answered, "While you are not able to serve men, how can you serve their spirits?" And he said, "We don't know about life; how can we know about death?" It is in this world that the human being must live and with other people that one must associate, Confucius emphasized.

Nevertheless, Confucius understood the importance of religious ritual for the state and was fastidious in carrying out its mandates. To achieve a proper balance in this regard is the mark of a superior man, he said. "Devote yourself earnestly to the duties due to men, and respect spiritual beings but keep them at a distance. This may be called wisdom."

Another key concept in Confucius's thought is that of the **sage,** or superior man. The sage represents, in effect, an ethical ideal to which humans should aspire. To achieve the status of sage, Confucius believed, requires having intimate knowledge both of change and of the order of things; it requires, more specifically, having a correct understanding both of human relationships and of the workings of nature. A correct understanding, according to Confucius, involves, among other things, setting right in thought, or *rectifying*, what is distorted or confused, and it especially involves the correct use, or **rectification,** of names. (This meant knowing, for example, when it is legitimate to accord someone a title or rank.) The sage or superior person, according to Confucius, puts this correct understanding into action and seeks the mutual cooperation that enables others to fulfill their own destinies.

Confucius: Insight on Life

At fifteen, I began to be seriously interested in study; at thirty, I had formed my character; at forty, doubts ceased; at fifty, I understood the laws of Heavens; at sixty, nothing that I heard disturbed me; at seventy, I could do as my heart desired without breaking the moral law.

I never take a walk in the company of three persons without finding that one of them has something to teach me.

The superior man is distressed by his want of ability; he is not distressed by men's not knowing him.

The superior man understands righteousness; the inferior man understands profit.

What you do not want done to yourself, do not do to others.

A man who is strong, resolute, simple, and slow to speak is near to humanity.

The way of the superior man is threefold, but I have not been able to attain it. The man of wisdom has no perplexities; the man of humanity has no worry; the man of courage has no fear.

According to Confucius, the sage's actions are superior to those of other men because his model of behavior is superior. Specifically, he patterns his behavior on the great men of the past. In addition, he constantly learns from his own personal experience. (Confucius said that, if he were able to study change for fifty years, he would finally be free of mistakes.) Wisdom requires constant learning, and constant learning allows the superior man better to know the measure of things and to perform his duty accordingly.

Thus, in the philosophy of Confucius, the sage not only thinks correctly but also lives correctly. Indeed, according to Confucius, for the sage no discrepancy exists between thought (or speech) and action. The sage does not think (or say) one thing and do a different thing: he matches word with deed.

Further, according to Confucius, the superior man is an altruist who provides impartial and equitable service to others. He is kind and benevolent; he repays evil not with evil but rather with uprightness. His concern is with reform, not revenge. And his virtuous behavior is a matter of habit that holds even in the direst crisis. For this reason, Confucius believed, the sage can be counted on at all times. His fairness makes him a figure of trust to all, including the rulers of state.

Now, the rulers of the Chinese states of Confucius's time did not entrust their affairs to superior men; nor did the rulers themselves merit this title. Instead, these states were dominated by military regimes that ruled by force and were constantly at war with one another and whose subjects lived in a state of dread. In the opinion of Confucius, the ignoble policies of such inferior rulers were based on four root evils: greed, aggressiveness, pride, and resentment, which singly or together cause a ruler to rationalize and to excuse the most odious behavior on his part. Further, according to Confucius, a ruler is invariably the model for the behavior of his subjects, and, as a consequence, societies ruled by vicious men are vicious societies (see the box "Confucius on Government").

By contrast, a state so fortunate as to be ruled by a superior man, Confucius believed, will be peaceful, secure, and prosperous. Because the superior man is

Confucius on Government

To govern means to make right. If you lead the people uprightly, who will dare not to be upright? Employ the upright and put aside all the crooked; in this way the crooked can be made to be upright. Go before the people with your example, and spare yourself not in their affairs. He who exercises government by means of his virtue may be compared with the polar star, which keeps its place, and all the stars turn toward it.

According to the nature of man, government is the greatest thing for him. There is good government when those who are near are made happy and when those who are afar are attracted.

Remember this, my children: oppressive government is more terrible than tigers. A ruler has only to be careful of what he likes and dislikes. What the ruler likes, his ministers will practice; and what superiors do, their inferiors will follow.

Guide the people with government measures and control or regulate them by the threat of punishment, and the people will try to keep out of jail but will have no sense of honor or shame.

Guide the people by virtue and control and regulate them by respect, and the people will have a sense of honor and respect.

Do not enter a tottering state nor stay in a chaotic one.

When the Way prevails in the empire, then show yourself; when it does not prevail, then hide.

Tzu-kung asked about government. Confucius said, "Sufficient food, sufficient armament, and sufficient confidence of the people." Tzu-kung said, "Forced to give up one of these, which would you abandon first?" Confucius said, "I would abandon armament." Tzu-kung said, "Forced to give up one of the remaining two, which would you abandon first?" Confucius said, "I would abandon food. There have been deaths from time immemorial, but no state can exist without the confidence of the people."

---

governed by the principle of the Mean, as a ruler he will be just and impartial and will seek to establish a fair distribution of wealth, which in turn will promote security and peace. And because his behavior will be emulated by his subjects, he will rule through virtuous example rather than by force of arms. Further, because he is conscientious in his service to all, he will act without fear or sadness.

Confucius's philosophy touched not only on the state and the individual but also on the family. In fact, for Confucius, the well-ordered family is a model for the well-ordered state and ultimately the world as a whole. The family, Confucius believed, should, like the state, be patriarchal and authoritarian.

Thus, the proper functioning of the family depends on the obedience of the subordinate members and the responsible governance of the parents (and ultimately the father) in accordance with the principle of the Mean and on the fundamental virtues of filial piety and brotherly respect. Together, these two virtues, according to Confucius, allow an optimal functioning of the five primary human relationships generally: those between ruler and subject, between parent and child, between elder and younger brother, between husband and wife, and between one friend and another. In the well-ordered family, because relationships are clearly defined, life will be stable and will provide the means for all members of the family to develop their capacities to the fullest extent.

PROFILE: Mencius (c. 371–c. 289 B.C.E.)

Mencius, or Meng-tzu, was born in what is now the Shantung province of China. He purportedly was taught by Confucius's grandson. Like Confucius, he lived in a time of political turmoil; he spent forty years traveling and teaching. His works became part of the "Four Classics" of ancient China and are based on his belief in the original goodness of human nature. These quotations reveal some of his insights.

The great end of learning is nothing else but to seek for the lost mind.

To preserve one's mental and physical constitution and *nourish one's nature* is the way to serve Heaven.

If you let people follow their feelings (original nature), they will be able to do good. This is what is meant by saying that human nature is good. If man does evil, it is not the fault of his natural endowment.

Humanity, righteousness, propriety, and wisdom are not drilled into us from outside. We originally have them with us. Only we do not think [to find them]. Therefore, it is said, "Seek and you will find it, neglect and you will lose it."

With proper nourishment and care, everything grows, whereas without proper nourishment and care, everything decays.

Those who follow the greater qualities in their nature become great men and those who follow the smaller qualities in their nature become small men.

That whereby man differs from the lower animals is small. The mass of the people cast it away, while the superior men preserve it.

The disease of men is this—that they neglect their own fields and go weed the fields of others.

Thus it may be said that what they require from others is great, while what they lay upon themselves is light.

Mencius

The work of the great Confucian philosopher **Mencius** [MEN-shus] (c. 371–c. 289 B.C.E.) is regarded as second only to that of Confucius himself. Mencius, like Confucius, was very saddened by the quality of life during his time. He spoke of princes who were deaf and blind to the terrible events about them that "boom like thunder and flash like lightning." Nevertheless, a central tenet of his thought, as with Confucius, was that human beings are basically good (see the box "Mencius and Thomas Hobbes on Human Nature").

According to Mencius, the natural goodness of humans had become perverted by circumstances. Still, he said, each person has the potential for becoming perfect: doing so is a matter of recovering his lost mind and forgotten heart; it is a matter of thinking and feeling *naturally,* a matter of following intuition and conscience.

Mencius never lost his optimism about the possibility of human betterment. For him, if anything is tended properly, it will grow and thrive. Therefore, human beings should nourish the noble or superior part of themselves so that it will come to predominate. Each person, however, will decide for himself whether he will transform his life for the better.

Mencius and Thomas Hobbes on Human Nature

Mencius was quite aware that, by and large, people in his time were violent, self-serving, inclined to stop short of the mark in everything they attempted, and successful only in bringing premature death on themselves. But for Mencius, this evil came on people because circumstances had not allowed them to cultivate their inherent nobility and to search out within themselves love, wisdom, virtue, a sense of duty, and self-perfection. Human nature, according to Mencius, is inherently good, and this goodness can be actualized if people would develop their potentiality—as would happen under a just and humane regime.

Among the many Western philosophers who have also viewed people as selfish and violent, Thomas Hobbes (1588–1679) is probably the most famous. In the state of nature, Hobbes wrote, the life of man is "solitary, poor, nasty, brutish, and short." But Hobbes, unlike Mencius, attributed the ugly ways of humankind to human nature. So Hobbes believed that only through force wielded by an absolute sovereign can humans be prevented from devouring one another: *Homo lupus homini*, said Hobbes, quoting the Roman poet Plautus (c. 254–184 B.C.E.): *Man is the wolf of man.* Mencius, in contrast, believed that a wise ruler will successfully call forth the goodness inherent in human nature through mild and benevolent leadership.

Whether their malevolent actions mean that human beings, although essentially good by nature, exist in a fallen state or whether they indicate that human nature is essentially bad is a question that has not been resolved. Perhaps it is not resolvable.

For the person who has chosen to seek it, the way to self-betterment, the way to a noble existence and the upright life, according to Mencius, can be found only within oneself. Conscience, for Mencius, is "the mind that cannot bear suffering [on the part of others]." The pathway to the upright life, however, must include *self*-suffering and difficulty, he said. "When Heaven is about to confer a great office on any man," he said, "it first exercises his mind with suffering, and his sinews and bones with toil. It exposes his body to hunger and subjects him to extreme poverty. It confounds his undertakings. By all these methods, it stimulates his mind, hardens his nature, and supplies his incompetencies."

Difficulty and suffering, according to Mencius, are to be considered privileges and opportunities to develop independence, excellence, mental alertness, freedom from fear, and quietude of spirit. He goes so far as to imply that prudence and the other virtues are hardly possible for those who have not suffered deeply.

In the process of perfecting one's own life, Mencius said, one is put in a position of benefiting one's family and, through teaching and leadership, society as a whole (see the box "Mencius on Virtuous Activity"). Indeed, true happiness, he said, does not consist in ruling an empire merely for the sake of power, the desire for which is the driving ambition of the inferior mind, the mind that, like that of an animal, contains no notion of what is great or honorable. True happiness consists in seeing one's parents and family alive and free from anxiety and in helping one's society. Further, he maintained, whoever is happy in this way is happy in another way, for he need never feel shame for his actions.

Thus, it may be seen that Mencius, too, like Confucius, was concerned not only with the person but also with the state (see the box "Mencius on Government"). Disorder in a state, he believed, is often caused by a ruler who takes no

Mencius on Virtuous Activity

It is said that the superior man has two things in which he delights, and to be ruler over the empire is not one of them.

That the father and mother are both alive and that the condition of his brothers affords no cause for anxiety, this is one delight.

That when looking up he has no occasion for shame before Heaven, and below he has no occasion to blush before men—this is the second delight.

In the view of a superior man as to the ways by which men seek for riches, honors, gain, and advancement, there are few of their wives who would not be ashamed and weep together on account of them.

Men must be decided on what they will not do, and then they are able to act with vigor on what they ought.

If on self-examination I find that I am not upright, shall I not be in fear even of a poor man in loose garments of hair cloth?

If on self-examination I find that I am upright, neither thousands nor tens of thousands will stand in my path.

I have not heard of one's principles being dependent for their manifestation on other men.

Benevolence is man's mind and righteousness is man's path.

How lamentable it is to neglect the path and not pursue it, to lose the mind and not know to seek it again.

Benevolence subdues its opposite just as water subdues fire.

Those, however, who nowadays practice benevolence do it as if with one cup of water they could save a whole wagon load of fuel which was on fire, and, when the flames were not extinguished, were to say that water cannot subdue fire. This conduct greatly encourages those who are not benevolent.

notice of conditions within his own state, a ruler who—again like an animal—is indifferent to all but his own selfish interests and petty ambitions. This indifference and selfishness is a form of blindness, maintained Mencius, and a state governed without vision, he said, inevitably falls into ruin and death.

Further, according to Mencius, the subjects of the state ruled by the inferior person follow the example of their leader and also become like beasts set to devour each other. In this thought Mencius echoed Confucius. But, unlike Confucius, Mencius held that killing such a monarch is not murder, for the establishment of a humane government is not possible under such an individual.

The good ruler, Mencius maintained, is benevolent toward his subjects as a father is toward his children and will seek to establish a good order and a just regime. He displays, in addition to benevolence, three other primary virtues or attributes: righteousness, propriety, and knowledge. Further, the good ruler is mild in manner and governs with mind and heart rather than with the strong arm. Because of his mild manner, he encounters no enemies, and because he is humane and his subjects accordingly have confidence in his goodness, he will have only little opposition.

In short, this superior ruler, who has himself suffered on the path to betterment, acquires the mind that cannot bear the suffering of others, and, because it is humane and just, his governance is the foundation of all present and future good within the state.

Mencius on Government

If a man should love others and the emotion is not returned, let him turn inward and examine his own benevolence.

If a man is trying to rule others, and his government is unsuccessful, let him turn inward and examine his wisdom.

If he treats others politely and they do not return the politeness, let him turn inward and examine his own feelings of respect.

Only the benevolent ought to be in high stations. When a man destitute of benevolence is in a high station, he thereby disseminates his wickedness among all below him.

Virtue alone is not sufficient for the exercise of government; laws alone cannot carry themselves into practice.

[In a state] the people are the most important; the spirits of the land (guardians of territory) are the next; the ruler is of slight importance. Therefore to gain [the hearts of] the peasantry is the way to become emperor.

Killing a bad monarch is not murder.

If a ruler regards his ministers as hands and feet, then his ministers will regard him as their heart and mind. If the ruler regards his ministers as dogs and horses, his ministers will regard him as any other man. If a ruler regards his ministers as dirt and grass, his ministers will regard him as a bandit and an enemy.

To say that one cannot abide by humanity and follow righteousness is to throw oneself away. Humanity is the peaceful abode of man and righteousness is his straight path.

All men have the mind which cannot bear [to see the suffering of] others. . . . When a government that cannot bear to see the suffering of the people is conducted from a mind that cannot bear to see the suffering of others, the government of the empire will be as easy as making something go round in the palm.

Humanity, righteousness, loyalty, faithfulness, and the love of the good without getting tired of it constitute the nobility of Heaven, and to be a grand official, a great official, and a high official—this constitutes the nobility of man.

Mencius's philosophy exhibits the humanistic concerns and faith in human goodness and perfectibility that characterize Confucian philosophy in general. Both Mencius and Confucius were aware, however, that in practice humans are often self-seeking and that their potential for goodness must be cultivated or nurtured. As may be seen in the boxes, Mencius offers much advice and sets forth many telling maxims that, in effect, constitute a method for cultivating the better part of human nature.

Hsün Tzu

Another important Confucian philosopher, who blended Taoism with Confucianism and added his own, rather more pessimistic conception of human nature, was **Hsün Tzu** [SHWIN-tsuh] (298–238 B.C.E.). He was rationalistic and realistic in his approach, believing that the hierarchical order of society was established by following unchanging moral principles. If moral practices, laws, and the rules of propriety were followed, then order, peace, and prosperity would inevitably be the result. If they were not followed, disorder and disaster would result.

Hsün Tzu's view of the basic nature of human beings is what makes him strikingly dissimilar to other major Confucian thinkers. He did not agree with Mencius that human beings are originally good and therefore naturally inclined to goodness. Hsün Tzu believed that human beings are basically bad but that they are impelled to compensate for and overcome this defectiveness, this badness, through education and moral training. Fortunately, the human being is perfectible. Through a study of past and present sages, a human being may develop a moral understanding based on the ultimate virtues of humanity and righteousness.

For Hsün Tzu, the state, like the individual, can lose itself in seeking profit. The result is strife, violence, lewdness, and rebellion. Such an inferior state must be reconstructed through moral principles, which must come to be embodied in the person of the ruler. Hsün Tzu's thought was the official creed during the Han period (c. 206–220), and it has continued to have an important influence on Asian societies to the present.

ZEN BUDDHISM IN CHINA AND JAPAN

Zen Buddhism is one of the Buddhist sects of Japan and China. (Buddhism, it may be recalled, originated in India.) *Zen* is Japanese and *Ch'an* is Chinese, and both words derive from the Sanskrit word for meditation, **dhyana.** When Buddhism first came to China, it emphasized the importance of meditation, rather than any particular scripture or doctrine, as the key to ultimate reality.

Although the heading for this section is Zen Buddhism, we discuss both the Chinese and Japanese traditions, Zen and Ch'an. It should be noted that other forms of Buddhism developed as well, but the Zen tradition is the one that has awakened the most philosophical interest in the West.

The growth of **Ch'an Buddhism** (Chinese Zen Buddhism) was slow at first, and numerically it always was one of the smaller sects. But over the centuries this sect spread throughout China and into neighboring countries like Japan and Korea. In the last century, it has taken root in the United States and Europe. Its current spread in the West seems to indicate that Ch'an Buddhism responds to a need in a highly complex, technological world.

Buddhism in China and Japan has a long and rich history. Here it will only be possible to look briefly at a few of its most original and profound thinkers, the sixth patriarch of Chinese Zen, Hui Neng; Murasaki Shikibu; and Dogen Kigen, the founder of the Japanese Soto tradition. The philosophies of these thinkers complement one another and give an overall perspective on basic elements in the Zen Buddhist tradition.

Hui Neng

Hui Neng [HWAY-nung] (638–713) lost his father in childhood and had to sell firewood to keep his mother and himself alive. He was illiterate.

One day, while delivering firewood to a shop, Hui Neng heard the chanting of the Buddhist *Diamond Sutra* (perhaps the most important scripture of Chinese Buddhism, in which Buddha strips his student Subhuti of his coarse views and allows him to see the fundamental oneness of all things and the immutability of perceived phenomena; *sutra* means "secret doctrines and sacred teachings"). Hui Neng immediately grasped the deep truth latent in its words. But not until some time later did a gift of money enable him to confirm his perception of truth by seeking out Master Hung-jen, the fifth Chinese patriarch of Ch'an Buddhism, at Huang-mei Mountain in Hupei.

During the first meeting with the fifth patriarch, Hui Neng did not hesitate to manifest the unshakable strength of his vision, and he was accordingly accepted in the Huang-mei monastery. For eight months, however, he worked in the kitchen without even entering the main temple.

At this time, the fifth patriarch was seeking a successor and asked the monks to write a poem showing the depth of their insight into truth. Only the person who has a direct intuition into the truth achieves peace of mind, the Ch'an Buddhists believed, and they also thought that each person must discover this truth for himself. That all is ultimately one was a basic precept of the fifth patriarch. This one reality was thought to be our true self-nature and was held to be immanent within human beings from the beginning. To see this ever-present truth exactly as it is would require going beyond the usual way of thinking, which breaks down ultimate being into distinct entities and classifies and relates them so that they are understood only in terms of the categories to which they belong and their relationships to one another. Hence poetry rather than a normal form of discourse would be required to express insight into this truth, for normal forms of thought and language can express neither the uniqueness of the individual entity nor the underlying oneness of all things. Perhaps you are reminded here of Heidegger.

Shen-hsui, the senior monk at the monastery, was the only one who dared to write the requested poem, and the other monks doubted their ability to surpass him in depth of understanding. His contribution, however, according to tradition, only showed that he had not seen the ultimate truth and had not escaped the confines of normal thought. Hui Neng, though illiterate, is said immediately to have sensed the inadequacy of the vision conveyed by this poem when he overheard it being recited by another monk and to have composed a reply to the poem on the spot.

The monks, it is said, were astounded by the words of this twenty-three-year-old illiterate, who had not yet even been admitted into the meditation hall. The fifth patriarch was moved as well and immediately recognized Hui Neng as his successor. Perceiving the possibility of jealousy and anger among the monks, he is said to have had Hui Neng come to him in the middle of the night to receive the robe and bowl symbolic of his new status as sixth patriarch and to learn the wisdom of the *Diamond Sutra*. According to tradition, Hung-jen, the fifth patriarch, convinced that the truth of the *Buddha-Dharma* (ultimate reality) would ultimately prevail through Hui Neng, instructed Hui Neng to leave the monastery immediately and to remain in hiding until he was ready to teach.

What is the ultimate **Dharma** (reality/truth/law)? Hui Neng gave it a number of different titles: the Self-Nature, the Buddha-Dharma, the Real Nature, and the eternal and unchanging Tao (note the Taoist influence implicit in the last name).

Hui Neng on Life and Truth

As mentioned in the text, Hui Neng sought out the fifth patriarch of Ch'an Buddhism, Master Hung-jen, who eventually confirmed Hui Neng's insight into the truth and appointed him his successor. On meeting the fifth patriarch, Hui Neng is said to have said: "I confess to Your Reverence that I feel wisdom constantly springing from my own heart and mind. So long as I do not stray from my nature, I carry within me the field of bliss."

Other interesting quotations of Hui Neng as to life and truth are as follows:

How could I expect that the self-nature is in and of itself so pure and quiet! How could I expect that the self-nature is in and of itself unborn and undying! How could I expect that the self-nature is in and of itself self-sufficient, with nothing lacking in it! How could I expect that the self-nature is in and of itself immutable and imperturbable! How could I expect that the self-nature is capable of giving birth to all dharmas [laws]!

The *Bodhi* or Wisdom, which constitutes our self-nature, is pure from the beginning. We need only use our mind to perceive it directly to attain Buddhahood.

One Reality is all Reality.

Our original nature is Buddha, and apart from this nature there is no other Buddha. Within, keep the mind in perfect harmony with the self-nature; without, respect all other men. This is surrender to and reliance of one's self.

Light and darkness are two different things in the eyes of the ordinary people. But the wise and understanding ones possess as penetrating insight that there can be no duality in the self-nature. The Non-dual nature is the Real Nature . . . both its [the Real Nature's] essence and its manifestations are in the absolute state of suchness. Eternal and unchanging, we call it the Tao.

All things, he said, are in reality one: there are no "things." Human thought and understanding, to make sense of a totality that cannot be grasped at once, impose categories, contrasts, and distinctions on reality (including thirty-six basic pairs of contrasts or opposites, such as light and darkness, yin and yang, birth and death, good and bad, and so on). But in truth there is only one thing, the Real Nature, and, as it is in itself, it exists prior to any distinctions or categorizations; it is (so to speak) beyond good and evil, permanence and impermanence, content and form. It is an absolute state of "suchness" that neither comes nor goes, neither increases nor decreases, neither is born nor dies. It is exactly as it is: it is reality and truth (see the box "Hui Neng on Life and Truth").

According to Hui Neng, though this ultimate reality or truth is in principle accessible to all, it remains hidden to many of us because we are focused on false attachments and selfish interests: in short, we lack a balanced, objective outlook. And, as a result of this imbalance in our perspective, our efforts, too, are one-sided in pursuit of our goals. Hui Neng made it his purpose to free humans from selfish, one-sided visions of reality. His recommendation was for a state of "no-thought" or "mindlessness," in which the mind does not impose itself on the truth but, rather, remains open and spontaneous—a mirror reflecting the wisdom inherent in reality, one that reflects but does not impede the flow of events.

To deepen one's spirit, he said, is to live in harmony with the true or "self-nature" of all things. When the mind is right, it thinks without bias or partiality and is thus considerate of the needs of each and every thing.

The blend of Taoist, Confucian, and Buddhist precepts is very much in evidence in Hui Neng's thought.

Buddhism in Japan

At this point, we depart China for Japan, where Zen was introduced from China. As you have seen, under Hui Neng, Zen emerged as a distinct and separate Buddhist sect that combined elements of Indian Buddhist and Chinese thought. When it spread to Japan, Zen was influenced by Japanese culture as well.

Japan is a serene and beautiful country, a collection of many islands dominated generally by volcanic mountains offering scant natural resources. Ancient legends see the Japanese as descending from the Sun Goddess, but more specific data indicate that the Japanese came from Central Asia (Mongolia today), from South China, and possibly also from the South Sea Islands of the Pacific. Because Japan consists of islands surrounded by water, it has remained relatively free of hostile invasions for long periods of its history. Its isolation has also allowed it to develop a unique style in almost every facet of life.

From early times, the Japanese borrowed ideas and practices from other cultures, often modifying them in the process. Confucius and Confucianism were particularly revered and implemented in various degrees at various times in Japanese history. Korean scholars introduced Buddhism to Japan around 552. Architecture, sculpture, painting, music, and poetry were all heavily influenced by this event, because China was the older, dominant culture of the region. The Chinese influence was furthered by the arrival of Zen Buddhism in the fourteenth century; more about this shortly. Only after the middle of the nineteenth century did modern Western influences make an impression on Japan.

Medieval Japan was a melting pot of philosophical and religious views. For men, the mixture of Asian philosophies probably was good enough, but its effect on women was less fortunate (as you will see). If there were a recipe for medieval Japanese philosophy, it would read as follows:

> 1 cup Shinto animism
> 4 Buddhist Noble Truths
> 1 yin
> 1 yang
> 1 handful Confucian virtues
> 1 Mahayana Buddhist doctrine of the void

> Mix all ingredients well, apply liberally to everyone. Prepares men for salvation. Prepares women for reincarnation as men.

This is intended to give a reader only a broad idea of some of the main elements in Japanese Buddhism at the time. By the late ninth century, Japanese culture reflected an unequal mixture of Shinto, Confucianism, Taoism, and Zen Buddhism (and its Mahayana branch, and *its* branches, Tendai and Shigon). What are these ingredients? You already are familiar with most of them, other than Shinto and Mahayana.

Shinto is an ancient native religion of Japan that, from the earliest times, has played a large role in Japanese culture and politics. Unlike most animistic religions, it persists even to the present day in what is now a modern society. Shinto is an animistic, nature-worshiping religion in which the sun, the moon, storm, and fire all are viewed as deities. Shinto is based on gratitude for the benevolence and beauty of nature rather than on fear of it. There are no iconic images and no angry gods to be mollified. There are also no sacred scriptures or moral codes to be followed.

Shinto related humans to the **kami,** or gods of nature, that created the universe. People were said to be just another part of the physical universe. The Japanese language did not even have a word for nature as something distinct from humans. People were regarded as "thinking reeds" completely identified with and part of the natural and divine universe. Such a view is called **animism.**

People's duties were derived through their blood relationships. One was connected to the gods of nature through one's ancestor's clan and through the divine clan of the Mikado, who was both national high priest and head of state. The Japanese word for government, *matsuri-goto*, means "things pertaining to worship." So there was no conceptual difference between religion, ethics, and government. And there was no conceptual difference between people and other natural objects.

Mahayana Buddhism was just a twist on Zen. It was introduced into Japan in the late sixth century, when Japan lost its territory in Korea and its ally, the Paekche Kingdom, suffered military defeat. Many Korean war refugees, most of them Buddhists, fled to Japan, where their religion gained acceptance among Japanese diplomats and aristocrats. Prince Shotoku (his name means "sovereign moral authority") made it the official religion of Japan, incorporating it into Shinto. Shinto connected one to one's historical, anthropological past; Mahayana Buddhism connected one to the present and to the future eternity. It incorporated the Confucian virtues of filial piety, veneration of ancestors, duties based on rank and position, honesty, and so forth. (Taoism, too, fit in nicely, with its views about the oneness of humans and nature, spiritual freedom, and peace—not to mention yin/yang emphasis on orderliness and balance.)

Mahayana saw humanity unified through spiritual enlightenment, in the worship of one god, who, as luck would have it, turned out to be the Mikado, the greatest earthly *kami*. This was the form of Buddhism adopted by Japanese aristocracy. The higher up the sociopolitical aristocracy one was, the closer one was to God— and thus the theory did not displace aristocrats.

This brings us to Murasaki.

Murasaki Shikibu

Murasaki Shikibu [MOO-ruh-sah-kee shih-kih-boo] (978?–1026?) lived at the height of the Mahayana Buddhist influence in Japan. And while all Japanese shared this philosophical heritage, not all shared social and political equality.

The Tendai sect of Mahayana Buddhism held that the closer one was to the Mikado, the greater was one's potential for moral excellence and for admission to the Western Paradise (heaven). But in Buddhism, women generally were considered to be of lesser moral worth than men. Women could achieve salvation or reach the psychological state of nirvana that would prepare them to enter the Western Paradise, but only after reincarnation as a male.

PROFILE: Murasaki Shikibu (978?–1026?)

Murasaki Shikibu, or Lady Murasaki, as she is sometimes called, is an important Japanese, Shinto, Buddhist, and feminist philosopher. Murasaki Shikibu is almost certainly not her real name, however. She was given the nickname "Murasaki" because the real author strongly resembled a character by that name in the book she wrote. Murasaki came from a literary family of the Fujiwara clan. In Japan at that time, it was forbidden for women to study Chinese characters (the original written form of Japanese language). Murasaki learned young how to read Chinese characters by hanging around when her brother was being tutored. She eventually entered court service in the entourage of the teenaged empress Joto-Mon'in Shoshi, to whom Murasaki secretly taught Chinese. Learning how to read gave Murasaki access to the forbidden literatures of religion and philosophy.

In addition to some poetry, Murasaki left two works: a diary, *Murasaki Shikibu Nikki*, and an epic philosophical novel, *Genji Monogatari*. Despite the fact that it was written centuries before the invention of the printing press, once it was printed, *Tale of Genji* (as it is also known) never went out of print. It has been translated into more than thirty languages. Murasaki's primary philosophical interest was with the moral status of women under Japanese Buddhist ethics.

The fact that one was a woman was evidence that in a past life one had been a male who was now making up for a past life lacking in virtue. In the Buddhist doctrine of reincarnation, a good woman can hope at best for reincarnation as a man. After a lifetime as a virtuous man, it would be possible to achieve salvation and enter heaven. Women, no matter their virtue, could not hope for salvation, as Murasaki says:

> But then someone with as much to atone for as myself may not qualify for salvation; there are so many things that serve to remind one of the transgressions of a former existence. Ah, the wretchedness of it all!

Murasaki's women characters illustrated just how hopeless life was for Japanese women, especially those who thought about things like self-identity, morality, free will and determinism, predestination and salvation. Judging from the popularity of her very long book, *Tale of Genji*, and the fact that it was initially circulated a chapter at a time among aristocratic women (obviously, many had learned how to read Chinese characters on the sly), a lot of Japanese women did care about these philosophical issues.

Murasaki kept the basic recipe we gave in the "Buddhism in Japan" section, but she changed the directions and added a few ingredients. Here is Murasaki's version of the recipe:

1 cup Shinto animism
4 Buddhist Noble Truths
1 yin
1 yang
1 handful Confucian virtues
1 Mahayana Buddhist doctrine of the void
1 lifetime of spiritual enlightenment

Mix all ingredients well with a strong, feminist hand. Contemplate for a lifetime with as much detachment from worldly distractions as possible. (Become a nun if you can.) Use as an antidote to determinist misogynist elements of Tendai. With lifelong use, women may achieve salvation.

Murasaki's version of the recipe added the importance of spiritual enlightenment and contemplation. She also emphasized the virtues of simplicity and detachment from worldly possessions.

In sharp contrast to the views of women present in Buddhism and reflected in Japanese culture, Murasaki's female characters struggled with the problem that, in Japanese culture and Buddhist religion, women existed only as predestined, natural objects.

Murasaki's main character, Ukifune (which means "loose boat," "loose woman," or "person with no direction and uncertain destination"—you get the idea), becomes so depressed following a rape that she attempts to commit suicide, but she is saved by a monk, against the advice of other monks who think she should be allowed to drown.

Everyone, especially other women, has told Ukifune that she cannot do anything about the rape and its social consequences; it is just her fate. There is no hope for her other than to become a prostitute. Ukifune rages against the double injustice: first, she is just an object to a man who forcibly rapes her; second, she is punished socially for having been wronged. Rather than accept her fate, she challenges her destiny through suicide, hoping for reincarnation as a man.

But her rescue, although also attributed by the monk to fate, leads her to a path of religious contemplation. Ultimately, she becomes a nun—but not an ordinary nun performing public service. Ukifune spends her life contemplating life's meaning and seeking enlightenment. Ultimately, a lifetime of contemplation will reveal to her that she can control her destiny through self-knowledge.

Murasaki's women characters struggle to become free, responsible moral agents who assert that they have natural rights. They also assume moral responsibilities to others. Although Murasaki rejected mainstream Buddhism's view of women, her philosophy represents a minority Buddhist view that women are moral agents who, instead of blaming fate, can assume moral responsibility for their actions. Murasaki held that women should challenge their *karma* (destiny) and take control of their own lives by engaging in what were then forbidden, illegal activities such as reading the *sutras* (secret doctrines and sacred teachings) of the great Buddhist monks.

Murasaki's personal decision to become a nun and to read the *sutras* was the product of a wager that was worthy of Pascal (see Chapter 13):

The time too is ripe. If I get much older my eyesight will surely weaken to the point that I shall be unable to read the sutras, and my spirits will fail. It may seem that I am merely going through the motions of being a true believer, but I assure you that I can think of little else at the present moment.

By understanding and living according to what Murasaki argued was the true meaning of Buddhism, women could achieve a state of contemplation that is compatible with reaching nirvana. Under Murasaki's philosophy, women need not be content to wait until they have been reincarnated as males to begin the difficult and long process of philosophical enlightenment. They can begin that process in this life by living, as do men, according to the teachings of Shinto and Buddhism. It should be taken into account that there have been more positive developments regarding women's status in Japanese Buddhism, especially recently.

Dogen Kigen

By age fourteen, **Dogen** [DOE-gen] (1200–1253) was already a monk. He eventually became dissatisfied with the decadent state of Tendai Buddhism, which, being egalitarian and anti-elitist in nature, adopted many popular rituals like chanting the name of Amitabba Buddha. **Tendai Buddhism** was a Japanese variation of the T'ien-t'ai School of Buddhism in China. It was introduced into Japan in the ninth century. Its basic notion is that all phenomena are expressions of the absolute oneness or suchness (*tathatā*). Dogen therefore sought out a Tendai monk, Eisei, who had twice traveled to China to study Ch'an Buddhism. Eisei died soon after the encounter with Dogen, but Dogen continued his studies for nine years under Eisei's successor, Myozen. Afterward, Dogen went to China himself to deepen his studies, and eventually he came under the tutelage of Ju-Ching, at T'ien T'ung Shan monastery. After five years, he returned to Japan in 1227.

Dogen continued to teach and write in monasteries in and around the old capital city of Kyoto until 1243. During this time, he came increasingly in conflict with the predominant Tendai tradition and eventually withdrew into the mountains to establish the Eiheiji monastery. To this day, Eiheiji is the principal monastery of the Soto branch of Japanese Zen Buddhism.

Many of life's numerous problems, Dogen realized, are not easily solvable. There is, for example, the problem of the impermanence of life. Life passes like the rush of a spring stream, flowing on, day after day, and then it is gone. Dogen therefore urged humans not to waste a single second. Time must be utilized in a worthy pursuit, a single objective that merits an all-out effort. The life goal must be nothing small, selfish, or narrow-minded. It must be chosen from a broad perspective and with an eye to benefiting others as well as oneself. Dogen's philosophy is, in essence, a prescription for an unwasted or noble life, a life of happiness here and now.

It is difficult, of course, Dogen realized, to choose how to live and equally difficult, if not more so, to carry out that choice. One lives in an uncertain and hurried world, and "our minds go racing about like horses running wild in the fields, while our emotions remain unmanageable like monkeys swinging in the trees." The rapidity of life and the uncertainty of its course makes people's lives full of torment and confusion. They do not understand its nature or how best to manage themselves.

Moreover, according to Dogen, the mind overwhelmed by a world not understood seeks safety in selfish and self-protective acts. Life is perceived as a succession of real and suspected dangers, and it is viewed in stark contrasts of good and bad, right and wrong, black and white. This perception of the world is what Dogen called the "Lesser Vehicle," and it arises out of ignorance and fear. The ignorant, fearful mind constructs a list of things deemed bad and to be avoided, and anger and resentment are felt toward perceived sources of danger. The individual caught in a dark and threatening world he does not understand finds little rest or peace, and doing violence to himself or others is a frequent consequence of his entrapment.

Dogen's Prescriptions for Virtuous Activity

Dogen, a Zen monk since early youth who traveled to China for further studies, gained a reputation as a strict teacher. His writings have had a profound influence up to the present day. Many of his works have been translated into English and have played an important part in the growth of Zen Buddhism. The following are his prescriptions for virtuous activity.

To plow deep but plant shallow is the way to a natural disaster. When you help yourself and harm others, how could there be no consequence?

Everyone has the nature of Buddha; do not foolishly demean yourself.

Even worldly people, rather than study many things at once without really becoming accomplished in any of them, should just do one thing well and study enough to be able to do it even in the presence of others.

While simply having the appearance of an ordinary person of the world, one who goes on harmonizing the inner mind is a genuine aspirant to the Way. Therefore as an Ancient said, "Inside empty, outside accords." What this means is to have no selfish thought in the inner mind, while the outer appearance goes along with others.

Emperor Wen of Sui said, "Secretly cultivate virtue, await fulfillment." . . . If one just cultivates the work of the Way, the virtues of the Way will appear outwardly of their own accord.

To practice the appropriate activity and maintain bearing means to abandon selfish clinging. . . . The essential meaning of this is to have no greed or desire.

Students of the Way, do not think of waiting for a later day to practice the Way. Without letting this day and this moment pass by, just work from day to day, moment to moment.

It is written (in the *Vinaya*), "What is praised as pure in character is called good; what is scorned as impure in character is called bad." It is also said, "That which would incur pain is called bad; that which should bring about happiness is called good."

In this way should one carefully discriminate; seeing real good, one should practice it, and seeing real evil, one should shun it.

Jade becomes a vessel by carving and polishing. A man becomes humane by cultivation and polish. What gem has highlights to begin with? What person is clever at the outset? You must carve and polish, train and cultivate them. Humble yourselves and do not relax your study of the Way.

There is a saying of Confucius: "You can't be apart from the Way for even a second. If you think you are apart from it, that's not the Way." He also said, "As the sages have no self, everything is themselves."

This state of malcontent, according to Dogen, in which the world is perceived in terms of stark and fearful divisions, remains with the individual until he or she achieves clarification about the true nature of things. But everyone, Dogen said, has the nature of Buddha. Everyone can see the truth and live calmly and peacefully in its presence. It is simply necessary to abandon the selfish and narrow perspective in favor of the broad and unbiased view, in which the mind is expanded beyond the limitations of divisive categories like good/bad and desirable/undesirable, in which greed gives way to generosity, self-serving to other-serving. It is necessary to see things as the ancient sages did, from the perspective of the universe or "Buddha-Dharma" or "universal Self." To do this is to practice the Great Way.

Understanding from this broad perspective, Dogen thought, also involves acceptance—going along with things, following the Way. This, he said, is the wisdom

Zen Buddhism in Japan

There are two major forms of Zen Buddhism in contemporary Japan: Rinzai Zen and Soto Zen. Over the centuries, each has mutually influenced the other. The difference between the two has more to do with method than with doctrine. Both seek enlightenment apart from the scriptures.

Rinzai Zen, named after the famous Zen monk Rinzai (785–867), seeks sudden enlightenment, as preached by Hui Neng. To achieve *satori,* or the enlightenment experience, *koans* are often used in addition to sitting in meditation (*zazen*). *Koans* are illogical, even nonsensical, puzzles that are designed to break the stranglehold of conceptual thought so that the absolute, indivisible truth or reality may be suddenly and utterly seen or intuited. Among the most famous of all *koans* is "What is the sound of one hand clapping?"

The **Soto Zen** tradition places less emphasis on sudden enlightenment and tends not to use *koans.* As exemplified by Dogen, enlightenment is to be found slowly through *zazen* (meditation) and also by performing all daily duties in the same state of awareness as when sitting in *zazen.* This tradition recognizes no single moment of *satori,* for enlightenment is believed to be possible in all moments.

of emptiness—allowing things to be, without exercising any preference or desire whatsoever. The similarity to the philosophy of Chuang Tzu is evident.

How does one acquire this perspective of the universal Self? For Dogen, the answer is practice—seeking to help others without reward or praise, caring for others as a parent would. If one makes a continuous effort to do all things with a parental mind and without seeking profit or praise, then one's life will be suffused with the attitude of a "Joyful Mind," in which life takes on a buoyancy and lightness that cannot be diminished by any external event.

Dogen endeavored to set forth a way to achieve permanent joy in *this* life, a way of living that enables the human to achieve a majestic dignity, uncompromisable nobility of character, and peace. "No one or anything could ever make merit decay in any way," he said. In his precepts, Dogen continued the tradition begun by Chuang Tzu, Lao Tzu, and Hui Neng. Life does involve suffering, pain, and transience. But despite the presence of these and of evil too, life, if lived according to the Tao, should be a joyful and fulfilling event. Dogen urged, "Rejoice in your birth in the world." If one does not escape the fears and insecurities of the small self, life is a torment. But if one lives as would the Magnanimous Mind, then one is living out the truth of the Way itself—the Way of the Buddha-Dharma.

THE PHILOSOPHY OF THE SAMURAI (c. 1100–1900)

Japan's warrior class, the **samurai,** were also the ruling class for long periods of time. Their wisdom was transmitted in the form of martial precepts, the earliest dating to the twelfth century or earlier. The precepts were handed down the generations with the class, and they were often used to train the samurai and to teach them the code of **bushido,** that is, the way of the samurai. According to William Scott Wilson's *Ideals of the Samurai,* the word *bushi* ("samurai warrior") is

A samurai.

first recorded in an early history of Japan dated 97 C.E. At the time, these educated warriors served in close attendance upon the nobility. The weakness of civil government, however, led to clans and private estates developing their own armies and to increasing involvement by samurai in government. Eventually, the warrior class actually replaced the court aristocracy, and the late twelfth century marked the beginning of warrior-class rule, which lasted seven hundred years.

The literature of the samurai tradition has influenced all areas of Japanese thought and behavior. Westerners who have wished to understand the basis of the Japanese economic "miracle" since World War II have looked to such samurai classics as Miyamoto Musashi's *The Book of Five Rings* and Yamamoto Tsunetomo's *Hagakure*. The writings concerning the samurai tradition have become popular and reportedly are widely read among business executives and in business graduate schools. The film *Ghost Dog* sought to apply the teachings of the samurai to American life.

One of the most famous samurai was **Miyamoto Musashi** [Mee-yuh-moh-toh Mu-sah-shee] (1584–1645), who was perhaps the greatest swordsman and duelist ever. Among Musashi's many accomplishments apparently was the single-handed defeat of an entire band of samurai from the most prestigious school of martial arts specialists. When he was only thirteen, Musashi fought his first duel.[4] Reportedly, his opponent was armed with a *wakizashi*-style sword; Musashi had only a piece of wood. However, Musashi was sufficiently proficient with his toy

---

[4] Said to be a reliable reference on Musashi is William Scott Wilson's 2004 book, *The Lone Samurai* (Japan: Kodansha International). Not surprisingly, there is much legend surrounding Musashi.

sword to slay his opponent. As you might expect from such reports, Musashi became the subject of many unbelievable legends, such as being able to walk on air.

Beyond this, Musashi was an accomplished sculptor and artist. But he also had a keen understanding of the art, methods, and strategies of fighting. Toward the end of his life, he withdrew from society and wrote *The Book of Five Rings,* the classic treatise on *kenjutsu* (sword methods) and the martial arts in general.

The famous book has played a role in Japan similar to that played in China by Sun Tzu's *The Art of War.* It became a principal manual of military, economic, and political strategy and might have something to do with Japan's rapid rise as an economic superpower. *The Book of Five Rings* is said to be required reading in some American business colleges.

Much in this book is about weapons and techniques and how to slash heads and so forth, material that may not be useful to the average business college student. But the work goes far beyond this and is something of a primer on life strategy. According to Musashi, study and practice are everything. He thought that even trifles must be deliberated upon and understood. Nothing should escape one's gaze. "There must not be one thing you cannot see," he wrote. To achieve invulnerability, one must anticipate every possibility and understand one's opponents better than they understand themselves. The ultimate goal is to achieve "unclouded vision" of events and people, without distortions introduced by fear, prejudice, or desire. This gives rise to an intuitive and instantaneous understanding of events, which enables one to react spontaneously and decisively. The price of not being able to see and foresee everything in an instant, what Napoleon called the *coup d'oeil* (stroke of the eye), is death. Clearly, some of this has application beyond the martial arts, at least to competitive situations.

Knowledge, however, according to Musashi, is turned into action only through training and practice. Life must be constant training, and training is the practical pursuit of perfection. Because perfection is never completely achieved, one must use it to spur oneself toward improvement. Further, both body and spirit must be trained, each preventing the other from becoming lax and weak. Those who fall short in preparation will never even realize their lowest potential, let alone achieve excellence.

Training, Musashi said, develops balance, rhythm, and timing, but to do so, it must be all encompassing. The trainee must become conversant with every art and must understand all disciplines, must comprehend both the ways of peace and the ways of war. The nature of human behavior must be understood thoroughly: people's outlooks, goals, strategies, and methods all must be comprehended. The trainee must master the various arts and sciences to such a degree that they become one with his being.

Training enables one to release one's full potentiality in action, Musashi thought. Generally, people are fearful, hesitant, indecisive, and lack confidence. Thus, their actions are constrained, clumsy, and wasteful and are either procrastinated or rushed. To attain invincibility, one's actions must become lightning fast and decisive, must arise from a resolute spirit, and must be performed without hesitation.

Takuan, the Zen monk who trained Musashi, taught the way of instantaneous, untainted response. According to this perspective, the real secret is to release one's spirit from the constrictions of fear. This is what Musashi called "becoming one with the supreme power," which he regarded as the true virtue and basis of all strategizing.

But how is the spirit to be freed from fear, lack of confidence, and hesitation? How can one avoid being a "bashful monkey"? Musashi said that, to attain extraordinary ability or miraculous power, the trainee must become free of all preoccupations with the self. Musashi called this state of perfect acting the "Spirit of the Void." When a person's spirit and actions are not in the least contaminated with considerations of the self, then that is the true void. Then the warrior is no-thing, and the universe itself is no-thing to the warrior. Then there is a perfect oneness of actor, action, and the enacted, what Musashi called "just being it."

Musashi also placed emphasis on ferocity. You "must strike with all your heart and all your soul." Because the struggle with an opponent is a matter of life and death, you must not be surprised or overwhelmed when the opponent resorts to extreme measures. Likewise, you, too, must be prepared and willing to use any means to achieve victory. It is a matter of "keeping your spirit tall and your resolve strong."

Fierceness of spirit must be developed in training, he believed. The true warrior trains fiercely and thinks fiercely. Following this prescription enables ferocity to become a matter of habit. This, in turn, means that one will act swiftly and without hesitation, which will make one a formidable opponent.

But training must also emphasize dignity and bearing, he said. In *The Name of the Rose,* Umberto Eco (an Italian novelist born in 1932) wrote, "Nothing gives a fearful man more courage than another's fear." Musashi was perhaps coming at things from the reverse angle when he emphasized the importance of using body language that expresses fearlessness. Although a warrior should always be courteous and considerate, his bearing must reveal ferocity and must be unnerving, even scary.

Musashi also discussed the best strategy to defeat an enemy. The main thing is to use knowledge of the opponent to keep him or her off balance. This will ruin his timing, shake his confidence, and make him vulnerable. And once he has been misdirected and shaken, he must not be allowed to recover.

If there is another person whose name is associated with the samurai tradition, it is **Yamamoto Tsunetomo** [Yah-muh-moh-toh Tsu-neh-toh-moh] (1659–1719). Tsunetomo served only a short time as a retainer before his master died; thereafter, he withdrew from the world and lived as a recluse studying Zen Buddhism. During the final years of his life, his thoughts on the essence of the samurai way of life were written down and preserved (see the box "Samurai Insights from Yamamoto Tsunetomo, *Hagakure*"). The ideals of the samurai tradition have endured and still determine to no small extent the life and thought of modern-day Japan.

The worldview expressed in Tsunetomo's *Hagakure* will be familiar to readers of the material on Dogen. Human life at best Tsunetomo sees as "a short affair." No time may be squandered without regret and loss. Yet brevity is not what makes life so difficult and painful; this effect comes rather from life's uncertainty. Humans exist in a world of constant and unpredictable change.

When these changes are not anticipated, the result is often disastrous. Therefore, a samurai must train himself to be ready at all times for anything that may happen. He must train to anticipate all eventualities and deal with them before they become a problem. A samurai precept is "Win beforehand."

According to Tsunetomo, not only is the uncertainty of events problematic, but also human beings themselves are often flawed, ignorant, selfish, and unreasonable. Accordingly, the samurai must learn to be self-reliant. He cannot and

Samurai Insights from Yamamoto Tsunetomo, *Hagakure*

Everything in this world is a marionette show.

[The samurai] remains undistracted twenty-four hours a day.

A samurai's word is harder than metal.

The Way of the samurai is in desperateness. Ten or more men cannot kill such a man.

With an intense, fresh, and undelaying spirit, one will make his judgment within the space of seven breaths. It is a matter of being determined and having the spirit to break right through to the other side.

If one will do things for the benefit of others and meet even those whom he has met often before in a first-time manner, he will have no bad relationships.

A samurai's obstinacy should be excessive.

It is natural that one cannot understand deep and hidden things. Those things that are easily understood are rather shallow.

Courage is gritting one's teeth . . . and pushing ahead, paying no attention to the circumstances.

There is nothing other than the single purpose of the present moment.

I never knew about winning . . . but only about not being behind in a situation.

There is nothing that one should suppose cannot be done.

One must be resolved in advance.

Human life is a short affair. It is better to live doing the things that you like.

If one will rectify his mistakes, their traces will soon disappear.

At a glance, every individual's own measure of dignity is manifested just as it is.

One cannot accomplish things simply with cleverness.

By being impatient, matters are damaged and great works cannot be done. If one considers something not to be a matter of time, it will be done surprisingly quickly.

A man's life should be as toilsome as possible.

People become imbued with the idea that the world has come to an end and no longer put forth any effort. This is a shame. There is no fault in the times.

When I face the enemy, of course it is like being in the dark. But if at that time I tranquilize my mind, it becomes like a night lit by a pale moon. If I begin my attack from that point, I feel as though I will not be wounded.

It is the highest sort of victory to teach your opponent something that will be to his benefit.

Win first, fight later.

There is nothing so painful as regret.

Money is a thing that will be there when asked for. A good man is not so easily found.

Meditation on inevitable death should be performed daily. . . . It is to consider oneself as dead beforehand.

does not depend on others to act properly. He knows that human beings will not always act either reasonably or justly. He is prepared for treachery and cowardice and awaits their arrival. Only by practicing alertness and bravery can a samurai avoid wasting his life.

Because of the uncertainty of the world and the unreliability of the human character, the samurai must learn the arts of war as well as the arts of peace. Human beings, like states, must be able to defend themselves. Kuroda Nagamasa (1568–1623), known as a great military strategist, wrote, "The arts of peace and the arts of war are like the wheels of a cart which, lacking one, will have difficulty in standing."

Courage and Poetry

Samurai warriors often sought to discipline their spirit and free themselves from fear by training with Buddhist masters. At various times, samurai and Zen monks both used poetry, especially short forms of poetry like **haiku,** to test the strength and validity of their insight into truth. At a critical moment, just before death, for example, a trainee was expected spontaneously to write a poem that revealed his perfect freedom under all circumstances, as well as the depth of his insight. He was expected to remain calm, clear-headed, and imperturbable even at the point of a sword. There are stories of captured warriors being spared death if they were sufficiently intrepid and their poem manifested deep wisdom.

The greatest of all the Japanese *haiku* writers was **Basho** [Bah-sho] (1644–1694). He was deeply involved with Zen, and his death poem is regarded as profound:

Stick on a journey,
Yet over withered fields
Dreams wander on.

Dogen also gives an example of the genre:

Scarecrow in the hillock
Paddyfield
How unaware! How useful!

Here are two more poems considered to reveal the deep insight and spontaneous expression of the truly free individual:

Coming and going, life and death:
A thousand hamlets, a million houses.
Don't you get the point?
Moon in the water, blossom in the sky.
　　　　　　　　　—Gizan (1802–1878)

Fifty-four years I've entered [taught]
Horses, donkeys, saving limitless beings.
Now farewell, farewell!
And don't forget—apply yourselves.
　　　　　　　　　—Jisso (1851–1904)

The samurai strives to realize Confucius's notion of the complete man, who is both scholar and warrior. Life requires constant training and learning. Without learning, a person would be ignorant of what is necessary; without hard training, he would be unable to put the necessary actions into effect quickly and efficiently. The samurai works hard to know where his duty lies and to carry it out "unflinchingly." To do this, he hardens himself to suffering. He welcomes death if it comes in pursuit of duty (see the box "Courage and Poetry"). He learns to abhor luxury and considerations of money in order not to be attached to them or to life generally.

An important part of the samurai's study is past traditions, particularly the Confucian and other classical Chinese philosophies, and Zen Buddhism. These determine and shape *bushi* and are in turn unified and synthesized by *bushi* into a single, effective way of life.

The Influence of Confucius

The model of the perfect samurai closely shadows the Confucian idea of the complete man. He is a scholar warrior, literate yet deeply knowledgeable about practical affairs. He knows that life involves change and that survival depends on understanding the inner workings of change. Although a few samurai teachers emphasized the art of war and the ways of increasing courage, more usual is the view of the *Hagakure*. Here the samurai is called on to develop his knowledge of whatever might be useful, "querying every item night and day." Above all, he must understand the Confucian principle of the Mean: more than merely the middle way between two extremes, the Mean is the universal standard that determines what is right and appropriate. The wise samurai reads the sayings of the ancients as the best way to find out what the Mean recommends and how best to follow it.

For Confucius, the three basic and interrelated qualities to be pursued are humanity, wisdom, and courage. According to the samurai tradition, these virtues allow those who have them to enjoy a useful life of service as well as a life free from anxiety and fear.

As Confucius also prescribed, the samurai should be filial, making every effort to respect and honor his parents; he should be polite, discreet in manners and conduct, proper in dress and speech, and upright and sincere. He must not lie. There is the story, for example, of the samurai who refused to take an oath because the word of the samurai is more certain than any oath.

In historical Japan, those who possessed these qualities exhibited enormous dignity. The samurai's dignity displayed itself in every action and in every word. His solemn behavior and resoluteness frequently struck fear in the ordinary observer. The samurai code sought to create a character that was flawless in behavior and taut in spirit.

Another samurai virtue had its roots in the philosophy of Confucius: the samurai was to be economical and, as noted, to avoid luxury. He was to save what he could, but only with an eye to using it on campaign when it was needed.

Because of his virtues, the samurai could be expected to establish and maintain an ordered state in the midst of the most chaotic times. His own steady and unshakable behavior would then serve as a model to be trusted and followed by all others. This, of course, is a Confucian theme.

The Influence of Zen Buddhism

It is slightly ironic that members of the warrior class in Japan went to Zen monks for training, for Zen monks dedicated their lives to saving all living beings. Kamakura, a Zen center that dates back as far as the thirteenth century, was especially noted for training samurai warriors. Perhaps the most famous instance of this relationship was the influence of the Zen monk Takuan (1573–1645) on two of Japan's greatest swordsmen and strategists, Miyamoto Musashi and Yagyu Munenori [YAH-gyu mu-neh-NOH-ree] (1571–1646). All three men produced classic works that were used in the training of samurai.

The samurai, recall, were warriors who trained themselves to be ready at any moment to fight to the death. The ability to fight, of course, is frequently hampered by fear; for fear, if it does not paralyze a fighter completely, may well prevent the lightning-fast response that may be the difference between winning and losing. Though samurai engaged in ceaseless martial arts training, a state of fearlessness sometimes escaped even the best of them. Some samurai, therefore, sought out Zen masters to free themselves of their own fear.

Fear, according to the Zen Buddhist, arises from an excessive attachment or clinging to things and to life generally, a perspective of possessiveness from which anything and everything is viewed as a threat. The remedy for fear—the samurai learned from the Zen masters—is to free oneself from attachments and personal preferences, to rid oneself of the desire to possess anything, including life itself.

The samurai was taught to overcome himself, so to speak—to free himself from all thoughts of gain or loss. He was taught to accept what happens without joy or sadness, without complaint, and even without resignation. This hard lesson was thought to require constant meditation on death so that the warrior was ready to "die completely without hesitation or regret."

In this way Zen training sought to rid the samurai of the self-imposed paralysis of fear. Both the Zen and the samurai traditions shared the same ideal: to attain *an unobstructed state of instant, untainted response.* For the samurai this state of mind was the key to total preparedness.

The samurai tradition therefore emphasized that, through a vigorous training of the body and the mind, the individual can perfect his character to respond immediately to any situation. Such training can create a resolute single-mindedness, in which the present moment is all there is and the present action alone is real, that is both efficient and powerful.

The ultimate goal of both Zen Buddhist and samurai training is the state of **mushin,** that is, the state of no mind, no thought. This is a state of awareness beyond calculation in which one moves "no-mindedly" in the here and now, doing exactly what is appropriate without any hesitation. This mind is the "secret" of the great swordsmen like Musashi and Yagyu Munenori.

The samurai tradition, together with Confucianism and Zen Buddhism, provided the Japanese with a noble ideal of character, a context in which the efficiency of Japanese society, and much of what is good and successful in Japan, may perhaps be understood. Certainly the vision of the noble person who trains all his life to be of benefit to others seems a fulfillment of the ideal of humanity put forward by Confucius, Zen, and the samurai. However, the chauvinist nationalism of the Japanese in World War II, the unquestioning obedience to authority, and the glorification of death may also perhaps be explained by reference to these same influences. It is interesting to speculate what these traditions might have yielded, what their effect on Japanese society might have been, if they had been stripped of their authoritarian and excessively militaristic qualities. Confucius seeks to delineate his notion of humanity (**jen**) in terms of what constitutes a superior human being.

Early in its history, Taoism had a relatively strong influence on rulers in China. But as Confucianism replaced it as the dominant value system within society, beginning with the T'ang dynasty (618–906), Taoism increasingly focused on religious functions, an area in which it eventually had to compete with Buddhism. More and more, Taoism came to encompass magic, soothsaying, and incantations for healing and for warding off evil spirits. To this day, Taoist priests perform ceremonies at funerals and on other important occasions. Reportedly, Taoist hermits are still living out the highest forms of Taoist practice in the mountains of China.

As Confucianism established itself as the dominant moral and political philosophy, the Confucian classics became the basis of civil service examination, and in this way Confucianism became even further embedded into Chinese thinking. Between the eleventh and eighteenth centuries, there was a significant Neoconfucian movement, one of whose major figures was Wang Yang-ming (1472–1529).

Confucianism received a severe blow from the Communist revolution in 1949, and Mao Tse-tung made it a repeated target for ridicule. This does not mean that Mao was not himself influenced by Confucius both in his style of writing and of ruling, nor does it mean that Mao was loath to use Confucianism to his own ends—for example, in transferring the individual's family allegiance to state allegiance. In any case, after Mao, Confucian thought is again making itself apparent.

Chinese Buddhism developed a number of different schools from the fourth to the ninth centuries. Ch'an Buddhism was especially powerful and innovative during the seventh to ninth centuries. Chinese Buddhist temples have provided religious services for the people from that time even until the present day. Further, the influence of Ch'an Buddhism spread to Japan, where Zen Buddhism and other forms of Buddhism have endured until the present. Currently, Zen Buddhism especially enjoys growing popularity in the United States and the West generally.

PHILOSOPHY EAST AND WEST

It's a delicate matter, at best, to generalize the principles of Eastern philosophy since Eastern thought in the various cultures contains distinctive differences. Indian and Chinese philosophies, for example, in some respects are as different from each other as Eastern and Western philosophies are. That said, and speaking very, very generally, we could say that Western society looks for and tries to prove truth while Eastern society accepts given truths from various sources and focuses on balance and social responsibility. Eastern philosophies are primarily derived from religious authorities who are not challenged, rather than from principles of logic, conceptual analysis, or a priori assumptions. There is no interest in proving statements asserted as truths.

Eastern societies are viewed as collectivist societies whose essence is an awareness of the connectedness of all things. People are viewed as fundamentally connected. All phenomena are considered manifestations of the unity of things and events and are experienced as part of a basic oneness, a cosmic whole. Everything is thought of as part of the same ultimate reality. In the various Eastern traditions, this oneness is referred to by different names: in Hinduism, it is Brahman. In Buddhism, it is Dharmakaya. In Taoism, it is Tao.

Life is considered a journey toward the eternal reality that is beyond our senses. The universe is considered circular, endless: everything continually recurs. All of the religious philosophies in Eastern thought postulate an inner world, often experienced through meditation, which teaches one to become free of distractions and to learn that inaction is a form of action. In meditation and in daily life, the self seeks liberation from whatever is false, and experiences truth as a wholeness. One's life is lived according to the ethics discovered through these practices and the given truths of the particular philosophy. The combination of meditation and right action in one's life is thought to be the way to realize oneself as part of the whole which is the ultimate reality. Duty toward others is a strong value in Eastern societies. One regards others as oneself, so material gains must be created without a sense of ownership or expectation of compensation. Simply performing one's duties and having concern for all beings becomes the virtuous life.

The key Eastern value is found within oneself. One is always striving to improve the inner life through self-development. One rids oneself of such negatives as anger or the desire for material goods, revenge, victory, or fame through self-control.

By contrast, Western philosophy—as mentioned above—looks for and tries to prove truth. Western philosophy, speaking generally, is *argument-based*. By this we mean that insights into human nature, the human condition, society, or

Bertrand Russell Wows Students With a Short Lecture

whatever, no matter how striking or profound in and of themselves, are generally not accorded the highest status, unless backed by argument. Argument is to Western philosophy what experiment is to natural science: it is what separates philosophy from conjecture.

Think back, for example, to the ancient Greek philosopher Parmenides (Chapter 2), the first philosopher to use argument in a big way. Parmenides' main contention—that being does not change—was not just thrown out as a pearl of wisdom for others to take or leave, but was deduced by him from a priori principles. As you may recall, Parmenides started with the premise that, if something changes, it becomes something different. From this, he said, it logically follows that, if being itself were to change, then it would become different. What, then, is different from being? The only thing different from being, he reasoned, is nonbeing—which by definition does not exist. Therefore being does not change.

Or consider, to take a wildly different example, John Locke's contention that every individual has specific, natural rights. Locke began with the premise that all people are created by God and are thus His "property." From this it logically follows, in Locke's view, that not only are we obliged to preserve ourselves, but also we may not take away or impair another's "life, liberty, health, limbs or goods," or anything on which these various items depend. This in turn logically implies, he reasoned, that each person has inalienable natural rights to these things. And from this yet another conclusion logically follows, Locke thought, that the legitimacy of the state rests on the prior consent of the governed. It does so, he said, because a person's natural rights would be violated if the state were to exercise its power over him or her without his or her consent. Now, the ideas of natural rights and government by consent are of course familiar to us from the *Declaration of Independence* and U.S. *Constitution,* in which document they are more or less explicitly articulated; but in those documents they are not argued for—which is why the documents do not count as philosophical.

An argument, of course, is only as good as its ability to withstand rebuttal. Thus it should come as no surprise that the premier method of Western philosophizing is the Socratic method, in which an argument is proposed, and a counterargument (a rebuttal) is sought—followed by a counterargument to the counterargument and so forth until only either the original argument or a counterargument is left standing.

Thus one might expect to find standoffs in philosophy, where argument and counterargument seem equally compelling. These are the notorious "dualisms" of Western philosophy—rationalism/empiricism; physicalism/idealism; objectivism/subjectivism; realism/nominalism—to list but few.

As far as specific content is concerned, Alfred North Whitehead once famously stated that all philosophy is but a footnote to Plato. There is more than a little truth to this, in that many of the major issues of philosophy were examined by Plato. Plato was certainly interested in several of the big questions, such as the nature of knowledge, justice, and virtue, the distinction between appearance and reality, the form of the ideal state, and many others. But there are philosophical questions Plato did not address, so numerous in fact that you could spend your entire life studying philosophy without having examined them all.

Another distinctive feature of Western philosophy is that it is both broad and, at the same time, minutely detailed. Anyone who will have read this book in its entirety will hardly dispute the former point, since he or she will have seen that philosophical discussion covers everything from the nature of being to the conceptual problems involved in giving and exchanging gifts. As for the fondness of Western philosophers for detail, no better example could be found than Bertrand Russell's *Introduction to Mathematical Philosophy,* in which Russell devotes two full chapters to an analysis of the word "the" (Chapters XVI and XVII). Western philosophers tend to use a high-powered magnifying glass when considering questions that interest them, so that no detail, no matter how tiny, is left unexamined.

Much Western philosophy has been devoted to conceptual analysis. Russell's discussion of the word "the" would of course serve also as an example of this. Another, quite different, example would be Peter Abelard's painstaking exploration of the nuances of the concept of sin. Sin, Abelard said, consists neither in malicious action nor even in evil desire, but in consenting to act on evil desire. A profoundly different type of conceptual analysis was that of Immanuel Kant, who attempted to ascertain the fundamental concepts, such as space, time, and causation, that are presupposed by the very possibility of experience.

The last example—that from Kant—discloses yet another feature of Western philosophy: its interest in really big questions. What is consciousness? What is the relation between language and the world? Why is there something rather than nothing at all? These are huge questions, which some would say it is pointless to try to answer. Western philosophy disagrees. Eastern philosophy, however, does not comment. It simply has a different agenda.

SELECTION 15.1

Analects

Confucius

Book I

CHAPTER I. 1. The Master said, "Is it not pleasant to learn with a constant perseverance and application?

2. "Is it not delightful to have friends coming from distant quarters?

3. "Is he not a man of complete virtue, who feels no discomposure though men may take no note of him?"

CHAP. II. 1. The philosopher Yû said, "They are few who, being filial and fraternal, are fond of offending against their superiors. There have been none, who, not liking to offend against their superiors, have been fond of stirring up confusion.

2. "The superior man bends his attention to what is radical. That being established, all practical courses naturally grow up. Filial piety and fraternal submission!—are they not the root of all benevolent actions?"

CHAP. III. The Master said, "Fine words and an insinuating appearance are seldom associated with true virtue."

CHAP. IV. The philosopher Tsa'ng said, "I daily examine myself on three points:—whether, in transacting business for others, I may have been not faithful;—whether, in intercourse with friends, I may have been not sincere;—whether I may have not mastered and practised the instructions of my teacher."

CHAP. V. The Master said, "To rule a country of a thousand chariots, there must be reverent attention to business, and sincerity; economy in expenditure, and love for men; and the employment of the people at the proper seasons."

CHAP. VI. The Master said, "A youth, when at home, should be filial, and, abroad, respectful to his elders. He should be earnest and truthful. He should overflow in love to all, and cultivate the friendship of the good. When he has time and opportunity, after the performance of these things, he should employ them in polite studies."

CHAP. VII. Tsze-hsiâ said, "If a man withdraws his mind from the love of beauty, and applies it as sincerely to the love of the virtuous; if, in serving his parents, he can exert his utmost strength; if, in serving his prince, he can devote his life; if, in his intercourse with his friends, his words are sincere:—although men say that he has not learned, I will certainly say that he has."

CHAP. VIII. 1. The Master said, "If the scholar be not grave, he will not call forth any veneration, and his learning will not be solid.

2. "Hold faithfulness and sincerity as first principles.

3. "Have no friends not equal to yourself.

4. "When you have faults, do not fear to abandon them."

CHAP. IX. The philosopher Tsa'ng said, "Let there be a careful attention *to perform the funeral rites* to parents, and let them be followed when long gone *with the ceremonies of sacrifice;*—then the virtue of the people will resume its proper excellence."

CHAP. X. 1. Tsze-ch'in asked Tsze-kung, saying, "When our master comes to any country, he does not fail to learn all about its government. Does he ask his information? Or is it given to him?"

2. Tsze-kung said, "Our master is benign, upright, courteous, temperate, and complaisant, and thus he gets his information. The master's mode of asking information!—is it not different from that of other men?"

CHAP. XI. The Master said, "While a man's father is alive, look at the bent of his will; when his father is dead, look at his conduct. If for three years he does not alter from the way of his father, he may be called filial."

CHAP. XII. 1. The philosopher Yû said, "In practising the rules of propriety, a natural ease is to be prized. In the ways prescribed by the ancient kings, this is the excellent quality, and in things small and great we follow them.

2. "Yet it is not to be observed in all cases. If one, knowing *how* such ease *should be prized*, manifests it, without regulating it by the rules of propriety, this likewise is not to be done."

CHAP. XIII. The philosopher Yû said, "When agreements are made according to what is right, what is spoken can be made good. When respect is shown according to what is proper, one keeps far from shame and disgrace. When the parties upon whom a man leans are proper persons to be intimate with, he can make them his guides and masters."

CHAP. XIV. The Master said, "He who aims to be a man of complete virtue in his food does not seek to gratify his appetite, nor in his dwelling-place does he seek the appliances of ease; he is earnest in what he is doing, and careful in his speech; he frequents the company of men of principle that he may be rectified:—such a person may be said indeed to love to learn."

CHAP. XV. 1. Tsze-kung said, "What do you pronounce concerning the poor man who yet does not flatter, and the rich man who is not proud?" The Master replied, "They will do; but they are not equal to him, who, though poor, is yet cheerful, and to him, who, though rich, loves the rules of propriety."

2. Tsze-kung replied, "It is said in the Book of Poetry, 'As you cut and then file, as you carve and then polish.'—The meaning is the same, I apprehend, as that which you have just expressed."

3. The Master said, "With one like Ts'ze, I can begin to talk about the odes. I told him one point, and he knew its proper sequence."

Chap. XVI. The Master said, "I will not be afflicted at men's not knowing me; I will be afflicted that I do not know men."

SELECTION 15.2

The Eightfold Noble Path★

Buddha

[*The Eightfold Noble Path is at the heart of Buddhist practice, ranging from moral mandates as to how to live to the experience of the ultimate enlightenment and blissful rapture.*]

The Fourth Truth
The Noble Truth of the Path That
Leads to the Extinction of Suffering

(S.56) To give oneself up to indulgence in *Sensual Pleasure,* the base, common, vulgar, unholy, unprofitable, and also to give oneself up to *Self-mortification,* the painful, unholy, unprofitable; both these two extremes the Perfect One has avoided and found out the *Middle Path* which makes one both to see and to know, which leads to peace, to discernment, to enlightenment, to Nibbana.

It is the Noble Eightfold Path, the way that leads to the extinction of suffering, namely:

1. Right Understanding, *Samma-ditthi*
2. Right Mindedness, *Samma-sankappa*
3. Right Speech, *Samma-vaca*
4. Right Action, *Samma-kammanta*
5. Right Living, *Samma-ajiva*
6. Right Effort, *Samma-vayama*
7. Right Attentiveness, *Samma-sati*
8. Right Concentration, *Samma-samadhi*

★"The Eightfold Noble Path," from *A Buddhist Bible,* edited by Dwight Goddard, copyright 1938, renewed © 1966 by E. P. Dutton. Used by permission of Dutton, a division of Penguin Group (USA) Inc.

This is the Middle Path which the Perfect One has found out, which makes one both to see and to know, which leads to peace, to discernment, to enlightenment, to Nibbana.

Free from pain and torture is this path, free from groaning and suffering, it is the perfect path.
(Dhp. 274–75) Truly, like this path there is no other path to the purity of insight. If you follow this path, you will put an end to suffering.
(Dhp. 276) But each one has to struggle for himself, the Perfect Ones have only pointed out the way.
(M. 26) Give ear then, for the Immortal is found. I reveal, I set forth the Truth. As I reveal it to you, so act! And that supreme goal of the holy life, for the sake of which sons of good families go forth from home to the homeless state: this you will, in no long time, in this very life, make known to yourself, realise and attain to it.

First Step
Right Understanding

(D. 22) What now is Right Understanding?

1. To understand suffering; 2. to understand the origin of suffering; 3. to understand the extinction of suffering; 4. to understand the path that leads to the extinction of suffering. This is called Right Understanding.
(M.9) Or, when the noble disciple understands what demerit is and the root of demerit, what merit is and the root of merit, then he has Right Understanding.

What now is demerit?

1. Destruction of living beings is demerit.
2. Stealing is demerit.
3. Unlawful sexual intercourse is demerit.
4. Lying is demerit.
5. Tale-bearing is demerit.
6. Harsh language is demerit.
7. Frivolous talk is demerit.
8. Covetousness is demerit.
9. Ill-will is demerit.
10. Wrong views are demerit.

And what is the root of demerit? Greed is a root of demerit; Anger is a root of demerit; Delusion is a root of demerit.
(A.X.174) Therefore, I say, these demeritorious actions are of three kinds: either due to greed, or due to anger, or due to delusion.
(M.9) What now is merit (*kusala*)?

1. To abstain from killing is merit.
2. To abstain from stealing is merit.
3. To abstain from unlawful sexual intercourse is merit.
4. To abstain from lying is merit.
5. To abstain from tale-bearing is merit.
6. To abstain from harsh language is merit.
7. To abstain from frivolous talk is merit.
8. Absence of covetousness is merit.
9. Absence of ill-will is merit.
10. Right understanding is merit.

And what is the Root of Merit? Absence of greed is a root of merit; absence of anger is a root of merit; absence of delusion is a root of merit.
(S.21 (5)) Or, when one understands that form, feeling, perception, mental formations and consciousness are transient, (subject to suffering and without an Ego) also in that case one possesses Right Understanding. . . .

Second Step
Right Mindedness
(D.22) What now is Right Mindedness?

1. The thought free from lust.
2. The thought free from ill-will.
3. The thought free from cruelty.

This is called right mindedness.

(M.117) Now, right mindedness, let me tell you, is of two kinds:

1. The thoughts free from lust, from ill-will, and from cruelty:—this is called the Mundane Right Mindedness, which yields worldly fruits and brings good results.

2. But, whatsoever there is of thinking, considering, reasoning, thought, ratiocination, application—the mind being holy, being turned away from the world and conjoined with the path, the holy path being pursued:—these Verbal Operations of the mind are called the Ultramundane Right Mindedness, which is not of the world, but is ultramundane and conjoined with the paths.

Now, in understanding wrong-mindedness as wrong and right-mindedness as right, one practises Right Understanding; and in making efforts to overcome evil mindedness, and to arouse right mindedness, one practises Right Effort; and in overcoming evil-mindedness with attentive mind, and dwelling with attentive mind in possession of right mindedness, one practises Right Attentiveness. Hence, there are three things that accompany and follow upon right mindedness, namely: right understanding, right effort, and right attentiveness.

Third Step
Right Speech
(A.X. 176) What now is Right Speech?

1. There, someone avoids lying, and abstains from it. He speaks the truth, is devoted to the truth, reliable, worthy of confidence, is not a deceiver of men. Being at a meeting, or amongst people, or in the midst of his relatives, or in a society, or in the king's court, and called upon and asked as witness, to tell what he knows, he answers, if he knows nothing: I know nothing, and if he knows, he answers: I know; if he has seen nothing, he answers: I have seen nothing, and if he has seen, he answers: I have seen. Thus, he never knowingly speaks a lie, neither for the sake of his own advantage, nor for the sake of another person's advantage, nor for the sake of any advantage whatsoever.

2. He avoids tale-bearing, and abstains from it. What he has heard here, he does not repeat there, so as to cause dissension there; and what he has heard there, he does not repeat here, so as to cause dissension

here. Thus he unites those that are divided, and those that are united he encourages. Concord gladdens him, he delights and rejoices in concord; and it is concord that he spreads by his words.

3. He avoids harsh language, and abstains from it. He speaks such words as are gentle, soothing to the ear, loving, going to the heart, courteous and dear, and agreeable to many.

4. He avoids vain talk, and abstains from it. He speaks at the right time, in accordance with facts, speaks what is useful, speaks about the law and the discipline; his speech is like a treasure, at the right moment accompanied by arguments, moderate and full of sense.

This is called right speech. . . .

Fourth Step
Right Action
What now is Right Action?

(A.X. 176) 1. There someone avoids the killing of living beings, and abstains from it. Without stick or sword, conscientious, full of sympathy, he is anxious for the welfare of all living beings.

2. He avoids stealing, and abstains from it; what another person possesses of goods and chattels in the village or in the wood, that he does not take away with thievish intent.

3. He avoids unlawful sexual intercourse, and abstains from it. He has no intercourse with such persons as are still under the protection of father, mother, brother, sister or relatives, nor with married women, nor female convicts, nor even with flower-decked (engaged) girls.

This is called right action.
(M. 117) Now right action, let me tell you, is of two kinds:

1. Abstaining from killing, from stealing, and from unlawful sexual intercourse:—this is called the Mundane Right Action, which yields worldly fruits and brings good results.

2. But the abhorrence of the practice of this three-fold wrong action, the abstaining, withholding, refraining therefrom—the mind being holy, being turned away from the world and conjoined with the path, the holy path being pursued:—this is called the Ultramundane Right Action, which is not of the world, but is ultramundane and conjoined with the paths.

Now, in understanding wrong action as wrong, and right action as right, one practises Right Understanding; and in making efforts to overcome wrong action, and to arouse right action, one practises Right Effort; and in overcoming wrong action with attentive mind, and dwelling with attentive mind in possession of right action, one practises Right Attentiveness. Hence, there are three things that accompany and follow upon right action, namely: right understanding, right effort, and right attentiveness.

Fifth Step
Right Living
(D. 22) What now is Right Living?
When the noble disciple, avoiding a wrong living, gets his livelihood by a right way of living, this is called right living.
(M. 117) Now, right living, let me tell you, is of two kinds:

1. When the noble disciple, avoiding wrong living, gets his livelihood by a right way of living:— this is called the Mundane Right Living, which yields worldly fruits and brings good results.

2. But the abhorrence of wrong living, the abstaining, withholding, refraining therefrom—the mind being holy, being turned away from the world and conjoined with the path, the holy path being pursued:—this is called the Ultramundane Right Living (*lokuttara-samma-ajiva*), which is not of the world, but is ultramundane and conjoined with the paths.

Now, in understanding wrong living as wrong, and right living as right, one practises Right Understanding; and in making efforts to overcome wrong living, to arouse right living, one practises Right Effort; and in overcoming wrong living with attentive mind, and dwelling with attentive mind in possession of right living, one practises Right Attentiveness. Hence, there are three things that accompany and follow upon right living, namely: right understanding, right effort, and right attentiveness. . . .

Eighth Step
Right Concentration

(M. 44) What now is Right Concentration?

Fixation of the mind to a single object, (lit. One-pointedness of mind);—this is concentration.

The four Fundamentals of Attentiveness;—these are the objects of concentration.

The four Great Efforts:—these are the requisites for concentration.

The practising, developing and cultivating of these things:—this is the Development of concentration. (M. 141) Detached from sensual objects, detached from demeritorious things, the disciple enters into the first trance, which is accompanied by Verbal Thought and Rumination, is born of Detachment, and filled with Rapture and Happiness.

(M. 43) This first trance is free from five things, and five things are present: when the disciple enters the first trance, there have vanished (the 5 Hindrances): Lust, Ill-will, Torpor and Dullness, Restlessness and Mental Worry, Doubts; and there are present: Verbal Thought, Rumination, Rapture, Happiness, and Concentration.

(M. 27) And further: after the subsiding of verbal thought and rumination, and by the gaining of inward tranquillisation and oneness of mind, he enters into a state free from verbal thought and rumination, the second trance, which is born of Concentration and filled with Rapture and Happiness.

And further: after the fading away of rapture, he dwells in equanimity, attentive, clearly conscious, and he experiences in his person that feeling, of which the noble Ones say: Happy lives the man of equanimity and attentive mind—thus he enters the third trance.

And further: after the giving up of pleasure and pain, and through the disappearance of previous joy and grief, he enters into a state beyond pleasure and pain, into the fourth trance, which is purified by equanimity and attentiveness.

(S. 21 (1)) Develop your concentration; for he who has concentration understands things according to their reality. And what are these things? The arising and passing away of bodily form, of feeling, perception, mental formations and consciousness.

(M. 149) Thus these five Aggregates of existence must be wisely penetrated; delusion and craving must be wisely abandoned; Tranquility and Insight must be wisely developed.

(S. 56) This is the Middle Path which the Perfect One has discovered, which makes one both to see and to know, and which leads to peace, to discernment, to enlightenment, to Nibbana.

(Dhp. 627) And following upon this path you will put an end to suffering.

CHECKLIST

To help you review, a checklist of the key philosophers of this chapter can be found online at www.mhhe.com/moore9e.

KEY TERMS AND CONCEPTS

QUESTIONS FOR
DISCUSSION AND REVIEW

1. Evaluate Mencius's idea that difficulty and suffering are opportunities to develop independence and peace of mind.

2. Do the subjects of the state adopt the ethical standards of their leaders? Or is it the other way around?

3. "Benevolence subdues its opposite just as water subdues fire." Evaluate this claim.

4. Are power and riches chains, or are they the keys to freedom and happiness?

5. What is the sound of one hand clapping? Is this an intelligible question?

6. How did Mahayana Buddhism reinforce sexism and elitism?

7. Why would suicide help a woman achieve salvation under Mahayana Buddhism?

8. How important is it to have a life goal?

9. Is it possible for a person completely to abandon selfish desires?

10. Based on your acquaintance with both, compare and contrast Eastern and Western philosophy. What do you think are the most important differences?

SUGGESTED FURTHER READINGS

Go online to www.mhhe.com/moore9e for a list of suggested further readings.

16

Postcolonial Thought*

Strength does not come from physical capacity. It comes from an indomitable will.   —Mohandas Gandhi

. . . The true criterion of leadership is spiritual. Men are attracted by spirit. By power, men are forced. Love is engendered by spirit. By power, anxieties are created.   —Malcolm X (el-Hajj Malik el-Shabazz)

In this chapter we encounter representatives of postcolonial thought in Africa, the Americas, and Asia. Postcolonial thought is an essentially modern phenomenon. Growing out of group experiences of colonialist domination on every populated continent, postcolonial thinking is shaping new work in ethics, metaphysics, epistemology, political philosophy, and every other subdiscipline of philosophy. Well-known postcolonial thinkers include Mohandas Gandhi, Martin Luther King Jr., Fidel Castro, Malcolm X, and Desmond Tutu.

Postcolonial thinkers have brought traditional and radical ideas together in a uniquely modern synthesis that opens up new possibilities of practical engagement for philosophy. Whether reflecting through a history of slavery, systematic marginalization, or overt repression, postcolonial thinkers do their work in recollection of deep cultural traumas that have occurred in the histories of their respective peoples, leaving indigenous traditions self-consciously compromised and needful of imaginative reconstruction from within. Postcolonial thought addresses this need by taking up problems of cultural dissolution and questioning previously unquestioned worldviews, just as any modern way of thinking must. As is true of recent Continental philosophy, postcolonial thought challenges the uncritical acceptance of the notion of progress.

---

* Revised and updated by Greg Tropea.

Postcolonial thinkers have long realized that direct appeals for justice, reasonable as they might be, generally are not sufficiently compelling to bring about change. This is why raising consciousness through philosophy has become such an important undertaking. It is one thing to affirm that justice is a social good and yet another to have an idea of what justice might be, what conditions might be prerequisite to it, and how the best intentions may be subverted by subtly conflicting ideological claims. Detailed analysis of these sorts of issues occurs frequently as postcolonial thought pursues the ideal of sustainable social justice.

Because the postcolonial style of analysis is closely tied to concrete historical conditions, the writing of history itself has become an issue for philosophical investigation. **Historiography,** which takes the writing of history as a matter to be studied and analyzed, typically begins with a preconception of causation in history, an overarching idea of why events happen as they do. Having such a preconception directs the search for facts and guides the selection of what is meaningful from the mass of data. Thus, individual elements can be assembled into a story with a definite logic and a point of view. Recognizing that there are no bare facts apart from a conceptual framework and that those who would report those facts would not have a "God's-eye view" to reveal them even if the possibility of perfectly simple atoms of truth existed, many postcolonial thinkers who take up the task of understanding history begin by making the choice of a conceptual framework within which the writing of history can have sense and purpose. **Perspectivism** is the idea that all perception and conceptualization take place from some particular perspective. In the twentieth century, some flavor of Marxism was the overwhelming theoretical perspective chosen by third world writers—even as Marxism was overwhelmingly rejected by first world writers.

Among the topics most intensively developed in postcolonial studies of history and justice has been the matter of domination. This theme has been known to extend beyond easy intuitive understanding since Hegel's discussion, early in the nineteenth century, of master–slave dynamics, in which the powerlessness of the slave was shown to entail numerous unavoidable consequences for the master (see Chapter 11). As the postcolonial program began to require an analysis of justice that satisfied both experiential and critical needs, the nature of the links between subjective perceptions and the systemic conditions under which people live began to come into view. For many thinkers, the international market system was the major force for injustice through a form of domination that reduces everything to a dollar value.

HISTORICAL BACKGROUND

The development of similar viewpoints in the work of thinkers in several different modern cultures has become less likely to be a matter of mere coincidence and more likely to derive from participation in those common social/cultural realities that began to emerge in the fifteenth century, when the Spanish and Portuguese shifted from thinking locally to thinking globally. This development in imperial thinking led the Iberian powers to pursue a comparatively simple strategy of colonization based on extracting traditionally valuable metals and other commodities from the areas under their control and taking them back to the mother country.

The Latin American pattern of colonialism was not precisely replicated in other colonial experiments. A different profile occurred when the British realized that their colonies could serve not only as sources of raw materials, exotic produce, and precious minerals but also as markets for manufactured goods. This changed everything. To support trade in manufactured goods, British colonies in the eighteenth century needed to be fully functioning economic entities. This plan determined that the social tone of eighteenth-century British colonies on the North American continent would be set by an unambiguously economic agenda that quickly supplanted the religious concerns that dominated in the seventeenth century. To a certain degree, the influences that shaped the self-understandings of the colonists worked similarly on Native Americans. The indigenous inhabitants of areas colonized by the British seem to have acquired their sense of Old World values less through religious missions than through trade and territorial expansion, though missionary activity certainly did occur on a significant scale. The colonial pattern of relationship between whites and Indians of North America, which was based primarily on economic exploitation, continued after the American colonies won their independence. According to most histories, colonialism came to an end in the United States with the surrender of the British at Yorktown, but from the Native American perspective nothing of the sort occurred.

Thus, colonial activity went beyond simple extraction of wealth to become linked to technological development for some imperial powers. At varying levels of integration, colonized peoples joined the world money economy whether they wanted to or not and had to face all the cultural changes that such a development implies. Among the most dramatic effects of these policies was the impoverishment of rural India, which most analysts attribute directly to British mercantilism. There, centuries-old patterns of labor and exchange vanished within a few decades, creating not only economic hardship but social dislocation as well. In Southeast Asia and some other areas where money economies could be sustained among the colonized population, the French instituted a colonial model that was midway between the Spanish strategy of simple transfer of valuable materials and the British strategy of constructing a dynamic trading system that had a reasonable chance of providing comparatively stable returns over the long term. Whatever the model, colonization entailed not only the violent physical subjugation of indigenous peoples but also the introduction of the colonizers' values and beliefs into traditional societies around the world. The reduction of existence to financial equivalences is a continuing theme in postcolonial metaphysical critiques.

During the intense colonial activity of the eighteenth and nineteenth centuries and the first part of the twentieth, huge populations were participating directly or indirectly in some sort of militarily enforced experience of cultural confrontation. Whether one was on the winning or the losing side, these events occurred on such a scale and with such intensity that reflective interpretation on all sides was virtually inevitable. The depth of this interpretation was not uniform by present standards, however. Some thinkers in the West, such as England's Herbert Spencer, pleased large followings in their own countries by celebrating successful military adventures as evidence of the natural superiority of the victorious imperial nation.

Others, whose peoples had endured colonial domination, inclined to more critical efforts to come to terms with their experience. These latter reflections, which consciously situate themselves within a history of subjugation and revolutionary impulses, constitute the substance of postcolonial philosophy. In the colonial and former colonial powers, postcolonial thought has often been marginalized, summarily dismissed, or even totally ignored. Just the opposite has been the case among subjugated and formerly subjugated populations, however, for whom the analyses and calls to action of postcolonial thinkers have resonated powerfully, providing ethical and metaphysical understandings that ring true to lived experience. Frequently, postcolonial thinkers have become social and political leaders in their respective countries; the roster includes Mohandas Gandhi in India, Sun Yat-sen in China, Léopold Sédar Senghor in Senegal, Ho Chi Minh in Vietnam, Kwame Nkrumah in Ghana, Paulin Hountondji in Benin, Václav Havel in the Czech Republic, and numerous others.

Postcolonial philosophy is a diverse genre, but its voices share an intentionally substantial engagement with the historical realities of third world peoples or those who have been systematically excluded from power in their societies. This critical commonality may be obscured at first glance by the variety of expression in postcolonial thought, a range of beliefs that includes advocacy of both violence and nonviolence, capitalism and utopian socialism, absolute standards and anarchic relativism, to touch on only a few of the categories. Further, postcolonial thinkers within their respective traditions frequently disagree among themselves in their valuations of events and situations; if one ever needed proof that radically different conclusions could be inferred from very similar historical facts, postcolonial philosophy would provide it.

In no small measure, though, postcolonial thought constitutes a distinctive category of endeavor because it consciously traces back to the ineluctable dislocations that ensued from encounters with conquerors whose imperialism aimed at nearly total domination. Although the invaders asserted both physical and philosophical superiority, their ideas have received at best a mixed reception in the lands they once controlled. Given the available historical and anthropological information, it seems most reasonable to believe that the commonalities of postcolonial thought around the world are not so much due to the conceptual similarities of the specific ideas introduced by different groups of colonizers as to the similarities among experiences of invasion and foreign domination.

AFRICA

In the philosophies of African cultures, as in the other major geographic groupings in world philosophy, certain themes tend to recur, although no single worldview or school of thought enjoys general acceptance. Very few universal claims apply accurately across the many expressions of the philosophical impulse in African cultures and their offshoots beyond Africa. Taken together, these expressions have come to be known as **Pan-African philosophy,** a term with a range of meanings in the early twenty-first century. Understood in this inclusive sense, Pan-African philosophy reveals itself to be many philosophies in both content and method, all united by a geographic reference point. Existing virtually side by side with contributions to international conversations on technical issues in semantics and the impact of technology on society are statements of ancient tribal memories and understandings transmitted by oral tradition. Of special significance, the centuries-long encounter of African cultures with powerful influences from outside Africa has inspired efforts in African and African American communities to preserve and extend originally African intellectual and spiritual resources.

After centuries of contact between African and non-African cultures, it is difficult to isolate a set of purely traditional African philosophical positions today. The most promising preliminary question to guide an inquiry into Pan-African philosophy is not what a purely African philosophy precisely is but rather *how philosophy has been done* in Africa and in the places outside Africa where Africans have resettled, whether voluntarily or by force. With this sensibility, contemporary African philosophy comes into view as a modern development in thinking, even as some of its exponents retrieve the most ancient traditional concepts extant on the continent where humanity originated.

Oral and Traditional Philosophy

Before any direct statement of abstract principles or any intentional construction of a rational system of thought comes the telling of stories of desire, of bravery, of ancestors, of trickery, of the unseen, and of all else that is important to people. In these narratives, which are often highly ambiguous, the world's cultures have developed their unique visions and voices over thousands of years. As thoroughly as in literate cultures, oral traditions have transmitted complex value systems and their rationales. Although continuing indigenous written traditions of philosophy exist only in the lineages of the Asian civilizations following China's lead and in the Indo-European civilizations ranging chronologically across northern Africa, India, Europe, and the European cultures of the New World, all cultures possess continuous oral and folk traditions. Here we describe a few themes found in African oral traditions, and their explanation by important Pan-African philosophers.

Person   Physically, the distinction between self and other appears to be given in the biology of organisms. In virtually all cultures of the world, this distinction has psychological and philosophical reality as well. That such a distinction seems to exist across species lines certainly does not mean, however, that different organisms possess uniform or even logically compatible senses of their own individuality. The same holds true for cultures. From our knowledge of human beings, at least, the sense of what it means to be a human being is something that must be created as much as discovered. One way philosophers have approached the matter of individuality has been to develop the notion of **person.**

What a person is cannot be adequately determined simply by observation or experiment. It is, rather, a metaphysical question, that is, a question whose answer is more a matter of decision about the general nature or being of something than of empirical knowledge about it. In other words, the idea of person, which can seem so self-evident, is more an invention of human beings than an inherent fact of nature. As such, the notion of person might be expected to vary greatly from culture to culture, and indeed it does.

Historiography   Poet, philosopher, and president of his native Senegal, **Léopold Sédar Senghor** [SENG-ohr] (1906–2002) almost single-handedly determined the issues and methods of philosophy in French-speaking Africa in the mid-twentieth century. From his studies in France, Senghor acquired an intimate acquaintance with the thoughtways of Continental philosophy. This background, demonstrated in close readings of the texts he considered foundational, also clearly informs his political writings, in which Senghor establishes a discipline far removed from the colorful rhetorical assertions that often take the place of thinking in the lives of nations. Senghor's hope was that Africans would find a way to adapt socialist theory to the needs of their postcolonial societies. Adaptation was necessary, in his view, because European ways and values were inadequate to the depth and richness of African understandings of life. To this end, he attempted to create a methodology that would work for Africans.

His doctrine of **negritude,** a concept that remains widely misunderstood to this day, sought to outline a distinctively African epistemology to explain the claim that there was an African way of knowing that was different from the European. Senghor's own method was phenomenological, that is, aiming to be dispassionately descriptive, but his claim that African cultures evaluate metaphors differently from European ones was widely treated as a simple opinion. A selection from Senghor appears at the end of this chapter.

The Nature of Philosophy   A series of articles breaking with past practice and proposing a rigorous program for the future of African philosophy brought **Paulin Hountondji** [hoon-TON-jee] (1942–) to the forefront of postcolonial thought in the late twentieth century. Hountondji has attacked *ethnophilosophy* (philosophy that takes into account ethnic factors), the concept of negritude, and other colonialist assumptions. Hountondji, whose career includes service as minister of education in his native Benin, brings techniques of French critical theory to bear on the question of the integrity of African philosophy, focusing especially on the task of deconstructing texts that, in his analysis, perpetuate a colonial mentality. He has been most concerned to dismantle what he sees as the destructive influence of two connected positions in the African intellectual milieu—namely, ethnophilosophy and the advocacy of the concept of negritude. Hountondji's claim is that both of these positions work against African interests by perpetuating related falsehoods. The problem with ethnophilosophy, which seeks to describe traditional beliefs, is that its practitioners violate the experience of those they describe by abstracting ideas from their practical contexts.

Ethnophilosophy's first offense, then, is that it imposes external categorizations on those it studies. Its second offense is more historical in that its practitioners have often justified their work in terms of its usefulness to those who would control African consciousness by the judicious manipulation of symbols and concepts. A critical view of ethnophilosophy sees that Africans who buy into the ethnophilosophic

PROFILE: Desmond Tutu (1931–)

Desmond Tutu became prominent as a fighter against police brutality in South Africa in objecting to the massacre of children during the Soweto uprising. He pleaded with then President Vorster to dismantle apartheid for the future of the children. He also gave an impassioned speech at the gravesite of Steve Biko, a leader of the Black Consciousness movement who was murdered on September 12, 1977. Tutu became secretary of the South African Council of Churches in 1978 and a leader in the fight against apartheid in South Africa. He called the South African government the most evil since the Nazis.

Apartheid, a system of racial segregation enforced in South Africa from 1948 to 1994, for Tutu, was "intrinsically evil" and had to be dismantled. He believed that no one could be neutral in this matter. "You are either on the side of the oppressed or on the side of the oppressor." To be fully free, Tutu believed, all must have freedom. He continually risked imprisonment traveling the world and condemning the brutal injustice of the apartheid system.

Tutu's method of fighting for liberation was through nonviolent action, a strategy with parallels to that of Martin Luther King Jr. This was initially also the method of the African National Congress and Nelson Mandela. However, the strategy of that organization changed in 1961 after introduction of the stringent Security Laws, which were seen to interpret nonviolent resistance as weakness. The new method was to use force to resist force. Nelson Mandela immediately began to organize the armed resistance, was captured in 1962, and remained in prison until 1990. The question of the efficacy and necessity of armed resistance versus "nonviolent" resistance remains one of the central issues confronting the contemporary world. Archbishop Desmond Tutu was a vice chairman of a group on "Christianity and the Social Order" at the 1988 Lambeth Conference, which adopted a resolution on South Africa stating that it "understands those who, after exhausting all other ways, choose the way of armed struggle as the only way to justice, whilst drawing attention to the dangers and injustices possible in such action itself."

Underlying the philosophy of Desmond Tutu is the concept of humaneness. Everyone must have the freedom to become fully human; apartheid prevented this both for whites and for blacks, he argued. "I lay great stress on humaneness and being truly human. In our African understanding, part of Ubantu— being human—is the rare gift of sharing. . . . Blacks are beginning to lose this wonderful attribute, because we are being inveigled by the excessive individualism of the West. I loathe Capitalism because it gives far too great play to our inherent selfishness."

story, which does contain an element of fact, are prone to mistake these facts for the whole truth and thus acquiesce to control strategies they would otherwise resist. The same problem afflicts the adherents of the negritude position, says Hountondji, when they valorize African soul and relinquish African intellect. Not only is this a bad trade, he claims, but it also is built on an ideological illusion that serves the purposes of the colonizing forces. The remedy Hountondji prescribes at this juncture in history is a sustained critical examination of the task of a postcolonial philosophy and, to avoid unconscious perpetuation of conservative traditionalist or colonialist assumptions, a renunciation of most notions of cultural pluralism.

The Good Life The question of what constitutes the good life is one of the oldest in philosophy. It assumes particular poignancy when the conditions of life are as difficult as they have been under colonial rule. Among the most painful realizations of postcolonial thinkers is the fact that colonialist regulations that provide a comparatively small economic or political benefit to the ruling class may cause a great deal of suffering among the colonized population. Over time, the consciousness of the people may become distorted through sustained brutalization, and traditional values and virtues may fall into obscurity. Countering the tendency to give in to baser motivations, especially once independence has been achieved, requires constant vigilance and personal discipline. In addressing this issue, some postcolonial thinkers recommend socialism, some recommend democracy, some recommend religion. All, however, unite in recommending justice.

Archbishop **Desmond Tutu** (1931–   ) is widely credited with helping to maintain civility and minimize bloodshed as one of the architects of South Africa's revolutionary transition to representative democracy from an authoritarian regime characterized by apartheid's rigidly enforced subjugation of the mostly impoverished black majority. Speaking out frequently against economic exploitation, official brutality, and broad application of the death penalty, Archbishop Tutu not only helped focus the eyes of the world on injustice in his country, but also articulated basic principles to guide his fellow citizens in what he saw as the inevitable shift to black control of the levers of power.

THE AMERICAS

The history of colonialism and subjugation of native peoples in the Americas properly begins even before the arrival of Europeans in the fifteenth century. On both continents of the Western Hemisphere, indigenous Americans from the Toltecs to the Onondagas engaged in vigorous campaigns of empire building. With the coming of the Europeans, however, imperial ambitions in the Americas were pursued from a position of technological superiority that the colonized native peoples could not match and with a sustained, single-minded acquisitiveness outside the experience of most tribes. Just as the numerically superior Dacians of Eastern Europe could not withstand the organized onslaught of Roman legions, so the Indians of the Americas were confronted by forces whose methods and ultimate objectives were utterly foreign to anything they had imagined in their mythology. Montezuma's destruction by a handful of Spaniards is just the most dramatic instance of a story line that played itself out numerous times on both continents of the Western Hemisphere. The final episode of this centuries-long European conquest of the many native cultures of the Americas is being enacted today in the rain forests of South America.

Upon the coming of the Europeans history turned inscrutable for Native Americans and has remained largely a sequence of unwelcome surprises. Buffeted by centuries of broken agreements and destructive coercions, the Indian nations have tried to maintain their integrity by negotiation, by violent resistance, by legal process, and by plumbing the depths of their religious and philosophical traditions. In the worst cases, whole tribes have disappeared. With first-person accounts of genocidal aggression still part of the experience of many

Hernán Cortés (1485–1547), Spanish conquistador and conqueror of Mexico.

Native Americans, the postcolonial philosophical response has only begun to enter the literature.

The African diaspora has resulted in establishment of populations of African descent in many areas of the world, but only in the United States has there developed on a large scale a distinctive and continuous thread of critical and normative philosophy growing out of the transplanted group's unfolding historical–cultural experience. Thinking on these things has developed into a multifaceted effort to come to grips with the everyday realities of African American life, in which racial factors figure in some issues for virtually all writers and in virtually all issues for some of them. Some would argue that this material is not philosophy at all, but given the problematics of postcolonial thought, drawing more inclusive category boundaries for the field of philosophy makes good sense. Some conventional conceptions of philosophy are challenged in this categorization, for unlike most academic philosophy, African American postcolonial thinking occurs not only in self-identified philosophical texts but also in story and song—wherever propositions are presented and explicitly considered or justified.

In Latin America, the colonial order established in the fifteenth and sixteenth centuries did not evolve uniformly in all areas. Spain did not relinquish Cuba until the end of the nineteenth century, and Britain still maintains a tiny foothold on the Falkland Islands. After independence, most nations of Central and South America continued to be controlled by small, wealthy elites supporting authoritarian regimes. These regimes tended to attract the support of positivistic thinkers, although there

Colonialism and the Church

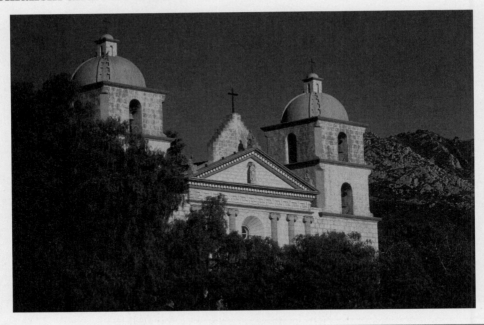

The Santa Barbara mission, founded in 1782 by Father Junipero Serra.

Many native groups, in the American West especially, still make a connection between colonial coercion and mission Christianity. The encounter of native peoples with Christianity cannot be categorized in purely negative terms, however, because in virtually all former colonies active indigenous Christian communities of varying size and demographics exist. Of special note, Latin American thinkers have taken the religious consequences of colonialism as a key issue and are actively debating the ambiguous legacy of Europe's highest ideals and most violent betrayals.

has been variation from country to country. In this regard, Latin American philosophy roughly paralleled that of Western Europe. Beginning early in the twentieth century, however, positivism's influence began to decline in Latin America as in Europe, but for somewhat different reasons. Positivism's close identification in some places with discredited political factions was partly responsible, as was the vitality of competing currents in French and German philosophy. The introduction of Marxism to Latin America, which occurred mostly outside the traditional academic circles, provided the first serious challenge to the hegemony of Roman Catholic metaphysics, providing conceptual support for the still vital commitment of Latin American thinkers to a discourse focused on the problematics of practical engagement (see the box "Colonialism and the Church"). Strongly influenced by intellectual advances made in Europe and, to a lesser extent, the United States, Latin American thinkers nonetheless avoided the style of European and American

Liberation Theology

Postcolonial thought in Latin America is closely connected with Christian social activism. Seeking to show how adherence to Christian principles can lead to a better life, theologians of **liberation** have become especially well known for their work in ethics. Epistemology has also been an important concern, however, because it offers methodological resources with which to address prevailing prejudices. Theologians of liberation, as other postcolonial thinkers do, lay great emphasis on knowledge derived from experience as the first line of defense against illusion. One reason postcolonial thinkers so often privilege experience is that, for generations, religiously inspired otherworldly hopes and a quasimedieval hierarchical understanding of society preached by conservative clergy functioned to disarm revolutionary sentiments that might arise among the large numbers of peasants. These sorts of claims may have been spiritually beneficial, say thinkers who are inclined to give the Church the benefit of the doubt, but they did not lead to sufficient nurturing of the people. Moving beyond the straightforward social gospel school of preaching that was popular among North American Christians seeking a just society, liberation theology not only has delivered the homiletic message of social change through Christian love but also has developed a complex critical–theoretical infrastructure grounded in Continental philosophy.

philosophizing. By the middle of the twentieth century, a major part of Latin American philosophical discourse had taken on a heavily religious cast; interestingly, this move, which has been studiously avoided by most philosophers in Europe and North America, has been almost uniformly celebrated among postcolonial thinkers (see the box "Liberation Theology").

This fact points up a little-recognized commonality among the expressions of postcolonial thought: in virtually all cases, except those in which Marxist materialism has been consciously adopted, the line between religion and philosophy seems very hard to draw. Whether the religion is the Christianity of Latin America, the pantheisms and myriad mythologies of Africa and the Americas, or the Hinduism of India, religiously metaphysical claims regularly serve as points of departure or elements of the presuppositional structures of postcolonial texts.

African American Thought

Social Justice   Decades after his assassination, the call for justice articulated in the writings of **Martin Luther King Jr.** (1929–1968), remains the single most powerful determinant in the American civil rights movement. King's basic message was a simple one, stated memorably in the oft-quoted dedication to *Why We Can't Wait*: "To my children . . . for whom I dream that one day soon they will no longer be judged by the color of their skin but by the content of their character." How to turn vision into reality was, for King, not just a matter of the mass organizational strategies for which he is often remembered but of personal responsibility. King was strongly influenced by the example and writings of Mohandas Gandhi in both setting his agenda and deciding on the appropriate methods to achieve it. Like Gandhi, King did not separate the two, nor did he minimize the difficulties of this comprehensive project. It is no coincidence that King's background was religious, for, as

PROFILE: Martin Luther King Jr. (1929–1968)

Martin Luther King Jr. was America's most famous civil rights leader. He helped end racial segregation by organizing nonviolent resistance to unjust law.

The son of the pastor of the Ebenezer Baptist Church in Atlanta, Georgia, King was ordained in 1947 and in 1954 became the minister of a Baptist church in Montgomery, Alabama. He received his PhD in 1955 from Boston University. In 1955 he led the boycott by Montgomery blacks against the segregated city bus lines; this landmark civil rights battle ended in 1956 with the desegregation of the city buses. King's passive resistance philosophy had won its first major victory, and King was catapulted to national prominence.

King organized the Southern Christian Leadership Conference, through which he fought for civil rights in the South and throughout the nation. Though he always advocated and used nonviolent methods, he was arrested and imprisoned many times and was, allegedly, the victim of a vendetta by FBI director J. Edgar Hoover.

In 1963 King organized the March on Washington. This, the largest demonstration in U.S. history, brought more than 200,000 people to the nation's capital. In 1964 King was awarded the Nobel Peace Prize.

By the mid-1960s, King's methods were being challenged by more militant civil rights leaders like H. Rap Brown ("Violence is as American as apple pie") and groups like the Student Nonviolent Coordinating Committee and the Black Panthers. At the same time, King's fight for justice was expanding; he became critical of the Vietnam War and concerned with poverty in general.

King was organizing a Poor People's March on Washington in 1968 when he made a side trip to Memphis, Tennessee, to support striking sanitation workers. There, standing on the balcony of a motel, he was slain by an assassin's bullet. James Earl Ray was convicted of the murder.

Martin Luther King Jr. was a philosopher who made a difference.

---

other thinkers in the postcolonial world found, commonly held religious sensibilities can provide a point of departure for ethical reasoning from a strong set of broadly accepted premises. King believed that right behavior leads to right consequences.

Feminism   In the late twentieth century, beginning in France and the United States, the feminist movement pursued a thorough revaluation of the traditional themes and methods of philosophy. Feminism is sometimes caricatured as a movement of political reaction, but from a feminist perspective, this constitutes a rather transparent strategy to undermine the philosophical authenticity of feminist thinking. Within philosophical feminism, several schools of thought have emerged, each with its own profile of insights and emphases. In the African American community, awareness of the successes of the civil rights movement and the rise of feminism in the white middle class combined with firsthand knowledge of a mostly unwritten history of the particular difficulties of black women, including a high incidence of domestic violence, to produce a variant of feminism that is especially sensitive to the social–ethical problematics of marginalization. In the view of **bell hooks** (c. 1952–   ), whose writings range from general-audience essays in popular magazines to highly nuanced discourse best appreciated by

PROFILE: bell hooks (Gloria Watkins) (c. 1952–)

Acknowledged as one of the most provocative essayists in America today, bell hooks has devoted special attention to the suppression of the voices of black women. Writing under the name of her unlettered great-grandmother to symbolize this very problem, hooks often takes up controversial themes that other writers avoid by design or oversight. Her mordant analyses typically begin by calling attention to something that has been missed or covered over. Her interruptions of the conventional flow of cultural conversation have discomfited nearly every sort of reader in one way or another, and hooks does not spare herself as she searches for the examples that will inspire, edify, and (even) entertain.

Among the thorniest issues hooks has raised is that of class distinctions in the construction of American feminism; specifically, she has argued that a feminism that emphasizes the concerns of

white, middle-class women with career plans does not do justice to minority women, many of whom must contend regularly with a very different set of economic realities.

bell hooks is the author of numerous books and articles, including *Ain't I a Woman: Black Women and Feminism* (1981), *Feminist Theory: From Margin to Center* (1984), *Breaking Bread: Insurgent Black Intellectual Life* (with Cornel West; 1991), and *Black Looks: Race and Representation* (1992). Her earlier writings are strongly flavored with Marxist ideology, but ideology seems to be less a concern for hooks than is finding ways to think and act inclusively.

The writing of bell hooks attacks domination that is sometimes obvious and sometimes hidden. She does not stop at critique but instead ventures proposals that promise not only to benefit a narrow constituency but also to create a more just society generally.

academically trained minds, it is important to make some distinctions within the feminist movement. Claims hooks, the feminism of the founders of the movement, at least in the United States, centered on careerism, a specifically middle-class concern. As such, it was liable to be co-opted by the existing power structure to perpetuate a culture of competition and individualism, which she analyzes to be antithetical to the best, inclusive impulses of feminism. The problems of the more thoroughly disenfranchised require a more radical rethinking, hooks and others have argued.

Afrocentrism **Afrocentrism,** a school of thought primarily focused on investigating the heritage and influence of African cultures, derives primarily from the work of **Chaikh Anta Diop** (1923–1986). Diop, an Africanist, brought his acknowledged expertise in ancient Egyptian history and culture to bear in arguing for a set of theses that ran counter to ancient history as told by Europeans. Diop's history claimed, among other things, that black Africa was the origin of Egyptian civilization and that Europeans who were not purely Nordic traced their ancestry back to Africa. The matter remains hotly contested among historians at this writing. Whether Diop's case prevails in whole or in part is a matter for archaeologists and historians to decide, but whatever the eventual verdict, Diop has inspired a school of cultural interpretation that is pursuing a revaluation of virtually all things African.

PROFILE: Cornel West (1953–   )

Deep questions confronting American culture, asserts Cornel West, cannot be addressed effectively if the society continues to think in conventional ways. Indeed, conventional thinking is precisely the barrier to a better quality of life. Lecturing and publishing frequently, West seeks to help chart the direction of genuinely beneficial change as he prophetically urges creation of a more compassionate society. Bringing about the necessary social reforms, he claims, requires changes in the way individuals live their lives, especially in the degree to which self-understanding develops. By living the examined life—here West sounds a perennial theme in the history of philosophy—one may progressively overcome the strictures of habit and prejudice. Now, says West, it is time to transcend the limits of Eurocentrism, multiculturalism, and all the other "isms" that keep people from perceiving the realities of life. This is not just a matter of intellectual clarity for West but also a challenge to a deeply personal commitment.

Always involved in the church throughout a career that has included appointments at Princeton and Harvard, West has consistently articulated philosophical positions that cannot be separated from religious insight. His major writings range topically from work in the critical history of ideas, represented by *The American Evasion of Philosophy: A Genealogy of Pragmatism* (1989), to the kind of personal statement represented by *Race Matters* (1993). In the realm of postcolonial thought, Cornel West occupies a position in the methodological mainstream by virtue of his explicit rootedness in social–historical experience, his use of religious tradition as a reference for thinking, and his critical analysis of current conditions and their causal antecedents.

Afrocentric thinkers hold to a range of not necessarily compatible positions, but something of a mainstream constellation of ideas has been articulated by its chief architect, Molefi Kete Asante (1942–   ), in numerous publications.

Social Activism   **Cornel West** (1953–   ), now at Princeton University, is among the most influential thinkers exploring the theological and philosophical vectors of social activism at the beginning of the twenty-first century. Although West's philosophical writings have dealt with a variety of issues, essays in which he combines trenchant analysis with positive recommendations for future action command his widest readership.

Latin American Thought

Postcolonial Latin American thinkers work in a context that is at once strongly influenced by European philosophy and powerfully motivated to move out from under the shadow of European domination. One feature that importantly distinguishes Latin American thought from most European philosophy is the sustained effort to explore the relevance of philosophy to problems of social justice. The concerns of Latin American philosophy encompass the full range of the philosophical spectrum, but its activity in postcolonial thought has concentrated on analysis of Marxist theses.

Ontology   Ontology is the branch of philosophy that concerns itself with the question of being. In the twentieth century, ontology was revived by the work of Martin Heidegger and Jean-Paul Sartre after centuries of dormancy. Although there is always a danger that orthodoxy will stifle thinking whenever the work of a philosopher is widely acknowledged, recent writings of Latin American philosophers demonstrate the possibility of interpreting Heidegger's work in ways that probably were not anticipated by either the politically conservative German philosopher or the politically progressive French philosopher. In an essay at the end of this chapter, Argentinian philosopher **Carlos Astrada** [uh-STRAH-duh] (1894–1970) takes Heidegger's thinking as evidence of the collapse of the bourgeois mentality that determined much of the course of colonial activity. Though Latin America's colonial pattern was more feudal than bourgeois, most historians agree that bourgeois influences from North America have played a great role in perpetuating unequal distributions of wealth inherited from colonial times. Postcolonial reality has brought with it the realization that surprises can overtake whole civilizations, including the awareness that longstanding patterns of wealth and poverty are not necessarily permanent fixtures in a society. Recent history, unfolding at the pace of technological change, plants doubts about the stability of existence. It should not be surprising, then, that a school of philosophy, existentialism, should arise that sees becoming as the fundamental fact of existence. For postcolonial thinkers, it is not surprising, either, that the wealthy would project the instability of their own power structures onto the existence of humanity itself. Astrada's essay demonstrates that works of existentialist ontology can be read as political–economic texts.

Metaphysics of the Human   For as long as we have been keeping records of our thoughts, human beings have sought a reliably firm foundation upon which to base ideas about ourselves, our laws, our destiny, and so on. Many promises of a final answer have been made, but outside of religious faith—a category of claims that arguably has its own distinct rules of discourse—no claims of foundational insight have stood the tests of time and philosophical investigation. In the sensibilities of postcolonial thinkers, though, the moral and metaphysical claims of the ruling elites of past and present demand constant vigilance and persistent critique. Marx called these dangerous claims **ideology,** meaning in his vocabulary a kind of self-interested delusion that infected the bourgeoisie and that they half-cynically, half-unconsciously passed on to the proletariat. Marx believed that the proletariat would eventually realize, as he had, that ideological claims were without necessity or merit and could, therefore, be contradicted. But, contends Peruvian philosopher **Francisco Miró Quesada** [keh-SAH-duh] (1918–   ), with the pragmatism that has become a trademark of recent Latin philosophy, contradicting the claims of one group with the claims of an alternative theory of reality does not solve the problem. Instead, it creates conflict, and conflict creates suffering. Quesada continues on to argue that humanity itself must be reimagined. His argument consists of two main parts: first, a critique of the truth claims of theories, which concludes that theories cannot reliably deliver the truth, and second, a consequentialist argument centered on the suffering caused by people who take theories too seriously. The eventual proposal is to divide the human race into those who are willing to exploit people and those who are willing to defend them from exploitation.

Gender Issues   The phase of feminism as a movement of middle-class European and American women began in 1959. Analysis of the early rhetoric of the movement suggests an underlying assumption among that generation of feminists that all women shared common concerns. It was not long, however, before women in more traditional societies began to assert that the universal claims of most feminist literature did not speak well to the conditions of marginalized peoples. From both unreformed colonial and postcolonial perspectives, a certain myopia afflicted mainstream feminism.

Two major expansions of feminist perspectives have been suggested from outside the mainstream. The first calls for more attention to issues of class. In this connection the argument is made that commonalities based in shared gender become functionally irrelevant when class-based exploitation determines not only woman-to-woman relationships but also the circumstances of domestic relationships. A woman living in grinding poverty has few resources with which to overcome traditional strictures and inequities, third world writers observe. The second major modification of feminist discourse suggested by several postcolonial writers was the abandonment of a black–white racial dichotomy. Because the majority of the women in the world are neither European American white nor black, the reasoning goes, feminists who fall into a black–white polarization not only exclude a large ethnic segment, but, more ominously, they exclude a wide range of situations from analysis as well. Sonia Saldívar-Hull addresses these problems in a selection at the end of the chapter.

SOUTH ASIA

The history of European colonial rule in Asia began in the early sixteenth century and continues to this day. It included such developments as British domination of large areas of India and other parts of South Asia; French control of Vietnam, Cambodia, and Laos; the partitioning of Ch'ing China by multiple Western colonial powers; and much more. Although the vast inland deserts of Asia and the rugged Deccan plateau of India remained mostly outside the grip of invading powers, most of Asia's population centers experienced alien invasion at one time or another. The reactions of indigenous peoples to these events ranged from the pacifism of Gandhi to murderous secret societies from Afghanistan to China, with the Vietnam War marking the bloody culmination of an era of highly confrontational violence. According to the majority of contemporary analysts, colonialism has been economically and socially destructive in the former colonies. A few, however, claim that the legacy of specifically northern European colonialism has been positive in terms of modern political infrastructure and value systems that facilitate success in a technological world. This is difficult to settle at a distance, but one thing is certain: the formerly colonized peoples of Asia have documented their own ideas of what counts as good over thousands of years. Postcolonial thought in Asia draws sustenance from these cultural wellsprings.

Unlike the cultures of sub-Saharan Africa, the nations of Asia have traditions of written philosophy that stretch back more than three millennia, longer than in the West by at least a thousand years. The ancient *Vedas* of India and the Chinese classics anchor their respective cultures with unmistakable gravity, testifying to resources beyond the grasp of any colonizing power. The shock of colonialism to Asia was deep but not so comprehensive for these cultures that their philosophers have felt impelled to the kind of sustained reflection and cultural reconstruction that has been so prominent in Africa. Certainly, colonialism wrecked the economy of the Indian countryside and changed China's self-image forever, but the effect on the discourse of Indian and Chinese philosophy seems to have been a relatively small dislocation. This does not mean that no serious reflection occurred, only that Asian cultures already had so much internally generated philosophical momentum that outside influences, even outside influences with the intellectual resources of the West, could not effect a significant change of course. Instead, outside ideas and techniques, from British aesthetics to Marxist political–historiographical philosophy, were appropriated and reworked to conform to indigenous values.

From another angle, Asian thinkers in the colonial era frequently regarded Western thought as crude, simplistic, or just wrongheaded. Even so, the Western presence was hard to ignore. It prompted thoughtful efforts not only to develop an appropriate sense of history but also to project an appropriate relationship with the foreigners. The result included such disparate expressions as the highly reflective Young India school of thought in the waning years of the British Empire and the cynically manipulative, sloganeering rhetoric of Chairman Mao.

Let's focus on India, which endured about two centuries of economic despoilment at the hands of the mercantilist–capitalist forces of Britain. It cannot be argued that the leaders of the independence movement relied on indigenous values to develop their notions of economic justice, for India had traditionally established rigid class lines that effectively excluded large numbers of people from the possibility of economic well-being. Ironically, the introduction of British values in India created the conceptual resources that Indians would use to remake their society—after figuring out how to expel the British. Gandhi looked to India's own traditions primarily in his quest for the contours of a future just society, but the majority of members of the dominant Congress Party believed with Jawaharlal Nehru, independent India's first prime minister, that the road to modernization also necessitated adoption of modern political–economic thinking.

The independence movement's greatest influence was certainly Gandhi, but many of its leading thinkers also mined the writings of modern socialists, including Marx. Drawing on Hindu psychology, which views grudging obedience to rules as a very serious problem, Nehru and his followers sought to avoid the imposition of socialism on a populace that was in part unwilling to engage in this transformation of Indian society. Though most of the early leaders of the Indian resistance to the British were convinced that socialism was the surest path to peace and justice, they also saw that domination of the minority by the majority, always possible in a democracy, had to be avoided. These thinkers consciously renounced the use of a colonialist style of coercion to achieve a postcolonial objective.

The topics taken up by Asian postcolonial thought are similar to those considered elsewhere in the world. As well, thinkers in the countries of Asia draw on indigenous thought forms to develop their inferences and expositions. Asian writers are the most likely of the postcolonial thinkers surveyed in this chapter to couch

PROFILE: Mohandas (Mahatma) Gandhi (1869–1948)

Mohandas Gandhi was the world's leading exponent of the strategy of active nonviolent resistance or non-cooperation—the attempt to change unjust laws through nonviolent civil disobedience to them. This philosophy, which Gandhi used successfully time after time to produce legal and political change, was the inspiration and guiding light for protest movements throughout the world and was adopted by many American civil rights leaders, including Martin Luther King Jr. Gandhi's life, like King's, was ended by an assassin—a Hindu fanatic upset by Gandhi's concern for Muslims.

Gandhi began his political activism not in India but in South Africa, where he was a successful lawyer and leader in the Indian community. While there, he gave up a Western mode of life and began living according to Hindu ideals of self-denial. It was there in South Africa, in 1907, that he organized his first campaign of civil disobedience, and this *satyagraha,* or "clinging to the truth," was so successful that the South African government agreed to alleviate anti-Indian discrimination.

In 1915 Gandhi returned to India a famous man. There he used *satyagraha* to advance numerous democratic reforms. He became known as Mahatma, or "great soul," and his influence was so considerable that he could exact concessions from the British government of India by merely threatening to fast to death. Not only was he the spiritual leader of the Indian people, but he was also a major political figure. He was the leader of the Indian National Congress and was a principal participant in the post–World War II conferences that led to India's independence and the creation of a separate Muslim state, Pakistan (although he opposed the partition). When there was violence between Muslims and Hindus, Gandhi used his influence to help control it, often resorting to fasts and prayer meetings. It was during one such prayer meeting that he was assassinated.

Gandhi altered the courses of nations: his extraordinary power came not through guns but through his ability to bring out the best in people by setting the highest standards for his own life.

their discussions in terms of the abstract principles and linear inferences typical of Western philosophy. This stylistic similarity is not a borrowing from Western thought, however, but a continuation of local traditions of discourse.

Satyagraha

Satyagraha, a concept closely identified with the social and political thinking of **Mohandas (Mahatma) Gandhi** [GAHN-dee] (1869–1948), has been translated as "clinging to truth." This definition immediately raises the question of the nature of truth. In traditional Indian philosophy, this issue had already received a great amount of attention. Thousands of years before Husserl's phenomenological method called for clearing the perceptions of prejudices, Indian philosophers were insisting on the same thing and developing a yoga, or discipline, to facilitate it. The discipline needed in the search for truth was not simply a matter of acquiring the tools of scientific investigation; one also had to practice such virtues as giving, nonattachment, and noninjury to develop mental purity. Gandhi is part of this tradition in his adoption of its rigorous demands for personal integrity.

PROFILE: Rabindranath Tagore (1861–1941)

Modern India's best-known poet was also in the vanguard of postcolonial thought. Rabindranath Tagore was not simply an advocate for an interest group but also a thinker who saw that philosophy and action must be unified in the life of the individual. Thus, his political claims were intentionally grounded in the traditions of Indian spirituality. As we have noted, postcolonial thought often makes use of traditional ideas and values in its critiques of the structures and methods of domination. It also tends to begin with concrete social situations; for Tagore, this translated into heartfelt advocacy of social reform as a task for Indians themselves, regardless of British policy. Tagore was himself inspired by the beauty and manifold possibilities of life, and he sought to share his vision as an artist through both the written word and the painted image.

Born to an upper-class family in Calcutta, Tagore's opportunities were broad, including a brief period of study in England. In later life, as he established a worldwide reputation, he traveled to Europe, the United States, and Japan. He began writing for periodicals while still very young and acquired a lifelong interest in education as a great hope for the betterment of the human condition. In 1901 he established a school in his native Bengal to put his ideas into practice. He continued to write and, in 1913, was awarded the Nobel Prize for literature. He promptly devoted the proceeds to his school. Knighted in 1915, Tagore resigned the title in 1919 in protest against the harshly repressive tactics employed by the British in maintaining their empire in India. Among his many works are *One Hundred Poems of Kabir* (1915), *Nationalism* (1917), *The Home and the World* (1919), *Broken Ties* (1925), and *The Religion of Man* (1931).

Gandhi is also a modern figure, however, a student not only of the classical texts of India but also of Thoreau and Tolstoy. Seeking what was best in his tradition, he repudiated the claims of human inequality by circumstances of birth that underlay the caste system. Declaring freedom from ancient caste laws marked Gandhi as a modern figure despite his notable adherence to ancient ascetic forms. Gandhi's uncompromising concern for the welfare of the people of India and his courage in the struggle for independence from Britain established him as a political leader. His devotion to Hindu ideals and the simple life he lived made him a spiritual leader. Hailed as a saint in his own time and acknowledged as one of the most influential thinkers of the modern age, Gandhi insisted that his way was open to any who would simply decide to follow it.

Metaphysics

To this day, it is common for Indian thinkers to hold the view that India's role in the international community consists at least partly in promoting a spiritual understanding of the human race and the issues of the times. Once Western cultures entered the Indian sphere of consciousness, they were evaluated to see not only how they met the standards of indigenous tradition but also how they might be recast to fit into the Hindu framework.

Around the turn of the twentieth century, while India was still a colony of Britain, **Rabindranath Tagore** [tuh-GORE] (1861–1941) developed in poetry and essays his sense of a possible modern Indian consciousness. For Tagore a realistic consciousness of the challenges and opportunities of the time can come only if the true nature of human beings is acknowledged and actions are carried out accordingly. Indian tradition provides a guide to the complexities of human nature and the behavior needed for a harmonious and enlightening life. The needed learning is not something that can be acquired once and then stored away for future reference. It must be examined and extended throughout one's life. In this way of thinking, humans must devote themselves to living the examined life. Tagore's thoughts remind us of this most central theme in the history of world philosophy.

SELECTION 16.1

On African Socialism★   *Léopold Sédar Senghor*

[*Senghor attempted to delineate the Negro African way of thinking, feeling, speaking. He differentiated it from the abstract European way of thinking based on the Latin* ratio *("reason").*]

Let us then consider the Negro African as he faces the object to be known, as he faces the Other: God, man, animal, tree or pebble, natural or social phenomenon. In contrast to the classic European, the Negro African does not draw a line between himself and the object; he does not hold it at a distance, nor does he merely look at it and analyze it. After holding it at a distance, after scanning it without analyzing it, he takes it vibrant in his hands, careful not to kill or fix it. He touches it, feels it, *smells* it. The Negro African is like one of those Third Day Worms,[1] a pure field of sensations. Subjectively, at the tips of his sensory organs, his insect antennas, he discovered the Other. Immediately he is moved, going centrifugally from subject to object on the waves of the Other. This is more than a simple metaphor; contemporary physics has discovered universal energy under matter: waves and radiations. Thus the Negro African *sympathizes*,[2] abandons his personality to become identified with the Other, dies to be reborn in the Other. He does not assimilate; he is assimilated. He lives a common life with the Other; he lives in a symbiosis. To use Paul Claudel's

[French diplomat, poet, and dramatist] expression, he "knows[3] the Other." Subject and object are dialectically face to face in the very act of knowledge. It is a long caress in the night, an embrace of joined bodies, the act of love. "I want you to feel me," says a voter who wants you to know him well. "I think, therefore I am," Descartes writes. The observation has already been made that one always thinks something, and the logician's conjunction "therefore" is unnecessary. The Negro African could say, "I feel, I dance the Other; I am." To dance is to discover and to re-create, especially when it is a dance of love. In any event, it is the best way to know. Just as knowledge is at once discovery and creation—I mean, re-creation and recreation, after the model of God.

Young people have criticized me for reducing Negro-African knowledge to pure emotion, for denying that there is an African "reason" or African techniques. This is the hub of the problem; I should like to explain my thought once again. Obviously, there is a European civilization and a Negro-African

---

★ From Léopold Sédar Senghor, *On African Socialism*, translated by Mercer Cook (New York: Praeger, 1964). Used by permission of Mercer Cook, Jr. and Jacques Cook.

[1] An allusion to the Age of Reptiles. [Trans.]

[2] In the French text, *sym-pathise*, literally, "feels with." [Trans.]

---

[3] Here again the word is separated, *con-nait*, literally, "is born with." [Trans.]

See Arthur Koestler, *The Lotus and the Robot* (New York: The Macmillan Co., 1961), p. 43:

The traditional Eastern way of looking at things is to deny that there *are* things independently from the act of looking. The objects of consciousness cannot be separated from the conscious subject; observer and observed are a single, indivisible, fluid reality, as they are at the dawn of consciousness in the child, and in the cultures dominated by magic. The external world has no existence in its own right; it is a function of the senses; but that function exists only in so far as it is registered by consciousness, and consequently has no existence in its own right.

civilization. Anyone who has not explained their differences and the reasons for them has explained nothing and has left the problem untouched.

Thus, I explain myself. However paradoxical it may seem, the vital force of the Negro African, his surrender to the object, is animated by reason. Let us understand each other clearly; it is not the *reasoning-eye* of Europe, it is the *reason of the touch*, better still, the *reasoning-embrace*, the sympathetic reason, more closely related to the Greek *logos* than to the Latin *ratio*. For *logos*, before Aristotle, meant both reason and the word. At any rate, Negro-African speech does not mold the object into rigid categories and concepts without touching it; it polishes things and restores their original color, with their texture, sound, and perfume; it perforates them with its luminous rays to reach the essential surreality in its innate humidity—it would be more accurate to speak of subreality. European reasoning is analytical, discursive by utilization; Negro-African reasoning is intuitive by participation.

Young people in Black Africa are wrong to develop a complex and to believe the latter inferior to the former. "The most beautiful emotion that we can experience," wrote the great scientist Einstein, "is mystic emotion. It is the germ of all art and all true science." . . . Now you will understand why, in my definition of Negro-African knowledge, I rejected abstract analysis on the European pattern, why I preferred to use analogous imagery, the metaphor, to make you *feel* the object of my speech. The metaphor, a symbolic short cut in its sensitive, sensual qualities, is the method par excellence of Negro-African speech.

Today, it is also, quite often, the style of European speech. . . . So, our young people should not repudiate the Negro-African method of knowledge since, once again, it is the latest form of the European method. *Participation* and *communion* . . . are the very words that ethnologists specializing in the study of Negro-African civilizations have used for decades.

SELECTION 16.2
The Sword That Heals*

Martin Luther King Jr.

[*Here King explained the power of nonviolent resistance in bringing about political justice as well as giving dignity, courage, and heart to those who practice it.*]

The argument that nonviolence is a coward's refuge lost its force as its heroic and often perilous acts uttered their wordless but convincing rebuttal in Montgomery, in the sit-ins, on the freedom rides, and finally in Birmingham.

There is a powerful motivation when a suppressed people enlist in an army that marches under the banner of nonviolence. A nonviolent army has a magnificent universal quality. To join an army that trains its adherents in the methods of violence, you must be of a certain age. But in Birmingham, some of

the most valued foot soldiers were youngsters ranging from elementary pupils to teen-age high school and college students. For acceptance in the armies that maim and kill, one must be physically sound, possessed of straight limbs and accurate vision. But in Birmingham, the lame and the halt and the crippled could and did join up. Al Hibbler, the sightless singer, would never have been accepted in the United States Army or the army of any other nation, but he held a commanding position in our ranks.

In armies of violence, there is a caste of rank. In Birmingham, outside of the few generals and lieutenants who necessarily directed and coordinated operations, the regiments of the demonstrators marched in democratic phalanx. Doctors marched with window cleaners. Lawyers demonstrated with laundresses. PhD's and no-D's were treated with perfect equality by the registrars of the nonviolence movement.

As the broadcasting profession will confirm, no shows are so successful as those which allow for audience participation. In order to be somebody, people must feel themselves part of something. In the nonviolent army, there is room for everyone who wants to join up. There is no color distinction. There is no examination, no pledge, except that, as a soldier in the armies of violence is expected to inspect his carbine and keep it clean, nonviolent soldiers are called upon to examine and burnish their greatest weapons—their heart, their conscience, their courage and their sense of justice.

Nonviolent resistance paralyzed and confused the power structures against which it was directed. The brutality with which officials would have quelled the black individual became impotent when it could not be pursued with stealth and remain unobserved. It was caught—as a fugitive from a penitentiary is often caught—in gigantic circling spotlights. It was imprisoned in a luminous glare revealing the naked truth to the whole world. It is true that some demonstrators suffered violence, and that a few paid the extreme penalty of death. They were the martyrs of last summer who laid down their lives to put an end to the brutalizing of thousands who had been beaten and bruised and killed in dark streets and back rooms of sheriffs' offices, day in and day out, in hundreds of summers past.

The striking thing about the nonviolent crusade of 1963 was that so few felt the sting of bullets or the clubbing of billies and nightsticks. Looking back, it becomes obvious that the oppressors were restrained not only because the world was looking but also because, standing before them, were hundreds, sometimes thousands, of Negroes who for the first time dared to look back at a white man, eye to eye. Whether through a decision to exercise wise restraint or the operation of a guilty conscience, many a hand was stayed on a police club and many a fire hose was restrained from vomiting forth its pressure. That the Revolution was a comparatively bloodless one is explained by the fact that the Negro did not merely give lip service to nonviolence. The tactics the movement utilized, and that guided far-flung actions in cities dotted across the map, discouraged violence because one side would not resort to it and the other was so often immobilized by confusion, uncertainty and disunity.

Nonviolence had tremendous psychological importance to the Negro. He had to win and to vindicate his dignity in order to merit and enjoy his self-esteem. He had to let white men know that the picture of him as a clown—irresponsible, resigned and believing in his own inferiority—was a stereotype with no validity. This method was grasped by the Negro masses because it embodied the dignity of struggle, of moral conviction and self-sacrifice. The Negro was able to face his adversary, to concede to him a physical advantage and to defeat him because the superior force of the oppressor had become powerless.

To measure what this meant to the Negro may not be easy. But I am convinced that the courage and discipline with which Negro thousands accepted nonviolence healed the internal wounds of Negro millions who did not themselves march in the streets or sit in the jails of the South. One need not participate directly in order to be involved. For Negroes all over this nation, to identify with the movement, to have pride in those who were the principals, and to give moral, financial or spiritual support was to restore to them some of the pride and honor which had been stripped from them over the centuries.

SELECTION 16.3

Existentialism and the Crisis of Philosophy*

Carlos Astrada

[*Here Astrada explained the death of the concept of modern man that has dominated Western thinking since the Renaissance.*]

---

* From *Latin American Philosophy in the Twentieth Century*, ed. Jorge J. E. Gracia (Buffalo, NY: Prometheus Books, 1986). Reprinted by permission of Jorge J. E. Gracia.

Toward a New Image of Man

The rationalist concept of man is dogmatically constructed on the peripheries of concrete humanity, of individual historic man, and of vital reality. Over against this rationalist concept, a real, living image of man is being raised, an image with blood and viscera, with earthly fluids and air to breathe.

A new image of man, man conceived according to other necessities and purposes, necessarily presupposes a new social order, a new hierarchical order of values to which the historical sensitivity of the age gives allegiance. The concept of man of rationalist humanism with its parallel postulate of progressivism is embedded in all the instances and sectors wherein it was able to gain preeminence, but even now, it is dead, though still hauled around on a declining verbal rather than mental plane on which are placed all the survivors of individual liberalism and its residual doctrinaire expressions.

This type of man, purely rational, antihistorical, and anonymous, is a ghostlike entity that eludes reality and struggles along a retreating front against the great events the future is preparing. It cannot be ignored, however, that this image of man has reigned for almost three centuries in the cultural and political life of the West, having shown that in the past it was an efficient reagent in the multiple aspects of this life. However, for the past three decades, this image of man is in obvious decline. It is barely a vanishing shadow that those adrift in the historical present vainly attempt to seize.

The completed man, conceptually constructed by rationalist humanism, that is to say, the isolated, completed, purely ideal man, without roots in a specific soil, with no vital ties to a nationality, with no connections to an instinctive and emotional repertoire of historically conditioned preferences—such a man does not exist. Neither is there an essential equality of all men based solely on universal reason as a constant and unalterable factor that would act independently in the psycho-vital, historical reality of national communities, classes, and racial constellations.

Having surpassed it, we are also far beyond the pseudoantinomy of *individualism* and *collectivism*. Our age no longer knows the individual as a social atom nor over against him the collectivity, considered as an aggregation of such atoms and billed as the leading actor of social and political history. It does recognize, however, opposing classes whose struggle, undoubtedly, is the crux of the economic-social process. There is also a growing awareness of the concrete historical man, the man who, without turning loose the bonds and surroundings in which he is implicated, stands out as a personal, psycho-vital unit, who affirms and gives life to his humanity as a function of his real goals, which are immanent in his particular becoming.

The Extinction of Modern Man

The unbalanced society of our age, especially the capitalist and mercantile commanders who are the possessors of political power, attempt in vain to live off the remains of the rationalist idea of man embodied in so-called "modern man," an image already in a state of desiccation. These commanders are the crusty bark oppressing and retarding the buds of a new idea of man of great historical significance that have been germinating rapidly in the deeper levels of contemporary life. Suppressed forces that are emotionally and historically articulated by a generation destined to place its seal on the future give added thrust and life to this idea of man with which the coming generation will impose a new *ethos*, affirming a particular political will and instituting also a different scale of evaluation for the culture, economy, and society.

Modern man is a cadaver that senescent human groups, adrift in the storm of these days, attempt vainly to galvanize, appealing to slogans and incantations that no longer have meaning. In a letter to Dilthey,[1] Count Yorck von Wartenburg said: "Modern man, the man who began with the Renaissance and has endured until our time, is ready to be buried."

This type man, the man of individualistic liberalism, the ultimate, valedictory expression of "modern man," imbued with vestiges of the rationalist ideals of the nineteenth century is the corpse to be buried. The present age is responsible for carrying out this task so the new man can cover the whole surface of history and thus affirm and give full meaning to the spiritual and political orders now germinating.

---

[1] Wilhelm Dilthey (1833–1911) was a German philosopher noted for his work in textual analysis and the history of ideas.

SELECTION 16.4

Man without Theory *

Francisco Miró Quesada

[*Here Quesada reviewed many of the pitfalls in trying to frame a theory as to what constitutes a human being.*]

The history of humanity is an impressive succession of complicated, yet false theories that man has woven around himself. . . . In the present, in this modern, troubled atomic era, the era of the machine and technology, we are aware nevertheless of what is really happening. We have a clear understanding that history is a succession of ways of conceiving the world and man, of ways considered absolute by men of different ages but that today are no more than vague shadows, difficult to understand. Our civilization, therefore, is the most philosophical of all, because none has had as clear an awareness of its limitation and relativity. In truth, our age is characteristically an age of search, of disorientation, and of acute consciousness of its negative traits. Contemporary man is one who experiences in his own flesh the failure of a great theory concerning himself: European rationalism, in all its facets, from the liberalism of "laissez faire" to Nazism and Marxism. . . .

Given this situation the inevitable question is "What shall we do?" The depth of the question does permit a dogmatic answer. Indeed, perhaps this essay should end here. However, to be human means to try unceasingly to overcome every "non plus ultra" and since we do not wish to deny our human condition, we have no alternative but to forge ahead. Yet, before continuing we wish to emphasize that what follows is no more than the point of view of a particular individual who, along with all other individuals in this age, is faced with an immense problem that by its very nature transcends any purely individual response.

The first thought that might come to mind, and perhaps a majority already favors it, is to commit our efforts to the reconstruction of the old theory, making it more comprehensive and adapting it to the demands of our modern circumstance. Or, should this not be possible, to elaborate a new theory that may or may not be related to the old or to earlier theories, but would constitute an organic system, capable of providing answers to the most pressing questions and have the scope and flexibility necessary to permit men of our day to work with the total range of their problems. In actual experience, the normal or spontaneous attitude always develops a theory. So we, although disillusioned by theories, in seeing ourselves in a bind, think of amplifying or creating theories, like men of other ages. In this day, however, there is a difference: men of previous ages were not aware of the relativity or limits of their theories, nor of the horrible dangers implicit in creating a complicated theory concerning man from which unforeseeable and mortal consequences were derived. Furthermore, they did not suspect that their theories ran the same risks as all preceding theories. Therefore they created under illusion, but in faith, and so their theories had "vital force" and served to resolve human problems since men believed in them and were convinced that all previous ages had been in error whereas they were in the truth. In this day, however, we are not convinced our position is unique, true, or definitive. Indeed, we know that whatever we do, our theory about man will suffer the same end as the others.

Yet, instead of searching for a new theory and instinctively following the destiny of Sisyphus, what if we assume a completely different attitude? Instead of inventing a new and dangerous theory, why not simply give up formulating theories about ourselves? Now this proposal may well produce a scandal and for two good reasons. First, because man is so accustomed to formulating theories about himself, to taking for granted that he knows what he is, to feeling himself at the helm of a world of structures and hierarchies, to renounce theory leaves him with the impression that he is giving up the possibility of finding solutions, that he is spineless and morally decadent, that he has given up the

---

* From *Latin American Philosophy in the Twentieth Century,* ed. Jorge J. E. Gracia (Buffalo, NY: Prometheus Books, 1986). Reprinted by permission of Jorge J. E. Gracia.

struggle for good and against evil. Second, because it is believed, more for theoretical than practical considerations, that no matter what man does he is condemned to theorize and that he can give up everything except formulating a complete concept of the world, of things, and of himself. It is believed that man needs theory to live, that without it he flounders and does not know what to hold on to, he is a lost soul on a ship without a rudder. For, although he may deny theory, implicitly he is always constructing a system of concepts for clarifying the meaning of his life.

To be sure, this second argument is much more powerful than the first. Its strength, however, lies in its inclusive breadth, for its detailed analysis of situations is slipshod. For example, if one analyzes all the elements constituting the world within which man includes himself, one sees there are various dimensions. One dimension is the surrounding world. This dimension, naturally, is undeniable. If man does not possess a well-formulated theory concerning the surrounding world he is not even able to walk down the street. The simple act of dodging an automobile indicates the possession of a rather clear concept of the principles of causality and the laws of dynamics. Further, our cultural crisis is not a crisis in knowledge of the natural world. The cosmic world, our surrounding environment, is known with increasingly greater certainty and vigor. It is perhaps the only part of our general vision of the world that at present follows a linear evolution. We have reached such a comprehension of what physical theory is, that the elaboration of that type theory is carried out in the awareness that in time it will be surpassed, and that it will be necessary to amplify it to include new facts. For this reason, it is possible that the nuclear emphasis of the old theory may be preserved intact and that it may be possible to consider it as a special case of a new theory. Some might believe that this procedure is applicable to the theory about the nature of man. However, given the complexity of all anthropological theory, this is not possible. Physical as well as mathematical theories are very simple, since they are based on broad abstractive processes. Therefore, this approach is not adequate for anthropological theory. But if we do not make use of it, we encounter the earlier objection, namely, that every theory concerning the surrounding world presupposes an integrated theory of the human being. And here we come to the crux of the issue. For, if this affirmation is true, then we will never be able to free ourselves from a theory concerning ourselves and we will always return to that monotonous, well-beaten path. This, however, we believe to be false, because even though it is undeniable that every theory concerning the cosmos presupposes a theory concerning man, it does not presuppose necessarily that the theory of the cosmos is complete. In order to grant validity to a theory about the cosmos, we must presuppose certain epistemological postulates, certain beliefs concerning the structure and organization of our consciousness, but in no way does such a theory necessarily include hypotheses about the moral life or destiny of man. . . .

However, man is so accustomed to living on the theoretical level that he does not conceive the possibility of refraining from decisions about his own nature and fundamental relationships with the surrounding world. Thus he always finds arguments that justify his use of theories. In the present case, those who deny the possibility of avoiding theory about man adduce that this avoidance is impossible because determining one's orientation in the world without language is impossible. To establish interhuman communication, whatever it may be, is impossible without speech, but speech is in itself a theory. The philosophical analysis of language shows unequivocally that every expressive system acquires its ultimate meaning from theoretical presuppositions about the nature of the world and of man. Thus the very possibility of language implies the immersion of the human being in a complete theory concerning himself, a theory that refers not only to his objective relationship with the environing world, but also to his norms of action and destiny. Philological analysis of the most trivial words reveals, in a surprising way at times, the immense background of cosmological, metaphysical, and ethical theory upon which all possible language rests. The argument, then, would seem to be definitive: man cannot live without an orientation in the world and to seek an orientation in the world requires a specific theory concerning the physical structure of the cosmos. This theory, however, cannot be elaborated without language, but language is the great, universal theory, the expression of what in the ultimate, collective, anonymous, and therefore inevitable sense man believes about the world and himself. Thus, it is impossible to live as a human being without presupposing certain theoretical axioms concerning our nature and our destiny.

SELECTION 16.5

Feminism on the Border: From Gender Politics to Geopolitics *

Sonia Saldívar-Hull

[*In this selection, Sonia Saldívar-Hull expressed her belief that feminism as found in first world countries oppresses and exploits third world women. She also noted that, in her opinion, some "Third World feminists" are really agents of patriarchy, capitalism, and imperialism.*]

Is it possible for Chicanas to consider ourselves part of this "sisterhood" called feminism? Can we assume that our specific interests and problems will be taken care of by our Marxist compañeros?

. . . Our white feminist "sisters" [must] recognize their own blind spots. When [Catherine] MacKinnon uses the black woman as her sign for all dispossessed women, we see the extent to which Chicanas, Asian-American, Native American, or Puerto Rican women, for example, have been rendered invisible in a discourse whose explicit agenda is to expose ideological erasure. Chicana readings of color *blindness* instead of color consciousness in "politically correct" feminist essays indicate the extent to which the issues of race and ethnicity are ignored in feminist and Marxist theories. . . .

As Chicanas making our works public— publishing in marginalized journals and small, underfinanced presses and taking part in conferences and workshops—we realize that the "sisterhood" called feminism professes an ideology that at times comes dangerously close to the phallocentric ideologies of the white male power structure against which feminists struggle. In her essay, "Ethnicity, Ideology, and Academia," Rosaura Sánchez reminds us of the ideological strategies that the dominant culture manipulates in order to mystify "the relation between minority cultures and the dominant culture." . . . She points out that U.S. cultural imperialism extends beyond the geopolitical borders of

the country, "but being affected, influenced, and exploited by a culture is one thing and sharing fully in that culture is another." . . . If we extend the analogy to feminism and the totalizing concept of sisterhood, we begin to understand how the specific interests of Anglo-American and other European feminists tend to erase the existence of Chicana, Puerto Rican, Native American, Asian-American, and other Third World feminists. Indeed, feminism affects and influences Chicana writers and critics, but feminism as practiced by women of the hegemonic culture oppresses and exploits the Chicana in both subtle and obvious ways. . . .

In our search for a feminist critical discourse that adequately takes into account our position as women under multiple oppressions we must turn to our own "organic intellectuals." But because our work has been ignored by the men and women in charge of the modes of cultural production, we must be innovative in our search. Hegemony has so constructed the idea of method and theory that often we cannot recognize anything that is different from what the dominant discourse constructs. We have to look in nontraditional places for our theories: in the prefaces to anthologies, in the interstices of autobiographies, in our cultural artifacts, our *cuentos,* and if we are fortunate to have access to a good library, in the essays published in marginalized journals not widely distributed by the dominant institutions. . . .

In the same way that we must break with traditional (hegemonic) concepts of genre to read Chicana feminist theory, working-class women of color in other Third World countries articulate their feminisms in nontraditional ways and forms. The Chicana feminist acknowledges the often vast historical, class, racial, and ethnic differences among women living on the border, but the nature of hegemony practiced by the united powers of patriarchy, capitalism, imperialism, and white supremacy promotes an illusion of an irreconcilable split between feminists confined within national borders. We must examine and question the First versus Third World dichotomy before we accept the opposition as an inevitable fissure that separates women politically committed in different ways from any common cause.

In her testimony, *Let Me Speak, . . .* Bolivian activist Domitila Barrios de Chungara acknowledges the separation between "First" and "Third" World feminists: "Our Position is not like the feminists' position. We think our liberation consists primarily in our country being freed forever from the yoke of imperialism and we want a worker like us to be in power and that the laws, education, everything, be controlled by this person. Then, yes, we'll have better conditions for reaching a complete liberation, including a liberation as women." . . . Her statement, however, is problematized by her occasion for speaking. As a participant at the UN-sponsored International Year of the Woman Conference held in Mexico City in 1975, Barrios witnessed co-optation of "feminism" by governments which use women and women's issues to promote their own political agendas. Barrios observed Imelda Marcos, Princess Ashraf Pahlevi, and Jihan Sadat as some of the conference's "official" Third World representatives. We begin to reformulate the dichotomy when we no longer choose to see these representatives as "Third World feminists," but as agents of their respective governments: agents of patriarchy, capitalism, and imperialism. Suddenly the First World/Third World dichotomy emerges as the arena where the split between the ruling class and the working class, between those in power and the disenfranchised, is exposed.

SELECTION 16.6

Satyagraha*

Mohandas K. Gandhi

[*Here Gandhi sought to explain his principle of social change, namely,* satyagraha, *as a truth-force and love-force. It is more than mere passive resistance and nonviolence. Through patience and self-suffering, it is a vindication and an insistence upon the truth by way of civil disobedience.*]

3: Satyagraha

For the past thirty years I have been preaching and practicing Satyagraha. The principles of Satyagraha, as I know it today, constitute a gradual evolution.

Satyagraha differs from Passive Resistance as the North Pole from the South. The latter has been conceived as a weapon of the weak and does not exclude the use of physical force or violence for the purpose of gaining one's end, whereas the former has been conceived as a weapon of the strongest and excludes the use of violence in any shape or form.

The term *Satyagraha* was coined by me in South Africa to express the force that the Indians there used for full eight years and it was coined in order to distinguish it from the movement then going on in the United Kingdom and South Africa under the name of Passive Resistance.

Its root meaning is holding on to truth, hence truth-force. I have also called it Love-force or Soul-force. In the application of Satyagraha I discovered in the earliest stages that pursuit of truth did not admit of violence being inflicted on one's opponent but that he must be weaned from error by patience and sympathy. For what appears to be truth to the one may appear to be error to the other. And patience means self-suffering. So the doctrine came to mean vindication of truth not by infliction of suffering on the opponent but on one's self.

But on the political field the struggle on behalf of the people mostly consists in opposing error in the shape of unjust laws. When you have failed to bring the error home to the law-giver by way of petitions and the like, the only remedy open to you, if you do not wish to submit to error, is to compel him by physical force to yield to you or

---

by suffering in your own person by inviting the penalty for the breach of the law. Hence Satyagraha largely appears to the public as Civil Disobedience or Civil Resistance. It is civil in the sense that it is not criminal.

The lawbreaker breaks the law surreptitiously and tries to avoid the penalty, not so the civil resister. He ever obeys the laws of the State to which he belongs, not out of fear of the sanctions but because he considers them to be good for the welfare of society. But there come occasions, generally rare, when he considers certain laws to be so unjust as to render obedience to them a dishonour. He then openly and civilly breaks them and quietly suffers the penalty for their breach. And in order to register his protest against the action of the law givers, it is open to him to withdraw his co-operation from the State by disobeying such other laws whose breach does not involve moral turpitude.

In my opinion, the beauty and efficacy of Satyagraha are so great and the doctrine so simple that it can be preached even to children. It was preached by me to thousands of men, women and children commonly called indentured Indians with excellent results. . . .

7: The Theory and Practice of Satyagraha

Carried out to its utmost limit, Satyagraha is independent of pecuniary or other material assistance; certainly, even in its elementary form, of physical force or violence. Indeed, violence is the negation of this great spiritual force, which can only be cultivated or wielded by those who will entirely eschew violence. It is a force that may be used by individuals as well as by communities. It may be used as well in political as in domestic affairs. Its universal applicability is a demonstration of its permanence and invincibility. It can be used alike by men, women and children. It is totally untrue to say that it is a force to be used only by the weak so long as they are not capable of meeting violence by violence. This superstition arises from the incompleteness of the English expression, *passive resistance*. It is impossible for those who consider themselves to be weak to apply this force. Only those who realize that there is something in man which is superior to the brute nature in him and that the latter always yields to it, can effectively be Satyagrahis. This force is to violence, and, therefore, to all tyranny, all injustice, what light is to darkness. In politics, its use is based upon the immutable maxim, that government of the people is possible only so long as they consent either consciously or unconsciously to be governed. . . . We have taken long to achieve what we set about striving for. That was because our Satyagraha was not of the most complete type. All Satyagrahis do not understand the full value of the force, nor have we men who always from conviction refrain from violence. The use of this force requires the adoption of poverty, in the sense that we must be indifferent whether we have the wherewithal to feed or clothe ourselves. During the past struggle, all Satyagrahis, if any at all, were not prepared to go that length. Some again were only Satyagrahis so called. They came without any conviction, often with mixed motives, less often with impure motives. Some even, whilst engaged in the struggle, would gladly have resorted to violence but for most vigilant supervision. Thus it was that the struggle became prolonged; for the exercise of the purest soul-force, in its perfect form, brings about instantaneous relief. For this exercise, prolonged training of the individual soul is an absolute necessity, so that a perfect Satyagrahi has to be almost, if not entirely, a perfect man. We cannot all suddenly become such men, but if my proposition is correct—as I know it to be correct—the greater the spirit of Satyagraha in us, the better men will we become. Its use, therefore, is, I think, indisputable, and it is a force, which, if it became universal, would revolutionize social ideals and do away with despotisms and the ever-growing militarism under which the nations of the West are groaning and are being almost crushed to death, and which fairly promises to overwhelm even the nations of the East. If the past struggle has produced even a few Indians who would dedicate themselves to the task of becoming Satyagrahis as nearly perfect as possible, they would not only have served themselves in the truest sense of the term, they would also have served humanity at large. Thus viewed, Satyagraha is the noblest and best education. It should come, not after the ordinary education in letters, of children, but it should precede it. It will not be denied, that a child, before it begins to write its alphabet and to gain worldly knowledge, should know what the soul is, what truth is, what love is, what powers are latent in the soul. It should be an essential of real education that a child should learn, that in the struggle of life, it can easily conquer hate by love, untruth by truth, violence by self-suffering.

SELECTION 16.7

Towards Universal Man*

Rabindranath Tagore

[*Here Tagore sought an alternative view of the human being to the Western notion of the survival of the fittest. In its place he would put the notion that human life is a spiritual journey toward self-emancipation and a rebirth into the infinite.*]

Nature, for its own biological purposes, has created in us a strong faith in life by keeping us unmindful of death. Nevertheless, not only does our physical existence end, but all that it had built up goes to pieces at the peak of achievement. The greatest prosperity dissolves into emptiness; the mightiest empire is overtaken by stupor amidst the flicker of its festive lights. We may be weary of this truism, but it is true none the less. Therefore, all our actions have to be judged according to their harmony with life's background, the background which is death.

And yet it is equally true that, though all our mortal relationships must end, we cannot ignore them while they last. If we behave as if they do not exist, merely because they will not persist, they will all the same exact their dues, with a great deal over by way of penalty. We cannot claim exemption from payment of fare because the railway train has not the permanence of the dwelling house. Trying to ignore bonds that are real even if temporary, only strengthens and prolongs the bondage.

That is why the spirit of attachment and that of detachment have to be reconciled in harmony, and then only will they lead us to fulfilment. Attachment is the force drawing us to truth in its finite aspect, the aspect of what is, while detachment leads us to freedom in the infinity of truth which is the ideal aspect. In the act of walking, attachment is in the step that the foot takes when it touches the earth; detachment is in the movement of the other foot when it raises itself. The harmony of bondage and freedom is the dance of creation. According to the symbolism of Indian thought, Shiva, the male

principle of Truth, represents freedom of the spirit, while Shivani, the female principle, represents the bonds of the material. In their union dwells perfection.

In order to reconcile these opposites, we must come to a true understanding of man; that is, we must not reduce him to the requirements of any particular duty. To look on trees only as firewood, is not to know the tree in its entirety; and to look on man merely as the protector of his country or the producer of its wealth, is to reduce him to soldier or merchant or diplomat, to make his efficacy the measure of his manhood. Such a narrow view is hurtful; those whom we seek to invest with glory are in fact degraded.

How India once looked on man as greater than any purpose he could serve, is revealed in an ancient Sanskrit couplet which may be translated thus:

> For the family, sacrifice the individual; For the community, the family; For the country, the community; For the soul, all the world.

A question will be asked: "What is this soul?" Let us first try to answer a much simpler question: "What is life?" Certainly life is not merely the facts of living that are evident to us, the breathing, digesting and various other functions of the body; not even the principle of unity which comprehends them. In a mysterious manner it holds within itself a future which continually reaches from the envelopment of the present, dealing with unforeseen circumstances, experimenting with new variations. If dead materials choke the path of its ever-unfolding future, then life becomes a traitor that betrays its trust.

The soul is our spiritual life and it contains our infinity within it. It has an impulse that urges our consciousness to break through the dimly lighted walls of animal life where our turbulent passions fight to gain mastery in a narrow enclosure. Though, like animals, man is dominated by his self, he has an instinct that struggles against it, like the rebel life

* From *Towards Universal Man.* New York: Asia Publishing House, 1961.

within a seed that breaks through the dark prison, bringing out its flag of freedom to the realm of light. Our sages in the East have always maintained that self-emancipation is the highest form of freedom for man, since it is his fulfilment in the heart of the Eternal, and not merely a reward won through some process of what is called salvation. . . .

Renounce we must, and through renunciation gain—that is the truth of the inner world. The flower must shed its petals for the sake of fruition, the fruit must drop off for the rebirth of the tree. The child leaves the refuge of the womb in order to achieve further growth of body and mind; next, he has to leave the self-centered security of a narrow world to enter a fuller life which has varied relations with the multitude; lastly comes the decline of the body, and enriched with experience man should now leave the narrower life for the universal life, to which he must dedicate his accumulated wisdom on the one hand and on the other, enter into relationship with the Life Eternal; so that, when finally the decaying body has come to the very end of its tether, the soul views its breaking away quite simply and without regret, in the expectation of its own rebirth into the infinite.

From individual body to community, from community to universe, from universe to Infinity—this is the soul's normal progress.

CHECKLIST

To help you review, a checklist of the key philosophers of this chapter can be found online at www.mhhe.com/moore9e.

KEY TERMS AND CONCEPTS

Afrocentrism 529	Pan-African
apartheid 523	philosophy 520
historiography 518	person 521
ideology 531	perspectivism 518
liberation 527	*satyagraha* 534
negritude 522	

QUESTIONS FOR DISCUSSION AND REVIEW

1. Does one need to appeal to a supernaturally determined standard to demonstrate that an act is good or at least permissible? Why or why not?

2. Is it reasonable for a philosopher to hold to a particular ideology? Is it possible for anyone not to have an ideology?

3. Should philosophy be done the same way in all cultures?

4. Is truth simply a matter of personal belief? Why does the answer to this question matter at all?

5. If Country A invades Country B, do the inhabitants of Country B have the right (or even the responsibility) to harass or kill any citizen of Country A they encounter?

6. If you believed that establishing an American colonial government in some country in South America would benefit the native peoples and help save the rain forests, would you have a responsibility to support colonialism under those circumstances?

7. Why would a physically stronger adversary refrain from destroying a nonviolent opponent? Try to avoid purely strategic considerations; instead, specifically address philosophical issues such as personal identity (or being), ethics, political philosophy, and so forth.

8. Can there be experience without interpretation?

9. What might it mean to me if I were to learn that many people speak of me in categories that I would not use to speak of myself?

10. Is there such a thing as a fixed human nature? Or does human nature change with historical circumstances?

SUGGESTED FURTHER READINGS

Go online to www.mhhe.com/moore9e for a list of suggested further readings.

17

Four Philosophical Problems

I am no stranger to working hard. I have done it all my life. As a result I have become accustomed to expecting success in everything I do. Some people call me lucky, but I know better.   —Donald Trump, *Think Big*

I do not believe in freedom of will. Schopenhauer's words, "Man can indeed do what he wants, but he cannot want what he wants," accompany me in all life situations and console me in my dealings with people, even those that are really painful to me. This recognition of the unfreedom of the will protects me from taking myself and my fellow men too seriously as acting and judging individuals and losing good humour.   —Albert Einstein, *Mein Glaubensbekenntnis*

We devote this chapter to four philosophical problems, or problem clusters, which cut across both analytic and continental philosophical traditions. Of course, other often-discussed philosophical issues can be found elsewhere in this book, presented in their historical context. Can God be shown to exist by rational argument? All major arguments purportedly showing the existence of God are set forth in Chapter 13. Do we have knowledge of the external world? The problem is covered in Chapters 6, 7, and 9. The main ethical frameworks of Western philosophy are discussed in Chapter 10. Do people have natural rights? This is examined in Chapter 12. The problems discussed in this chapter are not presented historically.

FREE WILL

Determinism is the idea that whatever you do, you were destined to do. Whether you are a success or a failure, rich or poor, saint or sinner, it is just a matter of luck. Yes, what you are is a result of the choices you made; but the choices you made, according to determinism, were the result of factors not under your control.

As you can see from the first quotation at the beginning of this chapter, Donald Trump, the real estate mogul known for his innovative hairstyle, doesn't believe this. Mr. Trump scoffs at the suggestion that his success was due to luck. It was due, he thinks, to his hard work. Now, determinism concedes that Donald Trump's success was due to hard work. The problem, determinism says, is that Mr. Trump was *destined* to work hard. According to determinism, Mr. Trump cannot take credit for his hard work *or* for his success. In the final analysis he was just *lucky* that he liked hard work, and lucky again that his hard work paid off.

Determinism startles people. It embraces the idea that whatever you do or become, you deserve neither credit nor blame, because ultimately it was not your doing. When they first hear this theory, many people regard it as bizarre, preposterous, patently false, and stupid.

Unfortunately, the arguments for determinism are not easy to dismiss. Albert Einstein, as you can see from the epigraph at the beginning of this chapter, accepted determinism.

Psychological Determinism

The three main arguments for determinism can be called the *forms of determinism*. First, there is **psychological determinism,** which is the idea that your choices are driven by your preferences, which in turn are created by—well, not by you.

Mr. Trump, for example, is a hard worker, meaning that on any given occasion he is apt to choose working hard over not working hard. Why would he do that? Obviously, because in some sense or other he *prefers* to do that. But—and this is the key question—did he *give himself* this preference? Did he make himself favor hard work? The psychological determinist says he did not. The psychological determinist says that Mr. Trump didn't *make* himself favor hard work—that's just the way he is. His fondness for hard work is something Mr. Trump just has, like his height or blue eyes. And since his predilection for hard work is not really *his* doing, his choosing to work hard is not his doing either. Logically we cannot praise him for choosing to work hard, any more than we can praise him for being six feet tall.

Is it really true that Mr. Trump's preference for working hard is not his doing? Well, consider any preference *you* have and ask yourself whether *you* gave yourself that preference. Imagine you see someone in need whom you can help with little cost to yourself. We will assume you would help the individual. That would be your choice, seemingly up to you to make or not make. But if you help the individual wouldn't it be because, in some sense or other, you prefer helping him or her? Now consider this carefully: Did you *cause yourself* to want to help the person? Did *you* create your desire to give assistance? The determinist says that if you examine the matter carefully you will have to admit that you have no idea how you came by the desire—it is just something you have.

Still not convinced? The determinist will challenge you to create within yourself even a *single* preference by an act of willing. Which do you prefer, McDonald's or Wendy's? Don't have a preference? Fine. Now make yourself have one. Take your time. Can you do it?

It is important, says the psychological determinist, not to be distracted by an irrelevancy. If we were to give Mr. Trump a chance to speak, he might say he does *not* prefer to work hard. He might say he doesn't even *like* to work hard. On the contrary (he might say), he prefers to take it easy. He chooses to work hard, he might say, *despite* his preference, which is for taking it easy. By an act of will, he might say, he *overrode* his preference for taking it easy, and deserves credit for the override.

This line of thinking, according to the psychological determinist, is hopelessly irrelevant. If Mr. Trump chooses to override his fondness for taking it easy, it is because he *prefers* to override it. The *operating* preference at this point (says the determinist) is the *preference to override*, not the preference for taking it easy. And this preference—the preference to override—is not something Mr. Trump can take credit for having.

So at the end of the day, according to the psychological determinist, whether Mr. Trump chooses to work hard because he is fond of hard work or because he desires to override his fondness for laziness makes no difference: either way his choice is an expression of a preference which Mr. Trump cannot take credit for having—and probably has no idea how he came by.

Still, everyone has had the experience of trying to *adjust* their preferences, of trying to make themselves (for example) prefer nutritious, low-calorie steamed broccoli over grease-soaked cardiac-arrest-inducing french fries. And when we perceive that we cannot just change our preferences by grunting hard and willing the change, we may well try to reprogram our preferences *indirectly*. Perhaps reading nutrition books will help, we think. Our perhaps if we see a physician he or she can scare us into liking broccoli. Or we might make a New Year's resolution or go see a hypnotist. We may even discover, if we do one or more of these things, that, Voila! We now like broccoli more than fries!

Notice however that this alteration of our preferences is something that *happened* to us. If our preferences are altered we were just *lucky* that the indirect methods worked. Equally important, if we attempt to adjust our preferences through the indirect approach, the attempt itself is just another instance of our desire to override our existing preferences. And it's just a matter of luck that we had that desire.

Let's take stock. Mr. Trump takes credit for having worked hard, but according to the psychological determinist he shouldn't. Yes, he chose to work hard, or chose to override his laziness, or chose to reprogram himself to relish hard work. It doesn't matter. In final analysis, his choices, whatever they were, were expressions of preferences he did not himself create or even has any idea how he acquired. He cannot take credit for them, says the psychological determinist.

Neuroscientific Determinism

Neuroscientific determinism is the idea that what we think and what we do are determined by unconscious neurophysiological events about which we have no knowledge and over which we have no control.

Now certainly, most would agree that something neurologically important happened when they made a decision—and anyone who is not a brain scientist would concede that he or she has no idea what exactly did happen. The possibilities seem to be either that the neurological event (a) caused the decision, (b) was caused by it, or (c) was not related to it in terms of cause and effect.

The last option (c) is far-fetched. How could it be that the neurophysiological event was somehow magically timed to occur precisely with the decision, yet had nothing to do with it? This option (first proposed by Nicolas Malebrance, 1732-1715) isn't impossible, but it has few adherents.

The second option (b) is almost as far-fetched. Neurophysiologists never invoke "decisions" or "choices" as causes of neurophysiological events. Neurophysiological events are fully explainable in terms of other neurophysiological events.

We are then left with the remaining option (a), that the neurophysiological event caused (or just is) the decision. This option, however, obviously supports determinism. Your neurophysiology isn't something you consciously control. What happened in your brain and central nervous system was not up to you—you probably don't even know what was going on there.

Supporting the idea that the neurophysiological event caused the decision rather than the other way around are famous experiments conducted by neuropsychologist Benjamin Libet in the 1980s. If a scientist discovered that your brain began moving your arm *before* you decided to move it, it would be a powerful reason for thinking that the *decision* did not cause the brain event, but the other way around. What Libet discovered wasn't quite that in so many words, and indeed the import of his work is controversial. What the experiments at least show is that electrical activity (known as the readiness potential) happens in the motor cortex of the (the part of the brain that generates neural impulses that control movement) a second or so before a subject makes a conscious decision to move his or her arm. This certainly could be viewed as the brain initiating movement of the arm before the conscious decision to move it is made. In any case it is a surprising experimental result that anyone who believes in free will must account for.

We do not need to ascertain the relationship between decisions and neurological events here; we go into this relationship in more detail in the next section. Let's just suppose that last night Mr. Trump decided to work late at his office, and let's ask this question: could he have decided *not* to work late in those circumstances? Popular opinion says yes, but determinism says no. Of course, if the answer really is no, then Mr. Trump's decision was just as fixed as his eye color.

But now let's revise the question ever so slightly. When Mr. Trump decided to work late, his brain and central nervous system were in a certain state. *Given that they were in that state, could he have decided last night not to work late?* Neuroscientific determinism says that, if last night Mr. Trump's decision had been different, then necessarily his neurophysiological condition would have had to be different as well. Now, what happens to Mr. Trump at the level of neurophysiology is not up to Mr. Trump (according to neuroscientific determinism). So, yes, Mr. Trump

Causal Determinism

Here are two beliefs dear to common sense. We hold the first belief thanks (in part) to the Atomists.

1. The behavior of atoms is governed entirely by physical law.

2. Humans have free will.

Do you accept both (1) and (2)? We are willing to wager that you do.

Unfortunately, (1) and (2) do not get along comfortably with each other. Here is why. It seems to follow from (1) that whatever an atom does, it has to do, given the existing circumstances, because physical laws determine what each atom does in the existing circumstances. Thus, if the laws determine that an atom does X in circumstance C, then, given circumstance C, the atom has to do X.

But anything that happened as a result of free will presumably did not have to happen. For example, suppose that I, of my own free will, move my arm. Whatever the circumstances were in which I chose to move my arm, I could always have chosen otherwise and not moved my arm. Therefore, when I moved my arm of my own free will, my arm, and thus the atoms in my arm, did not have to move, even given the existing circumstances. Thus, if (2) holds, it is *not true* that an atom must have done

what it did, given the existing circumstances. But if (1) holds, then it *is true*.

As the famous twentieth-century physicist Arthur Eddington said, "What significance is there in my struggle tonight whether I shall give up smoking, if the laws that govern matter already preordain for tomorrow a configuration of matter consisting of pipe, tobacco, and smoke connected with my lips?"

could have decided to not work late last night—but only if conditions not subject to his control had been different. His decision is as fixed as his eye color or his peak oxygen uptake according to neuroscientific determinism.

Causal Determinism

Presumably every event is caused by an antecedent set of events sufficient for the occurrence of the event in question. The same rule, of course, applies to the antecedent events themselves, and to their causes as well. This implies, if you think about it, that any event that actually happens had to happen, or at any rate had to happen given what happened in the far distant past.

From this it follows that, assuming human choices are events, they had to happen, given prior events (which themselves also had to happen). Mr. Trump's decision to stay late at the office is thus, according to **causal determinism,** the result of events that happened before the decision.

Another way of expressing causal determinism is found in the box by that name.

These three forms of (or arguments for) determinism have much in common, but most importantly all three lead to this conclusion: what you do, and what you are, are really just a matter of good (or bad) luck, akin to being tall or short or nearsighted. Jawaharlal Nehru is reported to have said, "Life is like a game of cards. The hand that is dealt you represents determinism; the way you play it is free will." To this, determinism says, "Wrong. The way you play it is also part of what you were dealt."

CONSCIOUSNESS

The problem of consciousness is the concern of the **philosophy of mind,** a vast area of primarily analytic philosophy that deals with the question of whether and how conscious experience can be reconciled with physicalism. **Physicalism,** or materialism as it is often called, is the idea that only physical entities exist. The approach usually taken in the philosophy of mind is to look at everyday psychological vocabulary—with its references to mental states of various sorts, including beliefs, desires, fears, suspicions, hopes, ideas, preferences, choices, thoughts, motives, urges, and so forth—and ask how it is to be analyzed. In recent years, these conceptual inquiries have broadened to encompass the research and findings of psychologists, neuroscientists, computer scientists, linguists, artificial intelligence researchers, and other specialists. The philosophy of mind is no longer the preserve of the professional philosopher.

Let's begin by noting that many—perhaps most—members of Western societies take the position that a person has a nonmaterial or nonphysical mind or soul or spirit associated with his or her physical body. *You* may well take this position, a position known as *dualism* and associated forever with René Descartes (but see the box on Oliva Sabuco in Chapter 6).

Dualism

According to the dualist, every existing thing (except for abstract items, e.g., geometric points, numbers, and brotherhood) is either *physical* (or material, these terms being used interchangeably here) or *nonphysical* (or immaterial or incorporeal, these terms also being interchangeable).

According to dualists, physical things possess physical properties (like density, velocity, charge, temperature, mass, and, most fundamentally, spatial occupancy), and nonphysical things possess nonphysical properties. These latter properties are difficult to specify, though dualists would say that only nonphysical entities can have conscious states or exercise volition. Both physical and nonphysical things can have neutral properties. For example, physical and nonphysical things both have temporal properties, both may be numerous, both belong to groups, and so forth.

A human being, according to the dualist, has (or is) both a physical body and a nonphysical mind (or soul or spirit). Further, according to the dualist, a person's nonphysical and physical components are *interactive:* if someone comes along and gives you a shove, you may become angry. In other words, the shoving of your physical body causes anger to arise in your nonphysical mind. Or—to run this in reverse—when you decide to do something, your body normally follows through; that is, your nonphysical mind causes your physical body to walk or run or speak or whatever it is you want your body to do.

Actually, a dualist does not have to believe that the immaterial mind and the material body interact, but most dualists do, so when we talk about *dualism* here, we mean **interactionist dualism.**

Now, to the extent that many people have ever thought about it, it seems pretty nearly self-evident that a human being has a nonphysical component of some sort, be it called a mind, soul, spirit, or something else. But the difficulties in dualism have led many analytic philosophers to doubt whether dualism is a viable theory at all, and they have cast about for more attractive alternatives. The most heavily subscribed alternatives have all been physicalist. They are *behaviorism, identity theory,* and *functionalism.*

Behaviorism

The word *behaviorism* is notoriously ambiguous. **Behaviorism** in one sense is a *methodological principle of psychology,* according to which fruitful psychological investigation confines itself to such psychological phenomena as can be behaviorally defined. *Philosophical behaviorism* is the doctrine we will now explain, which we are attributing to Gilbert Ryle (1900–1976). Ryle denied being a behaviorist, incidentally. Still, *The Concept of Mind* (1949) is regarded as one of the most powerful expositions of (philosophical) behaviorism ever written. (Hereafter, when we refer to behaviorism, we will mean *philosophical* behaviorism.)

According to Ryle, when we refer to someone's mental states (and this someone might be oneself), when we refer, for example, to a person's beliefs or thoughts or wishes, we are *not,* contrary to what is ordinarily supposed, referring to the immaterial states of a nonphysical mind. There is indeed no such thing as a nonphysical mind. There is, Ryle says, *no ghost within the machine.* A person is only a complicated—a very highly complicated—physical organism, one capable of doing the amazing sorts of things that people are capable of doing. When we attribute a so-called mental state to a person, we are in fact attributing to him or her a *propensity* or *disposition* to act or behave in a certain way.

For example, when you attribute to your friend the belief that it is going to rain, it might *seem* that you view her as having or possessing a nonphysical thing of some sort, termed a *belief,* a nonphysical, intangible, and unobservable entity that exists within her mind. But in fact, argues Ryle, to say that someone believes it is going to rain is merely to attribute to her a propensity or disposition to do things like close the windows and cover the barbecue and say things like "It's going to rain" and not to do certain other sorts of things like wash the car and hang out the sheets.

It is likewise when we credit someone with a thought or an idea. Thoughts and ideas, like beliefs, are not nonmaterial things, says Ryle. They are not even *things* at all. To be sure, "thought," "idea," and "belief" are words for things, that is, *thing-words*. But these thing-words are (to borrow an expression Ryle used in a different context) *systematically misleading*. Because they are thing-words, they mislead or tempt us into thinking that there must be things for which they stand. And because there seem to be no physical things for which they stand, we are tempted to conclude that they stand for nonphysical things.

In fact, however, when we say that someone has a specific thought, all we can really be doing is attributing to him or her a propensity to say or do certain things, a propensity to behave in certain ways. References to someone's beliefs, ideas, thoughts, knowledge, motives, and other mental "things" must be analyzed or understood as references to the ways the person is apt to behave given certain conditions.

Might not Ryle have strengthened his case by providing an *actual analysis* of a mental-state expression, a translation into behavioral language of a simple mental-state proposition such as "She believes that it is time to go home"? Indeed, Ryle could *not* strengthen his case in this way, for it is not his position that such translations could be made. According to behaviorists, there is no definite and finite list of behaviors and behavioral propensities that we are attributing to someone when we say, "She believes it is time to go home." Instead, we are referring in an *oblique and loose way* to an indefinite and open set of behaviors and behavioral tendencies.

This, then, is **philosophical behaviorism:**

- There is no such thing as a nonphysical mind.
- Mental-state thing-words do not really denote things at all. A statement in which such words appear is a kind of loose shorthand reference to behaviors (including verbal behaviors) and behavioral propensities.
- Statements about a person's mental states cannot actually be translated into some set of statements about the person's behavior and behavioral propensities, because the sets of behaviors and behavioral propensities to which they in fact refer are indefinite and open and depend on the situations in which the person happens to be.

Behaviorism nicely accounts for another problem facing dualism, namely, explaining why it is that brain scientists and neuroscientists just never do have to postulate the existence of nonphysical mental states to explain the causes and origin of our behavior. The reason they never have to postulate such things, according to the behaviorist, is because there are no such things.

Identity Theory

Another physicalist realm of philosophy of the mind is **identity theory.** According to identity theory, so-called mental phenomena are all physical phenomena within the brain and central nervous system. A thought, for example, according to identity

Is mind activity nothing other than brain activity?

theory, is in fact some sort of occurrence within the brain/nervous system, though we do not yet know enough about the brain or central nervous system to stipulate which particular occurrence it is. Among the many adherents of identity theory is the Australian philosopher J. J. C. Smart (1920–2012), who explains a version of identity theory at the end of this chapter.

Notice that the identity theorist does not say merely that thinking (or any other mental occurrence) is *correlated with* or *involves* a neural process of some sort. The claim is rather that thinking *is* a neural process. Just as light *is* electromagnetic radiation (and is not just "involved in" or "correlated with" electromagnetic radiation), and just as heat *is* movement of molecules, thinking and all other mental phenomena, according to identity theory, *are* physical states and happenings within the brain and central nervous system.

Beginning philosophy students sometimes have a difficult time distinguishing behaviorism from identity theory, usually, we think, for two reasons.

First, behaviorism and identity theory are both physicalistic (materialist) theories in the sense that, according to both, you and we and all other people are completely physical organisms: neither theory countenances the existence of the nonmaterial or nonphysical soul, spirit, or mind; and neither theory thinks that mental-state thing-words denote nonmaterial or nonphysical things.

Second, few theorists are *pure* behaviorists or identity theorists. Most philosophers who call themselves identity theorists do in fact accept a behavioristic analysis of at least some assertions about mental states, and most behaviorists do likewise accept identity theory with respect to some mental states.

But the two theories really should not be confused. *Identity theory* holds that mind-states are brain-states, that when we speak of a person's beliefs,

Monkeys Control Robotic Arm with Brain Implants

WASHINGTON POST

Scientists in North Carolina have built a brain implant that lets monkeys control a robotic arm with their thoughts, marking the first time that mental intentions have been harnessed to move a mechanical object.

The technology could someday allow people with paralyzing spinal cord injuries to operate machines or tools with their thoughts as naturally as others today do with their hands. It might even allow some paralyzed people to move their arms or legs again, by transmitting the brain's directions not to a machine but directly to the muscles in those latent limbs....

In the new experiments, monkeys with wires running from their brains to a robotic arm were able to use their thoughts to make the arm perform tasks. Before long, scientists said they will upgrade the monkeys' devices so they can transmit their mental commands to machines wirelessly.

The experiments, led by Miguel A. L. Nicolelis of Duke University in Durham and published today in the journal *PLoS Biology*, are the latest in a progression of increasingly science fictionlike studies in which animals—and in a few cases people—have learned to use the brain's subtle electrical signals to operate simple devices.

Until now, those achievements have been limited to "virtual" actions, such as making a cursor move across a computer screen, or to small actions such as flipping a little lever.

The new work is the first in which any animal has learned to use its brain to move a robotic device in all directions in space and to perform several interrelated movements—such as reaching toward an object, grasping it and adjusting the grip strength depending on the object's weight.

The device relies on tiny electrodes, each one resembling a wire thinner than a human hair. After removing patches of skull from two monkeys to expose the outer surface of their brains, Nicolelis and his colleagues stuck 96 of those tiny wires about a millimeter deep in one monkey's brain and 320 of them in the other animal's brain.

The monkeys were unaffected by the surgery, Nicolelis said. But now they had tufts of wires protruding from their heads, which could be hooked up to other wires that ran through a computer and on to a large mechanical arm.

Then came the training, with the monkeys first learning to move the robot arm with a joystick. The arm was kept in a separate room—"If you put a 50-kilogram robot in front of them, they get very nervous," Nicolelis said—but the monkeys could track their progress by watching a representation of the arm and its motions on a video screen.

The monkeys quickly learned how to use the joystick to make the arm reach and grasp for objects, and how to adjust their grip on the joystick to vary the robotic hand's grip strength. They could see on the monitor when they missed their target or dropped it from having too light a grip, and they were rewarded with sips of juice when they performed their tasks successfully.

While the monkeys trained, a computer tracked the patterns of bioelectrical activity in the animals' brains. The computer figured out that certain patterns amounted to "reach." Others, it became clear, meant "grasp." Gradually, the computer learned to "read" the monkeys' minds.

Then the researchers unplugged the joystick so the robotic arm's movements depended completely on a monkey's brain activity. In effect, the computer that had been studying the animal's neural firing patterns was now an interpreter, decoding the brain signals according to what it had learned from the joystick games and sending instructions to the robot arm.

At first, Nicolelis said, the monkey kept moving the joystick, not realizing her brain was now solely in charge of the arm's movements. Then, he said, an amazing thing happened.

"She stops moving her arm," he said, "but the cursor keeps playing the game, and the robot arm is moving around."

The animal was controlling the robot with its thoughts.

Experiments like these, in which monkeys control a robotic arm with their thoughts, seem utterly mysterious and incomprehensible from the standpoint of dualism.

From Rick Weiss, "Monkeys Control Robotic Arm with Brain Implants," *The Washington Post*, October 13, 2003, p. A1. © 2003, The Washington Post, reprinted with permission.

---

thoughts, hopes, ideas, and the like, we are in fact referring to events and processes and states within his or her brain and nervous system. *Philosophical behaviorism* holds that when we use our everyday psychological vocabulary to describe someone, we are really just talking in a shorthand way about her or his behavioral propensities.

Functionalism

Physicalist philosophers do not believe that people have nonphysical minds, and they deny that mental thing-words refer to states or processes of a nonphysical variety. But many physicalists cannot accept the idea that each distinct mental state or process is identical with a specific brain state or process. After all, inhabitants of distant galaxies (or even robots we ourselves might someday build) might also have feelings, hopes, and desires even if the matter that composes these beings is arranged quite differently from ours.

Functionalism is the idea that a mental state is defined not by some arrangement of physical matter but by its function: what it causes and is caused by in the network of sensory stimuli, behavior, and other mental states. On this view a mental state is like a garage door opener or word processor. Such things aren't defined by what they are made of or how they are assembled, but rather by their function. What is a mousetrap? The question calls for an explanation of what a mousetrap *does*. Likewise, if you want to know what beliefs or other mental states or processes are, the correct answer is in terms of their function—their role relative to sensory input, other mental states, and behavioral output. According to this view, although it is true that nothing nonphysical happens in your brain when you have a belief or hear a musical note or think about your mom, it is misleading to suppose these things are "nothing but" brain states.

Functionalism thus explains nicely why psychological talk—whether of the commonsense ("folk") or scientific variety—cannot be translated into neurology talk. It's not because mental states are nonphysical, but because they can be explained only functionally. Functionalism seems to provide a conceptual framework for psychological research that doesn't commit the researcher either to murky Cartesian metaphysics or to the implausible reductionist idea that psychology ultimately is nothing more than neurophysiology.

However, there are those who say that functionalism doesn't explain the most important aspect of mental life: *what it is like* to the person experiencing it. One of the more influential recent voices in the philosophy of mind is David Chalmers (b. 1966), who has refocused attention on the need for a theory of the "hard problem of consciousness," the problem of why and how the phenomenal or experiential properties of conscious states could exist in the first place; why or how there could be such a thing as what it is like to have a conscious experience. Many readers, we suspect, will sympathize instantly with Chalmers on this. Functionalism, behaviorism, and identity theory seem not to solve the hard problem of consciousness as much as to discount it as not worth thinking about.

Zombies

You know what a zombie is, right? Are you sure? Because there are actually at least three kinds of zombies, all of which are humanlike in some way but unlike humans in the most important way of all: consciousness. No zombie has it. This makes zombies very, very interesting to some philosophers, especially those who study the mind and its complex workings. But if zombies are mindless hypothetical creatures, and philosophers are all about thinking, what's for a philosopher to be fascinated by? Good question.

There are the zombies of Hollywood, the B-movie flesh-eating type. The zombies in *The Walking Dead* television series are a fine example. You will want to avoid zombies of this sort, because they will eat you. Philosophers pass on them as not having redeeming philosophical interest. Then there are the Haitian zombies found in the vodou (voodoo) belief tradition. These zombies are believed to have once been real people but have lost their souls or their free will as the result of the casting of a spell, so they are basically slaves who do the bidding of their masters. Those aren't the ones philosophers like to discuss, either.

It's the third type, the philosophical zombies (also known as **p-zombies**), that you will encounter sooner or later if you read articles on consciousness. Philosophical zombies are physically and behaviorally identical to humans but lack any form of conscious mind. If you stick one with a pin, it will say "Ouch" or, perhaps, "What do you think you are doing?" but it will not experience sensations. This kind of zombie holds fascinating possibilities in the realm of impossibilities, if you will. David Chalmers, mentioned above, has been joined by other philosophers and even some psychologists and neuroscientists who use the concept of the p-zombie to question physicalism, which (as you know) is the idea that consciousness—the mind—can in principle be explained completely without having to make references to nonphysical entities or processes. Chalmers uses his own "zombie twin"—Zombie Dave—to discuss such things. This, you will recognize, is a philosophical thought experiment. Zombie Dave's environment, physiology, and history are the same as that of Chalmers—but Zombie Dave lacks conscious experience. In his book, *The Conscious Mind*, Chalmers asserts that there is a logical possibility that zombies exist even though they are impossible from the standpoint of nature. The idea of zombie, he says, is internally consistent, and therefore there is at least a *possible* world where zombies do exist.

This "logical possibility" that zombies exist, according to Chalmers, can be used to argue against physicalism (which as you know includes behaviorism, identity theory, and functionalism): if there IS a possible world just like ours except that it's populated with zombies, then that would imply that the existence of consciousness in our world is a "further, nonphysical fact" about us. In other words, if p-zombies are logically possible, then there is more to us than our physical selves.

This, then, has been an overview of the philosophy of mind—the branch of philosophy concerned with the problem of consciousness. That "problem," although hugely multifaceted, boils down to the question of whether and how conscious experience can be reconciled with physicalism, the idea that only physical entities exist.

THE ETHICS OF GENEROSITY: THE PROBLEM OF THE GIFT[1]

How sweet, how precious is a gift, for which the giver will not suffer us to pay even our thanks, which he forgot that he had given even while he was giving it.   —Seneca, "On Benefits"

We are a culture of gift-givers. Most cultures are. We like to give and receive gifts, and we celebrate all sorts of occasions with the ritual of giving a gift—birthdays, weddings, graduation, religious holidays such as Christmas and Hanukkah, baby showers, anniversaries, good report cards—you name it, and someone is enjoying receiving or giving a gift to celebrate it. You may be surprised to discover, however, that this simple act has been the fascination of philosophers and other

---

[1] By Anne D'Arcy.

What could be more pleasing than giving (or getting) a present? But, is that pleasure morally deserving? The question turns out to be complicated, as you will see when you read this section.

thinkers across the disciplines for centuries. This is because the giving and receiving of gifts is not so simple as it appears on the surface. Consider, for example, the paradox that giving a gift to someone more often than not makes the receiver feel indebted. Is that really what we wanted to do when we presented the gift—to give something with a catch?

How do you feel if someone gives you a gift for some holiday, and you haven't thought to give them one? Do you feel awkward, guilty? Does it take away some of the pleasure of the gift itself? Do you then feel obligated to return that favor at some future time just to balance your personal books? Do you ever feel it's a duty to give rather than a delight? The word "gift" means "offering," but it also means "poison." What is a poisonous gift? Are some of these glitches in the gift cycle the poisoning of the gift? Is it possible to give a gift that is only positive without the negative of indebtedness? Is there any such thing as a gift without motive, without some expectation of return or of gratitude? In other words, is there any such thing as a true gift, a pure gift? Is it possible to remove giving from its social constraints by transcending ourselves in the space between self and other without losing our sense of self in the process? How does time figure into this complex circular equation? These are some of the questions philosophers ponder when they consider the gift.

All of the considerations mentioned above are part of what can be called the circle of obligation created by the act of giving: a gift implies a debt, which the receiver feels obliged to repay in some way. This phenomenon of the imprisoned gift, examined in all its complexities, is an ongoing focus of academics in anthropology, economics, social history, ethics, philosophy, deconstruction, and gender studies. Thinkers have been exchanging their views and constructing theories of gift exchange for all these years without arriving at any definitive answers. In fact, Alan Schrift (*The Logic of the Gift,* 1997) claims that the theme of the gift is one of the main focal points where all contemporary interdisciplinary discourses intersect.

We should mention a few key thinkers, any one of which would be fascinating to study in depth, to create a historical context. We could start with Ralph Waldo Emerson (1803–1882), the famous American essayist and poet. In his essay, "Gifts" (1844), Emerson posed an underlying question: when we discuss gift-giving, should we focus on the giver, the receiver, the gift itself, the relationship between the giver and the receiver, or the interconnections among all of these? This is an excellent way to frame our exploration of the ways the gift operates in our culture, what giving implies, whether and how a gift alters the relationship between the giver and the receiver, and how the implication of reciprocation makes the giver and the receiver feel. Emerson claimed that the only true gift is the gift of oneself because a gift must be a sacrifice, painful to give, must be unnecessary to the recipient, and must be excessive. In addition, both giving and receiving, he claims, run risks of various kinds of perversions. We can receive anything from love because that is just another way of receiving it from ourselves, but we never quite forgive someone who "bestows" a gift on us.

Marcel Mauss (1872–1950), a sociologist and anthropologist, in *Essai Sur le don* (1925), argued that although the gift may appear to be free, it is not. He analyzed the gift-giving rules in archaic societies, cultures that precede money as the unit of exchange, and detected obligation to return in the gift-giving cycle. His findings pointed the way to an economic anthropology. Many philosophers have written commentaries on Mauss's work, much of it critical of his failure to ask an important question: why does the donor give?

Intrinsic to Mauss's ethnographic studies of archaic societies is something unique: the *hau*. The **hau** is a kind of spiritual bond that exists in these cultures, a bond that crosses over from individuals to groups to the larger community and forms a pattern that makes the whole more than the sum of its parts in the cycle of gift-giving. There is a kind of surplus value in this view of the gift, a kind of self-lessness attached to the gift that transcends even the gift itself. It is a matter of collective giving, a social phenomenon, the product of community life itself.

Mauss is credited with opening the dialogue on gift and exchange, and his work is regarded as a classic in the study of the gift.

Georges Bataille [Bah-thai] (1897–1962), a French intellectual whose writing crossed the disciplines of literature, anthropology, philosophy, economy, sociology, and the history of art, is often referred to as "the metaphysician of evil." His writings were designed to repudiate everything that civil society values, so he exaggerated whatever would be unacceptable to discuss in polite society and took it to an extreme that is shocking and appalling. He thumbed his nose at what he regarded as the bourgeois view of eroticism, for example, so his works were full of topics such as excrement, deviance, death, sex, degradation, violence, blood, and sacrifice, all accelerating to an extreme that is often pornographic and certainly repugnant. He rejected traditional ways of portraying ideas in literature, which is one of the ways philosophers write for the general reader. Instead, he wanted to shock his readers into seeing society as he saw it, and this was his radical way of doing it. He was fascinated by the potential power of the obscene. For example, one of his texts was entitled, "The Solar Anus."

Bataille described "excess" that accelerates. His characters became obsessed, consumed with giving, and trapped in an endless, unproductive cycle of exchange, whether the exchange is a glorious one or is catastrophic. For example, in "The Story of the Eye," there is obsessive sexuality involving violent and repeated rape, necrophilia, coprophilia, fetish objects such as eyeballs, and numerous other types of deviance.

Are you curious about what kind of man would write of such things and become famous for it in the process as a philosopher and social commentator? We invited you to view the only TV interview of Georges Bataille ever made on YouTube, entitled "Georges Bataille: Literature and Evil." You may well be surprised to listen to a mild-mannered, soft-spoken man who appears to be the epitome of the French intellectual. Note, in particular, the reason he gives toward the end of the interview—we must face evil, confront it, in order to overcome it. We must not be afraid to explore the activities we have been taught belong to the dark side of human nature.

Well, perhaps, but how does Bataille's penchant for obscenity and pornography relate to the philosophy of the gift, you may well be asking at this point. The key word is *excess*. Everything Bataille wrote is of an excessive nature, regardless of the subject matter. And what is excess, if not a perverted form of generosity? And finally, what is the impetus of the gift? A gift springs from some form of generosity.

In *Thus Spake Zarathustra* (1891), Friedrich Nietzsche (1844–1900), the important German philosopher, cultural critic, poet, and philologist we covered in Chapter 8, reflected on the necessity of gift-giving. His character, Zarathustra, understood only too well that when you give, the gift can be regarded as a *pharmakon* (poison) because the receiver feels obligated to return the gift, yet cannot because they have nothing to give of equal value. Giving gifts is actually an art, said Zarathustra, because the trick is not to cause the receiver a feeling of indebtedness. Zarathustra complicated his remarks by pointing out that he never felt impoverished by his generosity and continued to regard gift-giving as the highest virtue. A good student, he pointed out, returns the gift by surpassing the teacher, but since the teacher never knows this, the gift doesn't return to the teacher, so it is not a counter-gift.

Martin Heidegger [HY-dig-ger] (1889–1976), the famous German philosopher we discussed in Chapter 8, took a different approach to the concept of the gift. His reflections on "the gift of Being" described the gift as not within a cycle of exchange, but in terms of time. Heidegger reconfigured the gift as "the forgetting of the gift-event of Being." He used the word "event" to indicate that the gift is a happening in time. According to Heidegger, a gift is impossible in time. A gift occurs only outside time.

Think of time as an unbroken directional thrust that is always moving forward. Now think of us existing as part of this movement. If the only true gift is outside of time as Heidegger insisted, then the only way a gift could exist is if that time directional is somehow interrupted or broken for a fraction of a second. Only during that break in the movement of time, which is still connected to time but is not actually a part of time, could a gift exist. Still not clear? Think of a baseball thrown up into the air. Its trajectory is in one direction: up. But at a certain point, gravity stops its trajectory, and the direction reverses. The ball falls until it hits the ground or is caught by someone. In that fraction of a second it took for the direction of the ball to reverse, you could imagine that time stopped. And in that brief nanosecond, there could be the gift.

Pierre Bourdieu [Bor-DYOO] (1930–2002), a French philosopher, sociologist, and anthropologist, in *The Logic of Practice* (1980), pointed out that the very question of whether there can be a pure gift can't be answered without reference to our social and political customs, both of which assume an economy of exchange. In the social sphere, acts of generosity and kindness, he said, tend to create lasting dependencies. Think of our welfare system, for example. People without income need to eat and have money for clothing, transportation, and necessary goods. Our welfare system provides food stamps and a stipend for them, but Bourdieu would have seen that charitable act as creating a generational chain of dependence on the social welfare system.

The question of the gift, Bourdieu claimed, is ultimately a political question because our political economy is entrenched in our system of money, banking, investments, loans, credit, taxes, interest, etc. In order to answer the question of the gift, we'd have to be able to think outside what we take for granted in our political economy. And how hard would that be? Impossible, according to Bourdieu. We have our reality, our habits of exchange, our social conditions, our symbolic goods, and the political philosophy that underlies it to contend with. We can't just think outside a box that encompasses our whole way of life. We would have to replace our existing economy with another frame of reference entirely, and that would be an invention, not a reality.

Bourdieu regarded the gift exchange as "the counterfeit coin of generosity." By this he meant that both on an individual and collective basis, our social practices are entrenched in our political practices. We pretend that the gift is virtuous, is an act of generosity, but in fact, it's part of our economic exchange system. The gift is counterfeit because we pretend, both as individuals and as a society, that it isn't, that it's real, free of self-interest, and is part of an ideal vision, but its true nature is to collect symbolic capital in the form of a counter-gift. The notion of the gift as disinterested generosity is a kind of collective hypocrisy that we've all bought into. As an example, Bourdieu told the story of a nobleman who gave his son a purse of gold coins and sent him out into the world to seek his fortune. The son returned after some time with the gold purse of coins intact, pleased with himself that he didn't spend any of it. His father was so infuriated that he threw the purse out the window. Why? Because it was an expectation that the son would return with coins or goods worth much more than the original value of the gold coins. In other words, he didn't spend the money to make money, didn't trade or invest it. He failed to make his fortune, failed his mission. This is analogous to our situation, according to Bourdieu. There is an expectation, based on our political economy of exchange, that drives our social actions, including gift-giving. The giving is not outside the system we live in. A gift expects a counter-gift. Since that's who we are, a pure gift is impossible.

Hélène Cixous [aay-LAYN seek-soo] (1937–), whom we discussed in Chapter 14, a French/Algerian philosopher, literary critic, and playwright, in *The Newly Born Woman* (1986) didn't believe there is such a thing as a pure gift. In her view, generosity was a value in itself, and the act of giving was pleasurable. Gifts should be freely given to the Other, who would then also be free to give. Giving, she said, springs from a desire for relationship. This relationship is comprised of Self plus Other, the giver and the receiver. In this kind of relationship, the act of giving without any expectation of return transforms the giver and the receiver; they become one. The one gives herself pleasure in the act of giving to the Other. Giving is an endless cycle, and there is plenty for all.

The one thing that distinguished the Cixousian concept of gift from all others is that, although she claimed there is no such thing as a pure gift, the possibility of taking can be given. What does this mean? It means that Cixous has invented a way around the trap of the gift cycle that causes a feeling of indebtedness. If you take something, if you steal it, it can no longer be considered a gift. But if the giver has allowed you to take it, then allowing you is the real gift. Cixous's theory transformed the nature of both the giving and the gift. The gift was no longer something that was already there. It's a stolen gift, taken with the permission of the giver. What was to be given is taken instead. This is why she said what must be given is "a gift to take."

Want an example? Let's say you want to feed the birds in your yard. You would get pleasure out of giving them seed and watching them eat it. But the birds are shy. They're wild creatures who are terrified of you. They aren't going to eat the seed if you offer it from your hand. So what do you do? You place the seed in a feeder, or you scatter it around the yard, where they can take it. Your seed is a "gift to take."

Luce Irigaray [e-RIG-uh-ray] (1932–), discussed in Chapter 14, a Belgian feminist philosopher, linguist, cultural theorist, sociologist, and psychoanalyst, saw the gift as having no object. She claimed it exists prior to being given, before there is any donor or donee. In *Elemental Passions*, she wrote: "The gift is given before any separate identities [of giver and receiver]. Even before the gift." In her view, the gift is therefore outside the circle of exchange. Giving, she said, is a part of offering oneself to the Other. In this process, there is a becoming as love changes the nature of the relationship between the giver and the receiver, that is, the "I" and the "You." The "I" [the giver] is not fixed as "not you" in Irigaray's model of the gift. They are not separate and distinct, not opposites. The "I" and the "You" become one in the process of loving. If there are no opposing parties in the gift, there is no circle of exchange, and there is also no loss of self in the giving. Love entirely transforms the gift relationship.

Need an example? Think of a pregnant woman, about to become a mother, which we regard as one of the most loving of all relationships. She shops for her baby before it's born, lovingly choosing pretty little clothes and toys. Are those gifts? Not yet—because there is no baby yet to give them to! Will they be gifts when the baby is born? Certainly the baby won't know, one way or the other. An infant considers itself part of its mother until it learns to distinguish between itself and the mother, usually many months after its birth. The baby that is literally a part of her before it's born will still be, in both the mother's view and in the baby's view, part of the mother after it's born. In Irigaray's model of the gift, the mother's all-encompassing love for her child exists before the choosing of any material gifts and continues afterwards. The gift of love is the real gift.

There are many others whose philosophy of gift we could explore (Aristotle, Kant, Levinas, Marion, Deleuze to name a few), but perhaps the most influential of contemporary Continental philosophers is Jacques Derrida (1930–2004), also French/Algerian. We discussed Derrida [day-ree-DAH] in Chapter 8. Building on Heidegger and Mauss, in *Given Time: Counterfeit Money* (1992), Derrida asserted that there is no such thing as a pure gift, that a true gift is not only impossible, but is THE impossible, as will be explained below. Derrida claimed that a true gift not only requires the absence of a counter-gift (a return), but that the gift must not even be perceived as one by the giver and by the receiver, "the donor" and "the donee." Even the simple intention of the gift, Derrida said, implies a return. The giver is paid back in "gratifying images of goodness or generosity" and "self-approval" (*Given Time*, 23). The true gift, according to Derrida, is unconditional, entirely gratuitous. It is outside the circle of obligation, the circle of commodity exchange. As soon as the gift is linked to thought, it enters that circle. So a gift must be spontaneous as well. It must also be outside the idea of generosity since generosity is the desire to give and involves conscious thought. As soon as there is any inkling of intention to give, there is no gift: it is annulled. And as soon as the gift is recognized as such by the donee, once again, there is no gift. Think about giving a present to a friend. Right now. As soon as you think about doing it, you have entered the vicious circle of the gift, and there is no escape.

In *Given Time,* Derrida referred to a brief story by Charles Baudelaire (1821–1867) called "Counterfeit Money," in which two friends leaving a tobacco shop encounter a beggar. The narrator of this little story gives a coin to the beggar. His companion gives the beggar a coin of a much larger denomination, which at first seems a most generous act. But the friend says the coin he gave the beggar is counterfeit! The narrator despises his companion for "doing evil out of stupidity." He might have forgiven him a mean-spirited act, but to do what he did without even realizing the consequences and feeling good about it to boot earns him the narrator's disgust. The giver has given a counterfeit gift—so is it a gift, or is it a poisoned gift? Let's consider some possibilities: If the donor knew the coin was counterfeit, then he knew he wasn't giving a gift at all, and the receiver of the gift may well end up in jail if he tries to spend it. On the other hand, the receiver may pass it off and get more money in change than the counterfeit coin's face value, in which case the "gift" would have multiplied: now is it a gift? What if the narrator's friend was lying, and the coin really wasn't counterfeit? Is there any way in which this changes the status of the gift? No doubt you can think of other scenarios that would complicate the question of whether or not this is a pure gift.

Derrida spent over half of his book studying the ramifications of this little story. How is this possible? It's because, as the world's best known deconstructionist, Derrida approached an idea from every possible angle, including all the sub-ideas it suggests. Every text, he claimed, already contains subtexts. He identified them, explored them, and when they collided or merged with other ideas, he followed those wherever they took him. Understandably, this kind of examination is a comprehensive, endless process. The process includes references to other thinkers and their texts in excruciating detail, asides, footnotes that take up more of the page than the text itself, and references to his other works. Reading a Derridean text is an exhausting and exhaustive task. But in order to understand Derrida's study of the gift cycle, we must read along with him through all the obstacles and twists and turns he discovered and not be impatient to find out where he stopped—because he never did. An idea in one of his books appeared again in another of his books with threads of ideas attached to that idea, and there were meanderings into multiple fields and disciplines where only scholars specialize. At the time of publishing *Given Time*, Derrida admitted to having been studying the gift in one way or another in his various texts for over twenty years.

This style of writing, the open circle of reinscription, that is, writing and re-writing and reevaluating, that he practiced, is similar to what happens to the gift in its cycle of exchange except that it is the opposite that takes place: once inside the circle, whether by motivated giving or by repaying the "debt" of the gift, the gift itself does not exist as such, according to Derrida. He literally turned his writing inside out to explore this phenomenon. Ultimately, he proposed three standards to determine whether a gift is pure:

- The gift must not be part of an exchange. There must be no reciprocation by the donee, not even an expression of gratitude. In fact, the donee must not even recognize the gift as such.

- There must be no motive by the donor of some return for the gift, no consciousness of doing good via the act of giving. In fact, the donor must not know (s)he has given a gift.

- The gift must be something outside the economy of exchange, that is, it must not be material.

A pure gift, then, is unconditional. If there are conditions, there is no gift. There can be no reciprocity, return, exchange, counter-gift, or debt. Even the simple intention to give results in a return payment to oneself, annulling the gift. Peter Leithart (1932–), a theologian, asked us to try this experiment to test out Derrida's conditions: a sleepwalking Harry hands flowers to comatose Alice. Has a gift been given? Both parties are unconscious of the action of giving and receiving. We would hardly think that there is a gift here because our cultural conditioning tells us that intention to give is a necessary element of giving. In order for the gift to be possible, Harry must wake up and Alice must come out of her coma. But by Derrida's conditions, the situation is different: as soon as they do that, they both recognize that a gift is being given, and the gift is destroyed; the conditions of the gift are also the conditions of its destruction.

With his three conditions, it is no wonder that Derrida claimed the gift is impossible, you might say. But Derrida wasn't saying the gift is impossible (opposite of possible); he was saying it is THE impossible. What's the difference? Ah, all the difference (*differance*) there is! The meaning of Derrida's "impossible" gift doesn't imply that it may become possible, but rather, that the impossible itself is possible. If this sounds like doubletalk, that's understandable. What he meant is that it may appear to be possible in terms of our normal comprehension and analysis, but it is in fact only possible in the sense that gift, as an event, exceeds our comprehension. Think God. Think heaven. Think grace. Think death. Think light years. Think parallel universe. Think eons. Think infinity. Think madness. Think any number of events or states beyond our immediate understanding, both as individuals and as humans, and you will begin to get it. The horizon of the gift that places it beyond our understanding is the locus of a rupture of the circle of exchange we've been discussing. That's where pure gift is located.

Now we begin to understand why Derrida insisted that the gift is an **aporia,** a paradox. Although a pure gift is outside the economy of exchange, it still needs that circle of exchange as a point of departure, if you will, a ground of possibility. Thus he asked us if the conditions of the possibility of the gift are not also the conditions of its impossibility. And, hopefully, we begin to understand the question. One may even ask, after the challenges and delights of exploring the works of Derrida in terms of the gift, if Derrida's gift to us is a pure one. Or one may ask if we are in his debt, and if that debt is inside or outside the circle of exchange. One may ask if it involves more than the two of us, Derrida and oneself as reader, or if something more has been born out of the process of our reading and exploring together. And one may hope to begin to answer.

WHAT IS ART? AND RELATED PROBLEMS IN AESTHETICS[2]

Unlike most other academic disciplines, philosophy is not confined to a specific subject matter. History concerns the past, biology concerns organisms, and education studies concern learning. In principle, it is possible to do the philosophy of X, where you may substitute anything you please for X. In practice, however, philosophers conserve their energies for topics of some importance. Philosophy of art, also called **aesthetics,** illustrates this process in two ways.

First, artistic achievement is a life goal for some people, and almost everyone values listening and dancing to music, reading stories, and looking at images. The value of art is obvious, but it is also puzzling. The point can be put abstractly: What sense could intelligent beings inhabiting an art-free environment make of our art? What could you tell them about the value of dancing, for example? The point also has a practical side: Why should public resources belonging either to the state or to private foundations be used to support the arts, especially when other needs are pressing? Puzzlement about art is one reason to do philosophy of art, and you may wish to study the subject because you care about art.

Second, art interests philosophers because philosophical questions about art connect to all the central areas of philosophy. Here is a sample. What is art (metaphysics)? What makes some art good (value theory)? How can we judge art good or bad (epistemology)? How is it possible to tell stories about things that do not

---

[2] Written by Dominic McIver Lopes, professor of philosophy and Distinguished University Scholar at the University of British Columbia. Currently he is president of the American Society for Aesthetics.

exist (philosophy of language)? What is creativity (philosophy of mind)? Doing philosophy of art is one way of doing philosophy. You may be surprised to learn that some philosophers of art are not great art lovers, and you may wish to study aesthetics only because you are interested in some of the toughest problems in philosophy.

What Is Art?

This question is the first a philosopher of art might think to pose. After all, a prudent first step in any inquiry is to fix upon what you want to understand, keeping in mind that what you decide will have an impact on how you answer other questions. The task for the philosopher of art is especially tricky because art and ideas about art have changed rapidly and radically during the past century. What is art? is not merely a philosopher's question. It arises for every gallery visitor and every pop music fan.

At one time, *art*—or *fine art*—referred to the sorts of pictures housed in art galleries, music performed in concert halls, and novels found in the literature department of the bookstore. During the past forty years, philosophers have embraced a more expansive conception of art, one that includes children's drawings, popular music, pulp fiction, B movies, and vernacular architecture. These items all fall within the extension of art—the class of things the term *art* picks out. Presumably philosophers and others noticed that comic books and television shows have certain features that qualify them as art.

One possibility is that these features define art. A definition is a statement of the features that are necessary and sufficient for anything to be art. A piece of writing, for instance, is art only if it has these features, and if it has the features, then it is art. Philosophers have devised several definitions of art. Plato thought that art is the imitation of objects and actions. Tolstoy thought that art is the expression of feelings that bind a community or culture. Clive Bell, an important early theorist of painting, thought that visual artworks express a special "aesthetic emotion" through arrangements of shapes and colors. None of these ideas is very convincing. Not all art is imitation (e.g., most instrumental music), and not every imitation is art. Not all art is expressive (e.g., Mondrian's grid paintings), and many expressions of feeling are not artistic.

Still, you may suspect that art must have something to do with imitation and expression. Sharing this hunch, some philosophers reject the assumption that the answer to the question What is art? should take the form of a definition (a statement of necessary and sufficient conditions for being art). Art is a cluster of items. Nothing is common to all works of art and nothing separates all art from all nonart. Some are imitative and not expressive; others are expressive and not imitative.

One day in 1964, the Columbia University philosopher Arthur Danto visited the Stable Gallery in New York, which was showing Andy Warhol's "sculptures" of Brillo soap pad boxes. Danto later wrote that the "Warhol show raised a question which was intoxicating and immediately philosophical,

Andy Warhol's work titled *The Brillo Boxes.*

namely why were his boxes works of art while the almost indistinguishable utilitarian cartons were merely containers for soap pads? Certainly the minor observable differences could not ground as grand a distinction as that between Art and Reality!"[3] Warhol showed that artworks can be perceptually indistinguishable from ordinary, nonart objects.

The lesson is that art cannot be defined as long as we assume that its defining features must be perceivable—that we should always be able to tell art from nonart

[3] Arthur Danto, "Art, Philosophy, and the Philosophy of Art," *Humanities* 4 (1983): 1–2.

just by looking. *Brillo Boxes* are art, but they look just like Brillo boxes. What makes them art is the way they are interpreted or the context in which they are made. Anything can be art if interpreted or made in the right conditions. In some contexts art is imitation, in others art is expression, and in others it is neither. Danto suggests a resilient definition of art. The features defining art have to do with interpretation and creation. The upshot is that we must find out what kinds of interpretations or creative contexts transform nonart into art. It means we must view art as a social phenomenon. Philosophers inspired by Danto's work have had a lot to say about this.

A Paradox of Fiction

Knowing what art is does not tell us why we care about art or what its value is. The capacity of artworks to arouse emotions is one source of the value of many artworks. Consider movies. Some movies are good because they deliver a strong jolt of horror. Others are tear-jerkers. Strangely enough, tear-jerkers are often "feel-good" movies. Aristotle noticed that the "tear-jerker" tragedies of his day must somehow bring pleasure, though grief, anxiety, and the other emotions that tragedies arouse are far from pleasurable—they are not emotions we normally spend good money to endure. Painful art is pleasurable to experience: this is a paradox that philosophers such as Hume, Schopenhauer, and Nietzsche have tried to explain away. But there is another, more fundamental paradox about our emotional responses to artworks, a paradox that makes us wonder how it is possible to have emotional responses to many artworks.

The following three statements all seem to be true:

1. We often respond emotionally to fictional characters and their situations,
2. Emotional responses to objects typically presuppose beliefs in the existence of the objects, but
3. We do not believe in the existence of fictional objects.

The first statement is manifestly true. We are saddened by the fate of Anna Karenina and cheer Road Runner as he outwits Wile E. Coyote, but Anna, Wile E., and the Road Runner are fictional and, as (3) says, we do not believe in the existence of fictional objects. The second statement requires some explanation. Many philosophers hold that emotions are more than bodily feelings. Anger and frustration, for example, feel the same because both involve a rise in adrenalin and stepped-up heart rate, but they are different because one is a reaction to a situation that is believed to be unfair or wrong whereas the other involves a belief that one's efforts are obstructed. Likewise, fear involves a belief that the situation is dangerous, and joy involves a belief that things are going well. Learning that the situation is not really dangerous dispels our fear, and learning that Road Runner eventually falls prey to Wile E. Coyote deflates our cheer, as learning that we have not been wronged defuses our anger, and learning that our efforts will succeed undoes our frustration. Emotions are not irrational; they are ways of thinking about and appraising our situation and they are revised as our beliefs change.

Rachel Steiner: *Vulture.*

The paradox is that, although (1) to (3) all seem true, at least one must be false. Suppose that feeling sad for somebody does involve a belief in her existence, and suppose we do not believe in the existence of Anna. That means we cannot feel sad for Anna—(1) is false. Or suppose that we do feel sad for Anna and believe that she exists. That means either that we do not know she is fictional or else that we believe in the existence of fictional objects—(3) is false. Or suppose that we do not believe that Anna exists, but nevertheless we feel sad for her. That means that emotions do not involve an element of belief—(2) is false. If any two of (1) to (3) are true, then the other is false.

How can we resolve the paradox? It is tempting to deny (3). Perhaps when you are reading or watching a fiction, you temporarily believe that what happens in the story is true and the characters in the story are real. The story evokes a kind of illusion (and the storyteller is a kind of Cartesian evil deceiver). This idea is problematic, however. We do not act, when we read the story, as we would act if we believed the story were true and Anna existed. For one thing, we quite properly take pleasure in her sadness, but we do not properly take pleasure in the sadness of real people. It is one thing to find a soap opera entertaining and another thing to be entertained by horrible things that befall the neighbors!

Another solution is presented in the most important recent book in aesthetics, *Mimesis as Make-Believe,* by Kendall Walton, a philosopher at the University of Michigan. Walton accepts (2) and (3) but amends them both slightly. We do not believe in the existence of fictional objects, but we do *imagine* them. Moreover, emotional responses typically presuppose beliefs, but sometimes imaginings will do instead of beliefs—particularly imaginings about the existence of fictional objects. Reading Tolstoy, you imagine Anna's suffering and so feel something like sadness for her. You do not *really* feel sad for her, because sadness is dispelled by the realization that the object of your sadness does not exist. Instead, you feel quasi-sadness, which is like sadness except it involves imagination instead of belief. Since quasi-sadness is an emotion, (1) is true.

Notice how this problem in aesthetics touches on epistemology (which is about what we should believe) and metaphysics (which is about what exists) and philosophy of mind (which is about the nature of our mental lives). At the same time, it touches on a mystery of everyday human life: we make artworks that engender emotional responses.

The Puzzle of Musical Expression

We feel sad for Anna because Tolstoy's story represents her as desperate and distraught. The novel expresses what she feels by representing her as acting the way a person acts when she is desperate and distraught. Many artworks, such as novels and movies, express emotions by representing objects and events. What about music, though? Much music does not represent anything (set aside music with lyrics and so-called program music), and yet it is expressive of emotion. How is that possible? After all, emotions are mental states, so to think of something as expressing an emotion is to think of it as sentient; but music is just structured sound—it is not sentient, and we do not normally think it is sentient.

This suggests we should find some sentient creature on whom we have good reason to pin the emotions expressed by the music. One ancient idea is that music expresses what the composer felt as she composed. The trouble with this idea is that the emotions we have good reason to attribute to the composer are not necessarily the emotions expressed by the music. While writing joyous music, a composer may feel only pride in her compositional cleverness or anxiety about meeting her publication deadline. Another popular idea is that music expresses feelings by arousing them in its listeners (we have just seen that artworks can arouse emotional reactions). This idea also faces difficulties. Some listeners all of the time, and most listeners some of the time, are "dry-eyed critics." Your unshakably morose mood need not render you incapable of detecting the joyfulness of a song—indeed, detecting its joyfulness while in a morose mood may simply annoy you.

Impressed by the difficulties facing these ancient and popular ideas, some philosophers propose that we attribute the emotions music expresses to a fictional *persona*. When we hear the music's expression of joy, we imagine that this fictional entity feels the joy. The proposal is especially compelling when applied to long stretches of serious classical music, where something like an emotional narrative unfolds (e.g., dread leading to grief leading to anger leading to resignation and finally hope) and it is natural to think of a fictional person as undergoing this emotional process. Do you imagine a fictional persona undergoing what is expressed by every jingle and ditty, however?

Boggs's Bills

J. S. G. Boggs makes exacting, life-size drawings of currency. On one side of each drawing is a rendition of a banknote embellished by amusing giveaways, such as the replacement of "ONE" with "FUN" on the U.S. one-dollar bill. On the back is documentation of the drawing, including the artist's signature. Most artists sell their drawings; Boggs "spends" his. Presented with the tab at a bar, he offers the bartender a choice between cash payment or a Boggs Bill. The Boggs Bill is offered at "face value"—if a hundred-dollar Boggs Bill is offered in payment for a sixty-dollar bar tab, Boggs expects forty dollars in change. However, Boggs Bills are now reselling at substantially more than face value. You can see, print out, and "spend" a Boggs Bill at www.jsgboggs.com.

The U.S. government charged Boggs as a counterfeiter. Boggs insists he is an artist raising questions about art and value. Who is right? Boggs? The government? Neither? Both? If Boggs is right, what is his artwork—his masterful handicraft or his culture-jamming transactions? Would you print out and "spend" a Boggs Bill, following the instructions at www.jsgboggs.com? Why or why not?

Other philosophers propose that we abandon the assumption that expression implies that someone has the emotion that is expressed. The suggestion gets some plausibility from the fact that it is possible for me or you to express an emotion though we do not feel it. My job interview smile hides my nervousness—it does not reveal inner happiness. Likewise, music may wear a sonic smile, which is an expression of happiness that nobody feels. Peter Kivy, a philosopher of music who teaches at Rutgers University, takes the metaphor of "sonic smiles" seriously. He suggests that the tonal structure, rhythms, and dynamics of a piece of music can mimic a human expression of sadness. Music sounds sad, for example, because its tempo mimics the slow gait of a sad person. The idea has some appeal for explaining expressions of garden-variety emotions such as sadness, joy, and anger, but how can music mimic an expression of hope or determination? Music is quite often emotionally expressive, and this is an important element of its value for us. Nothing could be clearer. Still, it is difficult to understand how music can be expressive in anything like the way people's faces and gestures are expressive.

Envoi

Theories of art, the paradox of fiction, musical expressiveness: this is a small sample of what interests philosophers of art. Like most topics in philosophy of art, they do two things: they go to the heart of our puzzlement about a unique human institution, and they demand all the skills and resources that philosophy has to offer. Why is a perfect forgery of a painting not as valuable as the original painting of which it is a copy? Why should our knowledge about artists' lives have any impact on our appreciation of their work? Does it matter that Leni Riefenstahl's acclaimed 1936 film *Triumph of the Will* is also a piece of Nazi propaganda? Does a work of music exist if nobody plays it or listens to it? Why bother to listen to it if you can read the score? The questions about art are seemingly endless, and that is where the philosophy begins.

SELECTION 17.1

Sensations and Brain Processes*

J. J. C. Smart

[*Here, J. J. C. Smart, an early and influential adherent of identity theory, presented and then rebutted objections to identity theory.*]

It seems to me that science is increasingly giving us a viewpoint whereby organisms are able to be seen as physico-chemical mechanisms: it seems that even the behavior of man himself will one day be explicable in mechanistic terms. There does seem to be, so far as science is concerned, nothing in the world but increasingly complex arrangements of physical constituents. All except for one place: in consciousness. That is, for a full description of what is going on in a man you would have to mention not only the physical processes in his tissue, glands, nervous system, and so forth, but also his states of consciousness: his visual, auditory, and tactual sensations, his aches and pains. That these should be *correlated* with brain processes does not help, for to say that they are *correlated* is to say that they are something "over and above." You cannot correlate something with itself. You correlate footprints with burglars, but not Bill Sikes the burglar with Bill Sikes the burglar. So sensations, states of consciousness, do seem to be the one sort of thing left outside the physicalist picture, and for various reasons I just cannot believe that this can be so. That everything should be explicable in terms of physics (together of course with descriptions of the ways in which the parts are put together—roughly, biology is to physics as radio-engineering is to electromagnetism) except the occurrence of sensations seems to me to be frankly unbelievable. . . .

Why should not sensations just be brain processes of a certain sort? There are, of course, well-known (as well as lesser-known) philosophical objections to the view that reports of sensations are

reports of brain processes, but I shall try to argue that these arguments are by no means as cogent as is commonly thought to be the case.

Let me first try to state more accurately the thesis that sensations are brain processes. It is not the thesis that, for example, "after-image" or "ache" means the same as "brain process of sort X" (where "X" is replaced by a description of a certain sort of brain process). It is that, in so far as "after-image" or "ache" is a report of a process, it is a report of a process that *happens to be* a brain process. It follows that the thesis does not claim that sensation statements can be *translated* into statements about brain processes. Nor does it claim that the logic of a sensation statement is the same as that of a brain process statement. All it claims is that in so far as a sensation statement is a report of something, that something is in fact a brain process. Sensations are nothing over and above brain processes. Nations are nothing "over and above" citizens, but this does not prevent the logic of nation statements being very different from the logic of citizen statements, nor does it insure the translatability of nation statements into citizen statements. . . .

Remarks on identity. When I say that a sensation is a brain process or that lightning is an electric discharge, I am using "is" in the sense of strict identity. (Just as in the—in this case necessary—proposition "7 is identical with the smallest prime number greater than 5.") . . .

I shall now discuss various possible objections to the view that the processes reported in sensation statements are in fact processes in the brain. Most of us have met some of these objections in our first year as philosophy students. All the more reason to take a good look at them. Others of the objections will be more recondite and subtle.

Objection 1. Any illiterate peasant can talk perfectly well about his after-images, or how things look or feel to him, or about his aches and pains, and yet he may know nothing whatever about neurophysiology. . . .

---

* From J. J. C. Smart, "Sensations and Brain Processes," *Philosophical Review* 68 (1959), pp. 141–156.

Reply. You might as well say that a nation of slugabeds, who never saw the morning star or knew of its existence, or who had never thought of the expression "the Morning Star," but who used the expression "the Evening Star" perfectly well, could not use this expression to refer to the same entity as we refer to (and describe as) "the Morning Star." . . .

Consider lightning. Modern physical science tells us that lightning is a certain kind of electrical discharge due to ionization of clouds of water vapor in the atmosphere. This, it is now believed, is what the true nature of lightning is. Note that there are not two things: a flash of lightning and an electrical discharge. There is one thing, a flash of lightning, which is described scientifically as an electrical discharge to the earth from a cloud of ionized water molecules. . . .

In short, the reply to Objection 1 is that there can be contingent statements of the form "A is identical with B," and a person may well know that something is an A without knowing that it is a B. An illiterate peasant might well be able to talk about his sensations without knowing about his brain processes, just as he can talk about lightning though he knows nothing of electricity.

Objection 2. It is only a contingent fact (if it is a fact) that when we have a certain kind of sensation there is a certain kind of process in our brain. Indeed it is possible, though perhaps in the highest degree unlikely, that our present physiological theories will be as out of date as the ancient theory connecting mental processes with goings-on in the heart. It follows that when we report a sensation we are not reporting a brain process.

Reply. The objection certainly proves that when we say "I have an after-image" we cannot *mean* something of the form "I have such-and-such a brain process." But this does not show that what we report (having an after-image) is not *in fact* a brain process. . . .

Now how do I get over the objection that a sensation can be identified with a brain process only if it has some phenomenal property, not possessed by brain processes, whereby one-half of the identification may be, so to speak, pinned down?

My suggestion is as follows. When a person says, "I see a yellowish-orange after-image," he is saying something like this: "*There is something going on which is like what is going on when* I have my eyes open, am awake, and there is an orange illuminated in good light in front of me, that is, when I really see an orange." . . .

Objection 4. The after-image is not in physical space. The brain process is. So the after-image is not a brain process.

Reply. This is an *ignoratio elenchi.* I am not arguing that the after-image is a brain process, but that the experience of having an after-image is a brain process. It is the *experience* which is reported in the introspective report. Similarly, if it is objected that the after-image is yellowy-orange but that a surgeon looking into your brain would see nothing yellowy-orange, my reply is that it is the experience of seeing yellowy-orange that is being described, and this experience is not a yellowy-orange something. So to say that a brain process cannot be yellowy-orange is not to say that a brain process cannot in fact be the experience of having a yellowy-orange after-image. . . .

Objection 5. It would make sense to say of a molecular movement in the brain that it is swift or slow, straight or circular, but it makes no sense to say this of the experience of seeing something yellow.

Reply. So far we have not given sense to talk of experiences as swift or slow, straight or circular. But I am not claiming that "experience" and "brain process" mean the same or even that they have the same logic. "Somebody" and "the doctor" do not have the same logic, but this does not lead us to suppose that talking about somebody telephoning is talking about someone over and above, say, the doctor. . . .

Objection 6. Sensations are private, brain processes are *public*. If I sincerely say, "I see a yellowish-orange after-image" and I am not making a verbal mistake, then I cannot be wrong. But I can be wrong about a brain process. The scientist looking into my brain might be having an illusion. Moreover, it makes sense to say that two or more people are observing the same brain process but not that two or more people are reporting the same inner experience.

Reply. This shows that the language of introspective reports has a different logic from the language of material processes. It is obvious that until the brain process theory is much improved and widely accepted there will be no *criteria* for saying "Smith has an experience of such-and-such a sort" *except* Smith's introspective reports. So we have adopted a rule of language that (normally) what Smith says goes.

Objection 7. I can imagine myself turned to stone and yet having images, aches, pains, and so on.

Reply. . . . I can imagine that the Evening Star is not the Morning Star. But it is. All the objection shows is that "experience" and "brain process" do not have the same meaning. It does not show that an experience is not in fact a brain process.

SELECTION 17.2

Free Will

Sam Harris

[*In this selection Sam Harris argues that our choices result from causes over which we have no control. Harris, who has a Ph.D. in cognitive neuroscience, has written widely in philosophy.*]

As Dan Dennett and many others have pointed out, people generally confuse determinism with fatalism. This gives rise to questions like "If everything is determined, why should I do anything? Why not just sit back and see what happens?" This is pure confusion. To sit back and see what happens is itself a choice that will produce its own consequences. It is also extremely difficult to do: Just try staying in bed all day waiting for something to happen; you will find yourself assailed by the impulse to get up and do something, which will require increasingly heroic efforts to resist.

And the fact that our choices depend on prior causes does not mean that they don't matter. If I had not decided to write this book, it wouldn't have written itself. My choice to write it was unquestionably the primary cause of its coming into being. Decisions, intentions, efforts, goals, willpower, etc., are causal states of the brain, leading to specific behaviors, and behaviors lead to outcomes in the world. Human choice, therefore, is as important as fanciers of free will believe. But the next choice you make will come out of the darkness of prior causes that you, the conscious witness of your experience, did not bring into being.

Therefore, while it is true to say that a person would have done otherwise if he had chosen to do otherwise, this does not deliver the kind of free will that most people seem to cherish—because a person's "choices" merely appear in his mind as though sprung from the void. From the perspective of your conscious awareness, you are no more responsible for the next thing you think (and therefore do) than you are for the fact that you were born into this world.

Let's say your life has gone off track. You used to be very motivated, inspired by your opportunities, and physically fit, but now you are lazy, easily discouraged, and overweight. How did you get this way? You might be able to tell a story about how your life unraveled, but you cannot truly account for why you let it happen. And now you want to escape this downward trend and change yourself through an act of will.

You begin reading self-help books. You change your diet and join a gym. You decide to go back to school. But after six months of effort, you are no closer to living the life you want than you were before. The books failed to make an impact on you; your diet and fitness regime proved impossible to maintain; and you got bored with school and quit. Why did you encounter so many obstacles in yourself? You have no idea. You tried to change your habits, but your habits appear to be stronger than you are. Most of us know what it is like to fail in this way—and these experiences are not even slightly suggestive of freedom of will.

But you woke up this morning feeling even greater resolve. Enough is enough! Now you have a will of steel. Before stepping out of bed you had a brilliant idea for a website—and the discovery that the domain name was available for only 10 dollars has filled you with confidence. You are now an entrepreneur! You share the idea with several smart people, and they think it is guaranteed to make you rich.

Free Press A Division of Simon & Schuster, Inc. 1230 Avenue of the Americas New York, NY 10020 Copyright 2012.

The wind is at your back, your sails are full, and you are tacking furiously. As it turns out, a friend of yours is also a close friend of Tim Ferriss, the famous lifestyle coach and fitness guru. Ferriss offers to consult with you about your approach to diet and exercise. You find this meeting extremely helpful—and afterward you discover a reservoir of discipline in yourself that you didn't know was there. Over the next four months you swap 20 pounds of fat for 20 pounds of muscle. You weigh the same, but you are fully transformed. Your friends can't believe what you have accomplished. Even your enemies begin to ask you for advice.

You feel entirely different about your life, and the role that discipline, choice, and effort have played in your resurrection cannot be denied. But how can you account for your ability to make these efforts today and not a year ago? Where did this idea for a website come from? It just appeared in your mind. Did *you*, as the conscious agent you feel yourself to be, *create* it? (If so, why not just create the next one right now?) How can you explain the effect that Tim Ferriss's advice had on you? How can you explain your ability to respond to it?

If you pay attention to your inner life, you will see that the emergence of choices, efforts, and intentions is a fundamentally mysterious process. Yes, you can decide to go on a diet—and we know a lot about the variables that will enable you to stick to it—but you cannot know why you were finally able to adhere to this discipline when all your previous attempts failed. You might have a story to tell about why things were different this time around, but it would be nothing more than a post hoc description of events that you did not control. Yes, you can do what you want—but you cannot account for the fact that your wants are effective in one case and not in another (and you certainly can't choose your wants in advance). You wanted to lose weight for years. Then you *really* wanted to. What's the difference? Whatever it is, it's not a difference that *you* brought into being.

You are not in control of your mind—because you, as a conscious agent, are only *part* of your mind, living at the mercy of other parts. You can do what you decide to do—but you cannot decide what you will decide to do. Of course, you can create a framework in which certain decisions are more likely than others—you can, for instance, purge your house of all sweets, making it very

unlikely that you will eat dessert later in the evening—but you cannot know why you were able to submit to such a framework today when you weren't yesterday.

So it's not that willpower isn't important or that it is destined to be undermined by biology. Willpower is itself a biological phenomenon. You can change your life, and yourself, through effort and discipline—but you have whatever capacity for effort and discipline you have in this moment, and not a scintilla more (or less). You are either lucky in this department or you aren't—and you cannot make your own luck.

Many people believe that human freedom consists in our ability to do what, upon reflection, we believe we should do—which often means overcoming our short-term desires and following our long-term goals or better judgment. This is certainly an ability that people possess, to a greater or lesser degree, and which other animals appear to lack, but it is nevertheless a capacity of our minds that has unconscious roots.

You have not built your mind. And in moments in which you *seem* to build it—when you make an effort to change yourself, to acquire knowledge, or to perfect a skill—the only tools at your disposal are those that you have inherited from moments past.

Choices, efforts, intentions, and reasoning influence our behavior—but they are themselves part of a chain of causes that precede conscious awareness and over which we exert no ultimate control. My choices matter—and there are paths toward making wiser ones—but I cannot choose what I choose. And if it ever appears that I do—for instance, after going back and forth between two options—I do not *choose* to choose what I choose. There is a regress here that always ends in darkness. I must take a first step, or a last one, for reasons that are bound to remain inscrutable.

Many people believe that this problem of regress is a false one. Certain compatibilists insist that freedom of will is synonymous with the idea that one could have thought or acted differently. However, to say that I could have done otherwise is merely to think the thought "I could have done otherwise" after doing whatever I in fact did. This is an empty affirmation. It confuses hope for the future with an honest account of the past. What I will do next, and why, remains, at bottom, a mystery—one that is fully determined by the prior state of the universe and the laws of nature (including the contributions of chance). To declare my "freedom" is tantamount to saying, "I don't know why I did it, but it's the sort of thing I tend to do, and I don't mind doing it."

One of the most refreshing ideas to come out of existentialism (perhaps the only one) is that we are free to interpret and reinterpret the meaning of our lives. You can consider your first marriage, which ended in divorce, to be a "failure," or you can view it as a circumstance that caused you to grow in ways that were crucial to your future happiness. Does this freedom of interpretation require free will? No. It simply suggests that different ways of thinking have different consequences. Some thoughts are depressing and disempowering; others inspire us. We can pursue any line of thought we want—but our choice is the product of prior events that we did not bring into being.

Take a moment to think about the context in which your next decision will occur: You did not pick your parents or the time and place of your birth. You didn't choose your gender or most of your life experiences. You had no control whatsoever over your genome or the development of your brain. And now your brain is making choices on the basis of preferences and beliefs that have been hammered into it over a lifetime—by your genes, your physical development since the moment you were conceived, and the interactions you have had with other people, events, and ideas. Where is the freedom in this? Yes, you are free to do what you want even now. But where did your desires come from?

CHECKLIST

To help you review, a checklist of the key philosophers of this chapter can be found online at www.mhhe.com/moore9e. The brief descriptive sentences summarize the philosophers' leading ideas. Keep in mind that some of these summary statements are oversimplifications of complex positions.

KEY TERMS AND CONCEPTS

aesthetics 566	neuroscientific
aporia 566	determinism 549
behaviorism 554	paradox of
causal	fiction 569
determinism 552	philosophical
determinism 547	behaviorism 555
functionalism 557	philosophy of
hau 561	mind 553
identity theory 555	psychological
interactionist	determinism 548
dualism 553	p-zombies 548

QUESTIONS FOR DISCUSSION AND REVIEW

1. Can *you* "reprogram" your preferences (desires and values) either directly through an act of willing or through indirect means? Defend your opinion.

2. Whose views on free will do you agree with, Donald Trump's or Albert Einstein's (see the quotes at the beginning of the chapter)? Defend your opinion.

3. If humans are purely physical things, can they have free will? Explain.

4. "My mental states are knowable by introspection, but my neurophysiological states are not; therefore my mental states are not brain states." Evaluate this argument.

5. When all is said and done, which of the theories of mind discussed in this chapter is the soundest? Defend your view.

6. What is a definition, and what is the purpose of a definition of art?

7. Suppose a song expresses emotions that it never arouses in its listeners—we always remain "dry-eyed critics." Is this a failing of the song? Suppose a song is so emotionally powerful that it is impossible to remain a dry-eyed critic. Is this a failing of the song?

Questions 8, 9, and 10. Reread the summary of the story, "Counterfeit Money" (by Baudelaire) that Derrida analyzes before answering these questions (see page).

8. Derrida's claim is that the act of giving creates a circle of exchange by obligating the receiver, thus negating the gift. Only a true gift, which would seem, by his definition, to be impossible, would actually interrupt that circle of exchange.

A pure gift would disrupt the exchange calculation, so there would be no exchange. In "Counterfeit Money," explore how this circle is/is not broken by the fact that the "gift" is phony.

9. Should the narrator of the story take his friend at his word that the coin is counterfeit? What if he were an even greater counterfeiter than the narrator thinks? What if he's passing off real money as counterfeit? And if that is the case, what could be his motive for doing so? If he actually gave real money but said it was counterfeit, does it alter the status of the gift as pure or impure?

10. Derrida says that as soon as the other accepts, there is no gift—even if the gift is subsequently refused. It is the act of recognition that creates the destruction of the gift. In the story, speculate as to whether the beggar's acceptance of the coin accomplishes the annulment of the gift or whether the fact that the coin is counterfeit changes the balance. Are there any other factors that could affect whether the coin is gift?

SUGGESTED FURTHER READINGS

Go online to www.mhhe.com/moore9e for a list of suggested further readings.

Credits

Index/Glossary

a posteriori judgment, 225
a posteriori truth vs. a priori truth, 214
a priori principle, 25
A priori principle: A proposition whose truth we do not need to know through sensory experience and that no conceivable experience could serve to refute, G–1
a priori structure, 166
a priori/a posteriori pair, 214
A priori/a posteriori pair: In the philosophy of Saul Kripke, an a priori truth is a statement known to be true independently of any experience, and its opposite, an a posteriori truth, is a statement known to be true through experience, G–1
Abandonment, 159–160, 167, 180–181
Abelard, Peter, 254–255, 510
  Historica Calamitatum, 254
Abolition, 424
Absolute, the, 135
Absolute, the: That which is unconditioned and uncaused by anything else; it is frequently thought of as God, a perfect and solitary, self-caused eternal being that is the source or essence of all that exists but that is itself beyond the possibility of conceptualization or definition, G–1
Absolute as spirit, 136
Absolute Beauty, 42–43

Absolute consciousness, 133
Absolute cynicism, 158
Absolute Idea, 311–312
Absolute idealism, 133
Absolute Idealism: The early nineteenth-century school of philosophy that maintained that being is the transcendental unfolding or expression of thought or reason, G–1
Absolute Idealists, 195
Absolute Knowledge, 311
Absolute realism, 143
Absolute reality, 135
Absolute Self-Consciousness, 312
Absolute thoughts, 133
Absolute truths, 150, 191
Absurdity, 158, 160, 162, 183
Academics, 77
Academics: Philosophers of the third and second centuries B.C.E. in what had been Plato's Academy; they had the reputation of maintaining that all things are inapprehensible, G–1
Accuracy problem, 219
Act utilitarianism, 268
Act-utilitarianism: A form of utilitarianism (subscribed to by Bentham) in which the rightness of an act is determined by its effect on the general happiness, G–1
Adler, Alfred, 153
Adorno, Theodor, 172
"Advice to Christian Philosophers" (Faith and Philosophy), 409
Aesthetics, 14, 361, 566

Aesthetics: The philosophical study of art and of value judgments about art and of beauty in general, G–1
Africa
  oral and traditional philosophy, 521–524
  postcolonial theory, 520–524
African American thought
  Afrocentrism, 529–530
  feminisms, 528–529
  King, Martin Luther, Jr., 527–528
  social activism, 530
  social justice, 527–528
  West, Cornel, 530
African diaspora, 525
African epistemology, 522
Afrocentrism, 529–530
"After the Death of God the Father" (Daly), 414–415
After Virtue (MacIntyre), 348, 350
Age of Reason, 95
Age of Technology, 95
Agnosticism, and antagonism, 399
Agoge (way of thought), 77
Agoge: Way of living, G–1
Albertus Magnus, 379
Alexander the Great, 61, 70, 249, 397
Al-Farabi, 470
Al-Ghazali, 470
Alienation, 316
Al-Kindi, 470
All Quiet on the Western Front (Remarque), 146
Allah, 470
Alterity, 170

Categorical imperative: Immanuel Kant's formulation of a moral law that holds unconditionally, that is, categorically; in its most common formulation, states that you are to act in such a way that you could desire the principle on which you act to be a universal law, G–2

Catholic philosophy, 84

Causa et Curae (Hildegard), 252

Causal determinism, 551–552

Causal determinism: The idea that every event is caused by an antecedent set of events sufficient for the occurrence of the event in question, G–2

Causation, 62, 128
  preconception of, 518

Cause, 386

Cause and effect, 7, 126, 392, 407

Cervantes, Miguel, 155

Chalmers, David, 211, 558–559
  The Conscious Mind, 558

Ch'an Buddhism, in China, 463

Change, 84
  causes of, 66
  nature of, 26
  source of, 62
  subject to causation, 132
  ultimate source of, 62

Character traits, 246

Charlemagne, 82

Chatter, 168

Chicana feminists, 542

Children's moral development, 430–431

China
  Ch'an Buddhism in, 463
  Confucianism in, 463
  Taoism in, 463

Chinese philosophy, 472

Chodorow, Nancy, 431
  The Reproduction of Mothering, 452–455

Choice vs. will, 397

Christian giants, 376–378

Christian philosophy, vs. realm of Forms, 83

Christian religion, 250

Christianity, 72

Christianizing ethics
  Augustine, 250–251
  Heloise and Abelard, 254–256

Hildegard, Saint (of Bingen), 252–253

Thomas Aquinas, Saint, 256–257

Christina, Queen, 97

Christine doctrine, 74

Chuang Tzu, 473, 479–482, 500
  profile of, 480
  on Virtuous Activity, 482

Cicero, 60, 248
  Disinterested Love, 254
  natural law, 291

Circularity, 35–36, 65–66. *see also* Form *circularity*

Civil law, vs. natural law, 303

Cixous, Hélène, 438
  early life of, 442–443
  Freud/Lacan period, 444
  The Laugh of the Medusa, 457–460
  "Laugh of the Medusa," 445
  literary criticism, 444–446
  The Newly Born Woman, 563
  phases of, 444

Clarity, 157

Class distinction within, 529

Class issues, 532

Class struggle, 314

Classes, 290

Classic liberalism and Marxism
  anarchism, 318–319
  Hegel, 311–312
  Marx, 311–317
  Mill, 308–310
  Smith, 307
  Taylor, 308
  utilitarianism and natural rights, 307–308

Classical liberals, 315

Clear and distinct criteria, 99

Clear and distinct criterion, 99

Clear and distinct criterion: René Descartes' criterion of truth, according to which that, and only that, which is perceived as clearly and distinctly as the fact of one's own existence is certain, G–2

Code, Lawrence, 435

Code Pink, 429

Code Pink: A third wave women's grassroots peace and justice movement that opposes any kind of military force, G–2

Cogito, ergo sum, 97

Cogito, ergo sum: "I think, therefore I am"; the single indubitable truth on which Descartes' epistemology is based, G–2

Cognition, 132

Cold War, 3, 147

Collective liberty, 301–302

Collectivism, 539

Collins, Patricia Hills, 427

Colonial order, 525

Colonialism, Latin American patterns, 519

Colonization, 518

Color blindness, 542

Comic vision, 154

Coming-to-maturity, 154–155

Common good, 348

Commonsense metaphysics, 93

Commonwealth, 328

Communism
  vs. communism, 318
  and Marxism, 317–318

communism, 363

Communism: (capital "c") The ideology of the Communist Party, (lowercase "c") an economic system, G–2

Communist Manifesto (Marx and Engels), 146, 313, 329–330

Communists, 363

Communitarian, 348

Communitarian: One who holds that there is a common good defined by one's society, the attainment of which has priority over individual liberty, G–2

Communitarian responses to Rawls
  animals and morality, 348
  MacIntyre and virtue ethics, 351–352
  war, 350

Comprehensive value system, 344

Compte, August, 146

The Concept of Mind (Ryle), 554

Concept of truth, 228

Conceptualism, 83

Conceptualism: The theory that universals are concepts and exist only in the mind, G–2

Conclusion: Epistemological Questions (Harding), 456–457

Condemned to be free, 160

Metaphysics and Epistemology

St. Anselm (c. 1033–1109)
St. Thomas Aquinas (1225–1274)
Julian of Norwich (1342–1414?)
Oliva Sabuco de Nantes (b. 1562)
Thomas Hobbes (1588–1679)
René Descartes (1596–1650)
Anne Finch Conway (1631–1679)
Benedictus de Spinoza (1632–1677)
John Locke (1632–1704)
Gottfried Wilhelm, Baron von Leibniz (1646–1716)
Catharine Trotter Cockk
George E

Moral and Political Philosophy and Postmodernism

Hildegard of Bingen (1098–1179)
Heloise (1098–1164)
St. Thomas Aquinas (c. 1225–1274)
Niccolò Machiavelli (1469–1527)
Thomas Hobbes (1588–1679)
John Locke (1632–1704)
Catharine Trotter Cockk
Charles Louis de Secondat, Baron Mo
Ja

Philosophy of Religion

Gaunilo (eleventh century)
St. Anselm (c. 1033–1109)
St. Thomas Aquinas (c. 1225–1274)
Julian of Norwich (1342–1414?)
René Descartes (1596–1650)
Blaise Pascal (1623–1662)
Gottfried Wilhelm, Baron von Leibniz (1646–1716)

Eastern and Postcolonial Voices

Murasaki Shikibu (978?–1026?)
Avicenna (980–1037)
Rāmānuja (b. 1027)
Al-Ghazālī (1058–1111)
Averroës (1126–1198)
Madhva (1199–1278)
Dogen Kigen (1200–1253)
Samkara (788–820)
Al-Kindi (d. after 870)
Al Fārābī (875–950)
Yagyu Munenori (1571–1646)
Wang Yang-ming (1472–1529)
Kuroda Nagamasa (1568–1623)
Takuan (1573–1645)
S

Continental and Feminist Philosophy, and Postmodernism